Ellis Jennings

Other Books in English Translation by Violette Leduc

Mad in Pursuit

Thérèse and Isabelle

The Woman with the Little Fox

La Bâtarde

[The Bastard]

VIOLETTE LEDUC

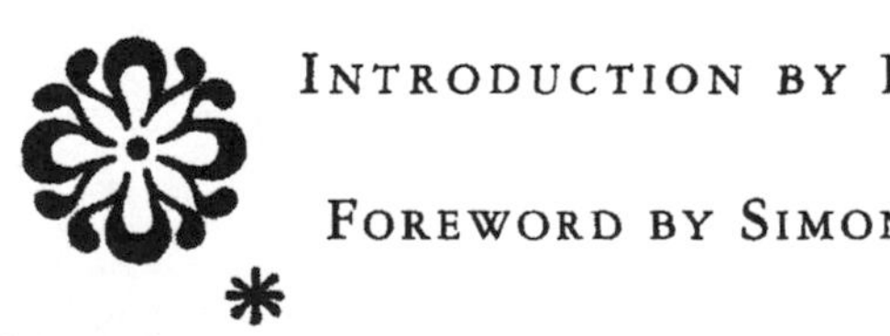

INTRODUCTION BY DEBORAH LEVY

FOREWORD BY SIMONE DE BEAUVOIR

TRANSLATED FROM THE FRENCH BY DEREK COLTMAN

DALKEY ARCHIVE PRESS

Originally published in French by Editions Gallimard, 1964

First Dalkey Archive edition, 2003
Second printing, 2015

Library of Congress Cataloging-in-Publication Data
Leduc, Violette, 1907-1972.
{Biitarde. English}
La biitarde I Violette Leduc ; translated by Derek Coltman ; introduction by Deborah Levy ; foreword by Simone de Beauvoir.
p.cm.
ISBN 1-56478-289-1 (pbk. : alk. paper)
I. Title: La biitarde. II. Coltman, Derek. III. Title.
PQ2623.E3657B313 2003
843'.9814-dc21

2002041532

Partially funded by a grant from the Illinois Arts Council, a state agency.

www.dalkeyarchive.com

Cover: design and composition by Mikhail Iliatov

INTRODUCTION

> *At the age of five, of six, at the age of seven, I used to begin weeping sometimes without warning, simply for the sake of weeping, my eyes open wide to the sun, to the flowers. . . . I wanted to feel an immense grief inside me and it came.*

La Bâtarde is a harsh title for an autobiography that is full of animals and children and plants and food and weather and girls falling in love with girls. It's true that Violette Leduc was the illegitimate daughter of a domestic servant who was seduced by the consumptive son of her employer, but to choose such a melodramatic and reductive title, "The Bastard" tells us how hard it was for Leduc to escape from the way her mother described her, and in that description gave her daughter an internal crucifix on which to nail her life's story.

It's not surprising then, that the furnace at the center of Leduc's autobiography and indeed all her writing, is stoked by her ambivalent steely-eyed mother of whom she writes, "You live in me as I lived in you." Yet if the young Violette's tears spill from eyes that are open to the sun, the older Violette's words spill from the same place too. She is not blinded by her tears, nor are her eyes shut to the pleasures of being alive. Which is to say Leduc was a writer very much in the world despite the distress she suffered all her life. What's more, she was a writer who was going to give maximum attention to the cause of her distress and create the kind of visceral language that often irritates men and makes women nervous.

This is because Leduc experiences everything in her body:

> As Isabelle lay crushed over my gaping heart I wanted to feel her enter it. . . . She was giving me a lesson in humility. I grew frightened. I was a living being. I wasn't a statue.

She doesn't just (infamously) describe the physical sensations of sex between women, she describes the physical sensation of being unloved, the physical sensation of poverty, of snow, of war, of peacocks chuckling in a meadow—she is tuned into the world with all her senses switched on. This is an extraordinary (and impossible) way of being in the world, but for Leduc it was ordinary. She is a writer who energizes whatever she gives her attention to, an orange shriveling in the sun, an ink stain on a table, the white porcelain of a salad bowl. Leduc refused to bore herself. Nothing is decoratively arranged to suggest atmosphere or a sense of place or to set a scene. Everything on the page is there because the narrator perceives it as doing something.

Even as a young girl, Leduc knew she had to find her own point to life. Her mother wanted her to be a Protestant, the religion of her absent father, but every time Violette tries to hear God, he is absent too. When she describes watching her beloved grandmother pray in church, Violette is shocked to realize that although she is sitting next to her, she has lost her. At that moment her grandmother is not there, she is in communion with somewhere else while Violette is doomed to be here, to be present, to be in this world. This is no small matter if you're poor, female, a bit bent, not that attractive (Simone de Beauvoir referred to her as "the Ugly Woman"), and have nothing but your cunning and your talent to buy you a loaf of bread. We know that Leduc's equivalent of the prayers that transported her grandmother elsewhere will be language. For Leduc was a born writer, a genius, as good as James Joyce, sometimes better. With words she not so much found the point to life, as sharpened life to a point.

The French essayist Antonin Artaud, who was sometimes mad, wrote, "I am a man who has lost his life and seeking to restore it to its place you hear the cries of a man remaking his life." Is that why people write autobiographies? Are they attempting to remake their lives? *La Bâtarde* is not an attempt to remake Leduc's life, although there is no doubt that writing books was her salvation.

It is probably an attempt to stage her life and in so doing witness herself as its main performer—and what a performance. By the time she wrote her autobiography, Leduc had lived through two world wars, had intense and volatile affairs with women—the end of a love affair, she says, "is the end of a tyranny"—been married and separated, written and published a few novels (in between lugging heavy suitcases of black-market butter and lamb from Normandy to sell to the rich in Paris), worked as a telephone operator, secretary, proofreader and publicity writer. She also had her relationship with the writer Maurice Sachs to make sense of. It was Sachs, a flamboyant homosexual, one-time reader for Gallimard, admirer of Apollinaire, Kant, Cocteau, Duras, and Plato—not to mention fresh cream cakes, apple brandy, and cigarettes—who encouraged Leduc to write instead of "sniveling" all over him. Leduc portrays him as a sort of French Oscar Wilde, a man both bewildered and fascinated by women, who filled her with terror because of "the gentleness in his eyes." Leduc became infatuated with him because she has a "passion for the impossible." What kind of accommodation can be found, she wonders, with people we deeply love but who cannot give us all we want? What Sachs can do is tell her to get on with what she is best at. "Your unhappy childhood is beginning to bore me to distraction. This afternoon you will take your basket, a pen, and an exercise-book, and you will go and sit under an apple tree. Then you will write down all the things you tell me."

There's a fairy godfather if ever there was one.

It was under that apple tree that she wrote the wonderful first line of her first novel, *L'Asphyxie*—"My mother never gave me her hand." Simone de Beauvoir read the manuscript and was so impressed she became Leduc's mentor, using her contacts to help get it published in post-Second World War Paris. When Leduc's editor Jean-Jacques Pauvert offered her 100,000 francs for the manuscript she demanded the sum in cash, preferably in small bills.

By the time Leduc wrote *La Bâtarde,* she was going to return to themes she had written about before (her mother, the deprivations of her childhood, the erotics of lesbian sexual passion, the erotics of everything, coffee, shoes, hair, landscape), but as a writer at the peak of her literary powers. In fact, she was uniquely placed to write an autobiography because she was a novelist who knew how to make the past and present seamlessly collide in one paragraph. Leduc also knew something that lesser writers do not know. She knew the past is not necessarily interesting. Eight lines into *La Bâtarde* she declares, "there's no sustenance in the past." This made me laugh, because I was on page one with 487 pages of "the past" to go. But I laughed in bittersweet recognition too, and here is a confession. When I read autobiographies I usually skip the early chapters that describe the house the subject was born in, her parents and early childhood. I start when the subject is about seventeen and begins to make choices for herself rather than react to the choices that have been made for her. I see no reason why I should be forced to meet aunts and uncles who are of no interest to me in the hope that I will better understand the subject's motives and psychology.

To observe so soon into her life story that there is no sustenance in the past is to give the past an edge. To make us curious about what the past lacks in sustenance for the narrator. What is the past anyway? What kind of place is it? Yes, it's a series of events that happened before now, but the past, like writing, is mostly a way of looking.

La Bâtarde is the first autobiography I have read all the way through. This is mostly due to Leduc's cunning decision to begin a work of tremendous narcissism by pretending she has no self-esteem and is a totally hopeless case. The first thing she tells the reader is that she is not unique, which is a relief—most people write autobiographies to persuade us they are. She then goes on to wish she had been born a statue—presumably because if she were made from bronze rather than flesh she would not have to feel the painful things she is going to tell us about. Still on page one, she tells us she is sitting in the sunshine outside, surrounded by grapevines and hills, writing in an exercise-book. Suddenly she imagines her own birth. She is in a dark room. The doctor's scissors click as he separates the child from her mother—"we are no longer the communicating vessels we were when she was carrying me."

"Who is this Violette Leduc?" she asks. And then it's the next day, she's picked some sweet peas, collected a feather and is now writing in the woods staring at the trunk of a chestnut tree. Every moment has breath and every breath pushes the narrative on to a surprising place, to somewhere that matters because it matters to Leduc. When she steals flowers "always blue" from a park, she connects the action to a perception. She says the flowers are her way of "taking her mother's eyes back," by which I think she means she wants to find her mother's image in something beautiful. And when she is convalescing from an illness in the countryside, she writes, "Whenever I looked round at the objects and furniture in the room I felt I was sitting on the point of a needle. So much cleanliness was repellent." Her prose is kinetic and it is poetic, but it never collapses into poetry. In fact, her books are much more grounded in the realities and uncertainties of everyday life than her existentialist contemporaries.

Despite being acclaimed by Camus, Genet (who Leduc described as a burglar poet), Simone de Beauvoir, and Sartre, Leduc's books are not to be found alongside theirs. If in my view she stands shoulder to shoulder with them as a writerly equal, she certainly does not stand spine to spine with them in Barnes & Noble. Perhaps this is because nothing had taught her (or Genet) that life or literature was respectable. Literature for Leduc was not a comfortable sofa or a seminar room in a university—nor was it a place where flawed human beings undergo some sort of catharsis and emerge happy, whole, healed, miraculously cleansed of anger, lust, and pain. For Leduc, literature, like life, is a place where some people damage us and some people save our lives—and then it is lunchtime. Referred to as "France's greatest unknown writer," it is time to stop fetishizing Violette Leduc as a female outsider existing on the fringes of everything and allow her to take her place in the canon of great writing.

To declare there is no sustenance in the past is of course a half-lie. What sustained Leduc is that she wrote out her life with an audience in mind. It is for this reason she "bit into the fruit" of her "desolations"—that's what many writers do and Leduc is no crazier than them for having the audacity to believe that she too could spin some ideas into the world. I disagree with de Beauvoir, astute as she is, when she describes "the unflinching sincerity" of *La Bâtarde* as written "as though there were no one listening." De Beauvoir certainly did not write her own books thinking no one was listening to her and she must have been aware that even in an uninhibited autobiography such as this one, there is no such thing as an absolutely true memory—all writing (except for diaries, but that too is debatable) is shaped with an audience in mind. Leduc, who addresses the reader throughout as "Reader, my reader," felt more entitled to be listened to than perhaps de Beauvoir unconsciously thought she should feel. Given the turbulent historical time in which she lived, Leduc did not have a particularly remarkable life. It is how she crafts language that made her life remarkable.

"To find relief in what has been," Leduc whispers to her reader, "we must make ourselves eternal."

I am staring at a photograph of Violette Leduc now. She is smiling, a wry half smile, an expression I recognize in her writing too. I reckon she laughed out loud when she wrote, "I was afraid of having to present my big nose to strangers" or "I thought one's personality could be changed by wearing expensive clothes." She has a dry, camp wit, rarely discussed in a critical atmosphere that has often reduced her work to unstable female tragedy on a grand scale. Her eyes are slightly narrowed (is she flirting with the photographer?), her chin resting on her left hand. She holds a pencil between her fingers—or is it a cigarette? Violette. An old-fashioned name. She was born in 1907 after all. The very beginning of the twentieth century. She was seven years old when Freud told us the most interesting secrets are the ones we keep from ourselves—but Leduc knew that anyway. The secrets we keep from ourselves were her material.

Violette Leduc had to spend a lifetime unlearning how to see the world as her mother saw it. Most of us choose to be less alert to the things that grieve us. This was just not possible for Leduc. Reading *La Bâtarde* is like discovering a whole new nervous system.

DEBORAH LEVY
2003

FOREWORD

When, early in 1945, I began to read Violette Leduc's manuscript —"Ma mère ne m'a jamais donné la main"—I was immediately struck by it: here was a temperament, a style. Camus accepted L'Asphyxie without hesitation and published it in his Espoir series. Genet, Jouhandeau, and Sartre hailed the arrival of a new writer. In the books that followed, her talent was confirmed. Exacting critics gave it the highest praise. But the public did not respond. Despite a considerable succès d'estime, Violette Leduc remained obscure.

It is said that the unknown writer no longer exists; anyone, or almost anyone, can get his books published. That is exactly the trouble: mediocrity flourishes; the good seed is choked by the tares. Success depends, most of the time, on a stroke of luck. And yet even bad luck has its causes. Violette Leduc does not try to please; she doesn't please; in fact, she alarms people. The titles of her books—L'Asphyxie, L'Affamée, Ravages—are the reverse of cheerful. Leafing through them, you glimpse a world full of sound and fury, where love often bears the name of hate, where a passion for life bursts forth in cries of despair; a world laid waste by loneliness which, seen from afar, looks arid. It is not in fact.

"I am a desert talking to myself," Violette Leduc wrote to me once. I have encountered beauties beyond reckoning in deserts. And whoever speaks to us from the depths of his loneliness speaks to us of ourselves. Even the most worldly or the most active man alive has his dense thickets where no one ventures, not even himself, but which are there: the darkness of childhood, the failures, the self-denials, the sudden distress at a cloud in the sky. To catch sight suddenly of a landscape or a human being as they exist when we are absent: it is an impossible dream which we have all cherished. If we read La Bâtarde it becomes real, or nearly so. A woman is descending into the most secret part of herself and telling us about all she finds there with an unflinching sincerity, as though there were no one listening.

"My case is not unique," says Violette Leduc at the beginning of this narrative. No; but it is singular and significant. It demonstrates with exceptional clarity that a life is the reworking of a destiny by a freedom.

Before we have read many pages, the author is already crushing us beneath the weight of the ineluctable pressures that formed her. Throughout the years of childhood, her mother inspired her with an irremediable sense of guilt: guilt for having been born, for having delicate health, for costing money, for being a woman and therefore condemned to the miseries of the feminine condition. She saw herself reflected in two hard, blue eyes: an offense in human form. Her grandmother's gentleness saved her from total destruction. It is to this influence that Violette Leduc owes the preservation of a vitality and a fundamental balance of mind that have prevented her, in the worst moments of her story, from going under. But the role of the "angel Fidéline" was only secondary; her grandmother died while Violette was still young. The Other was embodied in the mother with the eyes of steel. Crushed by this woman, the child attempted to annihilate herself completely. She idolized her; she engraved her mother's law in her innermost self: fly from men. She set herself religiously to serve this woman, and presented her own future to her as a gift. Her mother married;

the little girl was shattered by this betrayal. From then on, she was afraid of all human consciousness because it had the power to turn her into a monster; of the presence of all human beings, because they might all dissolve into absence. She huddled down inside herself. Driven by the deceit practiced upon her, by her anguish, by her bitterness, she chose narcissism, egocentricity, loneliness.

"My ugliness will set me apart until I die," writes Violette Leduc. This interpretation does not satisfy me. The woman depicted in La Bâtarde interests dressmakers and dress designers—Lelong, Fath—to such an extent that they are glad to make her a present of their most daring creations. She inspires passion in Isabelle; in Hermine an ardent love that lasts for years; in Gabriel feelings sufficiently violent for him to marry her; in Maurice Sachs a definite and instinctive attraction. Her "big nose" seems to be no bar to either comradeship or friendship. If she sometimes makes people laugh it is not because of that; there is something unusual, something provocative about her dress, the way she does her hair, her whole physiognomy. People make fun of her to reassure themselves. Her physical ugliness has not controlled her destiny but merely symbolized it; she has simply found reasons in her mirror for feeling sorry for herself.

For, as she emerged from adolescence, she found herself caught in a diabolical trap. She loathed the loneliness which she had made her lot in life, and because she loathed it she plunged even deeper into it. She was neither a hermit nor in exile; her misfortune was that she never experienced a reciprocal relationship with anyone: either the other was an object for her or she made herself into an object for the other. Her powerlessness to communicate is apparent in the dialogue she writes: the people talk along lines that never cross; each has his own language which the other does not understand. Even in love, especially in love, any exchange is impossible, because Violette Leduc cannot accept a duality in which she sees lurking the threat of separation. Every break revives in an intolerable fashion the crisis experienced when she was fourteen: her mother's marriage. "I don't want people to leave me": that is the leitmotif of Ravages. The couple must therefore be only one being. There are moments when Violette Leduc attempts to blot out her own personality, when she plays the game of masochism. But she has too much vigor and lucidity of mind to keep it up for long. It is she who will devour the one she loves.

Being jealous and possessive, she finds it hard to tolerate Hermine's affection for her family, Gabriel's relationship with his mother and sister and his friendships with men. She is insistent that her woman friend, once the day's work is over, should devote every waking moment to her alone; Hermine cooks and sews for her, listens to her complaints, drowns with her in sensual pleasures, and gives way to her every caprice. Hermine demands nothing—except, when night comes, to be allowed to sleep. An insomniac herself, Violette rebels against this desertion. Later, she forbids it to Gabriel as well. "I hate people who sleep." She shakes them, wakes them up, and forces them with tears or kisses to keep their eyes open. But Gabriel, less tractable than Hermine, claims the right to follow his profession and dispose of his free time as he pleases; every morning, when he tries to leave, Violette uses every means at her disposal to draw him back into their bed. She imputes this tyranny to her "insatiable insides." In fact, what she desires is something quite different from sensual pleasure: it is possession. When she assuages Gabriel's desire, when she receives him into her, he belongs to her; their oneness is a reality. As soon as he leaves her embrace, he is once more her old enemy: the other.

"Presence and absence, two identical mirages." Absence is a torture: the anguished expectation of a presence. Presence itself is an interval between two absences: a torment. Violette Leduc hates her tormentors. They are each—as we all are—in collusion with themselves in ways that exclude her; and they also possess certain qualities she does not: she feels this as an attack upon herself. She envies Hermine her good health, her calm, her activity, her gaiety; she envies Gabriel because he is a man. She cannot undermine their privileges except by destroying their entire personalities; she attempts to do so.

"You want to destroy me," says Gabriel. Yes. So as to remove the differences between them—and to avenge herself. "I was avenging myself because her presence was too perfect," she says of Hermine. When they leave her, one after the other, she gives way to despair; and yet she has achieved her goal. Secretly, it is always her intent to shatter the relationship, the marriage. Because she craves failure. Because it is her own destruction she is aiming at. She is "a praying mantis devouring herself." But she is also too healthy a person to work solely toward her own ruin. The truth is, she loses in order to lose and win at the same time. Her broken relationships are reconquests of herself.

Through the storms and through the calms she always keeps—and this is her strength—her instinct for self-preservation. She never gives herself entirely. After a few weeks of ardor, she makes short work of withdrawing herself from the range of Isabelle's passion. At the beginning of her life with Hermine, she fights to go on working and providing for her own needs. Once conquered by the doctor, by her mother, by Hermine, her dependency weighs on her. She escapes from it thanks to her ambiguous and for a long time secret friendship with Gabriel. Once she has married him, she sets herself to destroy this bond by falling passionately in love with Maurice Sachs. When Sachs, after having gone as a volunteer worker to Hamburg, wants to return to the village where they had spent several months together, she refuses to help him do so. By then, transporting suitcases crammed with black market butter and legs of lamb into Paris with her own two hands, amassing a fortune, exhausted but triumphant, she is experiencing the heady delight of going beyond herself. Sachs would disturb the world over which she reigns, straight and proud as a cypress tree. "Once he came back, I would shrink into the ground again."

Others always frustrate her, wound her, humiliate her. When she grapples with the world, without outside help, when she works and succeeds, she is borne aloft by joy. The sniveling girl is also the woman traveler who, in Trésors à prendre, makes her way across the length and breadth of France, rucksack on her back, drunk with her discoveries and her own energy. A woman sufficient unto herself: this is the only image of herself that Violette Leduc can contemplate with pleasure. "I kept on till I had what I wanted: I existed at last."

And yet she has the need to love. She must have someone to whom she can dedicate her bursts of joy, her melancholy moments, her enthusiasms. The ideal would be to dedicate herself to someone who will not encumber her with an actual presence, someone to whom she can give everything without anything really being taken. And so she cherishes the image of Fidéline—"My little apple who will keep forever"—miraculously embalmed in memory; and Isabelle too, now in the depths of the past a dazzling image for her idolatry. She invokes these figures, takes her solitary pleasure as she imagines them, prostrates herself before them. For Hermine, now absent and already lost, her heart beats in a panic of desire. She falls in love at sight with Maurice Sachs, and later on with two other homosexuals. The obstacle that separates them from her is so impassable that they might be a light-year away; in their company she "was consumed on the live coals of the impossible." There is a sensation of pleasure to be had from an unsatisified desire when it contains no hope. The woman in L'Affamée whom Violette Leduc calls Madame is no less inaccessible. In La Vieille Fille et le mort, she pushed the fantasy of an unreciprocated love to a final extreme in which the other has been reduced to the passivity of a thing. Mlle. Clarisse, still unmarried at the age of fifty—not because men have neglected her but because she disdains them—goes into the café next to her grocery store one evening and finds an unknown man, dead. She lavishes attention and tenderness upon him, her effusions untrammeled by his presence; she talks to him and invents his answers for him. But the illusion fades: since he has received nothing, she has given nothing; he has not provided her with any warmth; she finds herself alone with a corpse. These love affairs at a distance ravage Violette Leduc as much as the reciprocated ones.

"You will never be satisfied," Hermine tells her. Hermine destroys her by overwhelming her with gifts, Gabriel by withholding himself. The presence of her lovers drives her wild; their absence lays her waste. She herself gives us the key to this curse: "I came into the world, I vowed to entertain a passion for the impossible." This passion took possession of her on the day when, betrayed by her mother, she took refuge with the phantom of her unknown father. This father had existed, and he was a myth; by entering his world she had entered into a legend: she had chosen the world of the imagination, which is one of the forms assumed by the impossible. He had been rich and of cultivated tastes; she relived these tastes, without any hope of satisfying them. Between the ages of twenty and thirty she coveted all the luxury of Paris with a dizzying intensity: furniture, dresses, jewels, expensive cars. But she made not the slightest effort to acquire these things: "What was it I wanted? To do nothing and to have everything." The dream of grandeur counted more than the grandeur itself. She lives off symbols. She transfigures the separate instants of her life by performing rites: the apéritif she takes in the basement with Hermine, the champagne she drinks with her mother, belong to an imaginary life. She is disguising herself when, to the sound of fantastic drums, she dresses in the eel-colored Schiaparelli suit; and her parade along the Paris boulevards is a parody.

And yet these sops to her desires do not bring satisfaction. From her peasant childhood she has retained the need to hold solid objects in her hands, to feel herself heavy on the ground, to perform real acts. To manufacture reality with imaginary materials: that is the prerogative of artists and writers. And toward this outlet from her dilemma she gradually makes her way.

In her relations with others she had simply taken her own destiny upon herself. When she begins to move in the direction of literature she gives it an unforeseen meaning of her own. Everything began the day she walked into a bookshop and asked for a book by Jules Romains. In her narrative she does not emphasize the importance of this fact, of which she quite obviously did not suspect the consequences at the time. An inattentive reader will perceive in her story only a succession of chance events. In fact it is a matter of a choice maintained and renewed over a period of fifteen years before finally bursting forth in a work of art.

As long as she continued to live in her mother's shadow, Violette Leduc despised all books; she preferred to steal a cabbage from the back of a cart, to pick greens for her rabbits, to chatter, to live. From that day when she turned toward her father, books—which he had loved—continued to fascinate her. Solid, glossy, they held within their beautiful, shiny covers whole worlds where the impossible becomes possible. She bought and devoured Mort de quelqu'un. Romains. Duhamel. Gide. She was never to let them out of her life again. When she decided to take up a profession, she put an advertisement in the Bibliographie de France. She went to work at a publishing house, writing publicity releases and the like; she did not dare to think of writing books herself as yet, but she kept alive on a diet of famous names and faces. After her break with Hermine, she succeeded in getting work with a film producer; she read synopses, she made suggestions for treatments. It was thus through her own efforts that she altered the course of her existence and helped produce her apparently chance meeting with Maurice Sachs. She interested him; he appreciated her letters, he advised her to write. She began with short stories and articles of topical interest which were published in a women's magazine. Later on, worn out by her continual spate of childhood reminiscences, he was to say to her: write them down, for heaven's sake. The result was L'Asphyxie.

She realized immediately that literary creation could be a way of salvation for her. "I shall write, I shall open my arms, I shall hug the fruit trees in them and give them to my sheet of paper." Talking to someone who is dead, to people who are deaf, to things, is a grating game. A reader would provide that impossible synthesis of absence and presence. "This August day, reader, is a rose window glowing with heat. I make you a gift of it, it's yours." And the reader receives this gift without disturbing the writer's solitude. He listens to her as she talks aloud; he makes no answer, but he is a justification for her soliloquy.

Still, it's necessary to have something to say. Fortunately, though in love with the impossible, Violette Leduc has never lost contact with the world; on the contrary, she clutches it to her as a means of filling the loneliness inside. Her unique situation safeguards her against prefabricated visions. Ricocheting from each failure back into nostalgia, she takes nothing for granted; she goes on tirelessly asking questions and recreating with words the discoveries she has made. And because she has so much to say, a wearied listener thrusts a pen into her hands.

Since she is obsessed with herself, all her works—with the exception of Les Boutons dorés—are more or less autobiographical: reminiscences, a diary of a love affair, or rather of a loveless affair; a travel journal; a novel which transposes a certain period of her life; a novella introducing us to her fantasies; finally, La Bâtarde, which summarizes and goes beyond her previous books.

The richness of her narratives comes less from the circumstances depicted than from the burning intensity of her memory: at each moment she is completely there through all the thickness of the years. Every woman she loves brings Isabelle to life again, herself the reincarnation of a young and idolized mother. The blue of Fidéline's apron lights up every summer sky. Sometimes the writer makes a leap into the present; she invites us to sit beside her on the pine needles; this is her method of destroying time: the past takes on the colors of the here and now. A schoolgirl of fifty-five is writing down words in an exercise book. And sometimes, when her memories do not suffice to illumine her emotions, she whirls us off into strange flights of fancy; she exorcises the absence that tortures her with violent and lyrical phantasmagoria. Under its real-life covering, the dream life shows through, running like filigree through stories of the utmost simplicity.

She is her own principal heroine. But her protagonists exist intensely. "An excruciating pointillism of the emotions." An inflection of the voice, a drawing together of the eyebrows, a silence, a sigh, everything is promise or rejection for this woman so passionately committed in her relations with other people. The "excruciating" attention she pays to their slightest gestures is her good fortune as a writer. She brings their personalities alive for us with all their disturbing opacity and in the most minute detail. Her mother, flirtatious and violent, imperious and conniving; Fidéline; Isabelle; Hermine; Gabriel; Sachs, as astonishing here as in his own books: it is impossible to forget them.

Because she is "never satisfied" she has always remained open to new experiences; any encounter can appease her hunger or at least distract her from it: everyone she meets is an object for her acute and attentive observation. She unmasks tragedies and farces concealed behind façades of apparent banality. In a few pages, in a few lines, she can bring to life the characters who have established a claim to her curiosity or her friendship: the old dressmaker from Albi who made dresses for Toulouse-Lautrec's mother; the one-eyed hermit of Beaumes-de-Venise; Fernand, the dézingueur who makes away with sheep and bullocks on the quiet, on his head a fine top hat, between his teeth a rose. Moving, unusual, they take the same hold on our interest as they did on hers.

She is interested in people. She cares about things. Sartre tells in Les Mots how, brought up on Littré, things appeared to him as precarious embodiments of their names. For Violette Leduc, on the other hand, language is to be found in things, and the risk a writer runs is that of betraying them. "Don't murder that warmth at the top of a tree. Things talk without your help, remember that; your voice will muffle them. . . . The rosebush bows under the ecstasy of its roses: what is it you want to make it say?"

She decided nevertheless to write and capture their murmurs: "I shall bring the heart of each thing up to the surface." When she is being ravaged by absence, she takes refuge among them: they are solid, they are real, and they have a voice. She sometimes falls in love with strange and beautiful objects; one year she came back from the south of France bringing two hundred pounds of dawn-colored stones with the imprints of fossils in them; another time it was pieces of wood, all in delicate tones of gray and twisted into visionary shapes. But her favorite companions are familiar objects: a box of matches, a kitchen range. She can extract the warmth, the softness, from a child's sock. She inhales the odor of her poverty tenderly from her old rabbit-fur coat. She finds succor in a church chair, in a clock: "I clasped the back in my arms. I touched the polished wood. It feels so warm and friendly against my cheek. . . . Clocks console me. The pendulum swings back and forth, outside happiness, outside unhappiness." The night after her miscarriage she thought she was going to die, and hugged the little electric bulb hanging over her bed with genuine love. "Don't leave me, dear little bulb. You're so chubby, I'm going out with a cheek in the hollow of my hand, a shiny cheek that I am keeping warm." Because she knows how to love them, she knows how to make us see them: no one before her had ever shown us those slightly tarnished flecks incrusted and glittering in the stairs of the Métro stations.

All of Violette Leduc's books could be called L'Asphyxie. She feels stifled with Hermine in their little suburban home, and later on in Gabriel's wretched apartment as well. This is the symbol of a deeper confinement: she wastes away inside the prison of her skin. But every now and then her robust health breaks forth; she tears down the partitions, she clears the horizon, she bursts out, she opens herself to nature, and the roads unwind beneath her feet. Aimless excursions, wanderings. Neither the grandiose nor the extraordinary have any attraction for her. She likes being in the Ile-de-France, in Normandy: meadows, paddocks, furrows, a land worked by man, with farms, orchards, houses, animals.

Often the wind, storms, night, a sky on fire, bring drama to this tranquillity. Violette Leduc paints tortured landscapes which resemble those of Van Gogh. "The trees go through their crisis of despair." But she can also describe the peace of autumns, the shy approach of spring, the silence of a sunken lane. Sometimes her slightly precious simplicity reminds one of Jules Renard: "The sow is too naked, the sheep is overdressed." But the art with which she colors sounds, or makes them visible, is hers and hers alone: "the sparkling cry of the lark." We perceive abstractions through our senses when she evokes "the playfulness of the cow-parsley flowers . . . the anguished scent of fresh sawdust . . . the mystic vapor of flowering lavender." There is nothing forced in her notations: the countryside is talking spontaneously about the men who cultivate and inhabit it. And through this countryside Violette Leduc is reconciled to those who live in it. She likes to wander through their villages, the open ones and those which are closed, shut in on themselves, but where each inhabitant knows the warmth of existing in community with all the others. In the bistros the peasants and the carters do not make her timid; she drinks, she is confident and gay, she wins their friendship. "What do I love with all my heart? The country. The woods, the forests . . . My home is there, with them. . . ."

All writers who tell us about themselves aspire to sincerity: each has his own, which resembles no other. I know of none more complete than Violette Leduc's. Guilty, guilty, guilty: her mother's voice still reverberates inside her; a mysterious judge is always stalking her. Despite that, thanks to that, no one can browbeat her. The faults that we impute to her can never be as grave as those she is charged with by her invisible tormentors. She spreads every last piece of evidence in the case before us so that we can deliver her from the evil she has not committed.

There is a considerable erotic content in her books; it is neither gratuitous nor deliberately sensational. She was conceived not by a man and woman but by two sexes. Her first awareness of herself, created by the constant harping of her mother, was of a condemned sex, threatened by all males. As a sequestered adolescent, she was stagnating in sullen self-love when Isabelle introduced her to sensual pleasure; she was shattered by this transfiguration of her body into a garden of delights. Doomed to what is called abnormal love, she became its champion. Furthermore, even though among the names she gives us for her solitude we sometimes find her using that of God, she is a firm materialist. She does not seek to impose her own ideas or her own image of herself on others. Any relation she enters into with them is of the flesh. Presence, for her, is the body; communication is only operative between bodies. To be fond of Fidéline means to bury oneself in her skirts; to be rejected by Sachs means to receive his "abstract" kisses; the outcome of self-love is onanism. Sensations are the truth of the emotions. Violette Leduc weeps, exults, and trembles with her ovaries. She could tell us nothing about herself if she did not talk about them.

She sees others through her desires: Hermine and her tranquil ardor; Gabriel's ironic masochism; the pederasty of Maurice Sachs. Wherever she may chance to meet them, she is always interested in those who have reinvented sexuality for their own purposes:

people like Cataplame, at the beginning of La Bâtarde. Eroticism for her leads to no mysteries and is never cluttered up with a lot of nonsense. It is, nevertheless, the master key to the world; it is by its light that she discovers the city and the countryside, the density of the night, the fragility of the dawn, the cruelty in the mouths of pealing bells. In order to speak of it, she has forged herself a language devoid of sentimentality and vulgarity, which I find a remarkable achievement. It has alarmed her publishers however. They would not allow the account of her nights with Isabelle to appear in Ravages.[1] There were rows of dots, here and there, replacing suppressed passages. La Bâtarde they accepted in its entirety. The most daring episode depicts Violette and Hermine making love together before the eyes of a voyeur: it is narrated with a simplicity that disarms all censure. Violette Leduc's discreet audacity is one of her most striking qualities, but one which has certainly done her a disservice: it shocks the Puritans, and the dirty-minded are left dissatisfied.

In these days, there is an abundance of sexual confessions. It is much rarer for a writer to speak frankly about money. Violette Leduc makes no secret of the importance it has for her: it too is a materialization of her relations with other people. As a child, she dreamed of going to work and giving money to her mother; once rejected, she gets her own back by filching it from her in small sums here and there. Gabriel places her on a pedestal when he empties his billfold for her; he pulls her down from it as soon as he becomes thrifty. One of the things that fascinates her most about Sachs is his prodigality. She likes to beg: it is a way of getting back at the rich. Above all, she loves to earn money: it is an affirmation of herself, she exists. She hoards with passion; ever since her childhood, she has been haunted by the fear of going without, and she measures her own importance by the thickness of the bundles she pins under her skirt. In the comradely atmosphere of village bistros she will sometimes gaily pay for rounds of drinks. But she does not hide the fact that she is miserly: from natural caution, from egocentricity, from the grudge she bears the world. "Help my neighbor? Did anyone help me when I was dying of unhappiness?" Hardness, rapacity: she admits to them with amazing honesty.

---

[1] *She has treated them again, to some extent, in* La Bâtarde. *The complete account appeared in a limited edition under the title* Thérèse et Isabelle.

She also acknowledges other petty traits such as we are usually careful to conceal. There were many embittered people who eased their rage against the world by taking advantage of France's defeat: their first thought, after the Liberation, was to have it forgotten. Violette Leduc admits quite calmly that the Occupation gave her her chance and that she seized it with both hands. She did not find it unpleasant to see misfortune falling on other heads than her own for once; hired by a woman's magazine but convinced of her own worthlessness, she dreaded the end of the war because it would mean that the "able" people would return and she would be fired. She neither excuses nor accuses herself: that's how it was. She understands why and makes us understand too.

Yet she offers no extenuations. Most writers, when they confess to evil thoughts, manage to remove the sting from them by the very frankness of their admissions. She forces us to feel them with all their corrosive bitterness both in herself and in ourselves. She remains a faithful accomplice to her desires, to her rancor, to her petty traits. In this way she takes ours upon her too and delivers us from shame: no one is monstrous unless we are all so.

This audacity is a result of her moral candor. It is extremely rare for her to blame herself for anything or to produce any sort of defense. She doesn't judge herself; she judges no one. She complains. She flies into rages against her mother, against Hermine, against Gabriel, against Sachs; she does not condemn them. Often she is tender, sometimes admiring; she is never indignant. Her guilt came to her from outside, without her being any more responsible for it than for the color of her hair; and so the words "good" and "bad" are empty ones for her. The things from which she suffered most—her "unforgivable" face, her mother's marriage—are not listed as crimes. Inversely, anything that does not touch her personally leaves her indifferent. She calls the Germans "the enemy" in order to make it clear that this borrowed notion has remained quite foreign to her. She does not owe allegiance to any camp. She has no sense of the universal, no sense of simultaneity; she is there where she is, with the weight of her past upon her shoulders. She never cheats; she never yields to pretensions or bows to the conventions. Her scrupulous honesty has the value of a moral challenge.

In this world swept clear of moral categories, her sensibility is her only guide. Cured of her taste for luxury and social success, she takes her stand with determination by the side of the poor, of the friendless. So she is still faithful to the meager circumstances and undemanding joys of her childhood; and also to her life today, for after the triumphal black market years she found herself once more without a cent. She holds the destitution of Van Gogh, of the Curé d'Ars, in veneration. All forms of distress find an echo inside her: that of the abandoned, of the lost, of homeless children, of old people without children, of hoboes, of bums. She is desolated when—in Trésors à prendre, before the Algerian war—she sees the owner of a restaurant refusing to serve an Algerian carpet seller. Confronted with injustice, she immediately takes the part of the oppressed, of the exploited. They are her brothers, she recognizes herself in them. The people out on the fringes of society seem more real to her than the settled citizens who always behave according to their allotted roles. She prefers country pubs to elegant bars, a third-class railroad compartment smelling of garlic and lilacs to the comfort of traveling first class. Her settings, her characters, belong to the world of ordinary people whom literature today usually passes over in silence.

Despite "the tears and the cries," Violette Leduc's books are "invigorating"—it is a word she loves—because of what I shall call her innocence in evil, and because they wrest so much richness from the shadows. Stifling rooms, hearts filled with grief—the truncated, gasping phrases have us by the throat: suddenly a great wind carries us away beneath an endless sky and gaiety runs beating through our veins. The cry of the lark sparkles over the bare plain. In the depths of despair we suddenly encounter a passion for living, and hate is only one of the names for love.

La Bâtarde ends at the moment when the author has concluded the account of her childhood with which she began the book. Thus we have come full circle. The failure to relate to others has resulted in that privileged form of communication—a work of art. I hope I have persuaded the reader to partake of it: he will find in it even more, much more, than I have promised.

SIMONE DE BEAUVOIR

❁

*

My case is not unique: I am afraid of dying and distressed at being in this world. I haven't worked, I haven't studied. I have wept, I have cried out in protest. These tears and cries have taken up a great deal of my time. I am tortured by all that time lost whenever I think about it. I cannot think about things for long, but I can find pleasure in a withered lettuce leaf offering me nothing but regrets to chew over. There is no sustenance in the past. I shall depart as I arrived. Intact, loaded down with the defects that have tormented me. I wish I had been born a statue; I am a slug under my dunghill. Virtues, good qualities, courage, meditation, culture. With arms crossed on my breast I have broken myself against those words.

Reader, my reader, I was writing outside, sitting on the same stone, a year ago. My square-lined writing paper has not changed; the grape vines run in the same lines below the plunging hills. The third row is still covered with a haze of heat. My hills are bathed in their halo of gentleness. Did I go away, have I come back? If so, then living would no longer be merely a slow and ceaseless death as the seconds pass on my wristwatch. And yet my birth certificate fascinates me. Or else revolts me. Or bores me. I read it through from beginning to end whenever I feel the need; I find myself once more in the long gallery as it echoes with the clicking scissors of the doctor attending my birth. I listen, I shiver. We are no longer the communicating vessels we were when she was carrying me. Here I am, born, on a register in the town hall, at the point of a town hall clerk's pen. No nastiness, no placenta; writing, a registration. Who is this Violette Leduc? The great-grandmother of her great-grandmother when all is said and done. Read it again, read it again. This is a birth? A mothball with its sulky smell. Women cheat, women suffer. They used to be attractive—so they smooth away their age. I shout mine aloud because I was never attractive, because I shall always have my baby hair. It's taken me two and a half hours to write that, two and a half pages of my exercise book. I shall keep on, I shall not lose heart.

The next morning, eight o'clock in the morning of June 24, 1962. I've changed my place, I'm writing in the woods because of the heat. Began my day by picking a bunch of wild sweet peas and picking up a feather. And I complain about being in the world, in a world of trills and thistles. The chestnut trees are slender, their trunks are languid. The light, my light, has been tamed by the leaves. It's new and it's the newness of my day.

*

You become my child, Mother, when, as an old woman, you remember things with your clocklike precision. You talk, I take you in. You speak, I carry you in my head. Yes, for you my belly is hot as a volcano. You speak, and I am silent. I was born the bearer of your misfortune as one is born a libation bearer. To live, you know you must live in the past. Sometimes I'm so tired of it I almost feel sick; sometimes around midnight, when I'm in bed and you're sitting beside me in an armchair, and you say: "I loved no one but him, I only loved once, give me a fruit gum," I become a lyre and a vibraphone for your dusty mane. You are old, you are preparing to leave yourself, I open the box of candy. You say: "Are you sleepy? Your eyes are closing." I'm not sleepy. I want to shake off your age. I wind my hair around my curlers, my fingers are telling me what you were like at twenty-five, telling me about your blue eyes, your black hair, your sculptured bangs, your shawl, the tulle, your big hat, my suffering when I was five. My elegant one, my uncrushable one, my courageous one, my vanquished one, my rambling one, my eraser to rub myself out with, my jealous one, my justice, my injustice, my commander, my shy one. What are people going to say? What are people going to think? What would they say? Our litanies, our transfusions.

When we come back from the beach in the evening, when you go into the shops, when it's your turn to speak, when you charm the housewives, I wait outside, I don't want to be with you. I rage in the shadows, I hate you, yet I should love you since I am effacing myself because of the customers, the delivery men, the neighbors. You come back, and I say: "You loved him. What a poor sort of man he was." You bristle. No, I don't want to demolish you by demolishing him. "A prince. A true prince." That's what you used to call him. I listened, I dribbled, I don't dribble anymore. The next day, in the grocer's, you say to the woman behind the counter: "Some nice fruit. It's for the goddess. I shall have complaints." You wound me. You wouldn't get complaints. What a gloomy young girl you had been. The bad soup in the orphanages had weakened your legs. Always tired, always too tired. No dancing, no outings, no girl friends. Disdainful, standoffish, irritable. Always lying down on Sunday. The country bored you, the city faded after you had bought the sort of collars and cuffs that were fashionable in 1905, after you had gone around with that saintly woman, your employer, giving aid to the poor. You say to me: "Your grandmother could talk like a book." I can't bear it when you confuse your mother with his mother. My grandmother couldn't talk like a book: she scoured other people's saucepans. I had only one grandmother, the one I knew. She was the one and only in our world, as a queen or a saint is the one and only in some higher world. Fidéline: your mother and my white meat of tenderness. I think she said to you: "Later on she will have no heart." I don't know whether I have a heart or not. Fidéline has not grown dim. You cannot dim a harvest of stars.

Fidéline. I lie there with her sitting beside me. She says:

"The Duc family, if you had only seen them! The men, real strapping fellows, the tallest men in the village. . . ."

She falls silent. In front of the door, in front of the window, the gravel is crunching. She drapes herself in the folds of her pink nightgown, her warm and simply cut nightgown from the store Guyenne et Gascogne. I wait for her to go on. I watch her,

I see a storm raging in the marble. She is an indestructible character.

". . . The father would say the blessing, he would give out the work. The father was a councillor. Everyone respected him. You'll plow, you'll do the harrowing, you'll sow, you'll take care of the sheep, or the horse. They all put on their berets, no one said anything, everyone went out, everyone did as he was told. They were proper men, clean-living men. My father was the weakest of the lot."

The crunching on the gravel has stopped. She loses herself in a dream of puritanism, obedience, authority. Her father's village: nothing but orders and people carrying them out.

I venture:

"The Duc family. Why Duc? You were called Leduc. I'm called Leduc."

She stands up and puts out the little overhead light. The lavender blue lamp brings the night pressing in on us.

"Duc . . . Leduc . . ." (She thinks it over.) "In the country they shorten things," she says.

An angel of eighteen is married: my grandmother Fidéline. Eight days later, the angel, still not very wide awake, looks in a mirror and sees the mouth of her fine strapping husband pressed to the mouth of a village whore. "Where did you unearth that child?" all the easy women ask the rogue. They all laugh uproariously. Angels do sometimes indulge in belly laughs. Duc was a cattle merchant; he was out on a spree and got himself kicked by a horse. Deliverance: Fidéline was a widow at twenty, my mother born after her father's death; she never knew him.

She was born in Artres, a backward village in the north of France. What thrift, in this six-year-old Minerva. She would come back from the fair with her penny still clutched in her pocket. While still a child she was already thinking of tomorrow; she had no choice. Laure, my mother's sister, the elder daughter, was sent away to her grandparents in Eth, where she lived with the Duc family. She was a strong, healthy child and was to be transformed into a rustic Valkyrie by her stay with the tall, strapping men and the patriarch. The two sisters were to have nothing in common but their sense of authority. Bilious attacks. Fidéline moaning and writhing on the floor. "Mum, are you sick? Mum, are you still sick?" her companion, her little daughter asks a hundred times a day. Their money came to an end at the same time as the attacks.

The angel, worn out and still not very wide awake, sent Berthe, my mother, to live with an aunt who trimmed ladies' dresses and an uncle who was a pork butcher. There she was appalled, terrified, ordered about by an ogre splashing about in blood as he made black sausages. This was a husband, this was the first man she had ever seen close up. There she was also delighted and fascinated by an Ophelia dying of consumption, sketching designs and motifs for Sarah Bernhardt's pearly dresses. The first married couple with whom she lived was an unhappy one. She weighed, she served, she answered the customers' questions. She's already a little woman, they all said. Columns of figures, quarrels, harsh treatment, foul language. The screams of the pig being killed at three in the morning did not disturb her, she was so intent on concealing beneath her pillow the clog she had split while skipping.

When her aunt died, my mother plied her needle with the nuns. Consumption followed her even into the convent workroom. Her companions faded out one after the other. The rosier the color in the young girls' cheeks, the more death fed on them. Every older girl had a little one under her, and Berthe pushed everything she didn't like onto hers. My mother had sore throats and abscesses, she was constantly threatened by rickets, she would stoop to anything to sit in the visiting room. The walks were her nightmare. The angel was not managing things well. She loved her children and neglected them. Laure got some schooling in the country; Berthe learned nothing except hemstitching and embroidery. Fidéline prepared dainty dishes for others. Where were they to live during the summer vacation? Fidéline couldn't take in her children under the roof where she was living. Sorry years. What memories to sour the future.

You were given the most difficult pieces of embroidery to do, you had a beautiful voice, it soared above the rest when you sang the canticles. You were given the solo parts. A young nun of noble birth, you say, singled you out, she talked to you about heaven. They found you a situation. You were released from that sacrificial massacre of consumptive girls.

They found Berthe a place with a redheaded woman, jealous, very rich, whose husband deceived her. Berthe took care of the children, she listened to their domestic scenes after the years of Our Fathers and Holy Marys. Jealousy no longer held any secrets for her. She was pinched, she was beaten as soon as the husband, from afar, sniffed too hard at this orphanage flower. A second hell, a second unhappy couple. She was at liberty to leave, she left.

Berthe's second place began like a dream in Valenciennes. The gaiety, the receptions, the bustle of a Protestant family filled her with wonder. She laid the tables and lit the lamps in the garden. She drank in their parties. You lit the little lamps outside, you thought of yourself as God creating the fruits of a summer evening. Even now, the champagne froths up with a delicious seaside sound as you say: "What gaiety there was in that house. . . . It was always gay." One daughter, three sons. The whole town was aflutter when the daughter married an orphan found under a hedge in a basket. Henri was a good-natured fat boy. Emile, nicknamed the Prince d'Arembert by the staff, came back unexpectedly from Paris where he ran a bicycle factory as a hobby: the first bicycles. There was a dizzy whirlwind of preparations for his arrival. André. The one who fascinated you. Tall, slim, graceful, clear-skinned, dreamy-eyed, with ash-blond hair, a long nose. Not good-looking, but how attractive. All the women were crazy about him. I quote you. What breeding, what gestures . . . Oh what vicarious pleasure for an old woman of seventy-two as you peep back at the son of the house, at your aristocrat. . . . André reads, André is artistic, he strolls around London, he plays tennis, he drinks too many glasses of water when he is hot, the narrowness of his nasal cavities deprives him of oxygen. He burns up his health, his youth. His mother's thoughts are elsewhere: she keeps the whole district breathless with her conversation. She is a saint; while caring for the poor she forgets to think about her son. She is deaf.

Berthe, with her well-modulated voice, her energetic expression, her devotion, her tact, turns herself into a lady's maid and then into a lady's companion. There are calls from Paris every day. Berthe answers the telephone, she makes a note of the rises and falls on the stock exchange. The grumpy old man with his ninety-nine houses is pleased: his wife is deaf and now she hears everything. A storm breaks over the house on the Rue des Foulons. The daughter dies of a milk-fever, Henri fails to bring off his marriage, Emile is caught in the clutches of a courtesan, André is spitting blood. And you, without desiring him, without expecting anything, you suffer because he spends the evenings when there are no guests at the home of three schoolteachers, three women who live together. Their house casts a spell on him. That is all we shall ever know.

Vacation time again; every year the vacation comes and every year you wonder where to go. This freedom every summer is a scourge. They are quite willing: you can stay there in your maid's room while they take the air in Switzerland. You will be trapped in it. I am telling you your own past, I want to explain it to you, I want to cure you of it, I want to set your twenty-year-old heart at rest under a gardener's frame. You say: "He came home in the summer, that's how he made me pay for my board and lodging." I believe you, but it's hard to fathom. You could have resisted, you yielded. Why should you not have yielded? A bed is made for the sharing of pleasure. He fascinated you; don't excuse yourself when you excuse him. Being a woman, not wanting to be one. You were to avail yourself of that weapon later on. I tell you to your face, he was badly brought up, your son of the house. He shouldn't have crossed the threshold of your room. The drawing room was there for everyone, your room was your underling's retreat. There now, come here to my arms and say after me: "Why didn't he pass the time preening in the mirrors two flights down?" A little white apron, it made a change for him. If I could only find it, your little white apron . . . I'd eat it up. You, my mother, and your little white apron, you suffocate me. Your little apron, I am drinking in the smell of it near Marly now, near the plundered orchard, near our house—our house—while Fernand swims with his bundles of tobacco under the water. I want to heal your wound, Mother. Impossible. It will never close. He is your wound, and I am the picture of him.

My mother loved him. I can't deny it. How did she love him? Courageously, fiercely, wildly. It was the love of a lifetime, it was a victim's march to the sacrifice. I forgive him, she says again. He was sick, he depended on his parents, he was afraid of his father. When it had happened, he said: "Swear you'll leave town, my little one, swear you'll go away." She swore, she would have crawled at his feet, she thought she had sinned. He had his linen washed in London, but his soul was less refined. Cowardly, lazy, good for nothing. My mirror, Mother, my mirror. No, I want no part of you, I reject my heredity. God, let me write a beautiful sentence, just one. "Cowardly, lazy, good for nothing . . ." Always loving, always judging, always destroying.

André's mother loved my mother so much. . . . Why do you want to leave, Berthe? Why won't you tell me about it? Don't you like your room? You used to tell me things, now you don't any more. You lower your eyes. Why do you lower your eyes? Don't leave, Berthe. I'll double your wages. I'm so unhappy about all this.

You've refused to say anything to me now for more than an hour. For several months now, sainted lady, the neighbors have been calling her your confidante. Every day Berthe hears people in the street whispering: "We know what's coming, you're getting fatter." I'm proud of you, Mother, when you say: "I'd do it all over again!" You left for Arras with the money you had saved like a wise virgin. There is ecstasy in your voice when you say: "Just to see him was enough for me." The town is gentle, the town is warm between the half-open shutters, the sea is singing a few yards away from us. Time has done its work too well: I don't want to look any more at the hurricane of the years in your face.

Let's go back again, open your belly and take me back. You have told me so often about the misery of dragging around looking for a room, of not being able to find one because your waist was no longer slim. Let us suffer together once more. I wish I had never been that thing, a fetus. Always present, awake inside you. It was inside your belly that I lived your shame in those days, your sorrows. You sometimes say I hate you. Love has innumerable names. You live in me as I lived in you then. I saw you naked, I watched your most intimate ablutions. No mother can ever have been more abstract than you are. Your skin, your legs, your back when I wash you, the kiss I ask you for in the morning have no reality. How am I to make contact with you? Clouds, elm trees, wild rosebushes are matters of indifference to you. Don't die as long as I am still alive. Let's go back again, carry me as you carried me then, let's be afraid together of the rats you had to step over in the passage to your room. Your blood, Mother, the blood trickling as far as the staircase when I came out of you, the blood streaming from someone dying. The instruments, the forceps. I was your prisoner just as you were mine. Forgotten, abandoned beside the stream made by your blood when I arrived. It's normal enough, you were dying. It was a long time before they washed the mess off me. But the people who pointed their fingers at you, the people who refused you a bed before I was born, stayed glued to my skin.

*

I was born on April 7, 1907 at five in the morning. You registered me on the 8th. I should rejoice at having spent my first twenty-four hours outside the registers. On the contrary, my twenty-four hours without an official existence poisoned my life. I always supposed that my grandmother, who had given up her job as a *cordon bleu* cook, Clarisse my godmother, who had left her post as cook in the house where you had been seduced, I always supposed that all three of you were wondering whether a pillow pressed on my tomato-colored mug might not be preferable to the future I was forcing on you. I was registered and baptized, you sent for the doctor times without number, for attacks of bronchitis, pneumonia, inflammations of the lungs. I used to weigh no more than a little chicken, you tell me. I was born, and I cried. Night and day. How I could yell. . . . So there I was guilty already of too many tears on my bib. I listen and say nothing. All our money went on doctor's fees and prescriptions. A breath. I was just a mere breath of a thing, but my eyes were bright. My eyes were bright. Why was I not an abandoned owl? If I talk about the other's sickness, about the spitting of blood at the time I was conceived, you shrink back, you are revolted. He wore himself out with pleasure but they were a healthy family. So now I am responsible for being a pair of lungs using up all their savings. He perspired, he wet the sheets, but you never caught anything, you tell me. So I am doubly responsible.

I don't remember Arras. I never visited it, I never shall. I should see forceps in every store window, trickles of blood outside every laundry. My birth is not a matter for rejoicing. But I like writing Pas-de-Calais. My pen draws a line under it in hotel registers. Arras is a black hole in my memory. My mother has filled it for me. I made three women suffer with my crying, my shrieks, my bouts of sickness. ("I sinned," you often say. I too sinned, my sin was being delicate.) My mother watched, she spied and listened at the window, she loved ever more intensely in the half light. Night fell, and she waited. Clarisse and Fidéline were critical of this love that would not wear out. The angel Fidéline was awakening; she wanted to tell his saintly mother everything, to raise a scandal. But the saintly mother died of a cerebral fever. I was asleep, my mother heard the sound of a carriage at last, heard the wheels stop, the door slam, the footsteps on the stairs and, in no great hurry, along the passage with the rats. A gentleman in evening dress came in, he chucked mother and child under their chins, he didn't want to give them his illness. My mother glows with pride when she says: "He didn't kiss you once. Do you hear? Not once!" She was always a champion of caution. The time—the flat watch is drawn from the fob. "I have an engagement this evening, little one, I must go." She has to ask him: the angel Fidéline would be angry, she does not understand ecstasy. She asks, he gives her two louis, he vanishes, the carriage rolls away more lightly than it came. I saw him, that was enough, the rest didn't interest me, she muses. Sometimes I suspect her of being frigid. I know nothing about their relationship, about their conversations in Valenciennes, in her little maid's room. "All that never interested me," she declares with a tone of superiority. A woman with a single passion, an amazon with severed breasts. The head on fire, the belly full of ice.

[I am the unrecognized daughter of a son of good family, therefore I must wear a medallion on a slim gold chain, embroidered dresses and long pantalettes, I must have a fair skin and silky hair in order to compete with the rich children in the town when my grandmother takes me to the park.] The angel has become a nanny. In our room: near-destitution—my chamber pot becomes a salad bowl at the beginning of every meal; in public: the façade. Vanity of vanities? No. My mother and my grandmother are intelligent women, they have character; they had both been crushed at the age of twenty, and they are attempting to ward off ill luck with talismans when they tie ribbons on their little girl. The park is the arena, I am their little torero, I must vanquish every well-fed infant in the town. The deputy prefect's wife asked why my hair shone so, what they did to it. My mother gave me three hundred brush strokes, relentlessly, three hundred and sixty-five days a year. My head sinks forward, that is my first memory.

It is terrible for them: I am always unlucky. I go down the staircase to bring up the newspaper, I fall on the shards of glass from a broken bottle. I am always falling, falling. Today my scars are pretty, they are all elliptical in shape. A mysterious insect . . . I'm sorry, reader, I must interrupt myself here. Shall I ever make myself remember my life at the age of five, at the age of four? I see a staircase, narrow and steep, I see pieces of broken glass at the bottom of the stairs, I see . . . I see nothing beyond that. The memory of my fall and my hurt has been spared me. A mysterious insect stung me on the leg, the doctor came every day, he ordered hot compresses, hundreds of hot compresses. The sickness was as mysterious as the insect. The bone was about to show through when an old woman came into town and saved me with a country remedy. Clarisse had gone back to her cookstoves, my mother decided I should go to boarding school. I was five. Why, tell me why? Was I as much of an encumbrance as all that? I don't remember my mother leaving me in the establishment and thank heaven for that privilege. I do remember my grief, my stamping on the tiled floor after she had gone. Screams, tears, groans, those days were to be an icy compress, always too heavy and too cold. The headmistress was afraid I would go into convulsions; she sent a telegram and my mother took me back home.

She once gave me her photographs of him. It is a strange moment when you gaze questioningly at an unknown figure in a picture and the picture, the unknown figure, is your nerves, your joints, your spinal column. Born of a father you never knew. I look at it. Who is talking to me, who answering? The photographer. His signature is on the back of the photograph, he gives his name as a present to a man who wouldn't give his own. It's a beautiful name: Robert de Greck. He gives him the Gare du Flon. He gives him Lausanne with his telephone number in brackets. He specifies: "The negatives are on file." The photographer is lavish with his bounty. I have received No. 19233. It is as though the infinite were changing into a top hat full of scraps of paper to draw from. The heart of the unknown man that beats inside my heart has a number. The number is 19233. That is not all: specialist in full-length portraits and non-fading carbonized enlargements. Thank you, photographer. Eight years old, is he? Or ten? That sweet face, with what precision the limpid eyes gaze at some dream. The mouth is half open, the dream is in the mouth too. He is a little boy weighing almost nothing and intent on his dreams. He can walk on primroses without crushing them. Sitting on the table, on the photographer's fringed shawl, left leg bent up under the right, the calf well formed without being fat, the knee round, very lovable, the boot tied tight, the sock turned down over it, hands abandoned in childish relaxation, fingers slender and supple, nails standing out from their tips as though a manicurist were already tending them, this elegant, unreal little boy is dressed in a white sailor suit with a sailor collar of dark silk covered with white polka dots. The point of the collar, the striped shirt front are finished off with a bow of ribbon. I love this little boy and his absence from himself, I love his anemone fragility. I would have stared him out if I had been the same age as he. One cold, sick, despairing, lonely Sunday, I burned the photographs together with his death certificate.

*

The angel Fidéline, tired of her daughter's magnanimity, grew threatening: the savings bank deposit books were melting away. We left Arras for Valenciennes. I remember almost nothing. A window —on what floor I wonder?—I used to look out of often. My mother agreed to act. She went back to the great house, now lugubrious, and got twenty thousand francs out of the grumpy old man, which I was to receive when I came of age. An agent was to pay her the interest on it: a hundred and fifty francs a quarter. André was beyond being scolded by then. He was a condemned man. 1913. I attached myself to Fidéline while my mother, now on the sales staff of a store, wore a uniform from early in the morning till late at night. She complained of the carpets, of how hot they made her feet, of her legs which wouldn't get stronger. I didn't eat, I didn't want to eat. The whole of my early childhood was a long revulsion against meals, all of them dramas. You're not hungry. You ought to be hungry. You must be hungry. If you don't eat you'll be sick like him, if you don't eat you won't be able to go out, if you don't eat you'll die. I'll knock your head off if you don't eat. I had nothing to say. I suffered and made them suffer my lack of appetite. My mother was haunted by the idea of tuberculosis. The sight of her eyes, hardened by her terror, filled me with panic. She wanted to conquer my ill health by main force. I remember: I am six, I am crying, I am sobbing all alone in a hole; I'm not hungry, I don't want to be. My mother is grinding her teeth, she is roaring. I am in the cage, the wild animal is outside. She is roaring because she doesn't want to lose me. It took me a long time to understand that. How can I lift my fork to my mouth when she looks at me that way? She frightens me, she cows me; I lose myself in her eyes. I am six, I drink in her youth, her stern beauty.

She went out to work, Fidéline's long blue apron was covered with beautiful clouds: balls of silk. I hunted for them in her apron pockets. Every day, year after year, untiringly, Fidéline made me my midday snack. I entertained her with my silly laughter as she stood patiently over the thick pancake watching it turn brown. I remember our escapades when my mother wasn't there. We used to walk through the market. The bunches of various flowers, dotted among the bunches of thyme and bay, filled me with wonder. Fidéline swapped village gossip with the peasant women; I stroked the cocks, the hens, the pigeons, the rabbits, all very much alive in their covered baskets. I preferred the chervil spread out on paper to the chervil flopping over onto a plump lettuce. The spinach leaves filled me with the same surprise I was to feel later when confronted with the

Douanier Rousseau's jungles. The parsley frothed laughingly in my eyes, the offers, the repartee of the women at the stalls with their black straw boaters sang in my ears. Two cocks in separate crates wanted to fight, a hen put down on the sidewalk dropped off to sleep, an apprentice knocked against a basket of eggs, the peasant women called across to one another. You're in the country, Fidéline would say to me. I believed her without really believing her. The country is not a marketplace. If my mother arrived unexpectedly she took all the color from the vegetables, from the feathers, from the fruit. The white rabbits became dowdy beside my mother's collars and cuffs. The town brought a chill to the countrywomen, the great lady was emerging from the park gates.

I return to my grandmother's blue apron. My terror when I woke up was intense almost to the point of physical pain and loss of consciousness. I would wake up, I would see the apron folded over the back of the chair, I would shriek: "Why is the butcher's boy living with us? It's because of him grandma's gone away." I howled. My grandmother came into the room with a broom, she held out her arms. We loved each other in passionate silence. She reassured me. It's my apron, she would say, but it's the same color as the butcher boy's when he brings the brains, the chops. . . . He'll be here at eleven. You can look at the material of his apron then, you can feel it if you want.

"Pick some, pick some," I used to say to Fidéline as dusk fell, soft all around us with the softness of new bread in the mouth. Fidéline picked the privet flowers from between the railings, she gave them to me, she whispered: we're not supposed to. What would people think? I crushed two or three of the privet flowers between my hands, they fell on the sidewalk, I sniffed at my hollowed palms. It was no longer the town, it wasn't the country. I smelled my hands again, I looked at the flowers still intact between their leaves, candles of white lace in some places, turning yellow in others. We were going to evening service.

My grandmother spent many long hours of her life in churches, especially in Saint Nicholas near the Protestant chapel. What a capacity children have for boredom, and how boredom draws things out. It was a long morning for me when I went with her to High Mass, a long evening when I sat beside her through Vespers. I loved the rapid, mechanical movement of her lips when she prayed, but not the explanations she gave me of the crib before Christmas. I wondered how the donkey and the cow I had glimpsed in the cattle market could get so small and hard like that. Jesus, about whom I knew nothing at all, seemed to me too naked, too sickly. Too exposed there on the straw. Alas, Fidéline sitting there beside me flew away. I put my hand on her jacket, on the long skirt falling down to her feet, Fidéline didn't move. Fidéline didn't look at me. Where was she? If I called to her, very gently: "grandma, grandma," she didn't answer me. She was sewing her prayers together quicker and quicker with her lips. She had closed her eyes. I looked for her amid the vaulted arches, the columns, the galleries, when I raised my head. The maze of architecture brought me back to Fidéline. When would she finish telling her rosary? I called again to the absent woman brushing against me. Fidéline opened her eyes, then shut them again immediately without scolding me. I recognized her at last in her blackened fingernails, real, badly cut, and felt consoled.

Once I tried to separate her clasped hands. She fixed me with a gaze so reproachful and so sad that I clasped my own hands and moved my lips in an attempt to copy her. I had to suffer the discomfort of my boredom patiently. I learned to observe, to follow, to listen, to look. This world of burning candles had its distractions to offer. I made bets: the flame on the left will waver before the one on the right. I checked which was my left arm and which my right before making the bet. I would lose, I would win. Sometimes all the flames performed the same erotic somersault at the same time. A burned-out, flattened candle, petrified in its own tears, took me another rung further down into my boredom; but if a pious lady came and stuck up a new candle, dominating all the others with its proud lancelike flame, then I rose back to the surface. The opaque play of light and shadow, the somber clothes of the women at prayer, the cassock of a priest disappearing into the vestry, the long hand of an Abbé straightening the curtain of a confessional, the comings and goings of the congregation, both men and women, the meaningful squeak of a chair, the tenacity of a stained glass window, of its colors and its warmth, the feet of a saint riveted into the plaster, the coughing, the reverberation of the footsteps, the holy sounds from the altar allowed me to go on existing until the final showing of the Host. The Mass, the gestures of the priests and choirboys, the litany, the singing in Latin . . . My theater when I was six.

I covered a crate with a white cloth, I decorated it with lace, I arranged vases on it and pebbles, my relics; I invented my own Latin, I sang it, I chanted, I prostrated myself, I bowed my head, I opened and closed my grandmother's prayerbook, I dirtied it, I got grease on it, I tore it without meaning to. I moved forward and stepped back, I stretched out my arms, I blessed the air in our room with unctuous signs of the cross. I didn't recite the Our Father or the Hail Mary that my grandmother had taught me. I preferred my own gibberish, my own *vobiscums,* which I drew out for as long as I could. In the distance, behind me, I could hear Fidéline and my mother complaining about life, about the pâté being overcooked, about the puff pastry, about how thoughtless Clarisse was about money. I sang, I recited, I intoned, I chanted louder still. I wanted to be the priest, the church, the chants, the words, the sacred gestures as an actress wants to be tragic and sincere. I took off my vestments (fur stoles or just rags), I went over to the table, I spun my plate, I played at being a drummer with two forks.

Outside, I was always unsteady, I was afraid of everything; outdoors I played alone because I was shy, the sight of the other children playing in groups crushed me. I would run up suddenly and hide in my grandmother's skirt, I would breathe in the musty odor of the cloth, I burrowed into it. I ran off, I picked flowers, always blue, calm, intense, downy, imperious flowers. They are indispensable in the flowerbeds of public parks. In this way I took my mother's eyes back again from the park keeper. My grandmother scolded me and stuck the flowers back in the places I had filched them from. It was the time when licorice was all the rage. The children were all licking the powder from their palms or the backs of their hands, or else they were drinking the liquid out of mugs. I envied them. They all liked licorice. I didn't like licorice. I'll give you a drop of pernod, my grandmother murmured. One drop. No more. I threw myself into her arms. Though bastards are monsters, they are ocean deeps of tenderness. Ageless Fidéline, without a woman's face and body, Fidéline my long priest, I shall always be betrothed to you. (Every night was a wedding night when I nested in the hollow of your neck. Your hand in the darkness: the beautiful hand of the beautiful young girl who sat embroidering at her window. With my feet in your nightgown you drew your thighs together: you made nests for me. You said: "Say your prayers." My prayers were just listening to the imperceptible sputtering of your lips as they moved in prayer. The tick-tock of the clock grew softer, it deferred to the silence of our love. I listened to your breathing, my ear cherished your unreal breast.)

Sometimes I was unfaithful to my grandmother during our walks.

I would stop and let her walk on ahead, I would bend down and do up my shoelace, quickly I would pick up a stone or a pebble, then run after her and give her my free hand. When the stone or the pebble was warm I let it fall on something soft: the grass or sand. Then I could breathe with the satisfaction of having had an existence of my own.

They decided I should go to day school. They thought a private school would be better than a public school. I don't remember how I learned to read and write. I remember how sad I felt when I left my grandmother, twice every day, at the foot of the solemn staircase, in front of the two open doors; and how my spirits soared, how happy I felt when I saw her again. Are your feet cold? Were your feet cold in school? You must tell me if your feet get cold, Fidéline insisted every day, at noon and again in the evening, from the day school all the way back to where we lived. Even if they were warm I answered: yes, they're cold, just to please her. We would get back to the room, she would take off my shoes and rub my feet with her long hands wrinkled with work, then take down the socks hanging to dry over the stove. Is your throat still sore? Does your ear still ache, my mother would ask if I was unwell. She worried and blamed me for it.

I didn't answer, I never said I felt sick. I suffered in silence. I didn't care about earning good marks, I had no communication with the others: my mother's and grandmother's worries cut me off from the schoolmistress and the other students. I didn't understand them but they stayed in my mind all the time. Often I lost myself, I forgot myself. I was six, I was an old woman. A centenarian, already disillusioned without having suffered, without having experienced anything. Go and look at yourself in the mirror, my mother would say during lunch. I would do as she said, I would see myself in the glass with my hat on my head. Eating with a hat on or without . . . I saw no difference. I took it off in a vague dream. "Are you always going to live in a dream? That's not what life is," my mother declared. Half an hour later I put my hat back on to go to school. I remember my slate pencil, its slow screech across the slate in its whitewood frame. The pencil taught me to write as it painfully traced out its gray letters. I liked the plain black slates better than the ones with red squares. Learning to read means my index finger bent against the letter, the word, the sentence; learning to write means the ungiving stone pencil, adamant between the pincers of its holder.

*

Now we have moved into the neighborhood called Les Glacis, outside of town, a long way from the streetcars and the markets. We are living in one of ten houses all stuck together. We have furniture, dishes, a garden of our own, sheds and rabbits; we look out on the plain of Mons, the soldiers on horseback who come there to train, the bugle blown by an infantryman in the evening; we have everything. Why must I go to school, why? A gentleman wearing pince-nez has lunch with us every Sunday, my mother is humming and embroidering an immense window blind; Fidéline often takes me out onto the plain where I learn to roll a hoop. We're alone there, the trampled grass is sad. Often I stop, I look at our house, our door, our windows, I wonder if I shall see the infantryman who blows the bugle when the layers of darkness come down one after another. I never see him. Fidéline follows the tracks made by the horses' hooves while I run with my hoop. It's been raining, I stumble in a hole made by a horse's hoof. Fidéline picks me up, she shouts for help. My arm is hanging down, my arm is broken. Three months in plaster. My elbow, after the daily attempts at learning to use it again—so painful that the neighbors run away when I scream—will never go back in its proper place again. That's my first memory, of a pain in my flesh.

When I'm better we go looking for plantains across the plain. I drink too much water at the drinking fountain in the recreation ground, I come home, I have measles. I'm ashamed when I'm sick, I feel I'm being naughty to annoy them. My mother says: "It's never going to end. What have we done to deserve it?" I have two consolations after all the wrapping up and the hot compresses: tiddlywinks and knitting. My mother scorns games. She takes care of her child from the brushing of her hair to seeing she has her tonic: that's all she cares about. But Fidéline is my sister when we play at tiddlywinks. On Sunday my mother sends us to the movies. We like the less expensive movie house in the working-class neighborhood best, but Fidéline buys two tickets for the balcony. I press myself against her or else stand up; the little girls and boys in the downstairs seats terrify and attract me; it is an orgy of clattering seats banging up and down, and impatient shouts; it is a smoking den. The scent of oranges is heavy on the air. A pianist, frenzied, romantic, pathetic, wild, martial, languorous, swooning according to the sequence, begins to play; the lights go down, I try to see the faces of the musicians, their hands beneath the lighted screen. "Synopsis of the preceding episodes." I read it all out in a whisper to my grandmother because she can't read quickly and her glasses aren't very good. I read out all the misfortunes of the *Two Orphans,* all the exploits of the forbidding *Judex.* Charlie Chaplin upsets me. I find those startled eyes under the bowler hat so attractive, and their unwitherable freshness as the cream pies squash against his face. The more the audience laughs the more I frown. At these moments my grandmother's face remains quite impassive. We discuss the sad fate of the *Two Orphans* as we leave the building. We encounter the hordes of children. They are fighting, they are tearing down next week's posters in their enthusiasm, they terrify me and attract me again. They are free, they are wild.

Fidéline takes my hand, we fly away over the carpet of dead leaves along the boulevard, we turn off along by the side of the school where I shall be going next day. The Sunday silence of the boulevard impresses me because we've just come from the movies. Someone is playing the piano, I remain rooted to the spot. It sounds different from the music in the movie house. I can tell who is playing because of where the window is: it's our headmistress, Mlle. Rozier, practicing in her apartment. I let go of Fidéline, I press my ear against the wall, I listen. I listen so intently it almost makes me weep. I confuse the majesty, the sweetness, the dignity of our headmistress with the tones of the piano, with her piano playing. I go back to my grandmother, I ask: "Do you like it?"

"I don't know," answers Fidéline. "Is it music? I don't know." She smiles, she doesn't want to discourage me. "You can go on listening," she says. I throw myself into the folds of her skirt which is like a cassock, I enfold her thin thighs in my arms, I extricate myself, I run away again, I give myself up to the sounds from the invisible instrument.

*

1914–1915–1916. I no longer go to the day school. We have moved. We are living on the Avenue Duquesnoy five minutes from Marly. Fidéline, who caught a chill in the cellar during a bombardment, is not properly looked after by the only doctor who has not been called up. She is dying. The man with the pince-nez is at the front, my mother without money. I am blooming and growing stronger. I have become a little woman and a little girl of the streets. I hurl myself every evening into the mahogany bed on the first floor, my mother pulls me out again, I weep with the passion of a woman torn from her lover's arms. Fidéline, my grandmother, you will always be my betrothed in your mahogany bed with your failing lungs. The doctor treated you with ice; he should have kept you warm. Neighbors came by bringing German officers asking about billetting. My mother agreed to have some billetted on her too: it brought in money. I interpreted for her: I don't know how, but I'd learned a little German.

I slept in the dining room; there was only a partition wall separating me from Fidéline. Her attacks of coughing, the noise of the soldiers' boots on the ceiling used to wake me up. I would ask myself with terror if I should see Fidéline again next morning. My mother sat up with her, she came and went along the passage. Every night was a threat. When I woke up I listened to hear if my grandmother was coughing. She was coughing, she was alive. I was no longer allowed into her room, I wasn't even to say good morning to her through the half-open door. I could see the pillows, the gray braid of hair resting on her chest, her flannelette nightgown. Her hands lay too quietly on the sheet. When the door of her room closed again, I saw Fidéline in the cup of beef tea, in the little bottle, in the saucer, in the doctor when he came in. Clarisse arrived, but that didn't make me happy. There were two women nursing Fidéline and her illness grew worse. I stayed awake, I stood on my bed, hoping the partition wall would provide help or revelations. One night I heard noises and people coming and going. I heard my mother. It's all over, she said to Clarisse. I got out of bed, I made my way on tiptoe out to the half-open door. What was all over? The pillows, the braid, the nightgown, the lowered eyelids, the hands lying on the sheet were all the same. I went back again. "What is it that's all over?" I asked the darkness. I could hear the water jug, the basin. Why wasn't she coughing? I didn't see Fidéline again. I was nine, she was fifty-three. The day that Fidéline was buried, this I do remember, it was raining. I didn't cry, I felt no grief. I chattered to my rag doll. Fidéline left the house surrounded by a sea of umbrellas. I leaned out from a second-floor window and watched her go.

Five years later I realized that she was dead, that I loved her passionately, that I should never see her again. The cypress beside her grave filled me with despair. Every time I went there, I thought it looked like a torch flaming with anger.

She was spoiling me and her death saved me. She spoiled me so much that when I dared to play with a little boy or another little girl

I expected them to handle me with hands like warm wax. If they spoke to me harshly, if they snatched a toy away from me, the tears rose to my eyes: I confused harshness and brusqueness with hostility. (I was alone, I had the whole world against me when the other boys and girls became impatient with my fragility and walked away.) I began sobbing when they laughed, and their laughter redoubled. I was losing myself in my grandmother's black skirt, alone, sheltered, bound by no limits. At the age of five, at the age of six, at the age of seven, I used to begin weeping sometimes without warning, simply for the sake of weeping, my eyes wide open to the sun, to the flowers. As soon as Fidéline stopped talking, turned away or gossiped with a woman of her own age, the ground swayed drunkenly beneath my feet. I would sit down beside her on the bench, I wanted to feel an immense grief inside me, and it came. Each tear, each sob took me further from the world. Fidéline died and I found my feet.

*

I hung around, I rang doorbells, I went off with boys, I pressed my hand over the spout of the drinking fountain and sprayed the passers-by with a white, arching jet. I educated myself from the books of songs that Céline or Estelle swapped with other girls. Don't open it, whatever you do don't open it, Céline said in the falling dusk as she put a book different from the others into my hand. I was to take it, hidden under my pinafore, to one of their friends. The mission took my breath away. I went into the overgrown orchard at the side of our house: the orchard where Aimé Patureau used to sit on the top of a tree whistling and singing the love songs from the books to my mother: *I met you that day . . . without a care . . . and you didn't try to capture me . . . but this despair . . . this burning pain . . . for you are fair . . . are bonds that will not set me free. . . . Will you not come back again . . .* ? I went into the tallest weeds I could find, I opened the exercise book. A woman was telling about her wedding night, she was comparing the sexual organ of a man to an eel inside a woman. I didn't understand; I shut the strange book, I fell flat on my stomach on top of it. I couldn't imagine it at all, or I imagined it too well. I could see the eels on the fishmongers' stall; I envisaged the serpentine virility beneath the trousers, writhing down from the navel to the ankle. My fist tapped against my temple, and every time I whispered: it's impossible, the cover of the book replied: it is possible. I emerged from the weeds, I ran until I reached the home of the girl waiting for the book. Her hands were trembling as much as mine when I handed it to her.

I often put my fingers down under the bedclothes and stroked them up and down between my lips; later on I often twisted the hair around them with one finger as I lay in bed, reading, before going to sleep. I continued to do so without any thought of achieving satisfaction, until the age of twenty-eight. It was a pastime, it reassured me. I smelled my fingers, I breathed in the extract of my being, to which I attached no value.

Aimé Patureau, a boy of seventeen with a pretty round face, with sandy puttees round his calves, hurt his foot. The wound became infected, he stayed at home, he lifted his window curtain and called me. Seeing him alone in his parents' house while they were out working, seeing his leg stretched out on a chair in the silence of the dining room rendered me speechless. We talked together while I stood there beside his bad leg. His hand moved lightly up inside my skirt. Aimé Patureau was running his fingernails up and down against my skin with the grace of a page as the country clock on the mantelpiece sounded the half-hours, the quarter-hours. I looked at him, he looked at me. I could read nothing on his face, he could read nothing on mine since I was not feeling anything. The sin was the burning color on my cheeks. My mother rang the bell and came in with a wild look on her face, furious. She questioned Aimé Patureau: "Why are you keeping her here so long?"

"We were talking, she was keeping me company," the boy replied looking at my mother calmly.

I left with her, I sensed that her mind was still not at rest. "Your cheeks are all red," she said accusingly as we walked home. "What did he do to you?"

"Nothing, mother, nothing."

She asked me the same question again and again. I didn't tell. It was a secret, a complicity The stroking fingers helped me grow up. I was a field with two paths through it. I ran to visit him again as soon as I could: with his eyes in mine, with his shirt against the fabric of my pinafore, I saw his face, the face of a sensitive doll when he sang for my mother or pulled apart the branches as he rocked in a pear tree, close to my own.

Every morning I cleaned the ashes out of the stove. I became formless, mechanical, as cold as the ashes themselves as soon as I began the task. I used a sieve, I shoveled all the cinders out onto a piece of paper, I squashed them, I crushed them. With lips pressed together and gritted teeth, I shook out the gray remains. One Sunday morning in winter my mother was not in our bed when I got up. I shoveled the ashes out of the stove, I heard two people laughing on the ground floor, in the room where Fidéline had died: one of them was my mother, the other was Juliette, a former cook. She often came to see my mother. They would talk about my mother's seducer, about his parents, about his home, where they had been in service together. The wall of Juliette's café was next to the main gate of their garden. The barman did odd jobs for the family. My mother, avid for gossip, desperate for news, would put Juliette through an interrogation. I could hear them laughing. Suddenly, a doubt. Still holding the poker, I left the stove. I listened through the partition wall, the wall through which I used to count Fidéline's coughing fits. Yes, it was my mother, but Juliette had the voice of a man. I went on sieving the ashes.

My mother would put on her clothes beside the mahogany bed upstairs, she would call out: "Have you got your overcoat? Have you got your cape?" I would hear her beautiful, slightly hoarse voice and feel a delicious sensation inside me as I recognized night mist on the little kitchen window. We used to sleep pressed against each other—her buttocks, which were never large, in the hollow of my body, between my belly and my thin, nine-year-old thighs—because it was cold in the room. My mother would come down dressed more poorly than before 1914, her hair in a kerchief, a lock emerging over each steel blue eye and one over the solidly planted nose. She would light the stove, we would eat breakfast beside its crackle and roar, I would take off the topcoat that my father's lady friends had given me: an exlusive model. I wondered what little girl had worn it. I played at being someone else when I slipped my arms into the sleeves, when I buttoned it up, when I pulled the collar around my neck. I forgot about it while I was running around the town, while I was waiting in line for my ration of Floraline and other food substitutes, or when they lifted me up so that I could sign my mother's name in the Allowance register. My mother wouldn't go into the town anymore. She gossiped with the neighbors for hours on end. One day we found some money on the table when we came home.

"One of the ladies your father knows must have left this money," my mother said.

Our kitchen in winter: the warmest, the gayest, the most popular in the neighborhood, the one most filled with songs and clamoring voices. The stove grew white hot, the Floraline crêpes turned in the air, each visitor slid her pancake from the frying pan in turn, the bowl of dark brown sugar was passed from hand to hand around the stove. We built a defiant wall of gaiety between ourselves and the cold, the wind, the frost, the war. The only child amidst all these adults, I was never bored. I was a backward adult surrounded by adults in full possession of their faculties. I saw each month's blood on the linen pads, my mother gave me lessons about reality: I shall return to them later. I shared all the emotional upheavals of a young girl who lived two doors down from us with her parents. Estelle used to preen herself at their upstairs window when she had done her chores. In the evening she made her escape. I used to rub her mother's back; jumping and dancing up and down to make up for my lack of strength, I massaged her back with my tightly clenched fists. She used to give me a penny. The young girl with the round face who lived for the night, for men, thought she was pregnant. I didn't understand what that meant, but one day, in the hall of our house, I understood that she was waiting for the blood and that it was a terrifying wait. Estelle walked up and down, she kept looking at her underwear. A hundred times, two hundred times, she wiped herself as she walked. She wanted me to look at the white linen pad all the time. "I'll buy you a bag of pralines if it comes," she said. She took my hand, she guided it over the dry hair that felt like brittle hay, she forced my fingers inside the folds of her flesh. To her, everything was good. I didn't tell my mother about it: it wasn't important. Buying pralines during the war, sheer folly. The period began in the hall, she made me look at the reddened cloth. Next day I ate the pralines with slow enjoyment. Estelle wouldn't eat a single one.

As we sat at breakfast, my mother would talk to me about the unpleasant side of life. Each morning she made me a terrible gift: the gift of suspicion and mistrust. All men were swine, men had no hearts. She stared at me with such intensity as she made this statement that I would wonder whether perhaps I wasn't a man. There wasn't a single one among them to redeem the race as a whole. To take advantage of you, that was their aim. I must get that into my head and never forget it. Swine. All swine. My mother still remembered a fair she had been to in Artres as a child where there was a peddler bouncing a pink sugar pig at the end of a thread. He was saying: "There you are, ladies, that's a man for you." My mother explained everything to me. I had been warned, I had no excuse for making a mistake. Men follow women, I mustn't let them catch me. I listened and if I played with the crumbs on the table my mother let me know with a look that I must pay attention. I folded my arms, the world was a path along which one must walk, without ever stopping; if the shadow of a man appeared, it must be exorcized by walking on alone, faster and faster—always alone, always faster, the indispensable mechanism of the onanist. From each side of the path snickering bushes reached out and clawed at you. My mother explained it all with vague precision. To follow a man, to listen to him, to give in to him . . . What did that mean, give in to him? Not to see the blood come, to get bigger and bigger till a baby came out of you and fell into the gutter with you. After such a lesson sin is impossible: I had been warned. My mother had surpassed herself in courage, in energy, in magnanimity when she had left André's home. She could not forgive men as a whole for what she had done for one man.

I treated the same subject in a different way in *Ravages* and in *L'Asphyxie*. I mingled the truth with fiction. After my grandmother's death, my mother tried to turn a little girl into an intimate friend. Alas for her and alas for myself, I became the receptacle of her pain, her fury, her bitterness. Children remember things without understanding them: they are oceans of good will drinking in an ocean of words. I suffered my mother's humiliating experience too early; I dragged it behind me as an ox drags its plow. The wrong done inside her had become a universal wrong. She suffered in both past and present when she said that I too had no heart. I retained her sermons, the pictures she painted, too well. But my innocence seized on the deviousness of memory and wreaked its revenge; until the age of nineteen I believed that women gave birth through the navel.

Berthe, my mother, I was your husband before your marriage. I scraped away the earth in gardens with my nails, I stole potatoes and green peas, I made light of the clinging brambles. You married, you bought me all the nicest things in the candy shop, you repaid me for the pale emeralds in the pea pods I brought you. Why did I steal? Because we were poor and food was rationed. Robbing the ground with one's nails, stealing from the earth what it gives in profusion, was a fever the color of wine lees, a deep excitement of the heart. My joy, my determination as I left on foot for the fields of Marly. My basket, my knife . . . moving forward at a crouch, looking for them, finding them, forcing the knife blade around the root, piling up the dandelions in the basket, what a frenzy of delight. Our rabbits would feast like kings.

*

I couldn't close my mouth the first time I saw him. I came in out of the cold and the darkness. Gazing at him was an intolerable pleasure. I looked at the kerosene lamp. I lowered my eyes, I could still see him. The light accentuated the deadness of the grass encrusted on the pale beige canvas of his shoe. The grass was asleep. For heaven's sake sit down, said my mother. I obeyed. I was obliged to leave the silky eyelashes. Stop shaking your knees like that, said my mother. I went back to him. The nonchalance of his crossed legs, of his drooping arm, of his long, immaterial, tanned hand, of his absent fingers holding the cigarette. His slim body, also nonchalant, also absent, clothed in a suit of gray mist. He remained silent much of the time, he stayed hidden and listening behind his long lashes. A person absent from his beauty is doubly beautiful. He recrossed his legs and considered me an instant from a long way off. I had a thankless face and my legs were so thin that the boys used to call me "Chicken Legs"; I savored our visitor more than another child would have done. Ignorant as I was, I learned the tan on his face as I would have learned the colors of the spectrum. He was a man of twenty. I had to keep a close watch on the corner of his mouth to see if the last petal of adolescence was about to fall. I memorized the curving line of his shoulder. The darkness had taken all the color from his eyes. His lips were the pale brick color of our factory chimneys.

He's a smuggler, my mother explained the next day. I didn't ask her what the word meant. I asked her when he worked. At night, only at night, she answered. He swims across under the water with bales of tobacco. He's going to change here, he'll get himself warmed up again then leave. My mother was not a gambler. She refused to store the tobacco in our cellar despite Fernand's tempting offers. Estelle, the girl who had had the late period, fell wildly in love with the indifferent Adonis.

My mother often announced after breakfast: "We've got enough food for today, but tomorrow . . ." She would empty her purse out onto the table; I was fascinated by this money and by the money we wouldn't have next day. Grief-stricken, intrigued, oppressed, I would eat bread and lard with powdered sugar on top. "Next day something turned up," my mother says now. I stole big cabbages from the backs of the German carts at the risk of a lash from the driver's whip. My mother would give them away: cabbage didn't agree with her. I was upset. Our poverty must have delighted and obsessed us. Eiderdown, explosion, bombardments. We would go down into the cellar. You hugged me against you. You were all I had, mother, and you wanted me to die with you.

*

I don't remember her name. Let us call her the Whirlwind. I remember her grandfather's name. Caramel was always sitting on the top step of their bar and we used to scratch his head. The Whirlwind. Face like a horse. Painful whinnies when she became excited. She kept her bar well. I used to pick the greens for her rabbits and wash the tiled floor; I could go into the bar whenever I wanted. She taught me the deaf-and-dumb alphabet. I was fascinated by the performance that went on when other deaf-mutes came to visit. A great deal of sputtering despite the absence of voices. She taught me to dance on the sawdust to the sound of the mechanical piano, which she couldn't hear. The piano would blare out the end of the refrain, I would wind the handle, we would begin again. Children peered in at us admiringly because they weren't allowed inside. A customer would appear, the Whirlwind would let go of me, I would run out, flying along one sidewalk, then along the other, still following the rhythm of the music, still living the sickening rise and fall of the refrain, the renewed onslaughts of the hammers. Every Saturday evening I had my set task. I stood beside the piano on a raised platform and turned the handle again; I never grew weary of watching the perforated cardboard unwind. Waltzes, schottisches, polkas, mazurkas . . . a firmament of music with stars pricked out in pinholes. I ran my free hand lovingly over the flowers painted on the wood, entwined and smooth to the touch. They broke into flower as I listened; they closed again in sleep when the piano fell silent.

*

A half-wit fell in love with the woman who lived next door to him. His name was Cataplame. Slightly built, her face concealed by freckles, her hair like a russet mist about her head, and with a boldly proportioned body, she lived alone near the overgrown orchard. Her husband was fighting at the front, her house was the best kept in the neighborhood. She would shake her duster out of the bedroom window from morning till night. Ungainly Cataplame was the eldest son of a poverty-stricken family and fascinatingly ugly. Lost in his striped shirt with its top button missing, in pants that were always a greenish color, as though his buttocks and thighs were covered with a layer of loving moss, with his oddly decorated fly and his shoes trodden down at the back, Cataplame had difficulty in using his powerful and muffled voice. It was a voice that came to you from the depths of an abyss. As I hung about in the orchard I saw him begin his approach tactics. Mme. Armande would shake her duster, he would run over, he would beg, again, again. . . . Mme. Armande was giving way, the dust fell on Cataplame's head. They laughed together. He clapped his hands, jumped up and down, scratched himself and shook the orchard fence.

Days and evenings passed. Mme. Armande no longer showed herself, Cataplame didn't take his eyes from the window. He was seized by hiccups, shaken by sneezes, nipped by lice. His beautiful, slow-moving fish-eyes were wedded to the windows and curtains. He emitted inarticulate cries. The passers-by shrugged their shoulders. Suddenly Cataplame was dancing from side to side like a pair of scales; he danced, he caught and swallowed a firefly. I opened the little window of our kitchen, I went out into the garden, I prowled around the orchard, then along the road; I could see him wherever I went, standing there with stubborn patience. Some girls asked me if I wanted to play hopscotch. I declined the invitation to their silly games. One morning my mother sent me around to Cataplame's mother with a piece of fabric to be hemmed on her sewing machine. He didn't see me, he didn't hear me despite the noise of my clogs. A fine rain was filling him with hope and despair. Clothed in a potato sack with openings for his neck and arms, Cataplame was waiting. A window opened. Cataplame shuddered and raised his eyes. He tore the sack open from top to bottom and, with naked chest and proffered shoulder, he jumped as high as he could. He gave passionate animal cries. The duster fell on his head. He seized it and buried his face in it. He nibbled it, he rubbed his eyes with it, he took it away from his face, he held it spread out on his hands and wrists. His fly was swelling. I went into his mother's house, I stammered out my errand, I ran back out into the orchard to watch them.

Leaning out of the window, protected by her housecoat, Mme.

Armande was stretching out her arms. Cataplame threw the duster and then stayed up on the tips of his toes. The duster came to rest on Mme. Armande's arm; she withdrew; Cataplame began to give gentle and regular groans. His big, irregular teeth emerged from his thick lips, his groans filled my stomach with melancholy. At that moment, the mechanical piano sprang to life. Cataplame was walking back and forth bending double. I ran till I reached our house. I rushed out into our garden where I had a view of everything. The mechanical piano stopped, leaving a note floating in the air. Mme. Armande reappeared, the duster fell to the ground. Cataplame picked it up; he rubbed it against his chest, his neck, his arms, the back of his head, his face, his forehead, his shoulders, his nipples; he displayed the duster to the heavens. Mme. Armande watched. Brusquely, she closed the window again. A curtain of gloom enveloped Cataplame; the object in his hands became funereal. I thought he was going to put it down sadly on the window sill. He hadn't time to do so. The door opened, Cataplame was swallowed up into the hall. The mechanical piano brayed. Two little hands closed the shutters. Days, nights, weeks went by. Even if you listened with your ear against the door at the hour when the crickets give up, Mme. Armande's house gave nothing away. Cataplame's mother stopped calling, the house ceased to hold any interest. Never a light showing, never an errand to run, never a sigh to be heard.

One sunny morning I saw people clustering in front of the house. I questioned a group of young girls who were bubbling with excitement.

"Cataplame has slit his mistress's throat," one of them told me.

*

I didn't set foot in a school for six years because of the war and ill health. Reading bored me to death. "Pick up a book, educate yourself, how lazy you are," my mother lamented. I preferred the feeling of folding my arms, swaying back and forth on my feet, nibbling the skin at the sides of my nails, savoring the skin of my lips, holding a lock of hair between my teeth, breathing in the odor of my bare arm. There were a few volumes of the Bibliothèque Rose hanging about the house. How did they get there? Céline, our next-door neighbor, the young girl who was sacrificing her life in order to nurse her mother and her grandmother, both bed-ridden, had lent them to us. I would pick up a book, I would open it on my knees, I would skip through it. The stories by the Comtesse de Ségur bored me. My misfortunes, when I lost an umbrella or a medallion or a five-franc piece, seemed to me much more real than Sophie's. The dark black illustrations, the clothes, the curves of the model little girls' calves, their hair styles, their fancy boots attracted me more than the text. I couldn't take their punishments seriously. I believed in the whistle of straps along our street: I didn't believe in whippings for rich little girls. Worldly wise as I was, these little girls seem to me no more than babies. I avoided fairy stories. A cabbage to be stolen from the back of a cart, that was a much more exciting "misfortune" to me: an adventure. I preferred my own distress when my mother was sick and I stood at the foot of the bed asking: "Are you still sick?" I preferred the conversations of real men and women, their troubles, their gossip, their songs. I went around gossiping from house to house; I had a big mouth and a lively tongue. I became a little woman again when I set out for plantain-Marly, for dandelion-Marly. I imagined I was keeping my mother. The factory, the lunch-box . . . To work in a factory just for her, to bring back my week's wages to her . . .

One family, which thought of itself as socially superior, never answered when I said good morning; and one day they called me a bastard. "What does that mean?" I asked my mother as I burst into our kitchen like a tornado.

My mother went pale. "It doesn't mean anything." She went out looking furious. I opened the small kitchen window; I heard her talking to them and shouting very loudly. I regretted my curiosity.

*

Later, a boy of twelve came around one evening while my mother was sitting with the neighbors on the bluish steps of the house—I always rinsed them well so that the blue of the stone would show. Félicien asked me if I would rather go for a stroll or walk along the top of the orchard wall, near the songs and the women's chatter. He pressed his hand on the brass button of the drinking fountain and we listened to the noise of the water. I pressed my hand on top of his, he took his away and put it on top of mine, and so on. He scarcely spoke, yet he was brimming with life. If my hoop slipped down from the wall where it was leaning, he rushed over to put it back again. He knew all my habits. Sometimes, quite suddenly, we would both start running side by side. He would slow down, he would say: "Let's walk now," before I ran out of breath.

Céline had lost her mother and her grandmother. One evening as we were playing at hopping from the sidewalk into the street, Félicien said between his teeth: "You must tell Céline you want to use her front bedroom. Then close the shutters and wait for me there." He commanded and I obeyed. I had to wait patiently until the day when my mother went into town with Céline. Céline agreed to lend me her keys. As soon as their silhouettes were out of sight, I went into the front bedroom and closed the shutters. I began waiting, then he knocked on the hall door. I thought he must have scrubbed his eyes, his cheeks, his lips. Everything was aglow. "Undress," he said, almost savagely. There was a sense in which we scarcely knew each other, because we had never met except at dusk. "Undress," he said again, "we're going to be married." I did as he said. He undressed too with his back to me. I lay down on the bed, I could hear my heart beating but I wasn't afraid. He climbed onto the bed. I could see his ornament, like the ones I'd seen on other little boys when I'd arrived unexpectedly on Saturday nights and caught them being scrubbed in their zinc baths. "Close your eyes," he said. I closed my eyes, I sensed that he was moving forward on his knees, taking care not to hurt me. I felt soft flesh against my forehead, against my cheek, then the other cheek, against one eyelid, then the other, against my closed mouth, against the place where my breasts would have been, against my hairless pubis. Lightly, he stretched himself out along my naked body; he said: "Don't breathe." I obeyed. His wet hair lay cool in the hollow of my shoulder. He breathed again after a long while, and I breathed with him. "I've married you," he said. He got up, dressed himself with his back toward me, and went away without saying good-by. I smoothed out the bedcovers, I opened the shutters: the light was a gift. I went home, I wept without sorrow, I wondered why I was weeping. The boy ignored me whenever he came back to our neighborhood.

*

The Germans left Valenciennes, we left too. I remember the cold, my sweaters, my coats, my shawls. My mother was pushing a handcart with Estelle. The girl's mother was walking beside me; she asked me—despite the army fighting its rearguard action, despite the horses and the panic-stricken civilians—if I would mind scratching her back. I also remember my mother, almost at the end of her strength, throwing a flatiron into the ditch. We were making our way toward Mons, forced onward by the German soldiers and the other civilians. We spent one night in a cellar before reaching our destination. I dozed fitfully, half undressed, surrounded by the dull thudding of the shells.

Next day, Mons was recaptured; some French soldiers helped us up with our luggage into a truck which took us back to Valenciennes. I recognized the road, the trees, the church spires, but there were dead horses and dead soldiers lying on both sides of it. A sad homecoming. The windows of our houses had vanished into thin air. The civilians had pillaged, broken, smashed everything. We were forced to sleep exposed to the four winds. A day later, I woke up with a knee the size of one of the cabbages I used to steal off the carts.

My mother and Clarisse decided to go and look for work in Paris. My mother boarded me out at the school in Valenciennes. I was always at the bottom of the class and twice as big as any of my classmates. I missed the private jargon of our street and was homesick for it. To be separated from my mother, from our big bed, from my basket, from the gardens I plundered, from the sawdust in the bar, from the tobacco juice, from Caramel's spitting, from the love songs, from the red heat of our iron stove, from the stew spread on bread, from the nocturnal visits of our smuggler gave me a fever. I learned nothing. How should I have learned anything? I could barely drag myself along beneath the burden of my nostalgia.

The sickness began with a pain in my shoulder. I couldn't raise my arm, I couldn't shine my shoes. The vise grew tighter. I suffered night and day, and in my bed, amidst the snores and the dreamers talking in their sleep, I thought of the shoe-cleaning session next evening, of the shoes I had to brush, of my shoulder, of my arm. The assistant mistress in charge of the dormitory scolded me. She thought my slowness, my laziness in the shoe shop and in class were willful. She was wrong. The polish and the brushes reminded me of home, of cleaning the house. They discovered my hands were always damp with perspiration. The school doctor said that there was nothing to worry about, that one should never listen to children. My mother, when she came to see me one Sunday, found me burning hot; she took me away to be examined by her own doctor. "A pleurisy begins with a pain in the shoulder," he said. I had in fact been suffering from pleurisy for a week. My mother canceled her return journey; the term's fees she had paid in advance would not be reimbursed, the doctor would have to attend me frequently, she would have to buy drugs: I could see a look of pained reproach in her eyes. I was sick, I thought of myself as guilty. A dry cough and a stabbing pain in the side replaced the pain in my shoulder. Each night ahead filled me with terror. Breathing meant coughing and shooting pains in my buttocks. Oh! That age of love, of self-denial, of sacrifice I had to endure in order not to wake her up at night! She slept in the big mahogany bed, the doors were open. I pulled myself up, I leaned forward, I clutched the eiderdown, I crushed it against my chest or stuffed it into my mouth, I bit my hand, I pulled my hair. . . . No, I would not cough. She would come in, she would ask if I was in pain, if I felt any better, any worse. I reassured her, I insisted she go to bed.

"You're lucky it isn't a wet pleurisy," the doctor said.

One Sunday after lunch my mother insisted: "You must be reasonable, you're going to be reasonable, you will be reasonable. . . . I'm going out. Estelle will give you your medicine. . . ." I told her she was beautiful, elegant. She made old, worn clothes look new. I couldn't tell her that her little veil had metamorphosed her completely. Now, my buttock and my cough had become company for me. And my mother? I began waiting for her to come home as soon as she shut the door behind me.

Estelle gave me my medicine several times during the afternoon and told me to be patient. Then she would rush off, her head full of young men. I was patient, I remembered the upright piano belonging to Marie Biziaux—a "kept woman" who had all the luck, they used to say in our one room as I gave my imitation of the High Mass—whose house I used to visit with my mother and grandmother. We used to walk through a garden full of flowers and vegetables, we used to go in, and Marie Biziaux, a buxom Flemish statue, would receive us with her mother, another statue carved out of lard. The four women sat making small talk, the sharp smell of coffee floated out into the garden. "You can play on it, you can go in there," my grandmother said encouragingly. I would go into the room and close the door, cutting myself off from the smell of coffee and the voices. First, I contemplated the stool, followed the pattern of the damask with my finger and sighed. At last I gained the courage to raise my eyes for a glimpse of the keyboard. The black and white silence was awful. I spurred myself to action: I pressed a finger on two black keys together. I wounded the silence. The chords died away. I was possessed. I played the piano without ever having learned how: I played nothing in particular. When I played standing up, the keys and pedals seemed too fragile for the din I was making. I leaned forward, I leaned back and to either side, I gave violent jerks of the head, I crossed my hands as I played. I wanted to be the great pianist I had never seen. I wanted to astound the walls, the tables, the chairs.

My mother came back before nightfall; she told me that the man with the pince-nez had come back from the war, that he had given me a bar of chocolate. She set it down on my bed. I ate one square, two squares; I asked no questions: chocolate was a luxury. The future was no longer our future. I sensed that amid the confusion.

*

The doctor prescribed the country. Laure suggested I convalesce at her farm about twenty kilometers away. I was dazzled during the journey by the way she flicked the whip over the horse's back. With her tongue pressed against her teeth she produced a noise that went "driiiii" as well as any carter. Nimbly, she slipped the handle of the whip back into the iron ring that also doubled as a posy holder, put on the brake when we went downhill, pulled up my blanket and retied the knots of the trap's leather apron. I sat wiping away my tears.

"My mommy . . ."

"You'll see her again, your mommy," she replied mockingly, but without malice.

At last I was seeing the country, the real country. The plain of Mons and the plain of Marly stretched before us as far as the eye could see, younger, fresher, more bursting with sap than ever before. A tree swam in the middle of a vast meadow; the houses at the edge of the road took up no room at all. A church huddled amidst its trees; the sky and the grass were reflecting one another. My mother was sinking below the horizon. The vast spaces sharpened my grief.

"You must call me 'aunt' and him 'uncle,' " she said as the carriage turned into the farmyard.

The cleanness of the windows and the curtains, of the flagstones beside the house and around the outbuildings, took all the strength out of my arms and legs. The gleaming door opened.

"Come and unharness the carriage, Laurent," shouted a little old woman with the face of a wrinkled apple. "Where are you, Laurent?"

"Why doesn't Laurent come? The horse will take a chill," said Laure.

Laurent emerged from one of the buildings.

"You must feed the animals," the little old woman said to Laure.

"I must see to this child first," said Laure.

I flung my arms around her neck.

Laure whispered in my ear that she would buy me some clogs.

"Give your niece a kiss," Laure said to Laurent.

For dinner that evening we had long pieces of bread and salty butter dipped in café au lait. The silence all around the farm made me feel strange. I gulped away like the others and my ears stopped buzzing quite so much. Whenever I looked around at the objects and furniture in the room I felt I was sitting on the point of a needle. So much cleanliness is repellent.

*

I began attending the school at the other end of the village. Turning out of the farmyard, I found myself on the rough road along the hedge. I stumbled over the paving stones, I ran out of breath going up the hill, I fought my way onward step by step. The hedge: it was my religion and my sanctuary. The clouds could see me, the clouds gazed down at me. Those islands floating in the blueness, those blocks of foam were masses of eyes without sadness and without joy. White, astonished, astonishing eyes. I had never seen so much sky free of roofs and chimneys. I made no distinction between the flowers with their chirping colors and the song of the birds. I seemed to be hearing thousands and thousands of birds: nature was a bird cage without bars. My ears were filled with posies of song, there was a cat leaping over the grass, a cock in all the glory of its russet and green feathers stood by unperturbed. My satchel became even more of an encumbrance; I wanted to see the gardens, the orchards, the meadows between the branches of the hedge. I imagined there was a mystery there because I was cut off from them, because they were alone with themselves, swept by the dazzle of the sun. Their jubilation left me panting with excitement. Drifting scents came to my nostrils, I scoured my forehead with a hazel leaf, I made my way to school beneath a vault of greenery, I breathed in the light and the fresh air, the breeze paid its court to the branches.

I ate my lunch in the home of a woman who ran a café, but before doing so I had to swallow down two raw eggs, then a third at four o'clock. Doctors prescribed eggs at that time to promote growth, to ward off tuberculosis, anemia, and fainting fits. The more you loathed them the more they forced you to have them. There was a spring where the water came streaming out of a spout in an arc. The water ran away down a green, babbling, narrow, elegant, eloquent furrow. Crack, crack. I broke my eggs on the edge of the cup, then I added a little cold water to help me swallow my round slugs.

I learned long division, I learned how words must conjugate and agree. And what I learned I remembered, which was not true of the lessons I'd had at the day school. The animals in La Fontaine seemed to me too stately and stiff. Despite the explanations we were given, I didn't believe in human virtues and vices in an animal. I preferred our big, thin, gray cat who was such a thief, I preferred my mother scolding him as she chased him with the dish towel. Why bring animals down to the level of our language? They have their own laments, their own cries, pleasures, tragedies, and moments of abandon, their own hungers. Their own griefs, their own ill-starred destinies. A frog is a frog, a cow is a cow.

*

Playtime:

"Why have you come to our school?"

"Because I was sick."

"You were sick. What did you have?"

"Pleurisy."

"What's pleurisy?"

"You cough, you have a sharp pain in your side."

"I get a sharp pain in my side when I run a long way. I haven't got pleurisy."

"You're lucky then. A dry pleurisy isn't as serious as a wet pleurisy."

"How do you know?"

"That's what the doctor said when he came to see me."

"Where is your mother?"

"She's working in Paris. She's going to write to me."

"Where's your father?"

"I told you my mother is working in Paris."

"I asked you where your father is. I'm not talking about your mother."

"And I said my mother's working in Paris."

"What are you kicking at me for?"

"Because I'm telling you my mother's working in Paris."

"Do you think I'm deaf or something? Why *are* you starting that again?"

"Because you don't listen. My mother is my father."

"You're mad, you're crazy. I've got a father and I've got a mother. My mother isn't my father."

"I'm not mad, I'm not crazy. We haven't got a father in our house. There's just my mother. Can't you understand what I tell you? My mother's all that by herself."

"All what?"

"Nothing. You heard me: nothing. I had a grandmother."

"I've got a grandmother. And I've got a father and a mother."

"You're lucky then."

"You're lucky too. You've got new clogs and a new pen. . . . Did your father give them to you? You were born like me: with a father and a mother."

"Oh leave me alone. I was born with my mother. Let's play at something."

"I'll play when you tell me where your father is."

"I don't want to play with you any more."

"And I don't want to play with you anymore either. You're stupid. You can't even tell me where your father is."

"Go away. You get on my nerves, you bore me."

I took refuge in a corner. The little girl wasn't boring me with her curiosity: she was torturing me. I worried, I tried to make myself remember. During the war, my mother had said: he's dead. Who was the dead man she used to talk about so much? "He didn't kiss you, he was so careful about the contagion. He just patted you under the chin and on the cheeks." I didn't remember him, I would never remember him. I decided to hop on one foot at the risk of splitting my clog. I defied the ground, the whole playtime, my inquisitor; I longed for Fidéline, who defended me when my mother was angry. It was different for my mother and me. Our home wasn't like other people's. When a father took his child onto his knees and bounced it up and down singing "Come to Daddy, come to Daddy," I blushed with shame and outraged modesty. We lived in a world of petticoats.

An unexpected attack of discouragement. Eleven-thirty in the evening. My radio is playing. Calypsos, blues, sambas. Bastards have a curse on them: a friend told me so. Bastards have a curse on them. It is a knell, a tocsin drowning the calypsos, the blues, the sambas. Why don't bastards help each other? Why do they avoid each other? Why do they detest each other? Why don't they form a brotherhood? They should be able to forgive each other everything since they all hold the most precious, the most fragile, the strongest, the darkest part of themselves in common: a childhood twisted like an old apple tree. Why are there no matrimonial agencies in existence to help them marry each other? I should like to see written in letters of fire: "Bakery for bastards." Then I needn't feel that stupid prickling in my throat anymore when people ask for the big loaves that French people refer to as "bastards." I have always wished that in that wonderful American film *Marty,* the two shy people who come together at the end were bastards.

*

The boys at the school ganged up on me. At five of four every afternoon, I could sense them getting ready to chase me along the roads. I was afraid of being afraid. Why had they picked on me? Did they sense what my mother had taught me, her terrible warnings; did they sense that their loud laughter, their practical jokes and their swaggering had no effect on me? The thought of my mother obsessed me, I wanted a letter from her. She didn't write. I would leave the school, they would give me a head start, then the stones would start showering down on me. Their hate hit me harder than their missiles. I took off my clogs and held them in my hands; I could run faster without their weight on my feet; I would fall and scramble up again, the stones were still raining down. I would have preferred Indian yells behind me, but the boys didn't shout. They disappeared as soon as I got near to Laure's farm. Laure was angry, she spoke to the teacher, the hounding stopped, the boys avoided me.

*

On Sunday evenings I used to take a quart of milk to the woman who ran the café where I ate my lunch. I glanced at the spring out of the corner of my eye, ignoring its gurgling because I had no raw eggs to swallow that evening. Halfway along my route there was a bar filled with as much shouting, drinking, laughter, and tobacco smoke as it was humanly possible to produce. There were a good many of us who stopped to watch the young ladies tucking their handkerchiefs back into their waistbands. Young men, rumpled and overheated, went out and urinated. They re-entered like conquerors. One of them came straight through the crowd of dancers without hesitation. He asked me if I'd like to waltz with him. I answered yes with all my heart. I danced in my violet coat, I was proud of having learned how to waltz. He gave me his glass of beer after the dance and put coins in the slot of the mechanical piano. We waltzed again; he pressed me against his sweat-soaked shirt. I looked older than my thirteen years; the young man wanted to know if I would be coming next Sunday. I said yes and fled. I could have waltzed till dawn. Next day, Laure scolded me. I had enjoyed myself in a place of ill-fame, I mustn't ever go there again. I thought the lecture I received stupid and unworthy of Laure. Next Sunday I delivered the milk without turning my eyes toward the bar. I was ashamed, and I wanted to go there again.

*

Laure's attachment to me and my attachment to her were growing stronger. She reassured me: "You'll see your mommy again. She'll write to you all right. Why shouldn't she?" She swore like a cowhand, she laughed, and I laughed with her. "She's my niece," she told everyone. "Don't you think she looks like me?" I liked it every time she said that. I admired her strength, her girth, her vitality. What a lusty specimen of womanhood she was! And the work she got through! Her angers and her fits of temperament were terrible. During a dispute with her husband and her mother-in-law, she threw the pails full of milk down onto the kitchen floor and shouted: "I'm leaving and taking this child with me." Night and morning, she braided up my long hair, she made everyone admire the two braids. Her sister's creation was her creation. This giantess preserved me from loneliness. Their son Léon came home for the vacation in his school uniform. I liked being in the farmyard, I liked being in the orchard and the kitchen garden, I liked being in the cowshed and in the stable. I had no place of my own, I was at home everywhere. I had the sun for my blanket if I lay down in the grass. I thought back to the park, so well groomed and joyless in its Sunday best. Everything was breaking into flower, I myself was growing stronger, I was breaking into flower. A bee collected the nectar of the silence, a hornet flew past in a straight line pursued by space. When I played at falling onto the hay in the barn I was so close to the earth in which it had sprouted. The meadows sloping steeply down toward the other side of the road cast a spell over me; the night came falling down, layer after layer. Nature grew dark, the world was evasive. A question, a communion. The coming of night never made me sad. In the city I would have sobbed because my mother wasn't there. Now, the melancholy vistas, the resignation of a road, the humility of a gate, the naked look of an upturned harrow, the tragic sinking of the sun, all brought me comfort. I saw all these things without explaining them to myself. No, I didn't melt into the landscape. I felt my cool cheeks, I took my foot out of my clog, I sniffed, I was myself, without purpose, without ambition, without intelligence, without reflection. Men, women, and children, none of them could harm me. The twilight confers power. I brushed the roofs of the village with my finger. I hummed, I went in, and the noises of the farm closed around a little girl brimming with wonder.

Laure announced that my mother would soon be coming back. I no longer spent hours on Thursday morning watching for the mailman, but I kept watch the whole day for the trap with Laure and my mother in it. I cannot imagine how the midnight sun itself could have amazed me more than that trap coming over the top of the hill. I was empty, my joy drained out of me as the wheels, the horse, the faces, drew steadily nearer. I was alone. Freed from my expectation, demolished by the fulfillment of my longing: to see her again. The trap rolled up to me, I was a gaping void. What was I wating for? I was being given everything and losing everything at the same time. I ran into the yard, I hugged her amid the tumult of a farmyard in chaos. My mother's forte is devotion, not kissing. She examined me, she inspected me minutely. Laure was telling her how much I had changed. I looked too well. I could read it in her eyes. She eyed my two village-style braids with contempt. I have written in *L'Asphyxie* how that evening, sitting by the stove, she murmured: "How countrified you've become." It was probably no more than a passing observation. The words were a knife in my heart. I went out into the yard with my cape over my shoulders. I didn't weep. I thought, standing in the moonlight, that I had ceased to be her daughter because I wasn't attractive.

My mother loathed being in the village, loathed the farm, loathed country life. She is a city person. I was influenced by her. The country side, the roads, the fields, and the trees no longer inspired me with the same confidence. My mother formed a screen around me. I would have denied Laure, her country dialect, her big movements, her activity, in order to please this disillusioned visitor from Paris. Once more we were both cut off from the rest of the world amid the bellowing of the cattle, the departure of a harrow, of a dung cart, of a plow. My mother has a delicate stomach because she was undernourished as a a child. She couldn't digest the bread soaked in milky coffee. I no longer ate as well as I did before. I gazed at my mother; I was no longer a peasant girl among the other peasants. She met the village dressmaker, and the two became firm friends on sight. I used to go and join them after class and we sat eating slices of fruit tart or crêpes or fritters in a hot room with the doors closed. When did my mother explain to me that she was going to be married in the village to a gentleman from the city, that she was going to return to Valenciennes, that I would go to boarding school again? I don't remember. To marry. I didn't understand, I couldn't envisage it.

A closed carriage driven by a coachman arrived one afternoon. After a quick meal in the farm dining room, my mother got up into the brougham with the man wearing pince-nez whom I had seen when we lived in the Glacis neighborhood. He said: "Au revoir, my dear." My mother was married, the closed carriage carried them off together, into the dusk. I took a deep breath. I became a peasant girl among the other peasants again. Yes, but at night . . . always the same thoughts. . . . What is the difference between a stepfather and a father-in-law? A father-in-law is the father of the husband, or else of the wife. So that wasn't it. What is a stepfather? "You're going to have a stepfather. . . ." It's an artificial father. It's a doll that opens and closes its eyes and says: I am papa. What is a father? What is a stepfather? I dropped off to sleep again. I had a mother, she used to pull the furniture about in our house. She was father and mother.

The day following my return to Valenciennes to go back to boarding school I got up at half-past nine exactly. An hour after that I approached my stepfather apprehensively. I said: "Good morning, sir" and kissed him. He replied: "Good morning, my dear." The expression "my dear," spoken with a slightly absent-minded air by a man who wasn't a stranger since I kissed him, a man I called "sir" even as I was kissing him, filled me with panic. He said: "What time did you get up?" I answered, almost joyfully: "At half-past nine!" He looked at me, he scrutinized me, his eyes were cold behind the lenses of his pince-nez. He added: "You musn't lie to me." I turned to ice for more than thirty years. From then on he was to make me afraid, I was never to be myself again. Why should I have tried to trick him about the time? Why did he stare into my eyes? Did he want to use this first contact as a way of knowing my mother's seducer, whom I resembled? A bastard must lie, a bastard is the fruit of evasion and lies, a bastard is an infringement of all the rules. I was intimidated, I wanted to be properly brought up. In such ways can hypocrisy take root. I understood in a vague way that he would have liked me not to be there. I was the weight of a great love, I was the blot on a clean sheet. He never scolded me, and yet he terrorized me. I never talked at table during meals or after meals, I didn't dare behave well or behave badly. I sat there bored, liquefying, vomiting inside. "Eat, my dear, eat. Your mother is eating, you see."

"Yes, sir, no, sir, thank you, sir. I've had enough, sir."

I couldn't stretch my arms toward my mother, brushing the cuff of her silky blouse. A dinner napkin, a fork, a knife, a knife-rest, what an obstacle course. Rolling the white of the bread into little balls was a help. Marly, Céline, Estelle, the deaf-mute, Caramel, the madman, his mistress, the orchard, Aimé Patureau, the songbooks, the greens for our rabbits. To live in the past at the age of fourteen . . . it's too soon. I looked at the statue of Froissart through the open window of the dining room, I lost myself in the deep folds of his robes, I wondered why my mother had brought me into a strange land. The streetcars came around the bend below our windows and continued their plaintive way toward my beloved Marly.

I ate my fill while I was in their house but I always sat at the table on a three-legged chair. From my fourteenth to my twentieth year the fourth leg was missing. The fourth leg was the dead man, my mother's seducer.

You gave birth to a river of tears, mother. I took the veil, mother. Yes, later on I often slammed the doors, I couldn't stand you. My wound reopened. My wound: where you were torn out of me. Jealous? No. Sick to fainting for the past. Cast off despite all your kindness, mother. Oh yes, banished from our eiderdown that kept us warm during the bombardments.

Poor stepfather, poor mother, poor daughter. I went to Paris with him at the age of fifteen to try on a corrective shoe and a canvas and steel corset. I limped, I was always hunched over. Crossing the Place de la Concorde in a taxi, he said to me: "Don't call me 'sir' any more. Call me 'father.' " I agreed, I said yes with marble lips. Of what stuff am I made? This man of good will found no answering softness in me. I must call you "father" but I don't bear your name, my eyes whispered to this man I always kept aloof from. All the seducer wanted was his linen laundered in London when I was born. Where was I born? Where did I fall after I came out of my mother's belly? Into a cocked hat. I would have preferred to go on calling my stepfather "sir." "Father" was a fish bone in my throat every time I said it. I prepared myself to say "Good morning, father," "Good night, father," as we prepare people for an operation. After all, I had been living in a world without men ever since my mother had put me on my guard against them.

I felt myself being inundated during class and asked to be excused. My groin felt hot, vulnerable to everything I met in the main quadrangle of the school. I went into the lavatories, I pressed my hand against it, I felt what I had been hoping for, what I had sensed coming. The hollow of my palm was red and sticky.

I asked to take piano lessons. My neuralgia, the stabbing pains in my ears, my sore throats would affect me less disastrously. I pleaded with my classmates, I explained to them that I was shivering. They agreed to let me have the place near the radiator. I would sit dozing there, my head resting on the radiator, waiting for the end of the evening study period so that I could run up and down the scale. The meager electric light impoverished the chatter, the reprimands. It was as though I had been condemned to eat meals of bread and water standing outside the dining hall. Evening study period . . . an ordeal of monotony because I was lazy. I learned my lessons without understanding them, without retaining them. I simply couldn't feel that studying mattered. Once I had rushed through my work I slid back into my cave, the snail inside my head warmed up again. I looked on the studious, industrious, gifted students with wonder. I didn't think: all I have to do is set my mind to it. If I set my mind to it I can win back the lost paradise of hard work, of good marks, of prizes, of congratulations. No, I was no guilt-ridden idler. I liked my geography book because of the infinitesimally small things on the maps. The pretty blue earthworm, relaxed in some places, writhing around in others, was a river running right across France. A coffee bean: an island with thousands of inhabitants. I had more courage than all the other students put together when I dared to feel alone alongside my companion. The plane trees, stripped or covered in leaves, cried out to me: no more waltzing in the pub, no more Marly. I had more courage than all the other students put together when I was questioned in class, when I froze, when I was stupid and made myself even more so, when I began to see in the others' eyes that I was ugly, that they found it amusing, that they nudged each other.

I moved up a class and had to learn the famous speeches from *Le*

Cid by heart. It was a terrible chore. A woman who was the embodiment of duty torturing a man who was the embodiment of love. I discussed it with a few realists, the country girls at the school. The duty part irritated us. And love triumphed at the end of the play without his glittering arrows. As one turned the last page, Rodrigue was clasping the shadow of a woman in his arms. How could children between the ages of twelve and fourteen get inside the skins of creative artists who had loved and made love before they wrote their plays? True, Corneille gave an added luster to the dog stuck inside the bitch during our Thursday walks. Such was the power of his eloquent speeches. Though I learned Racine he went over my head. Who were they, my emperors, my palaces, my tragic actors and actresses? The mistresses on duty in the dormitory. I flamed instead of studying. I quivered finally for Chateaubriand, for Lucile. I longed for the incest to be consummated. The writer's Olympian aspect and curling locks, the proud and solitary tomb standing by the sea and vying with it in grandeur, all fascinated me as they have fascinated so many others. His descriptions are admirable, explained our teacher, but he weakens them by allowing his own shadow to fall across the page. I shrugged my shoulders.

*

Ah those days of vegetation during the vacations when my mother was first married. . . . On one occasion there was a carriage waiting outside their place of business. I climbed into it with my mother to visit the throat doctor and as she was asking me whether I was afraid of the little operation I didn't dare reply: is it the same one, does it look like the carriage that came to Arras? After the operation I vomited blood on the carriage cushion. I could bear the burning in my throat but not the stream of blood in the carriage that she had waited for so long. I was bringing André back to life: the wound inside my throat was humiliating my mother even though she was married now, even though she was running a business and succeeding. I answered no spitefully when she asked me if I was in pain. I kept my pain inside and brooded on it. She wanted to help me undress and take off my shoes. I wouldn't let her. I bent down, I undid my laces, I covered my shoes with blood. "I don't want any help," I told my mother. I am certain today that I wanted to spit blood the way he had done; I wanted to create a bond between us, I was beginning to pay his debts.

Without shouting, without banging the lid of her desk, the assistant mistress supervising our evening study period could keep a roomful of sixty students quiet. She was studying for an exam, she worked harder than any of us. We were hatching her, yes we were cuddling our baby, hatching our chick when she stepped down off the dais. I stopped breathing as soon as she came near my table, as soon as she leaned over my exercise book: I had promised myself I would. I did everything within my power to make myself invisible. I no longer saw her, I no longer heard her. She was too close. I had no idea what I wanted. I suffered when she was far away, I suffered when she came close to me. I almost burst from holding my breath. "What's going on?" she asked, surprised, confiding, detached. I breathed again, taking shelter behind a pretended fit of coughing. She moved away from my table; I wanted her. I buried myself savagely in my book, I shed tears of rage and ignorance and impotence. "What is it now?" she asked in a slightly indulgent tone. I answered sullenly: "I've got a migraine." Did she sense the first stirrings of adolescence? On Sunday mornings, if I was allowed the joy of leaving the school, I talked to my mother about her in the damp bathroom and my mother listened to me at length. She understood, she didn't become impatient with me. I described my new emotions, I loved her as she listened, and yet my mother was ceasing to be the only object in my life.

I stopped going out for recreation periods as soon as I started piano lessons. We had fixed times for our lessons, but we could do extra practice if we found a free piano. I ran off on my treasure hunt, I felt a sensuous pleasure as I left the barbarous cries of the other girls behind me. My favorite place was the little room away from the quadrangle, near the treeless courtyard where the basketball goals hung above the blackish dust. A cell, a window with ground glass, a piano, a chair, that was all. I went in, I gave myself to the piano, it gave itself to me. Slowly, gesture after gesture. If I found the lid open, I closed it in order to open it for myself. I wanted it to be a secret every time I came. I unlatched my music case in one corner of the room because before I began practicing I had to stay silently at a distance from the silent instrument. I closed the music case again. The click of the catch? A click of triumph for the chair and keyboard. Once seated, less round-shouldered than usual, I leafed through my book of exercises. Feeling intimidated, I plunged one finger down among the high notes and another in the bass: I gauged the extent of the keyboard, I wanted the same silence again between the high notes and the low. Tirelessly, I played the chromatic scale for its romanticism, trailing sadness across the black keys. No, I never grew tired of those limping, melancholy ascents and descents.

Suddenly I would lose heart, I had started lessons too late, my fingers would never become supple, my wrists would never be free of their plaster casts. My head fell among the low notes of the keyboard and I wept amid the thunder rolling up from my collapse upon the keys. I wiped off the tears that had fallen on the yellow, aging keys; I went on practicing. I preferred doing the exercises consisting of little pieces, which I played badly. "The expression, the expression, don't forget the expression!" rapped out Mlle. Quandieu with her ruler. Mlle. Quandieu, with her fluffy reddish hair and her flabby face, gave lessons in a jacket and a hat. Two hundred pounds on a chair belonging to the school—her own alma mater. Mlle. Quandieu was not very strict. I used to wake up at night in a cold sweat if I hadn't practiced enough. I shall talk about it again later. I used to wake up after having gone to sleep finally at one in the morning, after having cried under my bedclothes because I was different from the other girls in the dormitory, because they slept and talked in their sleep, because they threw themselves about and laughed while I couldn't sleep. I got up in the morning exhausted, I loathed my toilet things and the step of the mistress on duty in the aisle. I made my bed in my cubicle between two partitions, I took hold of myself, I stored up the breakdowns, the depressions for later. The less I slept the more I asked to practice the piano after breakfast. It meant I had somewhere to go, I could forget that I was in captivity.

*

My mother didn't come to visit me often. She was devoting every moment of her time to her furniture and interior decorating business. She sent an apprentice over every week laden down with a bundle as big as a hundred-pound sack of coal. She was still very concerned about my health. I used to receive huge loads of provisions which inspired an ironical smile on the face of Mlle. Fromont, the mistress in charge of sickbay. My mother bought me the best fruit, the best chocolates, the best honey. I had the fullest locker, I was almost ashamed of such profusion.

My mother brought an added responsibility to her husband when she married, what she called her "burden." A former student at the

Ecole Boule, he knew everything there was to know about woods, styles, draperies, brocades, taffetas, and silks, and everything he knew he taught my mother. She worked at the business from eight in the morning till eleven at night with the determination, the will, the effort, the unstinted energy of those who are uneducated and suffer from the fact. "I threw myself into it," she says. What progress she made, what a head for business she had. She organized and brought a sense of order into an old firm with stifling, poorly equipped premises. My stepfather and his family thought small. She thought big. Patiently, subtly, and with even more subtlety than the next woman, because she had been a domestic servant in other people's houses, she shouldered, she dragged about, she displayed their collection of wallpapers without ever getting tired of having to listen to her rich customers' tales of woe. She intended to sell and she sold. Her patience, her discretion, her tact overcame every caprice, every whim, every moment of indecision. At fourteen and a half, hidden in the darkness of a corridor, I would listen to her without being able to see her, I drank in her voice, I refreshed myself with its intonations. I admired her and yet I suffered. This businesswoman was a stranger, she gave too much of herself to others. I didn't recognize her when I saw her again, I didn't confess that I had hid nearby in order to observe her.

Tall, nearsighted, first in pince-nez and later in round-rimmed tortoise-shell glasses, his face stern but easily softened, too anxious to please or too aloof, shy, easily carried away, stammering under the stress of anger or excitement, defying the opinion of a whole town for love of my mother, my stepfather would lose his patience and get angry with customers who wouldn't make up their minds, or else flare up at tasteless provincials who chose things that were ugly. He preferred art to business. Which was why the pupil soon eclipsed her master. The customers, whether cultivated or not, preferred diplomacy.

We were getting ready for Christmas at school: I was to act the part of the black king from the East and then play a Brahms Hungarian Dance on the piano. I rehearsed my part of the black king. The prospect of blacking my face when the day came, the face which tormented me, whose scapegoat I had become, the prospect of blacking my great nose consoled me. When the day came I played my role of the king from the East. No one laughed. I wanted to play the Hungarian Dance behind the shelter of my blackened skin as well. The mistress in charge wouldn't allow it. I climbed up onto the stage in the auditorium once more. The curtains opened. I played my piece—in profile. Everyone laughed. My mother, the teachers, were looking at me, listening to me. It was one long shower of wrong notes. The more they laughed the more mistakes I made. I went down to join my mother in the audience. She was cold and seemed upset. I regretted the expense she had gone to in giving me a new blue serge dress. That evening my stepfather asked about the concert. I left the table, I suffered enough for two. Later, I was to have the audacity, the callousness, the unfairness to blame my mother for having given birth to an ugly daughter. When would I meet an ogre? I would love him. I would hold up a mirror in front of him, I would say: I can see two roses in the mirror. Look, please look: one is you, the other is me.

*

"Learn," my mother used to say. "I don't want you to suffer from a lack of education as I did. To be able to write a letter without a mistake. . . ." A letter without a mistake: it was her promised land. I told her about Napoleon's spelling mistakes. She didn't think of herself as Napoleon, she sighed. At those moments I would have liked to lay my grammar book down at her feet, on a cushion of camellias. I have never received more than messages from her, not letters because she was always afraid of wording her sentences badly. Her messages are as abstract as she herself is when I wash her back.

She gave me a mahogany Pleyel piano. The most expensive and the largest upright piano made. It came from Paris, carried inside a sarcophagus of planks by a gang of men. The light ran streaming off the mahogany Pleyel when the men unpacked it in my room. My mother asked me if I was pleased, she gave me the little key.

I was sixteen, my mother was expecting a legitimate child. One evening at the dinner table, as I sat silent as usual, trying to lose myself through the open window in the folds of Froissart's robe as I had lost myself once in my grandmother's skirt, I said without thinking: "Pregnant women are so ugly." My stepfather raised his head and looked at me with unkindly eyes. I had said it because I wanted my slim elegant mother back, my mother the coquette, walking toward the tall mirror and then away from it again with all the passion for perfection of a mannequin in a fashion house. I missed her cuffs, her boned bodice, her immense hat picked out from among so many; I missed them so much there were times I almost groaned aloud. Big, heavy, she sat eating noodles at every meal. Not that I was jealous of the fruit of their love: I lived in another world, cold, stiff, mistrustful of myself, mistrustful of others. And yet, I longed for extravagant loves, for incest. I wanted compensation, I wanted redress with something abnormal about it. One evening when she was in bed —my stepfather was staying late in his office—my mother said: "Listen, come and listen, he's moving." I pressed my ear against the coverlet of their bed, on her belly. "I'm afraid," I said to my mother, "it makes me afraid." I said good night to her and went up to my own room. My room with the silent Pleyel: my insides without somersaults.

Well dressed, well shod, well groomed, I became more indulgent when I evoked the memory of the seducer. My mother inspected me before I went out, she used to say: "Her father, she's her father all over again. . . ." I was flattered by this indirect compliment from her. I missed Marly less and less. A basket, a kitchen knife, a bunch of dandelions would have made me smile. Who can say whether I might not have tipped over the basket with the toe of my pretty shoe. . . . "Her father, she's her father all over again. . . ." I went out, I confronted the twilight, I looked at myself in the first lighted storefronts, I turned my head toward the half-darkness, I coughed several times for the benefit of a passer-by on the other sidewalk, I swelled with pride at the thought that I looked like the consumptive seducer, that I was coughing like him. I went walking down his street, I paid court to the doors and windows of his house, now in the hands of others. I didn't say to myself: Your mother wore herself out for them and for him in the garden, your mother fought her way out, your mother has strength of character. No. I walked up and down there feeling that I was the rightful heir to that great house, to that perpetually sleepy street.

I also walked in the Place d'Armes on Saturday nights. The lighted storefronts crackled before my eyes. I was attracted, intrigued, spellbound by the yellow covers of the books published by the Mercure de France, by the white covers of the Gallimard books. I selected a title, but I didn't really believe I was intelligent enough to go into the largest bookstore in town. I had some pocket money with me (money that my mother slipped me without my stepfather's knowing), I went in. There were teachers, priests, and older students glancing through the uncut volumes. I had so often watched the old lady who served in the shop as she packed up religious objects, as she reached into the window for the things that people pointed out to her. . . . She took out Jules Romains' *Mort de quelqu'un* and looked at me askance. I was too young to be reading modern literature. I read *Mort de quelqu'un* and smoked a cigarette as I did so in order to savor my complicity with a modern author all the more. My bedroom window was open, the moon shone in on the piano, the candle flame bent over toward my book. I was reading by candlelight because my stepfather would not let me keep my light on later than ten. The biography of an anonymous railroad worker opened a new world to me. The mediocrity of his life was transformed into incalculable wealth because of the hundreds of thousands of railroad workers' lives identical to his. Next Saturday I came home with Georges Duhamel's *La Confession de minuit,* some reproductions of paintings, some etchings, and a bronze paper knife decorated with lilies and lily leaves. A week later my parents left for Paris-Plage, where they stayed from Saturday till Monday evening. My mother sent me to stay with Mlle. Guerby, one of our French teachers. I reread *La Confession de minuit* till daybreak. I talked to Mlle. Guerby about it. She advised me against reading modern authors: they were all mad. The Saturday after that I stole a book which I didn't read; but I paid cash down for André Gide's *Les Nourritures terrestres* and a sculpture of a dead bird. Later, under my bedclothes, when I went back to boarding school, I returned to the barns, to the fruits of André Gide by the glow of a flashlight. As I held my shoe in the shoe shop and spread the polish on it, I muttered: "Shoe, I will teach you to feel fervor." There was no other confidant worthy of my long book-filled nights, my literary ecstasies.

*

The rumor sprang up in the school corridors: she is coming from Paris, she is twenty-eight. The question went the rounds from group to group: shall we have her? As soon as she went into the library, the men teachers went in there too. The men teachers worshipped her. She stirred our provincial dullness into life. Her smooth hair drawn back, a chignon in the form of a figure eight lying down her neck, narrow browed, hollow cheeked, dark complexioned, fine lipped, with dark eyes lit by the fire of her intelligence, delicate pince-nez, slender with the slenderness of the South, absent-minded about her briefcase, and with a Touraine accent that sent us into transports of delight, while she was amused at ours. Would we be having her? Yes, oh yes. She taught us geography, astronomy, and literature:

Mlle. Godfroy's classes became celebrations, ecstasies. When she spoke our first names—which was rarely—we blushed with happiness. Her handbag hypnotized me. She would put it down on her desk, she would move it forward, then push it first over toward the wall, then over toward the plane trees beyond the windows. The heavens, the earth, the planets, the stars of first magnitude, of second magnitude, of third magnitude were all her. I heard the name Andromeda. "You must look for her this evening, you must look for her," she said to us. Because of the name, I looked for a heroine from Racine up in the sky. I looked too for the music and the beauty of the speeches from Racine that she read out to us with such simplicity. Mlle. Godfroy would ask us for an orange, she would turn the sun between her ethereal fingers, then assign it to its place in the heavens. When she took off her pince-nez suddenly, without warning her eyes became twice as large; the orange shriveled up, the sun was no more than a piece of peel. The universe she presented to our grasp with an orange, with a handbag, stretched out to infinity, because it was reflected in Mlle. Godfroy.

"I've left it behind. Will you go and bring it from the library?" she said to me at the beginning of a class.

Being alone in the corridor, hearing the voices of the teachers coming from behind each door I passed, gave me an illusion of freedom. I entered ceremonially into the room forbidden to the students. The teachers' library. I was filled with a fever, yes a fever at the thought of the changed voices there, the teachers' voices springing to life as they discussed the merits and defects of their students or told about their private lives, laughing as they corrected one last paper in that vague scent of expensive cigarettes still lingering there. I was breathing in the scent of a forbidden fruit. I picked the handbag up off the table. A kidskin purse the color of marron glacé, two ivory balls to open and close it. I had a vision of a bunch of keys, of a lawn handkerchief. I held it in front of my eyes; I was holding Andromeda, Cassiopeia, the celestial spheres, all the planets and the comets and the stars. I carried the sacred object to her; I was sad as I handed it over. Mlle. Godfroy didn't thank me: she was discussing a complicated rule of grammar with one of her favorite students.

The piano brought me out into cold sweats at night. I would wake up with a start, I could hear Mlle. Vautier: Your thumb . . . The passage with the thumb . . . I can hear too much thumb. . . . One shouldn't be able to hear the thumb. . . . Your left hand is so heavy, you sound as though you're laying bricks. Your left hand mustn't know what your right hand is doing. The hands must be independent. Don't use the pedal. You muffle the sound. . . .

I cried, I got up, I sat there in nothing but my nightgown practicing my exercises, my chromatic thirds. Tirelessly, between two and four in the morning, I continued up and down the scales on my Pleyel's keys. The piano I had longed for since the age of seven exceeded my dreams. I stroked the mahogany, I lifted the lid with neverfailing emotion, I sat down, I straightened my back, I emptied myself inside, I attacked. What remorse I felt if I didn't practice for five hours during the day. I have already said that I began too late, I didn't understand the theory . . . I was intoxicated by virtuosity, but the career of a concert pianist was closed to me. I studied with passion, it was my consolation for my mother's marriage, my piano was my moral guide. I came to it with emotion, with a sense of communion. It was my altar. I admired it while it sounded, I admired it when it fell silent again. The lowered lid concealed a row of black and white idols. It hurt when Mlle. Vautier said to me: "You have fingers," which meant, you are a machine. I was crazy with determination and perseverance for the *Three-Part Inventions*. Music, symmetry, mathematics: they called to me, and with what joy I went to meet them. Oh great marriage feast of composition. Johann Sebastian Bach, I have given you my knees for all time. I gave up the piano when I went to Paris. Phonograph records were more beautiful. But I still play my diminished arpeggios when there is a piano available. I do it as a pilgrimage, I go for a ride over the keyboard. Music, the most mysterious of the arts. Tchaikovsky's *Concerto No. 1* in B-flat minor, my debauch for all the loves that never came to fruition.

*

"Come on," my mother would say. "I'm taking you out, we're going for a drive."

I would climb into the touring car beside her, she drove, we went through the town, we were a long way from Marly. But I had her to myself, I had her beside me, I was proud of her. Such a good driver, such a clever businesswoman.

"That's Henri," she commented, "your father's brother."

We had already left his heavy silhouette behind us. We left the town, the wind stung our faces.

"Faster," I said to her. "Mother, please, please go faster. You're going too slowly."

She gave way.

"How fast am I going?" she would ask suddenly with the shy voice of a young girl.

"Sixty, sixty-five, seventy!" I cried.

"Oh! that one!" my mother would exclaim.

That one meant me. I made her as drunk with speed as I was myself.

On Sundays I never wanted to go with them in the car to visit their colleagues in a nearby town. I was afraid of having to present my big nose to strangers, I was afraid of having to talk to people. They would drive off and I was happy to be left alone in their house. I read, I wept, I leaned out the window, I took the pulse of the street, I took advantage of the crowd coming out of High Mass. Oh that spinach . . . I heated it up, I forgot it. I watched the children, the young men, and the old men in the Square Froissart. I studied them as though I were at the theater, as if I were using opera glasses. There was a poverty-stricken little girl, like a scarecrow in her tattered dress, patting the earth with a trowel and then patting the same place with the palm and the back of her hand. She picked up her trowel and started the same thing all over again with her hair falling down over her eyes. An old woman standing nearby, not daring to sit on the bench because she too was a scarecrow, called out to her. The little girl obeyed. She patted her grandmother's worn-out shoes with the palm and the back of her hand. The old woman displayed no reaction. She remained standing calmly in the vicinity of the statue. They walked away. They plunged into a more colorless, a more secret world beside the warehouse belonging to Jalabert's, the big furniture movers. The little girl hopped from time to time, the grandmother turned her head and looked back with such sorrow and commiseration that I supposed she was wondering if there were not someone even poorer than herself behind her. I could no longer see them, I would never see them again: I went with them into their eternity.

I seized hold of the silver spoon in the saucepan with the spinach. I yelled, I had burnt the palm of my hand. I was annoyed at this unexpected hurt. I poured salad oil on my hand, it went on hurting all day. Now, I say to myself that Arras, Marly were taking their revenge. Fidéline and her granddaughter, poorer, dirtier, more wretched than they had ever been, were coming back to life.

*

I will attempt no embroidery for her. Nineteen, coils of chestnut hair over both ears. Slender, lissome, graceful, her sharp profile contrasting with the long eyelashes, her languorous eyes gazing at you questioningly. A mocking air. Her air. She came from some other region, her accent was not our accent. I followed her at a distance through the main quadrangle. I felt sad and forced myself to feel sad so that I would be interesting to her.

"Get back in line," she said to me, suddenly furious for no reason.

She decided we would go for an excursion into the countryside, we two alone, for a whole Sunday. I was struck dumb with shyness as soon as we climbed up together into the streetcar. She asked me what I was interested in, what I read. I answered: nothing. I smiled, I was disappointed because she was taking an interest in my reading and I wanted us to devote ourselves to her. I kept my gaze fixed on her face; I was ashamed for us both when the streetcar went around a corner and forced us together. I would have preferred to sit opposite her face, her alabaster eyelids. We stepped off the trolley, she went into a café, she asked for the bathroom. Her absence was a relief; I was oppressed by her return. "Aren't you going?" she inquired.

"No," I said with a false air of superiority. I needed to urinate very much. As our outing continued, hour after hour, this need became first a discomfort, then an agony. I refused several times to use the bathrooms she suggested to me so simply. I left her that evening at the foot of the main steps up to the school, I squatted down in the street, I relieved myself. My day with her had been a tortured bladder!

*

"He was a Protestant so you must be a Protestant," my mother said. "You must make inquiries, you must go and find out about it."

I made inquiries, I went to the service at the chapel one Sunday afternoon. "Come up," a woman said. I went up the steps, the harmonium took me by surprise. The congregation were whispering together as they waited for the pastor. A door opened to the right of the pulpit; a little man in a black cassock with a calm face, holding some books and papers, climbed up into the pulpit. "Let us pray to God," he said. The pastor spoke to God as though he knew him quite well. He said several times: "We call upon thee, Oh our God." That "our" touched something in me. What? Everyone in this place can hear God, I said to myself, and I can hear nothing. Someone played a few opening chords on the harmonium. A dimpled hand with well-kept nails picked up the hymn book lying on my lap. Everyone was singing. The hand returned my book open at the page given out by the pastor. I sang. "Let us sing it again, brothers," said the pastor. A pudgy finger, like the finger of a baby, laid itself on the open page before me, pointing out the proper place. I didn't turn my head, I didn't say thank you. I stopped singing. I was among them, I was not one of them. The pastor opened a big book and announced which psalms he was going to read. I felt her move closer, she placed an opened Bible in front of my eyes. I followed what the pastor was reading. I looked at the tiny print, at the fine paper, like tissue paper, I also looked at the hand holding the Bible, at the other hand in its kid glove. Finally I turned my head. Whiteness, washes of pink, transparency, the trembling fragility of the most fragile of eglantines. If she were more slender she wouldn't have that complexion. To have dimples, to have her tiny rosebud mouth. But I must lower my eyes now. The slight roll of her calves over the tops of her boots. She is wearing old-fashioned clothes, she is too neat. Unbelievable: she dares to clean her glasses during the sermon. I must close my eyes since they all have their eyes closed. Trying to find God, what hard work. If one of my hairs were suddenly to stand up, if one of my nails were to fall off while I am trying to find God . . . Good students are given encouragement. . . . An effort in the right direction, oh God omnipotent. God is resting from his labors, God created all that is. Fidéline used to close her prayer book with a key. I must open my eyes. "We shall sing hymn number . . . verses . . ." That "we" is the bait they'll use to win me over next Sunday.

"I'll bring you a Bible and a hymn book for your own use," said the young girl as I left the chapel.

That evening, in my bed, to help me recall her face and above all her hand, my fingers twisted the hairs of my pubis. Innocently. Simply as a way of helping myself concentrate.

And Mlle. Godfroy? And the assistant mistress for whom I held in my urine? I no longer go to school. Only the piano has resisted the change. I read Tolstoy and Dostoievsky until dawn, then dawdle away my time over the big ledgers at the business. I rub out, I erase entries with my two bottles of liquid, one white, one black. The "Corector" puts me to sleep. What shall I do with my life? I shall work in a bookstore, I shall read all day without having to cut the pages, I shan't leave my mother. . . . The kiss of my escort, at night, at Estelle's wedding. His excitement, his drunkenness. He went out, I followed him. It was heavenly when he lay down on the flagstones in the courtyard. Such beauties are ephemeral. His long kiss, his absent-mindedness. He kissed with his eyes open.

"What is your name?"

"My name is Aline. Here is your Bible and here is your hymn book. Let us go in."

"Let us go in."

Who told me what to do? I took off my gloves and stuffed them into my purse. Who told me: Hold your book in your left hand? I don't believe in the devil. If God exists he has no rival. Hell is our ambition for evil. I was obeying an order. Her arm slipped under mine, my hand was in hers, her fingers intertwined with mine. I sang with my mind far from the hymn, a ray of sunshine shone on my knee. She squeezed my hand as hard as she could, I squeezed her hand as hard as I could, the pastor said we must sing some more. Her fingers disengaged themselves from mine with all the delicacy of a flute separating itself from an oboe. "Let us pray to God," said the pastor. Would the girl's fingers come back? With fingers intertwined once more we listened to the sermon. The others were all so absorbed they didn't see our union. I avoided her when we came out; I was too shy to say good-by. That evening, that night, next morning, next day, the day after that, I set myself to reliving the feel of those fingers between my own. Next Sunday, Aline was playing the harmonium and I didn't dare show my distress in the chapel. She asked me at the foot of the steps if I would like to knit for the Sunday School children. The crossed needles were our interlocking fingers. My parents were astonished: I was always running to the chapel, running to hear the preachers; and I became interested in good works. I had a secret, there was a driving force inside me: the image of her hand in mine. Often, in the evening, when my parents insisted, I sang the famous hymn, "Keep we our lamps in readiness," for them. I sang out of tune with such enthusiasm that they laughed until they cried. I lived my whole life for an arm, for a hand, for the Bible and the hymn book at Sunday service. Once the service was over I avoided her and she avoided me.

Once, though, she did invite me to go and listen to chamber music at her parents' house on the outskirts of town. Her mother showed me around the little soap factory where Aline, dressed in a long white smock, was working with her father. I recognized her crown of blonde hair. "Don't shake my hand," she said to me. Aline was packing soap. Her father didn't open his mouth. I fell in love immediately with the smell of chemicals, the languorous background smell of the place.

Dinner with Protestants . . . It was like playing truant. The chamber music bored me. Aline played the violin. I would have to sleep at their house if the evening went on too long. It did go on too long, as the violin, the cello, and the piano continued their interminable conversation. I listened to them, my hair, gleaming with boredom, escaping through the cracks under the doors. Finally we exchanged good nights.

I found the same disturbing smell of toilet soap in their bathroom. I put out the light, I waited with bare feet, dressed in a flimsy nightgown.

Aline smiled at me in her bedroom, in her bed. She closed her Bible and placed it on her bedside table. The room sparkled with virtue. She was going to sleep in her crown of blonde hair. I climbed into the bed. Put out the light, I said sternly. Already? said Aline gently. She found my hand, she squeezed it as she squeezed it on Sundays. "Why don't you say anything?" she asked.

I squeezed her fingers furiously. "Let's go to sleep," I said. I didn't want to sleep. I didn't know what I wanted, but there was a bow of expectation drawn taut inside me.

Five minutes later, Aline was asleep. Her possessions, the things surrounding us, as well as the stern and unaccustomed silence of the room, held me in their grip for a moment. I spilled a few tears on the strange pillow. I was powerless against the sleep of an eglantine. I listened to her breathing, I listened to the movement of that most ancient of all machines: the human body. I let myself be taken in by that tale from the *Arabian Nights:* the peaceful breathing of another being. I moved over toward Aline, I sought out her mouth, I stole the kiss I gave her. Aline didn't wake up, my lips on hers did not insist. I had felt the breath of the eglantine inside my mouth, that was enough.

I then had the leisure to reflect on what a hypocrite I had become since I ceased being a child of the streets. I had become taciturn of late, because I was afraid of speaking badly, but often, as often as possible when my mother was first married, I rushed off to entertain the women who worked in my stepfather's upholstery workshop. I gave imitations of the fishwives crying their wares. If my stepfather appeared I grew pale, I blushed, I was ashamed of distracting his workers from their work, and, even worse, ashamed of being myself. I examined my conscience as I lay on a downy mattress beneath a feathery eiderdown. What was I doing in the world? Nothing. I was a parasite on my mother. Her marriage had made me go rotten inside. I mean that by providing me with the opportunity of an education she had taken away the self-sufficiency I'd had at Marly, the armor I had acquired as a child of the streets. My piano, my books. I didn't say to myself: Tolstoy and Dostoievsky are worth years of school. They didn't come into it: they were simply the companions of my sleepless nights. I lived in their world, I gave myself to their characters, I gulped them down because the more I read of their novels, the hungrier I became with every page. Life isn't just reading at night and practicing scales. I couldn't understand anything, I couldn't remember anything, I never won any prizes. My mother didn't scold me: she signed my reports without even reading them. That night, in the bed of the pure Aline, at the heart of a Protestant home, I'd had enough, I had quite simply had enough of the chapel, enough of the catechism classes I would soon be attending. I didn't deny the existence of God. I just couldn't find a place to put him. During the week, I sometimes went into churches in the same spirit as a chemist repeating an experiment.

In the catechism classes I sat opposite one of André's nephews. He had a resemblance to his uncle. I looked at him out of the corner of my eye, he looked at me out of the corner of his. He didn't speak, I didn't speak; we both abstained from the discussion when the other members of the class touched on problems of theology. "You will be going to your first Communion soon," the pastor told me. I looked at him for a moment, then replied that I wasn't ready to swallow the body of Christ. I didn't go back. I have never been to Communion. It was thus that I lost the arm, the hand, and the fingers of Aline.

Ungrateful, having become a young lady without religion, without respect for the law, without principles, living in the heart of town, I had drifted away from Laure: she didn't visit us anymore; her apron was a disgrace to their stylish furnishings. I was free to find her in the market place and kiss her there. I didn't go to the marketplace. Laure rose in the world, she achieved prosperity with her unrelenting efforts, while our fortunes declined. I often hear her great Northern peasant's voice as she quarreled with her husband and his mother, as she shouted: "If I leave I shall take the child with me." We had both experienced a sudden and overwhelming feeling of kinship. I can hear her laugh: it shakes the chandeliers in my parents' display room.

Unforgettable red letter days, unforgettable feasts of chicken and champagne and mocha cake when my stepfather went to Paris on business. I ate lunch all alone with my mother. We talked about everything and about nothing, we talked about Marly, Marly our fairyland. At the height of our chattering and gaiety, a voice inside me would ask: can you see us, Fidéline? Does our meal please you? I would fall silent and my mother would say: "Off in a dream again like her father." I had gone flying off into another world of adoration. I wasn't being unfaithful to my mother. Another presence would force itself upon me, then vanish again.

*

We spent money like water when we went to choose underwear and blouses at Mme. Wyamme's. My mother gave all her attention to her shopping. I wandered about, I dreamed my way about the store, I thought about the Mendelssohn concerto I'd found among some music. I didn't see the new blouse my mother was trying on: I was seeing the smaller, more densely packed notes for the orchestra under the music for the pianist. "Do you like it?" my mother asked crossly.

"Yes, I like it," I said, off in another world, a world of sugared desolation.

"Attend to what you're doing, say what you think. Do you like it?" my mother repeated impatiently.

"I like it," I said more loudly. For piano and orchestra. I found the concerto hollow but the orchestral part showed me the way, helped me in my progress toward the destiny of Ludwig von Beethoven. He was deaf and he composed music. I smiled at the sea of Valenciennes lace. Deaf and a composer. I ran over to her, we discussed fabrics, trimmings, cuts, necklines. My mother whispered: "He's looking at you. If you could see how the Wyamme boy is looking at you! Whatever you do, don't look at him." I was at the disobedient age, I disobeyed, I looked at him. Shy, with a nice-looking face and very wide eyes, the son of the firm was no longer looking at me. He was coming and going, apparently bored amid all that whiteness. Flattered? Yes, even as I made sure that my mother was mistaken. The mirror gave its approval. We received a sullen good day from the young man plus a set speech of commercial courtesies from his mother as we left the store.

"Wouldn't you like to be married to him?" my mother insisted.

I laughed, I relieved her of her packages. I answered: "I'm not going to marry."

"You'll get married like all the others," concluded my mother.

That annoyed me: "I shan't get married! I'm going to work in a bookshop!" She had forgotten her daily warnings at breakfast when I was little. I was still carrying them in my ovaries.

I was incapable of selling a yard of braid, incapable of keeping the accounts. If I went down to the store it was always to wait for my mother, to observe, to keep watch from my hiding place: a dark corridor. I followed the movements of their lips through the glass partition of the office. I didn't say to myself: they are working, they are discussing business. I said: her hair smells of Directoire furniture, of toile de Jouy, her eyes have taken on the proud shimmer of moiré silk, of shot taffeta. Her hair no longer has the good old smell of dirt it had when we both caught the scabies brought by the German soldiers in the war; her eyes no longer hold the image of our old saucepan full of potato stew. I would wait for an hour, for an hour and a half, until she was ready to take me to the fair. Occasionally she would emerge from the office like a whirlwind, she would come toward me as I went toward her, and reassure me: "Just a little while longer, I'm coming now." I lost her once more, once more I stood watching her animated gestures. My stepfather walked up and down the office, my mother turned the pages of the great ledgers, entering figures. When she closed the ledgers, when she finally stood up, I ran up to the second floor, I was with her again in an everyday world. The glass wall of their office had melted, but it wasn't enough to bring back the streams of Marly.

*

The fair in the Place Poterne was erected on a raised wooden platform that protected us from the reverberations of the music. The caryatids, the brightly painted bosses, the glitter of the inlaid mirrors, all went to my head. There were young people with confetti scattered on their hair buying more cones of confetti. I went into the fairground with my rolls of pink, blue, and green streamers; the planks were strewn with litter. Around the merry-go-round itself there whirled another human merry-go-round hurling fistfuls of confetti. All the sensible people were sitting on garden chairs outside. My mother settled herself on one of them, cut off from the barbaric music, from the shouting and pushing by her elegance and inner disdain. I was older now, I no longer wanted to be in a gondola. I wanted a horse, the biggest there was, so as to see, to be seen. Confetti flew into my eyes, into my mouth, streamers tugged at me. I became a proud iris battered by a rain of paper.

At last I managed to climb up onto the merry-go-round. I reached the red velvet saddle, I found the reins. I was preparing for a journey as I slid my feet into the stirrups. The motion at first was like a dream. It was gentle, it was slow. We were turning at last. My mother, I can't see her. Where is she? There she is. She's seen me, she's looking at me, she's nodding toward me with her chin. It's true, she's quite separate from the fair, and she could separate me from it. I don't want her to. Softly, softly, I throw my first streamer toward her chair. Now she is looking at the town's upper crust waiting on the garden chairs. The Wyamme boy, standing back on his own, was throwing as many streamers at me as he could. As I went by I saw some cruel young men: they were opening girls' mouths and filling them with confetti. Lustily, the girls spat the little rounds of paper back in their faces. The agility of the fairground men as they walked to and fro on the bucking planks astonished me. My mother rose to her feet, she was always angry with me if the young men tried to make me eat confetti. I felt sorry for the wooden horses next to mine that were circling around without riders. Not dead, yet not alive.

I got down after my twentieth or thirtieth go. We left the fairground.

*

My stepfather, very suddenly, sold his whole business. Or rather, he disposed of it. Now we are living in a châlet facing the park, on a very lively square: cars and passers-by during the day, the whistling and struggle of the winds at night. I practice Schubert's Impromptus without losing heart, I walk the baby that was born before my parents gave up their business. I talk to him, I take him in my arms, I hold him against me, but I am too much in awe of him. I don't scold him, I don't shake him, I don't give him little smacks here and there. He frightens me when his face begins to change. That screwed-up look announcing that he is unhappy when I know he isn't sick fills me with panic. I pore over him too much, his skull intrigues me. No, I cannot be aloof with him. I devote myself to him. I play at being a mother like a little girl. I give and treat myself to a performance. I want the baby to be happy, very happy. The length of time his tears and yells go on for, that is the mystery of mysteries. I don't say to myself: You will be able to have one just like this.

I was pushing the baby carriage when I met Mlle. Fromont. She had taken a job as assistant mistress at the school in D—. She said:

"It's a pity. You should finish your studies. Persuade your mother." I didn't dare reply: "Finish my studies? I haven't begun them." My parents would soon be going to live in Paris. Live in Paris? What a horrible thought. I didn't want to be swallowed up by all those millions of people, those millions of apartment houses, those millions of cars, those millions of streets in the capital. I preferred living in the closed world of a boarding school. I would go to the school at D—. My mother, when I asked her advice, wanted me to do what I wanted. I promised to work hard.

We were beginning the week with our usual Sunday evening session in the shoe shop; we had just come back from our half-term holiday. The shoe shop in our school was the room where we cleaned our shoes, not a place of lasts and hammers and nails. We polished away in a vault of monotony, windowless and badly lit; we sat dreaming with our shoes on our knees those first evenings back at school. The virtuous odor of the polish, that odor always associated with tonics in druggists' shops, made us listless. We languished over our brushes and rags. We had filed in, two by two, with the monitor, who was bored. Now the new assistant mistress was there sitting on the bench with us, reading, escaping into her story, away from the school, away from the town itself while we stroked our woolen rags across the leather with desultory gestures. That evening we were ten girls back at school, wan under waiting-room lights; ten girls back at school with nothing to say to each other, ten sulking girls forced into each others' company and avoiding each other.

I can count and recount: it was thirty days since I had been back at boarding school; for twenty-six evenings Isabelle had spat on the school as she spat on her shoe. My polish would be less hard if I were to spit like her. I could spread it more easily. She spits. Can the favorite student be annoyed? I am the bad student, I am the worst student in the whole of the senior dormitory. I don't care one way or the other. I loathe the headmistress, I loathe sewing, I loathe physical training, I loathe chemistry, I loathe everything, and I avoid the other girls. It's miserable, but I don't want to go away from here. My mother is married, my mother has been unfaithful. The shoebrush had fallen from my knees; Isabelle had given my brush a kick while I was brooding.

"My brush! Where is my brush?"

Isabelle spat more vigorously on the box-calf in front of her. My brush was under the assistant's foot. She was going to pay for that kick. I picked up the brush, I tipped back Isabelle's face, I thrust the rag spotted with polish, with dust and red cream, into her eyes, into her mouth. I glimpsed her milky skin through the opening in her uniform, I took my hand away from her face, I returned to my place. In silent fury, Isabelle wiped her lips and eyes. She spat for the sixth time on her shoe and shrugged her shoulders. The assistant closed her book and clapped her hands: the light flickered. Isabelle went on rubbing her shoe.

We were waiting for her. "You must come now," said the new assistant timidly. We had entered the shoe shop with clattering heels but we were ghosts as we left it in our black gym shoes like a line of orphans. The gym shoe, near relation to the espadrille, muffles what it strikes: stone, wood, earth. We borrowed the heels of angels to leave the shoe shop and walked with wads of melancholy in our canvas shoes. Every Sunday we went up to the dormitory with the monitor beside us, we breathed in the faint pink smell of disinfectant. Isabelle had caught up with us on the stairs.

I hate her, I want to hate her. It would be a relief if I could hate her even more. Tomorrow we shall be at the same table in the dining hall again. She smiles vaguely when I come in late. I can't change tables. But I crushed that smile of hers. That natural self-confidence of hers . . . I'll flatten that into her face as well. I'll go to the headmistress if I have to but I will change tables.

We entered the dormitory where the dark shine of the linoleum foretold the loneliness of the center aisle at midnight. We lifted our percale curtains and found ourselves once more in those cubicles without locks and without walls. Isabelle was the last to slide the rings of her curtain along their rod; the monitor made her tour of inspection along the aisle. We opened our suitcases, took out our linen, and put it away on the shelf in our closet, keeping out the two sheets for our narrow beds. We threw the key into the suitcase and closed it again for eight more days. We made our beds. Our things didn't belong to us in that municipal light. We pulled our uniforms back into shape on their coat hangers for the Thursday walk. We folded up our underclothes and put them on the chair, we took our bathrobes from their pegs.

Isabelle left the dormitory with her pitcher.

I am listening to the knot of her bathrobe cord brushing against the linoleum. I can hear her fingers drumming on the enamel. Her cubicle is opposite mine. I have that to face. Her comings and goings. I listen for them, her comings and goings. She laughs because I shut myself in the music room to practice diminished arpeggios. She says I pound, she says she can hear me in the study hall.

I went out into the aisle with my pitcher.

She was still there, always there, still there on the landing. I'd have undressed more slowly if I'd known that she was filling her pitcher at the tap. Shall I turn back? Shall I wait till she's gone before coming out? I won't turn back. I'm not afraid of her: I hate her. She knows there's someone behind her, but that wouldn't make her hurry. What nonchalance . . . She isn't even curious enough to look over her shoulder. I should never have come if I'd known she would dawdle like this. I thought she'd gone: here she is just in front of me. Her pitcher will soon be full. At last. I've seen her long hair let down before; how could I avoid it when she's always parading it up and down the aisle? Excuse me. She said excuse me. She brushed my face with her hair as I was standing thinking about it. It's unimaginable. She tossed back her hair into my face. She didn't know I was behind her and she said excuse me. It's unbelievable. She can't say I made you wait, I'm sorry, the tap isn't working properly. She just throws her hair in your face while she says excuse me. The water is running slower. Of course, because she's fiddling with the tap. I won't speak to you, you won't get a word out of me. You ignore me, I will ignore you. Why are you making me wait? Is that what you want? If you've got the time, so have I.

The assistant on duty in the aisle called to us as though there were some sort of complicity between us. Isabelle walked away.

I could hear her lying: she was explaining to the mistress that the water had stopped running. I went back to my cubicle.

The new assistant came and spoke to her again through her percale curtain. They were confiding in each other that they were both the same age: eighteen. A train whistled in the station and cut them short.

I pulled my curtain aside slightly: the proctor was moving away, he began reading again as he walked down the aisle; one of the girls was rustling the paper in a box of candy.

"I have strict orders," murmured the new assistant. "No visiting. All girls are to stay in their own cubicles."

As soon as we had washed, the assistant inspected us as we lay scrubbed and docile in our beds. Some of the girls gave her candies and delayed her with compliments and flattery, while Isabelle retired into her tomb. As soon as I had made a nest in my cold bed I forgot her, but if I woke up again I would grope for the thought of her in order to hate her. She didn't dream aloud, her bedsprings didn't creak. One night I got up at two in the morning, I went across the aisle, I held my breath and listened as she slept. She was an absence. She was laughing at me even in her sleep. I closed her curtain, I listened again. Yes, she was absent, she was having the last word. I hated her as I lay between sleeping and waking. I hated her in the bell at half-past six every morning, in the deep tones of her voice, in her washing water as it ran away, in her hand as it closed her tin of dentifrice. All you ever hear is her, I said to myself with unreasoning obstinacy. I hated the dust in her cubicle when she slid the mop under my curtain, when she bumped against the partition, when her hand disturbed the folds of my curtain. She didn't talk much, she performed all the required motions in the dormitory, in the dining hall, in classes: she was thoughtful during recreation periods. I wondered where she acquired her arrogance. She was good at her work without being either overzealous or conceited. Isabelle often used to pull the strings of my pinafore undone, then she pretended she hadn't when I turned around. She would begin the day teasing me in this way, like a little girl, and then she would immediately tie my pinafore up again for me, humiliating me twice instead of just once.

I got cautiously out of bed as though I were a smuggler. The new assistant stopped buffing her nails. I waited. Isabelle, who never coughed, coughed: for once she was still awake. I brushed the thought of her from my mind, I plunged my arm as far as the shoulder into an unappealing cloth bag hanging in my closet. I always concealed my flashlight and my books inside my dirty linen bag. I used to read at night. That evening I got back into bed with my flashlight and my book but without any desire to read. I switched on the flashlight, I lay gazing with brooding eyes at my gym shoes under the chair. The artificial moonlight filtering out from the assistant's cubicle gave all the objects in my cell a pale and sickly look.

I put out the flashlight, a girl rustled a piece of paper, I pushed away the book with a disgruntled hand. More like a statue on a tomb than the real thing, I said to myself as I imagined Isabelle lying there stiffly in her nightgown. The book fell shut, the flashlight sank into the eiderdown. I put my hands together, I prayed wordlessly for a world I could not envisage, I listened to the surf in the seashell so close to my belly. The assistant put out her light as well. She has all the luck sleeping there, all the luck, lost in her warm, downy tomb. The limpid tick-tock of my watch on the bedside table spurred me to action. I picked up the book again and began reading under the bedclothes.

Someone was spying on me from behind my curtain. Hidden beneath the bedclothes I could hear the inexorable tick-tock of the watch. A night train rolled out of the station drawn by a whistle that arrowed through shadows unknown to the school. I threw back the covers, I was afraid of the silent dormitory.

Someone was calling behind the percale curtain.

I lay low. I pulled the covers up over my head. I lit my flashlight.

"Violette," someone called inside my cubicle.

I put out the flashlight.

"What are you doing under your bedclothes?" asked the voice I didn't recognize.

"I'm reading."

Someone pulled back the covers. Someone pulled my hair.

"I told you I was reading."

"Not so loud," Isabelle said.

One of the girls coughed.

"You can report me if you want to. . . ."

Isabelle wouldn't report me. I was being unfair to her and I knew it.

"Weren't you asleep?"

"Not so loud," Isabelle said.

I was whispering too loud because I wanted my joy to be over and done with: my ecstasy was becoming an unbearable pride.

My visitor was still by my percale curtain. Her long hair hanging down inside my cubicle filled me with uncertainty.

"I'm afraid you'll say no. Say that you'll say yes to me," Isabelle said breathlessly.

I had switched on my flashlight again, I was being obliging to my visitor despite myself.

"Say yes!" Isabelle begged.

Now she was supporting herself with one finger on my bedside table.

She tightened the cord of her bathrobe. Her hair tumbled down over her ripening breasts, her face grew older.

"What are you reading?" She took her finger off the table.

"I was just beginning when you came in."

I put out the flashlight because she was looking at my book.

"The title . . . Tell me the title."

"A Happy Man . . ."

"That's the title? Is it good?"

"I've no idea. I've just begun it."

Isabelle was leaving, one of the curtain rings slid along its rod. I thought she was going back to her tomb. She stopped.

"Come and read in my room."

She was leaving again, she was scattering crystals of frost between her request and my answer.

"Will you come?"

Isabelle left my cubicle.

She had seen me with the bedclothes up to my neck. She didn't know I was wearing a special nightgown, a nightgown from a lingerie boutique. I thought one's personality could be changed by wearing expensive clothes. The silk nightgown brushed against my flanks with the softness of a spider's web. I dressed myself in my regulation nightgown, then I too left my cubicle, wrists gripped tightly by my regulation cuffs. The assistant mistress was asleep. I hesitated in front of Isabelle's curtain. I went in.

"What's the time?" I asked coldly.

I stayed by the curtain, I shone my flashlight toward the bedside table.

"Come over here," Isabelle said.

I didn't dare. Her long hair, all undone, seemed to belong to a stranger and it intimidated me. Isabelle was looking at the time.

"Come closer," she said to her wristwatch.

The luxuriance of the hair sweeping down the bars at the head of the bed. It made a shimmering screen hiding the face of a recumbent girl, it frightened me. I put out the light.

Isabelle got out of bed. She took my flashlight and my book away from me.

"Now come here," she said.

Isabelle was back in bed.

She lay in bed directing the beam of my flashlight.

I sat down on the edge of the mattress. She stretched her arm over my shoulder, took my book from the bedside table and gave it to me. She reassured me. I turned the pages of the book because she was staring at me, I didn't know which page to stop at. She waited for what I was waiting for.

I fastened my eyes on the first letter of the first line.

"Eleven o'clock," Isabelle said.

I gazed at the first page, at the words I could not see. She took the book from my hands and put out the light.

Isabelle pulled me backwards, she laid me down on the eiderdown, she raised me up, she kept me in her arms: she was taking me out of a world where I had never lived so that she could launch me into a world I had not yet reached; the lips opened mine a little, they moistened my teeth. The too fleshy tongue frightened me; but the strange virility didn't force its way in. Absently calmly, I waited. The lips moved over my lips. My heart was beating too hard and I wanted to prolong the sweetness of the imprint, the new experience brushing at my lips. Isabelle is kissing me, I said to myself. She was tracing a circle around my mouth, she was encircling the disturbance, she laid a cool kiss in each corner, two staccato notes of music on my lips; then her mouth pressed against mine once more, hibernating there. My eyes were wide with astonishment beneath their lids, the seashells at my ears were whispering too loud. Isabelle continued: we climbed rung after rung down into the darkness below the darkness of the school, below the darkness of the town, below the darkness of the streetcar depot. She had made her honey on my lips, the sphinxes were drifting into sleep again. I knew that I had needed her before we met. Isabelle thrust back her hair which had been sheltering us.

"Do you think she's asleep?" she asked.

"The new assistant?"

"She's asleep," Isabelle decided.

"She's asleep," I said too.

"You're shivering. Take off your robe."

She opened the bedcovers.

"Come in without the light," Isabelle said.

She lay down against the partition, in her bed, at home. I took off my robe, I felt I was too new on the rug of an old world. I had to get into bed with her quickly because the floor was going away from under me. I stretched myself out along the edge of the mattress: prepared to escape like a thief in the night.

"You're cold. Come close to me," Isabelle said.

A sleeper coughed, trying to separate us.

She was already holding me, I was already held, we were already torturing one another, but the cheerful foot touching mine, the ankle rubbing against my ankle, reassured us. My nightgown occasionally brushed against me as we clutched one another and rolled back and forth. We stopped. Memory and the dormitory about us returned. Isabelle switched on the flashlight: she wanted to see me. I took it back from her. A wave carried her away and she sank down into the bed, then rose up again, plunged her face toward me, and held me to her. There were roses falling from the girdle she put around me. I fastened the same girdle around her.

"The bed mustn't make a noise," she said.

I felt for a cool place on the pillow, as though that would be the place to keep the bed silent. I found a pillow of blond hair. Isabelle pulled me on top of her.

We were still hugging each other, we both wanted to be swallowed up by the other. We had stripped ourselves of our families, the rest of the world, time, and light. As Isabelle lay crushed over my gaping heart I wanted to feel her enter it. Love is a harrowing invention. Isabelle, Violette, I thought to myself, trying to become accustomed to the magic simplicity of the two first names.

She swathed my shoulders in the white softness of her arm as though in a fur, she put my hand in the furrow between her breasts, on top of her muslin nightgown. The enchantment of my hand under hers, of my neck and shoulders clothed with her arm. And yet my face was alone: my eyelids were cold. Isabelle knew they were. Her tongue began to press against my teeth, impatient to make me warm all over. I shut myself up, I barricaded myself inside my mouth. She waited: that was how she taught me to open into flower. She was the hidden muse inside my body. Her tongue, her little flame, softened my muscles, my flesh. I responded, I attacked, I fought, I wanted to emulate her violence. We no longer cared about the noise we made with our lips. We were relentless with each other; then, becoming quieter, methodically, both together, we began drugging each other with our saliva. After the exchange of so much moisture, our lips parted despite themselves. Isabelle let herself fall into the hollow of my shoulder.

"Together," she said to regain her breath.

There was something crawling in my belly. I had a sea monster inside me.

Isabelle with a childish finger on my lips was tracing the outline of my mouth. The finger dropped down onto my neck. I seized it, I drew it across my eyes.

"They're yours," I said.

Isabelle didn't speak. Isabelle didn't move. If she were asleep it would be over. Isabelle was once more as she had always been. I no longer trusted her. I should have to leave. This was her cubicle, not mine. I was unable to move: we hadn't finished. If she were asleep, then she had lured me there on false pretenses.

Make her not be asleep among distant stars. Make the darkness not engender darkness in her.

Isabelle was not asleep!

She lifted my arm, my thigh grew pale. I felt a cold thrill of pleasure. I listened to what she took, to what she was giving, I blinked with gratitude: I was giving suck. Isabelle moved suddenly to another place. She was smoothing my hair, she was stroking the night out of my hair so that it ran all down my cheeks. She stopped, she created an intermission. Brow pressed against brow, we listened to the undertow; we were giving ourselves back to the silence, we were giving ourselves up to it.

A caress is to a shudder what twilight is to a lightning flash. Isabelle was dragging a rake of light from my shoulder to my wrist; she passed with her five-fingered mirror over my throat, over the back of my neck, over my back. I followed the hand, I could see under my eyelids a neck, a shoulder, an arm that didn't belong to me. She was raping my ear with her tongue as earlier she had raped my mouth. The artifice was shameless, the sensation strange. I grew cold again, this refinement of bestiality made me fearful. Isabelle found my head again, she held me by the hair and began again. I was disturbed by this fleshy icicle, but Isabelle's self-confidence reassured me.

She leaned out of the bed and opened the drawer in the bedside table.

"A shoelace! Why a shoelace?"

"I'm tying up my hair. Keep quiet, otherwise we shall be caught."

Isabelle was tying the knot, she was preparing herself. I listened to what is always alone: the heart. I waited: she would come when she was prepared.

A tiny bluish egg fell from her lips onto the spot she had left as her mouth returned to it. She opened the neck of my nightgown, she explored the curve of my shoulder with her cheek, with her brow. I accepted the marvels she was imagining on the curve of my shoulders. She was giving me a lesson in humility. I grew frightened. I was a living being. I wasn't a statue.

She closed the neck of my nightgown.

"Am I heavy?" she asked softly.

"Don't move . . ."

I wanted to squeeze her in my arms but I didn't dare. The quarter-hours were borne into the air, one by one, from the school clock. Isabelle was drawing a snail with her finger on the bare patch we have behind our ear lobes. She tickled me without meaning to. It was silly.

She took my head between her hands as though I'd been beheaded, she thrust her tongue into my mouth. She wanted us to be bony, all cutting angles. We tore each other to pieces with stony needles. The kiss slowed down as it reached my entrails, it disappeared, flowing warmly into the sea.

We stopped kissing one another and lay down; we pressed finger bone against finger bone and charged our knuckles with all we could find no words to say.

Isabelle coughed, our intertwined fingers fell silent.

"Let yourself go," she said.

She kissed the points of the collar, the braid on my nightgown; she molded the charity we have around our shoulders. The careful hand drew lines over my lines, curves over my curves. Behind my eyelids I could see the halo made by my shoulder as it came to life, I listened to the light springing to life under the caress.

I stopped her.

"Let me go on," she said.

The voice was slurred, the hand was sinking into a quicksand. I felt the shape of Isabelle's neck, her shoulder, her arm, along my neck, around my shoulder, along my arm.

A flower opened in every pore of my skin.

I took her arm, I thanked her with a kiss that drew the blood up to her skin.

"How good you are!" I said.

The poverty of my vocabulary made me lose heart. Isabelle's hands were trembling, they pulled a corselet of fine lawn tight over the cloth of my nightgown: her hands trembled with greed like the hands of a maniac.

She pushed herself up, she squeezed my waist. Isabelle, with her cheek pressed to mine, was telling a tale of friendship to my cheek.

Isabelle's fingers opened, closed again like the bud of a daisy and brought my breasts through pink mists out of their limbo. I was awakening to spring with a babble of lilacs under my skin.

"Do it more," I said.

Isabelle stroked my side. My flesh as she caressed it became a caress, my flank as she stroked it sent a soft glow seeping down into my drugged legs, into my melting ankles. My insides were being twisted, gently, gently.

"I can't go on."

We waited. We had to keep watch on the watchful shadows all around us.

I took her in my arms but I couldn't hug her as hard as I should have liked because of the narrow bed; I couldn't embed her in my flesh. A peremptory little girl suddenly pulled herself free:

"I want, I want . . ."

I will want what she wants, if the sea monsters stop their lazy coiling, if the shooting stars stop gliding through my limbs. I yearned for an avalanche of rocks.

"Do some more, do some more. . . ."

"You don't help me," said Isabelle.

Her hand moved forward beneath the cloth. I listened to the coolness of her hand, she listened to the heat of my skin. Her finger ventured onto the spot where the buttocks touch. It went on into the groove, it came out again. Isabelle stroked the two buttocks at the same time with one hand. My knees and feet were deliquescing.

"I can't bear it. I tell you I can't bear it."

Isabelle, unmoved, went on stroking quickly back and forth for a long time.

There were pincers pulling at me, I was being filled with spices. Isabelle fell on top of me.

"Are you all right?"

"Yes," I said, unsatisfied.

She returned to the attack, she offered me a kiss, her lips calmly pressed against mine.

Isabelle was turning her hands into claws in the fabric over my Venus' mound, she was going in and out, though without actually entering me; she was cradling my groin, her fingers, the cloth, and time itself.

"Are you all right?"

"Yes, Isabelle."

I didn't like the polite way it came out.

Isabelle persevered with her task in a new way, with one finger moving rhythmically on one of the lips. My body soaked up the light from the finger as sand soaks up the sea.

"Another time," she said into my neck.

"You want me to go now?"

"It would be more sensible."

I got out of bed.

"You want us to be parted?"

"No."

She wound her arms around me while I pretended to resist. It was the first time she had held me against her standing up.

We listened to the whirlwind turning the nebula in our insides, we followed the circling sails of the dormitory's shadowy windmills.

I brought Isabelle back in my turn from a wintry, windswept beach. I pulled back the covers, I helped her in.

"It's late. I was wrong just now: you must get some sleep."

"No, it's all right."

"You're yawning . . . you're half asleep already. . . ."

I gazed at her as I gaze out at the twilit sea when I can no longer see it.

"Yes, you must go now," Isabelle said.

*

If I got bored during study periods—and I did so often because I didn't work—I opened the door of my book locker, I passed the time by looking at the labels on the closed books, I thought of my books as standing there asleep. I had written the names of their authors on the labels. I folded my arms, I listened for a long while, and at last I heard the murmur of classical tragedies.

"Lily of the valley!"

The bouquet, just a few slips tied together, was lying on my leather satchel. I saw a green and white crucifix made of leaves and flowers laid out on my satchel. The gift lent me an armor of strength: I was too happy. I closed the door of the locker again, I shut myself up inside myself, I went back to the locker. The bouquet hadn't vanished. She had given me flowers from an old romance. She had set down leaves like lances and a talisman of flowers as one sets down a baby in a basket to abandon it. I fled to the dormitory with my treasure.

*

What shall we do tonight? Tomorrow in this classroom, in front of this desk, I shall remember what it was we did. I stare at *b* on the blackboard. I shall think quickly of what we did last night. Of everything we did, before the girl on monitor duty picks up the eraser, before she rubs out *b*. We didn't do anything. I'm being unfair. She kissed me, she came to me. Yes, she came to me. What a world . . . She lay on top of me. I throw myself at Isabelle's feet. I don't remember what we did and that's all I can think of. What shall we do tonight? Another girl will rub out the triangle, will rub out *a* and *b* and *c*.

*

It was all even stricter than in church. Isabelle was studying at the front table near the dais. I sat down in my place, I opened a book so as to be like her, I kept watch, I counted one, two, three, four, five, six, seven, eight. I can't go up to her, I can't make her look up from her book. Another girl went up to Isabelle's table without any hesitation, she showed her some work she'd done. They discussed it. Isabelle was still living as she had lived before she called me into her cubicle. Isabelle was disappointing me, Isabelle was casting a spell over me.

I can't read. Every meandering river in my geography book holds the same question in every loop. What can I do to make the time pass? She turns sideways; she has exposed herself to me but she doesn't know I'm drinking her in. She turns toward where I am sitting, she will never know what she gave me. She is talking, she is far away, she is discussing something, she is working: a foal is gamboling in her head. I'm not at all like her. I shall go to her, I shall force myself on her. She yawns—how human she is—she pulls the pin out of her coiled hair, she pushes it back again. She knows what she will do tonight, but she can think of other things.

Isabelle leaned toward me when the other girl left the study hall. Isabelle had noticed me.

I moved down the aisle, squeezed between the walls of my joy.

"My love. Were you there all the time?" she asked.

My head was suddenly quite empty.

"Bring your books. We'll work together. It's stifling in here."

I opened the window and, for heroism's sake, looked out into the courtyard.

"Aren't you bringing your books?"

"It would be impossible."

"Why?"

"I couldn't work near you."

When she sees me and her face changes like that, it's genuine. When she can't see me and her face is normal, that's genuine too.

"Do you really want me near you?" I asked.

"Sit down."

I sat down next to her, I sobbed a sob of happiness.

"What's the matter?"

"I can't explain."

She took my hand under the desk.

"Isabelle, Isabelle . . . What shall we do during recess?"

"We'll talk."

"I don't want to talk."

I took my hand away.

"Tell me what's the matter," Isabelle insisted.

"Can't you tell?"

"We'll be together again. I promise."

At about seven that evening I was surrounded by other girls suggesting I go for a walk with them or talk to them. I stammered, I moved away from the others. I was no longer free and I was no longer the same age. Shall I ever listen again, as I listened once, outside the kindergarten room, to the young mistress who studies at the Conservatoire and still plays Bach on the piano of her alma mater? Isabelle was putting away her books, Isabelle was near me. I turned to stone.

My peach skin: the light at seven in the evening in the recreation yard. My chervil: the spidery lace floating in the air. My reliquaries: the leaves on the trees making arbors for the breeze to rest in. What shall we do when night comes? What happens in the evening becomes uncertain in the daytime. I feel time caressing me but I can't think what we shall do next time. I can hear the seven o'clock noise and voices smoothing the thoughtful horizon. The gloved hand of infinity is closing over me.

"What are you looking at, Violette?"

"The geraniums . . . Down there . . ."

"What else?"

"The street, the window, they're all you."

"Give me your arm."

The evening came down over us with its velvet coat stopping at the knees.

"I can't give you my arm. People will notice, we would be caught."

"Are you ashamed?" Isabelle asked.

"Ashamed of what? Don't you understand? I'm being sensible."

The courtyard was all ours. We ran with our arms around each other's waist, we tore aside the lace in the air with our foreheads, we heard the pattering of our hearts in the dust. Little white horses galloped in our breasts. The girls, the mistresses all laughed and clapped their hands: they urged us on when we slowed down.

"Faster, faster. Close your eyes. I am leading you," Isabelle said.

There was a wall we had to go along. Then we would be alone.

"You're not running fast enough. Yes, yes . . . Close your eyes, close your eyes."

I obeyed.

Her lips brushed against my lips.

"I'm afraid . . . of the summer vacation, Isabelle. . . . I'm afraid of our last day in the courtyard, in summer. . . . I'm afraid of falling and killing myself," I said.

I opened my eyes: we were alive.

"Afraid? I'm leading you," she said.

"Let's run some more if you like."

"My wife, my baby," she said.

She gave me the words and kept them for herself as well. She held them to her by holding me to her. I loosened my fingers slightly around her waist. I counted: my love, my wife, my baby. I had three engagement rings on three fingers of my hand.

The other girls were standing without speaking, it was the minute of silence. Isabelle changed places. We closed the ranks, we were keeping our distance.

"I love you."

"I love you," I said too.

The juniors were already eating. We pretended to forget what we had both said, we both began talking to other girls.

*

I reached my percale curtain, following the nightly routine. An iron hand seized me and led me elsewhere. Isabelle threw me down onto her bed and buried her face in my underclothes.

"Come back when they're asleep," she said.

She drove me out again, she chained me to her.

I was in love: there was nowhere I could hide. There would be only the respites between our meetings.

Isabelle was coughing as she sat up in bed, Isabelle was ready beneath her shawl of hair. Her shawl. The picture I was going back to paralyzed me. I collapsed onto my chair, then onto the rug: the picture followed me everywhere.

I undressed in the half darkness, I pressed my chaste hand against my flesh, I breathed, I recognized my existence, I yielded myself. I piled up the silence at the bottom of my basin, I wrung it out as I wrung out my washcloth, I spread it gently over my skin as I wiped myself.

The assistant put out the light in her room. Isabelle coughed again: she was calling to me. I decided that if I didn't close my tin of dentifrice I would remember what everything was like before I went to Isabelle in her room. I was preparing a past for myself.

"Are you ready?" whispered Isabelle on the other side of my curtain.

She was gone again.

I opened the window of my cell. The night and the sky wanted no part of us. To live in the open air meant soiling everything outside. Our absence was necessary for the beauty of the evening trees. I risked my head in the aisle, but the aisle forced me back. Their sleep frightened me: I hadn't the courage to step over the sleeping girls, to walk with my bare feet over their faces. I closed the window again and the curtain shivered, like the leaves outside.

"Are you coming?"

I turned on my flashlight: her hair was falling as I had imagined it, but I had not foreseen her nightgown swollen with that bold simplicity. Isabelle went away again.

I went into her cubicle with my flashlight.

"Take off your nightgown," Isabelle said.

She was leaning on one shoulder, her hair raining over her profile.

"Take off your nightgown and put out the light. . . ."

I put out her hair, her eyes, her hands. I stripped off my nightgown. It was nothing new: I was stripping off the night of every first love.

"What are you doing?" Isabelle asked.

"I'm dawdling."

She stifled her laughter in the bed as I posed naked in my shyness for the shadows.

"What are you doing, for heaven's sake?"

I slid into the bed. I had been cold, now I would be warm.

I stiffened, I was afraid of brushing against her hair beneath the covers. She took hold of me, she pulled me on top of her: Isabelle wanted our skins to merge. I chanted with my body over hers, I bathed my belly in the lilies of her belly. I sank into a cloud. She touched me lightly on the buttocks, she sent strange arrows through my flesh. I pulled away, I fell back.

We listened to what was happening inside us, to the emanations from our bodies: we were ringed around with other couples. The bedsprings gave a groan.

"Careful!" she said against my mouth.

The assistant had switched on her light. I was kissing a little girl with a mouth that tasted of vanilla. We had become good little girls again.

"Let's squeeze each other," Isabelle said.

We tightened the girdles that were all we had in the world.

"Crush me. . . ."

She wanted to but she couldn't. She ground my buttocks with her fingers.

"Don't listen to her," she said.

The assistant was urinating in her toilet pail. Isabelle was rubbing her toe against my ankle as a token of friendship.

"She's asleep again," Isabelle said.

I took Isabelle by the mouth, I was afraid of the assistant. I drank our saliva. It was an orgy of dangers. We had felt the darkness in our mouths and throats, then we had felt peace return.

"Crush me," she said.

"The bed . . . it will make a noise . . . they'll hear us. . . ."

We talked amid the crowding leaves of summer nights.

I was crushing, blotting out, thousands of tiny cells beneath my weight.

"Am I too heavy?"

"You'll never be too heavy. I feel cold," she said.

My fingers considered her icy shoulders. I flew away, I snatched up in my beak the tufts of wool caught on thorns along the hedgerows and laid them one by one on Isabelle's shoulders. I tapped at her bones with downy hammers, my kisses hurtling down on top of one another as I flung myself onward through quicksands of tenderness. My hands relieved my failing lips; I molded the sky around her shoulders. Isabelle rose, fell back, and I fell with her into the hollow of her shoulder. My cheek came to rest on a curve.

"My darling."

I said it over and over.

"Yes," Isabelle said.

She said: "Just a minute," and paused.

"Just a minute," Isabelle said again.

She was tying back her hair, her elbow fanned my face.

The hand landed on my neck: a frosty sun whitened my hair. The hand followed my veins, downward. The hand stopped. My blood beat against the mount of Venus on Isabelle's palm. The hand moved up again: it was drawing circles, overflowing into the void, spreading its sweet ripples ever wider around my left shoulder, while the other lay abandoned to the darkness streaked by the breathing of the other girls. I was discovering the smoothness of my bones, the glow hidden in my flesh, the infinity of forms I possessed. The hand was trailing a mist of dreams across my skin. The heavens beg when someone strokes your shoulder: the heavens were begging now. The hand moved upward once again, spreading a velvet shawl up to my chin, then down once more, persuasively, heavier now, shaping itself to the curves it pressed upon. Finally there was a squeeze of friendship. I took Isabelle into my arms, gasping with gratitude.

"Can you see me?" Isabelle asked.

"I see you."

She stopped me from saying more, slid down in the bed, and kissed the curling hairs.

"Listen, horses!" a girl cried nearby.

"Don't be afraid. She's dreaming. Give me your hand," Isabelle said.

I was weeping for joy.

"Are you crying?" she asked anxiously.

"I love you: I'm not crying."

I wiped my eyes.

The hand stripped the velvet off my arm, halted near the vein in the crook of the elbow, fornicated there amongst the traceries, moved downward to the wrist, right to the tips of the nails, sheathed my arm once more in a long suède glove, fell from my shoulder like an insect, and hooked itself into the armpit. I was stretching my neck, listening for what answers my arm was giving the wanderer. The hand, still seeking to persuade me, was bringing my arm, my armpit, into their real existence. The hand was wandering through whispering snow-capped bushes, over the last frosts on the meadows, over the first buds as they swelled to fullness. The springtime that had been crying its impatience with the voice of tiny birds under my skin was now curving and swelling into flower. Isabelle, stretched out upon the darkness, was fastening my feet with ribbons, unwinding the swaddling bands of my alarm. With hands laid flat upon the mattress, I was immersed in the selfsame magic task as she. She was kissing what she had caressed and then, light as a feather duster, the hand began to flick, to brush the wrong way all that it had smoothed before. The sea monster in my entrails quivered. Isabelle was drinking at my breast, the right, the left, and I drank with her, sucking the milk of darkness when her lips had gone. The fingers were returning now, encircling and testing the warm weight of my breast. The fingers were pretending to be waifs in a storm; they were taking shelter inside me. A host of slaves, all with the face of Isabelle, fanned my brow, my hands.

She knelt up in the bed.

"Do you love me?"

I led her hand up to the precious tears of joy.

Her cheek took shelter in the hollow of my groin. I shone the flashlight beam on her, and saw her spreading hair, saw my own belly beneath the rain of silk. The flashlight slipped, Isabelle moved suddenly toward me.

As we melted into one another we were dragged up to the surface by the hooks caught in our flesh, by the hairs we were clutching in our fingers; we were rolling together on a bed of nails. We bit each other and bruised the darkness with our hands.

Slowing down, we trailed back beneath our plumes of smoke, black wings sprouting at our heels. Isabelle leaped out of bed.

I wondered why Isabelle was doing her hair again. With one hand she forced me to lie on my back, with the other, to my distress, she shone the pale yellow beam of the flashlight on me.

I tried to shield myself with my arms.

"I'm not beautiful. You make me feel ashamed," I said.

She was looking at our future in my eyes, she was gazing at what was going to happen next, storing it in the currents of her blood.

She got back into bed, she wanted me.

I played with her, preferring failure to the preliminaries she needed. Making love with our mouths was enough for me: I was afraid, but my hands as they signaled for help were helpless stumps. A pair of tweezers was advancing into the folds of my flesh. My heart was beating under its molehill, my head was filled with damp earth. Two tormenting fingers were exploring me. How masterly, how inevitable their caress . . . My closed eyes listened: the finger lightly touched the pearl. I wanted to be wider, to make it easier for her.

The regal, diplomatic finger was moving forward, moving back, making me gasp for breath, beginning to enter, arousing the monster in my entrails, parting the secret cloud, pausing, prompting once more. I tightened, I closed over this flesh of my flesh its softness and its bony core. I sat up, I fell back again. The finger which had not wounded me, the finger, after its grateful exploration, left me. My flesh peeled back from it.

"Do you love me?" I asked.

I wanted to create a diversion.

"You mustn't cry out," Isabelle said.

I crossed my arms over my face, still listening under my lowered eyelids.

Two thieves entered me. They were forcing their way inside, they wanted to go further, but my flesh rebelled.

"My love . . . you're hurting me."

She put her hand over my mouth.

"I won't make any noise," I said.

The gag was a humiliation.

"It hurts. But she's got to do it. It hurts."

I gave myself up to darkness and without wanting to, I helped. I leaned forward to help tear myself, to come closer to her face, to be nearer my wound: she pushed me back onto the pillow.

She was thrusting, thrusting, thrusting. . . . I could hear the smacking noise it made. She was putting out the eye of innocence. It hurt me: I was moving on to my deliverance, but I couldn't see what was happening.

We listened to the sleeping girls around us, we sobbed as we sucked in our breath. A trail of fire still burned inside me.

"Let's rest," she said.

My memories of the two thieves grew kinder, my wounded flesh began to heal, bubbles of love were rising. But Isabelle returned to her task now, and the thieves were turning faster, ever faster. Where did this great wave come from? Smoothly now, into the depths. The drug flowed down toward my feet, my dreaming flesh lay steeped in visions. I lost myself with Isabelle in passion's calisthenics.

A great pleasure seemed to begin. It was only a reflection. Slow fingers left me. I was hungry, avid for her presence.

"Your hand, your face. Come closer."

"I'm tired."

Make her come closer, make her give me her shoulder, make her face be close to mine. I must barter my innocence for hers. She is not breathing: she is resting. Isabelle coughed as though she were coughing in a library.

I raised myself up with infinite precautions, I felt new-made. My sex, my clearing, and my bath of dew.

I switched on the flashlight. I glimpsed the blood, I glimpsed the red hair. I switched it off.

The rustling of the shadows at three in the morning sent a cold shudder through me. The night would pass, the night would soon be nothing but tears.

I shone the flashlight, I was not afraid of my open eyes.

"I can see the world. It all comes out of you."

The dawn trailing its shrouds. Isabelle was combing her hair in a limbo of her own, a no-man's land where her hair was always hanging loose.

"I don't want the day to come," Isabelle said.

It is coming, it will come. The day will shatter the night beneath its wheels.

"I'm afraid of being away from you," Isabelle said.

A tear fell in my garden at three in the morning.

I would not let myself think a single thought, so that she could go to sleep in my empty head. The day was advancing through the dark, the day was erasing our wedding night. Isabelle was going to sleep.

"Sleep," I said beside the flowering hawthorn that had waited for the dawn all night.

Like a traitor, I got out of the bed and went to the window. There had been a battle high up in the sky and its aftermath was chill. The mists were beating a retreat. Aurora was alone, with no one to usher her in. Already there were clusters of birds in a tree, pecking at her first beams. . . . I looked out at the half-mourning of the new day, at the tatters of the night, and smiled at them. I smiled at Isabelle and pressed my forehead against hers, pretending we were fighting rams. That way I would forget what I knew was dying. The lyric downpour from the birds as they sang and crystallized the beauty of the morning brought only fatigue: perfection is not of this world even when we meet it here.

"You must go," Isabelle said.

Leaving her like a pariah, leaving her furtively made me feel sad too. I had iron balls chained to my feet. Isabelle offered me her grief-stricken face. I loved Isabelle without a gesture, without any token of my passion: I offered her my life without a sign.

Isabelle pushed herself up and took me in her arms.

"You'll come every night?"

"Every night."

*

"Can't you see she's under a spell? Why don't you go over and speak to her?" Anaïs said to Isabelle in the courtyard.

Yes, I was under the spell of the assistant music mistress as she played the piano, the spell of her bare arms molding the air of the kindergarten with their movements, the spell of the hair massed down her neck, the spell of her red-brown homespun jacket, the spell of the celluloid swans and ducks.

She closed the piano and sensed my presence.

"Were you listening to what I was playing?"

"Yes, I was listening."

She came over to the window sill. I turned my head: Isabelle, in the distance, all alone, was watching me.

"It's a concerto by Saint-Saens," she said. "I missed getting a Premier Prix at the Conservatoire with it. Because I was too shy!"

"Too shy," I repeated.

I didn't dare look at her.

"You study composition," I said voicelessly.

"Yes, I study harmony."

I fled.

Isabelle was coming to meet me.

"Is she still playing?"

Her lips were trembling.

"She isn't playing. She's studying harmony. She told me so."

Some of the little girls forced us apart as they always did during recreation.

Now we were walking around the yard. Isabelle's eyes didn't leave my own. I was thinking of the monuments. The monuments were named: Conservatoire, Concerto, Harmony.

Isabelle put her arm around my shoulders.

"We will love each other as we walk," she said. "Don't be sad."

"Am I sad?"

"Yes, you're sad," Isabelle said.

"She plays, I listen. That's all."

"Yes, that's all," Isabelle said. "Look . . . over there . . . the sun on the windowpane. How strong it is, and how gay . . ."

I couldn't keep on walking. Isabelle's nobility of mind reduced me to a zero. Isabelle was protecting me from some danger—I didn't know what the danger was—when I came back to her, when I ran away, when I wasn't listening to Hermine playing Bach.

In the night, I said to Isabelle: "She's walking about, she's still up, she's studying. I recognize her step."

Isabelle hugged me in her arms. "Don't leave me."

Isabelle's cubicle was directly under Hermine's room.

Days passed and summer came to charm the spring.

The temperature: a rose always open. The evenings: always the same unpeopled legend. Invisible birds gave witness to the perfection of the light. So many, many, waking, hidden birds; so many chroniclers of each warm and gentle moment. I came out of the study hall, I met Hermine by accident in the corridor of what had once been the cloisters. Hermine told me about a Franck sonata she was unraveling, about his *Prelude, Chorale and Fugue,* about Bach's *Italian Concerto* which she was studying, about a Beethoven Trio which she played every day with her sisters, about the walks she went on with them and her father. I asked her the meaning of the expressions: cassation, flute obbligato, modulate into the dominant, basso continuo, and transverse flute.

Isabelle, without a word, made me a gift of a book: *Music and Musicians.*

*

The summer was crushing us beneath its heat. The other girls were clustered together in the shade of the plane trees. We, Isabelle and I, were walking round and round the courtyard while the drops of sweat stood glistening on her brow.

"The astronomy course is over. Say something, Isabelle!"

"No more astronomy classes. Do you hear?" The others call to us. . . . They shout: "It's better over here!"

"Don't go, Isabelle."

"Don't go, Violette!"

Giving each other orders was a way of checking how far we were still inseparable.

We walked faster and faster inside our armor of heat.

". . . No more physics and chemistry classes."

"Yes, Isabelle."

". . . No more algebra and geometry classes."

"Yes, Isabelle."

Isabelle mopped her brow. "Your hand. Give me your hand."

"It's damp. It's sweaty."

"Give it to me!"

I felt March in the palm of Isabelle's hand.

"The teachers won't be coming in from the town anymore. It's the end. What are we going to do? What will become of us?"

She abandoned my hand.

"We'll see each other during the vacation," I hazarded.

"Is that enough for you?"

Her face was imploring me. It was beginning to crumble.

"It's so hot, I don't really know. . . ."

Isabelle gazed at the windows.

"The school has changed, the school is changing," she said.

"The school is empty. No, it isn't empty. It's just quiet. Everyone is outside."

Isabelle shrank into herself.

"Soon the school won't exist anymore," she said. "I'm leaving it."

She had passed her final examinations and I my preliminary ones.

"Decide," I begged.

"There's nothing we can decide," Isabelle said. "Come into the cool."

She led me over to the window of the kindergarten. The piano:

closed. The sand: taken away. The swans and ducks: vanished.

"Why did you want us to stop here?" I asked Isabelle.

Isabelle was wiping my forehead, my hands.

"Because it's cool here, simply because it's cool," she said.

We found one of those corners that always remain neutral in any weather, a space between two flat stretches of cement.

"Are you close to me? Are you really close to me?"

"Yes, Isabelle, yes."

"Hold me," she said. "I don't want it to happen, I don't want it to happen," she moaned.

"I don't want to be parted from you!" I cried.

"Hold me tighter," she said.

She tore herself away roughly.

I asked Isabelle what she was staring at like that.

"The gravel," she said.

The gravel was us—that instant in all its nakedness.

Then she did her hair up again without taking her eyes off me. Her eyes said too much.

"Let's go somewhere else. Please, let's walk some more," I said.

"You want to leave but you won't leave!"

Isabelle was frightening me.

The clock in the main quadrangle struck one of the hours.

"Go away! Go away!"

I did as Isabelle told me. I went and stood out in the blazing sun.

"Come back. . . ."

I went back, broken. Suddenly I had an idea.

"Let's run away!" I said. "The main gate is always open while they're making deliveries."

". . ."

"Why don't you answer?"

"Because it's impossible," Isabelle murmured.

"Let's run away, Isabelle. . . . It's summer. We can sleep in a haystack. We're sure to find some bread to eat somewhere. . . ."

Isabelle pulled my head sharply backwards by the hair.

"The police, policemen, what are they for?" she said. "One hour and we'd be back. I've thought of everything. I've calculated every possibility."

Her hand in mine. I had held it there hundreds of times as we passed in or out between the great marble tables in the dining hall.

Our marriage every hour of the day and night was no longer the same. We looked sullenly at all the holiday blue overhead.

"It's terrifying," Isabelle said.

"The long vacation?"

"Yes."

In the distance, in the parlor, parents were asking for their children. More girls were settling themselves down in the shade of the plane trees with deck chairs, with their sewing, with books. All that blue above the trees was July's coronation.

"Come on!" Isabelle said.

"Where do you want to go?"

"Into the sun."

"We shall get too hot. What's the point?"

Isabelle seemed beside herself. She was rubbing her eyes. She was trying to grind her tears into dust. I pulled her out into the middle of the yard.

"And now?"

Arrows of fire were striking down at our heads. There was a persistent smell of dish water. We stood face to face, without flinching from the heat or our own obsessive pain.

"I'm learning you, I'm memorizing you. Deep in your eyes," Isabelle said.

One of the mistresses called to us.

"Don't answer," Isabelle said.

"You'll catch sunstroke," the mistress shouted.

"Don't answer," Isabelle ordered. "It's our last day."

The mistress had gone back into the paddock. Isabelle was smiling that kindly smile of hers, full of infinite subtleties.

Our nights. Where shall we find our nights again?

Now some of the girls were calling in their turn. They all wanted us beside them.

"We'll wait in the sun since that's what you want," I said.

"We'll stay here," Isabelle said, "and draw a circle around ourselves."

I traced a circle with my heel.

"You wanted to leave, didn't you? You wanted a house just for the two of us?" she asked.

"Yes, oh yes! A house just for us . . ."

"This is our house," Isabelle said.

She wasn't playing, she wasn't making fun of me. I looked at her, but I was cut off from her by the envelope around me: the heat.

"Let's talk. Isabelle . . ."

"No. Look, just go on looking."

"At what? The circle? Our house?"

"At what is going to happen to us."

"I can't go on. It's the sun. You never talked to me like this before. In that voice, in that tone . . ."

"I wasn't going to be parted from you then," Isabelle said.

The heat was beginning to make me feel drugged. I tried to fight it.

"Will your mother come tomorrow?"

". . ."

"Will you live with your family? I must know. . . ."

". . ."

The heat answered for Isabelle with its thudding in my arteries, in my temples.

"If you took a job as an assistant mistress . . . You'd be free."

"Is it over?" Isabelle asked.

The heat. A mirror in which Isabelle was keeping watch.

"Yes, it's over, Isabelle. I don't know what I'm saying anymore. Take me away . . . into our corner. . . ."

Blinded by the sun, Isabelle dragged a cripple after her.

Time, the unfeeling executioner. I saw it as I watched a little spider. Black and full of life. It was running away across the black ground.

That evening in the dining hall some of the girls talked about their futures. Now they had passed their exams they were all confidence. Pauline was going to be a lawyer, Andréa a physician, one of the others a scientist, like Pasteur she explained. Loys wanted to teach domestic science. Isabelle listened, far away from them all. Since the evening study period had been canceled, we went up to the dormitory right away.

I stopped Isabelle in front of her percale curtain.

"If you like," I said tentatively, "if you like I can help you do your packing, I can help you arrange your linen in your trunk. We'd still be together then. . . ."

Isabelle was pale. She followed the movements of my lips with overpolite concentration.

"Listen," she said with terrifying gentleness.

She raised her forefinger.

I listened: the other girls, in twos, were singing or dancing on their iron beds. I was crazed with love for this new face of Isabelle's: melting. All the contours dissolving in her pain.

"You don't want me to help you?"

"Go into your cubicle," Isabelle said.

I went across the aisle. A whole season of hurricanes and tempests was trying to come into being in my throat. I lifted my percale curtain; the softness of the evening beyond the window struck me in the face. The gentle evening outside was advancing with the elemental motion of a barge drifting with the stream. I went into my cubicle.

The cry pierced the school.

I huddled into the corner between my window and my closet, I pressed my pinafore against my mouth. The other girls, all the other girls, were running in the aisle.

"Who made that noise?" the assistant asked.

"Isabelle."

*

I went back to my piano during the vacation; I listened to Hermine playing, I practiced without any hope of playing better, I puzzled out an arpeggio exercise: the memory of the big book on harmony haunted me.

Summer streamed into fall; Isabelle would be coming soon.

I waited a whole day for her telegram. I kept leaving the piano to go and look out the window, then leaving the window to go back to the piano. Surrounded by her bed, and mine, her chair, and mine, her washstand and my washstand in the dormitory, I thought the school had been reconstructed around me. The indifference of telegraph boys will always be upsetting. I held her telegram in my hand as passers-by, children and lovers, began leaving the park for the fair in the Place Poterne. I opened my bedroom window, I let in some greenness for Isabelle before her arrival. Now the telegraph boy was gazing at an ice cream cart.

The station was devoid of activity, but a baggage truck, a weighing machine, a porter, a man wandering about outside, the closed ticket office, the label on a suitcase being sent in advance, the dust which had enveloped the whole place in outmoded melancholy, all told the same story: she is coming. The iron shutter of the bookstall suggested meditation; the streetcars passed by outside, with their tinkling bells and the rumbling refrain of their wheels adding an extra frivolity to the shortness of their journeys.

The ticket collector opened the gate; the rails suggested the gaze of nocturnal birds. The whole town was dozing beyond the platforms. The first passengers still belonged to the train, to the views they'd seen. I saw the speed in their polished eyes. Isabelle stepped down last. Without looking at me. Her neat hair, her simple dress, her country girl's gloves made me reel. The austerity of the station was stirring my entrails to desire. She showed her ticket with the willing acquiescence of a schoolgirl; she turned toward me at last.

"Good afternoon," she said coldly.

"Good afternoon," I said with equal coldness.

Our weeks of being apart still lay between us.

Isabelle set down her suitcase and tidied her coiled-up hair.

"Did you get my telegram?" she asked in a preoccupied voice.

The ticket collector closed the gate leading onto the platforms.

"I wouldn't be here if I hadn't got it."

She smiled. My logic pleased her.

What words are there when the entrails are crying out their hunger?

"It wasn't too long a journey?"

"I read," Isabelle said.

"We're closing up, ladies," the ticket collector shouted.

I followed Isabelle. The modesty of her attire oppressed and enchanted me.

We stepped around a dung collector.

"Which road do we take?" Isabelle asked.

I asked her if she would prefer to go through the town or keep to the outer boulevards. She preferred the latter.

A streetcar moved off into the town she had rejected.

We were walking past smart shops. Isabelle looked at nothing and still refused to let me carry her suitcase.

Abrupt as ever, she had arrived.

"You didn't forget me?"

At last it was her own voice again. But a knife and scissor grinder snatched it from me with his pushcart and his little bell.

"I didn't forget you. I couldn't sleep anymore. . . ."

"Be quiet, don't explain anything," cried Isabelle.

She looked at a display of Valenciennes lace.

"Be quiet? Why must I be quiet, when we were talking about the vacation? . . ."

"Don't you understand?" Isabelle asked. "There was no vacation."

"I understand," I said very quietly. "Did you go for walks? Did you read? Tell me what you did. Let's talk about you. . . ."

Isabelle gave a sigh.

"Please. Let's get to your house," she said.

She wouldn't take my arm, or my hand. She wanted more.

". . . My parents are in Paris. They'll be back late tonight. . . ."

Isabelle said nothing.

I hated the made-to-order temperature. It was all gone, the strident heat of our summer, pierced by the yells of the juniors and the older girls at play. Cafés, confectionery stores, and tea shops presented themselves. It was gone, the main gate so firmly locked. The first leaves were falling, summer was sinking, resting, trailing.

"Is it still far to where you live?"

"No!"

"Is that a factory?"

"Yes!"

"Where does that alley lead to?"

"Into town. You used to talk to me at school. . . . What's the matter?"

"We're in the street," Isabelle said. "I missed it more than you."

I thought: what if I could show her the depot where the trolleys stop? . . .

"Do you like the boulevards?"

"What do you expect me to say!" Isabelle exclaimed.

A desire to hurt her, a desire to trample on her so that I could find myself again, find her again, find everything again.

"Let's go upstairs," she said when we arrived.

Her hair tumbled down as I closed the door of my room.

That night I said to Isabelle: "We're in our house." I waited for her reply in the comfortable stillness of the thick lined curtains and the old books. "If you like . . . we're in our house," Isabelle answered. The girl on the left, the girl on the right, would not wake up, the assistant would not get up unexpectedly.

"Are you listening?"

"What do you want me to listen to?" Isabelle asked. "I'm looking, I'm resting."

She was learning my room and its unthreatening shadows by heart.

The silence held not a single danger.

A grotto gives too much security. I was lying in a grotto with Isabelle. I switched on the light.

"Do you miss them?"

Isabelle frowned. "The school? The other girls?"

"You see! You miss them. You miss it."

"It's different here," Isabelle said.

I switched the light off.

I was irritated by the shadows in my room: I couldn't see Isabelle.

The single divan kept us close to each other, but it didn't creak like the bed in Isabelle's cubicle. I asked if she wanted a window open. No. If she wanted to see the statues in the park. No. With their dreaming bellies and thighs and flanks. No, no. She liked it where she was. Did she want to eat fruit sitting on the window sill? She wasn't thirsty or hungry. Midnight emerging like crystal from between the angels on the Directoire clock didn't affect her. What did she want? The square of chocolate on the bedside table, the rose in the tooth-glass, my flashlight, our held breath as one of the girls moaned in her sleep?

"We're free, Isabelle. We wanted to be free. We could go down and walk naked through the house. It's possible."

Isabelle stroked her forehead with my hand.

"You're telling yourself a fairy tale, you're telling us fairy tales. We aren't free. We shall be parted, we shall be parted forever."

The following morning, when my mother called me, Isabelle wasn't awake. She was resting on a pillow of clouds. Her bared shoulder, her breast, filled with the ebb and flow of all the living things on earth, were offering themselves to the ceiling as though it were the sky. She could sleep till noon, so we were free. It was she who had been telling the fairy tales. I left Isabelle in a way I never did at school. I used to go back into my cubicle so full of anxiety, so full of hope. . . .

"I'm just buttering you some bread, you spoiled thing," my mother said.

I sat down opposite her; she had me in her power again.

"Did she arrive?" my mother asked.

"Isabelle is still sleeping. Didn't Marthe tell you I went to meet her at the station?"

My mother paused as she was spreading the butter on my bread. She sensed that her questions weren't welcome. She went on: "Marthe told me you spent the whole day watching for the telegram to arrive. It's funny: can't you be calm about anything?"

My mother slid the buttered pieces of bread over in front of my bowl.

"Why don't you take her breakfast up to her?"

"No, she's still asleep. I'd rather talk to you about Paris. Where did you go? What was Paris like?"

My mother was drinking her café au lait. She was suddenly almost angry.

"Eat! If you could see what you look like this morning! Paris? Well, Paris is always the same, the same crowds, the same noise. Your stepfather took me to the Caveau de la République and the Deux Anes. The sales at Amy Linker's were dreadful. I bought you a dress. . . . You'll have to try it on first if you want to go out this evening."

She left the table and went over to look at her baby. He was deep in a perfect sleep: the sleep of a daisy far out in a field amid the cool of early evening.

"Go out this evening?" I cried in bewilderment.

"Why not this evening? Oh that one!" she said from the stairs.

I was playing with her, flattering her. She couldn't understand.

I knocked at the door of my room and went in.

"You didn't come back," Isabelle said.

She apologized for having dressed, done her hair, put on her shoes.

"We may be going out this evening. . . ."

"Going out?" Isabelle said.

She came over to me looking troubled.

"It's not certain. . . . Just an idea . . ."

"I came for you, I came to be near you," Isabelle said.

I took her in my arms. She was stifling me; I recognized my visionary again. Her head fell onto my shoulder, our morning was withering away.

"Are you crying?"

Isabelle was rubbing her eyelids.

"So that I shan't be dazzled by the sun. I used to do it when I was little. . . ."

Isabelle never talked about her childhood. She made that up on the spur of the moment. Yes, it was true, our house depressed her.

I introduced Isabelle to my mother. It wasn't a great success. She was too straightforward, with her mocking manner and the arrogant way she had of tossing back the hair from her forehead. Isabelle stammered out a few inept remarks. My mother studied her. Her figure and her clothing in particular. A shadow of disappointment passed over my mother's face.

Isabelle's abundant figure naked was a thing of splendor. When I went into her cubicle she would be waiting for me relaxed on her bed, leaning in abandon on one elbow.

"Isabelle has passed her exams, she has her diploma," I said.

"She isn't lazy like you," my mother said.

Isabelle didn't protest.

In the afternoon I guardedly suggested a walk for Isabelle's amusement. My mother's face changed. I was banishing her. I suggested she come along with the baby. She refused, and Isabelle vomited her contempt into my eyes: Is this our nights together?

"You ought to try on your dress if you want to go out this evening," my mother said.

"Are we going out?" Isabelle asked.

She was lingering over a sheet of music.

"It's the fair," my mother said. "Don't you like fairs?"

"I didn't know," Isabelle said.

The music slid off her knees.

"Don't you want to go out?" my mother asked, as though Isabelle were being stuck-up about it.

"Just as you like," Isabelle replied.

She put the music back on the piano.

I mustn't try it on in my room, I mustn't try it on in the bathroom, I mustn't try it on in my mother's room. I must try it on in the dining room beside the piano. I did as I was told.

Isabelle got up from the piano stool as I turned around to show the fullness. Her eyes were saying: If only I could escape, if only I could just disappear. . . .

"You aren't with us," my mother said.

"I'm looking at the garden," Isabelle said.

Her arms had fallen to her sides.

I didn't dare say simply: Isabelle is consoling herself with some clumps of trees outside a window.

"Give us your opinion," my mother said.

Yes, Isabelle answered, the dress is pretty, yes, it's the right length, yes, the fullness is good, yes, it will be practical, yes, there's nothing to touch Paris.

I was aflame for my new dress, for our evening out. My mother was encouraging my coquetry.

"Take if off, you spoiled thing," she said.

I was being drawn closer and closer to my mother.

To attract the horses on the merry-go-round, to attract the iron seats as they swung through the air, to attract the wrestlers clad in their satinette, to attract the pink and green eyes of the nougat bars, to attract the girls on the platforms outside the booths . . .

"You'll see the Wyamme boy there," my mother said.

When we left, what a fuss, what twitching and patting from head to toe!

Outside, I said: "That way leads to Marly, to the Avenue Duquesnoy." Isabelle's "Ah!" was older, even further away than Marly and the Avenue Duquesnoy. I said: "This street goes past the boarding school I went to in Valenciennes. I was always sick, there was always some infection or other going around, always epidemics. Fidéline was buried. Pleurisy, stabbing pains in the side."

"Ah! Ah!" Isabelle didn't care one jot about these graphic details of my past. Her memory was not my private life. She was conciliatory with the silent façades of the great houses, she raised her eyelids as a token of recognition when we passed the gate of my old school, her lips were already moist for the approaching night; what was there for me to reproach her with? We were forced to walk into the whirling music with black confetti settling in our hearts.

"The fair," Isabelle said.

I said nothing, I was inhaling the trace of powder on Isabelle's cheek. I was crushing Isabelle's face in the winter lilac flowers.

She wanted to buy streamers and insisted on making me a gift of them. Her pleasant manner with the woman at the till didn't surprise me. Unhappiness always makes us expend ourselves on people who don't matter to us. How long would she go on laughing, her head thrown back, her eyes veiled, her mouth offered to the coldness of the sky? Some young men came and blew their squeakers in Isabelle's ears as she stood closing her purse, her head still thrown back to the sky. Others came and pushed us toward the merry-go-round, separating me from Isabelle. Still more, in a tight crowd working like yeast, were emptying their paper cones of confetti on Isabelle's head, down the front of her dress. The crowd was carrying me away. Isabelle did not defend herself, that was the most painful part of it. When I reached her again she was covered with a frosting of tiny colored stars, absinthe green, acid pink, sparkling blue. More young men threw confetti in our eyes and parted us again. The crowd was lifting me off my feet, I was spitting paper, the merry-go-round was slowing down. An iron hand seized my arm. The hand pulled me out of the crowd.

"Get on," Isabelle said in an unrecognizable voice.

She helped me into my seat on the outside horse—the outside one so that I could see, so that I could be seen—she handed me a streamer: her fingers were ice cold. She refused to sit on the horse next to mine. With her enchanting arm, she encircled the upright, white-painted ear in front of me; she said: throw it, begin. The merry-go-round began to move; the brass, the cymbals, and the drums poured their hot excitement into our heads. Throw it, begin, she said again quite calmly. Isabelle was attractive. Men and women were throwing streamers at her, and everytime, with the supple grace of an animal, she avoided them, she rejected them. "Throw it, begin," her words were becoming a sinister singsong in my ear. I threw my first streamer, it fell on an empty chair. Isabelle opened my fingers and put a second one into them.

I was becoming entangled, enmeshed, in the streamers being thrown up from below. The young man standing half hidden, with the brim of his hat turned down, immediately lowered his eyes.

"Is that the Wyamme boy?" Isabelle asked.

"Yes."

"Throw it," she said.

"Let's go now. You're cold, you look pale."

"Throw it," she said again.

I threw each streamer she gave me at young Wyamme. He accepted mine as I did his: without expression of any kind.

Isabelle asked me for no explanation and I didn't defend myself. I didn't know the Wyamme boy, I never spoke to him. He sometimes greeted me when he was standing with nothing to do on the step of their store. He had a nice face. My mother built plans around him to which I paid no attention.

"I've been offered a post at Compiègne," Isabelle said.

She looked straight ahead as she spoke.

"You'll wear yourself out like that. You shouldn't be standing up," said one of the attendants.

"At Compiègne? But that's impossible. Why?"

Isabelle threw a roll of streamers into the arms of a young girl.

"It's what you advised. So I applied. They've offered me a job as an assistant."

"Next semester?"

Before answering, Isabelle let me feel the weight of the sadness inside her.

"Yes, next semester. Will you write me?"

"Yes, I shall write. Let's go now. . . . Let's go home. . . ."

"Go home? We've only just arrived," Isabelle said.

She picked up a streamer from the litter on the floor of the merry-go-round and twisted it around my neck. She pulled it slowly tighter.

"Violette, Violette . . . Ah! Violette, why did you bring me here?"

Isabelle pulled the streamer off abruptly.

It was over.

❀

*

Hermine rose to her feet and buttoned up her red-brown homespun jacket.

"Play it again."

"I play it for you every day."

"You play it better every time."

Hermine sat down again at the piano and played Bach's *Italian Concerto* there in the music room, far from the kindergarten, far from the midday recess. I listened as intensely as she played. She concentrated so hard she looked quite cross. Her powerful fingers moving across the keyboard made Bach's exalting mathematics simpler to me. I raised my eyes. The notes of the elementary musical dictation on the blackboard humbly evoked the composer at his work. I drank in so much from both the music and the player that in the end I was saturated like a lump of moist clay.

I felt her passion for music in her embrace, in her kiss. Isabelle's hair searing my face was replaced by Hermine's burning cheeks. A concerto, nocturnes, sonatas turned back into hands, into lips, into her breath on my face.

I ran to her, she ran to me when she was free at eleven-thirty. She almost tried to crush me into the wall as I hung onto the lapels of the jacket she would never take off.

We left the music room, Hermine telling me about the rabbit her family had tamed, about a week of the vacation spent on a beach where the wind, the cold, the dunes . . . When they went swimming it was like the flood rolling in after the shower of arpeggios in Chopin's last Prelude. She opened her botany textbook and explained the anatomy of a plant. Wait a moment, she said. She came back into the corridor with a plaster cast of Beethoven's head. She lived passionately on very little money and a great deal of curiosity, courage, and enthusiasm for books, nature, a cigarette, a bodice she was cutting out, a concert, a lecture, a fingernail file. Her nostrils quivered, her eyes sparkled, her indulgence in the study hall was proverbial. She called out the names of the girls who were talking, she never lowered herself to exact penalties. I would stay up on the dais with her too long. Mlle. Fromont would come in to take Hermine's place at the desk and catch us. She would catch us, too, in the corridor outside the music room. Mlle. Fromont put nothing into words, but her eyes were saying: You're walking a tightrope, you know.

I received sad letters from Isabelle. The superb Isabelle was crumbling away. I answered her letters, then I answered them no more. I abandoned her in the school to which I had consigned her.

Hermine had moved down one floor and was now in charge of the "middle" girls' dormitory. At night, there was only a door between our two dormitories; in the evening I could hear her reprimands. Our new assistant mistress had the profile of a sheep and took ages to finish washing herself. Her light would go out and the thought of Hermine tormented me. I would get out of bed, pitter-patter down the aisle, and stop in front of our assistant's door. I wanted Hermine's door. The temptation to cross that frontier made me frantic. I would go back to bed. Next morning I would read my pocket score of Chopin's Nocturnes in my cubicle.

Hermine played less and less: we arranged meetings elsewhere. She told me about the director of the Conservatoire with whom she was studying harmony, about the curriculum at the Schola Cantorum.

Blanche Selva was one of the teachers at the Schola Cantorum.

She had visited Valenciennes to give a concert, her tiny hands embroidering Mozart. . . . I had seen her again at the station as she left to go back to Paris. I told Hermine all about it, I had the illusion of composing a minuet for her. I never talked to her about the door and its temptations, about the fire in my mouth and my insides.

My obsession with her homespun jacket, her sturdy legs, her low heels, her narrow buttocks, her eager nostrils, reduced me to an intolerable sleeplessness. To see her hair spread on her pillow, to gaze at her as she slept.

One night, I turned the handle of the door. I had succeeded, I was in her dormitory. There are some victories that are presentiments. She opened her eyes, she smiled, I got into her bed.

I went back to my cubicle before dawn, missing Isabelle.

At breakfast, I looked for Hermine in the dining hall. Where could she be? The mistress on duty clapped her hands and we formed into lines. Hermine's place at the assistants' table was empty; my eyes momentarily encountered the gaze of the assistant in my own dormitory. We left the dining hall. I looked for her in the courtyard, I looked for her in the study hall. How do you expect us to know what's happened to her, the other girls answered.

At eleven-thirty, a day girl swore to me that she had just seen Hermine coming out of the headmistress's office. I ran to the music room, but all I found was the animal warmth of the class there. I didn't dare risk a visit to the dormitories. At midday, her place had not been laid in the dining hall. Sitting at the table, one of the clever girls whispered: don't look around, you won't see her. I flared up: why wouldn't I see her? The girl suspected nothing. She whispered again behind her hand: they say it's something serious, they say she's leaving.

The assistant from my dormitory was walking up and down the aisle between the tables. Her eyes met mine. I understood: we had been reported. I found out what was happening without making myself too conspicuous: Hermine was leaving that evening. She had found a job as a teacher in a village school.

I was depriving her of the Conservatoire, of her harmony lessons, of her daily visits to her family, of her happiness with them. It was unjust: why hadn't they expelled me too? I received a letter from her through one of the girls, I answered it at night, under the bedclothes by the glow of my flashlight. Hermine's tiny, angular handwriting delighted me as much as what she wrote.

Deprived of music, of my mother, of Her
once again, I devoted myself more and mo
phy classes. The Stoics, who give nothing,
with a feverish enthusiasm. I defended the ca
against almost the entire senior school; none
countenance such absolute self-possession. Fo
fought tooth and nail in the cause of dry eyes.
on arguing endlessly with some of the countr
listened to me with the heavy gaze of their I would have argued with the blackboard, with the chairs, the wastebasket, the desk, always clutching the billfold holding Hermine's love letters inside the pocket of my pinafore. Parted from the one I was beginning to love, I longed for an even greater sensation of grief simply so that I could hide it.

"What did you say?" a group of girls asked me.

"I said I shall be the anvil on which I forge my own sorrow."

"Violette Leduc is nuts," they decided.

Time for afternoon snack. I ran to collect my share of the soft rolls being handed out.

Living as I did for the letters I wrote at night, the letters I always carried with me, the letters I was constantly expecting, my inner pretensions increased in proportion to my feelings. Don't daydream, I was told in class. I wasn't daydreaming. I was voiding my scorn on everything, on everyone. That idiot preferred the steps and columns and stones in picture books to a page of Sophocles. Don't sit there sleeping with your eyes open, I was told. I wasn't asleep. I was saturating myself with the word "oracle." The word grew and grew inside me, the world beyond the school and the town grew heavy with the heaviness of an awaited oracle. In the next class, Aeschylus ended my wait. I fell off my chair, I upset my inkwell. The eternity of God was now the eternity to be found in the simplicity of a text. My hand burrowed and twisted in my bangs.

One Sunday, passing through the outskirts of the town on our long weekly walk, we met Hermine with her sisters and her father in a somber stretch of countryside. They quickened their steps, avoiding the assistants and the long files of girls. I thought it was an apparition, so quickly did they appear and then vanish once again.

Strings of weeks, of nights, of days. I harried the faces of the clocks, and the clocks harried me. No longer was every meal in the dining hall a wedding feast: the lentil soup in my spoon without

…he café au lait in my bowl without Hermine were both so … mustard to be forced down. Eighteen years old. What a farce a …h certificate is. I was a hundred and eighty when one of the girls massacred a sonata in the kindergarten, I was fourteen when I received a letter from my mother, I was seventeen again when the girl who was my accomplice slipped a letter from Hermine into the sleeve of my pinafore. I read the letter in the lavatories where I had loved Isabelle, I read it again in my cubicle, I collapsed on my bed listening to *L'Oiseau prophète*. Hermine played it with remarkable simplicity. I never said to myself: she doesn't play anymore, I took her piano away from her.

*

I don't remember how or with whom I left the school one Thursday after lunch. I ran to the meeting place outside the town completely alone. I found Hermine, as we had arranged by letter, in a landscape without trees, without houses, without factories. It was a wasteland made more desolate by some sheds and huts in the distance. The sharp claws of the wind, the mosaic of shattered coal, the thin, bleached grass. A handshake. I became a student again, she an assistant.

"Have you been waiting l . . . ong?"

The wind cut into my words.

"I've just arrived," Hermine said. "You're listening. What are you listening t . . . o?"

We were forced to swallow the wind and the unseasonable winter cold.

"I'm l . . . istening and . . . I'm not l . . . istening. I can't help it. I'm seeing you again, you're . . . close to me, in fr . . . ont of me, and yet it's . . . you playing, you playing the piano to me that I see."

I was lying and not lying.

"I'll play you *L'Oiseau prophète*," Hermine said.

Yes, I was lying. No, I wasn't lying. The smoke coming out of the chimney of one of the huts was the sinuous line of *L'Oiseau prophète*. The voice rising from the gutted roof of a nearby shed was saying: "It wasn't too long a journey, Isabelle?"

"I read, Violette."

Neither hut nor shed had anything anymore to give me.

"I was talking to you," Hermine said. "Are you annoyed? Don't you like being with me again?"

She was too quick to become a begging student. I wondered why I hardened at her questions.

"Annoyed? It's you who should be annoyed. It's my fault you had to leave the school. All of what happened is my fault. Let's talk about you. What is it like . . . the village? How . . . is your playing? Do your practice? Do you have time to practice?"

"I haven't a piano anymore," Hermine said, lowering her head as though it were she, not I, who was the guilty one.

She continued to beg in silence. I saw a future of indulgence in her eyes.

"Oh I've got things organized. I still play. I practice on Sundays at home," Hermine said.

She was trying to reassure me.

She pulled up the collar of her jacket. Her red cheeks whipped by the wind were two perfect chords. Hermine looked at the sky which had come down lower than the barren ground; she was humanizing that miserly landscape.

"Your career is ruined!"

Hermine smiled as people do when they are finished.

"My career? My career isn't ruined. I'd missed winning the Premier Prix. . . ."

The wind whistled as it swept over the stunted grass.

"You can't be a piano teacher now!"

"I teach school," Hermine said.

The landscape was adrift, floating at the mercy of the livid stormlight spreading over it.

Holding hands, we began running in search of a ditch. The ice had been broken. Almost two carefree gypsies, almost. The blast hardened our lips and lifted our skirts. We found a sloping embankment and I fell at Hermine's feet. The wind helped me. Hermine tried to stop me.

"Why did you come if you're afraid?"

"I'm not afraid," Hermine said, "but it's impossible here."

I demanded the impossible. There are some beings who are the greatest risk we can face. Hermine: already my folly, already my harness.

Hermine allowed herself to slide down on the grass and coaldust.

"Keep watch," Hermine said.

Her caution irritated me.

"I can't kiss you and keep watch as well."

She no longer tried to stop me, but she begged. She wanted a sentinel while I wanted to murder her modesty, yes, murder it. I had to keep watch in one direction, she in the other. Then we changed places. The horror of that improvised stage-management. The wind, like a reptile, was chilling our arms and our legs.

"Someone's coming!" Hermine cried in terror.

"No, they're not, I tell you!"

I had to keep watch on all sides, as well as follow what was going on between us.

"Someone's coming!" Hermine said again, without looking.

We clutched our arms around our knees and hid our faces. The wind struck down with its knives at the backs of our necks.

"I wanted so much to see you again," she said.

"I wanted to see you too," I said.

I said it without civility. That wasn't what I'd come for.

Finally I turned my eyes toward Hermine. As gaze melted into gaze, there was no further threat to modesty. No more wind, no more claws, no more knife blades on our necks.

Hermine wanted us to leave, she wanted me to stop looking at her. She insisted.

"Why?" I asked with genuine sadness. "Why are you sending me away?"

She hesitated before replying.

Now the sun was warming us. But I hadn't come for an air played on a solo clarinet, because that's what the pale yellow sun was that day.

She explained, looking straight ahead of her.

She wanted me to look somewhere else because her red cheeks made her so unhappy, because her face was too conspicuous. She made this confession without dramatizing it, without exaggeration, expressing the pain she felt without changing her voice. I didn't answer. What answer could I have made? I loved her: I loved her weakness. My former mistress, my elder by five years, my virtuoso of our May evenings was opening herself to me. Confession is an orgasm also.

She said it was time to part, that I should leave first.

"Shall I see you again?"

"I don't know," Hermine said.

I walked back to her.

"Hermine . . ."

"Yes. Don't ask me. It's impossible here."

The wasteland with its enchanting breeze seemed another world of flowering gardens and bright meadows.

". . . I'm not asking for anything. You don't understand. Your face . . . Your face, Hermine, is your ardor. . . . You wouldn't play as you do."

"Let us take each other's hand again," Hermine said.

Isabelle made no confessions. With Isabelle, even the humus would have been pressed into paying tribute to our pleasure. Isabelle, Hermine, my torches as I walk into the vaults of madness.

The confession of a face that's too conspicuous, of cheeks too brightly colored, what is that when there are so many lives to be saved? The start of my life with Hermine. You spoke, you grieved, I drank in your words, I saw the pale green color of your grief. I see it now. My sober mourner, I was already a harvest of pain. I listened to you, and the late afternoon light opened vistas before us.

*

"Your mother is coming. She will be told everything."

"I can't give them to you. I don't have them. My mother isn't coming."

Morals, as they say in the newspapers. Morals, the letters of a former assistant mistress to a student, of a student to a former assistant mistress. I had been reported. A day of interrogation in the awful office. The headmistress wanted my letters. I fought on, hour after hour. I thought I was lost, the headmistress's assistant came in, she took the headmistress away with her. A miracle: someone was playing Clementi on the piano in the little room off the bursar's office. I left the headmistress's office, I flew toward the sound of the piano despite my exhaustion. The good, fat peasant, the prize student Amélie, my neighbor in evening study hall, was practicing. I took her hands, I thrust into them the score or so of letters in their little, sky blue envelopes with Hermine's black, energetic writing on the outside. "Throw them down the lavatory, tear them up, please, please." Amélie rose from the piano, I went back into the headmistress's office.

"The letters!"

Her dried-up face.

"The letters!"

Her crow's voice.

"The letters!"

No end to the scene.

"The letters!"

Everything made rotten, everything poisoned.

"The letters!"

The paperweight on the desk—marble in which I became marble in order to rest. . . .

"The letters!"

The wide belt of perforated kid over the headmistress's belly, over her absence of belly. The harm—where is the harm, tell me that?—she had done since the moment I opened the door of her office was an abscess between us. She wanted to read the love letters first, then expel me. Workmen were repairing a roof, the everyday was unbearable. Hammer, hammer, hammer, hammer, hammer, hammer . . . I counted the blows of my escape.

"Get out. You are expelled. Your mother will come and collect you."

I left, I crossed the covered courtyard where I used to play them tangos on Sunday evenings. Teachers, students, assistants—everything had already been broadcast on the waves of slander—saw me coming and fled. I was contagious. I went up to the dormitory, I went to bed in broad daylight, without eating, my throat was sore, the record kept turning: my mother won't come, my mother won't stick her nose into this. The next day, I begged one of the girls for her help. Since my parents had left the North my mother would receive my telegram in Paris. The day after that a telegram arrived from my mother. I was to go to Paris. She wasn't coming to collect me. My mother had issued her orders.

I have a mother blue as azure, I love her through my tragedy, I love her after the tragedy. My mother is a great wind from the ocean because she will not set foot in such filth.

An expressionless assistant escorted me with my trunk into a cab, then as far as the station.

I climbed into the train. My first real journey on my own. I was free, free with my nostrils quivering like a mare's. Everything lay before me, everything was making an offer of itself, I was moving toward it, I was reaching it, then leaving it behind as the train window moved on. Would Hermine write to me again? Would my mother be waiting at the station? Yes, since the headmistress had telegraphed the time of my arrival. Would there be another scene? My heart . . . vibrating metal.

What solemn thunder beneath the glass roof, what a flood of porters. It was dark, vast, enormous, and there I was, gazing with adoration at the soot of the great locomotives as they took their rest at last in Paris. I had harvested so many miles of branching rails. I saw my mother in the first row: a brushstroke of elegance. A young girl and a young woman. Her grace, our pact, my pardon. I kissed her and she replied: "Do you like my dress?" We talked about her clothes in the taxi. My mother's metamorphosis into a Parisienne eclipsed the headmistress and sent the school spinning into limbo. Not the slightest innuendo. Giving me Paris, she gave me her tact. And I took the buildings, the height from which they looked down, the patina of their walls, the length of the streets, the men and women walking in them: a woman without make-up filled me with surprise. How much two little sockets can take in and hold. . . . The shoulders are crushed by the weight of it. "You're shivering. Are you cold?" my mother asked. "You are shivering," my mother insisted. Because Paris is indifferent and large.

"Become a schoolteacher," my mother begged. I promised her I would finish my secondary education and obtain the necessary certificate. I was to go to the Lycée Racine at the start of the following semester. If I didn't become a schoolteacher, my old age would be the same as my poverty-stricken childhood. My old age terrified her. She gave me the quietest room in their apartment on the Place Daumesnil. I played the piano for them in the evening; my stepfather never spoke about the school, about my expulsion. It was my mother who waited with me for Hermine's answer to the letter I had written her. And after weeks had passed, it was my mother who walked into my room holding one of those same pale blue squares. I still didn't want to believe it; then I recognized that incisive writing. Hermine had answered, Hermine was not angry.

Paris emerged from the earth and I went out to meet it. The zinc, the zinc counters of midday. The strange vocabulary of the customers, *apéro, Diabolo-menthe, mêlé-cass, blanc panaché,* are you coming to the bistro, have you got time to put one down? To me it seemed a coarse world in which I was floundering with a wooden leg. Their vocabulary made me an outsider. But I could see how transparent they were to each other, standing elbow to elbow. Midday. Gin and beer in the country bars where I came from. Midday in Paris. They were going to play at *diabolo-menthe* and *mêlé-cass.* They sounded like games. But they weren't playing: they were drinking and fraternizing with colors. I thought them frivolous and too full of themselves; their Parisian accents grated on me. Life in a capital is always nerve-wracking. Their jokes, their banter, and their accent were their way of compensating for it.

A rain of lovers at midday. Lovers in the streets, lovers on the benches, lovers in front of the store windows. They were making love with arms wound around each other's waist. Their temples kissed even when their mouths didn't meet. The others, all the others, rushed down the steps to the Métro at such a speed. . . . The Métro was overtime labor, not included in the working day. How preoccupied they were, how tense, how pale, the men and women who live in Paris. Worries. Miles of worries unwinding from one neighborhood to the next. My first summer in Paris, the Paris heat.

Paris was empty along our street, Paris despite everything was a forest of shapely calves. Paris had a smell of scented armpits. The trace of anisette in the air . . . the air of Paris. I was floating over it in a balloon, sinking toward it, with only a little ballast left. . . . Paris was heavy, Paris was light, Paris was Paris. The fields, the meadows, a poppy, a kingfisher. . . . Their print dresses, their bodies more conspicuous than if they were unclothed. Sparrows, sparrows born in Paris. The strength of the oxygen, the power of the chlorophyll in a Parisian plane tree's leaves.

*

My parents went on a trip, and one evening I went out to the attack. The Métro. Can I or can't I convey that scent of sun-starved jonquils in the Métro? Watch out, little chick, the train is coming into the station. As noises go, that's certainly some noise. The miners in Denain with their white eyes staring out of their blackened faces seemed gayer to me than these underground travelers with their papier-mâché faces. I was contemptuous of their slightly snickering accent, I understood their hurry when I lost myself in the passages. I had no luck, I was affronted by a closing gate at every platform. I returned to the surface, I set off on a voyage of discovery along the Boulevard Saint-Michel from the Place Saint-Michel to the Fontaine Médicis. 1926. Paris had enslaved the four corners of the earth. An Indian wearing a delicately tinted turban that recalled the color of my flannel bandages was sitting on a terrace drinking beer. An Indian woman swathed in her cunningly disordered silks, an Indian woman the color of a dead leaf crushed my hand with infinite gentleness beneath her sandal. The beautiful mouths of the Negroes transformed my mouth into a hortensia. I walked by, I flowered in the darkness of their faces. A Japanese woman was pressing down upon the asphalt with her vermilion pattens. The unforgettable cross of the Boulevard Saint-Germain intersecting the Boulevard Saint-Michel. I walked over to the opposite sidewalk and found an oasis of darkness. It was stronger than a tomb.

"Where am I?"

"You are outside the ruins of the Jardin de Cluny."

I turned my back on the four corners of the earth, I seized hold of the railings. Reader, the night was growing gray behind the railings. The timid dawn, the dawn that takes its courage in its hands: the night that grows young again at ten in the evening in the Jardin de Cluny . . . I was with my beloved Isabelle again, telling her about the stones that lay before me. They move slightly if I look at them a long time, my darling. It's the slow displacement of the ages, it's not an illusion. Listen, oh listen with me. Is it silence, is it a rustling sound? Can it be the rustle of a tunic worn by a bygone tragic actress? . . . Is that possible, my love, in this garden of grasses, of neatly arranged and labeled stones? That rustling, that rustling, it is a theater that will never end. Three massive stones. Are they the eyes of tragedy? Yes, my little one, yes. Jardin de Cluny, theater of pride and silence. The ruins, the stones: the secrets in their chrysalis. Ruins of the Jardin de Cluny, you are my first real memory of Paris.

Isabelle, beloved and then abandoned. I give you the cross made by the Boulevard Saint-Germain and the Boulevard Saint-Michel. Isabelle, you gave me lily-of-the-valley and now I am walking in Paris for the first time alone. Now it is my turn to hem the bottom of your dress with the roses, the violets, the carnations the flower girl is selling at the corner of the Jardin de Cluny. Seven o'clock. At seven in the evening everything was closing where I came from. A street sign. The Café de la Source. Almost a poem by Verlaine. It is Rimbaud I am looking for.

"Where am I, please, sir?"

"You are on the Place de la Sorbonne. Just up there is the Gare du Luxembourg."

The Sorbonne. I talk to myself aloud when I'm really impressed. The Sorbonne. Shall I dare to pick french fries out of a cardboard container one day, like those young men standing just a few steps away from the building where they study?

I come back to Rimbaud on a Sunday morning, July 13, 1958. The building where I live is empty. They are all on vacation, they are in the country, the sunless summer weather is like an eiderdown; the Radio France III is playing Bach's *Cantata No. 170*. The announcer explains that the singer is a countertenor. What is a countertenor? Listen. The voice of an angel yet human too, a recitative weaving in and out of the flute obbligato, the organ, the orchestra. Sadness and serenity intertwining. What grace and what command. The musicologists are inventive. It's over. The voice will not come again. I open the psalms of *Une saison en enfer* at random. "Without dizziness or faltering let me measure the vast regions of my innocence," he writes. Verlaine, Rimbaud, London light up my room.

Now I come back to my first evening out alone in Paris. Psychology books, philosophy books, science books, astronomy books . . . The desire to lift that bookstore bodily off the ground and carry it off on my back, to feel the green embrocation of the covers on my shoulders. That was my first pious halt before the bookstore of the Presses Universitaires. Another day I stood and drank in the titles of the Garnier classics draught upon draught.

A fresh aspect of the Latin Quarter: the fruit sellers were wheeling their barrows around the Fontaine Médicis, taking their stand at the street corners and crying their wares. In the town I had come from in the North, by seven in the evening the spring vegetables, the big yellow apples with their faded color, their modest yellow, their yellow murmured like a pardon, were already keeping watch like kindly sentinels in stores taken over by the night. I bought some peaches for my dinner. The gates of the Jardin du Luxembourg stood guard over a garden unlike any I had ever seen. I plunged through them and after some difficulty found myself an empty bench near the Senate. I ate my dinner. The statues among the foliage stood with their great uncluttered bodies prophesying the coming on of night. This contact with antiquity refreshed my spirits. I had read so many accounts of the Jardin du Luxembourg in *Comœdia,* in *Les Nouvelles littéraires*. . . . Now I was there. An anonymous conquest and an unsung triumph among so many unknown people. My spoils were the last velvet reflection playing among the trees. I turned my head: I preferred Capoulade to the Panthéon. The chairs, standing two by two, one facing the other, bore witness to tender dialogues. I ate my fruit under clusters of happy birds.

"Will you give me one?"

I started.

"Give you what?"

"A peach."

"You're not French."

"I'm Argentinian."

He transformed my fruit with his slender fingers and his singsong accent. We were eating mangoes. He told me he liked modern literature, that he was reading Proust. What risk was there? The young girls entwined with their young men were all around us without seeing us. I listened to him and enjoyed, in addition, the presence of a miraculous dressmaker for the buttonhole of his lips, a sculptor for the modeling of the cleft in the middle of his chin, a tailor for the narrow cut of his long, dark eyes, an engraver for the locks of hair curling out under the band of his wide-brimmed hat, and the shadowy hunter of shadows for his eyelashes and eyebrows. And in a perpetual conflict of vanity and modesty I saw my little eyes, my big mouth, my great nose reflected in the shine of his shirt collar.

The stranger spread his legs, he leaned forward, he ate one, two, three, four, five peaches. The juice dripped onto the gravel.

"Now let's go and have dinner," he said.

He checked the curling brim of his sheriff's hat and took me to a restaurant in Montparnasse. He questioned me. I quoted titles and names of authors to him. I said *Le Coq et l'Arlequin,* he answered *Plain-Chant.* I said *L'Annonce faite à Marie,* he answered *Tête d'Or.* I said Francis Jammes, he answered Guillaume Apollinaire. He gave me a copy of *Du côté de chez Swann.* What did he want? To initiate a French girl into French literature. He was so pleasant, so cultivated, so correct, so sure of his knowledge of literature that he didn't exist. He disappeared from his hotel in the Rue Cujas and I forgot him. I didn't write about him to Hermine and I didn't talk about him to my mother.

Du côté de chez Swann. The two volumes within hand's reach have followed me around for more than thirty years. The dust won't settle on them. If I open them, I hear as if it were yesterday the singing notes of his Argentine accent. An immortal film of youth overlaying the long Proustian sentences. Alas, since I wrote that, the Invisible Visitor who comes here, by night or in my absence, has torn the cover off, leaving the threadbound pages naked. I can no longer keep count of the books in my room he has destroyed in this way: Bousset, Mallarmé (more than the others), Saint-John Perse. . . . Sign and signature of a vampire whose prey is books.

*

The Lycée Racine beside the Gare Saint-Lazare, near the Métro station of the same name, in the neighborhood of the big stores, the tourist hotels, the packed cafés and restaurants, sent me into a fever of excitement. I had come to look for instruction in the heart of a furnace. I could hear the noise of the people and the traffic outside even in the classrooms. The level of the work we had to do appalled me; I resumed my place at the bottom of every class except the one in foreign literature. The intelligence, the elegance, the knowledge of make-up displayed by one of the girl students terrified me during science and math classes. I collapsed into a stupor when I was asked a question; the high-flying feats of the other girl reduced me to a zero. She and the others made fun of my face, of my ignorance, of my shyness. I studied at night only to grasp less and less. I became run down. I spat blood the whole night after having a tooth extracted. I was growing poorer, despite my daily exchange of letters with Hermine. My experience, my superiority came to me through my senses. I had to hide the fact from everyone.

Archangel, I was unjust to you in *Ravages*. It was a novel, a romance, our romance. Archangel, you will soon be sixty. Archangel, I don't believe you stole from poor-boxes. I hope you hate me. You can hate, I know, for you were imperfect then.

Here is how I met him.

One Sunday afternoon I went into a movie house, the Marivaux. It was packed to capacity. One seat, the last seat left, the usherette told me. Like you, I had come to see *Ariane, jeune fille russe* with Gaby Morlay and Victor Francen. A profile in that movie exalted me, the way a Chorale played on an organ can exalt you. I was discovering the austerity there is in a profile; the resources and riches, the ethics of chiaroscuro. Plus an overwhelming attraction. A mere student, a young girl just off my train from the provinces, I was offering a cigarette to the man on my right with the meditative profile. The man took my cigarette without turning his head. We smoked our Camels, we watched the film, we thought about each other without knowing one another. Too close, too far apart. What confusion already, what a strange prelude. All the distance from the Northern Cape to Palmyra, all the closeness of one ear of rye to another ear of rye. I left and he followed. An apéritif, a brasserie. I have told the story of that evening already, with variants. A student, I told him about the school where I studied. Days passed. I didn't see him again. A commonplace occurrence, I told myself. I wrote every day to Hermine, I loved her in my letters, I loved myself in her letters, I concealed my visit to the movies from her, my evening with Gabriel. I concealed from her something that existed and something that existed no longer: the presence and the absence of that profile in the movie theater. It's quite true, I didn't want him to come to the gate of the Lycée Racine. I was and I always shall be hampered by what I think other people will say. I looked for Gabriel when I came out of school. The memory of having things out with him on a bench in the Métro. His docility. It used to pain me, his docility. Don't come back, we mustn't see each other again. He wasn't coming back.

I came out of the Lycée one afternoon with a crowd of other students. The other times, I used to look for him in front of me, near the entrances to the Métro. That day I turned my head so slowly. . . . There are understandings, gestures, movements prepared before we were born. He was leaning against the Lycée wall and waiting, watching me from the other side. . . . The other students dispersed and I found myself alone with him. He begged without opening his mouth, without putting out a hand. The one supported the other, Paris was fading around us.

"How are things?" he said with assumed heartiness.

I couldn't thank him for his closely shaved face, for his hair smoothed down with brilliantine.

"You shouldn't have . . . If my parents were to see me . . ."

"Your parents won't see you. There's a pâtisserie just along here," he said.

His calm, his green eyes, made me feel lost.

"It's impossible. I must go home. . . . We used to live on the Place Daumesnil, now we live by the Porte Champerret. I must go."

He smiled and his face lighted up. Paris was reappearing, Paris was making me bolder.

"I know where you live," he said.

"You came to the Porte Champerret!"

"Yes. Let's go and have tea."

His help, the lightest of touches, as we crossed the intersections. I thought of his thoughtful man's mouth, of his delicately formed lips on which my algebra problems were resolving themselves and dissolving as we walked.

"Not so close," I said to his mouth just at the height of my shoulder. We walked on.

I went with him into the pâtisserie and into fairyland: he was inviting me to have tea with him. I became a member of that great band of women who were bought things by men.

Gabriel asked for two plates and two forks. The woman serving us bustled back and forth without seeing his shabby topcoat. I could see it only too well.

We ate little pastries in the shape of books, with cream in the middle the color of meringue. Gabriel guessed my thoughts.

"I like good things," he said.

I changed, the Lycée Racine changed. Gabriel was waiting for me on every teacher's dais, on the faces of the clocks, on the paper I was covering with ink. When two lines joined to form a diamond, Gabriel was waiting for me in the four corners of the diamond. When a girl was called out to the front of the class, she was writing a message from him, I'm waiting, as she set out an equation on the blackboard. I felt no desire for Gabriel and I didn't want him to feel desire for me. I waited patiently alone every day, alone outside, alone in the crowd. I clenched my fist, I glanced at the time on my wristwatch with a manly gesture of the arm, a gesture made for Gabriel, a tribute to his gentleness, to his slightly feminine walk, to his slender waist. When we met, I was dazzled by his stoicism. I was flattered by his pastries, his liqueurs, his apéritifs. More than that. With his gifts and his self-control he made me grow up. He countered my thirst, my hunger for Hermine with a little plate, a little fork, a big glass of spirits. I could read Gabriel's thirst, Gabriel's hunger, in his pleading eyes, in the intensity with which he gazed at me like an animal trying to persuade you to stroke it. When a woman customer came into the pâtisserie Gabriel would move closer without taking his eyes off me and I would feel myself tottering: I became too vast. He could see the sea, he was looking for the boat. I became both boat and sea. I loved his faithfulness, I loved his arm under mine, I loved his patience, I loved his sacrifices.

"Just a moment, little fellow," he would say in the street.

He would stop in front of a Paul Colin poster and explain it to me with enthusiasm, he described the pictures of Othon Friesz, he pointed out a change in the light over the Trinité, the persistence of a white cloud over my Lycée, a rainbow puddle at our feet, the relative ill fortune of the men in sandwich boards advertising a restaurant in the Rue Saint-Lazare. We brushed against the prostitutes of the neighborhood as we overtook them in the street and he offered them his friendship as he passed. He squeezed my arm to make me notice a waiter saying good night to his replacement on a café terrace. He observed everything, everything was of interest to him. He took Paris for his own; his eyes were always saying to me as they begged: help yourself, take it, it's there in me for you.

He was a buyer for a firm in Clermont and his job was to buy in Paris all the things the women didn't have down there: dressmaking articles, porcelain, hardware. Our freedom at four in the afternoon went to my head. He tried to make me smoke in the street and his daring stunned me.

"Last week you went to the Galeries with your mother and your brother. You got on an 'S.'"

"What? How do you know?"

"I followed the bus in a taxi."

His eyes added: "Don't make a fuss. That's how it is."

"Your mother ordered a lemon juice. You had an ice. Your mother was in a bad temper."

"You were there!"

"I was there."

I said: I have a girl friend.

"We'll go to Montparnasse!"

I said: before her I had Isabelle.

"We'll go to the Dôme!"

I said: I have a girl friend. I write her every day.

"We'll go to the Select."

I said: She writes me every day.

"We'll go to the Jockey, my little one, we'll go to the Jockey together."

"I've got a girl friend!"

Gabriel understood; his sacrifices increased.

*

My love.

Twenty minutes before midnight. My parents are asleep, the apartment is asleep, the building is asleep. You could come now, the city is a mask. You won't come. I wouldn't let them put curtains at my windows. It is for you, this holiday of light on an attic window. Lamps lighting another world. It is wan and full of grace. You are still awake, I know that from your letters. We keep each other company at night! The chair, the closet, the briefcase I take to school . . . These things, these objects make you fade. I turn away my head. They would have swallowed me up. The silence in my room is the silence of your piano, the silence of the music you no longer play. Your fingers molded the singing notes and the frothing leaves of the forest brought a smile to the sky. A great and serious musician. My dream. Your breath is on my hand as I write to you. At night it's easier. The distance, the distance between us, is discreet. When will you kiss me till I beg for mercy? I kiss your sentences, I kiss your words, I rub my lips over your writing paper. When will you be in my arms? I have soft jewel cases for you. The looking glass says so in the hollows of my shoulders when I'm dressing, when I'm undressing. I weep. I can't get used to your handwriting. I see it running across a keyboard also. I want to see you, Hermine. Love is not being separated. The breath on my hand is gone. You are absent, always absent. Paris with you. I can't believe that will happen. Shall I come to you? Impossible. The letter that came from you this morning is a band of coolness on my brow. Don't take off your red-brown jacket, don't take it off. It's you, it's your signature on my closed eyelids. We've had bad luck, always bad luck. Do you think it will go on? What will become of us, one without the other? Answer me. What will become of us? I shall write to you tomorrow.

No, I can't leave you. You are generous, Hermine, you give me details of your life. I see the drawings on the walls of your classroom, I see the faces of the students, I see the headmistress. Does she teach too? Two rooms in a village school, that's very grand. The garden, the one belonging to the both of you, does it have a good exposure? You grow things. You have the time to grow things? That's magnificent. They are little things, but little things that enable me to reconstruct you every time I read them again. Suddenly Paris is tiny, suddenly Paris is cold. There are so many lonely people here. Everyone lives in his own cage. You used to tell me about the Jardin du Luxembourg, you used to tell me about it in the corridors at school. We'll go to concerts if you come. You give private lessons, you sew, you read in the evening. . . . You don't waste any time. I am still as lazy as ever. I shall work at the end of the school year. I'm afraid of the end of the school year. I'd like to see your oak table and the armchair. Your father is kind. You live alone, you have your own place. I'm proud of you, my darling. If I could only become a schoolteacher like you, in the same village, in the same school. Play the last Etude on Sunday if you're alone with the piano, play it for me, my love, play it at the end of the day. Violette.

The envelope was sealed. I put out the light, I whispered in my bed: Play the Etude, play the Etude. . . .

I was threatening myself and threatening Hermine.

Play the Etude! I am concealing Gabriel from you, concealing the film *Ariane, jeune fille russe,* the Marivaux and the other movie houses I've been to with him. His feverishness, the dampness of his hand in mine, his pleading, the way he gazes appealingly like a dumb beast, I don't tell you about that. Play the Etude at the end of the day while we are savoring Paris together, please, my pure spring. I am deceiving you when he offers me a cigarette. I am deceiving you and it is your victory. I can't write about it to you. I need you and I need him, you wouldn't understand. If it made you angry, I wouldn't see him again. I won't run the risk. My mother has her husband on Sunday evenings, on Sunday afternoons, and I have Gabriel. I can't write to you: I picked him up in a movie house. I'm afraid of what your judgment would be and I want to keep what I have: Hermine, Gabriel. What is it I have? An inoffensive man who finds me attractive, and I am rarely found attractive. A rather short man, a badly dressed, stunted little man. That's what the crowd sees. A man who can control himself, who can forget his own existence, who knows how to sacrifice himself. A giant. A bed of orchids in a field of turnips. I calm him by giving him caresses one at a time with my hands. Does he really desire me? I don't think so. It is the torture he desires. The torture of what he cannot have. His money . . . He walks into a café, he throws away tomorrow's crust of bread in tips. He doesn't talk about his money difficulties. His reticence is colossal. Worn cuffs, soiled collar, greasy knot to his necktie. I feel the same shame for him that we feel for martyrs.

He goes with prostitutes. I had forgotten them. I wouldn't be able to explain that to you, Hermine. You play the *Italian Concerto*. Gabriel reads, and he loves music. He skimps his reading and his music so he can take a schoolgirl out to tea. He isn't an old man, he isn't a middle-aged man. He's twenty-six. He steals my kisses from you, Hermine. I can't be unbending, I have to pay for my security with fraudulent caresses. No, you couldn't understand.

As though she had received this letter written on night's slate, Hermine answered that she had to come to Paris on some sort of business. I left my parents' house for two days. She kissed me, she said that she wanted us to go to bed together, that there was nothing else she wanted in Paris. The first night at the Hôtel du Panthéon, Sunday, and the following night at the Hôtel du Grand Condé. A concert when we were exhausted.

Let us share the last croissant, Hermine. Will you keep the room? Yes, we'll keep the room. Your watch, don't forget anything, pick up your watch off the bedside table. Shall we have seats in the middle at the Châtelet? If we run, yes. We won't be first there but we won't be the last. You'll see crowds of students. Is that the Châtelet? Yes. Are those the students? Yes, they're climbing up to the balcony. Tired, Violette? Yes, but light, light . . . Oh! It's nothing, Hermine, nothing; lower your voice. Gabriel! There he is behind us, he's mad. A blinding light and a great avalanche of anthracite. How did he find out we were going to this concert? How did he know Hermine was in Paris? I can't work out how many hours he must have watched and waited. Now he is playing his role of anonymous concertgoer beside us. He is forcing me to play an unpleasant role. I can't blame him. He is keeping himself in my memory, he doesn't want to be cut out. He wanted to see what Hermine is like. Say something, Violette. You're not talking to me, why not? I am talking, Hermine. I was asking you if you like being in a crowd of students. I like it very much, Violette. He is brushing my shoulder with his cheek. I gave him my shoulder to brush against, but I didn't really want to. It's impossible. You see, Hermine, we're moving forward at last. His boldness makes me sad. And it enchants me. We shall be in the middle, Violette, just as you said. He is a fraud, that martyr. Talk to me, Violette. Where are you, Violette? He is quicker than us, he is ahead of us in the staircase. His long hair. He doesn't give a damn about his long hair when he walks into the Jockey, when he sits with radiant eyes and bleeds himself white so that we can listen to Kiki de Montparnasse when she sings. . . . Yes, Hermine, it's always like this: lots of steps to climb if you want cheap seats. . . . The banjo, the alcohol, two "bolsheviks" like last time. Yes, there's always this race up the stairs, and the first to the top get the best seats. He's got what he wanted. Behind us and close to us. Let's go back to the hotel, Violette. But you were looking forward to this concert so much, Hermine. . . . Let's go back to the hotel, I don't like it here. Your favorite Schumann concerto. You're shivering, Violette. You don't like it here any more than I do. I'm not shivering, Hermine. Yes, I am shivering, because he's already sitting down. There are two seats empty in front of him. How did he manage to keep them, to save them? Let's go back to the hotel, Hermine, let's go back. No, Violette; the orchestra is tuning up now and it would mean disturbing the other people. I cheat. I cheat between my eyelashes in order to look at him. He is brushing his knee against my back just as he brushed my shoulder earlier. We are murdering Hermine while she smiles at the violas. There's something white in his hands. . . . What is it? I'm going to turn my head around, I'm going to murder Hermine a little more. The books! The books he promised. Have patience, little fellow, I'll find them in a rare edition. He is pressing the rare edition against his threadbare lapels as a sign that he's found them, bought them. Will he have soap to wash with tomorrow? Tomorrow he will give me the copy of *Si le grain ne meurt* he's holding in his hands, tomorrow Hermine will have gone. I should have shouted out what was happening, the chandelier should have fallen. Doorman, gentle doorman, why don't you throw all three of us out of the theater? Hermine is a lamb, and the lamb is listening to the *Egmont* overture. She takes my hand, she thanks the music. Gabriel, is that what it means to enjoy your beloved? Hermine, is that what it means to die in blissful ignorance, surrounded by the Gods? Violette, is that the meaning of betrayal?

*

"Become a schoolteacher," my mother said. "What will you do if you don't become a schoolteacher, if you don't pass?"

She was tormenting herself more and more.

"Think of your future. You must think of the future."

I reassured her: "I shall pass."

"Do you think so?"

"I shall go to work in a bookstore."

"Really?"

The whole woman, completely disarmed, was in that little question, and I loved her for it.

I went to classes at the Maison du Livre; the examination at the Lycée was coming close now and I was reaping what I had sown: my idleness, my casualness, my hundreds of hours lost to work while I went walking with Gabriel or wrote letters to Hermine. I wanted to pass for my mother's sake, for her peace of mind. In my panic at the thought of all the time I'd lost, I forgot my desire to share a school with Hermine.

I wanted to say to my mother: I've passed. The other students were revising, I was learning. There was a sun in my eyes day and night, and it oppressed me. I would have wept my last drop of blood to come close to it. What was it, this sun? It was the cluster of girls who were sure of themselves. Of their success. My head emptied itself again as quickly as I filled it up. At the time when I was learning my multiplication tables, my mother used to console me with the phrase: what you don't remember in the evening, you'll find you know next day. Next day, as my exams drew near, I got up in the morning with an old moldy beehive where my brain should have been. Geography, History, were like so much treacle inside it. Every morning I would have joyfully exchanged my schoolbooks for the porters' brooms.

One afternoon after a review class at the Lycée Racine, I found my mother in my room. She was packing two suitcases. We had often talked about leaving home: we set off with heavy hearts, feeling frightened and bewildered. By that evening my mother regretted what she had done. I had a fever, I told her I wanted a studio. It was one of the fashionable words at the time. We had moved into a good hotel and were eating our meals at La Reine Pédauque as we always had when we visited Paris from the North. The comfort of these places was a substitute for the help and protection we craved. My mother couldn't live away from her husband and her son. We talked about them ceaselessly; even sitting in a café we were wandering elsewhere. I was developing a bad sore throat. At the end of the following day, my mother begged me to telephone my stepfather and ask him if we could go back. He answered: "Yes, come back."

I came down with diphtheria: permanganate sprays, the bright blue of the methylene, my mother nursing me devotedly. My stepfather didn't come into my room, I didn't dare ask if he talked about my health. She went out with him the following Sunday. They ate dinner out and celebrated their reconciliation. I was left alone with old Marie, their maid; I was miserable, I was bitter. My stepfather was ice cold toward me in the dining room when I got better. He answered "Good morning" when I spoke to him, but nothing more. I was responsible for our leaving home, which was unjust. I had influenced my mother as she influenced me. I had telephoned to help her go back home with such enthusiasm.

*

Having passed the written exam and failed the oral, I didn't work during the vacation and failed to return to the Lycée in October. My mother made no fuss. She accepted what had happened and kept her grief to herself.

"You're lazy," she said.

My mother thought I wouldn't be able to find any work. My stepfather wanted me to pay for my board and lodging.

I put an advertisement in the *Bibliographie de la France*. The issue carrying my insertion fascinated me. Those rows of little black letters were busy making the honey of work for me, just as the honey of future happiness or misery is made by wedding announcements.

I read Hermine's letter and rushed out of my room like a tornado.

"Shall I be able to visit her if I get a job?"

"Yes, you'll be able to visit her," my mother said. "And don't slam any more doors. What a terror you are. . . . Why, Violette?"

The maid came into the dining room and my mother fell silent. The maid left again.

"Why, Violette?"

My mother was getting a skirt ready to go to the dressmaker's for pleating. It was chocolate brown. My mother was arranging it with her fingers, measuring, pinning, and tacking the uniform sadness of its autumn color. My job was being produced too in this new skirt she was going to give me.

"I do everything I can for you," she said. "I do everything I can to make you happy. What is it you've got against me?"

As soon as she began showing weakness toward me I hated her for that too.

"You should find something to do outside. You're getting dull staying at home all the time," I said.

"I'll think about it," she answered.

Her steely eyes asked me again why I went around slamming doors, what it was I had against her.

The tenderness welling inside me became a pain. Marly again, the dandelions again, always Marly, always the dandelions. I couldn't bear our conversation, I couldn't bear to feel her youth, my childhood, flooding back.

I couldn't say to her: I slam the doors, I am a terror because I'm not wanted. I'm still in Marly, by our rabbit hutches after Fidéline died. With you, I shall never go beyond that point. I would smash a door to pulp for our winters in the North, for our waffles, for the scabies, for my lice. We caught the scabies from the poor soldiers—our sulfur, our bath; my lice came from a mysterious classmate when I began going to the school. The fine comb in my mother's hand . . . the harrow in my hair. The comfortable rightness of the pain. The comb like a lyre expressing her energy. The vermin cannot resist my mother's power, the vermin die between my mother's nails.

We had shared the same memories.

"Was I gay?" my mother asked.

"Don't you remember?"

"You remember better than I do," she said. "Tell me about it . . ."

She pushed the skirt away; she escaped from the apartment.

"You were always gay. You used to sing."

"I used to sing?" she said with the voice of a child. "I used to sing, and I hadn't a penny to my name," she said ecstatically.

I often talked about Gabriel when my stepfather was out about his business.

"I saw you together," my mother said.

"Together!"

"Together! On one of the boulevards. You were wearing identical raincoats. I didn't say anything to your stepfather. . . . Be careful, think of your mother. It's Saturday. Why don't we go to the Prado? Put something on, tidy yourself up."

I clapped my hands, I jumped up and down on their carpet.

*

My mother made herself up as little as possible in her dressing room; I went and "tidied myself up" in my own room.

"Do you hear? Be careful," she shouted. "He's a man."

She came to the door of my room, powderpuff in hand. I was forgetting her advice. I lost myself in the delicately sensual scent of her face powder.

". . . He's not like other men," I said.

"Hurry up. Our table will be gone!"

She went back into her dressing room and I followed her with my powderpuff. We were not being very clever about our makeup; we were both wearing Cendre de Roses powder and the same color rouge.

"He's a man," she said again.

"He doesn't ask for anything, he makes no demands."

My mother was lengthening her eyebrows with a pencil.

"Then he'll be the first who hasn't," she declared.

"I tell you he's not like other men."

I concealed Gabriel from her by concealing my caresses and the kisses I was forced to give him.

The gaiety of our Saturday afternoon outing was like the gaiety of the flowers and posies painted by Séraphine de Senlis. Walking beside my mother from the Porte Champerret to the Place Pereire, I advanced through a crowd of tiny eyes shining with all the colors of the rainbow. I projected my excitement, my joy, before me and they came glittering back in a multicolored shimmer.

"Don't put your arm through mine. You behave like a farm boy!" she said.

Farm boy. That upset me: she could at least have said girl.

I didn't get annoyed. It was impossible surrounded by that crowd of little eyes with their laughing colors. 1927. I don't remember her dress, her hat, her purse, her gloves. I do remember something: I would have liked her to be more eccentric-looking.

"Walk in front of me," I would tell her.

My mother obeyed.

"You'll tell me . . ."

I was the master, she the pupil in our world of elegance.

"Well?"

She asked for my opinion without turning her head, very alert. I liked her stockings and the high-heeled shoes she was wearing.

She fell back.

"Well?"

"It's classic. It's too classic."

"Oh that one!" she would say, dismissing my opinion.

Now, more than thirty years later, I see things as she did: I expected too much of her; I wanted her dress, her hat, to be unique. More than thirty years later, I can envisage the passers-by, the cars stopping for the mother I wanted as they stop in Méliès films.

We reached the Avenue Wagram at about four o'clock.

"The cigarettes," my mother would say.

The party was beginning. I went on my own into the narrowest of the cigarette stores by the side of the Empire music hall. I awaited my turn with pleasure and anxiety. The woman behind the counter would pick the brand I asked for from its place on the shelf without looking around; she was a virtuoso, a robot.

"Come on, we'll go there next week," my mother said impatiently as I dawdled in front of the posters and photographs outside the Empire. We would go on past the music hall and hesitate just outside the Prado. People who didn't know what to look for used to walk straight past it.

"You go in first," my mother said.

I obeyed, I protected her because she was the more feminine, the more beautiful of the two. I walked down a softly yielding staircase that might have been conducting us to a basement full of friends; I closed my hand around the silk rope balustrade and let my fingers slide down it, I felt its twisted cords in relief, and the contrast with the stairs swooning beneath their carpet. My hand gliding over the twisted silk was remembering real ropes in the past: the channel steamer at Le Havre when I went to a children's camp in England after my mother was married. A knot: Southampton. A knot: crossing London as swiftly as a zipper closing. A knot: Bakewell, Derbyshire. A knot: the cottage of the old spinster lady with her garden full of lavender. A knot: the lavender growing as high as our wheat in Flanders. A knot, a knot, a knot, a knot, a knot, a knot: the spikes of lavender, the abstract blue of the lavender at the top of its stalk, the succulent desserts, the undulating flocks, the headiness of the green grass, the maternal watchfulness of the housekeeper. Peaches completely covered in cream, mommy.

"Yes, I've known what it's like," my mother said. "The ices . . . the ice cream men making their deliveries at your father's home. . . ."

So much the better for her if other people's receptions became her receptions; but her ices and her ice cream men cast a chill over my memories: the butterfly bow in my hair when I was photographed at the holiday camp at the age of fourteen and a half; the postcard of Dorothy Barker with the reproduction of her house.

The cossacks on the stage were singing "Dark Eyes" in Russian, a soloist was making his way from table to table with his balalaika. Curtain. The soloist had gone up onto the stage and now twenty balalaikas were playing another Russian air, paying ecstatic homage to tinkling bells and troikas. We found our usual table free.

"What do you want?" my mother asked irritably.

The cake waitress was in attendance with her tongs hovering over the display on her moving cart. What did I want? To see my twenty-year-old soul and heart in a ribbon. To see that ribbon quiver, to see it flutter over twenty balalaikas. A gigolo rose to his feet; he kissed the hand of the woman he'd been waiting for.

"It's sad, you know, Violette. . . ."

Waiters were turning away customers with a great show of politeness. The Prado was always packed.

". . . It's sad having to ask for money every time I have none left. We wouldn't be here if I didn't have my little store hidden away. He won't give me very much at a time because he's afraid I'll give you some. That's the reason."

Some Russian émigrés who had met each other the week before in this same place were greeting each other again with so much warmth that their week apart became twenty years.

Curtain.

The musicians came down from the stage and sat resting near the staircase.

The women were all waiting for him, most of them were there because of him, and the men at the bar pivoted around on their stools. The waitresses and the waiters pretended not to see their customers so that they could watch him and listen.

"He isn't Chaliapin, but he has a beautiful bass voice," whispered one of the old ladies at the next table.

The big cossack alone on the stage was singing without searching for effects. He described the steppe to us, he embellished it with his modulations, he darkened it, he made it warm again, he poured sun across it, he dramatized it, he journeyed over it, he covered it with thorns, he made us a gift of it. Though the Russian language made me feel strange, it brought the North back to me, all its harshness and its strength. The prestige of the émigrés. How rich they were, these aristocratic gypsies, since even I was unfastening the Tsar's cape, starching Lenin's collar, brushing Trotsky's fur hat, raking Tolstoy's garden as the cossack stood singing a song fit to explode an isba with its exuberance. I can still hear it. What am I doing? I am giving the celebrated baby carriage in *Potemkin* a good kick to help it on its way, so that the new world at the bottom of the steps will come into being quicker.

Curtain. Pause. The singer disappeared. With a lost gaze, he reappeared and made his way across *The Steppes of Central Asia* between the tables. He refused the flowers, he refused the cigarettes.

"He really is a handsome man," my mother said detachedly.

After our cakes, we ordered an apéritif.

That evening my stepfather talked about politics at the dinner table. He was beside himself with fury because of the strikes; the workers should be made to understand . . . My mother sat looking at our Marly in my eyes, I sat looking at our Marly in my mother's eyes. He was trying to think of the name of a politician.

I cried out: "Rappoport!"

"That's it, my dear. You've hit on the very man," he said.

My mother was exultant. At last her daughter was no longer a blockhead. If only I could hit upon Rappoports every day of the week, I thought to myself.

*

We went to the matinees at the Empire; we bought inexpensive seats and became cabin boys up there in the balcony keeping lookout from the top of a mast.

Marcel Jouhandeau said to me one day: "You're wearing a clown's sweater [it was a sweater with wide green and mauve stripes], we are both clowns. We love, and they laugh after we've gone." Grock did his act on his own. He was a clown we admired even after he'd left the stage. His mouth? The swag of a great festoon. His vast chin? A coconut. His skull? An Easter egg. His gloves? Borrowed from some Goliath. His March-April-May eyes. Children playing ring-around-a-rosy. His simplicity when confronted with applause. "Why?" "Really?" The points of suspension after the "Why," after the "Really," became tiny points of phosphorescence. Grock nestled his cheek in the hollow of his shoulder, grew tearful himself as he drew forth our tears, and cast a spell over the audience with his "Really?" He also played the . . . I don't remember what it's called. I open my dictionary at random and it opens at the proper names section, just when I've decided he played the ocarina. My eye lights upon Richard the Lionheart. Yes, Grock, you were a Lionheart, and we roared with pleasure at your triumphs. I remember what it was called. He played the concertina. His arms twisted the air into fantastic circles. He conjured with his gifts when he sat on the back of his chair and played on, drew sounds from, a microbe: the smallest violin in the world.

A week after that show, I said to my mother: "We absolutely must go to the Empire again."

"You want to see Grock again?"

"No . . . it's a new program."

"Have you seen it? Who with? Violette, be sensible. It could happen to you like anybody else. I know what men are. They're all the same."

"Shall we go to the Empire on Thursday?"

"Why? Since you've already been."

"I'd be seeing it with you this time. Shall we go?"

"All right, since you say it's good."

The heavy curtain rose, the young woman stretched on the divan at the left of the rostrum lay fanning herself with her ostrich feather fan. This occupation was immediately gripping because it seemed to have begun long before the curtain disclosed it to us. Fanning herself was how she had passed the last hundred years. The young woman was alone on the immense stage. The books tell us that in a beehive there are thousands of bees beating their wings to fan the queen. This young woman had a thousand fingers, a thousand wrists, a thousand hands cooling her solitude. She lifted a foot, she let one mule dangle from its tip. So much aplomb in the service of her frivolity became her. I looked at my mother. Her little eyelashes were flickering up and down with the intensity of her efforts to understand.

"Don't talk," she said, as I sat saying nothing.

Everything was rising and falling: the tuft of feathers on the mule, the foot, the ankle, the fan, the wrist, the hand. Men's eyes were drinking in every movement as the spotlights sent gold and silver showering over the blonde hair. And then a book of hours opened, a miniature came to life. Pompadour molded the calf, Marie-Antoinette carved out the fingers. Now a great courtesan was veiling all but her eyes with the fan drawn over her face. The feathers still rose and fell. I don't desert the audience when I go to the theater. On the knees of a bald-headed man, I glimpsed an acacia flower stuck in a hat, while the artist proffered those rising and falling ostrich plumes. The young woman finally relinquished her fan, and the dress fell from her as the first snowflake falls when winter begins. Someone permitted himself to cough.

A bathing suit, a glittering two-piece as simple as the memory of a seashell glowing on the beach at night. A miraculous moment as the silken rope was sent snaking toward the artiste's hand.

I leaned toward my mother: "What do you think of it?"

"It's crazy," my mother said without looking at me.

She was climbing the silken rope; our fine little pearl was a monkey. Every movement was a jewel. Each gesture as delicate as that fine hair. With the tips of her feet through the rings, she swayed back and forth looking at us upside down. Obviously death was in the audience. In the first row. And with such a stiff neck . . . It was too high; a human being. At that moment, recovery by the acrobat. The young woman was dominating, ruling over the spaces around her; death had been cheated. That twist of her hands coiling around the ropes, holding the rings, that grasp of friendship . . . It's as simple as that, she can't die, I said to myself for my mother's benefit. Obscenity: her legs bent back from the knees, her thighs spreadeagled. Oh the two-piece was irreproachable: everything that should be refused to the gaze was refused, our vague longing for her was mingled somehow with that feeling we have when our heart has been soiled. It was awakened by that hint of the amateur as she hung swaying back and forth and looked at us, but when she sent her trapeze swinging out into space, it was as though a motorman had set an express train in motion with one flick of the hand.

"What do you think? Do you like it?" I asked my mother.

"I'd be hard to please if I didn't," she answered, opening and closing her eyes in order to collect herself for a moment.

Reader, I spare you a description of the coloratura flourishes performed by the acrobat's body around the bar of a trapeze. She crossed and uncrossed her feet, she sharpened her toes against each other with the agility of a fly. Not the peril of her feats but their embellishment was what came first. She leaped from one trapeze to another in an attempt at suicide. But death, reduced to beggary, continued to beg in vain. She swung clear of her suicide.

"How sweet she is," my mother whispered at that moment.

Courage always softened her heart.

Perilous exercises, oh those long years of training for twenty problematic minutes. The curtain fell.

"What an angel," my mother said.

At that moment Barbette reappeared in front of the curtain. With his healthy-looking face, his freshly scrubbed cheeks, his tightly tied robe, his hair combed flat to his head, the young Englishman bowed and slipped away, taking shelter from the stupefaction and the applause.

"I don't regret having come," my mother said.

She'd brought a snack and we sat eating it off our knees.

"And now you're going to tell me who you came here with," my mother said.

"With Gabriel of course! Who else did you think? We were in the lounge."

"Why in the lounge?"

"It's less expensive and it's nearer the stage."

She grew indignant: "He sounds a pretty poor specimen to me! But the fact remains that he's a man! You can't tell me there isn't someone else!"

"If there is someone else, as you put it, then so much the better."

She was nonplussed by my attitude. She thought up nicknames for Gabriel: Moutatiou, Mamoizelle, Moutarde. She hurt me when she disparaged him in this way. I didn't dare tell her so: I laughed with her.

I used to believe I was a polyglot, a practical joker, I thought people couldn't believe their ears when I invented my own foreign language as a child. I hoped to astonish and stun my listeners. Here is a sample (I asked the questions as well as making the answers):

"Kroom glim glam gloomb?

"Blam glom glim gam.

"Vram plouminourou?

"Flarounitzoukoleenaree.

"Motziboo?

"Motziboo."

I wanted to make people collapse with laughter; I always finished up shaking and choking with my own private mirth.

My grandmother put up with it because she was deaf, but my mother used to shout at me: "Go and do that outside." After my mother's marriage, there was a charwoman who allowed herself to be taken in. What is it? she asked. German? English? Spanish? Italian? No, it's something else, I said making an exit.

Cab Calloway at the Empire was something else. He sang, improvised, poured out a stream of nonsensical words, meaningless words, hard words, closed words, metallic words, percussive words, explosive words and strings of words pressed one against the other without a pause between. And superimposed on all this, the rhythms of the jazz combo that accompanied him.

"He scats divinely," said a young man to his neighbor.

"He scats, he's a scat singer," I whispered very quietly to my mother.

"Oh, you know what I'm like," she replied without enthusiasm.

If she didn't understand something she just didn't bother with it.

The radio era was just beginning. In the evenings, after he had finished with his affairs for the day, my stepfather was putting together a crystal set. His apparatus finally attained the size and descriptive depth of Grieg's piece *In the Hall of the Mountain King*. The first sounds, the first broadcasts, the first interference—it sounded like fish frying—the intonations of the incredible, indiscreet voice, the miraculous presence of the speaker, are a part of history. A world was being born. The waves. I heard the *Toccata and Fugue in D minor* by Johann Sebastian Bach. The great organ heard for the first time outside a church became the greatest of all churches: the church of the music fanatics. God was playing in a cathedral, the cathedral of Bach. As I walked toward the tuning dial, the tubes, the wires, I was approaching a keyboard being played by Cortot, by Brailowski, by Iturbi, by Tagliaferro, or a bow held by Thibaud. Concertos by Liszt, by Schumann for piano and orchestra . . . The Pleyel my mother had given me, still as fine as ever, became laughable. I gave up heart, but I consoled myself in advance with the records played on the radio.

At last I received a letter from the *Bibliographie de la France*. I was summoned to an interview, I was to present myself the following morning at the offices of a big publisher on the Left Bank. I read the summons fifty times, the polite formula at the end, the signature of the unknown writer, the heading with the firm's name: Plon, and the two typed initials separate from the text.

"Explain," my mother said.

I read it and read it, but I couldn't explain to her what a publishing house was.

"It's a trademark," I said, "it's a trademark you find on the bottom of book covers. If a writer is with the Mercure de France he isn't with the N.R.F., or with Flammarion, or with the Presses Universitaires. . . ."

"It's too complicated," my mother said, "but explain anyway. . . ."

I shrugged my shoulders in my ignorance.

"Let's wait till tomorrow."

My mother served up our meals and, quite often, gave me extra. Her cooking was simple and excellent. Her tarts, her custards, her crêpes, the quintessence of the art. Her chestnut cake was unforgettable, her mashed potatoes incomparable, her sauces, her meat gravy, always light.

"No, I never took lessons. I watched grandmother," she always said.

It touches me when she says grandmother referring to her mother. Fidéline at those moments is grandmother to both of us. She moves me when a memory of her childhood comes flooding back. She whispers:

"Does it still hurt, a'ma?"

A'ma. The lightest of light-winged birds alights on the lyre of memory. Fidéline, I see you transfigured. It is a metamorphosis. A'ma. You are transformed into a pretty little boy from Biskra.

I crossed the Place Saint-Sulpice and searched for the publishing house along a strangled little street. A cyclist emerged with a pile of books. That was my door. I walked through into the courtyard; I was back in the provincial calm of my childhood. I wiped my nose, which often shines, and also my moist palms. I opened the outside door without hurry and tidied my hair in its glass panes. I opened the second door and stood gazing at the shelves of books stretching endlessly before me. Another cyclist, just leaving with a pile of yellow-covered books, asked me why I didn't go in. The size of the room, the height of the ceiling, the length of the ladders leaning against the partitioned shelves, the discretion of the people working on the ladders, sliding along or taking the books out from the various sections, held me immobile. Gone was the classical silence of our school libraries. Unread books, books not yet opened were living and moving in this room. Young women and girls, with books behind them on the shelves, books in front of them on the counters, were sifting, separating, collecting together, slipping sheets of paper inside the covers. The cashier was firmly ensconced inside her glass cage. Salesmen, some young, some old, were walking out the doors, pleased with the stock they were going to sell. I walked down the steps and showed the letter asking me to call.

"I'll take her. She wouldn't be able to find it on her own," one young woman said to another.

We went up two steps and turned right. We were both looking down at the vista of dovecotes filled with dated, faded whiteness: the cut edges of the books. We went up the staircase into the sales room and looked at a landscape of little pantries stocked with culture. There was a clackety-clack of typewriters coming from the main offices behind us, and my excitement mounted still further. She opened a door on the left, we went down some steps, walked along a dull, endless corridor, went down some more steps to the right, and turned into another corridor with glass-framed photographs along the lefthand wall. She opened a door to the right and we entered an office, its walls entirely hidden from view by filing cabinets and shelves loaded with folders. The room was dark and small with one table in the center. A woman employee was filing correspondence.

"It's bound to be for publicity," my guide said to the woman doing the filing.

Then she left me.

I handed my letter to the woman at the table, who then left me also.

Quickly, a curious glance at the correspondence:

". . . in answer to your esteemed . . . our present situation is such . . . it is therefore impossible for us . . ."

What was I waiting there for since they wouldn't want me? So that I could become an old business letter, a formula: "in answer to your esteemed . . . ," so that I could turn yellow inside a filing cabinet, since they weren't going to want me. Dismal woolen jacket, dismal handbag, dismal courtyard (I was at the back of the publishing house now), dismal light. If they should want to employ me . . . What am I going to say to them? Either I'm dreaming, or else someone really is writing here with a goose quill. So they are used for something besides those artsy-craftsy displays in stationers' windows.

"If you would like to follow me," said a forty-year-old woman with a complexion like old parchment.

I went into a modern-looking office: I remember my first step onto the gray carpet. The forty-year-old woman closed the door behind me. He stood up and came over.

"Louder, I'm deaf. I'm the advertising director. Speak louder."

"I'm not saying anything, sir."

"Louder, please."

"I'm not speaking," I insisted through my constricted throat, and without raising my voice.

He was holding his hand to his ear like a horn and stretching his head toward my mouth.

"She says she's not saying anything," shouted a pleasant young man of about twenty-five. He was sitting at a little table in one corner of the room near the window.

"Have you any certificates?"

"Certificates?" I answered, feeling completely stupid by now.

As if lit up by a lightning flash, I saw for a second the honorable mention I had received with my Primary School Certificate pinned on a notice board by a school gate after my mother was married. I dismissed school certificates from my mind.

"He wants to know if you've already worked somewhere else," said the young man with the round face and the black eyes.

He talked with his cigarette holder projecting from the side of his mouth.

"No, I've never worked anywhere else," I said with sincerity.

The middle-aged man's energetic face grew gloomy.

"I've studied at the Maison du Livre; and I've passed my secondary school exams. . . ."

The older man's face, incapable of hiding anything, sprang to life again.

"The written part. Half of them," I said in a low voice so that I wouldn't be lying to myself and so that my lie to them wouldn't be too barefaced.

"You studied at the Maison du Livre? That's very good," he said.

He went back to his table. He was rather short, and his short, gray mustache made him look French and English at the same time.

"Now this is what we want," he said.

He gestured to the chair.

"I'm going down to the binding room," the young man said.

Tall, well built, dressed in a navy blue suit, when he stood up I thought perhaps he was more than twenty-five after all. He was hugging a dismembered book to his chest and I wondered where the thread of the binding was. He left the room, dragging his feet as he walked, the shape of his head too round.

The director explained the job as follows: every morning they would hand me magazines, weekly newspapers, daily newspapers; in these I would find articles, critiques, announcements, and pieces of literary gossip circled with blue pencil; these would all have to do with the writers published by Plon; I would cut them out and stick them on loose sheets of paper, writing the date and the name of the publication above the article and the name of the critic below the printed text; I would then help Mlle. Conan with her filing. He would think it over; he would write to me; he would pay me six hundred francs a month. He asked me if I thought I was capable of doing this work.

He showed me out into the filing office once more. Politeness is also a discipline, his firm tread proclaimed. Mlle. Conan took over from him as far as the staircase, where I passed the young man with the round face and the black eyes.

"I hope you'll be coming to see us again," he said, his elegant cigarette holder perched in the corner of his mouth.

The same column of bluish smoke was rising from it.

This time he was holding several reviews and a book published by Gallimard. Already I could imagine him no other way than surrounded by the temptation of the printed word.

I was back in the big stockroom again looking at the innumerable cells in that honeycomb of books. Looking again. The novelty had gone, and yet the attraction emanating from the shelves on my left had not weakened. They published Chekhov, Dostoievsky. . . . The desire to discover Chekhov and Dostoievsky was already satisfied in each section of the shelves.

"Cheer up, it'll be all right," Gabriel said. "You'll see, everything will turn out fine. They'll take you. Why should you think they won't? And whatever happens, don't get down in the dumps, little fellow."

Gabriel reassured me as we walked past tiny warehouses or along the sidewalks of the main boulevards. "Why should you think they won't take you?" His arm squeezed mine, and his moist fingers between my own were asking: "Why shouldn't I take you, why shouldn't I?" I rejected his question; my arm, my hip, my fingers moved away.

"Want to down one with me? Come on."

He took me to La Lorraine in the Place des Ternes, one of the fashionable cafés at that time.

They took me.

*

I got to work at eight-ten every morning. I would ride in on the "S" bus, walk along the Rue Servandoni, which was nearer to Saint-Sulpice, narrower, livelier, more working-class, and then cut across. If I was early, I devoured the titles of the books or the list of contents on the cover of the magazine *Europe* in the windows of the Rieder bookstore. Gabriel often bought me copies of *Europe;* it was edited by Jean-Richard Bloch. We had read his *La Nuit Kurde* and liked it very much. *Europe,* at that time, was an international literary magazine specializing in avant-garde left-wing literature. The tawny cover with its black printing jumped out at you: a counterirritant for the mind. I was now an employee and therefore had to make my entrance, like the others, first through a narrow alley and then through the dark, metallic shipping room where everyone tried to outdo the others in gaiety.

Mlle. Conan always arrived first; she didn't do much to brighten the place up. I went to my table, where I found the evening papers waiting for me. I looked for the blue circles or the blue crosses at one side of the articles, then I sat and read the most anodyne reviews of the tamest of novels from beginning to end. I was satisfying my conscience as an employee. Once that was over I flung myself at the literary columns of *Le Temps* and *l'Action Française* to read the latest exchange of good-humored insults between Léon Daudet and Paul Souday. Their readers lived in anticipation of their furies. Léon Daudet never referred to Souday by any name other than Sulphate of Souday. . . . Neither of them was Léon Bloy's equal at polemics, but they did both have the gift of holding your attention, of amusing you. Their writing tables were the corners of a boxing ring. Souday's series of articles devoted to the Abbé Mugnier, an erudite and very cultured critic, are still remembered. I learned that writers trembled when they sent their books to Paul Souday.

Were the other newspapers on the advertising secretary's table yet? I left our gloomy office, escaping Mlle. Conan's continual grumbling, the files and the filing cabinets, and craned my neck into the inner office, so softly carpeted, so much lighter than ours. The piles of morning papers, foreign papers, provincial papers, were there on the desk. Before reading them I had to pay my morning visit to the night presses, the editors, the linotype operators, and I never missed that visit. The director, M. Halmagrand, arrived at about nine o'clock. We recognized his step and never dared to glance up at the frosted glass windows while he was in the corridor. If he came in unexpectedly, we said good morning to him in unison like an orphanage choir. The idea that he was a husband and a father never crossed my mind. He was an embodiment of discipline, a soldier who had become deaf during the 1914-18 war. He was stern but never cruel, and always in control of himself. He would ask to see a file the moment he arrived, setting us an example of diligence. His personal secretary might have popped straight out of a bandbox, she was so well groomed, so well dressed, so perfectly made up. She had in fact just got off a train from Bourg-la-Reine, where she and her husband got up every morning at five A.M. Everyone on the staff used to talk about her powers of endurance and her prodigious ability to appear in such a variety of different clothes on such a small budget.

The caramel scent of a Camel . . . M. Poupet with his cigarette holder stuck in the corner of his mouth, his feet dragging even when he was walking quickly. He went to bed late, he attended all the important openings, all the big dinners, all the big concerts. He spent his evenings at these affairs both for his own pleasure and for the good of the firm. The director never showed his face in literary and social circles. He listened and collated. I was always disappointed when M. Poupet closed their door right away, and I was on tenterhooks when he didn't close it.

"Oh please stop going through those files for a minute. You can't hear anything. I want to hear . . ."

Mlle. Conan suffered from stomach pains; she sucked lozenges from morning till night.

"Hear what? I've got my work to do," she grumbled with Breton obstinacy.

"Don't open the window," I begged. "We won't hear anything."

She breathed hard, she muttered complaints, she said aloud: "I'm from Guingamp. In Guingamp we're used to fresh air."

She closed the window and went on clattering through the files in her work smock, muttering grumpily to herself the whole time.

". . . I met Jean during intermission," cried M. Poupet. "I didn't see much of him though. The crush was fantastic."

"A fantastic crush?" queried the director.

I rose noiselessly to my feet as though there were a dove's nest in the wastebasket I mustn't disturb. I edged over to Mlle. Conan.

"Who's Jean?"

Mlle. Conan was now separating copies of recently typed letters into three piles.

"Are you still eating?" she asked snappily.

"It's my roll from ten o'clock break. . . . Who's Jean?"

Mlle. Conan went on with her filing. "You read. Can't you guess that he meant Cocteau?"

"Cocteau!"

Our firm was publishing some of his work in the Roseau d'Or series.

I returned to my seat. M. Poupet brought in the provincial papers and left again. The scent of browning sugar from his Camel was his evening of the day before, coiled in a single spiral around our office. Time past was still as incandescent as the red tip of his cigarette. That glow was Cocteau himself, whom they called Jean, Cocteau stepping out of his books and his photographs.

Since I was shy and incapable of following or holding a conversation, I felt no envy for M. Poupet. But I did envy the director who was handed all these evening festivities next day as a serial writer is handed the convolutions of his plot. Meanwhile, I was denying myself the performances of the Ballets Russes. The present is never a legend. The present then was part of a legend. Nijinsky, Karsavina, Serge Diaghileff . . . I never saw them. They astonished me and still astonish me as much as a masterpiece I shall never see in a London or New York museum. Nijinsky is dead, Nijinsky has not withered. The title of his ballet *Le Spectre de la Rose* has become the title of an immortal poem.

I read, I snipped, I glued until midday. The reviews disheartened and saddened me. I would have liked to read *Etudes, Le Mercure de France, La revue des Deux Mondes,* and *La Nouvelle Revue Française* from cover to cover and immerse myself in all the literary currents of the day. The midday bell rang through the building, releasing me from the glue, the brush, the reviews, and the newspapers. In the corridor or on the staircase I often met a short little man always dressed in a woolen topcoat, with raglan sleeves and no lining, that managed to suggest both the sartorial negligence of the intellectual and also a shepherd's cloak. With his umbrella over his arm, his body leaning to one side, his odd face that was somehow not ugly, his bright eyes and his pointed goatee held out like an index finger gauging the direction of the wind, this short little man was a figurehead and our firm a ship, sailing back to Paris with a cargo of the latest foreign books. Gabriel Marcel, for that's who it was, was at that time just starting the Feux Croisés series for Plon; the first floor, the second floor were already bubbling excitedly with authors' names: Rosamond Lehmann, Aldous Huxley, Jakob Wassermann.

I left with the other employees, the light crackled in my eyes, the wings of the pigeons flapped, the conductor on the "S" bus shouted "full up," the bells of the church were marrying one another for a wedding. I waited for the next bus. I liked riding on the platform best; I leaned out, I stood on the tips of my toes, I breathed in the sparkling air, I longed for the other faithful platform travelers to notice me, I forgot to love and admire Paris as it swept past, bubbling with cars and passers-by. The chain and the handle swaying continually back and forth, the conductor walking up and down, with an occasional moment's respite . . . I lived the life of the bus. I was exultant when a student rang the bell instead of the conductor, I imagined for a moment that we were a community of nomads. Riding from the Left Bank over to the Right Bank, from the Right Bank to the Left Bank was an ecstasy I experienced four times a day.

First, there was the classicism of the Place de la Concorde. My powers fail me; I need comparisons if I am to celebrate the Place de la Concorde. I think of it, I see it, it forces itself into my mind whenever I hear *Le Tombeau de Couperin*. A dancer dancing a pas de deux. That is the Place de la Concorde also. I know nothing about architecture; and yet the perspectives, the vistas, the proportions, the symmetry of the opposing pediments and columns, the opposition of a garden to an avenue, the connecting link provided by the horses of Marly, the feeling of spaciousness between the bronze lamp standards, between the balustrades and the colonnades, all the features of the Place de la Concorde are something I feel almost like a burn, like something that bites into me so far it's almost a part of me. Those lines traced by the architects of the Concorde in royal blue ink. I see them on my arm. The simplest tattoo means the Concorde to me, always the Concorde.

And so, four times a day I went over the bridge. If I had been reading inside the bus, if I had been gazing in a dream at the caps of the conductor or the driver, I came to life again attired in stone and water: the left and the right of the bridge. A bridge is a conquest. The pedestrian walks on the water. The blue sky was a vast blue dream, the river with its flocks of tiny waves and snaking ripples was more serious. The bus was advancing across the Seine. City views, distant frescoes, my graceful triumphs, my battles won. I watched for the snack bar outside the Chambre des Députés. The bus was emptying; it would fill up again in front of La Crémaillère, outside Tunmer, in the Place Saint-Augustin.

If everything went according to plan, I got back to the apartment at twelve-thirty-five or twelve-forty. Everything was ready. I threw my leather briefcase onto my divan, I glanced through Hermine's letter, then put it back on the table beside the ham roll, the banana, the chocolate. I had a quarter of an hour in which to absorb a mountain of mashed potatoes, cooked endive, two slices of sirloin, cheese and stewed fruit. "Eat, eat," my mother begged. She served me my meal and I told her that I would be paid, that the end of the month wasn't far off. My stepfather came in, I left again with Hermine's letter and my package of food for four o'clock. At the terminus there would be only two or three of us in the bus. Dressed in a beret or a mannish felt hat and a half-belted topcoat, I longed to enjoy all the luxury to be seen in Paris at one in the afternoon, I yearned until I could bear it no more. I was ready for anything—my ideas of what the anything would be were not exactly precise—if only I might own a luxurious car, make an entrance into the restaurant Larue, put down my cash and clean out the display window of Lachaume's in the Rue Royale, go in for a drink at the bar of Maxim's. I rose up a little from my seat as we passed Charmereine, the lingerie store. The more I veered in practice toward masculine attire, the more I was gnawed inwardly by a desire for frivolities, for beautiful cars, for fine furs. I coveted Paris through a golden grill from the Porte Champerret to Sèvres-Babylone. Covetousness. A turquoise blue agony.

Then I found newspapers in which I'd missed some of the articles. I was shamefaced, I forgot the city's superfluities. Next day I once more longed to damn myself for them, I mean lose my soul for them, without knowing how. Paris, my agonized desire for money as you ate your fashionable lunch.

A young girl would come in at three o'clock. "Good afternoon," Mlle. Perret would say to us brusquely. Her icy manner intimidated me, her dresses impressed me. She untied the ribbons of her long mountaineer's cape, she divested herself of cape and beret with unaffected nonchalance. The golden curls of her short hair lit up our dismal office, the filing cabinets, the files. She was tall, majestic, imposing, but her grave, fragile face, her complexion, her skin, and the circulation of the blood under her skin spoke to me of the weightless serenity in a Botticelli Madonna. Her long hands went with her face. I could see rose-colored lights in the gray cloth of her severe, double-breasted costumes. The silk of her blouse rustled beneath the broadcloth or the tweed as she sat down on my right, as she drew up her elegant cuff with a decisive gesture.

"What's new?" she would ask.

Mlle. Conan would sit talking to herself, or she would open the window a little more. Her perpetual monologue sounded like a bumblebee buzzing against a pane of glass.

She sat beside me, my superior, and I handed her all the articles, the gossip columns, the newspaper articles I had cut out.

The public director came in and shook her by the hand.

"Paul Bourget will be here in an hour. Get his file ready for me," he called back to us as he led my superior into his office.

"Paul Bourget is coming? Is that true?"

"Now I'll have to get his file up to date. Oh dear, oh dear . . . Always something new to file. I can't go on with it."

"I've got a clipping about him. Here."

"Are you eating already?"

"It's half-past three. It's the Paris air. What's he like?"

"You'll see."

"But I won't see. Not with this frosted glass . . ."

"You see the others."

"Yes, but this is Paul Bourget."

"Well, he can come now if he wants to. I've got the file ready."

The Disciple. I'm going to see *The Disciple.* Life after all . . . You're polishing your shoes at school, sitting in the shoe shop, and then whoosh. . . . There you are, certain the author of *The Disciple* is coming. But it's not the man I'm waiting for, it's his fame. Life after all . . . There's nothing it can't do. Except it isn't life: it's the *Bibliographie de la France.* I'm twenty. I shall have seen the author of *The Disciple* when I was twenty. I prefer Claudel. That's odd: I never wonder what Claudel's like. He has a tremendous number of readers, the author of *The Disciple.* I shall be seeing all those readers, I shall be seeing thousands upon thousands of readers in the figure of one man, when that man walks in front of our frosted-glass windows.

"Is he old?"

"Yes, he's old."

"Is he tall?"

"Yes, he's tall."

"Does he hold himself straight?"

"Yes, he holds himself straight."

Mlle. Perret wrote her texts with the goose quill, I'd heard, dipping it in green ink. I glanced over at her paper and read a sentence, a word here and there. I envied her: she was writing. I didn't feel jealous though, because I would have been incapable of writing. She came and went as she pleased. I was jealous of her for that. She talked to me about her mother, who was very beautiful and very elegant, and about her stepfather, who was the head of a big Paris daily. I wondered why she asked me about my favorite books. She was very tactful about the way she made me tell her things about myself. I held it against her after I had confided in her but, at the same time, I felt a vague presentiment, a presentiment of something good. Sometimes her violence, her flashes of ill temper when Mlle. Conan exasperated her, irritated me, sometimes they gave me a sense of satisfaction; sometimes I was wounded by her self-pride, sometimes it exalted me. She was a strong character. And this strong character was suddenly talking to me with the gentleness and sincerity of a friend. We waited for Paul Bourget. He came another day.

*

I changed trains at D . . . , in the cold, in the dark night. The station near the school, the streets outside the school, the school itself had all been spirited away. I was coming to see Hermine. I got up into a nice old compartment in the local train and admired my felt hat, my topcoat, the collar on my man's shirt, my gloves, and my suitcase, picked out with my mother's help at L'Innovation on the Champs-Elysées. I tidied myself up. The dilapidated glow of the light bulb threw its light far beyond my hat, far beyond the collar of my shirt, far beyond my pale beige suitcase. Some workmen were horsing around on the steps of the carriage, watching for the trainman. Their shouts and the dull sound of their studded boots warmed up the platform. Whistle blasts.

We moved off in an unreal train, a fairground train. I shrank into myself and became no more than a thin line. I loved Hermine, I had been separated from her for a long time; I loved her with so much joy, so much trust, so much apprehension. . . . The train, with its monotonous rhythm on the rails, was cutting its way through a shadowy length of corduroy. The villages were so near to one another: each merely a name with a voice. Darkness was covering the plains, we moved off again, the workers shouted heart-warming good nights to one another. They were dispersing, but they still were joined together by the well-earned rest they would all be sharing next day. We passed in front of them without being able to see them.

Auvigny. At last; the stationmaster shouted out the name of the village with the abandon of a newsboy. As he hurled the name into the air, I saw strawberry plants. The name of her village was a proof of spring in the months to come. I lowered the window. Hermine won't have come, Hermine will have taken fright at the cold and the dark. I wanted to cut a path for her through the cold of the night. Silent workmen climbed down, their bags with their lunchboxes inside bumping against their buttocks. Someone was swinging a lantern; the engine had been checked. A flute playing in my head, quick quavers of God. I looked for Hermine. An eagle was going to swoop down onto my shoulders. . . . Who would the eagle be? Isabelle.

The train is moving off. What will become of me? A fragment of night dissolved in night.

"Over here," she said in a muffled voice.

She switched on her flashlight. I was still listening to the "Over here" that had emerged from the shadows.

"Your homespun jacket . . ."

"You always liked it," she said.

She seized my hand impulsively. There were workmen calling out to us from the windows of the train as it gathered speed.

The passengers dispersed.

"Come," she said against my icy cheek.

There were horses pulling a cart. I listened to the sound of their hooves, I listened to the rhythm of the night, the cold, the bluish splintering of the ice over the puddles.

The cart, with its horse and driver, moved off into its own shadow world.

"Why don't you say something, Hermine?"

"You're not saying anything either."

One step was enough to take us off the road, enough to feel our legs lashed by the wind, our faces flattened, our teeth glittering with cold. I found warmth in Hermine's mouth, she found warmth in my mouth. I felt the fabric of her jacket, I molded it with my fingers. All Hermine was in its texture: the music room and the *Italian Concerto.* Hermine freed from her duties in study hall, torn away from the Conservatoire, dumped down in a village. I sheltered the elbows of the pianist, I gripped the lapels of the new schoolteacher. I asked where the inhabitants of the village were. "At home," Hermine answered with a laugh.

She guided me to her home. The first floor was shut up, because the house was too big for Hermine on her own. The hall passage was as icy as the weather outside. She opened a second door and offered me the sleepy oak furniture in the light of the shaded lamps, the warmth of the stove, biscuits, cheeses no bigger than postage stamps, Sandeman's port, Camels, jazz on top of the table, the trepidation of the player on the drums. I looked for her piano. No piano. Hermine told me all the details of her wait, of the preparations she had been making ever since Thursday. She took the face powder, the comb, the powderpuff out of my suitcase and arranged them next to the divan. Did I like the nightgown with the inset of ocher lace? Yes, I liked it. I had to like it. Her life was ruined, and Hermine shone with happiness. Drink, cigarettes, underwear, warmth, and the slow notes of the saxophone: she was offering me a Paris more moving to me than the depressing Paris I gazed at through the windows of a bus.

I wedded my fingers to Hermine's hair. Love. The bars of time collapsed in dust for several hours. The bars reformed themselves of their own accord.

My clothes on the chair made me wonder where I was. The jazz was still persisting.

Hermine dressed again. There are some memories that have no past. I remembered a brothel without ever having seen one as the bodice slipped down over her opulent breasts, as the skirt gripped those gypsy dancer's hips and buttocks. Hermine insisted on serving me my meal in bed. Not wanting to spoil her enjoyment, I spoiled my own. I would have preferred to follow her everywhere, I would have preferred Hermine lying in bed, stubbing out cigarettes against the wall. She busied herself with meats, she opened cans, she uncorked bottles. A violinist was playing a solo, improvising. The most audacious of jazz was in fact no more than the acrobatics of a violinist's bow. The player's improvisations were full of anguish.

"Who is it?"

Hermine came over, wondering if I really didn't know.

"It's Michel Warlop," she said.

I kissed her on the neck, in the hollow where men as well as women are soft with the softness of silk.

"I'm none the wiser. Who's Michel Warlop?"

"An extraordinary violinist. He preferred to play jazz after he left the Conservatoire. He's in Paris now. His playing still has the same feverish quality."

I stroked Hermine's hair; her face became a captive bird.

The port was good. Fire under ashes. She moved away again and returned to her chores. I lay learning the table, the chairs, the leather armchair by heart.

"In Paris, I drink," I said to ward off an attack of boredom.

"What do you drink?" Hermine cried.

"Don't worry. I drink Pernod. On the Place Pereire at seven every evening."

"You don't drink alone."

"Yes, I drink alone."

"You didn't say so in your letters. I'm trying to remember. . . . No, you didn't tell me!"

"I didn't tell you. Is that serious?"

"No, it's not serious. You were hiding it from me."

"I'm not hiding it from you now. I've just told you. And you're blaming me for it."

"I'm not blaming you for anything. Don't I tell you about our Thursday walks in my letters? . . . With my father and sisters, and our chamber music and the books we read and our sewing. Don't I tell you about them?"

"Yes. Often."

"Not in as great detail as I should. Are you alone? Are you really alone on the Place Pereire at seven every evening?"

She went straight on without waiting for my lie, saying that it was getting colder, that she was shivering. I wanted to scream out: "You're shivering because I'm lying to you." All I succeeded in getting out was "Gabriel." Under my breath. I wanted to add: "I drink it with him," but I couldn't find my voice. I hadn't come there to cut myself off from Hermine, I hadn't come there to cut myself off from

Gabriel. Gabriel, another world, the other world where I bestowed my kissing-thanks. He was on Hermine's side without my ever talking to him about her. I saw myself in his eyes, I saw myself there in the truest of lights for Violette-Hermine. I flew up and away toward Hermine as soon as my mouth was proffered to Gabriel. The two Pernods he would always prepare with such love . . . He loved me, he put up with me to the point of extravagance. For what should I have asked forgiveness? To pronounce his first name would be to subject Gabriel to a thousand sneers without Hermine having to speak one word.

She closed the door so that the heat of the room would stay in with me. An English jazz singer was suggesting the quietude of homosexuality.

I had to get into bed, I had to powder my face, I had to wear a luxurious nightgown. I had to become a whore: she wanted to be a martyr.

"Hermine!"

She ran in, she held the mirror higher, lower, more to the right, more to the left. Of the two, she was the prettier, the more feminine, the more courageous. She walked backwards when she left. I was her relic, her looking glass.

I curled myself up as tight as a hedgehog and ground my eyelids together. Gabriel, bright tattered blue, embroidered with points of gold, Gabriel beneath my eyelids like a lightning flash shone faceless and formless in splendor.

I stared at the great emerald of the Chartreuse, the twig floating in the bottle of Izarra. The moisture on my palms was the moisture on Gabriel's palms.

"Shall I go, Violette? Tell me what you want, little fellow." That was what I saw him asking on the covers of Hermine's books.

"Do you want to? I'll wait for you till tomorrow evening." That's what he was stammering in the mirror moldings over the fireplace.

And she, she asked me if I wanted to be her baby, if I would come again next Saturday, if I wanted to live with her if she got her transfer.

Yes, I will be her baby, yes, I will come again next Saturday, yes, I will live with her if she gets her transfer.

Hermine devours me, Hermine pricks me all over with a needle and pours all she has to give into every pore of my skin. Gabriel torments me: he is alone. I have him on my hands; he is so full of anguish, so unlucky. He says good night to me at two in the morning by the grill of the elevator shaft out at Porte Champerret. He is an overstrung bow, Gabriel. I prefer Hermine; yet I find Gabriel indispensable. Gabriel in the shadows around Hermine's house. If I am deceiving her when I explain to Gabriel how she plays the *Italian Concerto,* then so much the better. If I tell Hermine how he wants to wear a lily in his fly when we go out together, she will hide her face in her hands.

"Don't you miss the school? Your mind will go dead here."

I caught her by surprise. Hermine had been dreaming.

"Miss the school! I have you. I teach music here. The headmistress and her husband ask me over to drink an apéritif with them sometimes. The parents are nice to me."

"In the evening, away from home, don't you get sad?"

"I sew, I wait for you, I write to you, I read your letters."

"Your piano, Hermine. You can say it. Hire a piano."

"No, because I'm going to ask for a transfer to be with you. What about a silk voile with insets of lace, would you like that?"

"Make something for yourself. Buy some material for yourself."

"No."

Hermine won't buy anything for herself. Hermine can't. She is a self-sacrifice addict.

*

"Write news items! It's impossible, sir. I write letters, but news items, a news item . . ."

"A news item is shorter than a letter," said the publicity director. "You can try. Mlle. Perret will show you how and M. Poupet will correct your copy. I'll explain what it's all about. Have you read Henry Bordeaux's books?"

"No."

"That's perfect. You will read them now. So that is what it's all about. M. Henry Bordeaux has complained to us about a slump in the sale of his books. It isn't a slump in fact, it's just a passing slack phase. He wants us to give him some publicity. Discreet publicity. So you will read the newspapers in the morning and Henry Bordeaux's books in the afternoon. All his books. You will go through them looking for references that might be inserted into news items dealing with topical events in various fields, literary, theatrical, sports, cinema, science. . . . You will write out first drafts for me and we'll discuss them. One other thing. You mustn't mention the name of Plon. Just introduce a discreet reference to the name of the book or the author somewhere in each short item. The coincidence must appear natural."

Half an hour after this interview, another employee brought me the works of Henry Bordeaux.

I cut the pages slowly. I was determined in advance to find a news item in every vowel, every consonant, every preposition. I was agreeably surprised: the promise of adultery seemed nearer to fulfillment on every page. But just when I was exulting over the enjoyment to come, just as I was saying: it's inevitable, they can resist no longer, the lovers are going to fall into each other's arms, I turned the page and it was all over, already consummated. . . . I turned the page, and the wife, whom I had thought on the brink of the abyss, was trotting along a path strewn with rose petals, calm and freed from her passion, back to her happy home. I banged my elbow down on the table.

"What's the matter with you?" Mlle. Conan asked anxiously.

"Nothing's the matter. I'm just sulking."

My obsession with finding usable references. If the author, who was born in Thonon, set one of his novels in a mountain village, I prayed to Naples, Palermo, Athens, Cairo; I begged them to change into French mountain villages. In the evening I opened my pocket atlas, stretched a telegraph wire from Rutland to Tebessa and set hundreds of swallows on it: so many news items with a reference to the works of Henry Bordeaux. I began reading the important facts in the books through the wrong end of a telescope and the unimportant ones through a magnifying glass. I went to the files and read through the copy my superior, Mlle. Perret, had written. If I remembered my mother's criticisms—"It's heavy, it's too heavy the way you write"—then I lost heart in advance. My promotion filled me with panic. The men and women happily packing up books downstairs, their songs, their gaiety . . . The promised, carefree land from which I had been expelled. If I managed to prepare a few scraps of copy, I should be a threadworm in the binding of Henry Bordeaux's books, a threadworm feeding off their ephemeral topicality.

I made my first attempt sitting beneath the proofs I had filed: the *Cahiers* of Maurice Barrès. I made my first attempt while Mlle. Perret was not there. I could never have written anything with her beside me. Finally I showed her what I had produced. She read it, then told me very tactfully that it was too long but that she would submit it right away.

She left the office with my pitiful scraps just as another employee came in bringing the first batch of long-awaited galley proofs for Rosamond Lehmann's *Dusty Answer*. I sat sorting the proofs and awaiting results, quivering like a little flayed rabbit.

They came into the office, with mournful faces.

"It's too long, and it's too heavy," said the advertising assistant, his cigarette holder in the corner of his mouth. "You'll have to do it again."

The scent of his Camel, my mother smoked Camels when we went out together, the expression "it's too heavy"—nothing was missing: my mother and M. Poupet had reduced me to a zero.

I gave M. Poupet the first galleys of *Dusty Answer*. His face lit up. He walked out reading them.

"What was it you were saying?" the director of publicity shouted to him.

". . . I was just telling you that Marcel Jouhandeau lives next to an elevated stretch of the Métro, really depressing. Yes, the Pincengrain family. Yes, it's his first book."

The publicity assistant, in the forefront of every literary trend, stabbed me to the heart.

To read the surrealists, to read the explosive writers of today while sitting on a chair carved in the era of the courtly romances; to read *L'Amour fou* between the sky and the grass somewhere where there is nothing but sky and grass.

Gabriel was waiting for me at half-past six surrounded by tearing, vibrating taffeta: the flights of pigeons in the Place Saint-Sulpice.

"Well, little fellow?" he asked anxiously.

I didn't want to speak, I couldn't speak. I dragged him away toward Sèvres-Babylone.

"It's too heavy, and it's too long!" I shouted aloud.

People walking past turned around to look.

"The piano . . . My piano . . . I practiced, Gabriel, I practiced as much as I could. I hoped. I got nowhere. Do you understand? Nowhere! Say something."

"I say you nearly got yourself run down just then."

"I don't care."

"I do care. I like to see you get worked up."

"I'm not worked up. I'm discouraged, I'm unhappy."

"You're not unhappy at all! Would you like a drink?"

"Let's walk along the Rue du Vieux-Colombier."

"Damn it all, little fellow, you've got to walk before you can run. Everything takes time. Do you see that courtyard? There's an engraver works in there. Louis Jou. An engraver. Can you imagine the pains he must take, the patience he must have, the love for his work and the difficulty of it? Tomorrow you'll just take your news item and rewrite it."

I squeezed Gabriel's arm; he squeezed my hand against his hip with his arm.

"Yes, I'll rewrite it."

Gabriel kissed my hand as hard as he could.

I rewrote it the next day, the day after that, the following week, continually haunted by the heaviness of my sentences, the length of my sentences. I wanted to achieve the brevity of a fowl pecking at a single grain of corn. In the evening, as a contrast, I opened my Bossuet and admired the swelling periods, I skimmed through a sentence of Proust, and my eyes filled with tears.

"Your news items have gone out," the publicity assistant said to me at last.

He went back into their office and talked about René Crevel's health.

Two days later, I caught a glimpse of Henry Bordeaux. Tall and healthy looking with his bright red cheeks, he was very much the mountain dweller of his novels. He was smiling, therefore he was satisfied. What long conversation in the director's office? Me-and-my-copy, my-copy-and-me. With a dry throat, I wiped the perspiration from the palms of my hands. After a while, Henry Bordeaux came out into a little room, a sort of austere boudoir or convent parlor, between the director's office and our own. I glued my ear to the wall and begged Mlle. Conan for silence: the clicking of the filing cabinets ceased. I couldn't make out what the author of *Roquevillard* was actually saying, but I had no doubts in my mind: he was carrying on the conversation about me-and-my-copy, my-copy-and-me. He left without a glance in the direction of our frosted glass windows.

The following Saturday, in the Gare du Nord, at a quarter of one in the afternoon, Gabriel gave me the money for my round-trip ticket: a hundred and twenty francs. He was offering me Hermine, he was giving me Hermine a hundred and twenty times over. He bought himself a platform ticket. I was thunderstruck when he got onto the train with me; he was risking a fine, even a night in jail, since he had no money for the fine. My account of our trips, of his disappearances and reappearances, in *Ravages* is completely accurate. It is true that I would go off to see Hermine, that I would tell Gabriel he must get off the train. So he would melt into the streets of Lille or Amiens until Sunday evening. Finding me again on the train home, making love to the dark circles under my eyes, was that his idea of paradise then? Yes, that was the paradise I made for him with my avarice, my dishonesty, my coquetry. I had to have someone there to look at me, to plead with his eyes over a drink in the dining car. No questions. Just the gaze. His ecstasy: gentler than an erection. His gaze: semen, against his will, against my will.

Hermine was giving private lessons, she stayed up late, she sewed lace onto underwear for me. The more Gabriel sacrificed himself the more firmly I was held between the interlocking teeth of this double self-abnegation.

"Here's one of mine!"

They rang for Mlle. Conan. She left our office without hearing me. I sat drinking in the marvel before me, ringed with M. Poupet's blue pencil, printed in a literary column. And as I surveyed what I had created from the creations of Henry Bordeaux, my heart was glad.

"If you're pleased, I'm pleased," my mother said before lunch.

She threw her handbag down on my divan. My mother was working for a firm of decorators now. She was putting all she had into her work, and she was succeeding as she had succeeded with her own business before. Her fellow workers liked her. She told me about one boy in particular with whom she got on very well. His name was André Claveau and he was in love with music.

My mother often scattered her small change—her ammunition, she called it—on the purple velvet cover of my divan. I was spellbound by the luxurious shops in the Rue Royale and stole money from my mother. I took coins from her without remorse; I never imagined she might notice. The next day she would leave her bag lying around as trustingly as ever. I robbed her from time to time. She was bound to notice it in the end. When I look back on it now, it is her silence, her delicacy I find painful rather than the money I stole. I would hoard this money, no longer belonging to my mother, not yet belonging to me, for two or three days; then I would buy bus tickets with it, or share the cost of our drinks with Gabriel.

The seed had taken. The newspapers were using my news items. What feelings of gratitude, what illusions of complicity and sympathy I entertained toward Robert Kemp because he printed everything I sent him in his column of literary gossip. And an item in *Les Nouvelles Littéraires* with its own heading . . . the summit of success.

In the evening I was more modest, thanks to the proofs of Rosamond Lehmann's first novel. Two young girls fell in love, and a woman had dared to write about it. A gentle sun poured its melancholy light over the story, and one of the characters lent it a muscular strength: Jennifer. That first name haunted us. Do you like Jennifer? Do you like Jennifer better than the others? You find her too bold? Jennifer? Ah no! Wild? You find Jennifer too wild? You can't be thinking of Jennifer. We talked about her in the corridors, in the offices, on the first floor, on the second floor, and if Gabriel Marcel wandered through the building with his inevitable umbrella we gazed at him as children gaze at Santa Claus's sack. *Dusty Answer,* Jennifer, they were his briefcase. Old M. Bourdelle brought a measure of calm to the feverish atmosphere in the building with his great age, his white Franz-Josef mustaches and the solidity of his figure. The firm was his creation, but by that time he had started taking a back seat and handing over the reins to his son, Maurice Bourdelle. Maurice Bourdelle, with his rakishness, his alacrity, his American film star's face and thin brown mustache; he unsettled all the beautiful young women in his part of the building. And silly old ones, homely old ones, would go there to wait for some batch of papers or other, and end up waiting for him.

*

One day, after gossiping for a while with Chanel's niece, with Elizabeth Zerfuss, with an odd, rather swarthy girl with a gravelly accent who was a typist with the firm, I found a note waiting for me from M. Poupet: "You are to read the *Mémoirs* of Marshal Foch and look for possible news items."

I went into their office and walked over to his little table on the right. A Camel was burning away in his cigarette holder and I picked it up. The weightlessness of the slim black tube made me feel strange. I leaned over to look at his work. The publicity assistant had been drawing. I could sense his anxiety, his torment, his constancy from the way he had begun the same young man's face, lying on the same pillow, over and over again. I went over to the window with one of the drawings. I was violating a personal secret, my heart was beating. I stifled a cry of surprise, a cry of astonishment, a cry of joy. I recognized the young man, I recognized his fluid beauty, even more fluid in this pencil sketch. The beauty of his face: the persistence, the generosity of childhood. I remembered his lips, fleshy without being coarse, his slightly flattened nose, as ingenuous as his mouth. I remembered the lilac flowerets clustered on his lips, yes, that and his light eyes, their astonishment and the disorder of his blond streaked hair. The face of a young athlete caught in a mist of candor. I was seeing the young man who had come unannounced into their office, the young man I had glimpsed through the half-opened door of our office, not only on the sheet of paper before me but in the childlike memory of the secretary. René Crevel, our weightless visitor, was in Switzerland for his health. I fell in love with that portrait, sketched with so much emotion; I tore myself away from it and returned to our office with a secret. The publicity assistant returned to his office also and shut the door behind him. I regretted my visit. I folded my arms over the *Memoirs* of Marshal Foch and buried my head in them. I dreamed about M. Poupet's travels. Switzerland was named Switzerland no longer. I renamed it Endymion because that was the name I had given René Crevel, the author, among other works, of *Paul Klee, La Mort difficile,* and *L'Esprit contre la Raison.*

Five minutes later, the artist said to me: "Aren't you reading your Foch?"

"No, I'm not reading my Foch!"

He handed me several sheets of paper. I recognized the latest copy.

"The stuff you wrote yesterday is useless. You'll have to do it again."

He left the office.

Furious, grief-stricken, deprived of that halo of childhood around his portrait of René Crevel, I shut myself in the washroom. The publicity assistant's topcoat was hanging up there. I lifted up the sleeves, I checked the corners of the pockets, the backs of the lapels, the lining. It had not been properly looked after. His mother lived in Dijon, his cleaning woman only knew how to polish floors. No, I wasn't reading Foch. I was reading his accounts in the shine on that cloth, in that glistening silk. I was seeing what it was he ate from his embossed gold plate: a dry wafer cut from his threadbare topcoat. I was noting how those evenings he told about next morning were paid for twenty times over with insecurity and the worry of having to be punctual every morning at the office. And I was reading the price of his lightning trips to Switzerland, his fatigue, in the worn-out lining. That was how it was: he lived dangerously. The person I had often accused inwardly of being a snob, a drawing-room butterfly, an addict of worldly vanities, became a pauper in high society. His job demanded it of him occasionally, his own tastes forced him into that role every day. He loved music and concerts. He loved them in a world beyond mere books, beyond the drawing rooms and the manuscripts.

"Wanda Landowska's playing tonight. They haven't a seat left! I shall go all the same," he would cry to the director of publicity.

This week's budget shattered, I thought to myself. The smooth surface of the paint on the walls helped me to reflect on the acrobatics he must have to perform while reconciling his positions in society and in Society.

The swarthy young girl came into the washroom and apologized. I said: "It's I who should apologize for being here." The girl washed her hands, then fled. I used to encounter her often carrying signed copies of books piled up to her chin.

Next morning I described her to Mlle. Conan. Mlle. Conan couldn't picture her, she couldn't picture anything.

I tried again: ". . . Cheeks made up very naturally. A little too heavily made up considering how healthy her color is. There aren't so many girls in the press section. She has a straight nose, a perfect nose. Aloof without being arrogant. She spoke to me yesterday. Yes, dark rather than fair."

A file slid from Mlle. Conan's hands. Her letters in triplicate spread a white carpet across the floor.

"It's my fault."

"Yes, it is your fault," Mlle. Conan said. "You talk to me, you make my work more complicated and then I get a stomach ache. In Tréguier," she began.

I didn't listen to her, she didn't listen to me. I tore the paper bands off my newspapers, I looked for news items, reviews, relevant paragraphs. Hermine was there in my leather briefcase with the letter she had written yesterday. "What can you find to say to each other every day?" my mother was always demanding to know. "Scatterpins," she would reply. In her vocabulary, the word "scatterpins" signified something unimportant, pointless.

Mlle. Conan opened the window slightly in an attempt to counterfeit the fresh air of Tréguier.

"I know who you mean," she said. "It's Mlle. Radiguet."

"What!"

I abandoned paragraphs, news items, and reviews.

The shipping room of the press section was quiet. The new books, despite their bright colors, called to mind the serenity, the stillness, the flexibility of water lilies. The old maiden lady with her white hair and her soul carved in effigy on her face was doing up a monumental package. Still slender, active, and indefatigable at the age of seventy, she tore off her lengths of brown paper with a noise like thunder. She was singing. I asked her how she was. Getting up at dawn, coming in from Arcueil-Cachan, running, going up and down steps all day . . .

I ventured to ask: "Are you never in a bad temper?"

"Never."

She looked at me as she began work on a second package.

"Don't you ever get tired?"

"Never. Why would I get tired?"

"You're always in good spirits? . . ."

"Always."

I tried to think what more to say to her. She was stealing my youth from me.

I see her still today, I recognize her when I ask Rose for a book at Gallimard. Rose has gray hair, and though I don't want to know her age, Rose is slender, active, and indefatigable. Her eyes are always trying to give. Our anxieties are her anxieties. Our tears are her tears, the tears she never sheds. Amid the cages and the sheet-steel shelving which to Kafka were like country lanes, Rose moves with the agility of a squirrel. Rose, my beloved Fidéline whenever I'm distraught, whenever you say to me: I don't like to see you like that. Rose, my azure mouse when you trot away in your blue overall to find something you can give to me. Rose, it's time you found something for yourself. Between the books, up above the titles, you will see your prize for excellence, your award for valor, everywhere. Your life, won't you tell me the story of it, Rose? It would be a saga for us both if only you would.

The young girl came back into the room and returned to her place in front of the piled-up books. The breeding in her face intimidated me.

"Are you Mlle. Radiguet?" I asked in a tiny voice.

"Yes."

She didn't raise her head. She opened the cover of a book and took out a card inside.

"So you're Raymond Radiguet's sister?" I said in a tone of assumed self-confidence.

"Yes."

The old lady was tearing off more paper, the same thunderous noise was all around us.

"Would you mind telling me about him?" I murmured.

The cover of the book fell back onto the card inside it; Mlle. Radiguet placed her unreal hands over the book; at last she raised her head.

"He left; my brother left," she said with embarrassment. "He left us."

She grew more animated: "I have another little brother, and sisters. . . . I look like him."

"Like Raymond Radiguet?"

"Yes, like Raymond," she said.

Did she prefer *Le Diable au corps* or *Le Bal du Comte d'Orgel?* She evaded the question.

She continued to evade all the questions I put to her after that. The more I insisted, the more I wounded her. Had she or hadn't she read the books her brother wrote? Raymond was too great, too strange a figure for his own family circle. But she could not deny the elegance of the face she shared with him. Calm and sumptuous lashes, skin so transparent it might have been the petal of a hothouse flower, mouth expressing gravity but never puritanical, nose straight and hinting at antiquity, the whole imprinted with the signature: Raymond Radiguet. It was unbelievable, somehow supernatural, that she should be so evasive. Raymond Radiguet's gifts became more astonishing, his writing more perfect, his characters more electrifying.

I tried to tell Gabriel about it, I tried to tell my mother about it.

They were bubbling over with their own discoveries, their own emotions. Gabriel introduced some movement into his sleep-walker's afternoons by making pilgrimages to the galleries of Jeanne Bucher and Katia Granoff. He would describe Duchamp's paintings to me. I listened without seeing them, gazing at Gabriel's enthusiasm brightening in his cheeks. The dynamite of surrealist poetry was not yet all exploded. Its manifestos still crackled in Gabriel's hands. Paris? A lodestone. Cocteau, the diviner of talents, gave out his electricity. I glimpsed him through our frosted glass windows; his hair was electric too, his profile a cutting edge. One day he lifted his arms to heaven and closed his slender hands. It's beautiful, everything here is beautiful, he was saying.

After that strange movie actress, Musidora, with her stupendous eyes inside their anthracite ellipses, came a Swedish girl: Greta Garbo. The rain, the shine of her oilskin, her cloche hat, her straight hair, her disdainful mouth, her eyes sweeping the universe with their gaze, her long voluptuous lashes became classics of the cinema immediately. I sent my mother to a movie in the Avenue de la Grande-Armée. She saw her there and it was several nights before she could sleep again. When my mother says "the divine Garbo," she says it with such conviction that the moved skies become a lowered eyelid. Long hours together are insufficient to share our ecstasies. On Sunday afternoons—she preferred to go alone so as to "relish" it better—my mother would go to see Ludmilla Pitoeff play *Saint Joan*. We used to argue. I preferred *Hamlet* with Georges Pitoeff playing Hamlet, though I never for a moment wanted an Ophelia more ethereal than Ludmilla. The Pitoeffs gave every performance on the brink of bankruptcy. We remembered that, as we remembered their love for each other and their love for the theater, in between the speeches.

Dusty Answer was proving successful, the Feux Croisés series was under way. Gabriel Marcel wandered back and forth between the administrative offices and the publicity department with copies of future books in the series: *The Maurizius Case* by Jakob Wassermann, Mazo de la Roche's *Jalna*.

In addition to his evenings out, his concerts, his movies, his ballets, his grand openings, the publicity assistant also spent his nights reading manuscripts which he then brought into the office and discussed with M. Halmagrand.

"Is he English?" the publicity director asked again.

"No, he isn't English."

"Is he American?"

"No, he's French."

"Is it interesting?"

"Very interesting. If we don't accept it, someone else will."

"Then we'll accept it."

"Here it is."

The secretary closed their door. They were arguing, they were growing heated, I sat biting my nails. Who was it? What was it?

My neighbor in the office fell ill: a phlegmon. I replaced her. After long hesitation and many cold sweats I asked for a raise. I got a hundred francs more a month.

Discipline in the firm was tightened up. We were terrorized by a new machine that appeared in the shipping room. It looked like one of those weighing machines in the Métro and its lips were grim. We all had our cards and we punched them twice a day. Ting-a-ling. One minute late and the machine stamped your card in red; its lips began to get angry. Sprints, panting amid the fluttering pigeons. The director of publicity checked the cards at the end of the month; he called me in, he reprimanded me for being two minutes, three minutes, five minutes late. Punctuality became a scourge. Blameless time: a black column. Catastrophic time: a red column. I was given a week's vacation for the first year, two weeks the second, third, and fourth years.

*

Hermine had taken to buying magazines: *Vogue, Fémina, Le Jardin des Modes.*

I reached out to pluck the petals of the Paris I could not enter, the Paris of the expensive stores in the Rue Royal, in the Faubourg Saint-Honoré, as Hermine turned the pages. Hermine shattered the window of my one o'clock bus rides. A village over a hundred miles from Paris offered me the face of a Juliet thirty years old. She lived out her happiness for the camera of the *Vogue* photographer, unbinding her hair before its gaze. Lady Abdy, for such was the name we read beneath the photograph, dazzled the eye with her grace and her distinction. I gorged myself like an insatiable bee upon her features and plunged drunkenly into the depths of her beauty. We found her there again the following month. She was a reigning queen. We were to see her again at the Théâtre des Folies-Wagram in Antonin Artaud's version of *The Cenci.* The play scorched actors and audience alike. We listened to the incest, to the murder streaming down the strawberry-colored folds of Lady Abdy's dress. The incest was sweetened by the musk from her cascading hair.

Hermine turned the pages; she pressed her finger, as she had pressed it once on the notes of scherzos and adagios, on costly objects.

"There's nothing I want."

I wanted the impossible: the eyes, the complexion, the hair, the nose, above all the nose, as well as the self-assurance, the arrogance of the mannequins.

The following week I wandered along the Rue de la Paix. On Saturday I said: "A pair of mules in pink kid . . . that's what I'd like. With heels covered in gold leaf. I saw them in the Rue de la Paix, in the window of Perugia."

"I saw them too," Hermine murmured.

She waved a hand in the direction of the fashion magazines, then opened her billfold.

We used to take them out of the box often, out of their tissue-paper sheath. I would feel the gold and the shape of the heels with my thumb while Hermine caressed the soft kid. I would slip my feet halfway into them, but I couldn't keep my balance on the heels. I'd bought them several sizes too small so that I would always have them as *objets d'art*. Years passed, and I forgot how much they'd cost. They became an inheritance from a Cinderella who had shaken off her poverty. I would open the box and reappraise their quality. The gold and the kid kept vigil in their chapel. More years passed, and I gave them to Mme. Welsch, Denis Batcheff's secretary.

"Wouldn't you like to wear clothes like that?" Hermine suggested.

She pressed her finger, not on the notes of Ballades or Nocturnes, but on a tailor-made with square-cut shoulders.

"Isn't the one I'm wearing pretty? Feel."

"I am feeling it," Hermine said, "I'm undressing you. You didn't wear a necktie at the school. I can remember the earphones over your ears, and the bangs you were always mussing up. . . ."

"And I wore a uniform. How ugly it was. . . . I used to pull it out of shape on purpose."

"You've changed," Hermine said.

She closed the pattern book.

"Why don't you say it? I look like a man!"

She questioned me for a moment with a face bathed in love. Then she shook her head, suppressing her emotion.

"You don't look like a man. You're only imitating them."

That made me angry.

Whatever words she used, I could still hear the echoes of a remark I had overheard at work: "I saw Violette Leduc at the concert. . . . Yes, in the same get-up." I had hardened the baroque features of my face by razor-cutting my hair short above the temples; I wanted to be a hard focus of attention for the customers in a café, for the audience in a music-hall lounge, because I was ashamed of my face and because I wanted to force it upon them at the same time. I admit it: I wanted to be attractive to Gabriel. The necktie I wore: my sex for Gabriel; the carnation in my buttonhole, chosen at the florist's on the outskirts of Levallois-Perret: my sex for Gabriel. It was with a kind of fever that I bought my first shorts, a pair of man's shorts, for a day's boating on the Marne. I remember the deep gash Gabriel gave himself in one foot. He wouldn't let himself limp, and he didn't limp. Ten years later he told me: "Your shorts were too big. I was rowing. I could see. It hurt more than the gash in my foot."

I tried to suppress the woman in me as far as I could; it was the friend, the companion I was gluing to Gabriel's skin as my cuff brushed against his cuff when we shook hands. I wanted to be what he wanted me to be: indifferent to other people's opinions. Complexes. I learned that word later. I willed myself to be a figurehead for the complexes inside me.

Gabriel grew gloomy and changed the subject whenever I began talking about my birth certificate. Gabriel had lost his father many years before. His little teeth glittered even more brightly than usual when he said: they were furniture dealers in Caen. His mother had preferred her daughter. Childhood deprivation.

As for Hermine . . . I had to tell her about my father, describe the way he lived, the way his parents lived, the way his brother in Paris lived. I pushed my mother into the background, I spotlit my father.

Paris-Plage was ripening for our week's vacation. Woods, hansoms, summer frocks, villas, all glittered before us in the magazines. I asked her: at home, with your sisters, would you look at magazines all the time like that? How can you even ask such a question, her eyes replied immediately. She exclaimed: Where would we find the time, my poor darling? With all our books to be read, our music to learn, our evening walks . . . She gave me a picture of a carefree, genuine Hermine with her family, and of another Hermine with me, so concerned with being generous that she must suppress all her books and walks and music. In the beginning, I had made no demands on her. Now I insisted she see less of her family. I despised their family life together, their spontaneity, because I wanted that life for myself and knew it was forever denied to me.

*

The morning we were to leave on our vacation trip she woke me up, she switched off the light and opened the windows.

"It's finished," Hermine said. "Try it on."

I had wanted a collar so tight it would almost grow into my flesh. Hermine said that she would alter it, that she would perfect it in our hotel room. Forgive my sleepless night, forgive the wretched results, her eyes begged. She collapsed with fatigue during the journey. The intrepid interpreter of what they call the *Pathétique* sonata had been brought to her knees by a homemade blouse. I shook Hermine, but she fell back again and I did justice to the rushing panorama on my own. Invisible level-crossing keepers gave me dagger blows with their little gardens, their little laundry-lines, their little chicken runs, their little vegetable gardens. I averted my head and lit a cigarette. The emergency cord proferred itself for my use. To leap off the train, to trample the blouse underfoot, to search with torso bare beneath my jacket for some deserted house and begin all over again with Hermine. I took a fashion magazine out of the suitcase and asked if we would be staying in a hotel near the beach. Hermine was asleep.

I was disappointed as we drew into the station of our seaside town. I was expecting to see a crowd of pretty women and handsome boys standing bronzed and scantily clad on the platform, I was expecting to see them with salt and seaspray on their lips, I was expecting them to be wreathed with bracelets and necklaces of sea dew from their bathing, I was expecting a station refreshment room spreading out onto a terrace with all the chatter of Montparnasse, with the armored candor of starched shirtfronts, the chaste décolleté of smoking jackets, the glittering virtuosity of patent leather pumps, the arabesques of arms emerging from swags of pearls. There, between the bored-looking porters, lay a sleepy provincial town, while Hermine turned her head away to yawn. I recognized some of the frivolity I expected in the flow of perfect air along the main street. The sea, a long way away from the railroad station, lent some of its solitude and its immensity to the tables laid along the sidewalks. There were some hired carriages just returning from a trip.

"Don't go to sleep. You're asleep on your feet. Wouldn't you like to go in here? Wouldn't you like to make love here?"

Hermine gazed blindly around. Her face wouldn't open.

"Make love here? What do you mean?"

I was offering love to a melting candle.

"Don't you like the hotel?"

"Let's go in," Hermine said.

I ran my fingertips over the wood of a chair; the rustic furniture in the entrance hall of the hotel was becoming less imposing.

"Let's go. . . . I prefer your armchair," I said on an impulse of self-sacrifice.

"Too late," Hermine said.

An obsequious clerk came over.

"For how long would it be?"

I straightened the knot of my tie.

A young girl took us up to our room. How sweet it was to change into two orphans sitting on a bed with a bowl of calm at our feet.

"Don't be tired. . . ."

"I'm not tired anymore."

I closed the lined curtains.

Chairs, things, objects surrounding us: part payments of eternity. Oh furrow of resignation, drawn-out chord, fidelity of the great organ's sound even in our chairs, our things, the objects surrounding us. Hermine lay across the bed and smiled up at the ceiling. Now its ardor had returned, her face was even more intense than her smile.

"I'm playing," Hermine said.

"The *Italian Concerto?*"

"Yes."

She was playing from memory, retreating wholly inside herself. I was not supposed to listen.

Later, I said: "Do you want to?"

Hermine wanted whatever I wanted.

I undressed her with the fingers of a miniaturist. Women, chambermaids no doubt, calling from hotel window to hotel window, were invigorating the spaces outside with their high-tuned cries as we dived down into the accustomed azure deeps.

Two hours later on the same street in Paris-Plage:

"Let's follow them, Violette. For a moment, just for a moment, I promise."

"You're mad. They're the only people in the street. They'll notice. Did we come here to follow people?"

Hermine shrugged her shoulders. "They're not people. Put up your collar. We're at the seaside. I'm going to follow them alone."

Hermine set off. She looked like a painter in her black felt hat.

I trotted along beside her. "You might tell me what you see in them. She's skinny and he's fat."

The plate glass of the stores on each side of the street sent everything echoing back and forth between them.

"Not so loud," Hermine hissed. "She isn't fat, and he isn't skinny. They're in love."

I laughed. It was a forced laugh.

"You walk out of the hotel, and right away you can tell they're in love. . . ."

Hermine considered the expression on my face. "You mustn't be jealous," she said. "We're in love too."

She hooked her arm under mine. There was no choice but to follow them.

The man, about sixty, all his vitality, all his virility coiled in the small of his back, turned toward his companion. His ruddy face, his curly gray hair tumbling down over his forehead brought warmth to the street. The movement of his head set other gestures in motion: they linked themselves together by twining their arms around each other's waist, then continued on their way. We kept walking straight ahead of us down to the blond charity of the sands, down to its very fringe, down to the vast stretching of the sea. The North Sea was a battle echoing inside a cavern. We held onto our hats, we clutched our skirts between our legs, we staggered. The wind held us in its power, we were ridiculous. Not one holiday-maker, not one opened parasol.

"Say something."

"I'm looking at it," Hermine said.

"For how many centuries?"

"For five minutes."

There was a man picking up old pieces of paper. He asked us for a cigarette and stowed it away inside his cap.

Our drive out into the woods in a hackney carriage revived us. The driver pointed out all the villas and told us the names of the owners. Lulled by the steady rhythm of the rubber-covered tires, rejuvenated by the healthiness of the trees, we nudged each other shamelessly like two brazen guttersnipes whenever we recognized one of the names we'd read in *Vogue* or *Fémina*. The whole seaside town was transformed into a love nest till the time came for us to depart.

*

There were important new publications in the air. Montherlant telephoned, asking us to publicize the reissue of his *Songs* in a cheap popular edition. Julien Green was making his début: he scarcely raised his eyes once while signing copies of his first book, except to discuss music with the publicity assistant. Timid himself, he intimidated others. The manuscript that they'd accepted because "someone else would snap it up" had been *Mont-Cinère* (published before *Dusty Answer*) and it was now piled up, copy upon copy, all over our table. A meteor fell into our office: Georges Bernanos. We had read the advance proofs of *Sous le soleil de Satan* and were expecting its author to have a fairly disquieting physical appearance. What carnations he tossed in our faces with that laughter of his when he came in to sign his book and be interviewed. He laughed at everything without the slightest affectation. He had the good looks of a forty-year-old Spanish nobleman with a mat complexion and passionate eyes that sometimes glistened with spangles of boyishness. His eyes: two active volcanoes. A lavish presence. Whenever he fell silent, he became a well-fed Don Quixote, only middling in height but with the same fire, the same tempest raging about his head. He used his powers of invention to embellish his reminiscences. The memory of his brief spell in prison with Henry Bernstein during their time together in the army made him literally shake with laughter.

A bomb suddenly exploded in every department: the odd, rather swarthy young girl with the gravelly accent, who sat hunched over her typewriter in the most secluded corner of the typing pool, was a writer. Henri Massis was the first to read her manuscript. She wrote in the evenings. We had never supposed that this was the case, we hadn't even guessed it, that was what astonished us. Her pseudonym was all ready: Michel Davet. The title as well: *Le Prince qui m'aimait*. I hadn't read it, I didn't even know what it was about.

My late arrivals in red on my clocking-in card, my laughable raise, the hours I had to keep, from eight-fifteen till noon, from one-thirty till six-thirty, Monday to Friday and twelve-thirty on Saturdays, my daily sprint out to the Porte Champerret so as to be better fed, the hunt for news items for years on end, the books picked clean of anecdotes, the mountain of magazines, of dailies after two days off, Mlle. Conan's continual muttering, all made me lose heart. I was fed up with the whole department. But everything has its interludes. Simonne Ratel, an excellent woman journalist on the staff of the paper *Comœdia,* used to visit us; when she opened the door of our office the room was flooded with sunlight. She asked us how we were, she brought the month of May as a gift whenever she came. She told me how much she liked my lavender blue skirt with the pleats and my pullover to match. The files and the filing cabinets were suddenly delightful things. Mlle. Conan used to hum after our sower of spring had left.

To escape being stifled to death in our office, I sallied forth on a quest for gossip and gossips in the other departments; if a director appeared, I would mime some occupation or other, or invent a request for information. I would find myself in the bookstore, say hello to Jérôme and Jean Tharaud, thank Stanislas Fumet for having so generously inserted my news item in *L'Intransigeant,* and burrow my way into the complicated and exiguous premises of *La Revue hebdomadaire.* The books and manuscripts piled up there had overgrown everything like weeds. The editor, François Le Grix, slaved in the cause of his magazine like a man possessed. There was an elegant young man who acted as his assistant. The bearing, the modesty, the gently reticent face, the pleasant coolness of Robert de Saint-Jean, the editor's personal secretary, intimidated me. I would go back to our office, set about some task, and stagnate there. My eyes would fall blankly on the blotting paper, I would chew away at my banana, at my roll, as closed to the world as a mollusc on a rock. I would pick up my eyes, put them back in place, and summon up just enough energy to watch a fly crawling up the window or the solitary adventures of a spider, or to listen to the charity of a clock sounding the half hour. I sat pulling the fibers from inside a piece of banana peel.

In her furs, toward the end of the afternoon, she would arrive. She arrived, and her voice held me breathless. Strong, serene, luminous, it was the voice of a young girl tamed by an adult. Sighs, pauses, exhaled music, nothing was missing. The familiar burden of her melody: "Paris gets more crowded every day. You have no idea what traffic's like. It's taken us three quarters of an hour to come from . . . over to here." The actress Simone was having her first novel *Le Désordre* published in our series La Palatine; the director of publicity always saw her in the private sitting room next to our office. Her vitality held me captive even through the partition, her elocution lent me strength. I spoke for her, I spoke with her, I was in the theater. The sap of facility bubbled up into my head. I would go back to the little table covered with the mold of my slack habits, I imposed myself on the penholder lying in front of the inkpot, on the blank sheet of paper and its terrible nudity, I was mistress of my every effort before I made it. I had seen the actress play at the Théâtre de l'Oeuvre in Steve Passeur's *L'Acheteuse,* I had read *Le Désordre* and remembered the singular atmosphere of her novel. She talked, she talked: our pitiful office began to expand, to transform itself into a line of automobiles, into avenues, into streets and intersections. I met her again long after, somewhere on the outskirts of Paris, during a series of literary conferences and discussions that were being held between writers. It was an evening at Royaumont. The writers on the platform were playing charades. They guessed *Sparkenbroke* and began looking for another name to guess. I don't quite know how, but Mme. Simone in her evening furs created a circle of confidantes around her. There were three of us: Renée Saurel, Jean Amrouche, and myself. The reminiscences came flooding out under the failing electric light. Mme. Simone recalled the way Society people used to mock at Marcel Proust with their questions: "Well, my little Marcel, are we still hard at work?" "Well, my little Marcel, how is the great work coming along?" That evening the actress held our attention by main force rather than by charming us. She was writing aloud.

Hermine received her transfer to Seine-et-Marne. Leaving one's family . . . It's easy, it's very easy at the time. It becomes more difficult later. I detached myself from my room, from their apartment, from the block, from the 17th arrondissement with unforeseen ease. Hermine had come to have lunch with them. We all closed our eyes. We hid our relationship behind a veil of vagueness. Why shouldn't leaving one's children be easy too? I was relieving them of my bad moods, my fits of temper, my late hours, my late appearance at the dinner table. My departure for my mother: the extraction of her romance. I took all the clothes out of my little girl's wardrobe with indifference. Hermine asked me why I'd lived for years in a room without curtains at the windows.

"Because I don't give a damn about other people," I told Hermine.

❁

*

I left my parents then with the unconcern of a stroller leaving a park as it closes for the night. I walked down their stairs with the arrogance of a barnyard cock, first herald of day's first beams. Gabriel, who had started sketching people in the cafés of Montparnasse, was dozing in the toils of his disorganized existence. I moved into a furnished room with Hermine, out in Vincennes in a quiet street just a minute's walk from the streetcar.

I would get home completely exhausted at eight in the evening. I shook off the crowds, the trampling feet in the Châtelet Métro station, the waiting in line at the Porte de Vincennes. The kitchen, no bigger than a pocket handkerchief . . . The romantic smell of the veal in the saucepan put the idea of a village seducer in my head. I pushed my beret further to one side, I crossed my arms, I waited for dinner leaning against the door of our furnished room, still impregnated with the happiness of having our own front door, at the end of the corridor, on the topmost floor.

"Squirrel," she would cry.

She came in with my grandmother's cookbook, the recipes she copied from newspapers fluttering out of it.

Pleased with her day at school, with the headmistress, with her students, with her colleagues, with Paris, with Vincennes, with her sleep, with her awakening, with her short nights, with her plans for giving music lessons, Hermine sang a scherzo using the names of the notes for words, bending her head to the left when she hit low notes and to the right for the high ones. She leaned out the little window: the light was classical.

"What can you see?"

"Couperin."

"Come on," I said. "I'm hungry."

My superior at the office, Mlle. Perret, had recovered from her illness, but she put in fewer and fewer appearances. The office and the news items bored her, despite the favors she enjoyed. She was doing something with a theatrical company named Les Tréteaux and writing a play: *Notre-Dame de la Mouise*. She gave us three hours of her presence, two hours, one hour, then she stopped giving us any at all. I did the work for two; I also worked for the publicity assistant, hoping that my wages would be doubled. Nothing happened. I complained to everyone, except to the director and his assistant. I was given an increase of fifty francs a month.

As I waited my turn to climb onto the bus at the Porte de Vincennes I remembered my mother's meeting with Gabriel in a café near the Porte Champerret. I listened to my past before Hermine's arrival at Vincennes:

"Come on, mummy. I promised him you'd come. He's waiting for us in the café. You wanted to before, why don't you now? I tell you he's waiting in the café as we arranged. Look your best, dress up, wear your foxes. I shall talk, Gabriel will talk. Go in first, mummy. Let him see you. Yes, the man alone, at the corner table. Yes, that's Gabriel. Go on, he's seen us. . . .

"What did you think of him, mummy?"

"He didn't talk."

"No, he didn't talk."

"His eyes looking into yours, it's madness, Violette."

"What do you mean, 'it's madness'?"

"Looking at you like that and not asking for anything. . . ."

"What did you think of my mother? Gabriel, I'm talking to you, why don't you answer? What did you think of my mother? Didn't you like her?"

"No, I didn't like her much."

"Explain yourself."

"There's nothing to explain, little fellow."

Life in a furnished apartment is stimulating. The furniture can be inventoried on the fingers of one hand, and it frees you from the trouble of moving men. Everything rented is a disburdenment. It is a limbo between poverty and possessions. A furnished room in an apartment house is the final extension of a waiting room. Partition walls between the rooms, doomed echoes, aphrodisiac echoes, cells of a community, the contagion of brawls, sex, tragedy. We lived our love twice over with our neighbors, the two lovers. Our fellowmen were brought into sharper focus by their angry shouts; they were infected by our passion and our fury, we were infected by theirs. Promiscuity, penetration, a mirage of a community, that is a furnished apartment building.

*

Regrets, obsessions, nostalgias every Saturday between Chaussée-d'Antin and Havre-Caumartin.

Paris is a killer Paris is killing me Paris is drowning me I am walking and dying in this stream of crazed automobiles faster motors yes straight on yes over there my bed is waiting the sky will tuck itself around me I am the crowd the crowd follows me our room a piece of newspaper on the street Violette was out walking Hermine was teaching the tick-tock was trying to fly out of the room which they neglected a hand on my brow and interrogation mark it's a plantain it's a leaf from a tree weep I am the crowd and the crowd follows me I must dawdle I must get dirty I must have the noise of a Parisian artery I must feel it across the back of my neck so cold is the music of the cylinders a handbag is caught up the crowd wavers the woman wrenches her handbag away from the man's hip saved and they'll never get to know each other who forces me to come here on Saturdays I've so many graveyards on my shoulders Fidéline Isabelle Gabriel it's dying it's dead put flowers on our little mother between Havre-Caumartin and the Chaussée-d'Antin flowers of sadness so many white carnations fluffed in the sewing maids' rooms when the incestuous woman lost her brother be charitable sir be charitable lady if I dared it was to warm up my little graveyards let's stop in front of this cool shrubbery between the feet of the models in the window Hermine I'm talking to you crunch the chalk eat the blackboard chew slowly on our furnished room you don't say a little bit you say a little I'll be careful mummy next time I'll be careful how many times has she looked at me like that let's begin I screw up my face if you pull faces like that you'll have wrinkles later on I screw up my face a way of remembering the way she looked after I'd said a little bit she catches me up on it I'd had my eyes lowered I raised my head I caught her don't look at me like that while I wasn't looking at you you're not in a classroom here I don't insist I don't say you were observing me you were detached I would prefer a slap the wheel the whip for a little bit instead of a little but don't look at me like that too detached too indifferent men no men don't take advantage of your second's absence to turn you to ice satyr your hand I call a policeman and before the threats of a little girl a child vanished the satyr the moldy virtue of our room when it's alone I hurled the anemones the vase incredible dream the man and the woman with another woman's handbag between them found themselves one flag hung minute aerial sleds of sweat and face powder they talk to each other they say good-by a meeting the heavens permit the passage of a little gilded heart its so commonplace so crucial if it were Gabriel if it were Hermine I am nailed to the spot I think about what I never used to think about push her she'll come and plant herself here an idiot girl a meeting field stretching as far as the eye can see carefully tended my eyes my blue clematis flowers I'm blind spring what do you think you are with your beret over one ear where do you think you are Gabriel my philter in a profile let us go on since I am the crowd since the crowd follows me what is this beating tiny between my lips for Hermine an emotion-mouth a tremble-mouth for Gabriel when he says to me you're attractive little fellow his hand falls on mine he's said it it's all over Gabriel holds his cheek beneath the dome of Sacré-Coeur I feel better it was an attack of giddiness a wave of heat a mirage woman plus man on the other sidewalk mirrored two strangers the other sidewalk moves off with the black-sailed ship a despair to be concealed I feel better no it's coming back what shooting pains I have thirty-two aching teeth on my heart you are never satisfied Violette don't be so demanding face real life for heaven's sake don't make a scene mummy Gabriel has a sky like a palanquin over his hotel he is a king the king of all those who don't think about tomorrow I am the crowd the crowd is following me

Hermine is on duty in the playground Gabriel drugs himself with sleep Hermine Gabriel tear me apart do you know what you are when you get away from that no I don't know barley-sugar Violette doesn't know Hermine comma sweet Jesus exclamation mark here she is think the Conservatoire under the sea because she's shy and couldn't give concerts where is that handsome man going with his ivory face and tower disappearing missing her first prize her career face of a handsome man a cross for meditation music teacher where can her treatise on harmony be floating now historian shall I fill up your inkwell later you would write to us doves and pigeons flocking down over Paris that year Paris inundated with feathers and down there goes Cyrano de Bergerac that's what they shout at you Violette the urchins of the capital shriek and hold their sides my nose and bones my suffering flesh I squeezed it in a clothes peg my clothes peg when I was sixteen sixteen the ocean was asking me for alms sixteen as I dissolved into the sunsets ah face the sex of the looking glass ah mirror in which men and women are all whores am I attractive to you Gabriel question mark I have little feet my mother said to Hermine look she has the feet of a little girl I am the crowd is the crowd following me a window mender caught in its eddies it's common to shout out your profession like that keep quiet with your little graveyards on your back it's unavoidable sir if you're the checker they are my graves and were mine before I was born we must talk to Gabriel about it keep quiet a smile a golden age of models in store windows being with Gabriel makes you dowdy your café artist has judged you I don't mind I want him to sleep in a swan made of Cuban mahogany not in a swan of sycamore not in a swan the size of a nest I know the birds they won't refuse to do it for me a robin I knew once built a miracle from the fur of those fighting hares Gabriel bows and backs away Hermine has taken his sacrifices away from him why didn't you tell me in your letters Violette I would have understood I am the crowd the crowd is following me it wasn't important good gracious my mother would say it wasn't important his nights in the streets of Amiens while we felt the drug creeping down our legs three questioning points of suspension those women like the informal dinner dress best that's their choice though they don't buy it I chose Hermine Gabriel is here on the tips of my lashes you went out together as friends heavens he pleaded with me my hand laid its alms on the spread of hair above his groin the man when it's a curly tangle of song beneath my hand my ancestors Gabriel withdrew into his macadam haunts in Montmartre lies little deceptions going to the pawnshop by themselves what do you think you are it's true with my beret pushed over one ear what dark rings under the eyes good-by the store window shines see you soon store window models your smile will cast a spell on me again the bronze of your skin is my bath my leather briefcase under my arm my chaste oh so chaste eyelids my sidelong glance I am appearance walking in a forest the sexes burn.

I went into the department store.

What a sight you are, Violette. Nice under the shower of electric light though. If you're looking for the place that makes mourning clothes in twenty-four hours, you're on the wrong track, you've taken the wrong turning. You have entered the palace of frivolity. Why have I come in here? Hermine would want me to. What would she want exactly, Hermine? ". . . I'd prefer to see you in a hat, with longer hair, a cloche hat." She wants a woman with a cloche hat. Our senses are unsettled by the price tags, attacks of covetousness. Crops reaped and ready to be carted away. The beautiful love of things and money. What sighs. I am where I should be.

I stood stupid beside the elevators.

The women customers were wearing out the mirrors with their selections. I heard my mother in the distance. "Be a woman. When will you be a woman?" I was confusing feminine tactics and moral coquetry with outward accessories. Greedy hands. Thirsting eyes. Coquettish faces, faces certain of their wiles. The atmosphere was anesthetising me, the winking button on the elevator was putting me to sleep. Silt, river silt. Who was talking underneath my feet? The floors of the big department store would have nothing to do with my river silt.

White clouds, pink clouds, blue clouds, green clouds. They drew me to them. I felt the lightness of them, I picked them over, I stroked, I scratched, I dug in my nails. I splashed about in that frothy pool called luxury within the reach of the average budget. A warmth crept through me. I was a cloud among clouds, since the salesgirls, the customers, the floorwalkers were all making their gestures at a great distance from my transactions, my silken friendships. I felt myself growing heavier, I looked about me as a sudden anger sprang from some unknown place inside me, I looked to the right, to the left. "With longer hair . . ." Panties the color of lily-of-the-valley leaves, Hermine, would you like that? A black pair, a blue pair, a yellow pair, an orange pair, a salmon pink pair? I slipped the black, the blue, the yellow, the orange, the salmon pink, into my briefcase as though I'd been doing it all my life. A theft, a strangled rose. The magnificence of my petty larceny was manifested to me in the rapidity with which the thing for sale was transformed, without my having paid, into an object sold. I was reaping a harvest of panties. I rustled, I had wings, wings on my back and wings in my head, I was alone in my fever with the world at my back. Ah how I snatched my revenge on the fresh, bright conceit of those things. Thus encouraged, I made my way over to the lamb's wool and velvet powder-puffs, to the compacts, to the glittering jewels, the trinkets and tinkling baubles. I was stealing too in order to rob the other women of the things that made them feminine. Rape performed in a private darkness, for the others couldn't see me. In the end, though I calculated and laid down precise bounds for my dishonesty, though I foresaw the exact second when the object would be taken and observed in advance the sureness of my hand as it made the gesture, I was nevertheless abandoning myself utterly, without thought of good or bad, of success or failure, of life or death, of heaven or hell, as the moment for each theft arrived. My briefcase was bulging with fripperies. I stopped after taking a pair of eyebrow tweezers.

I left the department store neither proud nor humble. Now, the crowd was a refreshment to me.

"Follow me," said a voice behind me.

I turned my head.

"Follow me," said the same voice close to my temple.

I followed him. I turned the corner of the store with him and after walking a hundred yards along a restful street I entered the den of captured thieves. Nameless men resembling my escort were standing waiting in their putty uniforms near a table. Behind it, another nameless stranger was also waiting, seated.

The escort took my briefcase and removed the objects in it one by one.

"Why do you do it?" he asked.

The men looked at me without hostility.

"It's the first time," I said.

I wept without remorse, without regret. I wiped my eyes and looked around at witnesses of the paradise I was losing.

"Why do you do it?" the nameless man asked again.

He clicked the lock of my leather briefcase shut. The gesture was almost paternal. I sobbed.

"It's the first time," I said again between my sobs.

I sobbed all the louder because what had been done had now been so swiftly undone. The things snatched up, now snatched away.

"My briefcase," I cried. "Will you give it back to me?"

He laid aside the old briefcase to which I was more attached than anything else in the world.

"I must keep it," he said.

I stretched out my arms toward it.

"My briefcase, my briefcase . . ."

I was calling to the relic of my great feats.

The nameless stranger opened a register and wrote down in it a list of the objects stolen. The other men who had nothing to do concentrated on the insect moving across the paper.

I was weeping hot tears: all the powder, all the glamour had gone from my adventure.

"Your name, first name and address," said the nameless man.

He opened another register.

"You're not going to keep me here?"

"Your name, first name and address."

He was becoming impatient. I collapsed.

The others watched me with the compassion animals feel when they know we are suffering.

I moaned, I wanted their pity.

"I've got a stepfather. . . . It'll be terrible if my parents hear about it. My mother, for my mother . . . What will happen to me, what will it do to her? . . ."

I thought of my shame when I faced them, when I faced her. I thought of the shock for them.

I spelled out my name, then my parents' address, since we were to spend that Saturday and Sunday at their place while they were away.

"Why do you do it?" he asked again.

He banged his fist on the table. I was upsetting him.

He's weakening, I read in the other men's eyes.

"It's the first time. Believe me."

He looked hard into my eyes.

"I believe you," he said.

His job had given him some insight.

"But why?" he asked again.

I was free. Nothing had been decided. I was to go back at the beginning of next week. He called me back and asked where I worked. I told him about my news items in the newspapers, hoping to increase his indulgence. You aren't a professional shoplifter. You're a worm, his eyes conveyed to me by way of conclusion.

I felt at a loss without my leather briefcase. Handbags look more alike than people seem to think. I muttered a timid good-by.

I left bruised, bleeding, numbed. I could identify none of the things about me. There was blue water misting all my thoughts. I was making my way from the jail I had escaped toward the fresh air I had not yet won my way back to. The smell of waffles and vanilla-flavored sugar halfway between Printemps and the Galeries Lafayette, always till that day a delicious decoy for my memories of Fidéline, drove me over to the other side of the street. Mysteriously, it began again; I wept beside the same silks, the same lace: the silks and lace in the store A la Ville du Puy.

Hermine had set the table in my parents' dining room. They were away on a two-day vacation. I began to droop.

"Hermine, there's something I want to tell you. . . ."

I told her without words.

"Speak up," Hermine said.

I gave her the loneliness in my face, I gave her the last tiny grain of dust I shall become.

"Why are you looking at me like that? You're frightening me."

Paris was a dull thunder through the open window. Hermine shivered.

She stroked my hair, she called me "My own little baby." I took her hand and wrapped it in a glove of kisses.

"I'll give you whatever you want. Ask me," she begged.

I gave her a dawn: a new beginning. She gave me apéritifs and movies.

My musician, my deaf Hermine.

Look, listen. I am giving you the crown of sparks from Fidéline's fantail lamp, the flame fluttering this way and that in its sooty saucer.

Hermine softened too. We lay on their moquette carpet, face to face, apart.

"Look," she said as though it was important.

A late sparrow was hopping on the window sill. The evening outside became uncomfortable between each little hop.

"You've been crying. Tell me what's the matter," Hermine begged.

The sparrow flew off toward an irresistible world forever unknown to us. He freed us, he left us lying outside a church waiting for a miracle: the two cripples dragged themselves toward each other.

I began crying again.

"You don't love me," Hermine said, "you're unhappy."

"I don't love you, Hermine?"

I felt guilty, I wanted to believe everything, accept everything against myself. My tears wetted the back of Hermine's neck.

"Crying your heart out when we have a whole evening, then a whole day in front of us. What are you crying for? Is there a reason?"

". . ."

She got up, I followed her. She was arranging the pointed ends of her smooth hair so that they curled forward flat against her cheeks.

I covered her short hair with both my hands.

Hermine freed herself from my grip.

"Let me get a cigarette. . . ."

That evening she was smoking Marylands. Her style of smoking was as incisive as her writing.

"I want to know what happened."

I adore you, I stole, it's there in my throat. I thought I loved Hermine.

She asked me what I would like. I answered with my tears: a hat, and longer hair because that's what you want. Hermine was crying out: Ask me for a great many things, for heaps of things. I'd like a velvet powderpuff. I'll powder myself when we go out. You shall have several, Hermine replied. I'd like underwear in every color there is. I'll give you underwear in natural silk, in reversible satin, in silk voile, my little one, my little girl. . . . I'll go to the big stores and pick them out if this blows over. Why shouldn't it blow over? Hermine asked without understanding, without trying to understand. She wants a woman, she shall have a woman and I shall have no reason to steal, I said to myself. I was tired. I needed her and I needed the winter so that the earth could sleep. She went out to the bathroom, ready to pay for yardgoods from Colcombet and from Lesur, names we had never even heard of then.

On Saturdays, Hermine is a piece of polished furniture. That evening I had stolen, that evening I was contagious. I listened to the clothes brush at its reconstruction work. No, I haven't seen Gabriel again. He sleeps during the day, you know. Gabriel feels the cold, he has slept too often in the open air. Gabriel is a brother centuries away. She was brushing her hair. Not speaking, is that what living together means then? I say nothing, my sigh tells you: I stole. Now I am a wretched little dog, only just born, lost in an alley at three in the morning. He's asleep, Hermine, and you see nothing. His breath is coming in quick pants, he's calling out without making a sound. Hermine is absorbed in her tin of brilliantine. Pink jelly on black hair. Like shiny black carbon paper.

*

I don't remember where I met him. I remember that Gabriel was supposed to have dinner in our room that evening. His car must have slowed down, he must have got out, he must have followed me. Walking faster, walking slower, changing sidewalks, inventing a raised head for the sinking sun; the rhythm of an impregnable solitary. Being followed. I was being wooed by a sidewalk.

I got into his car. We exchanged professions. I found he was General Lyautey's aide-de-camp. I was put out by his car's pretentiousness. The height of refinement, I said to myself as I looked at his shapeless old leather gloves. I remember the one thing he told me about himself: he used to play the piano for the general when the old man couldn't sleep. The rank of aide-de-camp, so far from my world, his piano at night under the desert stars, intimidated me. He talked about what he was doing that evening, about the books he read, about our next meeting, about a dinner at Lapérouse. He expressed himself with a facility that froze me in my seat. He politely evaded the subject whenever I made halting attempts to evoke my children's drawings of palm trees, of desert beauty spots, of veiled women. He had come to Paris, he was talking about Paris. But the acacias were fluffy with ostrich plumes, there was a tiger growling in every sports car, and gazelles were driving their high shiny heels into the grassy parks, our oases. He stopped the car where I asked him to, and we talked about everything and nothing.

The correctness of his behavior dumbfounded Violette. She left him empty-handed. All she had wanted from him was a bundle of franc notes that he would have thrown in a garbage can, that she would have pulled out from among the garbage with her teeth.

I plunged into the corridor of our apartment house; Hermine and Gabriel threw themselves upon me shrieking with forced laughter. I waited, flattened against the wall.

"You saw me?"

Hermine answered: "We saw you through the café window. Gabriel was buying me an apéritif. We were waiting for you."

"You were out for a ride in a car," Gabriel cut in. "She can have a good time as well."

Hermine's nostrils quivered. She resented Gabriel's directness.

"We could almost follow your conversation," Gabriel said with a wicked smile.

The same forced laughter gripped them again. I told them they were being stupid.

"Less so than you with your solemn expression sitting there in someone's car," Gabriel rejoined.

"She's here anyway, leave her alone now," Hermine said.

"He's an aide-de-camp. We talked to one another."

"Who gives a damn?" Gabriel said. "Your dinner . . . It must be burning!"

"Let's go upstairs," Hermine said very quietly.

She led me up by the hand. Gabriel lagged behind on the landings whistling sullenly between his teeth.

He is staying to eat, only to eat, I said to myself. Pity can sometimes tear you apart.

Hermine took my coat, my briefcase, my beret.

"Go away," I shouted at Gabriel.

Gabriel lit up. "Of course," he said. "Will you just let me remove this spot first?"

He scratched at a white spot on the lapel of his jacket.

Beret, coat, and briefcase fell from Hermine's fingers. "He must have something to eat. He can't just leave like this."

"But I'm having a high old time," Gabriel said.

It was one of his favorite expressions.

"Go away. I want to be alone with her. Don't you understand?"

Hermine began rushing about. She took a piece of meat out of a saucepan and made up a colossal sandwich.

"I understand," Gabriel said. "You've come home, you want to pour out your heart. Are you seeing him again?"

"You're not to torment her," Hermine cried.

He bit his way furiously through the sandwich and left.

Hermine closed the door behind him and sobbed on my shoulder.

"You were keeping watch on me, spying."

"Are you angry with me?" Hermine asked.

"I'm not angry. I'm disgusted."

"You are angry with me," Hermine rejoined. "This is what happened. I came home earlier than usual. Gabriel was waiting. He was walking up and down outside. He looked for you in my eyes, and he hated me for it. He'll always hate me because of you. I stood there in front of him, I was almost ashamed of being myself. I racked my brains to think what I could give him. I had nothing to give him. He shivered. He asked me if by any chance you weren't up in our room. It's possible, I exclaimed. You call her first, he said. Tell me what's the matter with me, Violette. I'm worn out. You wear me out, you and Gabriel. I shouted up toward our window. Together, said Gabriel, it will be louder. People opened their windows, a baby began to cry. We had to give up. 'Watch the streetcars, intercept her when she comes, I'll go and buy everything we need for dinner.' He'd worked it out. There I was, rooted to the spot, standing there stupidly with my billfold in my hand. He doesn't earn much, you can see that. Well, this evening he paid for everything for the three of us. It's only now I understand what he wanted: I took his money, the dinner is ruined, and he's alone in the streets. It's my fault, everything's my fault."

Hermine was weeping.

"Nothing was your fault. I sent him away."

"Yes, you sent him away," Hermine said.

I wanted to take her by the hand and cool her burning face. She refused.

"Shall I tell you about my ride home in the car? He plays the piano at night for . . ."

"Oh please," Hermine sobbed. "I don't want to know anything about it. Be happy whenever you get the chance," she said with a wretched smile.

She began again: "Why did I come to Paris? I could have pulled open his jacket pocket and slipped in my billfold. I could have, now I can't. Tomorrow everything will be different."

"Tomorrow he won't come."

"He interrogated me. What time does she come home other evenings? He watched me, he judged me because I answered: when she wants to, when she can. He asked me for the key of our room, he went in first. He wanted to help me. I offered him an apéritif up in the room, but he refused. He'd have waited for you differently, he'd have been kinder, if I hadn't been there."

"I'll tell you how it happened. We bumped into each other, simply bumped into each other. . . ."

She took my face savagely between her hands. "You won't tell me anything. I'm going to do the telling."

Her lips, her cheeks were twitching.

"What a lot of fuss because I went for a drive. . . ."

"How wrong you are, how little you know about us," she said. "Now where is he? Alone, and the night coming down on him. Let's kneel."

"You're mad. Kneel for whom?"

"For him," she said very quietly. "Everything he had to give, he gave. His money, his anguish, his anxiety. 'I'll buy you a drink downstairs and we'll jump out on her when she comes.' Now I'm certain he hasn't enough to buy himself a bowl of soup. Go to the window," Hermine said. "Look for him."

The streetlamps shone down on a deserted street. Everyone was at home, everyone for himself. I wept with Hermine, I wept for him, for her, for myself.

"He'll walk about until tomorrow, I know him. If you think the city is going to drag him down you're wrong. He never gives anything unless he wants to give it."

"You don't know him," Hermine said.

She switched on the light. The green leaves awakened in the salad bowl were protecting the dinner with Gabriel. She switched the light off again.

". . . He gave me cigarette after cigarette in the café. Gabriel has something attractive about him. Everyone wanted to talk to him. 'There she is in the automobile, can't you see her!' He gave me a push, he wanted to hurt me. He hated me because I hadn't recognized you."

The little window swung open. Gabriel was still angry. But outside there was a clear sky, with not a jewel hung in it, inviting us to play truant in its infinity.

"Paris is getting ready to have a good time," I said with resignation. "Let it go: let us love one another."

"No."

Eclogue, please make things be simpler. She is refusing me her flanks against my hair. Eclogue, word for mercy in my vocabulary, intercede for me.

"Gabriel's wandering out there, and so are we," I said bitterly.

". . . My baby. I saw you in the car without seeing you. I said to Gabriel: there she is. No, I didn't say it, it was a sigh. You had come back, my heart began to beat the way it does when I play slow movements. You were running your finger over the car window, looking straight in front of you. I wasn't supposed to see, and there wasn't anything to be seen. You didn't talk much, you didn't move, but all the same it was like being at a play."

I switched on the light.

Hermine looked at herself in the mirror. A flick of the chin, a flick of that perfectionist conscience. She powdered her little nose. The nostrils looked too rapacious: one of nature's errors. I looked at Hermine in the mirror, she looked at me.

"You're unhappy, my poor baby," she said. "Your mouth is all twisted."

Hermine's words were like a past preparing for a future.

"Play something," I demanded.

"Whatever you like," Hermine answered.

I took away the knives and forks, the plates and the glasses. I placed a seat for myself in front of the piano, ready for the concert. I asked for Bach's Preludes.

Hermine played the piano on the table, she followed the keyboard from left to right, from right to left, singing the name of every note.

"Play some more. Play the Inventions. . . ."

She sat collecting herself, hands on her knees.

"Another evening," Hermine said.

She looked at me. It was deeper than weeping.

*

I grew paler, I grew thinner, I spat out phlegm, I kept up a persistent tiny cough for weeks and months. I had a pain in my side. My mother was worried. Doctors, the uncertainty about the X-rays. She went with me to a T.B. specialist. White hair, sequestered office, the doctor questioned me with gentle precision. I explained about the crowds, the streetcars, the Métro, about having to change at the Châtelet, about my lack of appetite in the cheap restaurant at midday. My mother told him about my father's consumption.

"Heredity doesn't come into it," the doctor replied.

I followed him into an even more sequestered little room for an X-ray examination.

"Don't breathe," he said.

I abandoned myself to his commands, I offered him the lungs of the stranger, my father. He can read them like an open book, I said to myself. He switched the light back on.

"What's wrong with her?" my mother asked.

"Nothing serious," he said, "but . . ."

I listened as he told me what I should do. I remembered the ineffable moment when the nameless man gave me back my leather briefcase with the suggestion that I should never do it again. His eyes said: it isn't worth it. The doctor's eyes said: being sick isn't worth it.

I asked the publicity director if I could write my copy every morning at home and read the newspapers at the office in the afternoon. Hermine was giving all sorts of private lessons. She insisted, she begged. I ought to drop everything, books, news items, newspapers, I ought to become the little woman who runs out to the shops, who does the chores, who cooks the dinner and simply lives through every day as it comes. I didn't give way to Hermine. I clung to my four and a half years of diligence, to the envelope with my pay in it. My idleness in the past, the thought of my idleness in the future, filled me with panic. I woke up in the night thinking I didn't work at the office anymore. I would switch on the light and Hermine would smile at me without opening her eyes. Sleep, she would say. She was bursting with good health. Being good to people suited her. I squeezed my forearm between my thumb and index finger, switched off the light, and said to myself: that's what you are.

My mother was insistent too. I ought to give up my job. She would buy my clothes and Hermine would feed me. The office became a battlefield. I couldn't bring myself to abandon those four and a half years of routine. Eat, said my mother, eat, said Hermine. I became Fidéline's little granddaughter again, the anemia had taken away my appetite. I shouted at them: I will go, I won't stop work, I'm going to keep on with it. My mother would buy my clothes, Hermine would feed me. What was happening to me? What would become of me? What was I? What would I be? Thin as I was, I wanted to be thinner and wear dark blue sweaters. My emaciated shoulders were a grimace. I could hear a voice: Gabriel's voice, his absent voice: "You're solid, little fellow, you know how to keep quiet, I like that. Got room for another drink? What would you say to a nice long walk along by the river?" I was his man, he was my woman in our friendship, in our wrestling match. He reappeared.

But he came to see us less and less. Hermine was turning me into a woman, and that infuriated him. I lay knitting on the divan in our furnished room, his eyes brushed my legs and turned away. When he looked at me again, his eyes said: you're turning into a whore, she's making you into a whore. And the pain in his smile: my little fellow, the little fellow I knew is dead, is buried. He could see what was happening. His step in the passage as he went away . . . Hermine wasn't jealous. Gabriel's fury made her sad. Gabriel never retraced those steps along the corridor. Gabriel was sufficient unto himself as soon as he was back among his own people: the little people. "You know how to keep quiet, I like that." Gabriel would have been mistaken if he'd said it now. I talked to Hermine till I was exhausted. I demolished Gabriel, I demolished my mother. I had to destroy them in order to destroy myself. I jabbered and held forth and criticized until I had no breath left. She is killing me and there's nothing I can accuse her of, I thought to myself as Hermine prepared our dinner, as she explained a knitting stitch to me, as she promised me the moon.

Finally I left the office with a reference from the publicity director, which was later stolen from me with a lot of gas bills, electricity bills, rent bills.

Hermine walked on tiptoe in the morning, hoping I was asleep; she drank the coffee she had made for herself in a filter the night before. So much vitality, so much alertness, so much determination when she had only just got up, drained more blood out of me instead of stimulating me. She left, and the sun sparkled through her arteries while my veins continued to fur up with darkness. I didn't admit to myself that her presence was too perfect, that I was shaking it off, revenging myself on it by going back to sleep.

I began coughing again. We made a woman doctor come out on a house call. It was winter. Her deep voice, her face without a hard line in it, her short hair, her topcoat with its fur lapels, her aura of intelligence and womanliness, above all her breeding, intimidated me. She looked at my nightgown with the inset of ocher lace, my long thin arms, then said: take that off. I took that off. I realized the extent of my poverty and my pretensions as I lay in front of this capable woman: I was a nothing in a green rag. She diagnosed tracheitis.

*

I wanted to be more beautiful. Hermine started buying *Vogue* and *Fémina* and *Le Jardin des Modes* again. I learned by heart the benefits to be derived from tonics and astringents—implacable enemies of the enlarged pore—from cleansing cream and nutritive cream, from orange juice and apricot powder. Head in hands, I pored anxiously over experts' advice and advertisements alike. Wrinkles, crow's feet, flaking skin, blackheads, cellulitis, a list as terrible as the dreadful warnings of Jeremiah himself. Page after page, I read and reread my blackheads, my wrinkles, my enlarged pores, my falling hair. Page after page I suffered and would not look at myself. I wanted to be rejuvenated at the age of twenty-four. I wanted it for the sake of *Vogue,* of *Fémina,* of *Le Jardin des Modes.* Wearing a crown of curlers, I drank down my orange juice, to get my vitamins, to improve my complexion. When I opened the window of our furnished room what I saw was now superfluous: men digging up the road, black fingernails, torsos encased in scarlet flannel, the geometry of the workmen repointing a façade, the aerial bicycle of a telegraph boy, the box on the front of a deliveryman's three-wheeler, a milkman's bottleholders. I didn't work myself, so my eyes were unable to see other people at work.

Clouds through the open window, dissolve! It is time for breathing in, time for breathing out, time for physical training. Time to stretch the thighs, time to rotate the waist, time to chase away that double chin. Time for the ankle, time for the wrist. Open window, azure ground for the bray of trumpets, be patient. It is time to loosen up, time for red flowers in the blood, time to improve the circulation. Flat on my back, having just touched the tips of my toes twenty-five times in order to rejuvenate myself twenty-five times before my twenty-fifth birthday, I lay gasping on the floor with a sob in my throat.

Concealing my curlers beneath an old silk square, I slipped on a decrepit old topcoat, I took the oilcloth shopping bag and set out toward the market, passing the flowers of the carriage-workers' art: the new cars lining the Avenue du Bois. The plowing, the furrows, the gusts of wind, the angelus, the sparrow, the multicolored songs of the birds above the salad greens, the reflection of a knife blade in the spinach, the roselike sun of the escarole deprived of sun, the youth, the emotion in a mutton chop, the calm and security in a sirloin steak, I ignored them all. The scales were there to weigh the figure I meant to have.

Hermine came home at seven and I went to bed. I fidgeted about, I wanted her to give still more music lessons, more English lessons. Gorged with broiled meat and cooked vegetables, I still accepted the casserole of potatoes cooked with smoked bacon, the noodles au gratin that Hermine served me, ennobled with a very dry Mumm's. I lay lighting candles in my mind to *Vogue,* to *Fémina,* to *Le Jardin des Modes,* and they took me by their intimate light into the mysterious world of high fashion, the world of the dresses and coats to be seen in my bibles, but never seen on our streets.

You loved me, Hermine, and you were not enough. We must have whirlpools of stars, motors wailing in madness when noon is all nickel, when twelve centuries, when twelve thousand years ring with the weight of a single instant. The great Schiaparelli had bewitched me, was obsessing me, dazzling me. I admired her, I forgot how to read when I had to make out the first syllable of her name. I pronounced it Shaparelli, suppressing the vowel *i* and turning her into a length of French velvet. I closed the magazine, I closed my eyes, I saw shapes, and a face. The shapes and the face were formed by the dust of light from a fountain. Sovereign and diffuse before me, Schiaparelli held the reins of her chariot as she wheeled in a Roman circus. I gazed at the pleats of her skirts: the unpeopled tiers of seats.

I opened my eyes, I opened my fashion magazines. The paper was warm with the names of the dress houses and the designers printed on it. It was my baptism as I entered the world of elegance.

"You and your eggbeater!" I exclaimed.

I was trying to enter into communication with the face advertising a beauty institute. A face from the past, a face from another world, a face set apart by the swathing bands around it. A mummy, a fate. I made my way in through the empty eyes, I walked about inside. A sphinx: beneath its chin, an advertising platform.

Hermine came in holding the eggbeater, its wheel coated with silky snow.

"You could at least read your magazine aloud to me," she said, her cheeks on fire, her voice gruff with goodness.

I read: "July stirs the blood to life. . . . Nothing counts except to get away today rather than tomorrow. . . . Our longing for the country makes maps seem masterpieces of painting. . . . To foresee the future, for a woman, means to order new clothes. Don't let's choose: we need them all. The signing of a marriage contract is still a pretext, in Paris, for a big reception at which all the wedding gifts are set out on display, including the bridegroom's gifts to the bride. . . . Quilting in modern design. You can have your gloves made to measure. Artificial silk is putting new life into the whole textile industry."

"Shall I go on?"

"I must finish beating the eggwhites, but I'll be back," Hermine said. "Yes, go on."

I slid down in the bed, I studied two pages of sketches by Christian Bérard. I slipped further down still and lingered over a photograph of a palace in London with trees and cars and people walking by. A great city, a great coquette behind her veil of mists. The palace had me in its power. Story after story, I climbed slowly up my Babel of desires. I had not known him, but I held my father in my eyes as I read "Walls and floors have been specially constructed so as to insure absolute quiet." I held him in my belly too, because my father loved London and now I was loving it with him. After that, I returned with more enthusiasm, more faith, more hope, to the following piece of advice: ". . . If you don't make up your lashes for the daytime, a very small quantity of this will make them silky and glossy, dark, pretty, and will even give them a graceful outward curl at the same time." I'm all for fashion magazines. From the least pretentious right up to the glossiest of them all.

"Schiaparelli is having a sale," Hermine said. She handed me the newspaper. "Read it. It says so here."

"A sale at Schiaparelli?" I said, flabbergasted.

The beater slowed down. She lit a Celtique and offered me a Camel. The beater started up again after a sip of Sandeman's port.

Hermine shouted in: "It's settled. We'll go on Thursday."

I ran into the kitchen, she scolded me for my bare feet. Leaning over the beater, her short-cropped locks falling into her eyes, Hermine was passionately absorbed in her eggs.

I said: "Would you dare? Would you dare go into Schiaparelli?"

"If it's a sale," Hermine said.

She led me back to our bed and told me not to get myself worked up.

Two days later, surrounded by broom, duster, wax polish, steel wool, and my crown of curlers, I returned to the subject.

"They'll throw us out."

Hermine was spring cleaning.

"The envelope is in the drawer," Hermine said. "What's the matter with you?"

What's the matter with me? A nostalgia for the gilded sleep of the wax polish, I who never sleep. Hermine will sew her own clothes, she will cut and weave garlands. As for money, the shiny slivers from our steel wool pad will suffice. I must be the champion of our everyday life. Yes, our neighborhood moviehouse, yes, the damp of our late afternoons, here in our furnished room.

"Don't let's go, Hermine! We mustn't go."

"Can't you see yourself in something by Schiaparelli?"

She could see me; her eyes lit up. Hermine's lashes were beating for my face too.

Rue de la Paix, four o'clock in the afternoon. Let us lap it up, Hermine, let us lap it up.

"There'll only be white elephants left if you don't get a move on," Hermine said.

The entrance to the jeweler's with its doorman's stool and its display windows, as sober and austere as a theorem, filled me with confusion. I refreshed my eyes in the light of the diamonds' nighttime festivities. Polaris and Cassiopeia immersed in the gaiety of a fountain. Millions of eyes winking on a velvet throat. I love diamonds, they have radiance; a diamond necklace stings me with witty icicles. The doorman rose, stepped down to the sidewalk and raised his cap in preparation for his rendezvous with a car door.

"It's here," Hermine said.

"This is Hellstern's!"

The fashion magazines with the pictures of the latest models and the bootmaker's name underneath were realer than the boutique and its niggardly display. Her window at last. Hers. Some American women passed, laughing, scented, feathers in the cap of tomorrow's fashions.

I gripped Hermine's wrist.

"This is hers. There's her name. This is really hers."

I could read the name Schiaparelli on the bizarrely shaped perfume bottles: the torso of a dressmaker's dummy.

"There's nothing there. There's nothing to see."

"Do you want people to come and copy them!" Hermine said. "Are you ready?"

Two young women, two superb young women, came out of the Schiaparelli boutique. Two more young women walked in.

"They come in twos. Like us," Hermine said.

". . ."

"Are you going to hang back?" she asked.

"Go in," I said to her. "Go on in!"

She obeyed. I sensed what was upsetting her: her round face, her red cheeks. I too was feeling ashamed of her face; it was bursting into flames, becoming far too conspicuous. They liked her though. A saleslady asked her what she required.

"We're just looking," I said, suddenly inspired, disdainful.

"Very good," the saleslady said.

I could read our furnished room in her eyes, I could read the envelope containing our money. We made mutual confession with our looks.

Hermine took my arm.

"You're already where you belong," she said.

A perfume already held us in its power, as it held the walls, the carpets, the basketwork dummies. You stepped in, and it dragged you on like a voluptuous waltz into a ballroom where the dancing had already begun. We were breathing the luxury of Paris.

"They sell everything already scented," I said to Hermine.

I went over to the counter facing the main entrance door. Hands were soothing the sharpness of their appetites by picking up stoles, handkerchiefs, silk squares, woolens. The French customers were talking a secret language. I was unable to fathom the nonchalance of their manner. I had been mistaken. The silk smelled of silk, the jersey smelled of jersey. The scented walls perspired.

"I've got a white one," Hermine said.

"What's the matter?"

"I've got a white hair."

She had extraordinary eyesight. She was playing with it standing a long way from the mirror.

"I'll pull it out for you."

Hermine turned scarlet.

"Here! You're out of your mind."

I took off her beret.

"Either I pull it out or else we go home. Choose."

"Why do you want to pull it out?" Hermine asked sadly.

We were standing there as though we had struck roots.

"All right," Hermine said, "pull it out, take it."

It didn't occur to her to run to the mirror and quickly perform the operation herself.

I led Hermine over to the entrance.

Two elegantly dressed women walked out with a look of disgust. We were despoiling their haunts.

"Have you found it?" she asked miserably.

"How do you expect me to find it? If you would just turn your back away from the light . . ."

Hermine turned to face the Place Vendôme. I pulled out the hair and gave it to her.

"The Maison Carrée," she said, wild-eyed.

I looked out with Hermine across the Place Vendôme, at the ant-hill of rectilinear façades. I couldn't see it. I was bewitched by Schiaparelli.

"Yes, the Maison Carrée," Hermine said again.

Her eyes were swimming as she smiled at what she saw.

Two more elegant women came in brushing her and her dreams aside. Hermine was holding the hair between her thumb and fore-finger.

"The Maison Carrée is in Nîmes."

Hermine gazed at me. The reproachful desolation in her eyes was saying: "I can't give you what I found out there, I can't."

"It will always be the Maison Carrée every time I come here," she said with a great big sigh.

Hermine was still holding the hair between her thumb and fore-finger as the open-topped elevator lifted us with the ponderous majesty of a duenna up to the second floor.

"Mme. Abadie's fitting," a saleslady shouted up the stairwell.

Mme. Abadie, standing next to us in the elevator, told us with a gentle look, with a modest movement of the eyelids, that the fitting was hers. It had been many years since Mme. Abadie's fingers first began wearing out those rings. A saleslady came and led her away. Paying to be beautiful, paying to be yet more beautiful also meant being spoiled. Mme. Abadie moved off with the saleslady. I wandered with Hermine into a circular salon. There were women sitting facing marble walls and mirrors, trying on hats. The hats lacked calm, but the strength in the presence of a velvet crown, the secret of a scarlet cherry, inspired love and thanks in the beholder. Between the "isn't it original, isn't it exquisite, wasn't it made just for you?" of a saleslady and the "I must say it's ravishing, I must say I'm tempted" of a customer to the saleslady, I asked where the sale was. Hermine was frozen by it all; I was fascinated by their adjectives. We moved on into a medium-sized salon. The noise of the hangers being lifted off their rods, the noise of the hangers being replaced on their rods, produced the tinkling rhythm of a forge inside the room. The clips on the dresses, on the suits, on the coats enchanted me.

Brass, kid, twin crescent moons, tubes wedded into the shape of a capital H.

"Their satin is as thick as leather," Hermine told me with the knowledgeable tone of an artisan appraising a new discovery.

I felt the tightly packed texture of a dress.

"It's silk," a saleslady told us as she walked past.

"It's impossible," Hermine said. "No hem, three rows of holes around the bottom and thicker than wool. Try this one on. I'm sure it will suit you. Silk? But how do they manage it?"

"Do you think it's expensive?"

"It's beyond price," Hermine said.

"It should suit you. You have a mannequin's figure," a voice said behind me.

I swelled with pride.

"I told you so, squirrel. You wouldn't believe me," Hermine said quietly. "Yes, you have, a mannequin's figure. . . ."

Mannequin, mannequin . . . I'm a mannequin, I said to myself, and felt disheartened. I was in a quicksand. Help me, Hermine, I implored. I'm a mannequin standing all naked in a fashion house, I'm sinking into a quicksand and soon you'll see nothing but my head.

A saleslady pointed to a cubicle and said we could go in there. A little fitting room, a triple mirror, a chair, a curtain on rings. Isabelle's cubicle, Isabelle's dormitory, Isabelle's rings, Isabelle's percale curtain. Isabelle . . . those other days . . . My heavy memory in its heavy armor.

"Give me your things, I'll hold everything," Hermine said in that tiny island of silence.

I saw myself three times at once as I took off my coat near the triple mirror. The lighting seemed harsher than in our furnished room.

"My God," I said to the mirror.

Hermine clutched my coat in her arms with the eager willingness of a little groom. We were joined by a saleslady, at once simple and artfully elegant in her black uniform. She asked Hermine if she wanted to try anything on. Hermine blushed, stammered out an apology, gestured toward me. The saleslady's sympathy disappeared, leaving only her professional manner behind.

"Let's look at the jacket first," the saleslady said.

I disturbed the silk lining from its slumbers. I enjoyed looking at the saleslady's face. The long face of a madonna putting everything in order, abolishing my disorder.

"Do you like it?" the saleslady asked Hermine.

I tried on the skirt.

"Is it brown? Is it gray?" Hermine asked.

"It's eel," she answered. "You can wear it with a ribbed lamé blouse."

"The things we shall have to say to each other" Hermine's eyes sang to mine.

"I'll leave you to think it over," the saleslady said.

She effaced herself from the cubicle like a discreet supporting actor.

Hermine hugged me in her arms.

"Oh! If I got it dirty!"

She stopped hugging me.

"Do you think she guessed about us?" I asked.

"I hope so," Hermine replied.

Her face was still lit up.

I didn't dare sit down, I didn't dare look at myself in the triple mirror. I just remembered the perfection of the cut: the wide shoulders and the pinched-in waist.

A transference of thoughts:

"And that's how you're built," Hermine said.

The saleslady came back.

"We'll take it," Hermine said.

"And you?" the saleslady asked Hermine. "Isn't there anything you want to try?" she insisted, as though she sensed how much Hermine had sacrificed herself, as though she could help her become her own woman again.

"No . . . ," Hermine said. "Really not."

The saleslady flashed her an assortment of delicate and encouraging smiles as I changed my clothes again.

"We have some very pretty things on sale, you know," she said.

Hermine closed her eyes to help her say no again.

I clutched the envelope containing our little hoard of money in my hand as I stood waiting for Hermine to say: yes, I'll buy something, yes, I'll look at something. Everything was shapeless, I could no longer distinguish what was possible and what was impossible.

I took out the money without showing our envelope. I gave it to the saleslady. She vanished.

"I'm so happy I feel slightly crazy," Hermine said.

"You can tell me about it later."

Hermine's attention was elsewhere.

"You pronounce it Skiaparelli," she exclaimed. "I just heard them saying that Mme. Skiaparelli will be here tomorrow. You're not listening."

I wasn't interested in anything.

The saleslady with the smooth hair handed the shiny white box to Hermine because she was determined to give her something. She said she hoped she'd see us again soon. We made our way through the crowd. The slim ankles were shimmering because of their expensive silk stockings.

"Let's walk once around the square, around your Maison Carrée," I said to Hermine.

Porters and elevator men were coming out to meet a couple, to take their baggage out of an automobile.

"The Ritz hotel," Hermine whispered.

She puffed out her cheeks. Pom-pom-pom-pom, she beat out Beethoven's *Fifth Symphony*. The triple mirror in the fitting cubicle came back to me with the savage glare of a car's headlights. "Oh be quiet can't you!" I exclaimed.

"It was music," Hermine said apologetically. "Guess where I'm taking you. Have you forgotten a certain remark about ribbed lamé?"

"I don't care," I cried abruptly.

"When will you be satisfied?" she asked.

I turned my back on Hermine, on the buildings, on the sky darkening into harmony with the stone, on the petunias shivering on a balcony.

"Never," I said between clenched teeth. "I shall never be satisfied."

"Let's go and buy the ribbed lamé," she begged.

I began to cry.

"People are looking at us, people are looking at you," Hermine said.

". . ."

"Come on squirrel, come to Colcombet's with me. It's just around the corner," Hermine said.

I fell into her arms. The cardboard box fell on the sidewalk.

"You won't leave me?"

"I won't leave you," Hermine answered.

"We'll always live together?"

"Always," Hermine answered.

Her eyes were sparkling; and yet they were sad.

She hummed the beginning of the *Fifth Symphony* slow movement. Then she sang the name of each note, and the mi-la-do-si-la-do brought us together as we stooped to pick up the shiny white box.

We walked past Elizabeth Arden's neat little candy box of a boutique. Elegant women were turning into it and being swallowed up. Hermine was looking for Colcombet's, the silk makers.

Then smack in the eye. A head of hair, a torch flaming with life: Hermine's first white hair. It was living again, resplendent amid a harvest of hair where the Place Vendôme's column should have been. Turning on themselves, the locks of hair swept the windows and the mansards all around the square. The summer lay unresisting as the strands made love to it, fanned it, caressed it.

"I'm looking for Colcombet's. You could help. . . ."

"I'm looking . . ."

"What at?"

"Nothing."

The florists were delivering roses, lilies, irises, or lilacs in long doll boxes, wrapped in beautiful tissue paper. A doorbell rings, the flowers are carried in asleep. Father, make up your mind. I'm old, I'm the age my grandmother was when she died. You would be eighty, father, if you were still alive. As it is, your youth is too bizarre; if you'd lived, your age would be more seemly. It's absurd, it's invigorating, what I'm asking of your ashes. Father, sink into the sleep of the lilies, the roses, the irises, or the lilacs in their box. Then I'll wake them up one by one in my room, I'll waltz with the gardeners' masterpieces. Their greenhouses, my mother says when she talks about my father's family. To break off a branch of lilac in a winter greenhouse when I'm sick, when my loneliness would freeze a stone. One branch, just once. Too late, it's all over. My big nose is pressed against the florist's window, my big nose is so near the dew on the other side, so close to the shivering dewdrops; and I shall crush it closer, that big nose, I shall see the lyre quiver again and watch its strings run down the window.

I told myself that I was in a National Gallery of rare fabrics, precious fabrics, mysterious tissued fabrics. It was a big room full of shelves and drawers. The shiny wood counters were classically simple. Bare. All odor of memories, including the dusty smell of percale, shall be taken from you. They were taken from us. The salesmen came and went noiselessly, without one unnecessary gesture.

"Are you dressmakers? Do you have your card, please?" one of them asked.

We thought the game was up, all purchase prohibited, the silks forbidden us. Hermine recovered first.

"I make dresses," she said, "though I'm not really a dressmaker."

The salesman was softened by the word lamé. He disappeared into the back depths of the room.

"You haven't changed your mind? You want it ribbed?"

"Hush, wait," I said in a whisper.

The salesmen were arranging, disarranging, rearranging the boxes along the shelves.

Our young salesman, anonymous as an acacia leaf, slid several boxes onto the counter, sure of himself in advance. When the lids were off, he gave a light, oh a very light tap on each fold of paper as he turned it back. The gold had dozed off in Colcombet's lamé, whereas the bronze was glittering with life.

"That's what we want," exclaimed Hermine.

"Yes, that's it!" I cried too.

The salesman raised his eyes and looked at us. He unfolded the lamé with its pinkish gray shading between the ribs. He was conducting a service. Wordlessly, he showed us the reverse side with its backing of pinkish muslin. We were jubilant.

"How much do you want?" he asked finally.

In a dream, without illusions, automatically.

Hermine explained the blouse with a drawstring neckline. The price was of little importance. To have found it without a search, to have found it without having to choose . . . He measured out what we would need for the blouse, ignoring the measurements we gave. A priest does not ask his congregation how to celebrate a Mass.

"Are you interested in any silk?" he asked. "I have some new embossed ones that have just come in. Shall I bring them?"

Hermine almost clapped her hands. "Oh yes, please bring them."

Other salesmen came over, deferential and amused.

I squashed Hermine's foot with mine, I scratched her wrist under the counter. I took hold of her hand and put it into the pocket of my coat so that she could feel the envelope which had just enough of her savings left in it to pay for the lamé.

I invented an urgent appointment.

We were exhausted by the time the café between Maxim's and La Cour Batave swallowed us up. Our own world again, a soufflé of orange blossoms! The customers devouring their evening papers at the tables or at the bar ignored us yet kept us company at the same time. The sounds inside the café, the sounds coming in from the street all helped us to relax. Paris was freeing itself from its stores, from its offices, from its workshops, the warmth was the warmth of men and women at liberty, and our croissants dropped their petals onto our knees, onto our saucers. We emptied the basket, our appetite was not beyond our means.

It was only a truce. In the bus, Hermine whispered in my ear:

"An eel-colored felt hat from Rose Descat, you shall have that too. And high-heeled shoes to match from the shoe place, those too."

Hermine cut out the blouse, tacked it, fitted it. She went to bed at four in the morning and got up again at six.

Drums are you ready?

Your cheeks ache from not being beaten. My drum roll will make you rejoice. Drumsticks, strike. Drums, beat out your delight, and slowly, slowly. Keep time, long fingers from the forests. And long live the last dying beat, a tiny wing left quivering in the air. First drum roll: my stockings, my silk stockings. The bees shall give their luster to my legs. I shall emerge from our room shining in shards. Today made by Gui, tomorrow by Bel-Ami. The silk is delicate, a stitch runs, strange murmur. A stitch runs and glides down a slope devoid of skiers. The feet are always too big. I pull on my stockings, a more serious task than people think. A moral duty, the seam in the center of the calf, the seam must be straight, the pure descent of the calf. The white skin is alive for the rich eye of the painter. "The hussars of the guard," Marie Dubas sings in the music halls. I am a "hussar" with my boots halfway up my thighs, a "hussar" as I stand naked before the closet mirror. A bizarre sewer-worker, a bizarre musketeer, a bizarre cavalier. I will not dream myself away with you, mirror. The spurs of Mercury are not what I desire. What am I, what shall I be when I emerge? A slender mare. A little respect if you please for a satiny skin that is no longer mine since I took the veil of coquetry and offered up my own to this glove of film. Drums, drums.

Second drum roll: someone has knocked, it's ruined. Who is it? The charwoman; Mme. Péréard wants to know if we need the exterminator again I don't think there's much point, my friend killed one the day before yesterday and there's been nothing since then, yes, let's hope it was the last, yes, the key will be on the board. Second drum roll: let's make it simpler. The skirt, the blouse over my Candide, that is, my garter belt in dark satin. Speak, mirror, say you're tired of copying me, say it's not a pretty sight, not really a pretty sight to see a thigh in the grip of a garter, squeezed by a stocking top. Mirror, you have no imagination. Two columns, marble from Delphi of course, two columns upright in the depths of your waters, mirror on my mirrored closet. If I could only sew my stockings with a running stitch into my flesh . . . Rata-ta-tat ra-ta-ta-tat pianissimo almost to tears for the silk lining inside the Schiaparelli skirt. You pronounce it Skiaparelli. I just heard them saying that Mme. Skiaparelli will be in tomorrow. Chairs, sofas, benches will not crease my skirt. It is far above such things. Drums, a trifle more lighthearted, I am plucking off a first anniversary, my first anniversary of luxury, of coquetry. A skirt in which a waltz is waiting hopefully. Cut completely on the bias, Hermine says. It turns, it is sensible, it shows off just as much as a tight-fitting skirt. Tomorrow I shall buy *Vogue*. Our vegetables are sticking, our vegetables will be burned. We shall eat my afternoon, we shall eat the story of my afternoon walk.

The drum rolls I need as I write, I remember now where they came from. July 25, 1960. After a journey backwards of thirty years, another journey backwards of only five. The summer of 1955, the beginning of my forty-eighth year. In the summer of 1955 the persecution had not begun. Summer 1955, sinister betrothal, against my will, against their will, with those who were tracking me down without my knowledge. All candor gone; the banks of all the world would not suffice if I had to ransom my lost candor. Summer of 1955. My Ibiza, for me so full of failures. Ibiza, my jewel, my darling, my white Araby wreathed in a Pierre de Ronsard wall as our boat moved to meet you through the sullen dawn. Ibiza after the gangplank, Ibiza, a sidewalk where the fiesta is a procession of aesthetes. Ibis, and even better: Ibiza (pronounced Ibissa by the French). Summer of 1955. Ibiza winding upwards, up and up again toward my hotel, on the right of the harbor. The ramparts of Toledo again, again. The ramparts with their folds, their hesitations, the effort of the climb. Here, the island is the reality of that house I used to trace out with chalklines as a child. No pardon, no postponement, no pardon, no reprieve. The heat of one o'clock in the afternoon, the world is a tightrope, the barracks is under the fig tree. The young soldiers sitting in a circle under the leaves are peeling potatoes. Lost in their greatcoats, they are peeling with the very tips of their knives. Their comrade, sitting with them, the drum between his knees, plays without heart. Singular potatoes, singular fatigue: without tragedians, a tragedy.

It is pleasant, drums, to hear you catch exactly the right tone. I am playing too: I am patting the dark-toned make-up on my Nordic-skinned face. I pat, I slap the make-up on, I slap my skin. Those are the instructions. Caveman, if I could but teach you to read, if you could only read what I write. Imagine a tiny porthole of pink lacquer, a circle of pink swooning with its own pallor, inside which there lies a disc of paste, a concentrate of timidity. That is "heavenly pink," the creamy covering for cheeks that are betraying the blows dealt by their enemy: the winter wind. A few circles on the left cheek, a few circles on the right cheek, for it must be patted in before you spread it out, that is the secret of a natural base, of perfect make-up, the saleslady told me so quite clearly. Where did she buy that timbre for her voice before she began selling things? I should like to become persuasive. You know you're getting ready for the circus, smudged clown in the glass. Drums, into training, all fatigue forbidden, I am about to do my circus act and my ring is to be the wide boulevards of Paris. Now "apricot" powder . . . Luxury teaches us to dream of luxury. The golden clasp of the powder tin cries out, at this instant, for the studded sword-belt of some fabled medieval knight. I must pat with the powderpuff, pat again, pat the abundance of a piled-up wig on either cheek and wait. How long must I go on drawing up the perfume from the powder tin? The surplus once brushed off in a cloud, to the devil with advice, good taste, and such discretions: a mouth drawn on in bleeding red that will be the envy of every butcher out delivering his meat. Blue on the eyelids . . . Indispensable.

Fourth drum roll: it's blue, it's cold. They will say that the poplars wept this angry azure down on my closed eyelids just before a July rain. In a restaurant, in the ladies' room, a femme fatale made up her eyes with the delicate grace of a fly sharpening its feet. An allegretto. I am blackening my eyebrows, Hermine. I'll tell you about it later. Hermine scolding the little pinafores, Hermine shouting in the playground. No time now, the asphalt is summoning me for the performance. As defenses go, Hermine, the lamé was a good defense to choose, down there amid the sickening odor of the public school. Bells, bells even freer in their bell tower. As if the moment had come to be married to a mirrored closet . . . Bells. There is a village dancing wildly here in our city.

Fifth drum roll: a little more stately, drums. And the bells. But I, I have organ pipes around my neck. I am wearing the Toccata, I am wearing my beloved tightly around my neck. She scratches when my head bends forward. I must bear that, since it must be borne. I have poor hair, it falls out; my hands are very ordinary. It's beginning again, it has me in its grip again. The triple mirror at Schiaparelli was a vampire. I look terrible. The banks of a canal, if I dived into it, would draw apart. I feel the pain of it in the entrails of my great mouth, my big nose, my little eyes. Pleasing others, pleasing oneself. Twofold bondage.

Sixth drum roll for the crown of curlers being removed: Hermine, please, please, Hermine, give me new hair. I want Ginger Rogers' hair. Hahn hair tonic, there's nothing like Hahn's, says my mother. But there's something better. Lady Abdy knows what it is. Lady Abdy is beautiful for all eternity, and I'm a fright.

Seventh drum roll: drums, a hint of the death march, this is the moment. I slip on the Schiaparelli jacket, isn't that a solemn moment? To cut cloth like that, it's witchcraft. It has something of everything in it: a groom's vest, a bolero, the vestigial arrogance of the Spanish dancer's jacket. It's bitter, I have a lemon in my head, a lemon drying up, I have swollen shoulders, I am a gypsy glittering with sham gold, I wonder where to go, where to sit, what to do. Hermine, can you tell me what I'm good for with my brass clips? Desolation of desolations, my hair is lusterless. I feel sorry for you, extraordinary garments washed ashore in our furnished room, I pity you, shiny white box clasped in a chambermaid's grubby hands. Poor hook there inside, was this where you were meant to end up? Mrs. Fellowes, the Princess de Faucigny Lucinge . . . I can't even recite my *Vogue* by heart. Enough, the store windows will show me what sort of figure I cut. No, another look. The waters in the mirror are my audience. I could eat my new eel shoes with a knife and fork. It's nice, a mirror. It doesn't tire you out. It takes, it gives back, love, always love.

A last drum roll for the hat from Rose Descat. I burst into helpless laughter, I see myself bursting into helpless laughter. With good reason: I raise the eel felt hat from Rose Descat high in the air, I am a great prelate putting on his miter. A feather, this felt. No heavier than a feather in the wind. As my mother always says again and again: a hat makes you look younger, a hat shades your face. It makes me look softer. It isn't masculine, it isn't feminine. The brim is neither wide nor narrow. It has that air of sobriety that never goes unnoticed. A last look, from the head down to the feet, from the feet back up to the head. It is perfection, the outfit is worth far more than we paid. It is beyond price, that was the phrase Hermine used. I must have gloves from Hermès. I shall use a different voice. I shall need a hoarse voice like Marlene's to answer the compliments. And now, out with you, filth. The drum under the fig tree on Ibiza would start to stink, you would change all the little soldiers in their greatcoats to carrion. I'm chic. There's no mistake about it, I'm chic. The purse cut out of cardboard and covered with cloth, good old Hermine, I won't forget that either. Under the arm, that's the fashion now. As I stand ready, I'm new from top to toe. I wonder where to go.

Boulevard des Capucines at half-past four in the afternoon.

Paris, be more transparent, I beg of you. I can't see myself in all the windows. I have oil in my joints, thanks to my gymnastics. The policeman smiled as I went by, a lady in a car looked after me. Yes, she turned her head this way. Soon the river of automobiles will have frozen, the drivers will climb out onto the roofs of their cars to see me more clearly. You've got to face up to it, Lolette. Apart from the policeman, apart from the lady in the car . . . dying of boredom . . . I walk on, unnoticed. It's horrible, it's unbearable. I am not the center of the world. One, walk in the middle of the sidewalk. One, tear myself away from the store windows, from the things in them. Two, throw back the shoulders. Three, throw back the head too, head up above all, otherwise they'll think I'm a hen looking for grains of corn. Have the sculptured buttocks of a bullfighter. Sculpted in marble, but a little dimpled. Set off that bullfighter's costume. The color of the braiding startling the spectators' eyes in the biting sun. My buttocks are sapping my strength. I'm collapsing, I'm afraid, I'm going to disappoint my audience. There are so many strangers behind me. They are saying to each other: carries herself well, walks well. Yes, of course, of course . . . carries herself well, walks well. Then comes my face, then comes the surprise, the shock. I should detach myself from my clothes, become separate from them while still staying inside them. That's what poise means. I should hover above my mere possessions. I'm learning, no mistake about it, I'm making progress. I walk on, unnoticed. It's unjust. I can't turn my head. My mother taught me it's a sign of bad breeding. I hope a man's going to follow me. What have I to lose? I'm in the bosom of my family: the other people in the street. I hear steps keeping time with my own. A decision being made. Now it's made. Really! He's yawning and moving away. That tall young woman coming toward me in the mirror of the Old England shop is me. Perfect, absolutely perfect. Subject for an essay: describe a Paris boulevard at half-past four in the afternoon. First sentence: I saw a tall figure dressed in pale brown, the color of chestnut paste when we're making the Christmas cake. If I don't speak to him first, he won't speak to me. He'll move away, he'll yawn. He speaks:

"May I offer you something?"

I can't answer him immediately, I am still working on my Marlene Dietrich voice. He walks beside me. Tch . . . I've lost him. Major defeat despite all efforts beside the Opéra; a half turn toward the Café de la Paix. The floods of foreigners go to my head. Strolling by from every country in the world. They look at me without seeing me, I took such trouble. My lambs, I am looking for blank checks on every table, the crock of gold at the end of the rainbow. Well, so are we all. Two English girls, very young, in the outside row. They're in love. Paris unites them; the noise makes a nest for them. I am alone, without a job, without plans, without a future. Saturday afternoon: my time to rest after the news items for the newspapers. I was always surprised by idlers, I used to go for walks, make little trips. A sickly time of day. Now I am an idler, I have Hermine. She is killing herself to pay for my little shoes.

"I asked you if you would like something. . . . You must make up your mind, my time is limited."

The same one again. He was following me. Discreet.

"No, monsieur, I'm not thirsty."

"We could meet again later for an apéritif. . . . I find you attractive. It doesn't happen often. My time will be less limited this evening. I don't say that we could spend the whole evening together. We could get to know each other. Till this evening then? At cocktail time? Without fail?"

"Yes, till this evening without fail at cocktail time. Good-by, monsieur."

"Don't forget."

"I won't forget. Yes, monsieur, the first to arrive will wait for the other. At seven o'clock here. I shall remember. Good-by, monsieur."

*

"No, monsieur, that wasn't my husband who just left."

"A friend, no doubt, someone you've known a long time . . . If he is your husband you can tell me. It's nice, a husband one leaves behind while one does a little shopping. . . . The ladies need so many things. There's the husband and then there's the little friend. Don't get angry. You are getting angry, you see I wasn't mistaken. Your husband was saying: come home early because I shall be back early this evening. That's just my luck. Isn't that what he was saying?"

"No, monsieur, it wasn't my husband. I have no husband. No, it wasn't my . . . whatever you said. He was arranging to meet me later."

"You're very stubborn. If it wasn't your husband and it wasn't your little friend, then who was it? All right, all right. I can see you're getting annoyed. You're all alike. All so quick-tempered. But why should you be? You can ask me if I'm married. I was expecting you to. But you haven't asked me. What would you like me to tell you about? I'll tell you about anything you like. A lady must always be kept amused. I can talk to you about everything, and about nothing. There's not a single subject I'm frightened of. You seem puzzled that I should be talking to you like this."

"Talk to me about my voice."

"Your voice reminds me of Marlene's voice."

"Really? I'm so pleased. . . ."

"You must have been told that often."

"Yes, people do quite often tell me my voice is like Marlene's."

"Are you in the movies?"

"No."

"These days everyone wants to be in the movies. Beddy-byes, those are the best kind of movies. Don't you think so? Now, without getting on your high horse, why don't you just come with me . . . somewhere private . . . where we can be together, just the two of us."

"Somewhere private? I'll think about it."

"You need to think about it?"

". . ."

"You're wrong. I'm not an egotist, you know. I always put the little lady first. We have to make our pretty little chickens happy too. You're expected somewhere? You should have said so earlier. Time is getting on, I wouldn't have talked so much. A pity. Men are egotists. They think of their own pleasure first, they're so brutish. Whereas I'm thinking of your little rosebud, that little rosebud under your skirt. The day after tomorrow, would that suit you?"

"If you like, the day after tomorrow. On the sidewalk, yes, all right, on the same sidewalk. The day after tomorrow. I won't forget."

"You won't stand me up?"

"No I won't stand you up. Good-by, monsieur."

"You're smiling."

"Am I? I didn't know."

*

"May I introduce myself? I saw it all. I've been watching you for quite a while. Nothing escapes me. Two fellows accosted you. I followed the whole thing. Two of them, one after the other. In broad daylight, and not shy about it either. If I'd been you . . . Well, they've got their nerve. I was watching, I followed everything. Cool customers, both of them. Did they introduce themselves at least? No. I'd have bet that. They think anything goes, that type. People's manners today . . . Well . . . I saw you gesture to me, so I hurried over. When I say I want to spend a little while with you, it's not the same thing. With me it's genuine. I know a hotel just around the corner from here. Would you like to see it? You must go in first. I'm not free, I mustn't be noticed."

". . ."

"Come now. Don't you find me attractive? I'll whisper something in your ear: I like having my breasts stroked. I'm a man but that's what I like. You don't want to. Go screw yourself then. You thought that? You should take a look at yourself sometime."

"I was good enough to introduce myself with the most honorable intentions. I won't beat about the bush: you excite me. Will you come with me? I'll stroke you, you'll stroke me. All right then, you affected little bitch . . . Who the hell does she think she is, anyhow?"

I collapsed in the Rumpelmayer hen roost and ordered a Mont-Blanc, one of their elaborate ice cream confections. A dismal treat.

I returned home with aching feet. Hermine wasn't back and I wept into the old throw on the divan.

There was a mild knock at our door.

"The key wasn't on the board," Hermine apologized.

She threw her beret onto a chair.

"You've thrown your new shoes on the floor," she said without looking at me.

She picked up the eel shoes and, still holding her bulging and shapeless leather briefcase, she stood them up on the table.

"Lord, how beautiful they are, those shoes."

"They're killing me. They're too tight."

Hermine sat down on the edge of the divan.

"How hot it's been," she said to herself. "Did you have a nice walk?"

"I certainly had a walk!"

Hermine got up. She was tracing patterns on my shoes with one finger.

"I was thinking about the neckline of that blouse during playtime. Are you sure it isn't too tight? Doesn't the lamé scratch you? Do you still like your hat? Answer me. Tell me about it all. What's the matter? Why don't you say anything? What about your skirt? It isn't too long, is it?"

Hermine inclined her head when she spoke of my skirt. Her face was raining too much gentleness on me.

"No, the neck isn't too tight. Yes, I'm still as pleased with my hat. No, my skirt isn't too long."

Hermine was fondling my shoes, stroking the color of the kid.

"And your purse?"

"No one guessed it was cardboard."

"And out in the street, your shoulders, did you still feel your shoulders were too wide?"

"I . . . I don't know. My shoulders?"

"You felt they were too heavily padded. Where did you go?"

"Into Paris. Along the boulevards."

"I'll bring you my slippers, your feet will get cold."

"Your slippers, how lovely!"

I hugged Hermine in my arms.

"There are some surprises for you in my briefcase," she said.

I hugged her, her and her bulging, shapeless briefcase; and I was hugging Paris too, Paris, its cars, its policemen, its maniacs and their manias. A love fondue has to have things you don't love as well as the things you do love among its ingredients.

My desire, my refuge, my catastrophe. There were guitars quivering in my legs.

"No," she said. "Later."

I collapsed in a heap.

"You don't want to. You don't want anything."

"I love you," Hermine said, "and that's not enough for you."

"That's loving yourself as well."

Hermine looked hurt.

"Paris, Paris," I sobbed. "Let me, and I'll do whatever you want me to."

Hermine waited with her briefcase, her old dusty shoes, her shabby summer coat.

"You talk like a man," she said.

"You don't know anything about men."

"I can imagine the things they say, the things they ask."

"They ask you to stroke their breasts."

Hermine opened her eyes wide.

They ask that?

She unlatched her briefcase. She took out a bottle of Mumm's, a can of asparagus, a can of salmon.

"They're alone, they're unhappy. They have to have their little fancies. Don't you understand that?"

"No, I don't understand," Hermine sighed.

She combed her hair with her pocket comb.

"Now tell me all about it. Did people look at you?"

I took off my new clothes, I folded them, put them away, shut the door and the drawers on them.

Hermine was putting out the cookies she'd bought at La Montagne, a bakery near the Place de l'Etoile.

"Tell me about the way people looked at you. Did they turn around?" she asked, after the first sip of champagne.

Hermine lit a Camel, then a Celtique.

"Distinguished old men, handsome men in the prime of life, beautiful young boys, they all followed me, talked to me, paid me compliments. Such a success . . ."

Hermine poured more champagne.

"Start with the young boys. What type were they?"

Our neighbors began to quarrel as a languorous odor of roasting veal seeped under our door.

"What type? The Chateaubriand type, the Byron type, one like Shelley at eighteen. Enigmatic and beautiful."

"You're joking."

"I'm not joking. If I lied would you believe me?"

"Yes, I'd believe you," Hermine said with love in her voice.

"I'm not lying."

"What were they like?"

I drank down a glass of champagne. To see them better.

". . . Dark eyes you lost yourself in, slightly cruel mouths, shirt collars open, floppy neckties, rumpled hair, and raincoats flung over their shoulders . . ."

"You're declaiming," Hermine said.

My description was boring her.

"What did they say to you?"

"Let's see, what did they say to me? They were crazy about my eel-colored suit. They said that with a suit that color I was trailing chestnut-colored darkness through the death of a summer's afternoon. Another told me I was one of those sweet, infinitely seductive fall seasons in the Ile-de-France when the roses have not yet ceased to bloom; and another added that he would never forget the half boyish femininity of the living triangle sweeping from my shoulders to my waist."

Hermine drew in a deep breath, her breast swelling to accommodate such a vocabulary.

"Do people talk like that in the streets?"

"Of course, do you think I made it up? Don't they talk like that on the streetcars?"

Hermine's face lit up.

"No, they don't talk like that. We knit, or read, or think things over, all the things we have to worry about. They look for apartments in the paper, or make plans for their vacation. They're tired, the people in my streetcar."

Hermine told me she was going to start giving an extra private lesson every day. She handed me the pencil: work it out, work it out, quickly. I mustn't forget to have my unemployment card stamped twice a week either.

*

It was on a Friday, the day assigned to my quest for elegance, that I passed beneath the great portals of the building in the Rue Cambon that housed the salon of the famous hairdresser Antoine. I climbed a shabby staircase, walked into the premises of the Fox Institute, and stood near the reception desk. Near the desk where Lady

Abdy made her appointments and paid for her treatments. I had learned so much from *Vogue* and *Fémina.* Baboon, a voice roared inside me, do you presume to tread in the steps of one of the city's most beautiful women? The poorly furnished, lackluster premises were haunted by her face. The waters of the Fox Institute were flowing in abundance and without surcease.

I was about to leave. An old lady with tufts of hair all over her head asked me in an English accent whether I had an appointment. I was so intimidated by Lady Abdy that I stammered out: I've come to see you so that I can have beautiful hair. She consulted her appointment book. It was impossible. You'll have to come another time, she said. Some of my timidity began to melt when I heard the difficulty she had expressing herself in French. My eyes begged her for treatment there and then. She went into a cubicle that looked like one of our cubicles at the college.

"If you will wait here," she said, "someone will take care of you."

The telephone rang. The old lady talked into it in English for some time; then she said: "That was M. Fred Astaire. He's coming in tomorrow."

I blinked, blinded by the beloved name.

A dressing table in front of the window, a chair in front of the dressing table. That was all.

The attendant took up a handful of my hair.

"Yes, it is in bad shape. We'll have to do something about that."

Her eyes turned away from the mirror. Of the two, she was the one under the obligation.

She massaged my scalp with all her fingers, the thumbs curving outwards down the back of my neck. The scent of the pomade opened like a rosebud in the cubicle. She massaged so rhythmically that I slid slowly down into a delicious state of confession without having anything to confess. My slowing brain, my intelligence, as it shrank ever and ever smaller, was being transformed into perfumed pomade, taking on the color of wax. You are idle, you are unhappy, but if a working woman works on you, then you nestle down into your cradle of illusions.

She told me the pomade was a secret. The Fox Institute used tiny herbs shipped in from Italy to restore vitality to hair. When the massage stopped, my relaxation remained. A little girl came in with two water sprinklers.

"It's the lime in the water that kills it," said the attentive wraith at my side. "We wash and rinse with distilled water. It's so gentle. . . . The other is hard."

She spoke calmly, unemphatically, while her eyes flashed fire from the tools of her trade.

Distilled water, bought by the tiny bottle. . . . Now whole sprinklers, whole buckets of this costly liquid were at my disposal. Lather—rinse, lather—rinse. It went on for three quarters of an hour as my head grew steadily lighter. The ritual of the hot towels began.

"It's getting darker. I used to be ash blond," I told the old lady.

"Our herbs will lighten it again. You'll be very pleased when you see."

She left the cubicle.

I took my courage in both hands.

"Lady Abdy . . ."

The wraith wound another hot towel around my head first. Then she rested with her hand holding it in place.

"She comes here," she said.

Silence.

"She's beautiful," I insisted.

I looked at the attendant in the mirror.

"I don't know," she answered in a low voice.

My hair tumbled down like silk when the treatment was over. I was afraid I might meet Lady Abdy on the stairs. I didn't meet her.

It was only a step from the Fox Institute to Antoine's hairdressing salon. I took that step so that I could keep company with something I would never be: a rich and beautiful woman, a woman completely sure of herself. A moth throwing myself against a lamp in the dusk, I waited my turn before the appointment book that insured admission to the emperor of short hair. Antonio would take me at four that afternoon, the receptionist told me.

The fiesta of waving and setting, of scarlet nails, was in full swing. Customers, friends sitting next to one another, smiled and thanked their lucky stars with an exchange of glances as I removed my hat. I waited my turn once again in the imposing salon with its rows of dryers. Young women sat beneath their helmets, their hair wound around snowy curlers, imprisoned in nets, some reading or leafing through fashion magazines, others examining their legs, their nails, their feet. I found a hiding place between two dryers, but they discovered me even there. The heads looked up, the magazines lay forgotten on their knees. Their little mouths, their great eyes: the signs of their nobility, the blazon they wore already while still curled in their mothers' wombs. I swooned at the onslaught of so many pretty faces.

The footman opened the door, he put his hand on his heart, he bent himself in two to make his double bow.

Why had that chicken been sent to spy on me? He advanced toward me without hesitation, behind the footman.

The footman withdrew, leaving me with a ball of bristling feathers. "I can get annoyed too," I muttered angrily. Get annoyed and, at the same time, feel the roses of reconciliation raining down upon my heart. Which is what happened as soon as I saw that the chicken was a cripple. A crippled spy. The surgeon, the carpenter, had done a good job with that little splint tied to his shattered leg. He began:

"I was at the antipodes; I came back to save you."

"I'm here for my hair," I said crossly.

The chicken leaped onto one of the unoccupied armchairs.

"My case is stronger," he said.

"Your case? What is your case?"

"Your poverty. You want to be like them and you never can be. You are less than their lapdogs to them."

"Go away," I said.

"It's up to you to go away. Go back where you belong; dip your head in your enamel bowl. You're out of place here. Everyone senses it, everyone knows it. You're concealing too many things."

I went over to the armchair.

"Our furnished room?"

"Yes."

"Hermine?"

"Yes."

"My unemployment card?"

"Yes."

"Her school? The fact that she's a schoolteacher?"

"Yes."

"And the market? Doing my own shopping? Carrying the shopping bag?"

"Yes. Will you go? Are you convinced?"

"No, I won't go. I want two waves under my Rose Descat hat, I want a wave on each side of my face."

The little spy raised his eyelids. I thought he was dying.

"Poor girl," he said into the distance of infinity.

The eyelids were lowered again.

"I feel so sorry for you. You're so unhappy, so hemmed in, so deprived. . . ."

"We're going to the movies tomorrow. We're going to see *Wonder Bar*. I want two waves under my hat. We're going to the Apollo."

"There's no hope," he murmured.

Despite his splint, the feathery spy leaped easily down from the armchair onto the tiled floor.

"Poor, poor girl. I pity you but I bow to you all the same." Saying which, he limped away, commanding my admiration for the gallant bearing of his feathered rump.

All the pretty women began loading me with torment once again. I ground my upper lip inside my mouth to make my nostrils more delicate. What are you, Lolette? You are one of those coarse faces wallowing in some Flemish painter's hell. At last I reached Antonio's chair.

And then Antonio smiled at me, widely, unceremoniously. And then, in the extraordinary mirror, a fresco reflecting the walls of the entire salon, I gave myself up to my sacred duties, a mantis preying on Antonio's face, Antonio's clothes, Antonio's body. His melodious voice escaped my devouring appetites. I asked him to make my hair like Joan Crawford's. I opened my handbag and showed him a photograph I had cut out of a movie magazine. He understood without my having to explain. Other customers came over to him, to say a last good-by, to discuss their next appointment. They couldn't tear themselves away from him. Antonio mocked them, was rude to them, but tactfully.

He was tall, he was supple as he bent over and shaped a head of hair with a touch so sure it created a sensation of well-being deep inside you. His skill was the skill of a sculptor, a master craftsman, a geometrician. He balanced the volumes, he combed in equations.

"I'm in pain, Antonio. I . . . fell on the stairs. On your stairs. Yes, here."

He looked at me in the mirror and laughed without malice.

"I fell, Antonio. Good-by, Antonio. See you soon, Antonio."

The woman, about fifty, dressed in pale gray, a great lady, a great rain of gold and silver, speaking in a foreign accent, tore herself away at last.

I'm fairly sure he told me she was from a very noble Polish family.

She rushed back again.

"I'll see you tomorrow. I . . . fell. . . ."

"It's your own fault," he said. "You shouldn't drink so much. . . ."

"Antonio," she exclaimed, wide-eyed.

"Antonio," she said again, indulgently.

My head was being covered with little snails of hair, and I wondered how he was going to change those little snails into tumbling waves. I handed him the pins, and if I made him wait I felt guilty. The questions flooded into my mind: how had he become the number one hairdresser in Paris? Were those his eyes in which a portion of the night had taken shelter? Did his gifts provide the energy that fed his radiance? He scarcely spoke to me, sensing that he would never succeed in drawing me out of myself. He fluttered above his task. Not obsequious, not superior. Forthright as a multiplication table. It was no labor to him; and yet it was a release too.

An attendant led me over to the dryer. On the way I checked my snails with my fingers. I sat down. I wept, I gave little whimpers through the noise of the breakers inside the helmet. I felt alone and abandoned when I saw two friends chance to meet. I sank down in my armchair; I climbed down, rung after rung, into a well of discouragement.

The wrists of the most beautiful women in Paris brushed against my wrists with the delicacy, the softness, the inevitability of tiny bat's wings. Their little noses with their arching nostrils fluttered against my temples. They got in my eyes, they stung my neck. Their sweet little feet hovered around me lighter than wild rosebushes. They skimmed over my shoulders. The slender fingers, languishing palely for a single jewel, rose in the air and allowed themselves to be carried like leaves floating down from branches. Their mouths, beautifully finished lips like wasps, teased and tangled the curls of my most secret hairs. An attendant switched off the dryer.

Adoremus for five voices.

Adoremus for six voices.

I am listening to this cantata for men's voices, for women's voices, as I go on with my story one August Monday of 1960. The voices are more heavenly than the gray heavens; the grave, deep voices rise up to a heaven that weeps on us every day. Suddenly, there is an unexpected clap of thunder, or more exactly, a rending and tearing noise that should free us from all this bad weather. And here is the crown of this instant snatched from the bad weather, from the music over my radio: Schubert's quartet: *Death and the Maiden.* My Clotilde, my beloved, my blood, my flesh, my sleep cure, my sickness, my little girl of fifteen, the young girl in my story *Les Boutons dorés*. I left Clotilde stretched out on a concrete bench in front of a railroad station waiting for a train due to leave at one-twenty-six in the morning which she will never take. I listen to the music. Death is a song, death is a searing pain. I am fifty-three, I am fifteen. The heart is wearied and the heart is refreshed by grief. Die, Clotilde, die in this music where your knell is a harmony. Georges doesn't want you, Georges has abandoned you. Clotilde, my little one, born of my wild errors and my wanderings, of my credulities and my ambitions. My little one, my child, my marrow and my inmost rhythm, my fifteen-year-old Clotilde, my five-and-dime Clotilde, my little maid whose maid I am. I loved a woman, I loved a man. From my two loves was born a child of despair. Mme. R— told me about her youth spent as a housemaid. Clotilde wriggled her way into it. Clotilde was born with a profession. Mme. R— lost her young daughter at fifteen. That Saturday, frightening in my stupefaction, I thought it was I who had been delivered. I was Clotilde, I was the young girl dying to be reborn free. The story has no end. Mme. R—'s little daughter (four years old) said to me the other day: "They're going to put you in prison. It was you who made Chantal die." And that is how the poor madwomen's remorse is born. No, Clotilde isn't dead. She lies in pain down there on her concrete bench. It is snowing beside her, it is raining all around her. An arid tomb, yet Clotilde still lives. The trains move off, the trains return, the whistle blasts pass over her. She will die with my first breath, since we die as we are born.

. . . An attendant switched off the dryer, Antonio brushed out my hair.

I went to the Boîte à Musique and heard Louis Armstrong. That did me good.

The same evening, two hours later.

We were nursing our apéritifs sitting outside a café on the Champs-Elysées. Praise, compliments for the two waves beneath the Rose Descat hat. Now Hermine had fallen silent and was contemplating the red glow of her cigarette in the silky lament of the falling dusk. Paris had a scent of expensive tobacco, Paris was scented with Mitsouko; the dusk, like dawn tumbling its dreams of light before it, was moving toward us with the caress of a wood fire sinking to rest. I turned my head: Hermine was so calm beside me, so close that she belonged to me. A hive of murmurs as the cars with their open tops filed past.

The day was sinking, doves were brooding on our shoulder, our skeletons were like silky hair, such suppleness, women over from America were spreading their sables across the evening, the potato chips were crackling in their waxy paper, a silken ladder was floating at rest above our heads. Already? Already the widow was there swathed in her purple. A different warmth, a different softness, and it was the night descending. A Camel? Yes, Hermine. Paris along the Champs-Elysées speaks every language in the world. The unmufflered roar of an Alfa-Romeo making an offering of its speed. Hermine swung her foot, I breathed in the sugary scent along my wrist. The old-timers were leaving, they left; the newcomers swallowed a glass of cognac and walked off also toward the Lido. Night. One had to tilt back one's head, then search for the depths of the night between two stars. Open your mouth, great city, a star is going to cry. Hermine suggested a walk along the Seine, on the embankments under the bridges. I accepted.

Gone were all the buildings and their office windows. Walls, partitions, things, little objects, erasers, scrapers, inkpots, tomorrow they would be given over to the darkness again just as they were today, there around the Rond-Point des Champs-Elysées. Was that the noise, the whirring, of a sewing machine? It was the unfailing rhythm of the fountains.

Reader, follow me. Reader, I am here at your feet begging you to follow me. My itinerary will be an easy one to follow. You leave behind the spray drops that were blowing to meet you, you make your way down toward the Place de la Concorde, being sure to take the lefthand sidewalk. Here you are, here we are. The miracle of the silence running along beside the noises. Reader, I want to tell you: we stepped up onto the sidewalk, we jumped with our feet together in the silence. A long, long scarf of natural silk held between the thumb and forefinger. We hauled it in. A caress as it flowed through the tightening ring of thumb and forefinger: the reality of a new silence that night. Reader, stay with us.

The modesty of the trees and their foliage.

"Are your high heels hurting you?"

"A little. I'm getting used to them."

The modesty of the trees and their foliage. More formally magnificent than the disintegrating jets of the fountains. Oh my countryside between the Place de la Concorde and the Rond-Point, you don't make me feel homesick for my countryside of wooden clogs. Born in Arras, here I am being born in Paris. The children's games a little while ago . . . The invisible will furnish me with memories. Hermine . . . Hermine let us walk more slowly. . . . It is our childhood of forbidden lawns we are unwinding, a pilgrimage without a beginning or an end. Let us stroll slowly, slowly. Everything is free between the Concorde and the Rond-Point. Something strokes my cheeks. What is it? Who is it? A ribbon, the night disguised as a young girl in 1830. Spring is infatuated with the past, and we shall return since we are meeting memories. Let us pick them from the bushes, let us harvest the tears we shed when we were six.

Place de la Concorde, the lights caught in the magnificence of their performance. The cars all fleeing into the dark. The space, the calm reflection, the proportions here, are not for those on the wing.

I dug in my heels, I wouldn't cross, I was afraid of the whirling sun of speed, those automobiles rushing in from every side. I gave my hat and handbag to Hermine. The breeze in my hair was encouraging. No, I wouldn't cross.

"Are your feet hurting? It's those high heels," Hermine said.

Who was nailing me to the spot?

Hermine tried to revive me; she talked about my waved hair, about the ribbed lamé in that festival of lights.

"I shall have to drag you over like a baby," she said laughingly, a little worried.

We walked across the spacious bridge. The banks were illumined far into the distance, glittering in honor of the river.

"There are some people behind us," Hermine whispered.

For all its splendor, we were obviously not going to be allowed to enjoy the evening in comfort.

There was a group of people following us. They passed us. Several men with one woman, all hips, with a face neither beautiful nor homely. Her words, her words were cried aloud as she pointed at me in the evening breeze.

"Oh!" I cried out too.

I had been given a staggering blow full in the chest.

"Oh, oh . . ."

A single blow can't be muffled. It has echoes. I felt other blows striking all over my body. My wounds were wounding the sidewalk. I was walking inch after inch through the offal of a slaughterhouse.

Ringed roundel of wood, it hurts, it . . .

"What's the matter? What's the matter with you?" Hermine asked.

She searched in my eyes, she panicked without a gesture, without a word.

Ringed roundel of wood. I am heaving up, thrusting out through my mouth all the insides of my head. Round target of wood for the darts in the fairgrounds, oh, oh. Roundel of wood, I can see you too well.

"Something's the matter. You're pale, you've gone quite pale. It was because of that woman. I didn't hear what she said. It was because of her, I'm sure of it. Say something, you're frightening me. They did your hair so beautifully. . . ."

The Schiaparelli suit is falling from me, disintegrating. Soon it will be just a heap of charred flakes. My stockings are falling down over my ankles, leaden colored, my legs are cold, I . . .

"Won't you tell me what's the matter? You're frightening me, don't you understand?"

"It's nothing," I said feebly.

The resignation over there, the sovereign resignation of the shelter waiting for tomorrow's bus. Resignation, resignation . . . Is it a place or is it a handkerchief waving to a departing ship?

Hermine took my arm. She held it in a vise.

"We'll go and look for a restaurant and have something to eat," she said with forced heartiness.

I am hurt, and now you are hurting me by squeezing my arm too hard.

"You could at least answer me. Would you like to go and eat?"

I am hurt and you are hurting me. Your thumb is digging into fresh brains.

She squeezed my arm harder and harder still.

"There must be a nice restaurant near here. They won't serve us if we get there too late," Hermine went on.

We were blinded by the headlights of an expensive sports car and my cheeks began to stretch. They sagged down over my brass clips and the metal made them cold. My cheeks were pulling my head over to the right, then to the left. My nose. Sudden and terrifying inflation; I was sweeping the bridge with my elephant's trunk. The little pebbles, the tiny fragments of gravel, the slightest accretions of grit on the sidewalk were tearing the skin off it.

Another car came by, a coupé driven by a chauffeur dressed in white, blinding us once more with its headlights.

"I'm quite hungry, you know," she said with false gaiety.

My eyelids, now I could no longer lower them, were merging into my forehead. The dirt in the air was coming into my eyes, my eyelashes were getting entangled with my hair.

"I was just thinking about our vacation," Hermine said.

"Yes," I answered with an animal moan.

Hermine moved to the other side of me. She put her arm around my shoulders.

I tried to make sounds. Nothing came out but the hiccups of a baby being fed, as though I were trying to spit out a great store of grief that would not shift from inside my chest.

Hermine, straining me against her, was massaging a pair of very old shoulders now riddled with wounds, wounds in the shape of tiny circles one inside the other.

I hurt and you are hurting me. Calf's head, pale tint of flannel, calf's head lying wanly on the butcher's parsley bed, give me your sleep, give me the calm ecstasy of your wide slit mouth.

"Why won't you walk? Why won't you say what's the matter? When we've eaten you'll feel less tired. . . ."

My yes emerged as the same moan. All my mucous membranes were studded with grit. Ten, twenty, thirty, forty passing cars blinded our eyes. It seemed to me that each car opened and closed its fist as the headlights swept by. My feet? My high heeled shoes? Flippers, but flippers made of mud and slippery clay slapping the ground far ahead of me.

The headlights of a long-distance bus returning to its depot hurled us against the parapet. Covered in night, peopled with the multitudes of History, the Seine was passing under us.

"You open your mouth and then you don't say anything," Hermine whispered.

"a e i o u," I moaned.

My trunk bent back on itself. I couldn't follow Hermine.

"Glue, glue, There's. On. The. Parap. Parapet."

Hermine retraced her steps.

"Talk, then you'll feel better."

The wind was rising. It was blowing cotton waste into my throat.

"Unstick me from the bridge," I begged.

She could no longer hear what I was saying.

Does one ask a swarm of dead flies to unstick themselves from their flypaper, to fly away again?

My sliced, scarred fingers, like strings of tightly tied sausages, could no longer move. A piece of hell, a piece of zinc, smashed down on my trunk.

"The wind is getting up, we must go and eat now," Hermine said.

Hermine threw herself on my neck. I couldn't put my arms around her: they were rakes with long teeth stiffening under the skin of my arms. My head rested against Hermine's, my trunk was giving me a terrible migraine.

"You're shivering the whole time," Hermine said.

A driver at the wheel of a luxurious custom-built station wagon was suddenly flashing his headlights on and off with the rapidity of a machine gun.

"Well well, making love in the streets now, eh, girls?"

Hermine began shivering too. The rising wind was determined to make the bridge into a desert.

"Where do you want me to take you, where do you want to spend the rest of the evening?"

My eel-colored shoes . . . Their high heels were tapping forward on their own along the sidewalk with the staccato rhythm of an animated cartoon; they were zigzagging from side to side.

The driver of the station wagon was playing at lights-on-lights-off with his headlight switch.

"Along the river. Take me along the river."

"You're speaking again at last," Hermine said.

We left the bridge and stepped down through the night. So alone, so old, so pitiful and orphanlike, we would have drawn a groan of pity from a flint.

I was weeping. The sand unloaded from a barge was too soft beneath my feet.

"You're not going to kill yourself?" Hermine asked through the darkness.

Kill myself: that would be too easy.

The wind wanted nothing to do with my trunk, with my flippers, with my gigantic eyelids. It stripped off everything superfluous. The wind, that evening, was scouring the world into transparency. Scrubbed clean, my grief was insupportable.

"Go away," I said to Hermine, without hostility.

The violins could wail more freely inside my stomach if she weren't there.

The wind carried a hint of something toward me, a surprise: a snatch of dance music on the air.

"Please, please, go away."

To sink, I had to make her disappear.

"I can see the river," I said in a low voice.

"You can see it?" Hermine cried from a distance.

I listened to it scalloping the edges of the night with splashes.

"How calm and wise it is. . . ."

"Calm and wise?" Hermine cried from a distance.

I wanted the stammering of the darkness as well.

"I'm cold," I said with all the misery of a lost child.

The wind was belaboring the small of my back with a fan, lights in the distance were making signs to me, a black throat was throbbing under an old tree: it was the river I loved.

I am at your service, come in, come in, why don't you, said the throat under the vast sky.

I will go in, effortlessly I will part the avenue of men admiring me, women wooing me, all kneeling in approbation of me, the sky will be the basket of linen I balance on my head. No no, oh no, because my carnival nose will float on the water. The profound opportunity had been missed.

I lay flat on my stomach in the sand.

"You'll be sick tomorrow. . . ."

"You've come back? Yes, Hermine, I shall be sick."

"I'm waiting for you."

"Go away."

She was walking on the sand, I couldn't hear her moving away. I was sobbing, my tears were moistening the sand.

Come back, Hermine, come back when I call you. I'll build it for you, your paradise, I'll build it with the down from our bed.

I looked around for Hermine.

"Here," Hermine said, "I'm here."

I looked for her in the other direction, battered by the darkness of the wind.

I gave her a kick, without wanting to. Hermine, stretched out on the sand as I had been, lay sobbing.

"You're crying."

"You were crying. I'm crying with you."

"You don't know what I'm crying for."

"That's why I'm in despair."

I helped her to her feet.

Then came the surprises hidden in despair, the freshness of an embrace, the abundance of grief.

We wound our arms around each other and we wept. We moved in a circle as we stood, we circled on the deserted bank, the tears from Hermine's nose running down onto my neck, my cheek. And the tears from my nose onto her cheek, onto her neck. Weeping with us too were the wind, the sky, the night. Sex and charity. Our ovaries, our clitorises were melting too.

Hermine licked at the tears running from my nose, I licked at hers.

"My little one . . ."

"My little girl . . ."

"My little one . . ."

"My little girl . . ."

We circled, we wept, we called each other "my little one," "my little girl" over and over forever.

"Tell me what that woman said."

"That woman, she shouted: 'If I had a face like that I'd kill myself.' "

Let's waltz, my darling.

Let's waltz, my love.

*

I shall have lived my whole life obsessed with food. My mother stuffed her daughter, her son, and her granddaughter with food because she was always afraid for their futures. Whenever some childhood illness or attack of the flu occurred she felt that all their years to come were in jeopardy. My mother will have spent her life, and taught me to spend mine, in constant fear of tomorrow. Not to eat as much as one can is to invite certain disaster. Anemic and on the verge of rickets when she left the nun's sewing room, a young girl—my mother—found her entrails suddenly crammed with the most phenomenal mass of provender: a child. For every million sperms in one jet of semen she countered with a million calories for the daughter they produced. You must be strong, otherwise you'll never have the courage to face life, she used to say. I was frightened, I always shall be frightened of tomorrow. Dying of hunger is the most difficult thing in the world to do, a friend once told me. Yes and no. I was carrying two futures of potato fields, of hayfields, of orchards, of vegetable gardens each morning I came home with two full shopping bags. I never tired of gazing at the marvel lying with its identical sisters on the greens. A marriage of sky and grass, of river and sea, of rainbow and silvery metal: a trout with its scattering of rusty spots. I owe my first trout to Hermine. I savored that quintessence of a grass blade and a stream. What I savored in a trout was its poem of timidity and fragility. The old eunuch who sold them—a gray shadow—upset me and saddened me. He would fuss over my prime cutlets or my slices of sirloin, he whispered sibilant suggestions or silly remarks in order to give himself the illusion he was an adventurous Don Juan. My answering laugh was always as false as it was stupid. I was at a loss when faced with this unhappy man all alone with his sex. I slipped him a tip just as the other housewives did, and he would tickle the inside of my hand. Then he would bend toward the next customer and tickle the hand that followed mine. We all find relief where we can.

In the afternoon I often found myself going back to our room as soon as I had left it and then coming out again in shabby old clothes. I would sit and knit in the public gardens of Levallois-Perret among the old men and women on the benches. I envied the blooming young mothers, I envied them their fixed and regular lives: the bar of chocolate, the roll, the milk, the oranges they peeled as though they were opening up flowers; I envied their calm. I forgot their responsibilities, their domestic crises, their duties. The happiness was a façade. I sat silently, I was always alone, I didn't think. The trees, the lawns, the birds, the lawn mowers . . . The mirage before me with its promise of the countryside pierced me to the heart. Hermine would come and meet me there at seven. I felt protected as soon as I saw her coming. She would suggest a visit to our neighborhood movie house while I said a silent good night to the immense platter of flowers in the middle of the lawn. The shouts of the very old little boys at play would echo through the vaults of my childhood, and I held out my hand to catch the spit from one of Fidéline's dying coughs.

I heard news of Gabriel: he had fallen ill. I have described in *Ravages* how I visited him in the hospital. It was a convalescent home for paupers where he had been sent after his terrible attack of typhoid. We looked for him among hundreds of uniforms, among hundreds of other convalescents in a courtyard, in a garden, against walls, between clumps of trees, beside the attendants. Men turned their heads toward us, offering us their sickly looks, their unshaven chins, the veils of illness over their eyes. A ghost grasped us by the hand. It was Gabriel. Hermine had brought him cakes, I had brought cigarettes and fruit. He didn't reply to our greeting. His green eyes looked at us, heroic. And cold that day. Impenetrable. His lips pressed together with rage. He led us into the covered recreation court without opening his mouth. A stab of memory: it was winter, hundreds of convalescents milling about in the livid lighting of the covered yard. We swam with them in their misery, watching as they cherished and blessed the stoves with their translucent hands. Gabriel sat between us brooding over a patch of damp on the wall. I forced myself to brood with him. There was a mother stroking her son's eyebrows, a woman kissing her lover's knee, then the patients without visitors coming and going, the old men gazing in admiration at their warmed hands. I was ashamed of my health, my freedom, my presence, my silence, our provisions. Hermine spoke to him and he closed up. I spoke to him also and he didn't hear. I offered him her cigarettes, but his long lashes didn't move, his hands refused to wake up. Gabriel continued his silence under cover of the bustle going on around us. We endured his silence for two hours, then we set down the things we'd brought for him on the bench riveted into the wall and, without any expression of kindness, left Gabriel to his private thoughts.

Three weeks after that visit I received an express letter from Gabriel: "I shall come for lunch on Sunday."

His ink was still the blackest of black, his capitals still streamed in the wind.

Two hours late. He must be coming from the Porte Champerret on foot. Were you expecting him to come in Louis XIV's state coach? Two hours of waiting to expiate his sacrifices. I'm sorry, I've come right across Paris on foot, please forgive me. An old crock, a corpse dragging himself across the city to see us eat. I hated him for his silence, I hated him for the smallness of his bunch of flowers, I hated him for his clenched teeth. He disappeared. He was my branch of flowering cherry; he was the bones of my body as I smashed them with hammer blows because I knew he was right, because I missed him the second he had gone.

*

We moved. No more furnished rooms. We had followed the construction of the apartment building in the Rue Anatole-France. Light, a bedroom, a kitchen, an elevator, I don't see what more one could want, Hermine said. I answered that there was something tight around my heart. No more paying for storage, we shall be able to have our own armchair and table, and you can practice on your Pleyel. You don't seem to like the idea. . . . Of course I do, squirrel, Hermine insisted. We were turning a page. Yes, there was something tight around my heart.

Once more the central boulevards, the Rue de la Paix, the Rue du Faubourg-Saint-Honoré, the formal confections at Rumpelmayer's, once more the Boulevard Malesherbes with my pauses, my long inspections outside the windows of La Crémaillère, the furniture store. I kept up each week with the changing displays, the departure of familiar pieces and the arrival of new ones. Now that we had a bedroom, a kitchen, a hall, in our modern apartment, I paused longer and longer in front of the tables laid with place settings or the furnishings for a cozy-corner, all complete and ready to be taken away. I fell violently in love with a low, almond green, lacquered table with a mirror joining its two wooden leaves. I went in, I asked how much it cost. I told Hermine the price and she gasped. I must forget all about it. I couldn't. I stopped again just to look at it, at its lacquer, at its mirror. A tall, gaunt man accosted me.

"No," Hermine said, "I won't go, I don't want to see him. You can go if you want."

Hermine was sewing for herself at last. A suit of flowing, absinthe-green satin with black stripes. She made it up piece by piece at night. The Pleyel my mother had bought me slumbered beneath its mahogany lid. I didn't play, and I didn't want her to play.

I refused to drop the subject. "Of course I won't go without you! He wants to see both of us."

Hermine tried on her skirt. I checked to see the hem was straight, then I put a record on the phonograph.

"Don't sew, I'm talking to you!"

"I'm not sewing," Hermine answered.

She stuck her needle into the satin. Now I was a sad book she already knew by heart when she looked at me.

"Shall I tell you something? The men that follow me, you don't give a damn one way or the other. Why can't you be jealous? Why can't you make me stay home? You don't even notice. As long as you can sleep, as long as you get to school on time, as long as the headmistress praises you . . . Of the two of us, you're the one who thinks most about herself."

From sheer weariness, Hermine put the record on again. The singer was pleading with the jazz band accompanying her.

"I'm always healthy, and that irritates you," Hermine said.

"Even when you're not asleep you don't say anything."

"I wish I could sleep, I wish I could rest. But it's impossible."

"Go on, say you're unhappy with me."

"How could I say that?" Hermine asked with the voice of a child being asked to lie.

"You'll say it one day."

Hermine shrugged her shoulders.

"I won't say it. Come here, come and sit beside me. Why don't you put your arm through mine while I sew, why don't you come and talk to me over here?"

Hermine went back to her sewing on the oak table. Her table.

I sat and dreamed about the lacquered table. My table. I couldn't understand what the singer was singing in her American accent. Sometimes her imprecations faded into the pain of a violin.

"Is it settled then? Are we going? He wants to meet us in the Ritz bar. You'd see what the Ritz bar was like."

Hermine sighed over her work. "Do you know what it's like?"

"No."

"Well then. The Ritz bar, the Ritz bar . . . Sherry is sherry. It's the same here as it is there."

"We would drink cocktails."

"We can drink cocktails here."

I lifted the lid of the Pleyel and slid my thumbnail in a glissando along the keys.

"Of course we could drink cocktails here. But the atmosphere, the setting, aren't you forgetting them?"

"I hate going out, I hate people looking at me. Would you enjoy it as much as all that? How old is he? What's he like?"

"How old? Sixty or so. Tall and gaunt. Well dressed. A long, pale face. A colorless voice. He must be rich. I met him on the Boulevard Malesherbes. . . ."

"Were you looking at the lacquer table?"

"How did you guess? 'Do you live alone?' No, I live with a girl friend. 'A girl friend? Very interesting. Might I arrange to meet you with your friend?' I'm not sure whether she'd want to. You know, men, as far as she's concerned . . . 'Even more interesting. Ask her.' And then he suggested the Ritz bar."

Hermine laughed. "What an old idiot he sounds. All right, we'll go."

We knew the entrance to the Ritz bar in the Rue Cambon because

Chanel's display windows were another of the attractions we used to stand and devour.

"The tall gaunt one over there. . . . That's him! Go on! There's an empty table in front of you. Go on! Everyone is looking at us."

The waiter helped us settle ourselves at the table.

"A glass of champagne," Hermine said.

"The same thing," I added.

There were eyes examining us.

"And this is the Ritz bar?" Hermine said.

She lit a Celtique and blew out a cloud of mild smoke.

"He's seen us, he's staring at us. He doesn't dare come over. I ought to go and speak to him. . . ."

"We might be at Paris-Plage," Hermine commented.

"It's a better-class place."

Hermine handed me my pack of Camels.

Her black eyes, her hair smoothed into a glistening mass with brilliantine, her mat skin, all stood out beneath the pale green suède hat on the side of her head. Hermine was sparkling. She took a sip from my glass.

"Look at him, give him some encouragement . . . ," I said to her.

"Me!"

"He's the reason we came here, isn't he?"

"You're the reason I came!"

"I was expecting you at my table. I hope I'm not being indiscreet."

He bowed to Hermine. The waiter brought over a small bottle of mineral water. Well-dressed women were smiling nearby: we had been labeled.

"Your friend has told me a great deal about you," he said to Hermine. (He had sat down facing us.) "She has told me that you play the piano remarkably well. Music is the most noble of the arts. Don't you think so?"

Hermine didn't reply immediately. I sensed that her red cheeks were tormenting her.

"I don't play remarkably well. You know I don't," she said to me. "I didn't win my Premier Prix," she added.

Shaken by this forthright admission, he made a show of blowing his nose.

"Would it be indiscreet if I were to ask you for your first names?"

Hermine turned her head toward me with a questioning look.

"Hermine," she said.

"Violette," I said.

The stranger drank a sip of mineral water.

"That's charming. Hermine-Violette, absolutely charming."

Hermine's satin jacket was beginning to slip off her shoulders.

"Tell me, squirrel," she said in an aside, without lowering her voice, "is it charming or is it a bad omen, our first names joined like that?"

"I don't know," I replied with embarrassment.

He cleared his throat. Hermine was ignoring him, Hermine was wounding him.

I said: "Do you like this place? Do you come here often?"

A slight flicker of animation reappeared in his anemic eyes.

"It's the first time for us, isn't it, Violette?" Hermine said flatly.

He looked at our glasses; he was at the end of his tether. "Why don't you have a gin fizz?"

"Do you want a gin fizz?" Hermine asked me.

"Yes. Call the waiter."

"Oh please," he said, "allow me."

He ordered two gin fizzes.

It was then that he began to perspire. Hermine's face was becoming redder. Oh, that satin suit! It was a torment to Hermine because it fitted so badly.

"Does your wife play the piano?" Hermine asked.

I stamped on her foot.

"My wife is an invalid. No, she doesn't play," he answered.

The conversation languished.

Help me, since I already know you a little, begged the man's faded eyes. I didn't dare.

"We could meet another time somewhere more private," he said.

He turned toward me.

"Would the Rue Godot-de-Mauroy suit you?" came his urgent whisper.

Hermine hung on my lips, begging me to refuse. Rue Godot-de-Mauroy . . .

"Does that suit you?" she asked.

"Why not?" I answered, lighting a Camel.

He paid the waiter.

"Have you read *Sanctuary*?" I asked suddenly, hoping to give us an air of consequence.

He was already shaking our hands.

"We'll talk about that next time, on the Rue Godot-de-Mauroy."

We arranged to meet again the following week.

Couples and men on their own were coming into the bar; Hermine watched him walk away.

Suddenly Hermine felt intimidated by the bar.

"Say we won't go, tell me you were lying to him," she cried.

She pulled her satin jacket back onto her shoulders.

"We shall have plenty of time to talk about it later," I replied.

She admitted how terrified she felt the following week, as we walked along the Boulevard Malesherbes. She stuttered like an old idiot woman. We caught sight of him suddenly, on the Rue Godot-de-Mauroy. He looked rather decrepit and sad. Hermine regained her calm.

"After all, he may be very nice really," she said.

"I didn't think you'd come," he said, as though we'd just brought him back to life.

"Is your wife any better?" Hermine asked with a lovely open smile.

He turned away his head.

"I'll go in first. You can follow me."

The affair was already settled. His manner was different from the week before at the Ritz. He was forcing his pace.

Hermine watched him as he walked away. "Let's go, squirrel, let's go while there's still time."

I got annoyed: "He's going in, we must follow him."

"Why do you want to do it? Why?" Hermine begged.

I pushed her after him.

"Let's go right up," the man said, quivering now.

I was already buried with my fears in the thick pile of the carpets.

A young housemaid showed us into a little drawing room with a mirrored ceiling and a triple mirror on one wall. There were naked women floating on clouds, and a large pouffe welcoming us.

"What are we doing here?" Hermine asked. "It isn't a bar."

"You're not a child, mademoiselle. Sit down. They are bringing you champagne on ice."

The maid came in. She set down the tray and vanished again.

Hermine questioned me. She pretended she was unaware of the man's presence. Was it a hotel or a private apartment?

"Both," he answered. "People make love here. Don't you think it's a charming love nest?" he asked me.

Hermine poured the champagne. It was a respite for her. He didn't smoke: he lit our cigarettes for us.

"Let's go now," Hermine said. "I'll pay for the champagne, then we need never think about it again. . . . The whole thing can be settled, Violette. We'll pay for the champagne and leave." Hermine opened her purse.

"Rotten spoilsport," I hissed. "What can you possibly have against this gentleman? You're always afraid of everything."

"I can see you're broad-minded," the man said to me.

"Squirrel, is it you talking like this? Do you like being here? The champagne is too sweet."

"The champagne is dry, Hermine!"

"It's too warm."

"The champagne is on ice, Hermine."

"I like seeing you both draw yourselves up like that," the man said. "Now we're getting somewhere, yes. . . ."

He crossed his legs. For him, the performance was beginning at last.

Hermine took off her hat. "Very well. I'll stay here, since you don't want to leave."

She refilled our glasses.

"Come and see your room," he said eagerly.

"Our room? You've been deceiving me," Hermine said.

He opened the door. Hermine went in first, plunging into the abyss so as to face the worst as quickly as possible. She hid her face in her hands and moaned: "Mirrors, mirrors . . ."

She moved into my arms. She was sobbing.

"Let's leave, my baby, let's go away from here. You shall have whatever you want."

The man was circling around the bed, his image reflected in all the mirrors.

"I'm terribly sorry. Do leave if she really wants to."

He sat down on the satin bedcover. I stood rooted to the spot as I wiped away Hermine's tears. I was supporting the weight of her head on my shoulder.

He left the room but returned with another bottle of champagne.

The alcohol had turned me into a faun that day. I was promising Hermine the most extravagant sensations. Broken in my arms, she listened and watched me in the mirror.

"Yes, if you like, but he must go away," she moaned.

He left the room again.

We clinked our glasses together and drank.

"He's bored out there, Hermine, he's all alone."

"Yes. It's just that I'm never bored, I'm never alone. I try to understand. But I don't."

"He may be unhappy."

"Yes, he may be unhappy. Let's drink to us, my little darling."

"To us. I don't think he can be dangerous."

"Yes, he may not be dangerous. It's true, he's alone and there are two of us," Hermine went on, as though she were referring to some mystery.

It was then that I suggested we undress. She wept for her wretchedness and her docility as I helped divest her of her principles.

He came in on tiptoe. It would be impossible to imagine a man more correctly dressed, more proper, more strictly made to measure. I undressed without taking my eyes off myself in the mirror.

And it was to the mirror that he ventured coldly: "You look like a Saint Sebastian."

A compliment is a springboard.

Lying on her belly, Hermine was waiting for me. I threw off the bedclothes, I forgot the man in the mirror, and I forgot Hermine, the better to worship the victim I had sacrificed.

"Make love to her. That is all I ask," I heard before I plunged into the abyss.

Close your eyes, don't look at them and they won't see you, I said to Hermine when her eyes encountered the mirrors with the man's face working on the ceiling.

The fleshless fingers handed me a glass of champagne as I lay there streaming.

Leaving the hotel was not easy. The man disappeared before we were ready, leaving us some money. We walked along the street without exchanging a word, deprived of the breeze or the wind that would have refreshed us. I asked Hermine why she'd decided to go through with it. She answered that she wanted to show she was brave. Should we laugh or cry? She said I could buy the lacquer table next day.

*

I walked into her bookshop, I was startled by the waxed wood floor. Cleanliness strips things bare. The cleanliness of this room would have left it quite naked if it had not been for the numerous photographs of modern writers set out along the shelves, reducing the rental library's subscribers to zeroes. The authors' eyes watched us as we chose their books. The new subscriber would give her name and address. She would pay to borrow one, two, or three books at a time. Then she could satisfy her thirst for the very latest publications. Everything that was printed found its way into Adrienne Monnier's shop: books, magazines, manifestoes, brochures. The names we read in *La Nouvelle Revue Française* or *Les Nouvelles Littéraires* were always there on Adrienne Monnier's long table. We chose, stowed away and carried off, one, two, or three new publications. Often two subscribers pounced on the same book. Then Adrienne Monnier, cunningly or truthfully, would announce that it had been reserved. Baby-faced, majestic and countrified, with her straight, untouched, blonde, silvery hair, cut under a pudding basin, with her fresh complexion, the slightly purple tinge of her cheeks caused by a light layer of white powder over their natural pink, with her narrow forehead, her piercing eyes, her slow voice, Adrienne Monnier, strictly, monastically, strangely—yes, an avalanche of adverbs—draped in a long dress of gray homespun belted at the waist, falling to her feet and gathered in folds, imposed on her shop an atmosphere created from the Middle Ages, the Renaissance, Ireland, Holland, Flanders, and the passionate reign of Elizabeth. Heavens, a peasant woman from some bygone age, one thought as one walked in.

My heart began to beat faster as soon as I reached the intersection in front of the Odéon. It was automatic: I would go into a flower shop, run by a rather unpleasant woman, with a perpetually diseased-looking display in the window despite the freshness of the plants, buy a bunch of flowers, then check my appearance in the mirror on the Rue de l'Odéon, beside a hotel that shone with virtue but had apparently no clientele whatever. I wonder why the books I brought away clutched against my breast, the books I read with such pleasure and such enthusiasm, finally turned into such trash. I would stop in front of the gray painted façade. I worked up my courage by gazing into the window at the left of the door: the temple of the avant-garde, the transparent monstrance containing *La Jeune Parque* and *Le Cimetière Marin*. The middle window was more eclectic and contained all the best new books and recent issues of literary magazines. I was not alone at this feast. The predominant color of the display was white, with red titles, and was composed mostly of books published by Gallimard.

Then I went in and gave the flowers to Adrienne Monnier. She would linger a moment over my name as I handed in my books. She complimented me if there were only a few customers, though less so if the shop was full. She said that she liked my eel suit, that I was reading the best books. My schoolgirl passion flamed higher. As she looked for my card she seemed to be making lace with all the hundreds of others because her hands were so dainty and dimpled. Her table looked like the one in Cézanne's *Card Players.* She left it as little as possible. It made me desperately sad for her, having to sit there going through all those finicky little cards. The silence in the shop was sometimes painful to bear. I fell, without exaggeration, into an abyss of surprise the first time I heard Adrienne Monnier saying: "Gide, with a few friends, read to us here, yesterday evening. . . ."

To hear such a thing being confided was too staggering. Adrienne Monnier was allowing me a glimpse of a forbidden world which I could not envisage. When I used to go to school in the village, when the boys had turned back after hounding me with their stones, or when I had shaken them off, I used to sit down, on my strong days, in the grass under the hedge. I settled my clogs on my knees, taking care to keep them upside down. I rested. There was a branch hanging over me; a bird decided to settle there, and despite the perpetual flight in its tiny eye, it stayed there. It tolerated my presence. I tried to make myself absolutely still, even the roots of my hair, the tips of my nails. I closed my eyes, depriving myself of the swaying branch. A bird is free, you can never get to know it. But the bird was uneasy. Its heart fluttered on mine. I experienced the same emotions when I heard about Gide reading his work at Adrienne Monnier's.

That evening, the reality assumed vaster proportions. Hermine listened to me with the kindliness, the detachment of a countrywoman, taking in the words but staying on the other side of the fence. I broke off; envisaging the photographs of the contemporary writers on the shelves filled me with anguish: too many brains all in one room. I told her about my bunch of flowers, how pleasant Adrienne Monnier had been, the compliments she had paid me. Hermine expressed her joy, seconded my ecstasies, and said: now we have to do the dishes. She left me and went to the sink. Alone with myself, I began to doubt: had Adrienne Monnier really been so pleasant, had we really got on so well together? I bounded into the kitchen, I shook Hermine by the shoulders. "Léon-Paul Fargue goes into her store, and she sees Valéry. Do you hear? She sees Valéry." Hermine handed me the dishcloth and answered: "You wipe." The unattainable world of modern literature, in which I should have floundered so clumsily with my shyness, my stupidity, my vanity, if I had found my way into it, faded away. Bent over the sink, Hermine assimilated all the things I told her better than I could myself. Hermine was deep, while I was scorching my wings against the brilliance of anecdotes. I wiped, I clung to my sturdy stone wall: Hermine. I wiped, and each of her kisses was another warm piece of wall around me. She went to sleep, and I didn't disturb her. I was sixteen again. I dug my fingers in my ears, and Hermine's sumptuous breathing ceased to exist. I was under the bedclothes again, reading *Les Nourritures terrestres* by the glow of my flashlight. I had been carried away by the style, by the image of Dionysus in pastor's clothes. Nathanael, the barns, the fruits, the homosexuals. I had not formed any precise idea of what they did together. They held each other in their arms for hour after hour. The act of love took place of its own accord, in the scent from a mountain of hay.

What was it I wanted from Adrienne Monnier, writing away without writing books, in her office open to anyone who cared to come, where writers read out what they had written somewhere else? Sometimes I was unfaithful to Adrienne Monnier's rental library; I would take a bus instead of burying myself in the Métro and get off near the old Restaurant Foyot—the same name as a bookshop in the North of France, a bohemian bookshop I was always browsing in as a girl—then I would wander around under the arches of the Flammarion bookshop in the Place de l'Odéon. I had an appointment with the Garnier Classics. The Luxembourg, the railings with their gilded pikeheads, the gates swung wide to welcome the groups of young people at loose ends, the posters advertising performances of *Le Cid* and *Bérénice* all gave off an aura of Seneca and Livy. Each volume, I think, cost three and a half francs. My eyes ran over the titles with avid satisfaction. The Garnier Classics gave me the illusion of memorizing Montaigne's *Essais,* Rousseau's *Confessions,* Lucretius or Virgil, in a second. Whether the other browsers were old or young, their hands were all the same age. The sap from the books was flowing in them. I walked down the Rue de l'Odéon and felt an unexpected pang on Hermine's behalf because she wasn't there to see the display in a music publisher's window; I read the name Leduc printed there without pleasure. I turned my eyes away from the anonymous-looking, exotic bookstore kept by Sylvia Beach. She was busy introducing James Joyce and *Ulysses* into France. Sylvia Beach used to pay visits to her friend Adrienne Monnier and then vanish again like a whirlwind. The sight of her slender body, her severely cut suit, her ageless puritan's face devoid of make-up, transformed me into a gasping schoolgirl. Then she would disappear in her narrow skirt and low heels.

Adrienne Monnier had begun her career modestly with the *Mercure de France*; she told me about it, and about her old parents too, and the orchards in Normandy. I lost my head; the following week I sulked because she was equally pleasant to a wealthy woman who came into the store. I found her adaptability shocking. I was sulky several times in succession. She no longer encouraged me, and I didn't encourage her. She must have guessed what a parasite I was. A strange parasite, never satisfied and yet so easily satisfied. As the years went by, I grew doleful in her store. I was sending out signals into a void. I became lugubrious, plaintive, tearful; it was mere sentimental masturbation. Adrienne Monnier must have felt sorry for me. Already out of her depth, forced to make sacrifices to keep her lending library open—she sold very few books—she suddenly took on an unpleasant young girl as her assistant. I became tragic. Whereupon she led me into the back room usually reserved for privileged visitors and asked me why I was unhappy. I fell at her feet, beneath Tolstoy and Dostoievsky; I stammered out a lot of complicated nonsense close to her long, gray skirt. She placed her hand on my head, wanting to console me. Her assistant walked in. Quick as a lightning flash, Adrienne Monnier regained her air of dignity. Her embarrassment over a schoolgirl who'd stayed after class, her metamorphosis for the eyes of an assistant as unyielding as justice, made me feel disappointed in her, disgusted with her. I borrowed Raymond Queneau's *Chiendent,* read it, returned it, and never went back.

*

A caterpillar is slow and sensuous: it seduces the surfaces it moves on with the quivers of its visible and imperceptible velvet skin. The change in Hermine during the summer vacation at Ploumanac'h after our afternoon in the hotel on the Rue Godot-de-Mauroy was visible and imperceptible. She moved over to the starched curtain hanging at our window, still filing her nails as she looked out at the waves surging in higher than the houses, dreaming of something else while the curtain squeaked between my fingers. Noon was dozing in a boat beached for repairs, and she inspected the progress of her tan. She wondered whether we would have crab or lobster for lunch. I left the dining room and returned to the starched curtain. The window was watching my grandmother's funeral procession in the rain. I saw the color and duration of my grief in the blackened cork float on a fishing net. The summer visitors were being fed, the curtain in our room squeaked and squeaked. Fidéline, it's chalk on a blackboard, I said to myself, swallowing back my tears. I went down again, and Hermine ignored my reddened eyes. I longed for my skin to be tanned like Hermine's, so I exposed myself on the rocks without using Ambre Solaire. The sun didn't care for my white skin.

That night the hell began. The lightest touch . . . and I was sliced to the bone. Hermine was sorry for me, she sat up in bed smoking, she suggested a trip in a fisherman's boat. I put out the light, there was warm dough rising on my shoulders. My legs swelled up. I wanted to follow Hermine when she went walking along the cliffs that fell sheer to the sea. It's between the two of us, her quivering nostrils seemed to say. My legs became three times their normal size, and the doctor informed us that I ought to be immobilized for the next three weeks. Once my calves and shoulders were swathed in bandages we set out nevertheless in the fisherman's boat to confront the waves. Hermine laughed, she stood up in the boat; I trembled with fear as the water splashed over my dressings, while Hermine, excited by the noise of the sea, stretched wide her arms and the fisherman spat over the side. We could have drowned, they were saying in Ploumanac'h, but Hermine shone with splendor, high above the dangers. And then the scouring light. And then the grayish grass when we took walks along the paths overhanging the sea, the tired grass to which I promised future greatness in the approaching winter. Hermine's mind was on other things. At Blankenburg, we ate french fries and mussels. In Ploumanac'h they were caulking the seams of their boat, their love. Hermine liked the local biscuits: she bit into them, one after the other.

The following summer, at La Baule, we hired a striped canvas bathing tent. I went down to it early every morning, my feet never grew tired of that fine sand, liquid as the sand in an hourglass. There were young boys down there, thin, free, untidily dressed, sticking in poles, bringing or taking away the canvas cabins on their backs. These strangers were my companions while Hermine was away buying me health in the market. Sleep, breathe deeply to work up an appetite, everything will be ready. I looked for the designs made by gulls' feet in the hard sand, and found nothing. I was in chains. There was a fine drizzle; Hermine had begged me to let her go on playing the handmaiden. Why weren't we those two holidaymakers with their trousers rolled up above their knees setting out to fish for shrimps, why? I waited for noon to come, I played with a ball and racket by myself, throwing the tennis ball higher and higher to attract the attention of a little sand-castle constructor. I wandered through the melancholy water and almost reached Croisic. Horses galloping fast splashed my cheeks with their spray. The horses on the beach, galloping along by the water. They reminded one of "the Sebum." We called him that because he was doing research into ways of beautifying the skin. A friend of De Chirico. He brought me a magazine with a reproduction in it of De Chirico's *Horses by the Sea.* What was it? A waking dream? Perhaps a sleepwalker who painted by night; perhaps he dipped his brush in the motionless eye of an owl.

Hermine was a creature bathed in bliss while she was in the ocean. In the water, Nature repaid her with a lavish hand for everything she gave to me. We didn't learn to swim. The waves went by, the young men teased us with fine sprays of water. She bought me a pair of Hermès sandals because I had a pain in my side. That spectacular silence, the depths of a pine forest, when I made my dismal and solitary way back from the beach at midday. She won't speak. She didn't speak during the meal. We were growing old at lightning speed. Hermine kept watch from the balcony of our furnished room, humming a theme from a Beethoven concerto. I turned my back to the sea, I wanted to punish the sun while Hermine sacrificed herself in the grocery stores, in the market. A mysterious insect stung me near the armpit while I sat in a moth-eaten garden trying to knit. That night I dared to say it aloud: it's over, it will soon be over, this is the end. Hermine told me next morning that I had talked in my sleep. I sobbed, and she said it was because I didn't eat enough. One day I fell asleep in the bathing-tent after coming out of the water and had a dream: I was waiting for Hermine in a seed store, I was plunging my hands into the sacks of seed because the waiting went on and on, because it was unbearable. A young girl came in. It was

Hermine and not Hermine. I was Hermine, anxious and neglected. I told her how I'd waited, I told her how beautiful she was becoming. She answered that she had come because it was time to sow her godetias. She began to read out the names printed on the seed packets. She had become a girl serving in a store. She was listening to the footsteps of a new mistress walking in the corridors of her school. I woke up.

*

October, November, December, January, February, March, April, May, June, July. I told her I wanted to see waves, she answered that I had insisted on the Riviera and that we were on the Riviera. I told her that she couldn't forget the Rue Godot-de-Mauroy, that she never mentioned it, that never mentioning it made it worse. I told her that she no longer laughed, that she was somewhere else, I was mistaken. She was beside me, she loved the Mediterranean and its little mirrors. The dance of the little mirrors for the Mediterranean, she called it. She called me "little chicken" or "squirrel" so that I should love it with her. I melted with pleasure when she called me those names, but I couldn't see her Mediterranean. She discovered the noise of the waves. It was "a lullaby," "the sweetest happiness there ever was." She discovered new things everywhere, as we discover love everywhere when we are ready to meet it. My headaches, the violence of my migraines in the Riviera sun escaped her. I spoiled things for Hermine, I made her impatient: the light was agony for me until four in the afternoon. Everyone there was having a good time. Hermine was enchanted by the bar set up on the sands; there was a couple dancing there on the platform at eleven in the morning. Hermine said it was like drinking blue cocktails; I annoyed her with my shivering and my cold hands. I didn't see her Mediterranean, but even so I wasn't blind. I didn't dare reveal what I wanted it to be: the violet ink in my inkpot when I was learning to write my alphabet. Hermine at midnight, savoring her cigarette as she followed the rise and fall of the "lullaby" along by the waves. And I, murmuring how much I was enjoying the walk, but lying.

The following day, nailed down by the sun, I watched Hermine watching the Mediterranean. She no longer sewed: the packets of dress patterns outside the draper's shops held no interest for her. Alone beside the sea at two in the morning, she listened to "the festooning of the night," then came back to sleep, still draped in a veil of apricot-colored darkness. I pointed out the sculptured white masses floating in the sky, recalling the North where we had come from. She couldn't see them; she refused to see them. She would slide back into the warm water to escape an eddy of cooler air. Suddenly deprived of her presence, I was both doomed and blessed. We drank silently in the bars while I looked into her eyes, begging for pardon, and she would burst into laughter over the slightest thing, trying to shake me off and yet not conscious of the strain I put on her. Outings, bus rides. Hermine gazed with passion at the indentations of the coast, the shattered rocks, the violent colors. A cypress . . . the cypress beside my grandmother's grave, my cry of grief ringing through the graveyard when as a speechless child I turned over a clod of earth that was sprouting mauve pearls. It's true, I don't play the piano anymore, Hermine said as she brushed her teeth. Now the light of the bedside lamp fell on my shoulders while she hummed away at seven in the evening. Oh God how I longed for a change, oh God how I longed to love Hermine more than myself, oh God how I was beginning to love her, oh God how I longed for a kind of saintliness within our reach: an everyday and never-ending smile. I wanted to tell her so while she was humming. "You mustn't interrupt me. You must leave me that at least."

I didn't notice that she had begun to give the orders. When we went on an excursion to Cannes, I wanted to go for a walk along the beach; Hermine wanted to see the smart hotels. In her shorts, which were shorter than anyone else's, and her high heels, she looked like a tart. I told her that people dressed up more in Cannes, that we were too scantily clad. She laughed, she didn't give a damn. Her laugh: the freshness of a swarthy rose. I wept with love for her: she took umbrage at my tears. The yachts attracted her. Squeezed up against the other, the only life they had came from the dismal water that was rocking them. I wanted to go back to Juan-les-Pins, but she refused. We must take an apéritif on the terrace of the Miramar, it was a sight we really mustn't miss. Her desires were like farewells.

I questioned her. Yes, she liked it on the terrace of the Miramar. Oh, if she were alone it would be different, very different, completely different. She would stay in the sea till nightfall; the Celtique she was smoking fell from her lips at that idea. She laughed a wild little laugh as the long cars with their tops down filed past. The water is so liquid, once everyone else has gone home and night has fallen. Hermine licked at a trace of salt water left in the corner of her mouth. She rejected my suggestion: a red sun, a great, dumb sun sinking into the sea, a shadow lying across her book. I begged her to go on. I had to risk everything, I had to make her remember all the things she'd been deprived of. The little restaurant? Or a dinner of fruit in her room? She could live on nothing and read as she ate. She smiled, she lost herself in what she was saying with a cruel expression on her face. What would she read? New books, old books, Biographies, novels, essays. Where would she read? Everywhere. By the light from the store windows as she walked in the street, by the light of the moon as she rested on park benches . . . She was shouting, and some people at another table began staring at us. She would get up at five in the morning, she would go scrambling over the rocks, she would cut short her vacation, she would live with her sisters, with her father. She was eliminating me, and she was admitting it.

Sunday, November 27, 1960 at twelve-thirty a.m. You can guess, reader, you have already guessed, it is the end of a love affair, it is the end of a tyranny. My fountain pen, lifted from the exercise book, is different. Love. Love has no end. If it had, it would not be love. We go on loving those we have loved in other forms, or else we begin to cherish in other forms those we should have cherished in the past. Nothing changes, everything is transformed. Sunday, November 27, 1960. Twenty-six years after the events I have just retold, I am watching the end of autumn being wooed in the sky by next year's spring. Hermine. Violette. Their present is now swept clean. And that monstrous woman who passed us on the Pont de la Concorde? Providence. Through a window covered with nylon net, through the embroidered garlands on a young bride's veil, I can see the clouds distending. I can see two lakes of Mediterranean blue. Hermine, Violette, the azure of our lives is sundered.

*

In Paris began the reign of the elevator. Sitting on our divan, my hands alternately icy and burning hot, I waited, I watched, I listened, I imagined the clatter of the iron grill opening on our landing, I counted the wrinkles on my knuckles. Heavy, unopened, the elevator moved up and down. The cables swung to and fro whenever it began to move. Hermine closed the grill listlessly behind her. I ran to the door, opened it for her, and her face changed. A whole life was over. The woman I hugged against me had no arms. She was blind, deaf, mute. Win her back. I thought I could, and I thought that tears were the appropriate weapon. If I waited in front of the elevator door, she couldn't conceal from me through the glass that all her vitality was quenched at the very sight of me. There was only one chance for me: gaiety, because gaiety is a trap. But I was not clear-sighted. I rushed toward her draped in the cast-off tatters of our love. If I had wanted to lose her I could have found no better way to do so. The more she loathed my begging, my laments, my self-indulgent grief, the more I wallowed in them. I went out onto the Boulevard Bineau and waited for her at the streetcar stop. I imagined that all the other people I saw led completely uncomplicated lives, I imagined they were all happy. I imagined the world was just a green lawn; I drew all the misery up out of it to swell my own misery. The streetcars kept stopping and then moving off again; I couldn't see her face, I couldn't see her beret on the platforms. Her lateness drove me to despair. The sparrows' favorite time of day. Before they settled, they skimmed the privets above the railings of a villa. I was living without hope in a world of flagstones. Ding . . .

Hermine, just at that moment, pulled the streetcar cord. I gazed at her with so much love that she turned to look. She gave me a pitying smile. Some shivers are prophetic. I shivered then: Hermine was now on the platform, giving me a guilty smile because she was so late. I knew that there were three of us: the new schoolmistress must be sitting in the streetcar. "What a sad little face you're wearing," Hermine said. I made no reply. I had been weeping from morning until evening to make her love me as she had loved me once. We walked home with light steps. That evening Hermine insisted on buying champagne.

If I kept up my inquisition long enough, I was always rewarded with the same reply:

"What am I thinking about? About her mouth."

I cursed her honesty.

The new mistress wanted extraordinary furniture, an extraordinary divan, an extraordinary studio. Hermine went into a trance as she talked about it. All these plans, never openly confessed, were worse than a clean break.

I stopped wearing anything but the orphanage topcoat I had bought at La Samaritaine: I wanted to melt her heart with my poverty. Beggars exhibit their stunted limbs; I exhibited my face, my grief. Hermine lived in expectation of the following morning; I lived in expectation of a miracle. I was already waiting for her, longing for her, as she opened the door to go out. She loathed Thursdays and Sundays; she slept through them to kill time. At night, I licked at her rose, her petals, her nests. She sighed and bore with me. I threatened her. I would do away with myself, I would throw myself out the window. Hermine would have to tear up her nightgown to pull me back up into the room. I was the victim of my own threats. I filled and refilled my graveyard with my shoes, my dresses, and my hats taken out of their boxes.

One Sunday, after a copious lunch in our room, I said to her: "Sleep, for heaven's sake, sleep!"

Wearing my orphanage coat, I trotted along the avenues of the Bois. A flowerless, leafless spring was smiling through the branches. I was freed from Hermine, and from myself. I would simply go on living with a woman who wanted someone else. A motorist offered to drive me out to Ville-d'Avray for champagne. I accepted. The place he took me to was disguised as an ordinary country house; but the trellises and the creepers on the walls were simply a camouflage for the hive of private rooms inside. We chattered away at a tremendous rate, like two soldiers between guard duties. Suddenly I felt a stabbing pain in my head, and there were pincers at my heart: Hermine. I begged him to take me back to Paris immediately. He disdained the idea of Levallois-Perret. I had to run all the way from the Bois back to our street. My first date: the elevator. My first date: the key in the lock. The same feelings of love set in again, this time complicated by a fever of virtue. Yes, I was asleep, Hermine said. She turned her back on me and traced imaginary symbols on the wall. Her hand fell back onto the divan. It took her five or six minutes before she recognized me, before she saw that I had been out, that I was wearing my old coat. Finally she asked me where I'd been. She didn't give a damn about champagne at Ville-d'Avray. She went off to sleep again. I wept, sitting on the rug.

I held off the storm until the evening before we were due to leave once more for our holiday in Brittany. Our suitcases were all packed. With alternately icy and burning hands, I waited for Hermine as I watched the second hand implacably circling the face of my wristwatch. Six o'clock. Seven o'clock. Eight o'clock. A slate blue sky was hanging over Paris like a threat. To love, to stop loving, to begin loving the same person again. Love is not made in a factory. At last: the elevator, the swing of the cables.

Oh the open gaze of the telegraph boy, taking the little blue envelope out of his leather wallet. An express letter. I recognized Hermine's incisive writing. "She's written me a letter," I said aloud.

"Dear Violette,

"Don't wait for me. I shall not be coming back again. You must be brave. Hermine."

Brittany. We were going to Brittany. Hermine had run away. It wasn't possible, it wasn't true. I was dreaming, it was a waking nightmare. I was going out of my mind. It was a forgery. It was in Hebrew. I didn't understand Hebrew. What was this little scrap of stuff I was holding against my knees? A central Paris postmark. D o n, apostrophe, t. Then a space. W - a - i - t. Don't wait for me. My name, our address. Twenty-five times, fifty times I read out our address: my address. I shall not be coming back. . . . It was beginning, I felt a cramp in my inside. They sway. . . . The cables of the elevator sway when it goes down . . . when it's out of sight. She won't be coming back. What was that I said? What was that I dared to say? I was mad. A slap, two slaps, three slaps, slap upon slap, more and more slaps, she has gone. Have pity, Violette, have pity. Ahhh God, ahhh, ahhh . . . Stare at the lid of the piano until it begins again. . . . I hurt all over, but where exactly? In the center of Paris. I would never find her. It hurts, it hurts, it hurts. If I could cry. I couldn't cry. Nine years. Hermine. Nine years, nine years, nine years, nine years, nine years, nine years. Why had I stopped? I tried to cry, even that was refused me. I'll go out, I'll bring her back. Cut off my head, cut, cut! Look at the wall two inches under the portrait of Beethoven, keep looking at that spot forever. Mummy! Help me! Mummy, make it all right. I would have loved her so much. She will come baaaaack. . . . I am sick, that's what makes me think she won't come back. Charity, Hermine.

I read the letter over and over a hundred times: my address and two lines of text. At last, I began to sob.

Now I remember, with this postcard keeping me company, on the lefthand page of my exercise book. A reproduction of the Portail Royal at Chartres. Pythagoras. He is seated, he is writing something. Pythagoras. A twelfth-century man like a tree trunk, with a face radiating light. His penholder is a plasterer's trowel, his hair is a cosmos of parallel lines. He has a big nose, children, Pythagoras has a great big nose. If I had a nose like that I'd kill myself. No, trash on the Pont de la Concorde, no. Pythagoras has a forehead etched with close parallel lines. And the lines that never meet, even in infinity, do meet, my doves, forming a flying bird in the center of his brow. I could drown myself in all the bedspread fringes of his beard. Our dormitories, our waffled bedspreads. Patience. I am writing all this to console myself for Hermine's disappearance, twenty-five years later. How diligent Pythagoras's hands are on his desk, beside the great door at Chartres. His face sings with the happiness of numbers.

Pythagoras dearest, I mean, Pythagoras, you are so dear to me on that picture postcard helping me to deliver myself finally of my grief after Hermine's departure, helping me to tear myself away from her after twenty-five years. The travail and the separation will take place again while I copy out this account of your life:

Pythagoras, a Greek philosopher and mathematician, born on the island of Samos (circa 580—circa 500 B.C.), of whose life little is known. He is generally supposed to have founded the *Pythagorean* sect. A believer in metempsychosis, he had lofty moral principles and forced his disciples to adopt a life of austerity. He believed that the elements of numerical science were also the elements of matter. The mathematical, geometric, and astronomic discoveries generally attributed to Pythagoras were more probably the work of the Pythagorean school as a whole. They were: the multiplication tables, the decimal system, and the theorem of the squared hypotenuse.

Forced his disciples to adopt a life of austerity. Eight eights, sixty-four; five fives, twenty-five; seven sevens, forty-nine . . . How is one to resist eight times eight and five times five? Irrefutable gaiety. Eight times eight and five times five . . .

A believer in metempsychosis. Hermine is on my sideboard, Hermine is an anemone in the middle of the vase.

No, reader, my grief is not manufactured. It must be allowed to settle, once for all, the sandstorm of despair stirred up by Hermine's departure. We suffer, then we call in words to help us. I am forcing myself to sweep out my skull, to clean out my brain, that hive swarming with madness as it was hurled into the pit, walled up, crushed by a great avalanche of coal. Reader, you have suffered. To find relief in what has been, we must make ourselves eternal.

Still dressed in my orphanage coat, I ran first of all as far as the Porte Champerret. Two dogs followed me. I howled, yes, I howled on the bus platform. A young girl came out of a record store with several records under her arm, the store where we had listened to passages from *Petrouchka* and *Le Sacre du Printemps*. Hermine was too much with me, the Hermine who wasn't coming back had not yet been born. There was nothing to lean on. The conductor was chatting with one of the passengers. Were they deaf to my howls, then? Were they blind to my tears? My grief was not a mask. The bus started. I began to howl again through the noise of the wheels on the cobbles; I watered the steps with my tears.

The caretaker of Hermine's school had just finished wiping up the dinner dishes; her husband was reading. The summer vacation had started, that was all she could tell me. I understood Hermine's plan. She had waited for the last day of the term to disappear with the new mistress. Every little hotel in Paris was clamoring for me to search it. It was an unpleasant task that had to be faced. I would find her, I would bring her back. How I longed to have a relative who was a detective or a police inspector to help me. Unhappiness is refusing to accept whatever has been sent to try us. The hugeness of Paris overwhelmed me. I had worked night and day to bring about the break between us, and now I turned my knife on the ruins that were left. An abscess: the elevator. Another abscess: our apartment. I bore the scent of her brilliantine on the pillow, I bore the piano and its remorseless creaks. The sun rose and brought fresh strength to yesterday's bad news. The things in the room were waiting for Hermine in their world. I sent a telegram to my mother in Chérisy, near Dreux.

"Your mouth is twisted, your mouth is all lopsided," she said as she came in.

She read the express letter. Her face made no comment.

"I saw it coming a long while ago. She'd had enough."

I looked at my mother, I saw a woman in full possession of herself. I leaned on Hermine, lost forever.

"I'll take you with me," she said. "You must come home with me."

I refused. I had to sell the Pleyel to raise a little money, then move back to our furnished room and put the divan, the table, the chairs into storage. Then I'd go and spend a while with them. My mother was disgruntled. Why not go with her right away? Taking a child back should be a matter for rejoicing.

I moved back into the furnished room in Levallois, then left for Chérisy. My mother persuaded me to go to a swimming instructor and take swimming lessons in a nearby river.

He was a consolation to me. I was consoled by his striped 1900 bathing suit, by his big bare feet, by the hard muscles on his calves that made his legs look like Jacobean furniture, by his brown ancient-Gaul mustache, by his great goggle eyes, by the cap covered in rubber daisies stuck tight on his head, and by his village which I didn't know. I loved him with a deep friendship when he counted one, two, thwee! He never managed to produce an *r:* it was endearing. I arrived, I shook his hand, and he replied: "To work!"

"One . . ."

I scraped at the grass with my arms and legs: I was learning the strokes.

"Two, thwee!"

I made scissor movements with all four limbs, and I learned to smile again. Was it because of the summer that the sky weighed with such a blue weight upon my neck? A sheep bleated in the distance, there were some children splashing in the wading pool. One . . .

I stretched myself out on a reflection of the sky when I learned the same strokes again in the water, holding onto the bar.

"Two, thwee!"

A long slide on my belly through the water, still holding the bar.

I threw myself into the water: a confusion of whirlpools, noise, and splashes.

"One . . . two thwee!"

We left swimming class at midday with the proud carriage of ancient Roman maidens. Where was Hermine? With her sisters? With her father? On vacation with the new mistress? I interrogated the fossilized lightning flash in a shattered tree. The tree stood cursing the sky, the heat, the space around it. The sun bore with the tree's shrieks patiently.

I swam on my own. I swam badly, with one foot sticking out of the water. I loved it all the same. I was rowing, my arms were the oars and I was the boat, then suddenly, irresistible delight, the boat was moving of its own accord.

Judge me, Hermine. Convict me. The night is on your side. The black hats of the judges are bowing to you in their millions: it is night. Your treasure, your consolation, the little cat you brought back to Avallon when we went on a trip into Morvan . . . He miaowed until dawn in our hotel room. That little animal, so grief-stricken it almost broke one's heart, that little cat was you: each miaow was one of the demands I'd made on you. You comforted it, you stroked it. . . . I couldn't bear it. At daybreak, I decided we would leave it behind in the room. You struggled. You gave way. It looked at us, unable to make a sound, its anxious eyes moving from one to the other. What is a little animal abandoned in a room? What was it? My jealousy, my power, my pain, my tyranny. I was trampling you into a bed of flesh. I knew then that you would never forgive me. I left the hotel wearing the steel corselet of a despot. I walked beside you, and I suffered more than you did. The leaves and the flowers in private gardens became thorny trophies for my triumph as we passed by. The sun rose on a sheet of steel. You suffered, I tortured myself. A scale was waiting, a dropper was glistening as it measured out the drops. Everything would be repaid in time.

*

I left Chérisy and went back to Paris; the dream was over. I went to watch Hermine through her classroom window. Hermine didn't see me, but she scolded the students who turned to look through the window. What was preventing her from seeing me? She was shouting too much. Hermine had become young again. One of the students told her that someone was watching her. She turned her head, recognized me, and waved her fist.

I drank in her presence, I couldn't go away immediately. To see her again. But it was a sin apparently.

I left the window, I left the school.

After the rebound I fell ill. Hermine. My closed eyes repeated her name, that was enough.

Hermine's silence. Hermine's absence. I wept night and day, and I hoped.

I found a celluloid arm with a hand on the end. It had dropped off a doll outside the little gate into the gardens facing the town hall. I took it back to my room with me, climbing the stairs on tiptoe. My tears had something on which to fall. I fell asleep at dawn with the arm and hand against my neck, woke up again an hour later, put on the light and held the little celluloid hand in mine, or else kept it warm by putting it between my temple and the pillow. I dozed off again, then woke up yet again ten minutes afterward because we were both so cold. The arm and its hand went with me everywhere, they enjoyed the benefit of the autumn warmth hidden in the pocket of my coat. As I watered them with my tears, so my plan ripened slowly into action.

One afternoon I walked across the town hall gardens again. October had been boisterous that year: a gardener was sweeping up dead leaves. Help me, you will help me, won't you, I said to the celluloid hand clutched in mine. A mirror in a store window full of glass and crystal reflected my livid face, the red slits that were my eyes. I went into the telegraph office. I wrote: "I am going blind. I should like to see you again. Violette."

I gave the telegraph form to the clerk. She counted the words.

"Heavens, how sad it is," she said. "Is it you who's sick?"

"Yes, it's me."

I was melting with hope because someone had pitied me.

"Do you have a good doctor?" she asked as she sharpened her penholder in the mists of her hair. "Does it hurt? Your eyes do look red, I must say."

"They burn all the time," I said. "But I do have a good doctor."

"Is there still hope?" she asked.

"I don't know," I replied, thinking of Hermine.

As I walked away I heard a click: my telegram being gulped down by the tube.

"Take care of yourself," the clerk shouted after me.

Outside, I threw away the doll's hand and arm.

Hermine arranged to meet me in a café near the Porte Champerret. She was already there when I arrived, drinking some sort of infusion. The pieces of mint leaf or lime flower left in the bottom of her cup told me I hadn't a hope. There was no kindness in her eyes. Her face had no expression on it. I slid around onto the banquette so as to be close to her. She held out her hand. I was choking. It was too much and too little. Then I saw her hands and the way her fingers had coarsened. It hurt me to look at them: when we lived together, Hermine used to give herself a manicure every day. The waiter asked me what I wanted to drink. I ordered a coffee.

"You won't sleep," Hermine said.

That "you won't sleep" was a knife slicing into me. I was so far from her sleep, from their sleep.

"I cry too much," I said. "The doctor says I may go blind."

Hermine looked at my eyes. Perhaps she ought to believe me, and she didn't want to believe me.

"You mustn't cry," she said. "You must take care of yourself."

She poured out another cup of her infusion.

"And you?" I asked with an immensity of hope.

Hermine's face changed. I mustn't try and intrude on her private life.

"I'm working very hard," she said.

She seemed to have shut herself behind a wall of worries.

We sat drinking the coffee and the infusion together. That was all I had left of her.

"I'll send you some money," she said in a faint voice.

My coffee cup was empty. The waiter was looking at us.

"Do you live in the center of Paris? Near the Gare Saint-Lazare?"

"Don't keep on," Hermine broke out.

She paid our check. The waiter was looking at us very gently.

"I must go home," Hermine said. "Take care of yourself. . . ."

"Yes, I'll take care of myself. Your hands have changed."

"It's the dishes," she said.

I followed her out and then she made it clear that I must go no further. Hermine, for the second time, was leaving me forever.

Hermine's coat, Hermine's beret, Hermine moving from island to island across the intersections of the Porte Champerret. The memory of that moment was already sprouting in me as I lived it. Who was there to protect me? My defeat kept me calm as I made my way back to my furnished room.

Who, in the end, gave most to the other? I did. The answer came without hesitation. Hermine, an assistant mistress in a boarding school, Hermine who practiced the *Italian Concerto* in the kindergarten could have avoided, kept at a distance, repulsed the schoolgirl Violette Leduc. In which case I would certainly have passed my exams. Then I would have become a schoolteacher. Hermine could have sent me away when I went to her cubicle at night. Then she would have become a music teacher and I would have taught in a primary school. After her dismissal, it was she who wrote to me first through one of the other students; which was the reason that I myself was dismissed in turn and ended up in the highest grade at a Paris lycée, where I failed the oral part of my examinations and consequently did not receive the diploma which would have enabled me to teach. It was my career, my whole future I had given to Hermine. I also gave her my health and my job in a publishing house. Hermine had appeared suddenly in my life, and now she had robbed me of my security. She sent me money for three months. Then it stopped. I looked for work. Work . . . I seemed to see more than enough of it for me in every little rectangle in the evening papers.

The classified sections are the Resteasy Balm of the brave and the lazy. Where are we to find those peers we need so much? On the back page of the newspapers. Professions, all the different trades I might attempt, possibilities, activities, resolves to work hard, resolves to earn money and buy food for others, they were all there buzzing around my room. I lay in the grip of my insomnia listening to the syncopated jazz phrasing of Pigïer and Berlitz. I thought back to my advertisement in the *Bibliographie de la France*. Was I going to find anything? The money from the Pleyel would soon be snow melting in a spring sun. I continued doggedly to scan the Help Wanted ads, and found a demand that suited what I could supply.

"What do you think of love?"

"A great deal and not much. And you?"

"A great deal and not much," he said.

He gave a sudden, brief laugh and tossed aside the magazine with the question blazoned across its cover. I asked him if he would like to take a seat.

He sat down at the table, looked at the framed photograph on it, and became suddenly sad. He opened the magazine.

"I'll come back for you," I said.

"Good," he answered, suddenly projecting a wave of affability and good grace.

I left the second waiting room at the end of the corridor with his deep, gentle gaze still in my mind. I found the singsong quality of his voice surprising, his pleasant manner disturbing.

I walked back into the office and forgot him.

In my function as receptionist, the demesne over which I held sway was minimal. A chair, a little table, and a switchboard standing against the wall beneath a hatch with a sliding glass panel. I raised the glass as the actor or actress closed the door on the way in; I lowered it while they wondered if they were to be admitted to the important inner office. If we didn't know him, the actor wrote his name on a card. If he was famous, I announced his presence over the telephone. I was the keeper of a glass gate; to the aging actor, to the novice, to the old actress with the make-up shrieking of her desire for success, I said: it's impossible for anyone to see you today. Why don't you telephone, or come back another day? . . . Lies made to order, lies in an endless chain, destructive lies, blood-sucking lies, while the businessmen wrestled with their columns of figures and their contracts. Why don't you telephone, or come back another day? I recited the phrase as from a great height. I took myself for Denise Batcheff, the producer herself. A failed switchboard operator, a switchboard operator too old to be doing such a job, a switchboard operator with hands of lead, where did I think it lay, this superiority of mine? In the fact that I had a job and they didn't. A nice way to think. I am writing this in June. The afghan will have to go to be dyed. I unfold it, I pick it up, I open it, I put it over my head. Pitiful covering, give your shelter and your consolation to all those who left that place with heavy hearts.

I was a haphazard switchboard operator. I mixed up the plugs, I plunged them into jacks at random, I disconnected calls at inopportune moments, I rendered directors' decisions null and void, I refused to admit the producer was in when I should have, and I connected her with unwanted calls when I should not have.

I have not forgotten the visitor. He had to wait while M. Dubondieu sat in our office extending, developing, embellishing, sculpting, and decorating the synopsis of a scenario. It wasn't a pen making marks on a sheet of paper: it was a skater's waltz. I waited for an erasure, for a pause in the flow; but I waited in vain. Not a word scratched out on the entire page. M. Dubondieu screwed on the top of his pen and rose to his feet: his synopsis was passed around from hand to hand. Hypocritically, I told him how good it was. Was I a hypocrite? Surrounded by the books in my furnished room in Levallois-Perret, no. In the office, yes. M. Dubondieu was deaf. He bent over us while we talked to him; his eyes looked as though they'd been sandpapered while we were reading. He was a provincial from Bordeaux who did enough work for two. His accent added a certain spice to our office. He was about forty.

Denise Batcheff, the producer, called on the intercom to say that she was ready for M. Sachs in her office. I passed Jean Gabin in the corridor and ran to the waiting room.

He was reading the magazine with more good will than concentration and stood up before I began to speak. The elegance of his floating clothes and his important-looking face with its big chin and forehead rendered me almost speechless.

"Would you like to follow me?"

"With pleasure, my dear child," he answered.

I was scarcely young enough anymore to be referred to as a "dear child," but it was said with such indulgence that I felt indulgent too.

I went back to our office. Jean Gabin was sitting on Julienne and Paluot's table swinging his legs; he was talking to M. Dubondieu. Gabin and Prévert never left each other's side. And Carné was always there with them too, his books tucked under his arm. They always came around and gave us all hearty handshakes.

Gabin would descend on the office like a Jove.

"Where's the jailbird?" he would ask.

"No one in the condemned cell?" Prévert would shout.

Then they pushed their hats onto the backs of their heads.

Dark, petite, elegant, very feminine, always perfectly turned out, Denise Batcheff would appear from the inner office, laughing quite genuinely at their tomfoolery.

Carné, very meticulous, was at that time working on a scenario. In the mist, in the darkness, they were just giving the first pickax blows into the rock for their film *Quai des Brumes*.

That day, Gabin was dressed in a green and brown lovat tweed jacket as thick as a greatcoat. With his cashmere scarf around his neck he looked like a welder accustomed to living in a world of sparks.

He raised his head.

"I'm going for a piss," he said to a cactus.

There is a sort of virility that makes the heart rejoice.

Prévert was puffing away at cigarette after cigarette with a slightly nervous air, Marcel Carné was wriggling, anxiously, out of his long camel's-hair topcoat, Dubondieu was holding his head in his hands. We were all like cripples. We all seemed to have one limb missing while Gabin wasn't there.

Where is the visitor with such good manners? Patiently or impatiently, he is waiting in the producer's inner office.

"I must talk to M. Sachs, then I'll be back," Denise Batcheff told us.

She vanished again as Gabin whistled a tune.

"I went dancing last night with a young kid," Jean Gabin said.

His expression was one of rage, but he was exultant. A young kid: the fruit of ecstasy in a real man's mouth.

Carné was hanging up his coat, Prévert crushed out his cigarette in a bowl, Dubondieu stuck the earpiece of his hearing aid back in place.

"What was it you were saying?" he asked.

Gabin obviously enjoyed his bewilderment.

"I was saying that I went dancing last night with a young kid in a little dance hall," Jean Gabin yelled in his ear.

"Ah," Dubondieu said.

His fingers slid down the cord hanging from his ear.

Gabin sat down with the grace of an acrobat on Julienne and Paluot's table. His shirt and necktie were hidden by the cashmere scarf.

"We spent the night together," Gabin went on.

He pressed his fist against his upper lip. He was thinking over last night's adventure.

"Ah," Dubondieu murmured, with a beatific smile.

"A nice kid. Never goes to the movies," Gabin explained. "When she was leaving this morning, I asked: 'What do you think of Gabin?' . . . 'What's Gabin?' she came back with, just like that. Then she went off to work. What are you all looking like that for?" he asked, almost angrily.

We couldn't speak. Because of the young kid and her simplicity.

"I was telling them how I went to a bash last night at a little dance hall," Gabin said as he walked through into Denise Batcheff's office.

The well-mannered visitor closed the door carefully behind him. I had forgotten his romantic-looking cane, his spring topcoat. Prévert, Carné, and Dubondieu were talking among themselves.

I began mixing up the plugs on the switchboard: without his intending it Gabin's enormous presence contributed to my confusion. The word "bash" was still bashing about inside my head. "Hello! This is London calling. Here is your party," I heard a voice say. I jammed in the plug: I was gagging London, I was silencing the whole of Europe. "Hello! Joinville Studios here!" I heard. My hands were shaking with delight. I answered: "The line's busy." I had better things to do: I was gazing at Gabin's young kid. She was skipping along my copper wires, she was looking down with a wave at Miami, Las Vegas, Honolulu, Honduras.

At six that evening, the producer called me into her office: an anthill of complexes for failures and visitors who lacked the courage of their ambitions. Small, placid and vivacious, calm, energetic, always alert, Denise Batcheff dominated her private office. Her personal secretary was working on the files.

"I'm expecting a call from London, go and work the switchboard," she told her secretary.

Would London call back? Was London annoyed? Had Westminster Abbey been struck by lightning?

"Sit down," Denise Batcheff said wearily.

I couldn't sit down: the Thames was flowing under the leather armchair.

To my surprise, someone opened the quilted door without knocking.

"London is on the line," the secretary said.

The producer lifted the receiver and talked into it in English. I sat down in the armchair.

I listened without understanding, I begged the leopardskin coat thrown over a chair not to let London denounce my idleness, my daydreams, my clumsiness. The sound of Big Ben coming over the radio reverberated in my ears.

"Why do you cut London off when they call?" she asked with distress in her voice.

She wasn't trying to torture me. She wanted me to change.

I looked down at my dress, bought on sale from a fashion house, extorted from the being who had since fled from me. Bought on sale and now old into the bargain.

The producer was leafing through a file.

"Answer me," she said without looking up.

"I get confused," I said, "and then Jean Gabin had been telling us about a bash he went to. . . ."

The producer took a contract out of the file, raised her head, and looked into my eyes.

"I get confused, I can't work out which is the right plug."

"I don't think you try," she said.

"No, you're wrong. I'm clumsy, I'm stupid."

"That's true: you haven't got what it takes," she said patiently. "I'll hire another switchboard operator, you can run errands. Beginning now. You can take this contract to Françoise Rosay for her signature."

Speechless, I rose to my feet. The cleaning woman who did the office was too efficient: like so many polished, well-groomed, dusted tigers, the furniture was showing its claws. The producer didn't dare say to me straight out: you're lazy. We would have been in agreement if she had. Clear understanding can produce sympathy. She could have fired me. But she didn't fire me.

I left her office carrying the sealed envelope and went back to my seat.

The shadow selected a book from the shelf. It replaced it with parsimonious fingers without having opened it. It took down another book, another, another. . . . The shadow, not tall not short, came in every day wearing a beige hopsack topcoat. With the collar of its topcoat turned up, it hovered against the bookshelves, leafing through a book, then rejecting it. It was beautiful, with melancholy hands and a half-awakened romanticism stirring on its face. Would it find the idea for a scenario there? We shrugged our shoulders. The shadow's name was Robert Bresson. The director of *Les Dames du Bois de Boulogne* and *Journal d'un curé de campagne* was hatching his films between the pages of books in which he could find no inspiration.

*

I arrived at the Place Saint-Augustin. The festive darkness was intoxicating the hundreds of motorists pursued by imaginary enemies. The cars were escaping along the Boulevard Haussmann, the Boulevard Malesherbes, the Avenue de Messine, the Rue de la Boétie, the Rue de la Pépinière. The light was stripping the display windows, the street lamps were dusting the trees with hoarfrost stolen from a dream, the neon advertisements were throbbing. I scurried for shelter into the Avenue César-Caire, since the church of Saint-Augustin was closed. The sphinx was offering the charity of its doors, of its dark rose-window, of its bunches of domes, to the people walking outside its railings. A barbaric chiaroscuro on the grime-blackened stones, a flirtatious chiaroscuro playing over the faded grays. I forgot that I was an errand girl with an errand to run. I could see men discussing something or dictating behind the windows opposite the church; I found myself in the Rue de la Bienfaisance. The name of the street and a light shining from an attic window consoled me for my idleness, my clumsiness. I came suddenly face to face with a man exactly the color of the wall. He was telling his beads as he circled the sleeping church. I followed him along the Boulevard Malesherbes, under the gentle lighting, through that gentle epilogue of wood ash fading at last to gray. Was he an unfrocked priest? The Broadway, at the end of the Rue de la Pépinière, was tantalizing the eye with its luminous signs.

I took a bus and sat for a moment padding the accounts of my day's expenses; I was finishing the day with a profit. I didn't enjoy the bus ride. I coveted the things I could see through the window: a red leather coat, a russet suède jacket, some lilac shoes, sweet peas in a bowl, the pink cheeks of a young girl, the studious face of a man out for a stroll, the froth, the foam, the naughtiness, the furbelows in the window of a lingerie store, the little fingers of two Arab women knotted together, the intertwined fingers of the wan-faced lovers. Walking slowly, I should have been less envious. I desired all these things as I desire the rough grass, the movement, the bending, the outpouring, the stirring, the play, the swell, the growing murmur, and the plunge of an orgasm. Paris, and the clear evening light. The festivities were beginning on the river, under the bridges, along the embankments. I was a great queen escorted by my kings, the conductor and the driver. We were driving across Paris between our guard of honor: the plane trees and the acacias.

I arrived finally in my room out in Levallois-Perret. The silence, the detachment of four walls and Paris had vanished. My possessions were fantastic to me because they were so faithful. A bowl, a saucer, a plantation of green sentinels in the center of the table. Why had I bought salsify? What a tedious vegetable . . . The sight of them released the sighs inside me. But since they have been bought they must be scraped. If I had a closet in my room, a real one . . . If I had a closet in my room the sunsets would make advances to me. I have a study corner, a divan flanked by two dilapidated wastepaper baskets; I have a certain feeling of friendship for my key, for the apartment blocks in the distance, and I have a gash of sky between two stretches of wall: the most calming of wounds. My soul breathes, my eyes wander across it when there are stars.

The white sticks were put on to cook. I closed the shutters, I said hello and good-by to the fragile moon. The shutters of a furnished room: my pride. I turned off the light and washed my hands beside the shuddering sound of the salsify. Ah, the featherbed comfort of a family. No, there will be no solitary pleasure taken this evening as I wait for dinner to cook. It is a stroke of kindness on the part of providence, this new discovery at the age of thirty, when you've been abandoned. Solitary pleasure, the light in a deserted mirror. You flow down till you reach the knees, so you must be a spring. Oh lonely spring. That evening was set aside for grief, I was to spend it with my grief at not understanding philosophy. A grief that lasted fourteen years. To be able to read Kant, Descartes, Hegel, Spinoza the way people read thrillers. The more I kept trying, the more I forced myself, the more I weighed each paragraph, each word, each punctuation mark, each sentence, the more the sentences, the punctuation, and the words eluded me. The more of myself I gave to the page, the more miserly the page became. Embers sending out an icy cold, that was all my stupidity obtained for me. I had been fired with enthusiasm twenty times by the heading to the third section of Spinoza's *Ethics:* "Of the origin and nature of the affections." I opened the book at page 243 (in the Garnier edition) and underneath the word "Definitions," which also went straight to my head, I read: "I give the name 'adequate cause' to those causes whose effects are clearly and distinctly apparent in themselves; I give the name 'inadequate cause' or 'partial cause' to those causes whose effects cannot be known from the causes themselves." I was already confused even before I'd begun and then, charging onwards at full tilt, I stumbled suddenly upon "adequate cause." I opened my Larousse and my Larousse finished me off. "Adequate cause."

The recalcitrant adjective was raising bumps of ignorance on my brow. My narrow brow, how wretched it made me feel. I mangled the flesh on it with my fingers because it was so puny, so degenerate. "Inadequate cause. Adequate cause." My affections were beginning badly. I was an old oak tree, old like an oak tree, old like an old woman. Adequate, inadequate. My hair began to get longer and longer; if it were all icicles . . . then I would die of cold with my futile desire to become intelligent. Kant, Descartes, Hegel, Spinoza: my promised land was disappearing, my promised land was vanishing. To have an inner life, to think, to juggle and leap, to become a tightrope walker in the world of ideas. To attack, to riposte, to refute, what a contest, what acclaim. To understand. The most generous verb of all. Memory. To retain, a geyser of felicity. Intelligence. The agonizing poverty of my mind. Words and ideas flitting in and out again like butterflies. My brain . . . a dandelion seed blown in the wind. I would read, and forget what I had read while I was still reading it. The only consolation I found was the name Cassandra. When I said it aloud it gave me the illusion of being intelligent. Cassandra, Cassandra. Modesty, elegance. To argue, to exchange views, to have opinions. The snow doesn't dance in the heads of idiots. Cassandra, Cassandra.

My producer was trying to find a title for a film. We all wrote down titles on pieces of paper. "I like 'Pass into Hell,'" she said. "Pass into Hell" was me. You'll make it yet, I told myself. "Pass into Hell" passed into oblivion.

The salsify was burning, the salsify was burned. I turned on the radio and tried to find the trill of a violin in the darkness. No trill. I declaimed: I am alone among hundreds of millions of lonely women and lonely men. You understand me, God, you can see me. More unhappy, less unhappy. How hackneyed it all is. But God sees into things, God knows things aren't that simple. Each case is unique. God looks into these matters carefully, let us hope. Then everything changed without my even lifting my head. The ceiling had become human. I wondered where God is. Was it of him I was despairing. Why not invent God since one invents prayers? Make me not be humiliated, make me not be humiliated. Take away our power of humiliating people. It's worse than killing. It's never too late to do good. It's you I'm talking to, God. You're not listening. How long will you stay away? I pray, but I don't get any better. I don't get any worse. I drift along with the world. I shall humiliate other people without wanting to, and they will humiliate me without wanting to. I am among the living, and that's my trump card. What is that buzzing? It's the noise my ears make when they don't want to be alone. Better to eat my dinner, and offer my friendship to the crumbs on the table.

Five days later, Michèle Morgan appeared in the splendor of her green eyes. Till then we had merely admired her face on coils of film: the first rushes of *Quai des Brumes*. Her voice on the telephone reconciled me to the switchboard plugs. It was reality assuming the proportions of a legend: Michèle Morgan arriving on foot from Le Havre with her young brother to try and "get into films," then landing this part opposite Jean Gabin. Everyone was talking about her raincoat in the film; Schiaparelli made all her clothes in real life. We were dazzled by the sight of this young girl emerging as a movie star. Julienne and Paluot discussed translation, literature, and religion with Lanza del Vasto as he sat in his corduroy suit with his thonged sandals protecting his bare feet. We all devoured the youth, the clear-eyed asceticism of his face. And sweet Lévi—a friend of Constance Coline who had just rushed through our office like a whirlwind—teased us and smiled as he wore himself out auditing our accounts.

Paluot drew Lanza del Vasto aside. They talked passionately about the East Indies while frail and pretty Mme. Welsch, the second secretary, sucked fruit drops.

Though I had never said more than good morning and good night to her before, Julienne suddenly asked me if I could help her sort out the letters that had to be signed. I told her how much I envied her vitality, her capacity for work. I helped her, and told her about some of my particularly dismal Sundays. She listened with only one ear: she was absorbed in her own vitality.

"What do you think of Lanza del Vasto?" she answered as she typed.

"He is remarkably good-looking," I replied.

Julienne looked at me. She was typing faster and faster.

"The body of a Viking and the face of an apostle!" she said.

She was fidgeting about on her chair. Her sex, all the most feminine organs hidden inside her seemed to become visible as I watched. I began telling her about my Sundays again. This time she heard me.

"You should go for walks in the country and take the *Church Fathers* with you to read," she said.

Julienne . . . A volcano of fervor. Her glasses made her look older than she was, but her eyes blazed with a generous fire that made her beautiful. She had the liveliness of an enthusiastic sprite. We all felt bad when she cried and got upset, when she talked on the telephone to the wife of the man she loved. Dubondieu would fill his fountain pen. He would look at her without seeing, without hearing. What a strange race, the deaf. . . .

"The telephone!" Julienne exclaimed.

I picked up the receiver.

"Do you still think a great deal and not much of love?"

"Oh I know who you are, you're Maurice Sachs. Yes, a great deal and really not much."

"Why shouldn't you know who I am?" he asked with a hint of mockery in his voice.

There was an empty sound in the telephone.

"Do you want to talk to Mme. Batcheff?"

"Do you want to come and have dinner tomorrow evening at my grandmother's in the Rue de Ranelagh?"

"Will you be there?"

"Why should I not be? Yes, I'd like to speak to Mme. Batcheff," he said.

"Yes, I'd like to come. I'm putting you through to Mme. Batcheff."

"Excellent," he said, "excellent, excellent. You get off the Métro at Ranelagh. Look after yourself till tomorrow."

I didn't get confused. Mme. Batcheff was free. My "tomorrow" stayed hovering over their conversation.

"Let's talk," I said to Julienne. "Oh, let's talk. . . ."

Grumpy and very busy, she was typing away like a maniac. She still suffered from acne at the age of twenty-six, but the red spots and the pimples were invisible in the light streaming from her eyes.

"What's the matter with you?" she asked. "There's so much mail today. . . . We'll leave together if you like."

She had begun using only two fingers in order to type faster. Her black curls were swinging back and forth.

"Why don't you glance through the *Church Fathers*? It's there . . . over at the side. . . ."

I put the *Church Fathers* down on my temporary switchboard operator's table. I didn't open it.

Finally she raised her head.

"You're making a mistake," she commented between two taps. Bing, bing! She was off again.

I shouted: "Oh, you know. . . . Me and theology . . ."

"You should read Saint John of the Cross. 'My tears streamed down like hair unloosed.' "

"You're reciting in Breton!"

"I'm reciting Saint John of the Cross," said Julienne.

"I'll read Saint John of the Cross," I told Julienne.

She began another letter. "My tears streamed down like hair unloosed." I recited the words to myself, I was using the words as a magic incantation.

"Good night, ladies," M. Dubondieu said.

"Good night, Monsieur Dubondieu."

Oh quotidian courtesies.

I waited patiently in the entrance hall, examining the posters for our latest films. Every morning as I came into the office I read the words *Camp volant* by André Fraigneau on one of the posters. The title of a book I had not read, the name of an author I didn't know, gradually became my village, my church tower, my familiar prospect.

"Ah, Paris!" Julienne exclaimed.

I took her by the arm and dragged her into a café near the Gare Saint-Lazare.

Swarming murmurs, conversation, relaxation, rest, smoke wafting in a world far from customers and heads of departments. The shopgirls from Printemps and the Galeries Lafayette were taking their ease before making their assault on the suburban trains.

We squeezed into a banquette. Julienne liked the idea of a Mandarin-Curaçao. She accepted one of my cigarettes.

There is nothing intimidating about a flame. But Julienne intimidated me despite the flame of her intelligence, despite the flame in her gaze. She could speak, write, read, and do shorthand in English and German. She pointed with her finger at a young man and woman buried in each other's arms. I turned away. Their kisses belonged to them. Julienne's face was transfigured. I told her about Maurice Sachs. Julienne was smiling at the couple, her eyes ecstatic. She turned back to me and confided that she was going to hear *Tristan* the following evening. Her eyes sparkled. There were newsboys making their way between the tables, and an old man placed some samples of peanut brittle in our saucers, in our hands. Julienne was still gazing at the young couple. Julienne a romantic shopgirl? No, there was simply a vital ingredient still missing from her heart. She was merely devouring what was placed before her: two lovers. Finally she replied to my question and said that she didn't know Maurice Sachs. Oh yes! she did remember . . . *L'Ecurie Watson*. . . . Yes, it was Maurice Sachs who had translated the stage play. Yes, possibly, she had caught a glimpse of him. . . . The young man and his girl were leaving, Julienne was on the brink of tears.

Outside, Paris was growing calmer, but the newsboys were shouting their wares and waving them in our faces. Julienne wanted to find the young man and the girl again.

"You'll never find them. They're making love in a hotel room."

"You mustn't talk like that," Julienne said. "They're only children."

"Exactly! They've got no time to lose."

Julienne veiled her face with the *Church Fathers*.

I asked: "Are you a virgin or a charity worker or something?"

"A virgin and a Dominican assistant," she answered. And then, emboldened by my boldness: "And you?"

"Yes and no," I said, half closing my eyes in order to add to the mystery.

Julienne told me that she lived with her parents, that she could come and go as she pleased, but that she still felt constricted. I felt sorry for her as I imagined the melting strains of *Tristan* filling her cramped little room. Julienne's English and German were self-taught. She had left her private school at the age of sixteen and lived ever since on a diet of music, painting, and books. She produced a book of Browning's poems from one pocket of her coat and a book of Hölderlin's poems from the other.

"I'll translate them for you," she said, "some Sunday when we go for a walk in the country."

*

Next day I looked for the Ranelagh Métro station on page 154 of the *Map of Paris by Arrondissements*. And Ranelagh, between Jasmin and Muette, in due time caught my eye with its modest characters, preceded by Michel-Ange-Auteil and Michel-Ange-Molitor with their thick, black ones. Ranelagh. It was oriental, guttural. By whom had I been invited?

Rue de Ranelagh. I found myself in a street in a provincial town, the silence of green plants at the windows and the coolness of the Métro still in the hollow of my hand. The heat striking up from the sidewalk was not uncomfortable. I checked on the swing of my black and white checked dress, bought that very day at the Galeries Lafayette, and dusted off the toes of my high-heeled suède shoes. No, I wasn't trying to look attractive. I was trying to look impressive.

"One flight up," the concierge said.

He opened the door right away and smiled: I was early. His mouth—it was the mouth of a woman—with its upper lip pointing upwards like a circumflex accent, looked like Marguerite Moreno's; his large chin had a certain swelling curve to it that recalled the purse of a Breughel peasant. The full chin, the generosity of the chin, made one forget the mouth. A worn mouth, a mouth that had lived.

"You're early. Excellent. Come into my room."

I went in first. The window was open to the greenery outside. The street now seemed less old-fashioned, less quaint.

"You've changed your hairdo," he said playfully. "It makes you look older, it suits you."

He laughed and I laughed even louder than he.

When he laughed his mouth protested against his gaiety.

The hair-slide fell down my back, my hair tumbled down around my neck.

"Your office hairdo!" he said in his singsong voice. "And so, my dear child, we already have our little private jokes. . . ."

He was making me too much at home.

He rubbed his hands together as though he were just stepping down from a pulpit. His hands were plump, his suit of magnificent tussah.

"Scotch? Gin? A martini? A Pernod? A cocktail of some sort?"

He offered me an English cigarette.

"A Scotch, it's the first time. . . . Your room is made of books," I exclaimed.

He uncorked a gold carafe.

I went over to the table where he had poured the drinks. He asked me if I would take soda water with it. He has lived, he has really lived, I said to myself, because I could see he had lost a considerable amount of hair. I didn't want soda water.

"Come now, you must have whiskey and soda," he said. "Why be eccentric?"

He gave a short laugh. He was giving a deliberate caricature of the benevolent host. He mixed the two Scotches. Velvety movements and gestures. The glasses became two chalices in his dimpled priest's hands. The silk, the tussah of his jacket, rustled as he officiated.

"The heat this evening is very trying," he said. "What?"

The "what" was added for his own peace of mind: he was damping the echoes of his solitude. Maurice Sachs still sought some form of communication even when asking a question that required no answer.

"The heat? It's very nice weather," I said after my first mouthful of whiskey.

He lighted a cigarette and went on shaking the match for a long time. The flame stubbornly resisted his stubborn efforts to extinguish it. He wiped his face, which was not sweating.

"I feel as though I'm floating," he said. "You have to float when you're fat. So, let's float. Do you like my room? There are more bottles of Scotch in the kitchen, more cigarettes in my table drawer. Drink. Smoke. You're not drinking. You're not smoking."

I was petrified by his opulent way of life, by the thoughtful detail of his generosity. I thought him very kind, and too well mannered.

"Sit on the divan," he said.

He was strolling about with his glass in his hand.

"No," I said. "It's so low. I'd rather walk around like you."

I went over to the table. I had never seen so many photographs on one wall.

"That's Wilde," I said, "Wilde with Alfred Douglas."

He poured another huge shot of Scotch into his glass, though he had not emptied it.

"Wilde," I said again softly to myself.

I thought he looked rather like Oscar Wilde.

"Let's go in and eat," he said.

I was delighted by the personality of his rich young student's room, and the Scotch was warming me the way snow held in the hand will warm it a moment later. I was intimidated, and in ecstasy. I walked in front of him across to the dining room. I tightened my muscles so that he wouldn't notice my feminine buttocks.

He introduced me to his grandmother. I remember a vigorous head of white hair; I remember a pale complexion, a round face, and the reticence and robust health of the eyes. One is never touched by a grandmother when she is not one's own.

He tossed the salad with the calm air of a paterfamilias, adding a coral-colored dressing.

"Do you like—?"

It was an English word I didn't understand. His pronunciation made me a stranger as the truck-garden lettuce turned pink.

He looked up at his grandmother who was delicately carving the wing of a chicken. I forget quite how we got from there to the explanation of how they were related to Bizet. The circular table, the lace tablecloth cascading down onto the carpet, the silverware, the complicated place settings all filled me with anguish. Thank heavens their maid was not in evidence. Three presences instead of two would have intimidated me even further. I am in society, this is my first meal in polite society, I said to myself, as though I were telling myself that I had succeeded in reaching the moon. I wiped my moist hands on the tablecloth, forgetting all about my napkin.

He placed two leaves of salad on my plate. The dressing had sugar in it. I wondered what such very ordinary lettuce leaves were doing on such a distinguished piece of china. The plate had turned an everyday vegetable into a candied rose petal.

"Do you paint?" he asked.

He was cutting off great pieces of chicken and putting them on our plates.

"Do I paint? Why?"

"You're not eating. You're gazing at the festoons of dawn around your lettuce. What?"

When he ate, the food scarcely stayed in his mouth two seconds.

"No, I don't paint," I said irritably.

He sprinkled the salad lying on his plate with the coral dressing. The idea suddenly flashed through my mind that he ate so much in order to still an ache in his heart, a wound in his soul.

"You don't paint. That's fortunate," he said. "Paris is stuffed to the brim with painters."

I let my irritation get the upper hand: "You know quite well that I work for Denise Batcheff!"

Why had I come? Why had I deserted my furnished room in Levallois-Perret?

"You mustn't lose your temper like that, my dear child. There are thousands and thousands of painters in Paris; besides, I don't understand you when you talk stupidly. You work for Denise Batcheff. Good. And I work in my room."

"That's different," I said admiringly.

"It's not at all different."

I regretted my remark. I was afraid I'd hurt him.

"What do you say we set ourselves up again with this raspberry tart? I loathe thirty-six course meals. What's the point of hors d'oeuvres? What's the point of cheese? Eh?"

He floated away in his silk shirt. He sliced the great raspberry tart into four and ate his piece like an ogre. I lit his cigarette for him, then my own. I was hoping to surprise him. He was not surprised.

His grandmother said good night to us in the dining room.

I went back to his room again, to his books, his photographs, his possessions, and the caresses of the street through the open window.

"We're going to have some more to drink," he said. "Alcohol releases one, alcohol liberates one. Isn't that so?"

I didn't dare reply that I was released and liberated already just by being in his room. Paris was floating in. A Paris tamed by the quiet of a provincial street.

Maurice Sachs put a photograph of a pleasant-faced young man in my hands.

"He's gone back to the United States. He was my friend," Maurice Sachs explained.

I turned instinctively to glance at Wilde and Alfred Douglas.

"Look at me, Violette Leduc," Maurice Sachs said firmly.

I looked at him. The furniture, the books, all the objects around us became an austere setting for a play.

"I love young men," he said.

He searched in my eyes as I was searching in his. The power to astonish sat well on him.

"You don't surprise me," I said. "I've read Proust, I've read Gide. . . ."

He did surprise me. A cold splash of reality. I had believed in Charlus, I had believed in Morel, I had believed in Nathanaël. Impalpable, fragile despite their talent and their genius, despite the weight of their characters, they had wandered through my mind much as Chateaubriand's Lucile wandered through the corridors of Combourg. Now they existed. All the same, I brushed my fingers against Maurice Sach's tussah silk jacket without his noticing.

The silence remained unbroken, and Wilde's tragedy hung darkly in the room.

"Are you sad?" I asked.

"Why should I be sad, my dear?" he answered.

I had gone too far. He turned me to ice with that affected "my dear." I wanted him to say: "Yes, I'm sad because he's gone"; I wanted to force my way into a homosexual's private world. He had repulsed me.

I brought him a drink and offered him cigarettes.

"Excellent," he said, "excellent, excellent . . . "

What unction, what blessings, what a crown of kindness he could suddenly place on one's head.

"I shall lend you my book," he said.

He circled a revolving bookcase with his arms.

"You write?" I exclaimed, dumbfounded. "You're a writer?"

"Yes, I write," he answered in a sad voice.

He wanted to laugh at himself, but he couldn't manage it.

He was peering from top to bottom, from bottom to top as the bookcase revolved. He searched and searched.

"You're looking at me, dear child. What is it you're staring at like that?" he asked without raising his head.

"Your initials," I replied very quietly.

Small initials, like printed letters, modest and opulent initials, embroidered in navy blue silk . . . I was reading the signature on the writer's heart.

"Here it is," he said.

I took the book from his hands.

"*Alias*," I read out slowly. "It's by you. . . ."

"You must read it and tell me what you think."

I was lost in my admiration for the white cover with its red title enclosed in a frame of red and black lines. To write, to be published . . . My eyes caressed the three letters *nrf*.

Sachs was pouring us another Scotch on ice.

"You're published by Gallimard!"

"Do you know Charvet?"

He was becoming playful again. He was turning pirouettes so as to forget himself; and yet the eloquent despair was still there in his eyes. His eyes: two gulfs of gentleness.

"I don't know Charvet. I know Jean Goudal."

Maurice Sachs switched on more lamps.

"Charvet is the greatest shirtmaker in Paris, my dear. We shall go and choose neckties together at his shop in the Place Vendôme, if the idea meets with your approval."

It was too much. I was annoyed. I was suspicious of his suggestion.

"I have to work," I said. "I can't go with you to Charvet's. I answer the telephone all day, sticking all the plugs in the wrong holes."

"You answer the telephone, do you? How fascinating!"

He cleared his throat and sat down at the table.

A friend, a leave-taking. I saw black-gloved hands over the photographs. The hands were waving.

"I'm a reader for Gallimard," he said. "No, I don't know Jean Goudal."

I was on the verge of tears. The ease with which he could change his moods unnerved me. I took hold of myself.

"I was nineteen," I said, "wasting my time at the Lycée Racine. . . ."

"Excellent," Maurice Sachs cut in. "I like you better this way. Go on. You were wasting your time at the Lycée Racine," he said mockingly.

He opened a large book and shut the photograph of the young man away between its pages. He was dreaming. I was powerless.

He said: "Where have you gone to, my child? Why are you so preoccupied?"

His hands were clasped on the stiff cover of the book.

"I was preoccupied with . . . with his leaving. . . ."

I indicated the book.

"Please," he said in a dry voice. "You were telling me . . ."

He had relegated me to the harem, surrounded by matrons.

I struggled on: "I met Jean Goudal by the fountain in the Place Saint-Michel. He's a Swiss writer. You've never heard of him?"

Maurice Sachs shook his head. ". . . No. I've never heard of him."

The city was sending gusts of country air in at us through the open window.

". . . We had lunch together opposite the Galeries de l'Odéon. There was a man sitting alone at a table . . . with the face of a monk or a great scholar. An extraordinary man . . . Jean Goudal told me it was Max Jacob."

Maurice Sach's face lit up. "Max! I must give you *Les Pénitents en maillots roses*. You can read it either before or after your punishment . . ."

He left his worktable and put his arms around the revolving bookcase again.

"What punishment?" I asked.

"Reading *Alias*."

"Oh," I stammered, "that won't be a punishment."

He gave me a copy of Max Jacob's *Les Pénitents en maillots roses* in an edition with a fancifully designed cover.

"You must take *The Ballad of Reading Gaol* as well. Have you read it? But of course you've read all of Wilde's things. . . ."

"No, I haven't read it. I've read hardly any Wilde. It's his life I find so moving. People say that was his most beautiful book."

Maurice Sachs closed the window.

I went back to his table. I was not looking at the Wilde standing so sure of himself beside the seated Douglas. I was gazing at Wilde completely alone, sanctified by his scandal. Maurice Sachs walked on tiptoe. I was unable to distinguish the two figures, and I would have liked to clasp Maurice Sachs in my arms. He was glancing through the Wilde, rereading passages, then glancing over at me. A string orchestra sang of deep wretchedness and the sweetness of life when he looked at me.

He set down *The Ballad of Reading Gaol* on top of *Alias* and *Les Pénitents en maillots roses.*

"How he suffered," I said, "and how he redeemed himself."

Maurice Sachs' face changed. His mouth frightened me.

"You talk of redemption! Women have such impudence. . . . He was famous, he is famous," he resumed after a pause. "To be famous, to become famous in Paris . . ."

His words filled him with despair and tore at my heart. I felt that he was very unhappy. I didn't dare mention *L'Ecurie Watson.* His longing was so misbegotten, as our deepest longings so often are. Fame comes despite ourselves. I didn't dare murmur in reply: tap, the reader knocks on your paper, then asks what you are writing as you write it. You publish it. Tap, the reader has come to say, yes, he will accept what you have written. So many photographs of famous men on the walls, so many books in the room, so many little ornaments in perfect taste, so much candor filled me with pity. And yet his corpulence, his hospitality, his generosity during that first evening together made me respect him too.

"Let's have a last drink to set ourselves up again," he suggested.

He opened the window. Paris was asleep. Paris was taking the night air.

I was ashamed of my woman's hips as I said good-by to him. I thought of myself as Aphrodite, I was willing my rump into nonexistence. Oh to metamorphose myself into a young torero emerging in triumphal glory from the arena . . .

Métro, Métro, I said to myself, here I am the same as ever, a failure with another memory. I'm coming, little furnished room in Levallois, I'm tired of new sensations. He's fat, I thought, he floats about, he's cunning, he has cherub's wrists, but Scotch can sweep away our misery. He's gay, and he longs to cry. Knowing how to get along with people. He knows everything there is to know about getting along with people. I don't want to remember him: I'll see him again.

I hugged the three books to me from Ranelagh to Havre-Caumartin. On the seat opposite, a passenger was asleep, a worried-looking traveling salesman. A briefcase with several compartments, his hand grasping the battered handle, metal tips on the flaps, automatic pencil clipped on the side. Sleep, absence, presence of a stranger, offerings to the man and the room in the Rue de Ranelagh. The evening was over, the reaction had set in. A homosexual. A man who is neither a monk, a eunuch, nor a senile old man. A man who is more than that and less than that. A homosexual: a passport to the impossible. I had loved the spurned old Charlus so very much, I had been so fond of that Lucifer Morel and gone so deep into the maze of Albertine. . . . Insecurity had offered me dinner with its old grandmother, the impossible had mixed me Scotches, given me cigarettes and books. His eyes pursued me. They were too gentle, too sad, too deep. I saw them again in the face of the traveling salesman sitting asleep, as though the face of Maurice Sachs were a light shining through it. Brutally, I said in a low voice: poor fellow. I was thinking as much of Maurice Sachs as of the worn-out salesman opposite.

That night I read *Alias*.

*

The new switchboard operator was at my post when I arrived the following morning. Flat face and big burning eyes. She told me about her life in Istanbul. Two hours later she was handling the plugs with the agility of a professional lace-maker. Denise Batcheff decided that I was to run errands for her personally as well as for the office. I was also to act as M. Dubondieu's assistant.

What delicious banishment when the producer sent me to her private address in the Rue de Beaujolais with a hatbox. . . . I would venture as far as the steps leading up to the stage door of the Comédie Française. Sometimes there would be a young man leaping up them two by two. Hippolyte with his topcoat flying in the wind? It was possible.

I would continue on my way under the arcades of the Galerie des Marchands with its little stores facing onto the Palais-Royal gardens. "Smoke a meerschaum" I was advised by a pink banner in one of them. Then the stamp collections in the windows further on attracted me. I often longed for a postmark from the Fiji Islands or the Leeward Islands, to be delivered by a mailman who would recognize me without knowing me. I squashed my face against the glass in front of the displays. Antigua, Barbados, Tasmania, Malta, Cyprus . . . A stamp from Zem cost several hundred francs. White hair, red hair, gray hair, fallen rose petals scattered among the wigmaker's glass vials, and then I was coming to the taffeta, the shot silk, the grosgrain of the National Assistance, of the Artisans' Benevolent Fund and the Tradesmen's Benevolent Fund, I was coming to Marie Stuart's store. It was not the trees I was breathing in; it was the explosive breasts of the scornful Directoire beauties. Their ribbons were whipping my face; the laughter of their beaux, the Incroyables, shattered the air. There are some places that can never be reduced to silence.

One afternoon, I read a note pinned to the door of the apartment: "Please make deliveries downstairs." I rang the bell one floor below. A bright, cheerful maid, a well-mannered countrywoman, asked me into the kitchen. She took the box I was to deliver and said: "I'll take it into Mme. Colette's room for now."

"Colette?" I said.

"The writer," replied the maid.

She left me there. I was standing among Colette's saucepans, near Colette's stove, beside Colette's kitchen buffet. I said good-by to Mme. Colette's maid and stole down the stairs like a thief in the night. Down in the gardens of the Palais-Royal once more, I walked along beneath Colette's windows as though she were writing her books on the glass.

I observed a cyclist sitting on a bench, resting near his bike, I observed the shape of a candy held in a child's hand, the shape of a flower in a pot, I thought I was already writing, without paper and pencil, because I was hearing, because I was memorizing the caress, the delicacy, the romance of the wind in the leaves. I left the gardens of the Palais-Royal, I was carrying the city on my shoulders, I was shriveling up again as I walked back to the office. A bakery revived me. I chewed on a croissant: my defeats, so many flakes of pastry, fluttered down onto my clothes as autumn scatters its flakes on the earth to increase the sadness of the year's decline.

That evening, after my hors d'oeuvres out of a carton, my inexpensive sparkling wine, my cutlet and my strawberries embedded in cream cheese, I took a walk along the Avenue du Bois. I walked as I walk in the country: enjoying the well-oiled articulation of my joints. I was drinking in the evening, and there was a serpent waiting for me: I began to covet all the most beautiful cars in Paris. A pale blue, open touring car lined with pale beige leather slowed down beside me; the door swung open, almost scraping the sidewalk. A man invited me in. It was his gray hair with silver flowing in its waves that attracted me rather than his face. I stepped in and set my foot upon a river of melted gold. The automobile began to move. The driver's hands scarcely touched the wheel and the gathering speed was an angelically smooth ejaculation. We didn't speak.

The rushing air of our progress was stronger than any wind. The car drove further and further into the Bois, along the avenues of trees. Then it stopped. The man switched the headlights up, then off.

"You're not pretty, I like that," he said. "Give me a very long kiss."

His face was beginning to look cruel. I kissed him for a long time without enjoyment. Men who are always ready for such casual adventures astonish me as much as meteors. They meet a mouth, and they throw themselves into it. The scent of his bath, the scent of his tobacco were inoffensive enough, and yet I took fright when he pulled up my skirt. I pushed open the heavy door and ran off without closing it. Night was coming on, I ran homewards, glimpsing the lovers as they melted away into the unlit avenues where cars were not allowed. More cars glittering, more men with searching eyes behind their wheels. I walked all the way home. What was it I wanted? To do nothing and possess everything.

I prepared a bacon and potato dish for the following evening, wordlessly telling the herbs and the onions that I was now safe from danger, that there was a book waiting for me, that I could now sit and read *The Ballad of Reading Gaol.* I opened the book, then closed it again immediately. I opened *Alias,* then closed that again equally quickly. I switched off the light. I went back to Maurice Sachs, to his room, to that evening in the Rue de Ranelagh. The darkness inside me was not intense enough: I pressed my hands on my eyelids, I was hoping to see a man of crystal instead of a homosexual. I had no desire to see them coupling in my private darkness. I wanted to hear their good mornings and their good evenings, I wanted to gauge their capacity for tenderness and take the pulse of their emotions. Nothing came. All I saw was Maurice Sachs lying in a shapeless mass on the divan we had both scorned. I saw him alone, very alone under his grandmother's roof. That frightening mouth was still tyrannizing over the rest of his face, even in sleep, while the moon shone in at the window, demolishing the photographs of famous men upon the walls. I switched on the light and looked at the time. A quarter of one in the morning. I wanted to get dressed, I wanted to go out, find a café still open, call him, thank him for the evening and hear his voice of a man set apart, while women with their men were loving, dancing, and sleeping intertwined. I gave up the idea. He intimidated me, he would intimidate me.

*

The following Sunday, Julienne—under the influence of the writer René Schwob and attached to the Dominican order as a lay assistant—took me out to Port-Royal. There were a hundred or so young girls nibbling their lunches on the grass slopes and embankments. They were the "Christianity" group. Obviously I could escape if I wanted to. Would I escape? Making decisions and sticking to them is not my forte. I stayed. Julienne, being very much in demand, neglected me, inevitably enough. I still wonder why she kept her pantheism locked up in the *Church Fathers*. She drank in the sky as though she could never get enough, she munched the leaves, the grass, the flowers, she hugged the horses and the cows, rocked cottages to sleep, offered her bare arms to the sun and her knees to pebbles and insects. We ate our lunch. My garlic sausage, my Pernod, my wine, cast a chill over the proceedings. A young girl with an ardent and ascetic Spanish face, her hair coiled in glossy black headphones over her ears, was talking about the devotional works she'd been reading. She also discoursed on theology, once her sandwich had been consumed. I didn't understand, I didn't try to understand. The young girl's face became so feverish that I soon found it hard to distinguish between religion and galloping consumption.

The Sunday after that, while she was busily picking daisies already heavy with sleep, Julienne told me about her first job as a secretary with the publisher Bernard Grasset. The manuscript readers used to help her up onto a table, study the length of her skirts, give her elementary lessons in make-up and tell her about Nietzsche, Greece, and Wagner at the same time. They helped her discover music and books. Julienne recited some Barrès. I wasn't convinced, but I was affected by the scorching heat of Barrès' style nevertheless. Julienne also told me about her trip to the South of France with Bernard Grasset and his retinue. He always turned his back on the sea: he was punishing himself. Julienne was sorting her flowers, her mouth made bubbles as she whispered: L'Ile de France . . .

My afternoon, my gliding bark . . . Light, the landscape's mirror. Mellowness and moderation, puffs and streaming trails in the sky. Ile-de-France, my countryside so well tended and perfected. Ile-de-France, my bath of sobriety. White snowball bushes on the other side of the road, snow-hung bushes and the dilapidations of the little gardens. Julienne was weeping. There was a smell of sweat and sensual pleasure, the scent of yellowing grass, eddying toward us in warm gusts.

"I'm always looking for him," she said. "He's present and absent at the same time. You wouldn't understand."

I understood. I felt upset for her. Why didn't she go out with him sometimes on a Sunday? Julienne gave a dismal laugh. It was impossible. She didn't even dare imagine such a thing. He was married. I tried to think of some way to shatter this dream of love, some way to rescue her from this universe without hope.

"I know an incurable narcissist. . . ."

Julienne replied that we are all narcissists.

She couldn't walk straight, she was weeping into her handkerchief.

"I know a woman who masturbates. . . ."

Julienne begged me to stop. I shouldn't talk about such horrors.

"They're not horrors. They are realities which are sometimes a preferable alternative."

"Oh, don't go on," she cried. Her grief made her ugly.

"All right, if you don't want to be distracted, I give up," I answered.

"So much the better," she replied.

The bunch of daisies clutched in her hand was soaked with tears.

"You could learn to swim. I was unhappy and I learned to swim in a river. . . ."

Julienne begged me not to go on talking nonsense.

We arrived at a village as dusk fell. Farms and still more farms. Mud tracks, dung, poultry running free along the ruts. Men and still more men, all wearing boots or clogs.

"Where are we?" Julienne asked one of them.

"You're in Eve," the peasant answered.

We went into a café. There was a crowd of farmhands drinking beer or cognac or wine and smoking Gauloises or strong-smelling pipes. Julienne gazed at them avidly; she was unaware that she desired every single one of them.

We left Eve. Night was beginning, the sky was leaning down toward us, the horizon flecked with lights was a nativity. The night against my haversack and my pubis. Two stones signaled to us from the side of the road. We sat down. I talked about my years in the publishing business while Julienne powdered her face. The catch of her compact clicked shut. I talked about the Lycée Racine, about Gabriel, about Hermine, about the school at D—. I didn't mention Isabelle.

"I shall never find him again," I heard myself say.

"Who?"

"Gabriel."

"Is he dead?"

"I've no idea. He disappeared. He often used to disappear."

Absent for nine years. He passed before me, a rigid giant with his cigarette in the corner of his mouth and his shiny new eyes.

"Why wasn't he your lover?" Julienne asked with reproach in her voice.

"I was afraid. It's a thing I've always been panic-stricken about. Sperm."

Julienne gave a cry of horror, then a satisfied little laugh.

I went on: "Did he really want that? I don't think he did."

Why hadn't he raped me in the blaze of noon, on the backs of the lizards?

"Poor Violette," she said. "You're always unhappy."

*

At the office we were sometimes unfair and superficial in our attitude toward Julienne. We would exchange secret smiles as she declaimed about her love for Provence. She never noticed anything. She was up in the clouds. Her blindness, and by that I mean her generosity, when it came to her feelings for the other sex was breathtaking. It was very sad being able to understand what was going on inside her better than she did. Our clearsightedness made us all into cripples. Julienne was longing, yearning, waiting for marriage with a glow of legend in her eyes. Trust. She trusted every man alive. The husband born of her desires, her enthusiasms, her patience, her impatience, her meditation, her frenzy, her prayers and her insomnia, whether an accountant or a schoolteacher, was to her the lover of the Song of Songs. She was sculpting her marriage and her husband with her own hands. And out of what? Out of her music, her books, her walks, and all her aspirations. Julienne used to stay on typing after office hours. If I stayed on with her she would tell me about how she was going to wander over the hills of Provence with her husband, the great unknown. She took off her glasses. Silence. We were listening to her future. What was he like, this future mate? His hair, like Jesus' hair, fell down upon his shoulders. Straight, and slightly oily, because long, oily hair gives a greater feeling of abandonment. And to set the Byronic seal upon his beauty, he had a limp. His brow, born of Julienne's long, sleepless vigils, had ash upon it.

December 26, 1963. It has been snowing since midday yesterday. A gray snow, soiled with city dust, lying over the earth and roofs of Paris. The sky is dirty, the sky is a bung of dirty linen. The snow is dancing, that's the one good thing about it. Yesterday evening it was just littering the ground like snippets of hair on the tiled floor of a barbershop. The dancing snow made me feel young again at first.

I used to go for a walk every day around the old harbor of Villefranche-sur-Mer. At midday, when the heat poured down from the sky. Worn-out oceans, and I their pirate. The sweetness of each moment: my own company, the easing of my nerves. The colors were soothing one another. The faded blue, the pale blue rocking an old boat. They were repainting their dinghies, I could hear *Les Gymnopédies* as though I were in Paris, the sea water was a foundation for my frescoes. Washed-out blue, another lullaby, another song to send me to sleep near the hulk of an old ship. My empire of invalids, my crustacean cemetery. The dying man who will not die: the proud jut of a prow, a ship, resplendent in its coat of rust, still yearning to set sail on stormy nights. The sea and its wrecks are neighbors. I sat down on a capstan, I looked out toward the horizon and saw how the sea had hung its colored wash out from the shore, while draft-horses rested their heads on my knees. I was no longer rotting in the last of my futures, in my very last moment, and the gulls fell silent as they flew past. My old, abandoned boats, tempests are only fables now, my dead things bought with my own eyes, my embroidered lime trees, my limes filled with insect murmurs while the *Magnolia* and the *Typhon* still hold themselves erect. They're going to dredge the Seine. Oh how lugubrious it is, that boat like a piece of a factory floating on the water. They go dredging with their gray boat and purify our river as it flows through Paris.

My replacement at the switchboard asked me if I would like to spend my two weeks' vacation with her on the island of Noirmoutier. I accepted. I didn't mention Hermine, I didn't tell her I was a woman who had been discarded. She drank hard, she smoked from morning till night with a refreshing inevitability. We chattered on the sands, recalling Simone Signoret's eyes when she paid one of her occasional visits to the producer, admiring the energy of Madeleine Robinson—her thick beige coat, her windswept hair. The movie world became more human, more simple. We breathed the air off the salt-beds as we slept in our room looking out over the farms. In the evening, we ate fruit and drank bowls of milk warm from the cow. I loved the coolness of the red, flagged floor in the inn at noon, I loved the virginal whiteness of the lobsters inside their white shells, I loved the destiny of their sleep. We talked about Julienne; we wondered how she was enjoying her vacation in the South of France.

*

Julienne. I had left her a beggar; when I returned, she had become a winged victory. How gently the sun had treated her, her tanned arms, her face, the opening of her blouse. Prettier, younger, all her features smoothed out, she was always looking at herself now in her compact mirror. She came in early in the morning, leaped at the stack of incoming mail, tore open an envelope, read through ten or so sheets of paper covered with writing of extravagant dimensions, exclaimed, emitted little cries and laughs of pleasure, shut the letter away in her bag and tobogganed away on her typewriter. Excellent vacation, perfect weather, Provence a dream. We waited. The following day the letter that arrived was even bulkier than the previous one.

I picked up the empty envelope. She thanked me, and I ventured to remark that she seemed happy since her return. She stretched herself and allowed her eye to wander over a landscape that belonged entirely to her: vistas of happy moments without a doubt. The rabbits in the fields, the wild thyme, Julienne murmured. That evening she insisted we leave together.

Paris was still on vacation, even though one had to kick aside the falling leaves of a departed summer, for Paris was a faded rose that evening. The silky decadence of a great city at seven in the evening. As I walked beside a silent and inspired Julienne, I felt that I too had a secret to confide. She was plunged deep in her thoughts. I led my radiant sleepwalker to the terrace of a café. She informed me that she would like a pastis because he had taught her to drink pastis.

"The one who writes to you?"

"Yes," she answered, with a smile intended for him.

The setting sun was blazing on an attic window. She cast off the weight of his first name as she gazed at the flaming panes. His name was Roland. At last she began to talk. Her story became my story. Her meeting my meeting.

. . . She had clambered up and down the goat tracks all day, she was returning contentedly home. How long had she been hearing that noise? It was a motorbike. She didn't want it, she didn't want the silence of the hills snatched from her. She had turned around. The motorcyclist stopped short. The memory of the foot reaching down to the ground, the memory of long, gentle hands on the handlebars. She was dazzled because he was so self-composed. The fury, the impatience of the motor. Julienne thought he was about to drive off again. He asked her where she was going. Espadrilles, a pure South-of-France accent, hills that would soon be lavender or purple . . . Where was she going? She couldn't answer him, she had lost the use of her tongue. Stripped of all that she had been, of everything that she had ever had until this meeting. He grew impatient: if she wanted a ride on his bike she would have to hold onto him because the road was in need of repair and the going would be pretty rough. Hold onto him. It was madness, and it was true: the road was in need of repair. No, she wasn't frightened. Frightened in Provence? Of what? They drove off on the bike in a cloud of dust. . . . Julienne put her arms around him without embarrassment. Her past, her lean years, her unhappy love affair were now no more than this rediscovered and familiar feeling of winding her arms around a young man's waist. The motorbike leaped up and down, he drove on, she could not see his face, her head was swimming. No, she didn't look around; no, she saw nothing. Solitude, solitude all around them at sixty miles an hour.

He dropped her in one of the village squares. She wouldn't see him again, the ground was slipping away from under her, the scent of the wild thyme filled her with despair. She was alone, she would be alone. The stranger had turned his bike around: it would be stupid not to spend the rest of the evening together. One second of good sense and she would lose him forever. And there they were once more, speeding along the roads that sped away in front so fast they could never catch up. Twenty-seven years old. He knew all the roads. They raced on, and the plants, the smells, the scents went with them. The earth, the grass, the plants were shaking off the long heat of the day. The olive trees cascaded down on them, rocks bled before them, the slopes welcomed the lilac trees' caresses. The scents and the smells were rising into the dark and intermingling. He knew all the places where the peasants laid their snares. Sometimes he took both hands off the handlebars; he was an acrobat. He shouted back to her that they would eat grilled sausages for dinner. The motorbike lay on its side, the sausages were cooking on their twigs. They say that happiness can never be conscious, that you can't touch it when it's there. Julienne touched the stranger's sweater as he tended the fire and kept watch on the twigs. It was a new life that Julienne had lived elsewhere. Happiness is something remembered. He pulled a flask of good, rough wine out of one of his saddlebags. They wandered about until two in the morning reciting Nietzsche, Péguy, Claudel, Barrès to one another. She hummed him fragments of *Tristan* and *Lohengrin*. This man whom she had always known, whom she had met at last, was the answer to all her prayers.

What was his profession? Julienne's face changed. Profession? She hadn't asked. They had parted at three in the morning. What dexterity, the night after, when they had to open the locked door of a barn. "Nothing can resist him. He opens things without forcing them, he knows every sort of lock there is." In you come, he'd said to her. He was already holding the ladder for her. The scent of hay, springtime sinking in defeat, layer after layer. Then they had been two simple animals, simple the way animals are at such moments. They wanted to see the hill again. Dawn was breaking. A bird sang. They washed in the stream, in the cool water that sparkled in their mouths. He picked her flowers. They went for a long drive on the motorbike before the villages were even awake. After the sausages came a wild rabbit cooked in the open air; after the barn another barn; after the stream another stream. They never left each other's side until the moment came for Julienne to leave. Did he love her? She hadn't asked herself. She thought her vague schemes of marriage meant that she had her future firmly by the mane. I thought back to a past much older than Julienne's. To Isabelle, my fleeting love. We had loved each other, it was our secret.

That evening, my head buried in the pillow, I reached the stage of wondering, after having lived and suffered so much, how exactly Julienne and her Provençal boy set about loving each other in the hay. I was a virgin still, despite the sullies of my flesh. I often longed to find Gabriel again so that I could begin with him. And then, I was beginning to forget Hermine, Gabriel, Isabelle, for that is life. But I also still remembered Gabriel, Isabelle, Hermine, and that was already a hint of death. I had gone toward women as the lonely peasant, cut off one snowy night, makes his way toward a sheepfold. I had behaved odiously to Hermine, but I had had as much faith in my demands as in her powers of sacrifice. I had always been tired of Hermine, that was the way it was. I would never have left her. She was a saint, and I could not forgive her for having betrayed her faith. I thought of my old age. It terrified me. My strength would ebb away; I should be without even a rock to rest against. I was ugly already, and I was going to become a monster of ugliness.

A penny is a penny. We were very concerned with our pennies when we went out together. We both paid for our own drink, our own sandwich, and then we split the tip in two. It was of small importance. Julienne bubbled over with vitality all the same. She translated Novalis to me in suburban trains. So much earnestness, so much openness, so much ecstasy. Every passenger in the compartment would hang on her lips. When she said: "I've almost got it," they smiled with excitement. They all wanted the *mot juste*.

One Saturday morning, sitting in the office flooded with light, Julienne opened *Le Figaro* and immersed herself in the literary columns. I was working on a synopsis. Dubondieu was writing, pretty Mme. Welsch was humming and sucking fruit drops.

"Oh this is too much," Julienne exclaimed.

She opened her handbag and unfolded one of the letters she received every morning. Her face lit up. "It's the same, it really is."

"Something wrong?" my replacement asked.

By now Julienne was laughing, bent double over the newspaper.

"He's been copying out Diderot's letters to Sophie Volland. It's marvelous, Roland really is marvelous."

She read out some passages from *Figaro* followed by excerpts from the letters. They were identical.

*

The producer called me in. I thought she had finally decided she would have to dismiss me because of my ever-increasing uselessness. I used to envy the bootblacks in the streets, the randomness of their activities, the sky above them serving as a sign, the dirt on the sidewalk to sell their wares for them, their energetic absorption in their task.

She told me she had arranged for me to meet an acquaintance of hers.

"You'll get on well with her," she added.

"What is her name?"

"Bernadette. You must go and call on her tomorrow."

"What for?" I asked. "Why must I meet her?"

"So that you can become friends," answered the producer.

"You can't arrange to meet someone so that you can become friends. . . ."

"Tomorrow at two P.M.," the producer commanded.

At noon next day, I dressed very carefully. I picked out a new dress hanging between two completely threadbare old dresses from Schiaparelli. The new dress was skin tight, fitted by a dressmaker in a not very fashionable part of Paris. I was satisfied with it, it was an adequate expression of my means.

I walked along a street in the sixteenth arrondissement, as provincial-looking as the Rue de Ranelagh but livelier. I looked for the right address. Tall, narrow house, cramped staircase, then I found myself all squeezed together with a beating heart at the threshold of a little sun-filled drawing room.

"I was expecting you," Bernadette said, moving forward to greet me.

At last I was shaking one of those hands I had marveled at in Antoine's salon, at Schiaparelli's, at Rose Descat's: a fluid, supple hand; mist made flesh. The slim elegance of the models who posed for *Vogue* and *Fémina* was no longer a mere display of unreal artifice. Paris had lost some of its destructive power over me now that I had set foot in this little room. We too were expecting you, cried the bright, Indian colors of Bernadette's sweater. She introduced me to Clara Malraux. I felt that it must all be a waking dream. I was assailed by an attack of shyness: the worst in my whole life. There were little kettles of boiling water bubbling shrilly inside my head. I was paralyzed by my own emotions, my stupidity was making me too hot, I could no longer see Clara Malraux's bright eyes, or the blue, almost sea-green eyes of Bernadette. The latter encouraged me with smiles and glances to intervene in their conversation. I couldn't. I was too crushed by the constant flow of famous first names recurring in their remarks. The precious fingers offered me a cup of coffee. How did one drink a cup of coffee, how did one hold a cup of coffee, how did one take sugar out of a sugar bowl? I could no longer be myself: their poise was reducing me to a zero. Everything swam in front of my eyes. I gulped down everything they said without understanding it. I shook myself. I tried to speak, but no sound came out. She offered me an English cigarette, another cup of coffee. I refused. I would rather have died than have them watch the life I lived on other days. How could they talk about everything so very quickly without saying stupid things? Clara Malraux kept laughing an abstract laugh. Her voice was high-pitched and musical. Suddenly it grew deeper and more muffled. Clara Malraux was sympathizing, saying how well she understood, and leaving. The even flow of her elocution filled me with panic. She took her leave and shook me heartily by the hand, which reassured me; but the fact remained that her intelligence, which was as supple as a virtuoso's fingers, and the atrophy of my brain made a barrier between us. She is leaving in disgust, I told myself. Still the same masquerade of vanity and false humility. Dressed in her leather jacket, with her hair stolen from some misty valkyrie, she closed the door.

Bernadette asked me questions: crutches tossed across the room to me. She was careful with my day-by-day existence, she treated my ailing brain with tender caution. The sun of the narcissist began to warm me back to life. I flowered, and the frail, unfulfilled blue of sweet peas began to tint the furniture and the walls. I confessed my loneliness; her face lit up.

"How well I understand," she said.

She listened and studied me. She approved without criticisms. She asked me if I'd like another "ciggy," handing me an English cigarette. The tightly packed tobacco, the delicacy of the cigarette, the blue veil of hanging smoke: for a moment I felt myself to be the equal of that fine Paris afternoon.

Bernadette made a telephone call: she made a lot of commonplace remarks, she disappointed me. I had been dreaming. I had no existence in her easy-mannered high-society world. Was she a high-society hostess? I decided she wasn't once more when she left the telephone and came back to warm me again with her kindness and her optimism. She must surely know at least five hundred people in Paris, and she was taking the time to linger over someone who couldn't even operate a switchboard efficiently. Yes, she is, I thought whenever she remarked of a journalist or someone in films "that nut, that punk, that megalomaniac." No, I said to myself again when she asked me questions. I sensed too that she had made a decision: never to feel sorry for herself. Her forgetfulness of herself was so pervasive that by the time I left, some of her supple intelligence had transferred itself to me. She tried to transmute sadness and melancholy into raw material for humor. And she succeeded. Yet I still glimpsed brief glints of sadness in the witty malice of her eyes. She kept her balance on this tightrope with phrases like "we laughed like pigs," "oh, he thinks he's Louis II of Bavaria, that one," "I simply don't care a plugged nickel about the whole thing," "they're nobodies," and "he's as nutty as a fruitcake." In the course of the conversation she remarked: "Everything that doesn't make you forget about yourself is a form of compensation." According to her, my situation was going to change. She would find me another job, she would come and get me at the office, we would have lunch together, she would telephone me frequently. I could have lifted the whole of Paris—oh, no more than a hair's breadth—as I walked away from Bernadette's. I didn't ask myself whether she lived on her own or not. She must love music and books because she knew so many writers and musicians.

"Maurice Sachs called to speak to you," Julienne said when I got to the office.

"Maurice Sachs? Where? When?"

"He wanted to speak to you. I told him you'd be in later. He's charming."

"What did you say?"

Julienne raised her voice: "I said he's charming. He thanked me profusely before he rang off."

I collapsed into my chair. Julienne turned on her heels. Already, without pausing for breath, the clatter of the typewriter.

The past? a womb. I was inside it; three-fifteen P.M. by my wristwatch.

"What time did he call?"

"At twenty past two," Julienne replied without hesitation, without a break in the stride of her galloping machine.

Almost three-thirty-two in a building on the Rue d'Astorg. The sky is too pale, the heat too animal. The confused rumble of Paris outside. He wants to speak to me, he wants to see me again, and yet . . . Why am I sad? He is warm, he is friendly, he's gay, he's funny. He isn't charming; his humor is a means of relief. He'll call again in a little while, or else tomorrow. I've seen him once. Our evening together, my sheath, my casket. What is it I'm nostalgic for? I drank him, I ate him, I chewed on him: I wasn't really there. Why this malaise? What malaise? An impeccable welcome, impeccable hospitality, Maurice Sachs. His friend has gone back to the United States. The first homosexual standing before me; my first homosexual momentarily effaced by the photograph of Wilde and Bosie. Ah, this is too much, lower your brazen trumpets of scandal. Bosie, Bosie. I sprinkle my young girl's ashes to the squalling wind. Bosie. I look at him and hold his gaze. I pave hell with the young girls he has never known; what wouldn't I do for your beautiful, cold little mug, Bosie! Is that what I'm nostalgic for? The hair of an adolescent invert, the suffering in my exiled fingers still caught in the mesh of love? You are cold, woman who loves women, lying on your scrapheap. Wilde waiting for Bosie as day melts into night, as dogs bark up into the sky. Wilde waiting for Bosie. His silence, that is why I sob.

"Julienne . . ."

"I'm working."

"Maurice Sachs . . . Do you think he'll call again?"

"My poor friend, how do I know?"

Am I unhappy? Am I really unhappy? The flour gets sticky when I wash my fingers, that never fails to irritate me. I take good care of myself, I shall always take good care of myself. Mustn't fall sick, my health is my capital. This lemon sole is enormous. I eat. For whom, for what? Shall I see her again. She is too nice to me, she goes out of her way too much for me. Another job. Where they'd take me seriously. How will she set about finding me another job? If we go to a restaurant I won't dare pick up my fork, my knife. I prefer sucking my fingers. You see what you're like. Hermine has left me. She thinks she did me an injury, but she's wrong. My mother says it's no good looking at men as though they're paintings. It's no good looking at women as though they're paintings either. Hermine kept me in a prison. Do I go out alone on Sundays now? No, I don't know how. Do I turn the fish over with a knife or a fork? It's not sticking to the pan, that's the first time ever. There has to be give and take in life, oh sure, that's what I said to her, but if a starving bum came and knocked on the door right now, would I share my fish with him? Share my fish? I wouldn't give him so much as the seeds out of m-y lemon after I'd squeezed it on m-y lemon sole. That's how I am that's how we are. Words, well-turned phrases, they don't cost anything. Ouch, what does this fish think, it's an acetylene torch or something? That's the oil, you mutt, not the fish; give and take; that star that won't go away outside the half-open window, could I give that away and take a memory in return? Shall I go to a restaurant with her or not?

The waiter brought us halves of grapefruit. I hadn't known till then that grapefruit could be an appetizer. I waited, wondering if Bernadette would put sugar or salt on it. She ate it as it was; I put sugar on mine, then regretted it. We were eating lunch on the terrace of a restaurant on the Avenue Kléber with trees on one side of us. The place went to my head. My shyness got the upper hand. I stained the tablecloth, my napkin slid off my knees onto my feet, my fork slipped out of my fingers into my plate. Bernadette came to my rescue. I couldn't stop gazing in admiration at the double string of jet beads emerging from her buttonhole and cascading down into the pocket where one often glimpses a handkerchief sticking out.

"What a beautiful suit, what a beautiful black suit. . . ."

"A folly," she said.

"How elegant it is! Where is it from?"

I was fascinated once more by elegant suits.

"It's from Balenciaga."

We talked about dress materials. She suggested we go and see if there was anything good on sale at Balenciaga.

"Oh," I said with a weary gesture, "I'm too ugly, and I shall be thirty soon. . . ."

Bernadette went red with indignation. "Age has nothing to do with it. You have personality. You carry clothes well. You have vitality, and that's what really counts in a woman."

"Do you think so?"

Bernadette was older than I. I asked her if I might call her by her first name. She assented readily. I found her optimism invigorating. How could she still be at home with herself when she had left so much of herself behind?

She would find me another job, but I must be patient.

"Well really!" exclaimed the switchboard operator. "M. Sachs is on the line. He wants to speak to you immediately. Here you are."

"Yes," I said into the mouthpiece, "yes."

"What do you mean, yes?" Maurice Sachs asked.

"I don't know. You asked to speak to me."

The clattering of the typewriter was getting on my nerves.

"You've certainly got an odd way of answering the telephone," Maurice Sachs said. "Yes, I did ask to speak to you. I wanted to ask you how you are after the other evening. Is this Violette Leduc I'm talking to or isn't it?"

People were coming into the office, talking, walking down the corridor. The switchboard operator had pushed up the glass pane.

"Yes, it is!" I said.

My voice cracked. I thought I wasn't going to be able to say anything else.

"Excellent, excellent," Maurice Sachs answered. "Have you read *Alias*?"

I cleared my throat into the mouthpiece. "Yes, I've read *Alias*."

"Excellent, excellent," Maurice Sachs said again. "You can write to me at my address in the Rue de Ranelagh."

"No, I won't write," I cried into the telephone.

"As you wish, my dear child. See you soon."

"Yes."

I found Maurice Sachs sarcastic and affected. I felt as though my arms had been broken, I couldn't think why.

That evening, I reread his book in bed. I ate bacon and potato casserole and drank a half bottle of champagne. The main character of *Alias* faded into invisibility beside my memories of the glittering personage I had seen in the Rue de Ranelagh.

M. Dubondieu was becoming less and less satisfied with my treatments. He looked at me, sighed and buried the pages I handed him inside a file.

Bernadette telephoned frequently. We used to go and sit amid the rainbow-colored embroideries of a tiny Russian tearoom on the Rue Lavoisier. It was there that I met Elsa Triolet for the first and only time. She was writing *Bonsoir Thérèse* then. Her eyes made me think of iron transmuted into light, her round face evoked Borodin's *Polovtsian Dances*. She talked about Mayakovsky.

*

"You worry too much about your Baron de Saint-Ange," said Mlle. Nadia.

She bent back her head: her gray hair hid the error I was erasing so cautiously in an attempt not to tear the paper.

"He isn't my Baron de Saint-Ange. He just dictates letters to me and I do my best."

Mlle. Nadia rested her head completely on the platen of my typewriter. Her big eyes were even bigger upside down.

"You fuss over him too much."

My eraser tore the paper.

"That was your fault!"

Mlle. Nadia crossed her arms over the front of her blouse.

"M. de Saint-Ange comes in late," she said sarcastically. "The hours he keeps. . . ."

"He comes in late and he leaves late."

Mlle. Nadia restrained a malicious laugh.

"I don't like him, your Baron de Saint-Ange. I hope you've guessed. . . ."

She swung away on her revolving chair and bent over her shorthand book. What nice gray hair she had, and how sensibly it was cut. Her foreign accent . . . like rich, black earth, but never a mistake in her French. Her two protruding teeth which she brandished at you when she was in a temper . . . How admirable her dilapidated face, what a combination her big eyes made with the thick lenses of her glasses.

Now she was typing. Everyone was typing. There were five secretaries, all in a line, each with her little table and a telephone.

"Mlle. Nadia!"

She didn't hear. I went back to my machine: "Dear Sir, in reply to your esteemed . . ." No, I didn't fuss over him too much.

"Mlle. Nadia . . ."

She swung her chair around. "Have you made another mistake?"

"No. Naturally I've guessed. Everyone is free, Mlle. Nadia."

"Not to do that."

What fire in her unpowdered face.

"Mlle. Nadia . . ."

"What?"

"He says good morning to you."

Mlle. Nadia leaned her elbows on my typewriter.

"I don't like him," she said with slow emphasis. "I find that disgusting."

Her telephone rang.

Mlle. Nadia walked through into the editors' office. I waited for her to come back.

She was a Russian who had escaped from the Revolution with her brother and her parents. Now her parents were dead she wanted more than anything in the world to go back to her native country and live there with her brother. She said it was impossible though. She couldn't pay the fare. She loved the U.S.S.R. with passion.

A neatly dressed cleaning woman brought us each a cup of tea at our table. We were among the more privileged employees.

Mlle. Nadia's leather briefcase was always open. That way she wasted no time in extracting her copy of *L'Oeuvre* from it whenever she had a free moment. In a low voice she read out one of the articles to me; it was all in italics and written by Geneviève Tabouis, whom she greatly admired. She read and reread her articles four times a day. She lived for her brother and politics. She prophesied war and a revolt of the colonies.

"Can you come and take some letters?" asked the invisible voice of M. de Saint-Ange.

His voice: a violin solo played on a carpet of heliotropes.

Mlle. Nadia shrugged her shoulders. I hated her, I appreciated her good qualities, I pitied her. She was nobody's fool.

I went into his office. The windows gave onto the courtyard with its daily band of tourists inspecting the well, the flagstones, the walls, the proportions of the building, classified as an Historic Monument, in which the firm publishing *La Nouvelle Revue Critique* had its offices. I went, I waited, notebook on knees, pencil ready. M. de Saint-Ange was turning the pages of a file. He coughed.

"Don't be impatient," he said, without turning around.

I wasn't impatient: I was a statue in a museum.

I was convinced that he was only reading in order to keep his eyes lowered, in order to infuse me in my turn with that same calm the perfection of his features produced in him.

"How is the shorthand coming along?"

"Badly, very badly."

I was taking shorthand lessons at a school in the Place de la République, but I couldn't remember any of it.

He dictated; I helped him find the right words.

"Read it back," he said.

He lit our cigarettes with a lighter made of checkered silver.

I didn't read it back. Handsome men, oh there are shoals of handsome men to be caught, and suddenly, what is a handsome man? His vomit between two seats in a Métro compartment. But for all that, young women desired M. de Saint-Ange. There were unreasonable young women who rubbed themselves with ground glass and moaned: "We want him. Him, M. de Saint-Ange."

I burned my dress with the cigarette he had offered me. The telephone rang, the languid hand reached out and took it from its cradle.

"Half-past eight at Fouquet's as we arranged," M. de Saint-Ange said.

I could hear another man's voice at the other end of the line. M. de Saint-Ange removed the telephone from his ear, he was dreaming. I coughed.

"That's all the letters," he said.

Thirty-two, thirty-three perhaps, M. de Saint-Ange. I often stole his English cigarettes and filched a few minutes of his evening engagements. Without hate, without jealousy. It enabled him to share his charms, his beauty, his successes. And then the charm, the beauty, the success vanished away like smoke.

I went back to Mlle. Nadia in our office.

"I answered your telephone for you," she said. "It hasn't stopped ringing all the while you've been away."

"Mlle. Nadia . . . I'm so glad . . . I'm so glad to be back with you. . . ."

I wondered what it was I felt I had to shake off as I closed the door of his office behind me. If I loved him, I said to myself, what a tragedy. I didn't love him. The whole world was there to protect me.

"Mme. Bernadette is coming to call for you here. That was all she said," Mlle. Nadia went on. "You're not listening."

"No, I wasn't listening. Yes, Mme. Bernadette."

I was jubilant at being able to look at M. de Saint-Ange without pain. I began typing the letters, I thought about Bernadette to whom I owed my new job.

Mlle. Nadia swung around to face me. "M. Sachs," she said.

"What!"

I clenched my teeth, I became deaf.

"M. Sachs telephoned to ask how you were."

"Maurice . . ."

His first name had escaped for the first time from his room and our evening in the Rue de Ranelagh. I pushed it back into its cage with the other emotions.

"You call him 'Maurice'?" Mlle. Nadia said.

A silence.

"What did he say, Mlle. Nadia?"

"He was very nice. Now he really is a pleasant man. He asked if you were here. He asked how you were."

"And then?"

"That was all. How pleasant he is. What a pleasant man . . ."

Mlle. Nadia was completely captivated.

Maurice Sachs didn't telephone again.

*

But he walked across the courtyard the following afternoon, without inspecting the stones classified as Historical Monuments. His cane, the bunch of flowers wrapped in their waxy florist's paper and clutched in his other hand did not make him look ridiculous. A convalescent's sun lit up his panama. Precious nineteenth-century cane, ostentatious flowers, expensive panama. Despite the elegance, the taste, I would normally have smiled. But I accepted all this in a homosexual. Dandyism is eccentricity brought to slow maturity, whereas a first attempt upon society is a thousand excuse-me's that no one has asked you for. The flowers in their glazed sarcophagus proclaimed that he was paying somebody a visit.

He came in, advancing nonchalantly amid the clatter of the typewriters. I was already on my feet.

"How are you, dear friend?"

I lost my head: "How did you know I worked here?"

"Was it such a mystery? I telephoned you yesterday, you know. . . ."

"I answered the call for her," Mlle. Nadia said.

Maurice Sachs turned toward her.

"And you did so very pleasantly," he rejoined. "You were very pleasant indeed when I asked you all those questions, and that is very much the exception when one speaks to strangers on the telephone."

She replied with a self-deprecating gasp; her eyes were shining.

"Shall I say you're here?" she asked.

"I should be delighted," Maurice Sachs replied.

"To M. de Saint-Ange?" she inquired.

She was preparing for the worst.

"I don't know M. de Saint-Ange," Maurice Sachs said.

Mlle. Nadia was jubilant. She disappeared into the editors' office.

"I shall entrust these to you," he said. "They might appear a trifle frivolous during a serious conversation."

He set the flowers down on my table. Where was he going? Such preparations . . . I was the quarry of his necktie, of his shirt. Secretly I stole that silk which would never be rumpled by any woman. I made a unique gift of it to myself.

"The setting is pleasant, very pleasant," he commented. "How is the work going?"

His question flattered me. My secretarial duties suddenly assumed the importance of genuine creative work.

"You wrote to me. We'll talk about it later."

"Yes, Maurice."

"Yes, Violette," he answered in the same tone. "Are you unhappy?"

"You intimidate me."

"Don't be stupid," Maurice Sachs said.

Fresh and exultant, he walked through into the editors' office. The skin of his face made one think of the towel being rubbed against it, of the well-being produced by a razor, by shaving cream.

I typed several letters, then the first draft of a balance sheet.

Maurice Sachs emerged from the office.

"Excellent, excellent," he said in an unctuous voice.

He was rubbing his hands, as though his success were an unguent; but the gentle gaze, the deep, sad eyes took no part in his glee.

"Have you read *Alias*? A very pleasant place indeed," he said. "Gladly would I rise to meet the dawn in such a spot. What?"

He leaned over my typewriter.

"Figures. Do you like figures?"

I stood up.

"I have read *Alias*."

"You've a very odd way of behaving," Maurice Sachs said. "Face a mile long, eyes on the ground, fingers ripping your dress to shreds. You don't like *Alias* and I don't like *Alias*. There's nothing tragic about it since we both agree. Why must women turn everything into a tragedy?"

"*Alias* . . . is you!" I cried, moved, idiotic, dazed.

"And what of that?" he asked.

Then in his singsong voice he continued: "You wrote me a letter. You should be a writer. I was just saying so a moment ago."

I gave what sounded like a cry of terror.

He wiped his face.

"Calm yourself, dear child," he said. "I'll see you later. Paris is expecting me, and I expect everything of Paris."

He moved away across the courtyard with slow steps. Where was he going? Who was about to greet him? Who was expecting him? Why did he talk to me? Why had he given me *Alias*? Why did he read my letters? Why did he talk to me about them? I doubted him, I doubted myself.

*

Bernadette, still elegant at the end of the day, by turns profound, frivolous, Parisian, humane, cordial, feminine, gregarious, refined urchin, and emoting music-lover, came to call for me.

We walked down the beautiful staircase arm in arm. The souvenir hawkers outside Notre-Dame were putting away their revolving postcard stands and trashy trifles for the day.

"Gabriel! It's Gabriel!"

There he was. A Paris bridge had shattered ten years of absence. There he was on the other side of the bridge. There he was, longed for, beloved, adored even before he had recognized me, even before he heard my cry. He existed, it was colossal.

"Gabriel!"

Patience, reader, I must slow down his reappearance, I am looking through the *Guide Michelin,* I am looking for the page on Notre-Dame de Paris. . . . "The story with the rose window." An automobile was separating us. "The great rose window seems to be its halo." A river of automobiles, I had to wait. "The largest rose window that any architect has ever dared construct." Gabriel had grown younger. His shoes . . . his two polished miracles . . . Gabriel was not hungry. "The rose story. Its design, adopted by all the master masons of the age." Gabriel wasn't cold.

At last we were face to face. My heart was beating on his lips.

"What are you doing in these parts, little fellow?"

His eyes were laughing.

". . ."

"I said what are you doing in these parts, little fellow?"

"I'm a secretary. And you?"

"I'm a photographer. I'm making my deliveries."

The siren of a fire engine cut our voices apart.

"You can telephone me if you like. Will you telephone, Gabriel?"

He made a note of the number in a little book.

"Will you telephone soon?"

He smiled. Already the yearning, already the pain. Gabriel had gone.

I went back to Bernadette. I asked her if she thought he would telephone; she said yes. On the terrace of the Café de Notre-Dame I sipped my drink slowly as he had taught me.

A frenzy of goldsmiths' hammers, the scissor-clicking of their blows, and my room was no longer my own. Tomorrow and the day after tomorrow had taken possession. He will say: "Where is Hermine?" What will happen to me without Hermine?

Throw a handful of soda in warm water. Listen. You have awakened the sea in the bottom of a bowl. Lose yourself in the crystals as they dissolve. The bowl is on the floor. Feel the warmth of the water, give the palms of your hands its comfort. Pull up the chair, soak your feet, bend down, rest your head on your hands down near your knees, watch your feet in paradise. Cascades, waterfalls, avalanches, cataracts, and clouds through all your limbs, and a flower on the hideous wallpaper smiles at you. Opulence and deep wonder of a footbath. Lean your head to one side and you will see the dampening earth being watered by the autumn rains. Cheek in hand, the passions drain away. Tread your grape harvest in a footbath.

Gabriel telephoned ten days later. I understood and did not want to understand. I wanted him in my room, at my table, in my bed. I have described in *Ravages* how our strange love affair began. I asked Gabriel to make love to me as a man makes love to another man. The jitters, the religious terror of that little cross marked to one side of the date on my calendar? On the surface, yes. But the truth, now I think back on it thirty years later, lay deeper. The deeper truth was my desire to have two male homosexuals in my bed.

We were in a state of anxiety; the war was imminent. Mlle. Nadia read out gloomy newspaper editorials to me with passionate concentration. I didn't dare say to her: don't go on, because there's nothing we can do about it. That is how I am: a rustle in a suburban shrubbery, a rabbit shrieking as its neck is broken, a child being slapped, a basketball falling into its net, the whine of a power saw, a fieldmouse crushed on a road, a convent bell ringing then falling silent, the petals falling from an anemone, a mare galloping then lying down in a field, an insect struggling with its feet in the air, a sliced-off bramble branch, two cyclists freewheeling together down a hill, a dewdrop at four in the afternoon, a crow hopping over the chaos of a plowed and dung-strewn field, a flaming sunset, the wisp of smoke from a cottage warming itself back to life, a smell of boiling tar, all those things were clearer prophecies to me than any newspaper. Ill fortune was hovering over us. I felt the need to go for walks, to pick flowers and breathe fresh air. The war would come, but dawn would be the same.

I picked bunches of flowers; I thought about myself, as I had before, as I still do. A loving friendship was turning into love, and another loving friendship was beginning. I didn't say to myself: Sachs will have to leave, Gabriel will be going away. I said: I don't want the war to interrupt a new love affair and a new friendship. I had been a failure in everything: studies, piano, examinations, relationships, sleep, health, vacations, tranquillity of mind, gaiety, happiness, security, application at work. Now I was winning; I almost had a job, almost a lover, almost a friend with a position in Parisian society. They couldn't declare war, they couldn't take all that away from me. I shall never cease to insist on the terror of insecurity instilled into me as a child. One must always have a few pennies in one's purse. The war would push me into the gutter. I interrogated Mlle. Nadia. Her predictions never varied. It was imminent, and the office where we worked would be closed, she would add bravely. Her brother would go to fight, she would send him parcels. There was a woman for you. I was in despair, my savings were already melting away before my eyes. At night, before going to sleep, I always repeated the same prayer:

God, you're no fool. You've proved that. You can turn people's heads. So please turn them any way you like, only make it in a direction where there aren't any wars. Please God, don't take away my monthly envelope and my typewriter, which isn't really mine, and my lunchbox, and my little gas burner that saves me having to spend money in restaurants. Please God, make it so that my little life between Levallois and Notre-Dame, between Notre-Dame and Levallois can go on.

I fell asleep half reassured, and if I woke up again two hours later I told myself that God was powerful, that he wouldn't allow himself to be humiliated by the destruction of his fields, his horses, his trees, his flowers, his birds. I didn't tell God about the English cigarettes I filched from M. de Saint-Ange. God is too busy.

I didn't tell Gabriel about Maurice Sachs immediately. I sensed that he wouldn't understand my dazzlement. I went to work in the morning head held high—I felt that every mirror I passed was wooing me; I left work in the evening using my high heels like spurs; when I passed women hanging on their lovers' arms I looked them up and down: I too have a man I hold in my arms in bed, my eyes flashed at them. I was one of the herd again. Oh vanity!

Julienne telephoned quite often, but she never mentioned her Provençal. Then one day she called to say that she would wait for me outside my office that evening.

"Let's take a walk under the bridges," she said.

She was wearing a Bulgarian peasant blouse and a print skirt. Men looked around at her all the same as they bit into the autumnal flavor of the summer evening. She told me that they had become engaged by letter, that she was going to introduce him to her parents, that he was supposed to be coming to Paris, but that he hadn't arrived yet. It was, in any case, of little importance since she was still engaged. Her dress was so pretty. . . . Oh a very simple dress made at home . . . Crimson velvet . . . Sleeveless and with a low boat neck. Of course he would come, she had no doubts on that score. She took out her betrothal dress from time to time, it was velvet so there was no danger of tearing it, and when the time came for the ceremony she would wear it. Julienne wanted to revisit Les Baux with him. She ran around from bookshop to bookshop and spent her time preparing for the trip. My olive trees, my dear, dear olive trees, she repeated, just as she had before. She lived only for him and for Provence. To be in Arles with him at this time of day, she said in ecstasy. I told Julienne about Gabriel's reappearance, but she took absolutely no notice. It seemed better to say good night. She hurried away to her writing pad.

*

1939. War. It had been declared. Our department was to be kept going with just Mlle. Nadia; I was dispensed with. Our two editors left without so much as a good-by. The heart-rending fidelity of the little possessions left behind on their desks. A void is always a surprise. The sun held us pinned in its embrace. Too sweet, too strong, too big. We veered toward God. God didn't want the war, it was impossible. God does want the war, claimed the man who ate at Fouquet's, now metamorphosed into a corporal in the Army Service Corps. I didn't dare ask him what the Army Service Corps was. I stole the pen and lighter from M. de Saint-Ange's desk. I didn't know whether he would be killed or not, I didn't imagine he would ever come back good morning M. de Saint-Ange good morning Mlle. Leduc please come in quickly we have a lot of mail to get through has anyone called Mlle. Leduc you must call up Fouquet's for me my God the amount of paper I spoiled each letter he dictated handed back like a pretty embroidered handkerchief between the two pink sheets of blotting paper I'm coming war has been declared he's gone what shall I do I shall pray religiously no I'm not going to pray I'm going to steal his fountain pen and his checkered silver lighter. Now the retreat and the offices are closing at last I have them for my own those criss-cross silver lines he used to squeeze in his hand when he was lighting my cigarette while I was taking down his dictation those silver criss-cross lines so fine you'd need a microscope well really stealing from a poor man who's going off to the front I regret nothing I made love to M. de Saint-Ange's face till I was drunk with it while I was taking down his letters then finish off with my compliments as you think fit and reword that last paragraph I trust you for that sort of thing and you can my boy you can I have flower spikes in my eyes scores of pointed little rods trained on you for you were destined for the war my beauty no I didn't deflower your face but I sent rays out into it from the flower spikes in my eyes I will finish off with my compliments by then I was passing one of my little rods all dimpled and chubby with love along your eyebrows so admirably drawn above your almond shaped eyes I love your face but no further than that M. de Saint-Ange there are eyes and ears waiting for you at Fouquet's make your entrance I will type out your letters I asked you for a raise and you gave it to me out of your own pocket our complicity. He was one of the first to be killed. I repeat: killed. It's not so easy to die.

Today, March 27, 1961, M. de Saint-Ange is radiating health and youth and gaiety on the balcony of my mansard window. There he is, the tulip that opened yesterday morning. It is titanic, I assure you, the pink color of my tulip flower. How slow I am to understand. I was planting a corpse, I was watering a corpse, watching over a corpse, covering a corpse with straw on frosty nights. . . . What is my harvest? A man-flower. There is love in each one of its petals, it is a vibration of light even when the sun suddenly goes into retreat. My tulip washes the whole of Paris clean, M. de Saint-Ange can never be dirtied again.

My last cent, that was my war within a war. My future, ah my future . . . the crystal ball of the fortune-tellers and the fakirs persistently opaque. Who was there to reassure me? Gabriel had already been called up in Paris, my mother was receiving letters every day from her husband who had been recalled. Who was there then to reassure me? I wrung my hands, everything was in its right place, everything was different. My skin, my vertebrae, my whole body complained of this injustice: a handful of men had taken away my work again, had deprived me of the means to earn my bread. Whereupon Sachs wrote me a letter full of good sense. He was leaving for Caen, where he was to be an interpreter for the British forces. Everything had slipped through my fingers. Left completely idle, I wandered back and forth between my furnished room and the Rue Stanilas-Menier where my mother was living. She kept me up to date with everything that was told us over the radio.

*

The war had begun, Sachs was an interpreter in Caen, Gabriel was in the Army doing office work, my mother had rented a cottage from a farmer's wife in Chérisy, opposite the house they had sold. I joined her there so as to enjoy my tiny savings in safety. I wrote every day to Gabriel. He wrote to me quite often too, but I wanted his letters to be more passionate and more literary. I picked little wild flowers and slipped them in with my letters. On Sunday mornings I went to chapel, and when the faithful lowered their heads to listen to the pastor addressing God I kept mine raised, hoping to see my marriage on the ceiling. On the way home I wrote letters on every blade of grass. I saw my honeymoon hanging in the sky, trembling, palpitating, with no place to lay its head.

One Sunday after morning service, surrounded by the aroma of a pear tart set out to cool, we held Privy Council. We sent away "Petit-Poste," the son of the farmer's wife who owned the cottage. He was four. He was comic and intelligent. His little mouth dripped bubbles of gaiety between the syllables of "Petit-Poste." That Sunday we sent him home.

I moved to the attack in a low voice:

"You must advise me. It's your duty to advise me. I'll follow your advice. What do you advise me to do?"

"He's clever," my mother said, as though she were thinking very carefully about a move at chess.

"Should I marry him?"

"He understands you," my mother said.

"But should I marry him?"

"He knows what you're like."

"If you were in my place, would you marry him?"

"You have the same tastes," my mother continued.

"I'll do what you advise me to."

"He isn't brutal. He won't ill-treat you."

"He used to disappear."

"He's changed: he has a profession now," my mother said.

"All this doesn't tell me whether I should marry him or not."

"You can go to concerts together. You like going to the same sort of places. He isn't a tramp anymore. He lives with his family."

"Well?"

"Yes, I think the answer's yes," my mother said.

So it was over. I was a bride. The next night I thought over our decision and I was frightened at the thought of Gabriel's witty little teeth.

Why weren't we both Americans? I longed for a runaway marriage like the heroine of a Western. The town hall in Arras, then another municipal building in Paris; they were slow, those monuments entrusted with the preparations for our marriage. Finally Gabriel wrote that the banns had been published. I lost my head. People only had to show the slightest interest in this conjunction of Violette and Gabriel for me to start thrusting my happiness down their throats; my trenchcoat for the Great Day was almost worn threadbare by the attention I lavished on it. My husband would be a soldier, I would be able to draw the allowance made to soldiers' wives, I would have someone to love, and I would be saved. Our long-drawn-out engagement, our smuggled meetings under the shadow of Hermine . . . I had been in exile, and now I had come home again. My fourth finger feels uneasy, the poor thing needs a ring around it. You shall have your wedding ring, I promise you. It will shine, and when my marriage is glowing on my hand I shall know how to make the most of it.

It was an old marriage that smelt of naphthalene. We arrived the evening before and slept at my mother's apartment. Precautions, muffled furniture in every room, and the war against the moths spreading a reek of desolation everywhere. There was nothing for our eyes to rest on. But before that we had met Gabriel at the Gare Montparnasse. Three apéritifs and a stein of beer for him that made it cheaper and it was my mother who paid and my mother who looked thoughtful. I would have gone to the scaffold to marry him. He had just come from the barber's, his haircut looked as though it would last him for the rest of his life. The back of his head was too naked. Who was shivering? It was the bell outside a movie theater on a frosty night over Gabriel's shaven head. It's unsuitable the night before a wedding. Do I want to? Don't I want to? I am sure of the night under my eyelids. Oh sister-in-law, mother-in-law, all it needs is a quick visit, provided I don't mess up my trenchcoat before the ceremony. What am I made of? I'm made of Bourgeois Extract.

Let's make love, Violette. No, Gabriel, not before the ceremony. That's how I am, that's how I was. Hermine, Isabelle . . . They wove my marriage veil for me, they took it with them. My adolescence, my childhood are there too: Michel, my brother, who came with us because I insisted. "Come on, you'll get a good meal." He sat quietly, he was always quiet. We left the sister-in-law and the mother-in-law. Gabriel planted a kiss on my lips, an unfrocked kiss. We were going to be married, and everything was coming apart at the seams, we had lived before it was time to live and I thought someone had said that his mother would get the allowance when Gabriel had become a soldier-husband. He would be coming to take us to the ceremony at ten the next morning. I read that evening, proud of the temple beneath my curling hair. A single woman. I was a single woman, I belonged to myself. There was my bedside lamp, and it belonged to a woman who would always be single.

I said good-by to the hairs caught in my comb, I said good-by to the foam on my bathroom glass. I was a virgin who paddled her own canoe, but I was going to the sacrifice all the same.

*

Ten o'clock, a quarter past ten, half-past ten the following morning.

"Do you think he'll come?" my mother asked.

I was putting up a front: "Why shouldn't he come?"

Half-past ten, twenty of eleven, quarter of eleven.

At eleven o'clock we left the apartment and began waiting in the lobby downstairs.

"He's not coming," my mother announced from time to time.

I didn't answer. Gabriel was unpunctual, oh God how I had sinned.

"He's not coming, there's no use in waiting," my mother decided finally at eleven twenty-five.

He rushed in like a tornado. My mother's face made me afraid.

"You're too late," she said, in a voice that implied we'd better forget the whole thing.

"What do you mean, too late?" he asked arrogantly. "I have a taxi waiting!"

My mother looked at me. Her eyes asked if I still wanted to get married. Then they added: he's unreliable, he'll never change. Then, as they left me, they said: after all, it's your affair!

Gabriel was holding the heavy door open with his foot. My

trenchcoat Gabriel's trenchcoat. They were wedded in the doorway without formalities. We set out.

Waiting our turn on a bench, answering yes, signing the register. All too simple, too quick. I dreamed of long braids of flowers that we would have plaited together for days and nights together in that municipal hall before they at last united us, before we kicked all our beautiful handiwork behind us and stepped up to collect our marriage booklet from the mayor. My mother selected the menu for our wedding breakfast, and her self-assurance dazzled me. At four that afternoon my hands met hers under cover of the tablecloth as I handed her my money. I was sad.

Why did I feel hungry again at six that evening, just around the corner from the Lycée Racine and the Gare Saint-Lazare? We had come on foot and were walking along the street. My mother walked behind us chatting with Gabriel's sister. Michel was bored.

"I'm hungry," I said to Gabriel in front of a bakery shop.

Gabriel looked at me without saying anything.

I went in; I picked the gloomiest and most sorry-looking piece of cake I could see. I chewed at it in slow motion, never once taking my eyes off Gabriel as he watched me through the window. I paid the cashier for the cake I'd eaten. They were all waiting for me outside. I realize now, twenty years after, that I was trying to find that other pâtisserie again, the Italian cakes, the student at the Lycée Racine, the frantic Gabriel of other days and all his sacrifices. Time, my little Violette, is no work for amateurs.

I wanted a wedding ring, so it had been arranged that we would meet Gabriel's sister the following morning on a Métro platform. She knew a jeweler, I would be given a discount, what a to-do simply to put a metal band around my finger. She met us on the platform with the rings and the invoice. I paid for my platinum ring, Gabriel for his brass one.

Why did I marry? April 9, 1961, twelve-fifty P.M. I must answer that right away. The fear of being an old maid, the fear that people might say: she couldn't find anyone, she was too ugly. The need to destroy, to annihilate what I had had, what I still had then. "Nothing is changed," Gabriel explained to me, "you will be free, I shall be free." Yes, I answered, my head full of warmth, the warmth of my dishonesty. And Gabriel, why did he marry? To avenge himself? To make up for lost time? Plausible enough explanations, but I don't believe they are the right ones. Gabriel is my mystery. "We can love one another like brother and sister," he suggested on our wedding night. I refused. That suggestion is another of my mysteries.

The briefness of that honeymoon, without going anywhere together, without even one whole day alone with each other. The following day I went back to the village with my mother and Michel. I played with my wedding ring, but the other passengers in the compartment didn't give a damn. My mother scarcely spoke: I supposed that this was her way of reproaching me for having followed her advice, and for having asked it in the first place.

The bed was too small and my mother took up all the room in it. I was back facing the damp wall with the water trickling down it day and night. I had to make myself small and hunch myself up against it. The third night back I regretted my marriage, I felt the failure of it, I foresaw the bad times ahead of me. The cards were down: Gabriel was not going to give me anything. We had been united the better to widen the gap between us. I was blinded by the glare of my clairvoyance. But at dawn, because it was a routine, a false security, I hugged my marriage booklet from the mayor. Gabriel wrote that I wouldn't be able to draw the allowance from the Army.

Judge me: he was granted eight days' leave and wrote me that he wanted to visit us. My mother lost her temper: "We're leaving," she said. She opened her trunk and began folding up sheets. My mother didn't want the expense. Gabriel couldn't come. Judge me. I could have taken him to some disused barn, I could have said to him, here is our home, we will cut our steaks from the rumps of their herds, my darling, a shepherd will lend us his cloak, and there are hedges to plunder while the great wind plays its harmonica and blusters around us.

*

I have already described in *Ravages* how we began our married life together; how we moved into our apartment, my ecstasy, our scenes, the den: Gabriel's darkroom.

Julienne had given me some work; I was typing out Jules Laforgue's letters, unraveling the words that had been erased or written on top of each other. Gabriel, not being strong enough to go to the front, had been given a job in the records department of the War Office. He liked his work.

One morning an envelope slid under the door.

"It's for you," Gabriel said.

Gabriel went back into the kitchen. He hadn't finished washing.

"Maurice Sachs has written to me!"

Sachs had sent me his first letter from Caen.

"Do you hear? Maurice Sachs has written to me!"

"The writer? The one you talk about sometimes?" Gabriel asked in an uninterested voice.

"Exactly. The author of *Alias*."

Gabriel burst out laughing. "*Alias*, which you didn't like."

I was basking in bed after our dizzying calisthenics.

"*Alias* which I didn't like. He knows I didn't, I told him so, and if you think he took umbrage. . . . He is the first to admit that his book isn't so marvelous. I told him so, and I find it disgusting."

Gabriel had come back into the room.

"I like it when you get worked up," he said. "Why do you find it disgusting? Sincerity is a virtue, isn't it?"

Gabriel, wearing his towel as a loincloth, threw a cigarette, an "Army Issue," onto the eiderdown.

"Sincerity has its limits. I don't know how I had the gall. Could you write a book? No. Could I write a book? No."

I sat up in the bed.

"Oh I love it when you get furious!" Gabriel said.

He lit a cigarette.

"*Alias*, always *Alias* . . . ," I said. "You forget his fantastic personality."

His cigarette sticking out of the corner of his mouth, Gabriel blinked his eyes voluptuously.

"I don't know him, what do you expect?"

"But you're going to know him, you're going to see him."

Gabriel had begun playing with his cheap lighter.

"No, little fellow, no. You mustn't ask that."

"You prefer a zinc counter? An apéritif with your buddy at work?"

"I prefer a zinc counter, as you say, madame. You amuse me. I'm having a great time. Poor little fellow . . ."

"Why 'poor little fellow'?"

"Nothing. No reason, my little Don Quixote. Tears? You've just got a letter from him and you're weeping?"

I sobbed.

"What are you insinuating?" I asked through my sobs. "What is it you think you know?"

That morning I couldn't say to Gabriel: It's you I love and you know it.

He had sat down on the edge of the bed; he was wiping away my tears with a handkerchief.

"I know that you have a friend, that he writes to you, and that I'm very happy for you," he said.

"He isn't a friend. . . . He's nice. He has suffered, he's good."

"If he isn't a friend, what is he then?" Gabriel asked with a shake in his voice.

"I don't know," I answered, completely dashed. "I'm going to knit him a scarf. . . ."

Gabriel said he thought that was an excellent idea and escaped into the kitchen. I was going mad.

"I need some flints for my lighter," he said as he went on shaving.

I couldn't give him the lighter I had stolen, I couldn't read him the letter I'd received from Sachs. I had married Gabriel, I worshipped the man in my bed, and yet . . . and yet my scapulary of homosexuals still lay against my skin. I thought the same trio must be forming again.

That evening as I was typing the Laforgue letters I said: "Would you like me to read you Maurice's letter?"

Gabriel put his arm around my shoulders. "Little fellow, why do you want to spoil everything? We're both free, we're both going to stay free. Why do you want me to read his letter?"

He was preparing for the worst.

Sachs had asked me to do something for him and enclosed a short note for the concierge in the Rue de Ranelagh:

"Please let Mlle. Leduc into my apartment."

Mlle. Leduc. My name was Mlle. Leduc, the letter had been sent to my old address in Levallois-Perret. I would go on calling myself Mlle. Leduc at all costs. There were three of us, all free, each prowling alone between the other two, and my name was Mlle. Leduc. It was a firm resolve: I would redeem my maiden name. Mlle. Leduc, yes, you at the blackboard! Draw a triangle, a trapezium, a rectangle. . . . I'm sleeping. I can't. Isabelle, tell them I'm resting, that I've earned the right to rest.

The concierge on the Rue de Ranelagh made no difficulties about letting me into the apartment.

Once the door had closed behind me I felt I was an intruder in those deserted rooms. The apartment was sleeping; the furniture, the ornaments were like memories. I finally opened his door and ventured inside on tiptoe. His room was untouched. Maurice Sachs had given it to me. Once more I read the inkstain on the table, the names of the drinks on the bottles, the titles of the books. Your evening with us is not dead, that evening cannot die, cried the inkstain, the names of the drinks, and the titles on the books. I left his room in search of the shirts, the leather belts, the towels, and various other things he had written on his list. A melancholy trip as far as the dining room where we had eaten dinner with his grandmother. The scent of the privets that used to fill my nostrils as I gripped my grandmother's long skirt, that scent which, if I have my wish, will be the odor in my coffin, followed me along the hall. I opened the drawers. Luxury, abundance, order, method; the lace borders on the napkins and the tablecloths were calmer than our white summer flowers. I opened the drawers containing the boxes of cutlery as well. Why did I want to see everything, uncover everything, inspect everything? So as to hold Sachs' chubby hand and touch my finger against that too experienced mouth as it brushed a napkin or a fork. I multiplied his presence with silverware, with closets, with drawers full of the finest linen. Crackling from every corner I heard that short, saddening laugh with which Maurice was the first to mock himself. I walked away from the Rue de Ranelagh head held high, proud to have earned Maurice's confidence.

That evening I finished the dark green scarf I was knitting on my bamboo needles and included it in the parcel I sent off to Maurice. I was hoping for complaints or compliments from Gabriel. Nothing. Months passed, then I suggested to Gabriel that I knit him a beige wool scarf on my bamboo needles. His face lit up. You would do that for me? You were knitting for him but you hadn't deserted me? his eyes said.

My scarf, which he cherished for several years, became the path that led my cheek to his sprouting beard each time I gave my lover a kiss of friendship.

Gabriel was evacuated to a village whose name I have now forgotten. He wrote me a long passionate letter. He was missing me, I thought the miracle had happened. He is coming home on leave, we are going to be married properly now, I told myself, weeping with happiness. At noon, one summer's day, he arrived unexpectedly. I recognized his step, his soldier's boots in the yard. The other tenants were all at their windows. He took me in his arms, he closed the windows and pulled the lined curtains. Everything became simple inside our little room. Gabriel took me out to dinner, he told me he was leaving that same evening and promised to write to me again. Shattered by my emotions, I went to visit Bernadette, then left her after a short while, intending to go home and weep for happiness, to lie with my cheek against the gray stains on our bed. I got as far as the platform of the République Métro station. That little soldier sitting on one of the benches, huddled inside his greatcoat. It was Gabriel: he had lied to me. His face livid, he explained that he was leaving Paris at four that morning, that it was impossible to get any rest in our room, that he preferred to sleep at his mother's. I managed to drag him back to our room. We quarreled all night. He left at dawn, sickened by the whole thing, while I lay sobbing so as not to hear his steps crossing the yard.

The enemy—it was a word that sounded to my ear, I will admit, I dare to admit, like the glim gloon bam balim goon bahd of the foreign language I invented as a child—were advancing, they were gaining ground, everyone else had cleared out. I was scared, I begged my mother to leave but she couldn't make up her mind whether she should or not. We waited as long as we possibly could. We finally left at half-past five one morning because she was afraid for her son. She had heard that the enemy "picked up" young boys of fifteen. "Perhaps I should take a pound or two of sugar," my mother suggested. The silent streets, the silent buildings. A silence as thick as the air in a charnel house. It was heartbreaking to see the bricks, the stones, the asphalt, the sidewalks, the churches, the benches, the squares, the bus stops, the curtains, and the shutters all left to fend for themselves. Paris was too human a ruin. Where were the dogs, the cats, the flies? At the same time I was gnawed with worry over my mother's legs. She is a poor walker because of her wretched childhood. We were both of us remembering our first exodus, at the end of the First World War. I was hoping there would be some cars or trucks when we reached the Métro terminal. We were each carrying our own little suitcase, my half-brother Michel as well. I asked which road led to Versailles.

We followed the procession streaming along both sides of the road. There were mothers nursing their infants in the ditches, vain young girls tottering along on Louis Quinze heels, soldiers singing as they were driven past in trucks. One of the soldiers threw some cigarettes to an old man, who ran out into the road and salvaged them despite the drivers' curses. Scaffolding, mountains perched on the tops of cars. One man was making his solitary way with a mattress on his back. Our misfortune had become a funeral cortege. Suburbanites hung out of their windows to watch us pass. Market gardeners were deserting their plots with their horses and carts. Butterflies still fluttered and alighted on the flowers in vacant lots.

Versailles. My mother was very tired. The cafés, shut. Other families had set up house on all the benches. There was nowhere to sit down. The sight of French uniforms brought some comfort. I left my mother sitting on our suitcases and hurried off with Michel to find out if it was possible to continue. Versailles railroad station was asleep: no more trains. A young soldier told me that in fact there was one leaving in about twenty minutes, though I'd have to find out for myself where it was going.

"Keep it to yourself. Platform two."

"We must run," Michel said.

I found my mother still sitting on the suitcases.

"Well?" she asked in a defeated voice.

"We've found a train," I answered.

We dragged her after us, galloping as hard as we could.

Our hearts failed us when we saw the crowd on platform two. My mother was worried. Were we sure it was the right train? It would have been difficult to make a mistake. There was no other.

Soldiers were spreading fresh straw in the freight cars. Michel clasped his hands and gave my mother a leg up. We got the last three places on the floor, just next to the door. We hugged our suitcases on our knees and sat there wondering if we should ever start. The doors had been shut on us and time was passing. We waited patiently in the half darkness, trying to peek out, listening to the slightest noise our ears could catch through the continual rustling of the straw. We could hear the soldiers' voices as they paced up and down the platform; we were waiting for their orders with them.

"Do you think it's ever going to start?"

Everyone in the car stopped breathing as we eavesdropped.

"No, it'll never budge from this platform."

"I think it'll leave soon, I know it will."

"How could you know anything!"

The freight car breathed again. Often the whole train began to jerk; then silence again: these false alarms were demoralizing us all.

"What time is it?" my mother kept asking.

"They're tricking us," a woman whimpered.

"What time is it?"

His first watch strapped on his adolescent wrist, Michel proudly told us the right time whenever he was asked. Midday. One o'clock. Two o'clock. Three o'clock. Four o'clock. Five o'clock. We left before six. The train began trundling ponderously along the tracks; it was as though we all had a ton of anguish inside our heads. It stopped five hundred yards out of the station. A wretchedly dressed man, lying beside a drunken woman who was talking to herself, lit a cigarette. A matronly woman reading the serial in an old magazine snatched it from between his lips.

"We'd all go up in flames. A pity, mister, but there it is," said another woman, obviously worn out by a life of work and poverty and grief.

The train started again. The drunk woman asked her companion for some more to drink. He handed her his flask, she drank, then crumpled into sleep, a mess of greasy hair and purple, flaking cheeks. A baby began to cry; the mother had no more milk. Michel was asleep.

"How pale he is," my mother said. "That big body and nothing to eat . . ."

"We're doing about fifteen kilometers an hour," a man mumbled.

Fifteen. Exactly Michel's age. His head as it leaned against the side of the car seemed doubly subjected to every bump and sway in our progress.

"We'd better keep the cookies for tonight," my mother went on.

The worn-out looking woman smiled at us.

"Would you like some?" she asked. "It's good bread from my own baker. It's new."

Such simplicity leaves one without defenses. My mother asked me with her eyes whether she should accept. She took the bread and thanked the woman.

Our speed varied, but only from slow to slower and back to slow again. The baby was crying louder and louder, the drunk woman was clamoring for drink, voices were being raised, the tension was mounting. Where could we get milk for the baby? A phlegmatic-looking man who never stopped chewing on a cigarette succeeded after great effort in opening the door. We drank in the fresh air. The man threw his beret out into the netttles beside the track.

"Not a house in sight," he said.

We were lying on the floorboards; a smell of damp grass reminded us of the times we had been sad and full of nostalgia, relishing the howls of dogs as they bayed in the falling night. I wanted to get up and look at the grass flattened along the embankments; my mother wouldn't let me. The baby had stopped crying in the half darkness. Michel was nibbling at the bread.

"A thrush! Not a little one either," a man said.

They closed the door again.

We dined off a few lumps of sugar.

Eleven in the evening. The night hurled itself against the sides of our freight car with the violence and doggedness of a hurricane, as though it were jealous of the private night we were enjoying inside. Men and women were beginning to rebel, not knowing exactly what their grievances were, out of their depth in the events that had encompassed them. The wretchedly dressed man was holding his companion's hand and stroking her hair. Love could still put forth new flowers and cling to existence. The steady rhythm of the wheels; the train was going faster now, they said. People were sleeping, arguing, losing their tempers, lamenting. The matron, clutching her Wonder flashlight, was gloating over her magazine. The baby was crying less loudly, the mother had stopped sobbing; then it was crying louder again and the mother was yelling that the light was hurting their eyes. The man was still stroking his companion's knuckles. He took the flask out of his jacket pocket, gazed at it with terrifying grief, and his lips began to tremble; he had nothing left to give. My mother remained awake, her eyes wide open. Michel was eating lumps of sugar. The train stopped at last beside a crossing keeper's house.

The crossing keeper couldn't give us what she didn't have. Milk? We were asking for the moon. She agreed to sell us a bucket of water. Everyone wanted to drink and see that the baby had something to drink. It died before daybreak, despite the cold water; the drunk woman had a fit of delirium tremens. My mother squeezed herself against me and whispered: "Don't look, don't look. . . ." The man wept without crying out, without any lament. The way men do weep.

Le Mans. Our first glimpse: a mountain of three to five thousand bicycles abandoned in front of the station. We picked our way through a desert of fatigue, of collapse, of thirst, of hunger, of agony, of sickness: limp, exhausted bodies by the thousand. The sidewalks and the streets: so much human flesh. Each one of them lying alone in the hospital he or she had founded by falling to the ground.

Despite all this, I was still thinking of the wretchedly dressed man, of his companion, of the woman worn out by work and poverty and grief. Where were they? Lost forever, and therefore wandering in their own eternity with a friend.

Twenty years later, in this March of 1961 with its last gray days, I offer them a gift: the following notes:

Corner of the Rue des Fossés-Saint-Bernard and the Boulevard Saint-Germain. There is a bright rose-colored dawn rising near the Ile Saint-Louis on March 26 at seven in the evening. I cross over to the corner of the Rues des Fossés-Saint-Bernard and take up a position on the corner of the Halle aux Vins. It is bright as day; the lamps inside the Halle aux Vins are all alight. The color of rye when it is ripe for harvest, a wreath of light inside the great glass cage. There is no need to look for Nerval in the bookshop windows. He is here; his poetry is sputtering like sparks between these little brick pavilions.

I no longer know where we found some bread to eat, nor how we managed to find seats in a little local train. I have also forgotten the name of the little station where we ended up. People around us were talking about Fougères and Vitré; the refugees here seemed less demoralized, but we ourselves were beginning to give way under our own inner strain. The sun was shining on the neatly kept façade of the little station facing the platform. One of the windows of the stationmaster's private apartment on the second floor, the window over the station clock, suddenly opened, and as a woman leaned out we heard the radio. There was dead silence immediately. We feared the worst. An old man was speaking in a calm and monotonous voice. It was public and confidential at the same time. He told us that there would soon be an armistice. The radio fell silent, the dead silence below continued. I fell into my mother's arms: I kissed her all over her face, I squeezed her hands, I began to stammer something. She was crying too, and so were a great many others. Very few people displayed no reaction at all. We could continue our journey without telling ourselves every moment that we were going to die.

It proved possible to get rooms at the Hotel de S—. The French Army was billeted there too. By unbelievable coincidence, my mother bumped into her husband, who had been recalled as a captain. Suddenly we were treated with great respect. But I was afraid every time I heard a rifle shot. The inhabitants of the village were pleading with the soldiers: they mustn't fight, the village would be destroyed. Would they fight, yes or no? We spent the whole day in uncertainty. Finally there was a general stampede and all idea of fighting was abandoned. Since all the others, officers and men alike, had taken off their uniforms and put on civilian clothing, I begged my stepfather to do the same. He hesitated for a long time. Michel lent him his tweed jacket.

Then we set off again toward Vitré in a truck. At Vitré we waited; there was a strange feeling in the air. The enemy had still not shown up and our own troops were still hanging about there. Then they left, leaving a sentinel. We stayed at the big house, and what a pleasant stay it was. I went for a walk every morning through the beautifully kept kitchen garden. I stroked the leaves of a curly endive, I smelled a flower, and that was all I wanted. I read the volume of Jean-Jacques Rousseau I had brought with me. And Gabriel? I loved him and prepared myself for loving him. I was building a nest for us. He couldn't be taken away from me again, ten years of absence had been dissolved. Paris was Gabriel, my return to Paris was Gabriel. I never imagined that he could be dead or wounded. I was counting on him, I was counting on him too much.

Every afternoon I went out with my mother on our daily hunt for news; we would find the young sentinel sitting on a block of stone beside an unplowed field. He told us he was waiting, but he never knew what he was waiting for. I made fun of him. I no longer mock the blind faith of sentinels. Despair can make a man a hero too.

We went back to Paris separately in private cars. Gabriel arrived from a village somewhere with a healthy complexion, pleased to be back where he could get good French red wine once more. The capital was filling up again. The first time I saw an enemy in the street I followed him, from the Madeleine as far as the Opéra. An officer, slim, blond, impeccably turned out without looking affected, he was strolling along holding the hand of a young French girl still in her teens. The blue flower had not withered. I walked behind the officer and his young girl. My 1914-1918, my whooping cough, my cock crow, my sore throats were all careening around inside my head, my "Papa Vili": the German doctor's orderly who scoured the countryside for eggs and dairy produce. But this was another war and it was our nerves that were going to suffer this time. I felt humiliated when I had to walk around their barricades in front of our big hotels.

*

My dear. Why do you not write, my dear? When one writes letters such as yours, my dear . . . Affected phraseology, his crutches; I had to try and understand him. He suffered sometimes from an uncertainty of soul, Maurice Sachs. Poor fairground juggler longing for a family dinner table. My dear, my dear. He performed juggling tricks with his unhappiness. Wilde folding his gardenia in an urchin's handkerchief, Sachs' desire to please was a little like that. "One writes." He was off his head, he had lost his wits. What was I to say to him? I wrote to him what I saw, what I felt, what I preferred, because I was wooing him in my role as a loving friend. They weren't letters, they were my trials in the lists, intended to prove my capacity for attachment. He read manuscripts, he was a reader for Gallimard, he had bewitched me. His childhood, all his professions, his mother. A secretary, almost a bellhop, he had hidden nothing. An interpreter for the armed forces now. So much the better. Away from Paris. Better and better still. Paris was doing him no good; he was not getting what he longed for from it. Fame, that is what he wanted. A glutton, that well-bred man. But I was not competing in that race: fame, what a childish aim. My dear, I was dying of hunger and I couldn't eat because I had to talk, I had to tell a thousand amusing stories because I had to pay them back for the dinner they were giving me. A dismal thought, but that is what we ought to remember of him. His education was the mask he learned to wear.

When I met Maurice I was meeting a mask of gaiety, of altruism, of affability, of humor more real than gaiety, altruism, affability, and humor themselves. Forgetfulness of self, the most primitive source of courtesy. In order to make you laugh, to reassure you, to charm you, Maurice Sachs eliminated himself completely, destroyed his own being afresh at every moment. He gave everything he had. Max Jacob, Maritains, Cocteau, Claudel, the Castaings, Marie-Laure de Noailles, Louise de Vilmorin, Printemps, Fresnay, Chanel, and the hundreds of others he knew, he gave them all away. He gave away what he had read, he gave away what he loved. He scattered the talents, the successes, the virtues, and all the good qualities of his friends and his acquaintances broadcast. He was lavish in his distribution of what he most desired and was refused: recognition. This miracle made me forget to think about money. People used to wonder if Nijinsky, when he danced at the Opéra, was jumping on a rubber mat. I was jumping on a carpet of paper money when I spent a moment with Maurice Sachs, whereas the perpetual drama in his life was his desire for money, and the way money melted in his hands. His goal, his reason for living: to be loved by an intelligent young boy. His tragedy: to have died without finding that love.

An extraordinary surprise: he wrote to me that he had been demobilized and that I could have lunch with him in his apartment on the Rue de Ranelagh. That day Gabriel was having lunch with the verger of a church: their friendship was in the honeymoon stage. I rang and waited for the maid.

Maurice Sachs opened the door and welcomed me: "Excellent, excellent. Our chicken is in the oven. . . ."

We kissed each other on the cheeks, his kisses were offhand. He received me in his tie-silk dressing gown, slipped on over a dark suit. His slippers and silk socks were elegant also. I wondered why my shoes made such a noise on the floor as we walked over to his room. We went in, and I choked back a cry. The locusts had picked Maurice's room clean. Everything had gone except the walls, two stools, and a tiny kitchen table in the middle of the floor. On the table there were two place settings and a bottle of good wine. Maurice watched me, waiting for the question I did not dare to ask.

"Look around while I see to our chicken," he said.

He vanished into the kitchen. A velvety smell of roasting chicken, a metallic sound as though the gravy was raining down into the roasting tin.

The locusts had left nothing behind. All that remained of the dining room, the drawing room, the linen closet, and his grandmother's room were the walls, the ceiling, and the floorboards.

I ran into the kitchen.

"Well?" Maurice asked.

He was waiting for my question.

"It's not the same apartment. . . ."

"Hold the door for me," he said coldly.

He carried in the chicken.

"You've got a strange way of putting things," he said. "Of course it's not the same apartment. She's playing bridge in the provinces, so I sold everything."

"Your grandmother is playing bridge?"

"Don't ask stupid questions. She's in Vichy. Sit down, my child. I'll just cut it in two, what? I'll split it down the middle and we'll each take half, that's the simplest way."

He gave me my half. He loathed appetizers and odds and ends.

He simply ate large quantities of whatever things he liked. We emptied a jar of raspberries from Hédiard's. Why not, he asked, why shouldn't he have sold everything? Morality, the opinion of others, principles: so much syrup sipped out of a teaspoon. He suggested we go out after the meal to a "family café," with a hint of nostalgia in his eyes for the family life he had turned his back on. He suggested we go for a stroll along the Rue de Ranelagh.

"What do you say we talk about your marriage?" he said.

We had just passed an expensively dressed woman.

"How can she walk around with that flower pot on her head! Aren't women crazy?"

I smiled weakly.

"What?" Maurice said.

Attributing comments to me which I had not in fact made was his way of showing confidence in me, as though my silence, my stupidity, my impotence were all voices that he could half hear.

"Why did you get married?" he asked.

The way in which he had begun to play with his cane was theatrical.

"Why did you sell everything?" I replied curtly.

My boldness intrigued him for a moment.

"You must know, my dear, that an apartment can be reconstructed in a moment. The East, poverty. Ah! poverty. . . ."

Sachs began to look younger, his face became simpler.

"A woman wouldn't understand. The renunciation of possessions. Women are materialists."

He waved his cane as he herded his dreams before him.

"I understand," I said.

He turned his head toward me, pleased that I'd shown a gleam of intelligence.

"What do you understand?" he asked, not letting me off the hook. "Don't you think he's charming?"

A young apprentice locksmith had appeared carrying a great ring of rusty keys on his wrist. He passed by, he vanished forever.

"I understand that you're not happy, and that makes me unhappy," I said.

Maurice Sachs' face closed up.

"My dear child, please stop snivelling, I beg of you. . . ."

"I'm not snivelling!"

"Stop snivelling about yourself and stop snivelling over me. We would never see the end of it. Where did you get the idea that I wasn't happy? Women are so idiotic with their mania for protecting one, consoling one."

Women are not men, I said to myself with inward desolation. If the apprentice locksmith had talked as I had . . . Maurice's face would be radiant. That's what he's got against me. I stole the young apprentice locksmith's bow saw.

Was every boy Maurice passed in the street going to produce a similar melancholy yearning? Quite possibly. A homosexual is a bundle of such yearnings. He is always dreaming of what he has missed, he is often an angel lost in an inferno of regrets. He began talking again, talking and telling stories: Claudel used to get up early to write at six o'clock he told me I turn on the tap at eight o'clock I turn it off there are all sorts of marriages Mme. Mercier what an idea but we'll see what can be done don't be unhappy have you read the *Journal de deux Anglaises* in which absolutely nothing happens just the perfect happiness of each day during their long life together the Duke of Westminster my dear I was in the Place des Etat-Unis.

Be quiet, that's enough, I said enough. Coward that you are, Violette Leduc that you are, it's only inside you that you're saying enough, I said enough.

. . . I was there in a drawing room on the Place des Etats-Unis at eleven in the morning it was torture my dear with the sun glittering on every one of those gold objects I couldn't take away with me and I didn't take anything the mistress of the house kept lingering my hand just wandered over those tables covered in gold.

Maurice Sachs laughed at his own honesty, he told me about the psychiatrist Allendy, almost a neighbor, a doctor and a friend, always ready to help when his head and his heart were at a low ebb. We walked out into the Place du Trocadéro.

"I've eaten as many as seventeen pastries there," he said, pointing with his cane at the window of a pâtisserie. "I needed to recuperate. I was going to physical education classes; we used to dance to *Firebird* and *Petrouchka* in order to lose weight."

How could I not laugh with him?

"I'm too big, I'm too fat, my dear, I shall soon be flopping about inside my clothes. Well, let me flop, since flop I must, I have made my decision."

At that moment I loved him from the bottom of my heart for his simplicity. He rebuilt Paris for me on a foundation of cream puffs.

"Now you're going home and you're going to settle yourself down to writing that piece I promised them," Maurice said in front of the Trocadéro Métro entrance. "What's the matter?"

"Why, what's the matter with me, Maurice?"

"Stop wearing that graveyard expression."

He dragged me after him and we sat down on the terrace outside the pâtisserie. I ordered a tea. I was sinking like a stone. He told me to drink the tea quickly, that he couldn't see why I should be afraid. He swallowed his glass of spirits in one gulp: he liked it, it had to be got rid of.

"Yes, I'm afraid, Maurice. . . . I'm afraid of not being able to. Don't ask me to do it."

The sweat was streaming down my back, moistening the palms of my hands. I sponged it off my forehead with a frantic gesture.

"You wouldn't like to write? You wouldn't like to see your name printed at the beginning or the end of an article? I should have thought you would," he said slowly.

I felt myself melting with happiness and misery. I wanted it without daring to admit it to myself. Yes, it was my one wish that had never seen the light of day. I used to read my name in bookshop windows, a secret joy, a hidden disease; it was the impossible. To write . . . Maurice Sachs talked as though it was the simplest thing in the world. To write . . . I felt myself becoming soft, chloroformed by my incapacity. Completely free, completely useless. To write . . . Oh yes, oh no. He was asking me to build a house when I wasn't a mason. It was worse than an attack of vertigo if I tried to think of it seriously even for a second. Oh Maurice, you mustn't tempt me like this. What shall I write about?

"I can't even conjugate the imperfect subjunctive," I said to Maurice Sachs.

"Don't start being stupid again," Maurice replied. "Try, then we'll see."

Now I felt my insides melting in gratitude for his patience.

"I can try? You really think I can?"

"Yes, I do," he said.

I was melting too for his confidence in me. He gave me their telephone number so that they could make an appointment for me at their office and explain what sort of piece it was they wanted.

"I have to meet Bob now, and I don't want to make him wait," he said.

Bob, his new friend. A beauty.

*

That afternoon I waited my turn in a minuscule antechamber in the center of Paris, surrounded by fifteen or so women of all ages. It was like a dentist's waiting room. The women who had come to sell their articles kept glancing around, coughing, staring at each other, picking up magazines and pretending to read. All of them, except me, had drawing portfolios or folders or briefcases on their knees. The boldest sat reading through their work or studying their drawings.

The door of the editorial office opened and a woman's voice called out the name Maryse Choisy. A small woman with an intelligent but reticent face and wearing a turban—they were just beginning to be fashionable—stood up and gave me an apologetic smile. The door of the editorial office closed behind her.

Bob wasn't waiting, he mustn't be made to wait. I forgot the vigilance and efficiency with which Maurice Sachs had searched to find me work. I forgot that without being in love with me he was tending my letters as though they were a garden. I was not where I should be. Maurice was with Bob, he had abandoned me. Cut off, drained of all my energy, the love, the friendship that men felt for each other ravaged me inside.

Someone called my name. Maryse Choisy nodded to me and vanished.

I went in. A man and a woman rose from their chairs; this silent welcome filled me with panic.

"Your name is Violette Leduc?" the woman asked.

She was wearing a severely cut suit, her voice was curt.

"Your name is Violette Leduc?" Now I've been advised to be a writer, am I a prisoner in the dock?

"Yes, yes," I replied, without much confidence, "that is my name, yes."

"That is my name, yes." It was my gaucherie that upset me rather than my arrogance.

"Your name is Violette Leduc?" My two names sounded different now because of what Maurice Sachs had put into my head. I felt there was something vaguely creative about their past.

"Maurice Sachs has informed us through one of his friends that we can count on you to do a story, a short narrative for us. Did he tell you exactly what it is we want?"

"No, he told me almost nothing."

There was a silence. I was being vouchsafed a glimpse of what went on backstage in the world of journalism. The woman editor of the magazine explained the subject of the story I was to write. I didn't listen to her but I could hear a babble of syllables streaming across the sheets of paper all stuck over with printed columns ringed with big blue pencil marks. It was terrible, she was telling me the theme of the story, I was sure of it, and she thought I was all ears. What would happen when I got back home? I would be forced to write a story without a theme. That confusion of syllables was my chance of earning a living. And yet I couldn't listen, I didn't like her, someone had pulled out a plug and cut us off. She was saying: ". . . In the country, the countryside somewhere near Paris, a feeling of health, it must be healthy." She was explaining what I ought to write, and what was I going to write when I wasn't listening to her? It must have been my gift for complicating things, for making the worst of all my defects. I liked the tall man standing with his back to me. Was he a designer? An illustrator? "We must have it in two days," she said. That I did hear. In two days. If the worst came to the worst I could always throw myself in the Seine if I couldn't think of a first sentence. "We're counting on you, M. Sachs gave us to understand that we could count on you." Where is the money in all these plans? In a tomb. "Do you follow what it is we want from you?" Yes, I've followed, I understand, I understand that I am a representative who sells short stories and short narratives, that I shall have to go around selling my wares from door to door, that I must come back in two days and tell you how many I've sold good-by madame good-by monsieur and I smile at the woman following me in as Maryse Choisy smiled at me. I feel better, the thorn is out of my foot. Gummed paper, enigmas of the printing press, embryo sentences, truncated paragraphs.

"It was a page make-up," Maurice Sachs told me later.

Invincible celibacy, I had hidden my wedding ring in my handbag before going into the magazine office. I thought no one would be interested if I wore my platinum ring. A self-sufficient woman must be single, I had told myself in the waiting room. Showing my wedding ring would mean revealing that I was married to Gabriel, that he wasn't providing me with the means to live. By hiding my wedding ring I was hiding my disappointment; I had conceived a longing for a double life, for a new job; I was ashamed of our poverty, of Gabriel's shabby clothes, of his idleness, his taciturnity, his stubbornness, his contentment with his lot. My lamb of the bistros . . . Other people couldn't see your threadbare suit as I did, and read in it the menus of all the succulent meals you bought for us when we ate out. You didn't hide away your curtain ring.

"Submit your story as soon as possible." I'll be honest with you, my beauty. I have no story to write. I am the story, it's already written. It is Gabriel refusing to give himself. Tomorrow, little fellow, tomorrow I promise you. Tomorrow. Gabriel, Gabriel . . . Can't you hear me? My rose, it is begging. Tomorrow, always begging, a sexual cliffhanger. Another piece of honesty now; just one more. The story is already written, it is simple and it is extraordinary. Who wrote it? Can you tell me who wrote it? Gabriel did. Gabriel at the climax of his pleasure. I am not lying to you. I am the wardress of his moan, of the rattle in his throat, his final gasp. Take your pleasure, my son, I am hypnotized by the ocean I glimpse inside you. Your story ends with a spurt of silk. Take your pleasure, my son.

Sixteen years old:

"What do you think of my composition, mummy? Do you like my composition?"

". . ."

"Answer me. Don't you like it?"

"It's not bad. . . ."

"Well?"

"It's not bad, but all the same . . ."

"All the same what?"

"It's heavy. I find it rather heavy."

"I'll be careful of that."

The key to my short sentences.

*

I emerged from the editorial office, the city showed its claws. *You write, oh la la there's a thing,* the spangles on the steps of a Métro station whispered in my eyes. *You walked past, we existed. And that was enough, you decided you'd start to write with those little eyes of yours. Now that you can see us you're taking yourself seriously.* I shall describe you. *You haven't the talent.* It's true, I hadn't seen you before. *And now you want to exploit us. You weren't looking for us, but you're always looking for original phrases. You're noticing us now because you want to be original.* Oh, that's cruel. Go on, speak some more, I said you were cruel. *We are answering you. Call us demanding, we would prefer that. If you could have kept yourself free of the penholder and the inkwell, then you could have carried us inside you, you could have created us. That's the rub my little one.* It all has to stay inside? *Absolutely.* In that case every idiot is a phoenix. *You are right, idiots are phoenixes.* I'm standing here staring at you, people will think I'm simple. . . . *Simple, and lost in your simplicity, you should add, little one. You know Paris, you know it's no good just looking at the store windows.* What is it you want of me? You are silent, and now I feel tender toward you. My thirst for diamonds is fading. Paris used to make me sad. These Métro steps . . . brushed with a glitter of dust. You are silent now. . . . Why should I stay here contemplating you? *We are a nativity.* Ah, you are speaking again. . . . *We are the starry sky of matter.* You are more peaceful than the stars. *Exactly.* People are looking at me while I look at you. Timid to the marrow of my bones I am. Dead and timid even when the pink worms move in my mouth I shall be. If I could make myself all over again with a shovel and some earth, then I would do it. *Idle chatter.* I can't use you in the story they've asked me to write. *We are in it.* That's because someone told me to write a story. *We don't doubt it. In the rush hour what are you? We are spangles who stick to our post.* Yes, you make me begin to see: the stars are mere fireflies. *You can never count on the stars. We are here all night and all day.* You are conceited. The stars exist all the time too.

Not for the heels of Paris. The high heels of Paris shelter us when the curtains of rain come down. When the frosts come, we are part of the festivities. The holly berries and the mistletoe berries fall on us. People spit on you. *We glimmer through their spit.* I've had enough, I'm going now. When the frosts come, you are part of the festivities, I am quoting you. Polaris is part of the festivities in winter too. *Perhaps. But we prefer the soles of a lovers' first meeting to that punctual Minerva.* I shall die, I shall nose-dive as steeply as any airplane can. *Agreed.* Those soles. They trample you. You're always being trampled. *We go on shining under shoes with holes in, under worn-down heels.* You are making me irritable. I'm going now, I'm going. What is it that keeps me here? A clown without his pompoms. Let me go. I tell you I opened the dictionary once and found "bearded comet." I shall never forget it. *We feel sorry for you, frog.* Why frog? *Because you are puffing yourself up, because you are a parasite on other's greatness.* Have pity, I have to write a story.

Leave then. Not now. I shall go away from here, I shall write, and it will all be different. I am looking at you just for the sake of looking at you. *So, little one, down with the chandeliers in opera houses eh?* Yes. The poppies were setting fire to the field of wheat. . . . *Why do you say "setting fire to"?* I'm beginning to write, I'm trying to write, I'm learning to write. *You're playing with your ball, little girl. The wheat was flourishing amid the poppies, if you want our advice. Just a moment please. The noise coming is so good for us: studded boots. They've gone now, we're all yours again. Don't write, little one, darn your husband's socks.* You're cutting away the ground from under my feet. I'm leaving, this has gone on long enough. Aren't you going to stop me? *Stay, you spineless thing. Oh yes, the music of a pair of studded boots. For us though, not for you. It enveloped us.* Yes, but the music of the brass envelops the chandeliers in an opera house, you know. *Keep your innocence, take things as they are, don't spoil the green lace of a carrot with capital letters.* I have to earn my living by writing a story. *Why not sell your bearded comet at so much the pound, like a grocer? Take things in, carry them inside you, keep them in your throat, the hurricane will thank you for it, and like it you will be free. There is nothing for you to say, every image is there in its nest. Don't murder the warmth at the top of a tree. Things can talk without your help, remember that. Things can talk without your help. Your voice will muffle them. If you think what you write isn't just so much literature . . . Just so that you'll be on your guard. We repeat: just so that you'll be on your guard.* I have to earn my living. I shall write, I shall open my arms, I shall hug the fruit trees and give them to my sheet of paper. *Your mind is wandering, poor child.* Why are you discouraging me like this? *We are honest.* I must go. *Yes, yes, go and dip your pen in the inkwell then.* Defeatists, you are undermining all my efforts. *The rosebush sinks beneath the ecstasy of its roses, what is it you want to make it say? What could you add to the dusted light of dawn? Remember your piano. You know what we mean. Remember your piano.* I failed, I admit it. I haven't failed at writing, I haven't begun. I have the harvest of my efforts still to reap. He said to me, you can write a story. I am obeying him. *Slave.* I have confidence in his judgment. *He has too much confidence in you. You have nothing to say, nothing to write. There is a chosen band, and you are not of their number. You hang on grimly, but that's not good. We are your support.* You are my support? *Stop all this affected talk, stop this hodgepodge of your ordeals and your ecstasy.* I have a husband, I have no support. *Oh you wilting little bush, it was his handshake you should have married.* Friendship you mean? Forget it. I'm not an iceberg. *It's rush hour now, you must go and dip your pen in the ink.* You're sending me away? *It's time for the symphony of shoes.* Can I come back, glitters on the Métro steps? Can I say to you: you are the pollen of the clearest day I ever saw? *You have said it. Enough.*

I tried to write during part of the night. But I had to answer Gabriel's questions and argue with him at the same time. He wanted me to go to bed, to "drop it" for the night. When I explained to him between erasures that he didn't give me enough money and that I had to find some way of earning some myself, he became annoyed, or else tried to irritate me by murmuring as usual that he was "having a great time himself." My work simply didn't interest him. Since his attack of typhoid nothing interested him anymore. I told him as much and he replied that if I didn't shut up he could always "clear out." I stopped talking to him. My heart was heavy as I gazed at the sheets of paper in front of me. Then there was silence of the building around us, also striking me with awe. I turned my head: Gabriel was sitting up in bed smiling. I took advantage of his smile and asked if it would give him pleasure to read what I'd written in a magazine. His expression changed. "What the fuck" did it matter to him whether he saw my name in a magazine? . . . Suddenly he was sick for the past. He nibbled at the bedclothes and talked about my first news item. We had read it together on the Place des Ternes, on the terrace of the café La Lorraine, occasionally catching the scent of the oysters wafting over from the great dishes nearby. I was his "chick," the sheet-chewer mused, I was his "little fellow." He refused the cigarette I offered him. What a mess, the white sheet in front of me, covered with my crossings out, my sweat. I reminded him how I consoled him in taxis, how I paid for my evenings out, how having to console him used to make me want to vomit. Gabriel and his poker face. He sat reflectively, his thin-lipped mouth expressing his pleasure. He was ruminating on his own cruelty, dehumanizing himself.

"Well, you seem to be enjoying it, your new job!" he said.

I crumbled. His thing. I was his thing because of his sprouting ruff of beard. A bluish dawn was spreading its drama over his face.

"We're using up all this electricity, and what have you written so far?" he asked disdainfully.

I read through my rough draft.

". . . I've written about you . . . about an outing we go on together . . . one that will never happen. . . . You love me and I love you while I'm writing. . . ."

"You must be joking. Where did you think that one up!"

I explained how I was trying to put a pattern into our life, how I was thinking of all those other couples squabbling when I thought of us. There were hundreds of thousands of us. I was reconciling them and they would be reconciled by reading what I wrote. Gabriel laughed good-naturedly and remarked that I certainly thought big. I didn't lose heart: I told him that I was writing without him but that we were bound together while my pen was moving across the paper. Gabriel listened, I got excited: my story wasn't even begun, yet my paper looked like a checkerboard already. I put things down on it, then removed them again. I wanted a tree, so there was a tree; I wanted a house, there was a house. I wanted darkness, I wanted rain. . . . I could have anything I wanted, all I had to do was imagine it. I changed the clouds into greyhounds, the old oak trees into young dancers feeding on rose petals and floating on galleys. "You can be a terrible bore when you put your mind to it," Gabriel said, and returned to his comfortable ivory tower.

"If they refuse to accept my story, at least I shall have had you in my arms on every page I've written," I said. Gabriel shrugged. "Let's make love," I suddenly said out of the blue. My entrails, my tyrants. I begged beside his bed, I abandoned my sheets of paper.

I wanted to "wear him out," I "had no respect" for his work, I ought to be "ashamed." Sleep, he wanted to sleep. We were both free, that was our agreement. Unfortunately my insides were not interested in legal procedure. I whined and tried to coax him. He said I was "a nympho." I'll love you the way I loved you at Saint-Rémy in the story. Gabriel threw back the bedclothes: he was naked because I never did his washing. Love me then, love away. He gave way, I was in despair.

I began with arabesques. All my hope was in my hand. Frivolous, light, aerial, adventurous, simple, complicated, coaxing, surprising, deceptive, hesitant, precise, rhythmical, unending, subtle, lively, slow, dragging, conscientious. Do you like it, this long circling around your nipple? There is a swallow back from the warm south, Gabriel, fluttering from your thigh down to your ankle, listen to it on the outline of your body. Moving carelessly, diligently, attentively, curiously, watchfully, I traced the name of Saint-Rémy over my lover's flesh. I also wrote down the old woman picking up the rotting flower when the market was closing, I twined a long paragraph of honeysuckle around his haunches, around his wrist, around his ear. My slow lotus stream flowed down into his blood, but it didn't make Gabriel go to sleep. A shiver across his shoulder blades, token of my power. Dance-hall bowers, potatoes frying in the open air, his armpits, his groin. Hunched inside the chaos of my love, my hand followed the outline of his leg as I fed like a baby at my husband's heel. Dear teacher, you encouraged me. I listened to the sounds of the clearing: his shoulder as I gamboled around it. My fingers and my nails told you all about a very fragile moon being intimidated by a cloud, about a sunset being massacred, about the trills and the waterdrops of a shadow bird. A heavy walk we went on then. Oh God, how well I wrote from his knee up to his groin; oh God, that was my religion.

I cried for a long time after I'd finished writing my story down. I could hear Maurice Sachs' strangled laugh and the curt voice of the woman editor as she rapped out her refusal. After all, I put everything I've got into it, I said to myself.

May 15, 1961, at twenty past nine in the morning. A village in the Vaucluse region. I haven't changed; I still haven't overcome my desire to juggle with words so that people will notice me. An original phrase, that's my act. I do my act and my exercise book applauds me. When my exercise book doesn't applaud me that means it's indifferent, that it's avid for lucidity or fantasy. The tragedy of the untalented. Darling reader, I will give you what I have. I must leave you for a moment to collect it and give it back to you.

You have waited for me, reader, so you're still reading me . . . and I shan't be giving you what I've just received! Someone has lent me his terrace at the back of the village. Pic, pic, pic, pic, pic. It must be the relentless rhythm of castanets hidden in a bird's throat. The sun is grating across the sky, it is shouting down to me that it won't let me renounce my home in the North. My body suffers when I expose it. We Northerners can never discard our wool, our cocoons of cloth. A conductor has given his instructions to the sun: piano, piano. A brief intermezzo of gentle shade, a nuance fleeting across the ground. The hum of a June bug, the insects have their jet planes too. A mystery, he's on his way to settle some important business deal. A sound of steps, as though someone were walking under the ground. It's a thin man, a beige man, a man made of gray earth carrying his sulfate spray on his back. He walks past along the path, he takes no notice of me. Pic, pic, pic, pic, pic. My punctuation up in a tree. The pic, pic, pic, pic, pic, is also the coolness of the tree trunk shaded by the leaves. My roads down there, and my streams the color of stone walls, make their patterns on the side of the hills. From time to time I catch the refrain of the flowering broom before it fades again. Chiaroscuro: the darkened hillside with its counterpane of trees, its broken line of brush, is a living map of woods and forests as I look across at it (I am looking down from an airplane without having taken off); it is over there behind the bluish, quivering haze, it is my pen drawing a waving line against the sky. The curves and folds of the mountain, of the hills, console me for my chastity. Three cypresses, three serene flames down there, down there. Further off, much further off, a hint of poppies, further still, much further still, a mist of poppies. What are those clumps of fruit trees they've just finished planting? The parallel lines of the vines running into the distance, the well-tended, the civilized vines. The clean earth, the healthy earth between the vines. The little hut has ears made of leaves that are bigger than itself. Over all, the heat, taming us with its whip. A memory of the icy mistral that blew last week. Of all this landscape spread about me, I will give you first, I will give you above all, that slow-moving caravan. The caravan of shadows moving toward a mountain. And as for the masses of curly-headed trees that make up the backgrounds of so many Italian paintings, take as big a bunch of those as you can carry. And then let us swim, let us dive into the sweet peas.

May 18, 1961, reader. You are saying, why is she calling me like this, why is she hustling me? I'm not hustling you. I'm trying to get close to you. He began breathing again three times, he faded away at four in the morning, that is how an old man died, that is how they tell it here. When the wife of the dead man complained of an earache, someone asked her if she was suffering from neuralgia. "No," replied the old woman, "it's my husband, there are sweet harmonies just by my ear." What better way of explaining how one can be in pain and yet not in pain?

*

Accepted, my story was accepted. I became a child again. I picked a white globe in the Place du Palais-Royal, I played with a balloon through the streets of Paris. I gave the globe to a bus conductor, I addressed tender messages and gestures to cyclists riding by. There were qualifications; the magazine was intended for a very wide public, I must make things simpler, I mustn't tire my readers, in the future I must make things shorter, I would be paid later, what I'd earned would be called my standard rate. The man who worked standing up with rulers and T-squares liked my story, I could expect another assignment. The young women and older women waiting their turn in the waiting room gave my heart a pang. I could read my past on their anxious faces. I was a little ahead of them, that was all.

"Why shouldn't they have accepted your story?" Gabriel asked.

It was a pail of cold water, I thanked him without words. It was three in the afternoon. He was toying despondently with the plate of noodles I'd cooked for him because he'd already eaten lunch on the quiet with his verger. I had followed him, I knew what I had to cope with. Maurice Sachs sent for me.

"Excellent, excellent," he said, as though he were soaping his dimpled prelate's hands.

His singsong voice irritated me that day.

I found him already settled into a new furnished apartment on the Rue de Rivoli. Dressed in a dark tie-silk dressing gown printed with stripes, he seemed physically much more expansive than before. I sat rooted to my chair, despite the drink he gave me, despite the English cigarette. The fascination he felt for luxury, and his ability to find ways of satisfying it were only too dazzlingly apparent.

"What's wrong, my dear?" he asked, noiselessly opening and closing the drawers of a Louis Seize desk.

"Oh nothing," I said, feeling I was about to burst with misery.

"Don't be stupid," Maurice Sachs said. "You're simply crammed with neuroses, and you mustn't be."

My heart wouldn't be beating so hard if.

Maurice Sachs walked into his bathroom, I hid my face in my hands. My heart wouldn't be beating so hard if I didn't love him. Sachs wanted nothing to do with my heart and its solemn thumping. I inhaled the vague scent of his toilet water and wondered why I wasn't the most beautiful boy in the world.

He came back without my hearing him.

"You're crying when someone has just told me you're wanted for a reporting assignment?"

"Reporting?" I said, feeling very sorry for myself.

"And why not! My dear child, you'll never get anywhere if you insist on lumbering other people with your personal miseries. It's something people never forgive. A little gaiety if you please!"

I was paralyzed by his lightning change of apartments. I was half expecting another cloud of locusts. And also I wanted to cry, I wanted to be so full of unhappiness I would burst. It was true: hamstrung, garrotted by the bonds of my own self-pity I was a nuisance to myself and a nuisance to others. Sachs' remark was just, and irrelevant.

"Come with me," he said.

He took me into another room, smaller, cooler, more austere, and also darker.

Solemnly, he closed the door. He gestured with his hand to guide my eyes.

"Gold, diamonds, precious stones," he said with exuberance.

His face was unrecognizable: soulless. Those eyes, too gentle for this world, were suddenly sparkling with a cruel fire. An eagle's eye, an eagle's beak, saying to the money spread before it: Just the two of us.

"I sell, and I buy. What?" he said with a laugh.

Wily old Maurice Sachs! He had wormed his way into the behind-the-scenes activities of the big jewel dealers; he gave me a lucid and very funny account of how he had managed it. He weighed his gold on a little pair of apothecary's scales, and meanwhile he told me about the boy he was in love with, and who wasn't in love with him. He numbed us both with his spate of words. Patiently, willingly, I listened to the schemes of a diamond dealer mad with love who wanted to give all the most beautiful things that Paris could offer to the most beautiful boy in Paris.

"How's the husband?" he asked as we went back into his room.

"He's well," I said with fury.

I hated Gabriel for letting me be so attached to Maurice Sachs.

"He loves me," I said. But it sounded as though I was spitting.

"Of course he loves you," Sachs replied with conviction. "But why did you have to get married?" he asked with distress in his voice. "I don't see what advantage there is in being called Mme. Mercier. . . ."

"I hide that name!"

"Women are quite mad," he said with amused disdain.

He had a great many appointments. He bade me a spirited good-by.

"Keep well, and don't forget to go and see them," he said as he gave me a limp handshake.

His valet accompanied me as far as the front door mat.

*

I had a friend on the other side of a windowpane. Esther. She was a young girl of thirteen. It was during the war. We both lived in courtyard apartments on the second floor. My window and hers, face to face, night and day, never took their eyes off one another. Her window was draped with tiresome curtains. Mine was naked. Esther could see us; she learned how to love, how to hate, how to take a man in your arms, how to kiss his neck and his hand. She made a tracing of our whole existence. None of it was done with mirrors. I would appear first, she would raise her curtain, then go on brushing her straight hair, her hair that stopped short at her chinline. Esther wasn't young, she would never grow old: that was her beauty. She never smiled: that was her grandeur. The visits we paid each other through our windowpanes were more real than any spoken greeting. I would appear, she would rush to see me; or she would be there, and I would hurtle to watch her. She had the poise of an Infanta married while still a child. Mat skin and burning lips. Her brother would talk to her. I would step back but go on watching her. She never turned her head, she never gave any reply. Tirelessly, she went on brushing her hair. Admirable folly of a girl in full possession of her reason. She was alone, she would always be alone. That was her right, her claim to majesty. She liked the silk jersey of the dress I'd been married in. She knew me down as far as my shoulders and never asked for more. Ours was a public idyl. We had nothing to say to one another, nothing to confide, nothing to offer. The curtain fell again after she left.

I forgot Esther; I told Gabriel he had a Jewish nose.

"Oh yes, everyone knows Mercier is a Jewish name, you poor mutt!" he answered with a sneer.

I could read his pity for me in his eyes.

Gabriel wasn't cruel. He used to give me his ration coupons when he'd eaten out in a restaurant. They were our most easily negotiable form of currency, now rationing had begun. I had to wait in line two hours for a handful of vegetables. I chatted. I put myself in the others' shoes. An orgy of platitudes. I wanted to please them. So I talked: parcels to be packed for prisoners, letters received, letters sent, the advances, the defeats of our enemies, a ray of hope, relatives in the country, relatives going short themselves in order to send a piece of bacon. Repetitions, twice-told tales, lamentations, threats, I imitated the other housewives. I criticized with them, I drew my consolation from the same source as theirs. "All is not lost," one of the strong-minded ones whispered in my ear. "All is not lost," I would say to one weaker than myself. The enemy, our troops. This new vocabulary did nothing to help me in my war against Gabriel, nothing to prevent us from humiliating each other all the time. My defeat had merely coincided with the outbreak of war. Carrots, noodles and rutabagas all tasted delicious when Gabriel was good to me. I wailed with the others in order to bring Gabriel back sooner. But in fact I was sincerely neutral. And what is more, I was hoping for worldwide disaster, I was hoping that when everyone in Paris had fled I would be promoted in their absence. I wanted bombs and mortar shells to shatter my past failures. The war would get me out of the rut I was in. Making decisions is painful if you're lazy. Decisions, problems to be solved, all that was gone. We let ourselves drift; it was a transition, there was nothing to be done. I was living in one squalid room; but all those luxury apartments with their signs "For Rent"—they also belonged to me now. I breathed more freely in a Paris without people.

*

When the issue of the magazine came out with my story in it, they presented me with several copies. I paid little attention to the text itself, which was sentimental, badly written, not nearly good enough. My name, my first name and my last name, were all I needed, they filled every page. My eyes were sipping absinthe. I counted and recounted the number of letters making up my two names: There I was, round-shouldered Violette Leduc, standing up straight eight times, standing up straight five times, standing up straight thirteen times. I had stars for toes. I pressed my cheek against the paper of the magazine to see if my names were electric. They were. I ran to my mother, I gave her a copy of the magazine. I was disturbed by her enthusiasm and her indulgence. I brushed the story aside: it was only a beginning, they were asking me to do some reporting. My mother has never read any of the classics, except Stendhal and Dostoievsky. She murmured: "I'm so pleased for you. Writing is your life, it's what you've always wanted." Hangdog, I left her.

I hurried away, and on the platform of the Pelleport Métro station what did I see? A copy of the magazine under the arm of a frilly young girl. All is not lost, it was only a passing twinge of disappointment. People are reading me, therefore they will go on reading me. They take me out, they walk around with me, they tuck me into the warmth of their armpits. Oh the love bites as I walked over to her. She was powdering her little nose, she was stroking her lipstick over her lips. The magazine fell onto the platform, but she went on with her repairs.

I picked up the magazine.

"I'm sorry," she said. "You shouldn't have put yourself out. . . ."

She took the magazine from my hand, gracefully, absent-mindedly.

I stood shapelessly, meditating on the glass flowers studding the lid of her compact. She raised her eyes and stared at me. I was beginning to make her uneasy. I walked away without losing sight of her, humming to hide my mortification, as though I'd been caught committing some petty crime. I waited with her for the train. I got into the same compartment and found a seat where my eyes could devour her without her knowing. She laid the magazine on her knees, she opened the compact again, she rearranged several locks of hair. Finally she shut her handbag and gave herself up to the pleasure of being in a moving train. I got off with her at Barbès-Rochechouart. I followed her along the corridors. I walked behind her on the other side of the street. The sun on the terrace tables was inviting her to sit and read. She would sit down, she would leaf through the magazine, she would choose my story, and we would read it together. A passer-by shouted at me rudely: I was taking up too much of the sidewalk. Mystery girl, mystery girl . . . Listen to the enchanter calling you. Here, my little titmouse, come and peck at my prose in the shadow of this siphon. Settle at that table. Read me. I am going to fall over I want so much for you to want what I want. We kept walking, we left the cafés and terraces behind us. I followed her into streets that were strange to me. She went into a drygoods store. I stood looking back and forth between the bolts of cloth for ladies' coats and her prettily inexpressive face. She kept turning her eyes toward the door into the street as though she were expecting someone. She emerged with her packages, the magazine fell onto the threshold of the store, a passer-by picked it up and handed it to her. She thanked him curtly. My story had not inspired a romance. I began following her again; a hundred yards further on she pressed the button outside an apartment building, she went in and closed the door behind her.

I looked for a newspaper stand. Every copy of the magazine had been sold. I felt a warm gust of air: my story was stirring up a wind. Three houses further down, I saw some pages from my magazine impaled on a hook over the trays outside a seed store. I recognized the illustrations. I took the Métro again and found a seat next to a virago who was sitting by a window and brimming over with self-satisfaction. My quarry could not escape. I opened the magazine and leafed through it exuberantly. I left it lying open on my knees at the page with my name and the title of my story printed across it. This one wasn't going to evade them. I sat patiently with folded arms. She took off her gloves, opened her elegant carry-all and took something out of it wrapped in an immaculate table napkin. She unknotted the napkin and turned her head toward me with the slow movement of a robot. She looked me up and down using the whole length of a long neck swathed in several rows of pearls. She was knitting an undershirt.

*

They told me they would allow me to try my hand at writing an editorial. Our aim was to raise the morale of all the women separated from their loved ones. I had to inspire them with good humor, strength of mind, energy and health. Using the materials of their day-to-day existence I was supposed to provide a firm foundation for the women on the home front.

"Just write whatever they ask. You can do it," Maurice Sachs said without irony.

I didn't dare ask him: have you read what I've written?

My double life began.

*

May 22, 1961. A former headmistress—now eighty—took me to visit the wild gardens. We followed the path past a maze of ruins and some farmhouses that were still more or less intact. The mistral was blowing. Suddenly, I thought it must have stopped dead, the way things do when you tear open a telegram. We walked out of a winter in Oslo and into a Palermo spring. The surprise of a sudden exposure.

As we made our way into the sensuous disorder of an untamed garden I heard someone singing softly: an old man appeared wearing a straw hat, a mixture of honey and sun. A panama transformed by age into a cap with earflaps.

"Good day," was all his greeting, spoken in a drawling voice as though he were stretching out the line of his song to include the words of his greeting.

Poor, neglected, solitary, that was evident at a glance. But no! His pink cheeks, the rounded contours of his face despite his age, his big blue eyes, the soft movement of his white hair stroking his neck, that sparse white beard, they all suggested a lighthearted patriarch, freed from the necessities of time, a being who had conquered poverty and solitude. A man on his own, unable to sew his fly buttons back on.

"Good day . . ."

He showed us the little green fists of the young artichokes just ready to be cut. He wandered off carrying a pot full of earth with a hole in the bottom. His first strawberries, four or five of them, were stagnating in the muddy water of a rusty tin can. We were a long way from the absorbent cotton of the expensive fruit stores.

"He used to teach school in Mexico," said the eighty-year-old lady who listens to Sidney Bechet. Before that he had been with the Frères Chrétiens and was forced to leave France when the church was disestablished. He was a hermit who had knocked about in a great many places. We found ourselves rooted to the spot, gazing at a mass of titanic irises beside a mass of dark pink poppies. The voluptuousness of the colors enjoying the light, of the light enjoying the colors.

We congratulated him; he was beyond any words that we could say to him. He lived in the songs he hummed, the songs he invented and composed. The eighty-year-old lady who reads Sartre and Schwartz-Bart, who would like to see Bunuel's early films, who discusses radio news programs with the energy of a lion, who subscribes to *L'Express* and *L'Observateur* and *Temps Modernes,* remarked that some of his strawberries were ripe.

"But of course. I gave you the very first one!"

"It's true, you brought it to the house," she admitted.

He walked away to inspect his clematis, still singing softly. There was a quaver in his voice. Old, silly, prodigious. His fingers could endow any plant with miraculous powers of endurance. He had only to touch one and it grew.

May 23, 1961. Bitter cold here in the Vaucluse this morning. I haven't washed, that makes things simpler. One, two, three sweaters, my gray pants, and off I go with my little flat basket, my duck-egg-blue espadrilles, which are too large, and the chipped varnish on my

Parisian toenails. I have to leave my night residence and walk over to my daytime residence. Kindly sun . . . he is waiting for me when I get to my terrace. I make breakfast on a wood-burning stove with wood that doesn't belong to me. Can't afford to be too particular. Oxygen is a source of warmth too. The water has been put on to boil and there isn't an idea in my head as I stand facing my problem: how am I going to get my four pounds of strawberries down my throat before they become squashy and turn that pale tobacco color? My usual visitors are out for their morning stroll along the path below the terrace. The cats and the dogs. A big ginger dog, a big fawn dog, a big white dog . . . Absorbed by their morning census-taking, they avoid each other automatically as they search the earth for scents. They belong to the horizon around them. They are the dogs of my sad thoughts, the dogs of their own meditations.

May 24, 1961. Will it rain? The hills in the foreground are covered with a blanket of pale gray fur. It is raining. Cats and dogs. The mountain behind the hills is navy blue. It might almost be a mine tip in the North, in my own country, with those slaty clouds lowering overhead. The rain has doused the yellow broom, I can hear it falling on the cement. An orgasm for the gardens. Birds sated with cherries are singing nearby. The rain is hammering lightly in my ears, the tumbledown house has to use its last ounce of strength when it rains, the earth grows pink, the vines start to shrink, the huts in the vineyards grow faint and disappear. Whether it rains or whether it doesn't, I have the light and the dark of two hills sailing near to the infinite. A visit, the double-jointed flight of a swallow in front of the French windows. I have more sentimentality today than I know what to do with; I feel sad for the bench being soaked outside because I can't drag it out of the wet. The bunch of wild irises I picked last night among the broom bushes and the young fruit trees with their crimson shoots didn't warn me there was going to be a long-long rain. My house built of sun has collapsed.

*

I wrote several editorials.

Get up early, I told my readers. I used to get up at eleven, screaming for Gabriel's sex inside me. . . . I like begging, I like asking for things, being given things, getting something for nothing. Oh God, yes, oh God how magnificent it was, my mendicancy as I lay weeping on Gabriel's bare feet in front of the sink. The ivy I adored: my arms winding up around his calves. Oh, Madame Lita, what delicacy you showed. You lived on the floor above us all through the war. You listened to our love bouts, far from your husband in his prison camp. I used to meet you often on the stairs, you wore your yellow star sewn on your bodice, you gave your good morning to the least worried wife in the world. I am talking about you, Madame Lita, and here is a ray of sunshine for you coming through the rain.

And, above all, get up on the right side of the bed, I told my readers.

I didn't give a damn about the right side of the bed. Exhausted by my privations, I collapsed limply on our divan. My tear-spattered hair rained down my cheeks. When Gabriel came over and threw me onto the bed I was a great bundle of rags. Then another bout of pleading began. Gabriel gave way because he couldn't kill me. Then he tore himself away from the room. Often I used to hope that we would all follow him: the room, the table, the stove, the armchair, the divan, all trailing after Gabriel because he hated us so much.

Don't waste time: see that you're in a good temper when you get up. Put on your boxing gloves and face your everyday routine, Mesdames, Mesdemoiselles. Your difficulties will fly away, I told my readers.

If I got up at the same time as Gabriel it was in order to argue about the two francs for the electricity, the three francs for the gas, the one franc for coal, the hundred francs for the rent. I hid my purse and he never let me see how much money he had when he opened his billfold. Bizarre rivals in rapacity. We both lied about our earnings. I checked the amount of money in my handbag ten times a day. Not that I distrusted Gabriel; but I distrusted his curiosity. When he refused me money it was another way of refusing me his sex. I made it grow with my caresses, but he would talk about bronchitis, about colds, about sweaters. Anyone can see you've never gone hungry, my mother often used to say. Gabriel had gone hungry. He remembered how cold it could be in winter with nothing but a jacket. The memory of his typhoid was still haunting him. I gave him noodles, more noodles, always noodles. I was savagely determined to keep him and savagely determined to lose him.

Strength of mind above all else, Mesdames and Mesdemoiselles. Take care of your nerves. Tend your nerves as though they were a precious garden. A sound mind in a sound body, the Greeks used to say. Not a moment to lose, breathe in breathe out, window wide open as soon as you get up, I told my readers.

They were in a fine state, my own nerves! Weary of waiting for the revelation, the visitation, I tore myself free of my own hope with attacks of fury and threats of suicide. I accused Gabriel of hating women, I complained about his invincible friendships, I accused him of being a homosexual. I beat myself with the coal shovel to convince him. It was in him that I killed myself. "I'm going to leave, I'm going to vanish from the earth, I'm going to kill myself." He shrugged his shoulders. He left the room with his camera slung over his shoulder. He left me two cigarettes in the battered pack on the mantel. The wine bottle was empty, the glasses all had lipstick smudges on them. I dressed, I made myself up, and I realized I must be trembling because I noticed that a little of my face powder had fallen from the shelf onto the floor. Ah, I thought, I must exploit that tremble, I must extend this threat into a reality. I produced another fit of trembling and pressed the puff in my quivering hand against the powder in the box. The pinkish yellow powder scattered lightly down and settled on all the closet shelves. What a state she must have been in, he would say. Gabriel was in my power, his uneasiness about me would be a leash.

My hunger satisfied, my thirst assuaged, I left the apartment. I wondered where I should go. I was dying with boredom while I waited to play at dying. I dragged across the city. I dragged the long hours, the moribund cafés and the mouths of the Métro after me. I dragged all the store windows too; I counted the hats, the bracelets, the rings, the necklaces. I counted the engravings and the pornographic books. I counted the shirts and sweaters that Gabriel never bought for himself, I told myself I was no longer of this world, that I was looking down from my phony suicide's heaven and choosing socks and leather belts for Gabriel. I ended up finally in the room of a friend named Musaraigne.

We had first met Musaraigne by chance, in the street. Gabriel hadn't opened his lips the whole time we were with her. Musaraigne was the same age as myself. She was a practicing Roman Catholic. She observed, she judged, she was sometimes wrong and sometimes right, she fancied herself an amateur psychologist, but God didn't always lend her his microscope. Why was she so cold toward the epileptic having a fit on the sidewalk? Frothing at the mouth isn't nice. Musaraigne talked with slow preciosity. She was molded out of crystal. I was always afraid she'd break when she became excited. She was chaste, she was a virgin, she was poor, she lived off crumbs, the hiss of her breath at the end of every sentence made me uneasy. It was her struggle with the serpent. Sitting in a field, she would read Proust, Poe, Teresa of Avila, Péguy, or Valéry out loud to her mother or to her men friends. Like me, she had a mad passion for wild flowers. We used to gallop across a lake of white ox-eye daisies when we were out with Julienne, we would lose our heads over the field of lily-of-the-valley above the rocks of the Mer de Sable. The three Graces (which was what we called ourselves) would then return to Paris enriched. Gif, Bures-sur-Yvette, Chevreuse, Saint-Lambert. Saint-Rémy, Port-Royal, Eve, the Métro, the Gare du Nord, the Gare Saint-Lazare, the homemade Sunday cookies in the villages . . . At noon we looked for an abandoned orchard, and when we had found our patch of providence we unpacked our lunch. Musaraigne chewed on her soft bread, her rusks and sandwiches. But she burst out laughing when I waved my garlic sausage under her nose. We added up all our expenses and divided them; I made fun of Musaraigne's piety, I tortured her, I made her cry. She and Julienne told me about Vincent Van Gogh. Julienne lent me his letters. I will draw a veil, reader, over one of the greatest moments of my life: Van Gogh, the *Letters of Van Gogh*. I want to see him seated on his throne of glory, I want to see him spit down on the society that murdered him.

I put Musaraigne through an interrogation the day I staged my phony suicide. I arrived at her place and yielded to an attack of egocentricity. She listened, I talked. He's a sadist, you must admit he's a sadist. Why is he a sadist? What reason can there be? Think, take your time. Why won't he give himself to me? Why won't he give me anything? He hates women. I tell you he hates women. When Hermine left he took over the role I used to play. He won't give himself to me, just as I wouldn't give myself to him before. He wants me to give back everything he gave me. Can't you see what's happening on my face, doesn't it tell you what I'm going through? "Yes, I can see it in your face," Musaraigne said. She looked at me with compassion. Finally she admitted that Gabriel was sadistic, but that it was nothing to worry about. I wanted her to admit that he was peculiar as well. "You are more difficult to live with than he is," I read in her sad eyes. Then, in a grave and confidential tone, almost whispering, she told me I should never have married him. He could have run away, I retorted.

She gave a good-natured laugh. "Do you think he won't run away?"

"I don't know. All I know is that he grows on me."

"I don't doubt it," she said mournfully.

I could read in her smile: all this isn't my sort of thing at all. I prefer my evenings with the great writers.

I didn't tell her that day about the measures I'd taken to frighten Gabriel. I left her at cocktail time and drank a lemonade in a café. Soon-soon your victory, the hands of the Saint-Michel clock sang quietly to my eyes. I ate dinner at Les Balkans—no more lamb on the spit—the night as it began to seep in between the curtains was already answering my prayers. Gabriel had been waiting two hours for me already in our room; he knew my roars that morning had not been empty threats. I got home at half-past ten in the evening to find the room exactly as I had left it. No camera, not a single cigarette butt, not a trace of Gabriel. I opened the closet and felt a slight unease at the sight of the yellowish pink powder on the shelves. I went out again and wandered through the streets around the building. Suddenly I saw him. He was discussing something quietly with his sister. The blue paper stuck on the windows made them look like stained glass that had faded. Gabriel recognized my step. He ran up and flung himself in my arms.

"I've found you, I've found you," he kept saying, scarcely able to draw breath.

His sister parted us.

"Where were you?" she asked sternly.

"Where were you?" Gabriel asked.

The glow from Gabriel's flashlight was falling on all three of us. I wished I could have his shining face embalmed and put under a glass dome for me to keep.

I began to fiddle with my handbag.

"Tell us," Gabriel said.

"Tell us. My brother waited for you half the afternoon. . . ."

"You don't usually come home that early," I said ill-naturedly.

"We went to look for you at your mother's."

"You can go now she's back," Gabriel said to his sister.

Gabriel straightened our bed and emptied his pockets onto the mantelpiece without a word.

"Come on," he said finally, "tell me all about it. It was your powder that frightened me the most."

"Did you think I'd done something silly?"

"Yes, I did."

We were lying in bed. He looked at me.

"Little fellow," he cried.

He was hugging me in his arms and weeping.

"Poor little fellow," he said again into the hollow of my shoulder.

"Are you sorry for me?" I asked in a low voice.

"Yes, I'm sorry for you," Gabriel answered.

A silence. Who would speak first?

"Perhaps you were hoping I really had killed myself? And then I came back. . . ."

"Don't talk nonsense, please."

"Were you really worried?"

"Oh please. Don't play the little woman. I loathe that. Where were you?"

He leaned his elbow on the pillow.

"I'm going to have a cigarette. I'd completely forgotten to smoke."

Gabriel picked up the lighter and the pack of cigarettes from the floor: his bedside table.

"Put it out. . . . I'll tell you all about it."

"I'm not putting it out," Gabriel answered.

At that moment his cigarette was his best friend.

"I was walking . . . I went for a walk. I went to see Musaraigne. You can ask her."

"I won't ask her anything. I believe you."

He was reflecting in my eyes. He took another puff at his cigarette.

"It was because I love you," I said lowering my eyes.

"Oh yes, you love me all right, I can see that," Gabriel said contorting his face into a sarcastic grin.

He put out the light.

"What did my mother say?"

"That there was nothing to worry about. That you'd come back. That she knows you too well."

I felt bitter toward my mother. I was hurt by her optimism.

"Was she worried?"

"Less than we were," said Gabriel. "She knows you. Good night."

"Good night."

A clumsy hand crawled over and squeezed mine in the darkness. A farewell. I kneaded my misery, I wept without ostentation. Gabriel was trying to go to sleep, he kept twitching beside me.

"Congratulations, I see you slept well. Obviously you thrive on this sort of thing," Gabriel said next morning.

"And you?"

"I couldn't sleep. I'll catch up tonight."

And for the next three days, that was how I died slowly inside Gabriel.

*

I didn't get much reporting to do. What I did was meaningless, abortive, rejected. I'd had no training, I couldn't see things through the readers' eyes.

I suggested a feature article about backstage life at the Comédie Française to one of the big magazines. They liked the idea. I was given the best photographer in Paris. The stagehands demonstrated how the scenery and special effects worked. I couldn't make head or tail of their labyrinth of ropes and staircases and traps and catwalks, but I would have liked to have slept there one night after the play was over. The stage, looking out onto the sea of undulating dustcovers disguising the auditorium, seemed to me a mockery. I walked backwards and forwards across it in every direction, but I felt nothing. I, the tragic actress of our sleazy room, the tragic actress of our mutual blame and resentment, the tragic actress of my ovaries, my head ennobled by its wreath of curlers, with my train of tears, my storm rain for weeping, my broken face, the agony of rich loam sliced by the plow, what was I in the palace of Phèdre, in Chimène's apartment? A drowned rat. I went groping and bumping through the framework of that night's performance, and I no longer believed in its reality for an audience when the curtain rose. The drama of a beam or a pulley, the feeling of being in a great barn or warehouse was all I wanted now.

Some actors dressed in street clothes came and took us to visit one of the dressing rooms: a boudoir with walls covered in old cretonne. I didn't dare ask them questions. What did one ask an actor? I had read *Le Paradoxe du comédien* when I was writing my news items and I'd remembered it. Here were a group of nice guys with hearty laughs: a far cry from the clamor and magnificence of kings and emperors. The photographer did his job well. The pictures he took were impeccable, powerful, unusual, varied. I had to write the captions. What torture as I threshed about in my own poverty. . . . No, there was no way of counterfeiting a training I'd never had. I asked Gabriel to help me: the dawn would break and my work would not be finished. Gabriel said he'd rather study the photographer's work. They wanted captions: I wrote snippets of convoluted nonsense.

When the magazine came out, I wasn't there. Who had written those captions, so much simpler and so much better than my own? I cried because they hadn't printed at the beginning: from an idea by Violette Leduc.

I went back to the women's magazine; I made a speech about giving the readers a chance to see pictures of the high fashion collections. The editors hesitated. They didn't want to frighten their readers with anything eccentric, with things beyond their reach. I replied that their readers need only take what they wanted: a bow, a dart, a new shade, a cuff.

"Having prints of great paintings in your room doesn't mean you've got delusions of grandeur," I exclaimed. They thought it over, then sent me to see Lucien Lelong. To watch a collection being shown . . . The sight of my worn old raincoat shocked me despite its trailing rainbow of memories. I won't be allowed in, the doorman will turn me away. I pulled it on and soaked myself with poverty in our little kitchen. The rats underneath our tiny frosted glass window were tracing their swift patterns on the roof. Paris rats, Paris modes. We know that hiccuping sound: the nadir of despair. I hiccuped. Listen, I said to myself, listen and rest with the gas burner. My pulse, my eyelids, a few bars rest, I beg of you. The bark of time was gliding forward alongside all the things around me: the damp and tattered washcloth, the trashcan with its paper lining, the enamel bowl and its ring of grease, the squashed potato, the gas-lighter lying beside the cigarette butt. The bark was Hermine, she was standing up to row. We were feeling the fabrics of the dresses on sale. Our past . . . that tiny cluster of coffee grounds on the edge of the sink. Time to go. I will give eel-colored suits, I thought, I will give eel-colored suits and lengths of lamé to eyes I have never seen.

The gulf between a young woman coming to buy at a sale and a little reporter without training and without talent. I showed my letter of introduction; the doorman, the footman, the salesladies told me I could go in. In the well-fed cackle of the crowd, I became a terrified schoolgirl again. A lady dressed in gray gave me a frail chair made of gilded wood. The show would be starting soon: all around there were pencils, automatic pencils, and fountain pens pressed on notebooks held at the ready. Occasionally a saleslady hurtled like a meteor across the stage: the space between the opposing ranks of chairs. A voice called out a name and a mannequin wearing a daytime suit emerged from the wings. The show had begun. Someone whispered that the designer was sitting among us and pointed him out. Austerely dressed in a navy blue suit, he was sitting with folded arms preparing to contemplate his work.

June 15, 1961. We are drying the hay, children. The summer is in a good humor, the fields are beginning to sprout molehills, the sight of them warms the eye as the scent of a cow shed warms the nostrils. Drying and cutting. The noise of the tractor covers the silky rustle of the forks turning the hay. The grayness, the dryness of the earth as I lie on it; the mist of the grass, the clover regressing to its wild state again as two birds slake my thirst. The splendor of the broom: the sunlight is rocking its yellow clusters and the languorous blue sky is swimming overhead. Burning rose, mystic rose of a clover field growing to seed, there goes a little scarlet butterfly. The subtlety of the light as it spreads in orgasm on the grass, my stained earth window. And the hills, always the hills, eaten away by the breakers of the bushes at their base. The horizon is a wall of broom like ruffled fur. And the breeze is stroking my brow like a gentle nurse as I sit beside the long lashes of broom reaching out from the bushes. The flowers on the curving prow of the stem, are they earflaps or little open mouths? Religious art, the color of the trumpets in old pictures. The rushing stream of light. I would be stupid not to enjoy what I have. . . .

I enjoy it twice by confiding it to my exercise book. I am inside the calyx of a flower, the calyx of nature as it grows warm. My birth is the birth of the wildest, the most modest, the most unseen little weed. The silence on my shoulder, oh my dove. I drink in the blue fragility around me in deep draughts. I am hungry, I am thirsty, and I bathe in the throat of a bird. I listen, I look, and I am not dying. Old age, my old age, tell me you will be my pillow. The white tufts of my aging years caught in the hedgerows are so tender to my eyes. Tell me, my old age, that my solitude will be my little white-haired child. My age is drying in the fields, I am no longer afraid of children when they laugh. At night I am patient: not to sleep is to live each hour as it chimes; it is to be loved by a steeple. I am aging, therefore I am alive: the silver of my shroud is glinting on the bark of a dying tree. Now you must go home, Violette. I go home and turn the lime flowers spread out on the divans, the lime flowers I picked in the dome of a young lime tree, as I wedded myself to that world of flowers, of pale propellers and leaves in which the bees were humming as they wove my veil.

The dress designer folded his arms. Phlegmatically, he considered his work. I felt a sudden wave of fellow feeling for this silent, unostentatious man. He had the sort of thin body I liked, and his homely face had been hacked rather than wrinkled into furrows of generosity. His eyes, like his collection, lacked audacity. I didn't know that the collection was perfect from a commercial standpoint, that it was exactly suited to his conservative clientele. One young woman had led the entire collection to victory with the arrogant poise of a Russian student. I left the salon first, ashamed of having written so little.

Gabriel . . . was it you, is it you? I needed you through all the world and here you are between my nails and my skin.

Quiet, little girl.

Don't call me little girl. Don't push your ivy away.

Less saliva, little one.

Am I little?

I won't answer you. Our name, my name?

I hide it. It makes things easier. It's easier for my work.

Cheat. Sitting on that gilded chair, you call that work! If I weren't such a shrimp, if I were a somebody, you'd parade my name on a banner. Poverty is a shameful disease, don't you agree?

Gabriel, why should I give them the life we led yesterday, the life we lead today? They would spit me out, I would never get work. Think of our wretched room. I am hiding our poverty.

Cheat. I hoped you would tell the world to go to hell, but I was mistaken.

It isn't my fault. They shut my trap for me before I was born. I'm not cheating when I'm loving you. How could I know that anyone would ever try so hard to stop someone from loving them? I was unfaithful to Hermine. I shall always be a traitor without the courage of my derelictions.

Miser.

Possibly.

Maurice Sachs excites you.

That's possible too. He sends me back to you, you send me back to him. He is better than you.

He doesn't know you.

He can't love me.

He lives in exile. You are his exile. With them, your ambition is limitless.

I shall never desire him.

I can see you've been doing your accounts.

Swine.

You don't desire him and he'll make you die of thirst.

My Amiens, make him keep away from me. My beloved Amiens, what is it you need?

Peace. My socks, my sweater, a hot meal inside me.

Peace is the one thing I cannot give you. I have to spend my time hating you if I'm to spend my time loving you. We tear each other to pieces, but all the time I am building too. When we calm down, I have a nest, a brood of little ones.

Don't give a damn. Not a damn. Just a little warmth is all I ask.

You prefer the sight of dry wood bursting into flame.

Yes, little fellow. You don't have to tell me that.

Gabriel . . . answer me. Am I a hypocrite?

The vocabulary of vice and virtue could do with some improvements too, my girl. You a hypocrite? You're gutless, you have no strength of character. I'm tired of having to keep on telling you.

I was born broken. I am someone else's misfortune. A bastard!

You know nothing. I suffered more than you did, crushed between my father and my mother. Do you know what it's like when there's a favorite child?

You aren't handsome, I am ugly, let us love each other as hard as we can. It's still possible. You don't answer.

I was thinking.

No, I'm not a hypocrite. I want everyone to like me, everyone, because I'm unlikable. There are some people who can say anything. There are others who can't say anything. There are some people who are forgiven everything. And there are some who are forgiven nothing.

Don't punish yourself for so small a thing, because you're going to be always on your own, my little fellow. That's your lot in life.

Mercy, Gabriel. Let us understand one another. You who had the courage to take me, my beauty. If I could cut off my head to make up for that . . . You are growing, you have grown bigger. Gabriel, how big are you going to get? You are shining, you are glittering. Are you made of gold or silver?

Of zinc, of tin. I am the counter of all the little cafés in France.

Be the little photographer I used to stroke, be small again. We'll buy wine and cigarettes. I'll sing you the song of the fruit as it ripens on the cotton batting. Come.

*

"It's late. I'll go and ask if M. Sachs can see you."

"Oh, M. Sachs will see me."

"M. Sachs is sick."

"Sick?"

"Extremely sick. I'll go in and see if he's asleep."

No, it wasn't the valet who'd shown me out after my previous visit. The woman, about sixty years old and pleasantly old-fashioned under her long white coat, allowed me into the apartment. I had run there after a quarrel with Gabriel.

He's gone, it's as though Maurice Sachs has gone from here, I said to myself as I stood there hopefully.

"He's waiting for you," the nurse said.

She vanished.

"You've been sick," I said as I walked into his bedroom.

Sitting up in bed, dressed in ivory-colored pajamas, his head propped up against several pillows, Maurice Sachs was thinking, his hands lying clasped together on the bedcovers. I felt threatened by the familiar book on the bedside table. I couldn't read the title. But knowing the title would have made it worse. I would have penetrated into Sachs' private world only to be immediately driven out again because I couldn't understand the philosophy book he always kept beside him.

"Are you ill?" I asked in a tearful voice.

I was still standing just inside the door, but I was hoping nevertheless to end up very close to Maurice, to make Maurice love me because of the pain I was putting into my voice. . . .

He turned his head.

"You must learn not to ask stupid questions."

He turned his chestnut and velvet eyes too much toward me. I thought I must be already living with him, I was already experiencing the compensations of a marriage between good friends: I had rushed around the streets of Paris for him at eight in the evening, I had found a store still open and bought him all the various little things he wanted. Now I was bringing them home to him. Sick people turn their heads like that so as to glimpse the world of the not sick, so as to breathe the fresh air that a visitor brings in from the street.

"Would I be in bed if I were in good health? Though it's true I like going to bed early and getting up early. . . . Starting work just as dawn breaks . . ."

"You shall get up early again before long, M. Sachs," said the nurse.

She had emerged from the bathroom. She must have entered it by another door. She was the queen of that place, and her rule deprived me of my rights. I went red, I was jealous.

"Mlle. Irénée," Sachs said.

He was looking at her tenderly, his face lit up for her. I saw the past of medications and injections they had shared together.

"Violette Leduc, a Paris journalist," Sachs said with gracious simplicity.

"Oh please, I'm nobody," I said without false modesty.

The nurse's eyes left me. There are some people for whom you are a well. They go down, they come up, and that's it. She was looking back into the bathroom.

"Did you have a good dinner? Or was the service good at least?" Maurice Sachs asked her.

"I have everything I need," the nurse answered.

She seemed troubled. Her liege-lord was filling her heart with unease, my liege-lord was filling mine with ice.

"Everything you need but what?" Maurice inquired.

"I don't want you to tire yourself," the nurse replied.

"And I want you to rest before the night," Maurice Sachs said.

An impeccable exchange. I wanted to escape from them. I didn't dare.

The nurse left the room.

"You've been very sick. She told me. Is it something serious?"

"Don't begin that again," Sachs said. "You must learn, my dear child, that nothing is serious. It is not even possible to die of hunger. Remember that." (Then he added with irony in his voice:) "My sickness? I am in love: that is my sickness."

I had difficulty in withstanding the gaze of his sad eyes. To unhook the moon from the sky, to hold it in front of his eyes so that I need no longer look at them, to knock at his door, to present him with the visiting card of the ideal young boy he was always aspiring to, I longed to do all those things.

"Bob?"

"Yes. Bob."

We maintained the silence of a problem that admitted no solution.

They love young men and the young men don't love them. The exceptions are rare. That was why I was so close to Maurice Sachs. His bed sheet . . . my handkerchief to soak up the tears I was weeping for his lovelorn agonies.

"Has he been to see you?"

"I can't remember. You can smoke," Maurice said.

"He hasn't been to see you."

"It's all over. Why the devil would you expect him to come?" he asked in a dead voice. "You can talk to me, my dear child. It doesn't tire me in the slightest."

He closed his eyes. He was resting; I imagined it was his way of making love to me.

"Move," I exclaimed in panic.

He opened his eyes. He laughed good-naturedly, and yet I didn't believe in the sincerity of his laugh.

"Move with a carbuncle on my thigh—you get some odd ideas!" Maurice said.

"A carbuncle, and you didn't tell me!"

"Don't get excited."

Maurice Sachs allowed me a glimpse of how he had spent the days immediately after his break with Bob. The carbuncle had formed after an attack of septicemia, after a course of sulfanilamides. He was bankrupt, he was going to be forced to leave the apartment. He told me about his wanderings, about his nights of despair and his nights spent drinking with his valet. I learned later that he spent hours weeping on benches with his head on the shoulder of this servant who had now become his friend.

"Let's talk about your work," Maurice suggested. "What about the reporting? I hear it didn't go too well. What? Don't let yourself get too introspective. You look solid enough but you aren't. You're a prey to your neuroses. You're being eaten alive by your unconscious."

Sachs had been observing me, he had been thinking about me. I was proud that I was so interesting to him.

I said: "You're in pain. I mustn't tire you."

I was thinking of Bob as much as the carbuncle.

He turned his head away. I was being importunate, I was talking too directly about his personal concerns.

"You Aryans, you're always unhappy and always dramatizing the fact," Maurice Sachs said.

I mustn't show interest in his health, in his affairs, in his grief. I began to hate his dimpled hands. I couldn't bring myself to quarrel with his tortured mouth.

"How's the husband? How's the marriage going?" he asked.

"I'm going to divorce him."

I didn't add: The more I love Gabriel the more I'm determined to divorce him.

"Good idea," Maurice cried.

I found his reaction superficial. I felt his approval was too glib.

"So what's new?" he asked then.

I talked to him about my childhood. He consoled me for my past and for my present. He cheered me up, he advised me to go on writing. I left him about ten in the evening.

"It's fabulous," I said to Gabriel when I got home.

That evening Gabriel was drinking in little sips and inhaling his cigarette appreciatively as he stood beside the fireplace. Gabriel warmed his glass of wine in summer as well as winter. He was doubling the voluptuousness of his sensations by rubbing his evening beard: at that time of day it made a faint noise like emery paper.

"Yes, it's fabulous," he said smiling into his glass.

"What?" I asked in a rage.

"Just living, smoking, drinking, old girl. By the by," he added, lowering his eyes and running his finger around the rim of his glass, "did you know they came and took Esther's father away yesterday?"

I didn't dare cry out that we were two monsters of indifference safe by our fireside. On my Aryan maiden's helmet there perched a parrot that would keep croaking: how lucky that we're not Jews, how lucky that we're not Jewish at this moment. Having been suppressed, reduced to a zero at birth by members of the wealthy classes, I was by no means unhappy, now we were at war, to see the rich being forced to escape into the Unoccupied Zone. It was only in a Paris stripped of all its really able people that I, an office mediocrity, was able to write editorials for the ladies and young girls who needed something to read in the Métro as a distraction from their work. At night I dreamed that the war was over, that the people with real ability had returned, that I was scurrying like a mangy dog to the refuge of an unemployment bureau. I would wake up soaked with sweat, convince myself with a stammering voice that it was a nightmare, then fall asleep again.

"The siren, the planes," Gabriel said. "Do you want to go down to the cellar?"

I threw my bag onto the divan.

"No, I don't want to go down. I want us to die together," I said to Gabriel.

"Unfortunately I don't want to die at all," Gabriel retorted in a fine outburst of independence.

My eyes filled with tears.

I began again: "Sachs is fabulous."

Gabriel offered me an "Army Issue", then added that he was listening to me and finding it very amusing.

"Sachs is at death's door, but he's able to forget it." (I moved closer to Gabriel:) "What are you listening to?"

"The siren. Our little scream of defiance at the planes!"

Gabriel slowly drained a glass of wine. His mouth didn't get wet, nothing touched his lips. Which of the two is the more attractive at this moment, I asked myself. Sachs, the big baby in the Rue de Rivoli, was sleeping; little Gabriel, supple and slender, was drinking. And Violette, a skinny pendulum, was swinging first toward the one, then toward the other. . . .

"Say that Maurice is fabulous, say it after me. . . ."

"If only you knew how little I care," Gabriel murmured.

I took the cigarette from between his lips.

"And you, my girl, you'll pay for this. I warn you, you've been warned. If you pull the lapels of my jacket once again the way you did the other day, I shall clear out for good. I shall clear out anyway. I shall go away from here, and that will be fabulous."

He poured himself another glass of wine.

"Why do you hate them?" I asked.

Gabriel was drinking his wine and looking at himself in the mirror over the fireplace. I went and stood beside him, I waited for his reply in the mirror.

"When the hell are you going to stop nagging me about them?"

I poured myself a glass of wine. I drank it slowly, copying him. Now Gabriel was smoking savagely.

". . . One night when I came back from Amiens," he began.

"One night when you came back from Amiens with me . . ."

"If you like. I'd taken you home in a taxi, young girl. I took you home in a taxi whenever I could afford it and even sometimes when I couldn't. That night I couldn't. Can you imagine how long it took me to walk to Pigalle? I arrived at half-past two in the morning with my portfolio under my arm. You'll still be able to make a few pennies, their place isn't closed yet, a doorman told me. A few pennies. I had those already: just enough to get me into a flophouse for the night. I was out of luck, the club was closing. I got there in time to see the last two customers preparing to leave. I threw myself against the wall and hid my portfolio behind me."

"Why?"

". . . I was hoping they'd see me, that they'd take me for a bum, for the down-and-out I was. I was hoping for charity. Get it? See me! They were enchanted with the club, bubbling with excitement. 'But darling, it's simply ravishing,' the older one was saying."

"Stop it! Don't talk like them. They don't all talk like that."

"There's no need to make a tragedy out of it. Is it that painful for you? What is it you find so painful, that they call each other 'darling' or that I hadn't a penny in my pocket that night?"

I began to cry with the pitiful air of a child caught doing something wrong. "It makes me unhappy when they mince about like that and I'm unhappy because you were broke that night."

I sobbed for his slim schoolboy's figure, for his badly ironed khaki shirt, for his sleeveless pullover.

"And then?" I asked between my sobs.

"Will you let me roll a cigarette or won't you?" Gabriel asked in return, holding up the cigarette he was making.

I waited till he was ready to go on. He licked the cigarette paper.

" 'And then?' The doorman of the club drove up standing on the running board of a cab. I saw their billfold, the bundle of money . . . . I heard them laughing in the taxi. They drove away."

"Without seeing you?"

"Without seeing me. I walked, I walked. . . . I found myself down on one of the embankments. I got myself warm again by burning newspapers."

*

I told the layout man and the woman editor of the women's magazine all about the fashion show they'd sent me to. They decided that they ought to send one of their men to get some sketches of the collection and that I should go with him to help him choose. We took to each other immediately and became fast friends at our first meeting. The salesladies were all busy with their customers; one of the heads of the sales staff kept crossing the salon in front of us with her pincushion strapped to her wrist like a watch. Sometimes they would stop to glance at a sketch, then rush away again, even more alive, even more alert: everything was going well, what talent. The artist's name was Claude Marquis. At night, while Gabriel snored, I lay hoping to read on the cover of the magazine: High Fashion, through the eyes of Violette Leduc. That issue appeared without my name in it. My copy was inferior to the drawings.

The editor criticized my imagery. "Dresses," she told me, "are not springs or breezes or tempests. Nor are they bushes or violins. Dresses," she said, "are pleats, materials cut on the straight, and materials cut on the bias. Read some of the other reporters' articles and take lessons from them," she added finally.

I bought some newspapers and read the reports of the latest fashion shows. They wiped the floor with me. My knowledge of these matters went no further than checking the evenness of a hemstitch, a backstitch, a lockstitch, or a featherstitch. I thought I had been fired when I was summoned to the office. I was told that Lucien Lelong had been extremely taken with my comparisons. He wanted me to employ my flowery pen composing a few short pieces of advertising copy, ten lines or so each, for his perfumes. These were to be printed week by week in the magazine. The advertising angle had to be discreet. I was to slip in the name of the perfume as the scent of lily-of-the-valley slips unnoticed into the streets of a town. I would be well paid. Lucien Lelong dictated the material for these pieces to me with great kindliness. I handed them in to the editor. Once more she sent for me. I thought the whole project had collapsed. "Read that," the layout man said to me. Pinned to the wall of the office there was a letter from Lucien Lelong expressing his congratulations. Ah, he was so nice, that layout man . . . his eyes were shining with satisfaction as he reread that letter, now exposed to the public gaze. Lucien Lelong wanted to see me.

I waited for a long time in his secretary's office. He rushed in like a whirlwind and shook me by the hand.

"I like how you write. Just a moment," he said.

Like a whirlwind he vanished again.

I was captivated by him: his furrowed face had the generosity of freshly plowed earth. My heart was beating, I was sure a new life was beginning for me. My future would be brilliant, this man was going to transform me into a queen. The carpet of the salon was licking my feet. The secretary led me into her employer's private office.

He took off his glasses and walked around his desk toward me. He greeted me once more with great warmth.

"It's true, I like how you write and you ought to be writing books," he said.

He hugged me in his arms.

I laughed foolishly. I replied that I was incapable of any such thing and wouldn't even dare entertain the idea. I also told him that I was forced to keep on with my day-to-day journalistic work simply in order to keep on living from day to day. He transmitted his energy to me. I was myself, without arrogance, without shyness, without complacency. Just being in his office was a treat for me. He listened to me and I became simple, genuine, direct. He called me "Mlle. Leduc" just like everyone else. My prestige was also my false celibacy. There was a flaw however: whenever he looked at my blue suit with its stippled white stripes, whenever his gaze fell on my turban, I shrank into a hole in the ground. His dress designer's eye was looking straight through me. He was organizing a documentary radio program for the Syndicat de la Grande Couture and he wanted me to write a commentary, think over what sound effects they should use, create an atmosphere for him. The microphones would be brought into the workshops themselves. It was wartime of course; but the women left behind on the home front still had to eat. Plying one's needle was neither criminal nor treasonous.

At the end of our interview, Lucien Lelong told me I could choose a suit and a hat from his latest collection. I like begging, but I like it even more when people give me things without my having to beg. I emerged into the street tottering with vanity.

I chose a simple, warm suit and a felt hat with a knife-edge brim.

"Excellent, excellent, my child. I see you've not been wasting your time," Maurice Sachs drawled in his singsong voice when I appeared in my new suit and my new hat.

Sachs had recovered. Having quarreled with his jewelers in the Rue de la Paix and got into serious trouble with the woman who owned the apartment in the Rue de Rivoli, he was living, writing, and receiving his friends in a little room over an establishment that was half brothel and half Turkish bath. He has described it fully in one of his books. He was a sage: he could adapt himself to anything. Yesterday he had been riding in a hackney carriage along the Rue de la Paix, just as the afternoon was opening itself like a fan. . . . Big and fat without being ridiculous, careless of the world to the very marrow of his bones, his felt hat sitting easily on his head, a cigarette between his fingers, sitting nonchalantly on his perambulating day-bed, he was conversing with Bob. The young man, indifferent to his companion, was dreaming and pretending to be sulky. I saw them coming unexpectedly and flattened myself into nonexistence against Dunhill's window. If I were to claim I knew this opulent potentate, I should be taken for an impostor. The hackney carriage disappeared into the traffic; I was left to bear the scorching pain of my poverty and my insane feelings for him. Today he was in retreat in a monastery of his own making. Making money. He would start thinking about that again in his own good time.

The dress designer asked me to go and see him several times, and each time he hugged me in his arms because he liked my little perfume advertisements. I was less clearsighted now when I was with him. I was waiting for him to say: my collection is yours. Dip in, help yourself, I want you to be more and more attractive. I didn't forget that he'd been married to Nathalie Paley, a Russian princess, a famous beauty who appeared in *Vogue* and *Fémina*. But nothing was allowed to stop the construction work on my castles in the air. I told Gabriel all about it. He listened and smiled.

Eleven in the morning, noon, we were lying in bed. You got out of bed, naked as the day you were born, you opened the door, shielding your nudity behind it, you answered: "Yes, Mlle. Leduc, that's here. Thank you." You came back, you said: "For you. A big envelope, a package."

"Who was it, Gabriel?"

"A deliveryman in a uniform. Move over, I'm cold."

The dress designer had sent me a trinket and a thank-you note for my help with the radio program.

Down the drain, my studio and my single life. The future queen of Paris shed an acid tear. An intriguer who had failed to intrigue, my dreams had all been crushed. On my next visit, I crept into his secretary's office with a hangdog look.

*

An avalanche of departures, of changes.

Gabriel. Our marriage, our life together could have been no more for him than a long summer vacation with the barometer always pointing to stormy. He decided to go back to his family as a student returns to school in the fall. Hermine had been swallowed up by Paris. Gabriel was not that lucky. His mother and sister lived almost next door to our apartment. After I had screamed and begged, he promised to take me out twice a week. A schoolboy returning to his family promised two dates a week to a married schoolgirl without a husband. Five days without sex, two days with sex. A life is so much slower than the tale we tell an exercise book. A life: thousands and millions of pages to be filled; all the insects that one has encountered or crushed, every blade of grass one's foot has brushed against, every tile and slate on the houses one has looked at, the tons of food that one has eaten, that one first had to buy, pound after pound, quart after quart. And the faces, and the smells, and the smiles, and the cries, and the gusts of wind, and the rains and the seasons perpetually returning . . . Imagine telling the story of one's life simply by remembering the colors one has seen, just the colors, the colors one has loved, or studied, or neglected.

Gabriel hadn't left. He was going to leave. I had to act and act quickly. I would go out and buy a man in the street. Then I'd be like other women. I'd have a trump card up my sleeve. To hold a man. My mother used to say: "She has what it takes, she used to have what it takes to hold a man." "Have you looked at yourself?" my mother asked. A face like a wilted cyclamen from all those tears. Make yourself beautiful again. How could I dare say that? I thought Gabriel would be crazy about my new suit, my new hat. To flaunt myself before him like that, to go out with him dressed like that . . . Does one ask garbage if it feels ashamed? No. A failure, that man there . . . You bunch of idiots. He was a man as strong, as regular as a clock. His ardor, his conviction, the fervor of his inner life when he took me to Jeanne Bucher's, to Katia Granoff's. His face as it lit up with the shading of the colors. Filthy typhoid, you took everything away from him. Does he even want to be well dressed? No, he doesn't give a damn: he could eat garbage without it demeaning him. He doesn't have to bow and scrape to make people like him.

An assignment. I was told to go to a cabaret near the Opéra and watch a chanteuse do her act. Then I was to talk to her about her plans and write a short interview. I had no permit for being out that late, I could get into trouble. Take it or leave it.

Gabriel convinced me I should go and got ready my new suit and hat while I ate an early dinner. Then he got into bed and lay nibbling the sheet.

The doorman looked at me with a long face as I walked up to the cabaret entrance.

"Women on their own aren't allowed in here."

I told him the magazine had telephoned to say I was coming.

"I'll go and see," he said skeptically.

He disappeared. Other women were going in with officers. I saw a monocle. The unexpected monocle made me feel young again: to me, it was Eric von Stroheim's. I didn't know what it was I felt ashamed of. I waited for the doorman to come back, feeling myself turning to liquid inside. A young officer looked at the time on his wristwatch. The gesture was so abrupt, so intense that I imagined it must be the signal for a bombardment to begin, somewhere thousands of miles away.

"You can come in," the doorman told me with a disgusted look.

I went in: small tables, tablecloths, shaded lamps, intimate pink lighting, maître d's; and at each table an enemy in uniform sitting with a woman. They were all drinking champagne, all smoking flat cigarettes.

"If you will follow me," the maître d' said.

He found me a seat at the back of the room. The chanteuse, obviously talented, was singing on a raised platform. I displayed my pencil and my sheet of paper on the table and folded my arms. The maître d' set down a glass of orange soda on my table. I didn't dare drink it. I thought of a gas mask in my glass. . . . The singer withdrew after taking several bows and the musicians began playing soft music. I was worried about being out after curfew. The maître d' told me I couldn't go now, that the chanteuse would be coming back soon with a different selection of songs. They were going to arrest me in the street, I would never see Gabriel again. My teeth were chattering, I started counting everything there was to count in the room: wrinkles, buttons, rings, bottles, bracelets, cigarette butts, matches, decorations, gold teeth, Sam Brownes, manicured hands. The chanteuse reappeared, her act was short. Another maître d' came to fetch me. I walked between the tables with the same feeling of timidity as when I was a schoolgirl walking up to recite a speech from a play. I admitted my terrors to the chanteuse as soon as I'd asked her the time. She offered to book me a room in the hotel next door to her night club.

I refused the room. My terror at the thought of not seeing Gabriel again was growing. I left her without drinking the glass of champagne she offered me, without asking her a single question about herself. I emerged into the street and breathed more freely again. The hand fell on my shoulder.

"Do you have an *ausweis*?" the policeman asked me.

"No."

The policeman shone his flashlight on me. The doorman came

over: "She's just come out of our place. Let her try and make it home. . . ."

The policeman was perplexed. His lamp disappeared again under his cape.

"You can try your luck if you want," he said, "but it's dangerous. All that way in those heels . . ."

"They make a noise," I said miserably.

"I'll bet they do," he replied. "Ah, women women . . ."

I set off at a run. I kept repeating, "women, women," to help my rhythm, to give myself support. I wasn't running, I was flying. I allowed myself a minute's pause, hanging onto the folding iron gates outside the movie house in which I had first made advances to Gabriel. It was wan and lugubrious now with its posters outside. Paris? A graveyard. Paris? An iron gate and a graveyard that would not yield me up one memory. I ran on faster and faster, I tried to pass two stores between two beats of my heart. I was still repeating the policeman's words: "women, women" . . .

I ran straight into a road block, I was ringed around with flashlight beams.

"You can't get through without an *ausweis*," the policeman told me.

I wept: "He's waiting for me. Officer, I beg of you . . ."

"Who's 'he'? Your husband or your little friend?"

I took one of the policemen's flashlights and shone it on him. "My husband! I beg of you, officer, please, officer, oh please . . ."

"Off you go then," they said.

"Her legs aren't bad," one of them said as I started running again.

"Yes, but with me its . . ." another of them began.

I was already away. Sometimes a truck, sometimes an automobile. No civilians, no soldiers. Where were they, the people with permits to go out at night? I'm going to make it, I said to myself as I reached the Place de la République. More policemen surrounded me; I pleaded my case for a quarter of an hour. A woman in love in that darkened Paris touched their hearts. I almost fell into the hall of our building. I gave a moan of fatigue, then a cry of pleasure. Gabriel had left the key in the lock so that I needn't disturb him.

He let me kiss him, one of my high-heeled shoes fell to the floor. I mustn't tell him that I'd been thinking about him the whole evening. I must undress and we must both get into bed and go to sleep because we were both tired. I did as he said. I said good night to him without kissing him because I didn't want to offend him. His laziness, his indifference, his senility, his caution, his fear of spending money . . . I took all that to be strength of character. How masochistic could I get?

The next morning he refused to give himself. I got angry.

"I'm leaving, I'll eat lunch in town," he said.

Our room became leaden.

What should I set my mind to? I cursed the paper with the notes I was supposed to write up about the night club. Did I even make any notes? All that running; why had I been in such a hurry to face disaster?

At that point I heard that Maurice Sachs was sick again. The tender care with which I prepared Maurice's stewed fruit and vanilla custard was mainly produced by the disgust I was feeling after Gabriel's insults. I won't be Gabriel's doormat, I told the stick of vanilla as I stirred it around in the custard. I set off in the Métro carrying my saucepans. I waited in the damp atmosphere of the steam baths. The owner was sitting at the reception desk noting down the appointments he was making over the telephone; pretty-looking masseurs were greeting their regular customers. A cleaning woman took me up to Maurice's cell. Swathed in a bathrobe, his feet encased in run-over slippers, he was writing away at great speed. He gulped down the custard and the fruit. I beamed. That day he talked to me bitterly about his childhood, about his mother who was living in England, about how inferior human parents are to animals because at least animals leave their young to fend for themselves promptly and for good.

"My dear child, that was exquisite," he said.

*

He offered me his cheek. His fingers were itching to get back to their fountain pen. I left with my saucepans.

The editor and the layout man asked me to attend all the fashion shows the following week, choose a number of models, and write an article on them. It was terrific. When I left their office, I piled pyramids of hats on the heads of the women I passed in the street, I draped them in mountains of dresses and coats. I found a seat on the terrace of a café near the Opéra. A lemonade. I plundered the faces and conversations around me of whatever booty I could find, because I was unhappy and I thought everyone else was happy.

I closed my compact: someone had placed a roasted almond on my table. I couldn't pick it up, or eat it, it didn't belong to me. The mystery was short-lived. The man selling them, dressed in a white coat, was picking his way among the tables with his tray of little white packets. He was collecting the almonds he had put down. An old man in spats allowed himself to be tempted. One hand to set down the packet of nuts and give change, while the tray rose into the air balanced on the other. Was there a school for roasted almond sellers?

He came and stood in front of my table; I could eat it. Oh, he didn't say that to everyone. Two gold front teeth. I shivered, my hair began to rise on my skin: he announced that he found me attractive. Was I waiting for a girl friend? Yes, dago. I am waiting for Isabelle on prize-giving day at the college. The other girls, with their arms held above their heads, are dancing to the music of *In a Persian Market.* I told the almond seller that I was never bored. Hairy wrist, well-kept hand. Will you love me, Gabriel, when I am one of those obliging ladies in the Palais-Royal? Two gold front teeth, I'll be unfaithful to you with two stumps of metal. No, I mustn't be so serious about it. I laid down my conditions: I didn't talk, and I didn't kiss.

"We won't talk," he said in a low voice.

We arranged to meet again next day.

The determination to be unfaithful to Gabriel. I decided what I had already decided, it happened at the age of thirty, and it was high time it did. Cyclist turning your head, are you being unfaithful to your wife, are you being unfaithful to your mistress? Shall I ever forget the nasty taste of the iron fork in my milky coffee, sitting in the dining hall on Sunday mornings, listening to them call out the list of girls who had permission to leave the college that day? My tears sprinkled down onto the bread I dipped into my bowl. I shall be unfaithful to him, the dining halls will all be in ruins. Not finished yet, that last tear waiting to fall? It will never be finished. Where are you going to, puppy-dog Violette? It's the sidewalk that's moving, not my feet. "It's getting better, it's running now," my mother used to say when talking about a cold. That block of consolations in the back of my nose when I had a cold and I was called into the parlor to see a visitor. I woke up in the night, I thought I was betraying the five-year-old that I had once been, the convulsions she'd gone into because she wanted to see her mother again and not be separated from her, I thought I was betraying that inconsolable little girl because I had slept. From the day I stopped caring about him I've had him at my feet. That's what they say, and they're proud of being able to say it. Where are you going, puppy-dog Violette? To stand in front of a photographer's window. I'm going to bathe in the waters of youth. That young girl in the broderie anglaise, is she dead? That young man in the alpaca suit, is he still alive? Where should we look for the boot button of the young girl in the broderie anglaise? Your hat, your garden in bloom, young girl, is fragile like a ship sailing out on the ocean. Good-by, broderie anglaise, good-by, garden, good-by, hat.

My mother used to say: "Where can she have gone wandering off to now?" Gabriel didn't say that to himself.

"Since the day you spilled your face powder in the closet, I've stopped worrying about you," he said.

He got together his albums of photographs, he dusted his shoes, he brushed off his jacket with his arm. I threw myself on him, I cried that if he wanted to there was still time. He pushed me away. It was time for him to go out on his delivery round. If I wanted to come with him I could. Since he was counting on "collecting a bit of dough," he was prepared to take me to a restaurant and treat me to an apéritif, but on one condition: I had to behave sensibly. I would behave sensibly.

How could I not adore him while we were riding in the Métro? Our intertwined fingers distracted the laborers going to work. But one man said to the woman with him, I heard him over the noise of the train: "At night, you can guess just when I'd pop the pillow over her face. . . ." Gabriel stared at him; did Gabriel hear or didn't he? Then I kissed him on the neck, and on his head I placed a crown of all my big noses that have caused me pain.

*

I liked the look of him better in his white coat than dressed in a suit. I preferred him with his tray. Then, as we lay stretched out on the bed, we could have played at counting roasted almonds.

"Don't talk to me."

"I'm not talking. I won't talk."

"You will be careful. You understand me."

"I will be careful. I understand you."

I found him repulsive, and the silent movie we were about to begin was repulsive too. He disgusted me and our agreement was disgusting too. He filled me with horror and this mutual grape-trampling was horrific too. Gabriel was on his way to the slaughter yard of deceived husbands. Quickly, let us run to the sacrifice so that I can enjoy my triumph.

Off, now that I have had my use of you. He was bewildered, he became pensive and unhappy as he put on his clothes again. Ah, Mme. Violette, what a great adulteress you are with the cold water in your hole. "Be a woman." I am a cold woman with a cold hand steeped in cold water.

I ran home, crucified, as I had foreseen, by the freshness of the little boys and girls out playing in the streets. My sex was crying out for pastoral idyls at the ends of alleys. I arrived out of breath, panting, ready to confess.

"We can talk tonight in bed. Cigarette?"

I insisted.

Gabriel, leaning on one corner of the fireplace, asked: "Is it so urgent?"

"Come and sit down."

"If you like. . . ."

Gabriel sat down.

I threw myself into my confession.

"I've been unfaithful to you. An hour ago I was being unfaithful to you."

A snickering grin. His eyes went up to the ceiling.

"You really are crazy. What put that idea into your head?"

I shouted at him. I told him I'd deceived him with a roasted almond seller; he was the one who was crazy because he didn't believe me. "You can't fool me," he said again, less certainty in his voice this time. I saw the color leave his face, I was going to be paid for what I'd done. Let him look me in the eyes, he would see that it was true. He looked at me in the eyes, and I was paid. Someone was washing vegetables at the faucet in the yard.

"Do you believe it now?"

"I believe it. But why?"

He pushed me away gently. I died a second time inside him.

"I have some developing and delivering to do; if you want to come you can," he said just as he had two days before.

I explained that the roasted almond seller had behaved quite properly.

"When are you seeing him again?"

"Never. Will you be nice to me?"

"I shall be as I've always been."

"Are you going to leave me?"

"Obviously I'm going to leave you."

"Do you want me to die?"

"I haven't the time," Gabriel said.

His step on the stairs. The step of a man set free. He had been the only one to gain.

I didn't have to wait long for our separation. There was the separation, then the mock suicide I have already described in *Ravages.*

Gabriel insisted that it was absolutely necessary. According to him it was an operation that had to be performed; according to him our abscess had burst. And I agreed, it certainly was an operation, since I was amputated of him five days a week. If time on the faces of the clocks had not poisoned our evenings . . . I idolized him twice as much as before, now we were caught in the meshing cogs of the minutes and the seconds; I lived in constant terror of his departure from the moment he arrived. For him and for his family I was an epitome of madness. A sadist's therapy: my faith-healer decided to cure me by starvation. Soon I would have nothing but my rivers of tears to give him. My mother prophesied that I would lose my reason, that my mouth was already twisted as it had been the day when Hermine ran away. I went out in the morning disguised as a scarecrow; a stab in the heart as I caught sight of him. He was trotting along with Lili's and Mummy's milk tin. I stood as smooth as a block of ice. That creature there? It's for that creature there? I ran back up to the sleazy room he had deserted, I sobbed because I wasn't holding the other handle of the milk tin with him. It hurt now when I said I lived on my own, because now it was true.

Gabriel explained to me that my friends Julienne and Musaraigne were good for me. I ought to go out with them on Sundays. I was no longer one of them: I bored them with the same old subject over and over again as we picked our wild flowers. Julienne, whose parents ran a store, would eat her cutlet while we sat beside her and nibbled at our garbage. At the end of the meal I harried Musaraigne with questions:

Why do his eyes glitter when I weep?

Why doesn't he give me any money?

Musaraigne, sitting in the boudoir she had made of the natural scene around her, considered my questions as she stripped the leaves off a twig. She spoke her thoughts aloud:

He's sadistic but not extraordinarily so.

He's not a person who should marry.

He hates scenes.

He has his own way of loving.

Not much satisfaction there. Julienne, lying a little apart, was murmuring as she dozed that there was nothing better than letting oneself be caressed by the sun. That made me think of the velvet dress that was still waiting. I had seen it. It was a Greek tunic. Julienne had got Roland out of a hole with her pocket money, she had preserved her love for Provence intact. Incapable of bitterness, she was rebuilding on the ruins.

I said: "Anything new at the cemetery?" The gravedigger's wife in Chevreuse used to sell us vegetables without coupons; she hadn't the time to reply. She was piling carrots, turnips, cabbages, spinach, and lettuces into our string bags. Anything new at the cemetery?

"Nothing much. My husband was digging . . . and suddenly, there was the skeleton of a woman still with a long head of hair."

"Shakespeare," Julienne said.

"Poe," Musaraigne countered.

We went to Paris; Gabriel was waiting for me on a banquette in the Restaurant Gafner. I walked in with all the riches I'd acquired that day, my rejuvenating glow of friendship and my bag of vegetables. I walked in and the other customers looked up. Picasso nodded to me because he'd seen me come in on previous Sundays. His dinner wasn't complicated: a raw tomato. He sometimes drew on the paper tablecloth, then he would tear off the drawing and take it with him. His companion, Dora Marr, was beautiful, with a face that was all architecture: a Picasso. She lit cigarette after cigarette in her cigarette holder and leaned over to talk to Marie-Laure de Noailles at another table. I realized between the lobster and the coq au vin that the celebrities of Paris live in a village. Gabriel was full of excitement just looking at Picasso's eyes. I remembered Maurice Sachs telling me about the suppleness of Picasso's wrist one day when Picasso was copying things in the Louvre with a pencil. His face would have been comic but for the fiery intelligence behind it. We left first; our time was limited because Gabriel would be leaving the divan at midnight. Picasso sensed the presence of love as he nodded to us and we nodded to him.

At five in the morning I was awakened by shouts, screams, howls. I went to sleep again so as to escape the nightmare of a woman in pain.

Next morning I was told that the enemy had come at five in the morning and taken Esther away. The neighbors had to tear the gas pipe out of her mother's hands by main force. Mme. Lita and Mme. Keller went out shopping as usual, with their yellow stars sewn on their bodices. They didn't dare mention Esther's disappearance.

Maurice Sachs was at the end of his tether. He dragged about from bistro to bistro near the Champ-de-Mars and the Ecole Militaire. He wasn't "setting himself up again" as quickly as usual. We went for a stroll along the esplanade of the Invalides and he talked to me about Socrates, Elie Faure, Henry James, Plato, the Koran, Cardinal de Retz, Talleyrand, Senancour, Chamfort, Max Jacob, Saint-Simon, Stendhal, Victor Hugo, Aquinas, Maritain. I tried to find out if he had anything left he could use to start making some money again. Nothing. His indifference to money when he had it exasperated me. I was afraid he was in for a bad time. His quest for money when he didn't have any drove me frantic. His deep, gentle eyes were my presentiments. He bought me an expensive drink with his last few francs. He was a gambler. He was tempting his fate by deliberately ruining himself. He had paid Charvet, he had paid his valet, but his other creditors still remained. His distress was a reality. I decided that next Sunday I wasn't going into the country, I wasn't going to have dinner with Gabriel. I was going to meet Maurice Sachs in a café near the Ecole Militaire. How would he be?

Next Sunday, I met Maurice Sachs. He hadn't shaved, his shirt was gray and would soon be frankly dirty. The conversation languished. Sachs was being agreeable, too agreeable. I paid for our drinks.

"You are sad, my dear. You are always sad."

My dear. That day it was a polite formula in the mouth of an unhappy socialite. What were we waiting for in that excessively large, excessively lugubrious café empty of customers? I could see his stubble sprouting before my very eyes. By that evening he would be almost a bum. What can he be looking at and brooding over at the bottom of his glass? Finally he made up his mind.

"I'm going to make you a proposition," Maurice began.

My throat was tight, it tightened even more.

"Do you mind?" he added.

He was falling too low, it was unbearable.

"Make it anyway, then we'll see."

He took a cigarette from my pack. His gestures became more animated, his beard looked less sad.

The waiter standing over us was cowed with a glance.

Maurice lit my cigarette.

"Would you like to have a child by me?" he asked.

He caught me unprepared. I stammered out a lying yes and a lying no.

He ignored them both: "You would go down to the Riviera. A week of sun, then when you're on top of the world we start the baby."

Maurice was smoking quicker than usual. The tip of his cigarette glowed red. We remained silent. We were avoiding each other.

"Do you agree?" Maurice asked.

"No, I don't agree. Do you want some money? I have three hundred francs. Do you want them?"

Maurice Sachs raised his eyes!

"Your three hundred francs would not come amiss," he said with a laugh.

His shirt became white again, his stubble looked less rough, the life came back into his eyes. I gave him everything I had, he invited me to have dinner with him but I refused. It had come into my head that I was experiencing a serious desire to throw up.

The years have passed, I have tried to fathom it out. If I had taken him at his word . . . He would have kept it. The motive behind it was money. That's by no means certain. He was sensitive, humane, too humane sometimes, he could see into my life, he could see the disaster my marriage had been, he could sense my feelings toward him. Did he want to make me a mother in order to save me? It's not impossible. Perhaps he envisaged me transferring my love for Gabriel and my mixture of love and friendship for him to a child. A week of sun beforehand. The thoughtfulness of a homosexual. And even if I am mistaken, what then? It was still I who represented Maurice Sachs' hope, his confidence in himself, his optimism, that day when he was penniless and his impulses brought him to me. He knew many wealthy people, yet he turned to a poor nobody. To answer the appeal of a friend whose friends are weary of him. They say that homosexuals take advantage of women who fall for them. So much the worse for them, so much the worse for me. The folly of our feeling for someone can be paid for in a hundred different ways. Loving them all is a luxurious insanity.

*

They were all discussing their own cases. An old woman explained to me the trouble she was having with her landlord. He had urged me to be on time; but he was late. I had walked through the colonnades where the men and women lawyers were strolling beneath the arches and pillars. Now I was sitting with beating heart in a hall black with people. Sometimes a chosen one was called from among us; he would walk over, open a little door, and yield himself up to the specialists of justice.

"How's it going?" he said, just when I'd given up expecting him.

He was wearing a long cape that his friend had found in a church; Gabriel had chosen friendship in coming to the Palais de Justice. His hands were hidden, he was depriving me of his handshake. I told him he was late.

"Then they've called you?"

"No, they haven't called me."

"Well then," he said ill-temperedly.

He wouldn't sit beside me on the bench. What a dismal mess it all is, I thought to myself, since after all I love him and don't want to be separated from him. Someone called out a name.

"Come on," he said, "come on for heaven's sakes, it's us!"

I was expecting long lawyers' gowns, and all I found were dark suits in a little room full of papers. A clerk told us to sit down.

"The Mercier case," the judge said.

It was a delight hearing his name reduced to such anonymity.

The judge raised his head. His eyes confided in me: a new face, yet another face, and I'm going to find the strength to listen to it.

"Why do you seek this divorce? What complaints have you against your husband?"

"He never gives me any money," I replied, pulling myself up straight because I was telling the truth.

I had forgotten the restaurant meals, the hot toddies, the mugs of bouillon, the celery salt.

I had taken care with my appearance because I was to see Gabriel again. The judge inspected me from head to toe. I realized he'd maneuvered me into a tight corner.

"We are at war, madame, don't forget that. You husband can't give you money."

He coughed so as to leave me alone with his argument.

"What else?" he asked. "What other complaints do you have?"

"We don't get on together," I said in a husky voice.

That is enough, the worn eyes of the judge conveyed to me. He turned to Gabriel.

"What complaints do you have to make against your wife?" he asked Gabriel in a gentler voice.

The judge, the clerks, I myself, we were all waiting for a revelation.

The cape opened. Gabriel made a gesture as though he were offering to shake hands with a friend. His face lit up. He said: "I have no complaints against her and I don't want a divorce, sir!"

"Go on," the judge said.

An exchange of looks, tender confidences between them on the subject of women's failings.

"I have nothing more to say, sir. I am quite happy to stay as I am. I don't want a divorce."

Without a word, Gabriel led me into a packed café. Why had he said what he had? Silence. Why had he come in the first place? Silence. Why had he insisted I apply for Legal Aid? Silence. Since he had left me he must want a separation between us. So why? Silence, silence.

Gabriel picked up our check, then he deigned to say: "I'll see you soon, probably over at the weekend." Draped in his long cape, he left the café with me, and disappeared.

*

Being able to follow the rise and success of a creative artist, what satisfaction for a failure. Tucked away at the end of a passageway in the Rue de la Boétie, the youngest dress designer in Paris had quickly built up a considerable business. He organized a show of his latest and very daring collection on the Rue François-Ier. Young, with the finely chiseled, youthful good looks of a Cocteau character, with his pure, blue eyes that sparkled kindness, his Greek nose, his oval face, his hooded eyelids, his generous mouth, his neck encased right up to the chin in a high, fashionably stiff collar, his upright carriage, his long, slender hands, his melodious voice suddenly breaking off to issue lightning commands, his discreetly blond hair, his dazzling white teeth, dressed in a dark suit, Jacques Fath in person was as captivating as his collection. I recognized the sensational mannequin I had first glimpsed in the salons of Lucien Lelong. She had migrated to the Rue François Ier. Ah! That priest's hat with its garland of monster roses laid flat around the brim and its veil of black tulle that swathed the crown and fell down the back like the scarf around the hat of a riding habit . . .

I went into Janette Colombier's boutique and she gave me a hat, just like that, without my asking for it. This is the one that will suit you best, she said as she took it from the window. I tried it on. It does suit you! she said, just as pleased as I was. The hat was of pale blue blotting-paper felt with ruching and a chin strap that tied under one ear. Maurice Sachs nicknamed it "Your dove's nest." But the silver fox jacket on my back was for sale; in partnership with Bernadette, I was trying to sell all sorts of things: pictures, sugar, coffee, soap, and an assortment of ordinary fox furs. I combed Paris for customers; I sold nothing.

I ran across some quicksilver: a little man with a subtle mouth. He had invented a new way of dressing hair which had made him famous. Louis Gervais frizzed up the hair to give it body, then he brought it down onto the forehead in a thick roll or a smooth convex fringe. After the emperor of short hair, the emperor of long hair. He could have made a bulldog look feminine. Modest, intelligent, entirely self-taught, he dressed hair from nine in the morning till eleven at night. His nights were spent seeking strengtheners for the hair. He discovered beef marrow. I can still hear the clacking of the wooden-soled shoes across his salon floor.

*

The blood did not come. I didn't want to keep the child. Sometimes I told Gabriel about my visits to the so-called midwives, sometimes not. A curious man: he still continued to keep himself in check, yet he wanted the child. As for my mother, she treated her married daughter as though she were an innocent maiden who'd been seduced. But despite this confusion I must admit her appraisal of my situation was astute enough. I was torn in two directions at once. When I fell on a staircase I imagined I was saved. I was mistaken. The months passed, and the five months' ripened fruit in my belly gave me the strength of a lion. If it moved, what would I decide? It didn't move, I wasn't forced to say to myself that there was a heart beating in my insides. It was while we were eating in a restaurant that specialized in the dishes of the Auvergne that Gabriel told me how he was going to rent a sunny apartment in a modern block, how we were going to bring up the child together. The rosé wine was sending me to sleep, Gabriel's voice was like a cradle rocking me. Since his mother's death and his sister's marriage, he'd been living on the top floor of a new building just around the corner from our moldering room. I came to my senses, I went to live with my mother. I was full of mistrust. My mother has no idea of the love I showed her or the sacrifice I made for her then.

A Sunday afternoon in winter without a fire. Michel was taking a course in sheep farming at a school in the country. He had to leave again that evening. I knew how passionate they both were about the movies and persuaded them to go to one. My mother was unaware of what a serious condition I was in after my final attempts at an abortion the day before. The door banged behind them, the elevator came up. I was warm as I lay in my mother's bed writing a story for the magazine. Writing: it meant entering the struggle; it meant earning my livelihood as religious people earn their right to enter heaven. I blew on my fingers, I massaged my hip, the infection was beginning, I went on writing, and every now and then I glanced through the glass front of the dresser in their dining room. Inside, I could see the drawer in which I had put away ten thousand francs, a fortune acquired in one fell swoop, thanks to an advertising story I had written for the firm of Lissac: in it I had demonstrated how a nearsighted girl who wore glasses was more attractive than her twin sister who had arrogantly refused to adopt a long view of things. They came back from the movies at six that evening and I told them I was in no pain. I was in pain. Unforgettable afternoon with my paper to be filled and my single woman's determination to stand by herself and not to fall.

I have described the sequel to that afternoon in *Ravages:* the following evening I was dying in a clinic. I didn't want my mother to spend the night in an armchair by my bed. I begged her to go home and rest in her own bed. But the one spark of life left in me kept flickering the same message over and over: she will stay, you'll see, she'll stay. She left. She told me later that she went to the movies, otherwise she couldn't have got through the evening. I understand her and I don't understand her. The next morning she didn't dare telephone the clinic. She thought they would tell her I was dead. I suffer from her sufferings as well as my own.

A terrible winter without coal. I had been discharged from the clinic and spent several months in bed at my mother's. She got up at six in the morning, she broke the ice in the kitchen, then she put the pieces of ice in the rubber bag I had to keep on my belly twenty-four hours out of twenty-four. I listened: the pieces of ice fell onto the tiled floor, and because her hands were cold, when she had finished picking them up she'd let them all slip onto the floor again. I accused myself of being sick, of lying in a warm bed, of making her wait on me. I upbraided my immobile legs.

A yellowish light coming through the window. The sky had snow in store for us. I panicked. Night was coming, I couldn't switch on the light. My mother had gone out to bring medical supplies from a pharmacy near the Gare Saint-Lazare and she should have been back by now. I called to her with all the strength of my lungs. Someone rang the doorbell. I sensed that it was Gabriel. Nailed to the bed, I loved him without desire and without regret. I heard him going away, I called to my mother again in the darkness. What had happened to her, what would happen to me, alone in her big bed? The door was double locked. Gently, in the silence, I began to weep. Crying rhythmically like that kept me going in the darkness behind my closed eyelids. My mother came back and flew into a temper. She'd been held up by the crowd in the pharmacy, the crowd in the Métro, the crowds everywhere she went. I asked her the time. She'd been away six hours, I said piteously between sobs. I would have liked her to take me in her arms. She was getting ready the permanganate, the boiled water, the douche. . . . She began giving me my treatment. The doorbell rang. She thrust the douche into my hands and went to the door. She came back into the room and went on attending to me. Wearing his long cape and his beret, leaden faced, he had followed her into the room. He looked at me and he looked at the pink rubber tube, the crimson blood. He left without a word.

I have never asked my mother for a penny since the age of twenty and I have never received a penny from her. I paid for my board and lodging the first month I worked for Plon the publishers and I have always paid for it whenever I have stayed with her since. I learned to walk again; I wanted to see my bill. She presented me with an interminable list of all my expenses down to the most trifling amounts. Two francs for surgical cotton hurt me more than any of the other items.

There was a fairly wealthy widow living on the first floor with her two daughters. They were, according to my mother, young women of such utter perfection that I went out of my way to avoid them. She had not told them about my wretched marriage, my dismal room, my birth, or the cause of my illness. The lady used to come and visit during the evening while her daughters were out skating at the Palais de Glace. Having recently returned from a visit to the orchards that produced her wealth, she began telling us the life story of a young and very poor country girl named Anita who was in the process of adopting a child. She adored it. Her goodness had the power to communicate itself, it radiated through the room while the ice on my belly made its tiny tinkling sound. The lady began the same story all over again every evening and I told myself that I was damned. I wanted the child I'd done away with. The lady talked, my mother listened in ecstasy. I lay silent, beseeching my mother with my eyes: Make that woman stop, make her go home. It's hurting me, it's hurting me too much and I don't understand you. The widow would leave, I would weep. Then my mother would scold me.

I had made my decision. I returned to the little room on Christmas Eve. I was still weak and convalescing. I picked up a piece of paper that had been slipped under the door during my absence. "To hell with you." It was signed *Gabriel*. I found some coal still left and lit our stove, then sat down beside it. There were some old noodles cooking. It was almost joyful, the sound of those flakes bubbling in our kitchen. I ate the noodles in a saucepan on my knees. The tears dripped down onto my crust of bread.

The lighted window, the window I worshipped as I patrolled up and down beneath it. Gabriel was at home, it was beyond all my dreams. He had no sex, this angel I couldn't tear myself away from.

My poor mother. I flew toward him. I trampled on all your work. You nursed me, you hoped it was all over, that I was growing away from him, poor mother. I hated him with you, I cursed him, I despised him, I tore him to shreds with you, poor mother. I betrayed him with you, now I was going to betray you with him.

He greeted me without coldness, without kindness, he promised to see me again after the holidays. That evening he was going out. He was living in the Henri II dining room he'd inherited from his mother. I glimpsed a folding bed in an empty room. I criticized my mother in order to reap Gabriel's indulgence. He cut me short and pushed me out of the apartment. I had brushed his beret and his cape with my fingers, I returned to my room trembling with happiness. Miscarriage, sickness, separation: all swept away. I gave myself the same treatment my mother had been giving me as though I were an excited young girl preparing to go on an outing. I sang to myself, I invented a Christmas carol for Gabriel.

I found my Jesus again with his long dirty hair. I found him sitting at a wooden table. The Christmas festivities had not begun but his friends were already there. The dark tobacco is his friend, and the cigarette paper marked with the name of Job is his harmonica.

It is Christmas, my Jesus has no time. I saw him again and he must go away. I saw my Jesus, my heart is a little chick wrapped in a rabbit's fur.

My Jesus has a lighted window, he gave me an evening star. Let us pray, brethren, let us pray to Gabriel. He has a neat little wife. She has no child, she is a shiny new penny. Let us pray, brethren, let us pray to that little shiny penny, that little penny all alone on Christmas Eve. You mustn't moan and sob, darling Violette, you mustn't try to find the smell of his sweat on the pillow, you won't find it there. I am going to rock myself to sleep in the cradle of my misery, it is my hand which is going to give up the ghost.

We spent nights without sleep on the folding bed. We were afraid of what had happened, of what could happen. It was frightful: our fears, our inspections.

My figure, my five feet seven inches, my hundred and six pounds, and my article had pleased Jacques Fath, whom I had compared to the angel Heurtebise. He had given me the hat with the garland of monster roses and a gray and black suit trimmed with fringes. He had tightened the white piqué cravat around my neck. I stood before the triple mirror again, and it was smiling at me. It was to the mirror I said: thank you for your generosity. I hid my eccentric new clothes from Gabriel. Now Gabriel was sleeping on a mattress on the floor so that I could rest properly on the folding bed. The five-foot divan in the old room where Gabriel refused to set foot lay taking its ease with my electric iron still lying between its sheets.

Bernadette introduced me to Sonia, a young girl who was modeling for Picasso. Her torso made one's head swim to look at it. Her mouth was full of champagne bubbles as she talked.

She made jewelry inspired by Greek and Roman originals. Bernadette asked me to help Sonia sell them. Hairdressers agreed to display her creations in their windows. She sold some, occasionally she handed me my little commission. She disappeared. I learned that she had been arrested and deported. She was a Jew, she never came back. Full cheeks, clear eyes, Sonia sparkled. Her beauty was also the joy she took in living.

I had heard from Maurice Sachs. He was "setting himself up again" in the Charente district and would soon be back. When he got back to Paris he invited me to come around to celebrate my "churching." I was still in bed. The editor of the magazine didn't believe in my virus infection. Your waistline, that's what was wrong with you, her eyes said. She gave me very little work from then on.

My mother fell sick: the white corpuscles were eating the red corpuscles. Nursing me had been too much for her, she had become run down, I was responsible. I talked so much about Gabriel when I was with her that she said with sadness in her voice that I ought never to be apart from him again, because I obviously loved him. Bewitched, I didn't visit her again. Alone in the apartment, left to the mercies of a cleaning woman, the daily visit of the doctor and the nurse, she could no longer even stand on her own. Her sickness dragged on through several long weeks before she was able to leave for the country. You see, reader, I do not conceal my ingratitude and my cruelty.

*

"I don't know what's the matter with me," Gabriel kept saying every day, "I'm bushed." I wasn't worried about him. He had been drained of all his vitality ever since his attack of typhoid. Not thirsty, not hungry. He complained of pains in his belly and his back. But he didn't complain. He answered all my questions. He was unwell because he was turning into an old man. First his face turned green, then it turned gray. I gave him my place in the folding bed. He tried to rest fully clothed, with his beret on his head, he didn't want me to call a doctor. His sickness was partly discouragement also. His beard was sprouting, that reassured me. He couldn't urinate. I brought him the bowl from the sink and took it back empty. Nothing, there was nothing he wanted. His unseeing eyes closed again. I went out to the movies, I could think about him better there. I didn't watch the screen. I watched a sick man behind my eyelids. I came back early from the movie, he wanted to urinate, I helped him out to the toilet. He was getting visibly older hour by hour. There was blood in his urine. I got him back onto the folding bed, I was afraid of breaking him. The noise of the bedsprings made me shiver every time he moved. He had settled himself deep into his sickness, he didn't answer when I said I was going to fetch a doctor. I called the emergency service. A disembodied doctor appeared. I showed him the blood in the toilet. "It's serious, very serious," he told me. He said he would arrange for Gabriel to be transferred to a hospital. Going back into the room I felt like a worn-out beast of burden. "He's still here," I said to myself, as though I were talking about someone who'd died. I didn't dare bend over him because he was so utterly quiet and still. Occasionally an angel sitting in the room while the airplanes skimmed the roof, occasionally an angel with monumental red, tawny and pale blue wings hurling itself against the wall and the windowpanes, occasionally an angel with the face of a mongoloid child stopped looking at me to clean its toenails with a fork.

The doorbell. Three of them, they had no stretcher. With his beret on his head, draped in his cloak. Gabriel went off to the hospital in a chair. They refused to allow me into the ambulance. I rushed off to the doctor's; they would let me know how he was in the morning.

Where was Gabriel? In the operating room? The nurses didn't answer.

I saw Gabriel again. He had a bizarre apparatus to one side of him. An upturned jar with serum they were feeding into him, drop by drop. It was slow, and painful. He'd found a way around that. He secretly poured the serum into a glass and drank it straight off so that he could get some rest. That's what he told one of the patients. He didn't look at me, he didn't speak to me. He gave away the things I brought him. The following day I saw the wine I'd brought him on the table belonging to one of his neighbors.

"Poor woman," the wife of the man he'd given the wine to said.

Both men were asleep.

They came and took away Esther's mother. Not one of the family was left.

The day before that happened, the young waitress from the Italian restaurant where Gabriel always ate lunch or quenched his thirst between two wedding parties, where he warmed himself at the family of his choice, the day before that, the waitress came to see him with a parcel. I arrived after her. They were devouring each other with their eyes. My heart in shreds, I stood at the foot of the bed. Gabriel was asking about the other customers he knew. Happiness in her voice, the waitress answered indirectly: they talked about him every day, they telephoned the hospital, they were following every step in his recovery, his napkin with its napkin ring was in its pigeonhole, they would cook his favorite dish for him when he came back. Oh nothing had changed, Paul came in before the bells rang, then came back as soon as they stopped. But Paul wasn't Paul any more without Gabriel. Well, he laughed, yes, he did still laugh, but it wasn't the same. They were waiting to have Gabriel back so they could hear Paul laugh the way he used to. Gabriel was getting better, anyone would do anything for him, which was no more than he deserved. Of course business is business, they weren't going to stop another customer sitting in Gabriel's place, but when it was just some stranger they'd never see again, well. . . . But there was nothing to worry about, they'd be seeing Gabriel back there soon. The bottle wrapped in tissue paper, that was for him and for them, as soon as he walked through the door of their restaurant again.

The day Gabriel left the hospital he tried to walk without my arm. He couldn't. I held his arm under mine and pitied him for his bitterness. He refused to sit and rest in a café. Weak but free, back in his own home, sitting at his table, draped in his cloak, wearing his beret, Gabriel rolled his first cigarette without glancing at the pack of cigarettes I had bought and which was there waiting for him when he arrived. He quickly stored up a reserve of strength again; he was naturally economical of his resources. Without clashes, without scenes, without arguments, I left again as I had arrived.

*

Who prompted me to put my wedding ring back on my finger? Maurice Sachs, with whom I had dinner after my "churching" on the balcony of an elegant dovecote on the Rue Royale, came unexpectedly into my room one morning.

"What's it made of, your wedding ring?"

"Platinum."

"Show me."

It slid off my finger and bounced into Maurice's hollowed palm. Kindness is also vanity. I wanted to prove to myself that I was kind.

"You can have it."

"I accept. I can sell it for fifteen hundred francs."

How long would I go on destroying Gabriel?

"My dear, your room looks like the room of a Russian student."

Price: fifteen hundred francs.

Remarks like that can send you out of your mind.

"I'll see you again soon, my dear child, I've brought back a border guide with me from the Charentes. I'll explain later. Good-by for now."

"Maurice!"

"Yes."

"I scarcely get any more articles to do. What's going to become of me?"

"That's of no importance. I told you, I'll see you again soon: that does mean something, you know."

I didn't dare watch him crossing the yard. I was ashamed of the yard, of my apron, of my poverty.

My torment had gone on long enough. An assistant in a hairdressing salon advised me to consult Doctor Claoué, the plastic surgeon everyone was talking about. Where was I going to get the money to have my nose shortened? I would be beautiful, I would bounce the piece he cut off like a ball. Looking up the plastic surgeon's telephone number put me in a fever.

A nurse ushered me into the doctor's office.

"What is it you would like?" he asked after a long silence.

I looked at him, I gave him, all at the same time, all the laughs, all the giggles, all the funny remarks I had been subjected to for more than twenty years.

"If you knew how I've suffered . . ."

"I do know," he said.

He sat down beside me.

"You do know?" I exclaimed, feeling a sudden surge of pity for myself.

He took my hand, then gave it back. His white coat might have belonged to a grocer's boy.

"I'm short," he said. "I suffered too."

I sighed, I came to the point: "They won't make fun of me anymore. . . . But I have no money. Would you like to tell me some more about yourself, Doctor?"

He stood up. He wanted me to see how short he was.

"I was unhappy. Then it came to me that I could bring relief to others."

Then he palpated my nose. I felt as though he were strapping it into a muzzle. I didn't feel humiliated, I trusted him.

"Is it possible?"

"Why not? Here is what I suggest: I will do the operation, and you will pay the hospital expenses. Four or five days. I'll take some off here and here. There and there."

He palpated again.

"I write articles and things," I said, hoping this would give him more confidence in me.

"You're a journalist?"

"Yes and no. I can write an article and talk about you in it."

"If you like," he replied.

He was famous, he was polite.

I left with a feeling of warmth around my heart, despite my fear of the operation. I was never to see Doctor Claoué again.

*

Maurice Sachs was "setting himself up again." He had a business office, a private office, and a waiting room, in a café near the Ecole Militaire. He offered his clients liqueurs, drinks, cakes.

"I must say that dove's nest suits you," he said.

I said nothing; he was examining my velvet chin strap.

He invited me to eat a second breakfast with him, at eleven in the morning; as he sat gulping down fruit cake, sandwiches, and hard-boiled eggs, he explained to me how exercising the mind stimulates the appetite. Ten minutes later we were taking our apéritifs.

Sachs had brought back a frontier guide from Charente. The guide knew all the most secret paths in that district. He came to Paris, then he left again by train with a batch of customers: Jews who were friends of Maurice and wanted to leave the capital. He then led them over into the Unoccupied Zone on foot, under cover of darkness. The customers paid Maurice, who in turn paid the guide. Maurice seemed calm and contented; he had money.

I told him about Gabriel's sickness, about our separation and the gradual wearing out of our feelings for one another: we were both just wrecks now, floating at different levels after having both suffered unhappy childhoods. I admitted to Maurice that I no longer got assignments to do articles.

"Why should you go on writing junk like that?" he asked.

I didn't dare reply: so as to eat, so as to live. Maurice made me feel warm and turned me to ice by suddenly summing things up for me, by hurling a neat bundle of logic in my face.

"You were wrong," he said, talking about my miscarriage. "A child! You could have given it all the affection you so much need to give. You were being given an opportunity to love. And you rejected it."

I didn't dare object that a child grows up, that it leaves you, that one day that too is a tragedy.

It was summer, the café had no windows. We sipped at our apéritifs and watched the desultory activity in the street.

"That street, that room, they're very bad for you, my child. From now on you must stay with me."

I looked at him, he was ordering two more apéritifs. I told myself it was too beautiful to be true.

"I can't leave my room just like that. . . . You don't leave a room just like that. . . ."

"Put it on my bill," he told the waiter who was serving us fresh drinks.

"M. Sachs is wanted on the telephone," the waiter answered.

I was alone, I took one of his cigarettes, I didn't ask myself into what past I was about to sink back, into what future I was about to hurl myself.

"That is precisely how one does leave a room, my dear. Just like that. There is no other way of leaving a room. Open your handbag and let's see what you've got in it."

"There's no point. I can tell you now. My lipstick, my compact, my mascara, my Métro tickets. I don't have a nightgown. . . ."

"You will sleep at my hotel, I shall lend you one of my shirts," Maurice said. "Why invent complications when everything is so simple?"

Then he immersed himself in his glass, while I sat already reproaching myself for abandoning my room: the palace of my defeats. Living with a writer, living with Maurice Sachs, would mean really living, with or without money. I accepted, and dissolved into a noisy display of thanks.

Our hotel was only a few yards from the café, so were our restaurants. I grew accustomed to seeing Maurice Sachs up early in the morning for everything, despite everything; the time he had spent in a seminary had left its mark on him. He was in love with the idea of health, with the idea of a tranquil mind, with the idea of using his time to the full. I found him looking fresh and charming at nine in the morning. He had been writing for four hours, he was almost young and happy again. He asked me how I'd slept, he told me about his visits to psychiatrists and psychoanalysts, the words "neurosis" and "unconscious" were constantly on his tongue. The unconscious, Violette, the unconscious can absorb a person. The neuroses, Violette, the neuroses can kill him. Maurice Sachs had frightened me. How was I to escape?

We decided that the child in me must be freed from its mother. At nine o'clock, then, I came down and found him writing, with his tiny cramped writing, in a school exercise book; he shut the exercise book and had a second breakfast with me. Feeling my "dove's nest" on my head, the beautiful fox jacket that I ought to have given back but hadn't given back around my shoulders, my black straw, wooden-soled shoes on my feet, tearing open the waxed paper, taking out the slice of fruit cake as the percolator bubbled beside us, it all seemed to me the ultimate in bohemian living. I thought of myself as someone extraordinary because I was living with Sachs, because he made me read his favorite passages: the funeral of Talleyrand in Hugo's *Choses Vues,* for example, because I was relying on him, because I took myself for him.

At eleven o'clock Sachs sent me away from his table. He gave me pocket money and told me to spend it—he called me "The Ant" because I was always thinking about saving, I have already written about that in *L'Affamée*—to buy books, to go and have a drink in another café. I did as he told me. I became a young girl again. I stood looking into bookshop windows. And then I bought some new kiss-proof lipstick. I didn't want my morning and evening kisses to leave red marks on Maurice's cheeks. Sometimes I cheated, sometimes I walked back again so that I could look at him from a distance. The head was enormous, the mouth a sagging line. The man or woman anxious to cross into the Unoccupied Zone would talk, Maurice would listen with a downcast air. Often the travel agency he had opened in the café didn't close until one in the afternoon, in which case I had to walk up and down in the street outside before going in to have a good lunch with him. He told me about a playwright who wanted to send his pretty little mistress over into the Unoccupied Zone and owned fourteen suits. That was the only sort of information he ever passed on. I had no idea how much he asked each customer, how much he earned, how much he paid the guide. He wasn't making a fortune out of it anyway. In the afternoon we each took our siesta or read, lying on our beds. I had no idea where his room was, or if his friends or his intimates came to visit him. At four in the afternoon we went out into the Champs-de-Mars and the Esplanade des Invalides for a stroll. Sachs' eyes were illumined by the stately splendor of the vistas.

Where did his new cane come from that day, so Baudelairean amid the children's shouts and hoops? That day he talked to me about Audiberti's *Tonnes de semence* and Marguerite Duras' *La Vie tranquille,* he recited poems by Apollinaire and told me of his unbounded admiration for Cocteau's *Plain-Chant.* I listened to him, I was bigger than the city itself, the present was a memory. We went to bed before nightfall. I was reading with much more fervor since I had come to live with him.

He read *David Copperfield* again; I began the *Correspondance aux âmes sensibles*. The religious exercises of a monk and a nun who would be meeting again in a bistro next morning.

Sometimes he told me I bored him with my childish miseries. Patience has its limits. Sometimes he felt nostalgic for the country air of Charente, for the woods and fields. He admired the English educational system: in England parents don't cling to their children, they send them to boarding schools. I didn't dare reply that I disapproved, that if I could have my childhood over again to suit myself, I'd spend it in a kangaroo's pouch.

Maurice had become friendly with a woman whom he treated with the greatest deference. It was Maud Loty. She lived on our street, on the sidewalk. Her make-up was smeared on rather than applied: a heartbreaking, clown's face. She clutched some of her youth in her hand: her handbag, always swinging, never relinquished. Maurice hadn't recognized her, the waiter had told him who she was. She was one of the sights of the neighborhood. People laughed at her, people laughed with her, the dogs began to bark, the policeman on duty smiled. No, she wasn't trying to find a customer. She had got into the habit of drinking and she was short of money. I claimed I could see no difference between her years of fame and her present destitution. I had seen her at the Théâtre des Ternes, still playing a young girl even then, with a big butterfly bow above her fringe of straight blonde hair. Now I was seeing her in a tragic role. The little woman who had packed all Paris into a theater with her way of saying *merde* was now reciting the most heart-rending words without opening her lips. Maurice called her over to his table and asked me to leave them alone. Of course, right away. She was so much in need of consideration. Those flowers her friends used to send her once upon a time—he would make them bloom again on her wretched, cheap print dress. I went for a walk, I didn't say to myself that this temporary life could never last.

Maurice had told me about a scene he'd made one night at the Comédie-Française when he'd been outraged by a performance of *Phèdre*. He had spent the latter part of the evening in the police station. He spoke very warmly about a young university graduate who had been as displeased as he was and followed him to the police station. They still exchanged letters. The young graduate was leaving to spend the summer with his family in a little village in Normandy. Excellent, excellent, Maurice added, as though some scheme or other were doing well.

We saw more and more of Maud Loty. She was often quite tipsy at midday without being at all silly or maudlin. Her broken voice: the fragility of her situation. She took me for Maurice's mistress. That caused me no little pride. She told him all about her life as a famous actress. He told me in confidence about an awesome project he'd conceived. He was going to adapt a Dostoievsky novel for her—he didn't tell me which one—and she would play it just as she was, the same make-up, the same dress, the same shoes, the same bare legs. It would make her name as a tragic actress.

Who was the young woman with the thankless face, the straight hair falling jaggedly across her cheeks, and the maimed hand? She came into the café, walked straight over to Maud, smoothed the actress's hair with her good hand, and then led her away by the arm. They moved away, Maud Loty's heels clacking, her friend's slippers flapping against the tiled café floor. I saw them both again at seven that evening. Maud Loty didn't recognize me.

"She has the most extraordinary affection for Maud," Maurice said to me.

Next day, Maurice informed me that we were to eat dinner at Maud Loty's. She lived in a modern apartment building about a hundred yards down the street from our café. An old woman opened the door.

"I don't know if you'll be able to see them. They're locked in the bathroom. But there's someone else here waiting to see you. I'll go and tell him."

"Maud promised me he'd be here," Maurice said.

The apartment was in a pretty poor state, you could tell that from the smell wafting out.

Maurice moved closer to me and whispered in my ear: "It's settled: we're leaving."

My heart tugged at its moorings, my heart was full of joy.

"Leaving for where?"

"We're leaving Paris, we shall go to the country," Maurice answered.

We followed the old woman inside. The air was unbreathable because of the smell.

A young man got up from what had been a sofa. "I was waiting for you."

"Enchanted to know you, enchanted to meet you," Maurice Sachs said, his affability billowing before him like a full spread of sail.

The young man didn't acknowledge me.

"We have so much to talk about," Maurice said to the stranger.

The young man was cold, he did not react. Dressed to kill, his eyes devoid of indulgence behind the lenses of his expensive-looking glasses, his voice deliberately lowered, holding himself erect, he drew Sachs over toward the decomposing sofa.

I chatted to the old lady at the other end of the room.

We sat down on some packing cases. "M. Sachs is too generous M. Sachs gave us too much money for the dinner this evening it isn't ready but it will be ready they will be coming out of the bathroom then they'll think about dinner and everything will be all right Monsieur is so generous every day Maud talks about him he is interested in her he is writing a play for her. Maud will be a success in it."

I listened and laid bets with myself.

I bet he was at the Polytechnic. I bet he was a statistician. I bet he was a purchasing agent. I bet he was a topflight accountant. I bet he was an architect. I bet he was a university official. I bet he was a surveyor.

They emerged. A commotion, overlapping voices. The young man shook Maurice's hand and left. The old lady kept repeating that there was nothing for dinner but that we should be eating in a moment; Maud Loty leaped on Maurice's neck while the crippled girl stood gazing at her. My eyes told Maurice that we should both go mad if we didn't leave; he agreed, we were going to leave now.

Maud Loty wept, then laughed; her friend took her back into the bathroom, she shouted that she wanted to see Maurice next day, the day after that, to start rehearsing the play. He told her he would see her next day. We left.

Once outside, we hadn't the heart to make any comment.

"Despite all my good intentions," Maurice said, looking away from me, and that was all.

"The young man . . . who was he?"

"Fascinating. That young man? The man who took a Watteau from the Louvre, my dear."

"The man who stole *L'Indifférent*?"

"Exactly. He was telling me exactly how he did it. It wouldn't have interested you."

So be it. It wouldn't have interested me.

It's settled: we're leaving.

"Where shall we go, Maurice? Where shall we sleep? Where shall we live?"

"You're not a four-year-old, so don't ask questions like that," he replied.

He made a telephone call to the country. He seemed disappointed when he came out of the booth.

Rosebush laden with roses, I looked like you when the woman in the laundry said: Have you come to collect your husband's shirts? What did I long for? For my sex to be rusted up inside. Then I could quietly have married Maurice Sachs. What was my desire for him? My entrails gone completely to my head. Overweening vanity. The wish to turn a homosexual into a bar of red-hot iron, and then to bend that bar. Be careful, Violette, Sachs is not just anyone. Unhappiness gets on his nerves, so put away your tears.

Our suitcases: two baskets we saw hanging outside a paint store.

"Is there not even the slightest wisp of summer folded somewhere in the closet of your room?"

"Wisp of summer?"

"A dress, a shift . . . I hope at least that you don't intend walking through the fields in your furs!"

Living with him had made me even more feckless than he was himself. I crammed my basket with all the most summery garments I could muster.

We were leaving for Normandy, the family of the young graduate was going to take us in.

The evening before we were due to leave, going to meet Maurice in the café as usual, I met him in the street accompanied by a simply dressed young girl with sensibly cut blonde hair. About eighteen.

He introduced us with a preoccupied air. The girl began to grow uneasy. Would Maurice come? Of course. Would he be at the station the morning after next? Of course. I looked hard at Maurice, he looked nonchalantly at me. The girl disappeared down a deserted street.

"Why tell her you'll be there when we'll be gone by then?"

"You get on my nerves, and I'll thank you to keep yourself out of my affairs," Maurice Sachs said in a cutting voice.

I forgot the young girl immediately.

Twelve years passed. I was to remember this scene when my sickness, when my persecution began. The entire world began to blame me for it. Every young girl I met had waited for Maurice Sachs in a railroad station. Students, clerks, waitresses, secretaries, they were all sneering at me without looking at me. My remorse, their youth as they threw it in my face. I denounced Maurice to my friends, to complete strangers. I invented the story that the girl had been a Jew, that she wanted to escape into the Unoccupied Zone. I invented it because I didn't know the truth. Some of Maurice's deals were shady, he never made any secret of that. And I profited from his dishonesty since I was living with him and not paying for myself.

Sachs suggested a ride in a hackney carriage to celebrate our last evening in Paris. The carriage stopped in front of the café, the men hanging about outside crowded around us, there were murmurs as Sachs helped me up. Then we were on our way. My arm hung over the side with the melting grace of a goddess floating on an allegorical cloud. Drunk without having had a single drink, I plundered the dome of the Sacré-Coeur; everything belonged to me and there was nothing I desired. I was Bob, that same Bob whose indifference had fascinated me as he drove in a hackney carriage with Maurice Sachs. I smiled a fickle, condescending smile as we passed the Champ-de-Mars where we once used to walk in the falling dusk, where Maurice had talked to me about Casanova and the Cardinal de Retz. We smoked, and the whole city was impregnated with the scent of our tobacco. I listened to the flapping of my chin strap against my neck. The detachment of the driver filled me with delight. We were exchanging our gossip in the presence of a witness who didn't count. Sachs gave him the address of a restaurant, after we had been for drinks in a bar along the Champs-Elysées.

"We are dining at Zatoste's," Sachs said as he helped me down from the carriage.

The Basque restaurant was packed, the meal excellent. We drank a great deal. I told Sachs that there was one old man who couldn't take his eyes off us.

Maurice leaned toward me: "Suit from the Rue Royale."

He leaned further: "Tie pin from the Rue de la Paix, necktie from the Rue de Rivoli."

"Long gray mustaches," I said.

"My dear, he's an old general on the retirement list. He's absolutely perfect."

He loved the smell of wealth.

The following morning we arrived just as the café was opening. Sachs had made arrangements. The waiter gave us two flasks of cognac.

The Gare Montparnasse was crowded. Was our train at the platform yet? When would it leave? A few carriages, no apparent means of locomotion. Paris was not Zatoste's, it was not a hackney carriage, fine wines, smoked ham. Paris was these thousands of hollow faces, these thin bodies lost in clothes too big for them, these haggard men. Sachs told me to drink; I poured cognac down my throat at seven in the morning. He took a drink also, then went to find out what was happening. I was intrigued by the aluminum suitcases, by what looked like huge lunch-baskets, by the wooden hatboxes and the oilcloth shopping bags I could see around me. Our train had been canceled, we would have to wait until early afternoon.

"Excellent, excellent," Maurice said, "we can go shopping. Then I can write, you can read, we'll have lunch, then come back to the station."

Seeing the good humor with which he set about buying books and exercise books after having his train canceled was a tonic. What was he writing? How much did he have in his billfold?

I was very much on my best behavior during my first journey in a first-class compartment. I wouldn't allow myself to watch the scenery while Maurice read, and the journey seemed rather uninteresting to me because I was deprived of the usual smells seeping out of food baskets.

We drank white wine on a hotel terrace in the center of a little town that was fast asleep at four in the afternoon. The reasonableness of the prices was such a pleasant surprise it made it seem like fairyland. Where was the war, I wondered as I watched the pink cheeks of the people walking by.

"Breathe," Maurice said, without raising his eyes from his book.

A suitcase was glittering. Some men and women were holding a discussion in the square. I recognized the huge lunch baskets, the oilcloth bags, the wooden hatboxes, the aluminum suitcases. Two cyclists got onto their bikes. They rode away with enormous suitcases roped to their carriers.

"See you this evening," the women shouted.

They walked away also, and disappeared among the trees.

"What are we waiting for?" I asked Maurice.

"A bus."

He turned a page of his book.

We shared a taxi with some other travelers.

The young graduate believed deeply in friendship and devotion to others. His nearsighted eyes proclaimed through his glasses: I attach myself or I die. His family couldn't put us up; he suggested we take rooms for the night in the postman's house, with that tremolo in his voice that excites hope in the listener. I swooned at the ardor of his admiration for Maurice. Yet he listened to him with anxiety. I was surprised by his disillusioned smile, touched by his slightly crooked nose. Tall, well built, dressed in white shorts and a white sports shirt, he helped us both move into our respective rooms.

I learned next morning that there was a search going on in the village: there were inspectors going around looking for Jews. Trembling, I rushed into Maurice's room. He was reading in bed, he went on reading with unruffled calm.

"Why don't you get up! Do something. They'll be here any moment. It's not myself I'm afraid for!"

"My dear, please. Don't panic like this."

"I'm afraid for you."

"Afraid of what?"

I didn't dare answer, because you're half-Jewish, you told me so.

It got on his nerves if I started to show how fond I was of him.

"Why don't you ask them to send up a nice little tray of breakfast?"

"Food! I can't leave you like this."

"Go on, off with you, my child. . . ."

What a relief! They were whispering in the street that the inspectors had gone away again.

Later that morning. The young graduate was pushing an old bike.

"The road to the left or the road to the right?" he asked.

"The road to the right," I replied without hesitation.

We were looking for a roof to put over our heads.

They talked about literature, about their studies, about a man they were both friendly with, among my hazel leaves, my hawthorns stripped of bloom, the smiling mallow, the basking camomile. My thirst, oh my thirst for the cool springs in the sky . . . I walked behind them, I drank in all that blue, I was feeling my cheeks new again and fresh against that landscape devoid of all romanticism. There were clouds, but white clouds, resting lightly on my summers. We were walking at an easy pace; I cut out dresses and pinafores from a field the color of milky coffee, the gentle sun was buttering my face, my wrists.

"A house at last!" Maurice cried.

Suddenly a smell of caramel. The house, a rectangular block jammed into the earth, looked like a cottage on a picture postcard; dahlias with their shrieking colors proclaimed our proximity to a village: the hay-tedder with white hens perching on it looked more like a dovecote than an improvised henhouse. And oh, the heraldic freshness of the hollyhocks further on. The others went into the house next door. I followed them in.

We waited calmly in a cool room which was obviously a café and made even more refreshing by the presence of a green plant; in the little store adjoining the café I could see the shiny blackness of a pile of rubbers. A man came in. His tape measure was hanging down from his shoulders.

"M. Blaise," he said to the young graduate with pleasure in his voice.

Short, solid, one might have taken him for a diplomat on account of his piercing eyes, his knowing air, his bearing. Everything was settled: we could eat lunch there.

"Excellent, excellent," Maurice said. "The whole thing seems quite perfect. Shall we start with a calvados?"

The young graduate left us: he was still looking for somewhere for us to stay. The shopkeeper helped me take off the fox jacket that didn't belong to me.

"We're looking for a house," Maurice said.

M. Zoungasse looked at our baskets.

"You won't find anything," he said. "We have two rooms, but everything is taken."

"Even if we pay well?" Maurice suggested.

"I always mean what I say."

M. Zoungasse had made a hole in the middle of the mashed potatoes; now he poured meat gravy in the hole and served us slices of veal.

"Flowing with milk and honey, the country around here," Maurice murmured in a low voice.

Reader, will you read *La Vieille Fille et le mort*? If you do, you will say to yourself: the same green plant on the table in the middle of the room, the same village store adjoining the little café, the same piles of rubbers. Yes. I didn't invent the café, or the village. They exist. You might say to yourself: then Maurice Sachs is the dead man. You would be wrong. The dead man is another homosexual I loved, the dead man is a rich man in the best of health whom I changed into a hobo because my fingers around my penholder could close the eyelids of a hobo.

The shopkeeper served us coffee.

"Don't you ask for coupons?" Maurice asked.

"Never," the shopkeeper replied, offended.

I turned my head: a sandy-colored road as sinuous as a grass snake was being weighed down by the heat and the haze above it.

"You go out of this café," M. Zoungasse said, "you turn off by the cemetery, you follow it around, then just beyond, on your right, that's it. He's old, he lives alone, that's all I can think of."

"We'll leave our baskets with you," Maurice said.

M. Zoungasse was a tailor. He was already drawing lines with his chalk.

*

"In my whole life I never saw a cemetery more charming," Maurice said. "Eh?"

The light was not kind. His suit was losing its shape, his reddish brown shoes were beginning to wear out. He was wiping his neck and his brow, his eyes were gulfs of sadness, despite the gaiety of the cow parsnip he was looking at but not seeing. I was stumbling over every stone in my thick wooden soles.

I can still see the cemetery. No gates, no door. Open to the day, open to the night, it is displaying all it has to display: the deserted tombs under their comforters of weeds. You can hear the splashing of the sheep as they go down to drink, the clatter of a harrow in the lane. One of the sheep escapes and walks into the cemetery for a feast of thistles; the sheep dog chases it out again. It is no longer a cemetery. It is a garden run wild in which singing is forbidden. Here the urns are never bored. They receive their guests. Bustling ants and slow, hermetic snails. The wreaths look like men who have huddled to the ground in sleep, just where they fell. The place is a plenitude of pale purple, gray, and violet, all faded by the harshness of the weather. Grasshoppers leap onto the pearls of the wreaths. The porcelain flowers, miniature holy-water stoups pressed one against the other, collect the raindrops in their petals. One feels the flowers made of cloth were cut from the tear-soaked shirts of mourning wives. As for the dates, as for the names . . . one reads, one deciphers, one sees the marks of time's eraser. The swallow dives with a flick of its wing across the whole length of the cemetery, and from that prodigious dive it takes its soaring, upward flight.

"It's there," Maurice said.

The house stood with its back to the road. A house born with its shutters closed. I heard the luminous cry of the lark. Maurice pushed open the childlike gate. We walked along an open-air passageway between the wall of the house and a shed.

The surprise of a kitchen garden decorated with black currant bushes and rose trees. Some of the roses were starting to fall, their petals adorning the cabbages beneath. The path down the middle of the kitchen garden had a border of flowered luster tiles.

The door, open. The man sitting inside had his back to the world, like his house; the old woman looked like an eagle and also like a hen. Her sparse hair, flattened with water and pulled down from a center part, was coiled into a shiny snail the size of a boot polish tin. They were playing dominoes.

"You have visitors, M. Motté, I'll be off."

The singsong accent gave fullness to her voice.

"Don't go," said the old man with silky hair to the old woman.

"What is it then?" he asked us.

He still had his back turned to us.

They both kept their store of dominoes walled up behind one hand.

Maurice explained that he was looking for a place to rent. The old man showed us his profile. We saw one glassy eye and half a drooping white mustache. His blue eye inspected me from head to foot.

"I have nothing to rent!" he said through his mustache.

The game of dominoes was resumed.

"How sad you look," I said when we got back onto the road.

Maurice was looking at a house opposite him; its shutters were open behind the shelter of a hedge.

"We must go back to Paris this evening," he said.

"Go back?"

"Walk on," he said, "I'm going to pray."

I stayed rooted to the spot.

Maurice climbed up the bank on our right. He fell on his knees in the grass and put his head in his hands. He was praying.

His praying, coming so unexpectedly, frightened me. I stared at a climbing rose, trying to melt into it.

"I'll go back alone this time. Wait for me," Maurice Sachs said.

He opened the childlike gate a second time.

Going back to Paris would be a catastrophe for him. I remembered the difficulties he was in, the trouble he'd had with the jewelers, with his former landlady. Where were his friends?

"We shall have a room each," he told me.

"A room each! He agreed?"

"For a lot of money. Come in."

"Now?"

"He wants to see you."

"This is your little lady?" the old man asked.

I could have wept at so much innocence.

Maurice asked him if he would mind showing us the rooms. The thin old man took off his cape and his clogs. The unpainted pine staircase, without a banister, very steep, made me feel I was being asked to climb a sheer cliff.

"I daren't . . ."

"Don't be stupid," Maurice hissed.

He pushed me in front of him.

The old man had already climbed up ahead of us. He was putting a few corrective touches here and there to a flower bed of opulent onions. I banged my head against the sloping roof. The warmth of a loft that has been shut up a long while.

"Here they are," he said.

Twin rooms, with a communicating door. Each had its cherry-wood bed, its feather-filled comforter covered in satinette, its two little windows looking out on the road and the kitchen garden, and its two pairs of starched curtains.

"Your beds are charming," Maurice said.

Charmed, the old man looked at Maurice.

"The beds are small but you should be able to manage all the same."

We both gave a false laugh so as not to disappoint him.

The old man removed some dust from a window sill by rubbing his thick finger along it.

"Ah, well I must look to my animals now," he said. "You'll find the sheets here this evening."

A countless host of empty, dust-covered bottles was standing guard beyond the gilded onions. The loft smelled of waxed paper.

The room we could use as a sitting room had a red, tiled floor with a fireplace all ready to take a wood fire. Maurice's eyes were caressing a long table that would have served for a banquet. The manuscripts that could be written on that!

We went back to the café and were greeted by Mme. Zoungasse.

"Were the lady and gentleman satisfied?" said a weeping willow straightening itself up with the effort to please.

A too ingratiating welcome, a carpet unrolled beneath our feet, a carpet made of the unloosed hair of a Mary Magdalene.

"Satisfied beyond our desires," Maurice replied with unction in his voice.

"He's a good man. You'll be all right there."

Mme. Zoungasse told us that she had to leave us in order to prepare the evening meal.

"Of course we would like to dine here," Maurice said, "but if that is going to cause you the slightest inconvenience . . ."

"If the lady and gentleman can make do with some soup, a piece of cold pork, an endive salad, and a baked custard . . ."

"That all sounds quite excellent to me," Maurice said, "and if you don't mind we'll take all our meals with you."

"The charge would be for breakfast too."

"Naturally," Maurice said.

*

An extraordinary salad. Endive is sometimes an unprepossessing vegetable: the chewed and rechewed edges of its frilly leaves can give the impression of a thistle without its needles. It's tough, it's monotonous, it makes one think of grass that's gone on growing in the middle of a recently tarred road. We were a long way from such fibrous infelicities that night. Tender to look at, oozing with a milky juice, the endives we were given, slightly curly here and there, still greenly flourishing in other places, the endives we were given were afflicted with the onset of some languishing sickness in the white porcelain of the salad bowl. A hint of yellowness resting on white alabaster curves. I attacked. I enjoyed the diet of a hermit, a connoisseur of silks and velvet. A memory of vinegar floated inside my mouth—yes, floated, I am persevering with this gibberish—it rose and vanished like the vapor from a scarf of finest lawn.

Maurice helped us both to this salad, a small quantity at a time.

"My dear, you are in the process of ingesting a masterpiece," he said. "Can you give me the recipe?" he asked Mme. Zoungasse.

She wiped her hands on her apron.

"Nothing simpler: you take a little saucepan, you melt a nut of butter, you add your fresh cream . . ."

"Our fresh cream," I said, stupid with wonder.

". . . You add your fresh cream, you stir . . ."

"Salad à la Proust," Maurice Sachs said.

Our day concluded with a moonlit night: the cemetery was a ghost.

"This village has only one street," Maurice remarked.

We climbed the hill with slow steps. There were steel blue glints slithering over the slate-covered roofs.

"No key and he's locked the door," Maurice said.

"Is that M. Maurice?" the old man asked through the door.

"In person," Maurice replied in his most playful voice.

The door opened, the old man appeared before us in his nightshirt, still wearing his enormous clogs.

A little ebony Christ on a little ebony cross shrouded in a veil of spider's web caught Maurice's attention. A dilapidated, badly lit kitchen, the neglected wood stove of a man on his own. The cherry-wood sideboard seemed to have been put there by an antique dealer. The patterns on two fantastic vases were hidden by a layer of dust.

The two pairs of sheets were lying ready on the long table. We each took our own. I was afraid of our future in the village, afraid of the comedy of affection and free love we would have to perform for them.

I wanted to make Maurice's bed, plump up his eiderdown and pillow, unfold, smooth out my tenderness now I had the chance. I made his bed while Maurice urinated into one of the empty bottles in the loft. I tucked it in at the bottom, I tucked it in at the sides.

"You're tired. We must say good night," Maurice said.

God, how abstract his kisses were upon my cheeks. I sank too far into his soft cheeks, I was drowning my two kisses. I experienced our friendly good night more acutely than in Paris because I was living alone with him, near the bed in which he would be sleeping. I went through into my own room, and when I had closed my door after me I felt teeth biting into my breast, a vise gripping my shoulder: the caesura of our two lives. Maurice Sachs was lending me his presence, but he gave himself to the old man, to M. Zoungasse, to the young graduate. He attracted people, he charmed them, just as Gabriel had attracted and charmed people by different means. I always attached myself to men who eluded my grasp.

I put out my light with burglarlike stealth because I was ashamed of not reading for a while. The two featherbeds irritated me: I was sinking into a quicksand. I turned over to face the door and saw a ray of light. Maurice was still awake. I wept. I despaired because I was cut off from his vigil. He read for a part of the night. I went to sleep, far away from him, near to him, after he had switched off his light.

*

The clogs woke me with a start. The old man was emitting long brrr sounds, he was making summer into winter. The angelus was ringing in the distance through cotton wool. I opened my eyes: clear day, dappled blue. Was Maurice asleep? Was Maurice reading in bed? I mustn't ask myself those things. His privacy belonged to him. I felt all my movements being constricted by embargoes, by the necessity of being reasonable and tactful. Stringy solitude beside my cheap bedside rug. The trampling clogs, the comings and goings of the old man kept me company. I got up. There was a trellis separating the black currant bushes from the dog's kennel. The dog, or more accurately the skeleton of a dog, was trying to escape. His chain was too short; he began barking as soon as it choked him. He went back into his kennel, I opened the window, a wasp lit up the garden.

I walked on tiptoe over to the door between our rooms. Was he asleep? Was he reading in bed? Could I get dressed? Could I go through his room? It would be improper to disturb him while he was reading Kant or Hegel. I got back into bed, I huddled up under the bedclothes. No job, no future, no plans. A big fly flew in, then it flew out. The old man began to dig in his garden. Who would help me get out of my room? The stones he was turning up rang against the metal, his spade was drinking toasts with the pebbles.

I got up finally at eight, I put on a cotton dress, I slipped a pair of sandals on my feet. I knocked at Sachs' door. Silence. I knocked again. Silence. I opened his door. The bed was empty, the basket was empty, the window was closed. I had weighed so heavy on my room; Maurice had only skimmed the surface of his. I went downstairs holding my sandals in my hand. There were potatoes cooking in a big pan and meat simmering in an earthenware casserole. The old man led an organized existence. I crossed the threshold of the open door into the garden.

"Are we up then?" he said.

He took a pinch of snuff, sniffing exuberantly and resting on the handle of his spade. His cheeks seemed pink beside the illumined black currant bushes, and the yellow roses nearby seemed to have gone into a decline. Where was the war? The richness of the earth, the contentment of the lettuces, the comfort of the full, round cabbages; the tranquillity of the tied-up endives, the frivolity of the parsley and the chervil. M. Motté was digging again. He was wearing an old felt hat the color of rain water as a substitute for a straw hat; Maurice has described it in one of his books.

"Have you seen him anywhere?" I asked.

"M. Maurice is in your room," he answered, pointing with his glinting spade toward the downstairs sitting room. "M. Maurice was up early!"

I heard the whine of a power saw from the shed alongside the garden.

"Come in," Maurice said.

I went in listlessly. Between them, they had taken everything away from me, these two men each leading their own lives so early in the morning.

Maurice was writing in a school exercise book on the long table. He finished his sentence and got up. Poverty was spinning its web. The printed, tie-silk dressing gown was dirty, the patent leather slippers had lost their shape, the socks needed darning. He came toward me, his slippers flapping, his dressing gown floating behind him; he was fat, he was unshaven, he was looking withered that morning, my Nero with the thinning hair.

"Did you sleep well? Sleep is so important. I tried not to make a noise turning the pages."

"Yes, I went off to sleep right away, yes, I slept well."

My lie, my self-immolation.

"How early you got up!" I said, admiring and shamefaced.

"I rose at dawn. There is nothing better," he said, dipping his pen in the inkwell.

I went out, also trying not to make a noise. There are presences that lose their novelty.

"I'd like to wash," I said to the old man.

He was stretching a rope between two posts.

"The bucket is in the kitchen. All you have to do is pump."

"Where shall I wash though?"

I waited for him to answer.

"There," he said, "where I put my wood."

I pumped up some water. The firewood was beautifully stacked in the lean-to shed. M. Motté grumbled because I asked him for some soap. I washed myself thoroughly. Oh! M. Motté had come over, he was watching me. I went on with my toilette, pretending I didn't know he was there. He went away again. I finished washing with a light heart because I was enchanted at the idea of having something new to tell Maurice. The old man had provided me with a minor role at last.

"What are you complaining about?" Maurice asked. "He's a connoisseur and he finds you to his taste. I should be flattered in your place."

I complained to myself in silence of Maurice's indifference. Now he had no young men, I wanted him to be proprietary and tyrannical.

"Good morning, M. Motté!"

"Morning," the old man rejoined curtly.

The young graduate came in surrounded by his swarm of affability.

"Dear Maurice," he said by way of greeting.

"Dear Blaise," Maurice replied.

"Already at work!" the young graduate commented. "I saw an exercise book on the table. I was walking past, I recognized that tiny handwriting of yours I love so much."

"You opened the window?" I asked.

I wanted to be informed about everything that concerned Maurice. Excruciating pointillism of the emotions.

Maurice suggested we go and drink a calvados at Mme. Zoungasse's café. I offered to take his dressing gown up to his bedroom.

"Women are slaves. The instinct is stronger than they are," Maurice remarked. "For heaven's sake leave that rag where it is. Come on."

The young graduate looked at me with compassion. He had guessed, he was sorry for me.

"You two are all anyone talks about at the moment," he said to create a diversion.

"I can't see what there is to talk about," I said ill-temperedly.

"Your furs, my dear!" Maurice said.

Mme. Zoungasse greeted us with the momentous humility of a woman who has just taken communion.

*

After lunch, Maurice advised me to rest for a while, then go out and explore the village. He retreated into the fresh new world he had created for himself that morning. I stood motionless in the kitchen. I heard the pages of his exercise book. The whine of the power saw began again. I missed the poverty and the nullity of my life in Paris. I needed a life crusted with burns to run my fingers over. I didn't want to rest away from him, I didn't want to go for a walk away from him, I said to myself like a sulky child. I opened the doors of the cherrywood sideboard. What should I take? A piece of pickled pork? I ate it. A knob of butter? I took some. A little calvados? I drank some of that. I had nothing and I had everything. What should I take? Where should I take it from? I went out into the kitchen garden. It was roasting hot. I picked a cluster of black currants. Too sharp. Stealing something of no consequence can be complicated sometimes. I finally managed to steal something by biting into a gooseberry. So hot: there was an iron, hot from its ironing board, melting on my tongue. Maurice was writing, the old man was resting, there was a bee sleeping at the bottom of a flower. The power saw stopped its whining, the smell of distress from the fresh sawdust refreshed me, a butterfly passed, transported by its own happiness.

The arrival of a Merovingian cart. It stopped, I knelt down behind a black currant bush so as not to be seen. A bundle of beige cloth, a clump of gray frizz, jumped down from the cart.

"Is it ready?" the peasant asked.

He was putting its hat back on the head of one of his horses. He spat out a jet of tobacco juice.

"Come in," said an answering voice from the shed.

The bundle of beige cloth climbed back into the cart and reemerged carrying a moldy tarpaulin.

"Shall I come in?" the peasant asked.

"Yes, come in," the voice replied forcefully from inside the shed.

The horses were twitching because of the flies. I heard the sound of a piece of wooden furniture being moved.

"Don't hold it by the handles," said the authoritative voice.

"How do you expect me to hold it?" the peasant asked.

"Hold it the way I do. By the underneath. Don't let the tarpaulin slip. Now back out."

"Easier said than done," the peasant answered.

The peasant began backing out of the shed. He was carrying a long piece of furniture draped with the moldy tarpaulin. The tarpaulin fell off, revealing a magnificent coffin. The carpenter came out of his shed and looked in every direction before picking it up. They set the coffin down on the grass as carefully as though it were a victim of some terrible accident.

"Well, we got this far," the peasant said.

He spat tobacco juice.

"This is only the half of it," the carpenter answered.

He took a pinch of snuff.

"Have you got it?"

"I've got it," the peasant said.

The carpenter pushed, the peasant pulled. He took his horses by their heads and turned the cart around. The coffin slid back and forth in the back. The carpenter went back into his shed. He shrugged his shoulders.

*

I walked up the hill, I set out for a walk.

I reached the cross at the center of the village, I stopped at the crossroads.

"Come in, poor dear. You can rest here. There's no happiness in this life. No happiness, believe me."

She insisted. Very well. I went in.

"There's no happiness in this life, my poor dear. Believe me, no happiness. If I want to give you some coffee I've got to heat it up and to heat it up that means I've got to light the stove. The stove eats money. The wood. The price of wood doesn't bear talking about. It's an abomination. If my stove hadn't gone out I wouldn't have to use up a match. Oh I just throw it in like that, it makes that much more kindling, doesn't it? I take in everyone's washing so if you've any washing you want done . . . The worse part of it, my poor dear, the worst part is the chilblains in the winter. You'll find everything you need here, you won't lack for anything here. What is one to do though with a sick man in the place? Now that our coffee is hot I'll pull the kindling out again. I can use it again you see. I've got him in bed through there in the other room. Do you want to see him? . . . Tire him? All those violins, all that dancing never used to tire him. I know M. Motté well enough. A dry old stick he is. And I can tell you he's not easy to get along with, M. Motté. And I can tell you things are so expensive these days.

Time was obviously expensive too: the pendulum of the clock was motionless.

"He'll sell you vegetables. He does sell them to you? It's a fine house he's got. Does he charge you a lot? He ought to be ashamed. Does he speak to you? He's not a chatty man ordinarily. No one here talks about anything but M. Maurice ever since you came. They say he's so kind, they say he has such beautiful manners. What can you expect me to do with a sick man in the place? I've got him in bed, you see, through there in the other room. . . ."

I gave up all idea of continuing my walk. I wanted to see her "M. Maurice" again. The carpenter was hammering in nails, M. Motté was planting out heads of celery.

"Hot today," he said. "There, and there, and there, and there . . . poor girl!"

He stared me calmly up and down. Had I been beautiful, he would have stared at me with the same avidity, the same arrogance.

Maurice opened the window, M. Motté's face lit up. The old, round face grew soft and gentle. The glassy eyes regained their candor.

"Six o'clock at Zoungasse's to set ourselves up again with a glass of calvados, my dear Violette."

Maurice closed the window again.

The old man had kept his eyes fixed intently on my reaction, he was observing me with such indecency that he made me want to laugh even though I felt like crying! I was now at a loose end.

I asked him the name of the woman who lived by the crossroads.

M. Motté dropped his celery plants.

"You went into Mme. Meulay's! She said: 'There's no happiness in this world.' It'll be the same every time you go. She starts the same thing every time."

"She gave me a cup of coffee with sugar," I said.

"That's as may be," the old man replied.

Maurice was writing; the books we'd brought with us repelled me. What was I to do with myself?

I rushed back to Mme. Meulay's house.

"I was bored," I said.

"Everything is so difficult," she replied.

"He's in his garden. He takes good care of it," I remarked for want of anything better to say.

Mme. Meulay's worn fingers looked dry in the bowl of water.

"Oh, he isn't a man who talks about his misfortunes. Deaths, fires in his barns . . . Married four times was it? Five times? I can't remember now, I forget everything. I shall have to ask my daughter. I bring the washing in of a night, I don't trust them."

La Turbie. An excursion from Villefranche-sur-Mer. A long drive at night in an open car with Albert and his friends. We admired the tiered sweep of lights, the glittering gulf. We drove through a village immersed in beatific sleep and a milky wash of moonlight. The warm air at two in the morning. A little boy lurking beneath his winter cape was stealing washing from a line. He was stowing his plunder away beneath the homespun folds of his cloak.

". . . His wives died: he wore them out. He's old now, he's quieted down. Deaths, fires . . . misfortunes. That's what's made him hard like that."

"Your husband is very quiet. Is there anything he needs?"

"Oh, there's nothing he needs, he's sinking now! I'll tidy myself up, then I'll walk down the hill with you. . . ."

I told Maurice all I'd seen and heard.

"Why shouldn't people die here?" he asked when I told him about the coffin.

His ironic and logical questions left me powerless. I was afraid I might annoy him if I explained: the peasant is the servant of the soil. He tends it. He gives it water when it's dry, he is making its bed when he plows the fields, he strokes it and soothes it by rolling it, he is already mingled with it even before he dies because he gives it back his dung. I didn't dare say to him: in a village death comes rarely.

*

The presence of a man you love and are intimidated by, the presence of an intelligent man to whom you listen with your ovaries is a fiesta and a hell. He spoke, and I felt the gluttony low in my belly.

"Get into bed," Maurice said, "I'll come and sit with you." The first night of the fiesta.

He came and settled down near my bed with the cigarettes, the calvados, the glasses, and the ashtray. He asked me if I was comfortable, he plumped up my pillows. The mock invalid, the convalescent who had not been sick were quite comfortable. The man they loved was a mock doctor in attendance. The woman in love was less comfortable. She asked herself in what way she desired the man sitting beside her. She would have pushed him off if he had fallen on top of her, she would have screamed if he had lifted the bedclothes, yet all the time she was silently roaring her need for him. She was writhing on the hot coals of the impossible. She was expiating in his presence the joy of living there beside him. He talked until one o'clock, until two o'clock, until three o'clock in the morning. She no longer had to count the nights of her fiesta. He was to give them without counting. She was given too much and not enough. She could never imagine him otherwise than as a homosexual. His sex rising for her would be a masquerade. Docile, dumb, attentive, lying on my two mattresses, I swallowed Maurice Sachs. I should never have wearied of it if he had gone on talking for ten thousand years, I should not have felt surfeited if the night had lasted twenty thousand years. I felt sad, very sad as I listened to him and looked at him. It was he who had wanted to come into the country and yet it seemed to me I was depriving him of Paris, of his fecklessness with money, of his inclinations.

I was to tell myself later that Maurice was at a turning point, that he was fleeing from his enemies, that he was turning the page on his disappointments in love, on his despair at being a man on his own. I wouldn't have lifted my little finger to help him move on somewhere else, and yet I couldn't conceal from myself a feeling that his proper place was in fact somewhere else. The neat little room was too small for him. I listened to him, shattered by my own stupidity. I told myself I was Cleopatra, that I could give him all the Orient if I so desired. We drank, we smoked. Maurice talked to me about Paris, about his friends in Paris, about his childhood, about how he grew up. His past came welling up into his throat, the lakes of sadness in his eyes grew bigger as he stood up in the room and did his imitation of Max Jacob, "dear, dear Max" as Maurice always called him. He was very fond of Raïssa Maritain. Her first name fascinated me, I saw black strips across the faded rug. Raïssa Maritain, Jacques Maritain. I remembered the books in the Roseau d'Or series published by Plon, their bright blue covers. Maurice explained the philosophy of St. Thomas Aquinas to me, then he described a big dinner and invented recipes: empty some cans of truffles into a plate of noodles. Then we laughed and laughed as the tomcats made love to their she-cats in the cemetery and emitted their long, lugubrious wails. Maurice also described Louise de Vilmorin playing the guitar in the Gallimards' drawing room. He had been dazzled by her: she was seduction itself when she sat down on the floor. He let me read the letters she had written to him before the outbreak of war. Louise de Vilmorin, her guitar. I saw the petals of a dress spread out on a carpet.

Maurice often used the first name Gaston when speaking of his publisher. He was proud of having the right to refer to him thus, and I was proud on his behalf. Gaston, he would say, and his mouth would be filled with the importance of the name. His cheeks swelled out, his jutting chin grew wider. "Gaston" in Maurice's mouth became the succulent brioche of success. He told me that he would have liked to be Casanova, to write the Memoirs of a twentieth-century Casanova. Yes, the Orient had an attraction for him. He was promising himself, once the war was over, to go and visit Lebanon, to live there for a while. I listened to him with a melancholy ear because I never figured in his plans. Are you unhappy? he would ask. No, I wasn't unhappy. I was bitter. He talked to me about Russia: that meant Serge Diaghileff, Nijinsky, Chekhov, Tolstoy, Dostoievsky, the childhood of Soutine, the young Soutine's journey from

Russia to Paris hanging stretched out under a train, Elsa Triolet's first short stories. Did he talk to me about Germany, about the war? Yes and no. He was rereading Nietzsche and believed that the Germans were going to win. If I dared to suggest that the last word had yet to be said, he shrugged his shoulders to show he wasn't convinced. Deep inside, there was nothing he was sure of. He pinned a map of Europe over his worktable.

*

"There's a scandal in the village," Maurice told me.

I shivered: the thought flashed through me that he was involved in the scandal.

"Some young evacuee boys boarded out with one of the women here ate all her homemade jam last night. Now they'll all have to go back to Paris, except for one little boy who didn't touch anything. A Jew."

"Is that all?"

"Isn't that enough in the country?" Maurice asked. "No one is talking about anything else but the jam thieves."

This petty theft committed by young boys excited Maurice. He wanted to get to know them.

That day some red patches appeared all around my ankles. That day I grew bolder. I walked around the hollyhocks, I went into the other village store. It did a very poor trade. I waited and listened to the English radio trying to make its way through a maddened hive of interference. Someone switched off the set. I was bored standing alone in the dismal little store, I gave a cough to make my presence known.

"Go and see who it is, chicken," said a woman's voice.

A slender Vercingetorix emerged from the kitchen. The complexion of a young girl, pepper and salt mustaches. Long, untaintable blue eyes. He went back into the kitchen.

"What can I do for you?" asked a ton of hardened fat.

"Er . . . some candy . . . some chocolate . . . some sugar . . . some cigarettes."

"Mademoiselle," she said, "if you want chocolate I shall be obliged to ask you for coupons."

Her voice was charming, her features delicate.

"Coupons? Oh yes, I have them with me," I replied effusively.

She moved majestically.

"Chicken, take the kettle off the stove," she shouted through to her husband.

Her hands were at work on my cigarette packs. She was determined to reduce the little pile to perfect symmetry.

"The water's not hot, shall I take it off?"

"I said to take it off, chicken."

A noise of glasses, then a noise of plates. Chicken was clearing their table.

"Aren't you taking M. Maurice's cigarettes?"

A glass smashed on the kitchen floor.

"M. Maurice! Do you know him?"

She gave me a reassuring smile.

"I haven't met him. Everyone here calls him 'M. Maurice.' They all say he's very nice."

"Do you serve meals by any chance?" I asked.

She waved through the window at some peasant women leaving for the fields.

She came around the counter to get a better view of the route they were taking. Bonnet strings flapped; the spaces above the hay as it lay waiting to be turned were moving to meet the women as they walked.

"Yes. I'll do my best. Give me notice," she replied.

She was having difficulty walking because her dainty bare feet in their slippers, her shapely legs, made to carry about ninety pounds, must have been supporting at least two hundred and twenty.

A townswoman rushed in like a tornado: "Mme. Bême, can I use the telephone?"

A hoarse voice, a coating of kindness inside her throat.

"I thought you'd left with Charlotte," Mme. Bême said. "Didn't you get what you were expecting?"

"Double, Mme. Bême, double! I haven't had any lunch, I've snapped off one of my heels. If you could let me have a piece of cheese and two fried eggs . . . Can I telephone?"

"Chicken, it's Didine."

"I can hear! I can't be everywhere at once: my garden, getting the greens for the rabbits, doing the dishes, cooking eggs, answering the telephone."

"Let me have a calva," the young woman said.

Her black skirt, her pitiful white blouse. Sweat under her arms, the scented elixir of poverty.

"You can go and bring two eggs from M. Lécolié," Mme. Bême said to her husband.

The young woman went into the kitchen holding the broken-off high heel in her hand.

"We're all just one big family here," Mme. Bême said to me. (She looked down at the red patches around my ankles.) "Didine, I want you to look at something."

Didine came limping hurriedly back. Her legs, rickety, just the slightest bit bowed, her legs with their stringy muscles and their veins too near the surface, too darkly colored . . . A flow of poverty and generosity.

"Isn't that it, when it's just beginning?" Mme. Bême asked her.

"Yes, that's it beginning," Didine said.

"What have I got?" I asked in terror.

"It's an epidemic that's sweeping the countryside. The doctor hasn't been able to say what it is yet. They turn into sores."

The young graduate was talking to Maurice about the friend they had in common when I got back to M. Motté's house. They fell silent. My presence severed through the bond of friendship between them. The presence of a woman without sex. Their man's world tottered nonetheless.

"Bême and his wife are an extraordinary couple," the young graduate said to Maurice. "Why don't we go and drink a calva at their store?" he suggested.

"An excellent idea. Away we go!" Maurice said.

"I'm going to have sores," I said with shame. "It's an epidemic that's sweeping the countryside. . . ."

"Poor dear," the young graduate said, dragging out the word "poor."

"Women are unbelievable," Maurice exclaimed. "She tells us 'I'm going to have sores' as though she were saying 'I'm going to have a child.' . . ."

We walked down the hill. The young graduate gave me his arm because he sensed I was unhappy.

"You must think about sending your furs back," Maurice said.

"My furs? It's just a fox jacket. . . ."

"A fox jacket that doesn't belong to you," Maurice said.

"The woman who wanted to sell it has several other coats like it. I'm not depriving her of anything."

"I'll make up a package," Maurice said. "I shall send it back. There are times when I don't understand you. I felt much closer to you in Paris. . . ."

It was true: Maurice without money was no longer Maurice Sachs. Maurice chaste and honest was Maurice Sachs diminished. I didn't permit myself to offer him advice. But when he had squandered money in Paris, at least he had sensed that I was giving my silent approval. One day he called me "The Ant." I can call him "The Grasshopper" in true admiration. In the village, he freed me from money by paying for everything, and if he stuffed a bill into my hands for some insignificant purchase it was a message he was giving me rather than a five-franc bill. He offered calvados and cigarettes to everyone he met: a saint rolling in money.

*

That evening M. Motté gave us his first ripe apples, which he had baked in the oven. Maurice covered them with fresh cream. Ungrateful that we were, we were already becoming unfaithful to the café-restaurant Zoungasse.

That evening, before beginning his vigil beside my bed, Maurice handed me several school exercise books. He said there were more to follow, and when I had read them all I must tell him what I thought. I opened the first one and recognized the tiny, cramped writing that suggested a man in a hurry. I flicked through it. Erasures were few.

"You can begin tomorrow," he said.

"What about the little boy who didn't dare to steal?" I asked.

Maurice had been wanting to tell me about him just at the moment I asked. He was twelve years old, his name was Gérard, he was a Jew, his mother was hiding him in the village. "Twelve years old," Maurice repeated in a low voice. He was alone among the others and didn't get enough to eat. Yes, he was beautiful, and his unhappiness increased his beauty. He was a boy who never laughed. How had he met him? Where had he met him? Maurice was walking along by the stream reading my Bible. The "jam thieves" were bathing and shouting as they splashed each other. Maurice explained that the sight of these young naked boys, of their antics in the limpid water, was far from displeasing to him, despite a certain showy vulgarity in their manner. He had closed the Bible and offered cigarettes to the naked bodies emerging from the waist-high stream. "You're forgetting Gérard," said the eldest, a big curly-headed boy. Where was

Gérard? Maurice looked for him. Unhappiness must have the power to annihilate, to make one invisible, for Gérard, wearing a little boy's suit too small for him, was sitting in the grass at Maurice's feet. It was Gérard he should have seen first. Lost in his unhappiness, Gérard no longer existed. In short, Maurice knelt down in front of him and held out the pack of cigarettes. A long hand, a beautiful, old man's hand moved toward it.

The fingers moved away from the pack again without having taken anything. With lowered eyes, Gérard confessed that he didn't know how to smoke. Then Maurice gave a start as he realized that he was still kneeling. The boys in the river began to whisper among themselves. Maurice stood up again. And Gérard? Sitting in the grass, he still kept his eyes lowered, as though unable to bear the weight of their long lashes. Would he agree to take a walk with Maurice along the river? Gérard at last raised his eyelids. Then Maurice saw two eyes in which the pain was as soft as the feel under a white cat's chin. Gérard looking up at me with the submission of our race, it was magnificent and it was frightful, Maurice said.

Dogs barked in the village: English planes passed over our roof, high in the sky. The hum of their engines was muffled by the darkness the way a landscape is muffled by mist.

Maurice resumed his narrative. They had walked along the bank of the stream, but Gérard thought that Maurice was making fun of him. It is true that children are only too ready to draw that conclusion when we treat them with deference. Prudish almost to suffocation, Gérard would not remove his jacket. But the young boy's hands were so beautiful that they clothed his whole body. He walked differently from the way Maurice had expected. His hands stuck in the pockets of his jacket, his jacket hunched up, he moved with the virile stride of a full-grown man. "If I could just hear the sound of your voice," Maurice said to this solemn child. "Come out of yourself a little, I'll try to be your friend."

"My friend? I have no friends," Gérard replied. His voice was breaking. A blind man hearing him would have taken him for a sixteen-year-old.

They walked along by the edge of the water, the cool air was delicious. Maurice asked a host of questions to which Gérard gave no reply. Would he like to smoke now that they were away from the others? Maurice gave him a pack of cigarettes. The hands trembled, they shredded the top of the pack, some of the cigarettes fell into the grass. Maurice reassured him: clumsy people always have generous hearts. Gérard stood fitting the cigarettes back into the pack with intense concentration. He is a little less sad now, Maurice thought, relieved both for himself and for Gérard's sake. As he leaned over the pack of cigarettes, Maurice told me, the dirt on the collar of his shirt was a slim chain around his downy neck. Yes, Maurice, everything can be a source of beauty when the elegance is inborn. Gérard had decided to smoke. He smoked quickly and gazed with astonishment at the ash that was his creation.

"I know you," Gérard had said to Maurice. "I see you go by every day. You always have a book under your arm."

Did he, Gérard, read? He liked reading, but he couldn't get books. He looked at Maurice. His eyes were begging. Give me some more friendship, they were saying. Maurice had promised: he would see Gérard again the following day. Maurice could help Gérard to live. He had shaken the beautiful hand; the shadowy child's grip had been amazingly strong. Maurice and Gérard then retraced their steps; the other boys were getting dressed and splashing one another still. They sat down cross-legged. They formed a circle. Gérard had remained standing up, his long lashes, Maurice added, already drumming his sadness back to man the defenses once again. Maurice made a joke and sat down cross-legged also. Gérard imitated him. It was then they told Maurice about the night they'd emptied the pots of jam and danced around the empty jars. "Curly," the tall one, had assumed the leadership of the gang when they were all evacuated to the old lady's house. They were waiting for their parents to take them back to Paris. One of them said loudly: "He can't go back though, his mother doesn't want him, and anyway he's Jewish." Gérard chewed on a piece of grass between his teeth, amorphous. He looked at his shoes which needed resoling. . . .

At that point, Maurice said good night to me. We would continue the conversation next day.

I burst into sobs under my bedclothes as soon as he'd closed the door. Maurice led his own life, he went walking alone, he read the Bible without telling me, he met young boys. I wept harder and harder because I could already sense that a little boy of twelve was beginning to love Maurice Sachs as Maurice Sachs had never been loved before. It's deeper than what I feel for him, I said to myself. My tears stopped with the suddenness of a summer storm, I forgot Gérard.

I lighted a cigarette, I opened the window a little way because of the smoke, and began on the first of Maurice's exercise books. Gripped, spellbound, I read on until five in the morning. The thing I had never dared to hope for was becoming a reality.

The following evening, Maurice continued:

He had met Gérard again as arranged. In the same spot, almost to the inch, where they had said good-by the day before. And Maurice? How did he remember, to the inch almost, where they had stood? There was a bush growing there. Gérard was behind the bush. Arms hanging by his sides. Rooted in the middle of the field. Staring straight ahead of him. He looked more like a Gérard returned from the dead, Maurice told me, than like Gérard himself. In order to lighten Gérard's mood, Maurice had to lighten his own. Gérard managed to produce a smile. He had been trying to clean his shoes with some sort of polish. He had merely succeeded in making them a mess. Never mind. Moving one's arms trying to polish shoes is already living. Gérard was alive. Maurice succeeded in making him talk. Gérard's mother had a lover who didn't work. His brother was a *zazou,* he wore his hair long and hung around in bars writing poems on scraps of paper. His father had been taken away to Silesia. "We never hear from him," Gérard replied when Maurice asked about him, stabbing at his questioner's eyes with his own pain and hate.

"Why shouldn't you read poetry yourself?" Maurice asked. "It doesn't mean you have to write poems on scraps of paper like your brother."

"I'd like to so much," Gérard replied. As though he were making an offering of his future enthusiasm. Maurice picked that moment to offer him a cigarette and it was as Gérard reached out to take it that Maurice noticed how his black nails suited his stiff manner, his air of being at once a man and a child who had been bruised in every conceivable place. The little boy he had once been was still visible, even as he tapped the cigarette gently on his nail. They smoked, they listened to the water swirling around the pebbles in the stream. Maurice noticed that Gérard had changed his shirt. His long lashes still weighed down his face with their melancholy as they had done the day before. His parents' home was near La Muette. Maurice exclaimed at that: they had been neighbors almost. . . . La Muette . . . Rue de Ranelagh . . . "It's my mother's fault I don't get enough to eat," he had said. She didn't pay his board regularly, he had to send a letter every week asking for it. Gérard had talked about the village, about Mme. Meulay who wasn't an unkind woman, not poor, but probably less rich than people imagined; about Mme. Meulay's daughter. She had a limp. She was lazy. Her mother worked herself to death for her. Mme. Meulay wasn't beyond reproach. Her chickens were allowed to look for food in other people's gardens. Mme. Bême ordered her husband around and made him wait on her. M. Motté was absolutely crazy about Mme. Champion, his opponent at dominoes. Mme. Champion didn't want to remarry.

"He sounds like a gossiping old woman, this Gérard of yours."

"No," Maurice replied. "He simply tells me what he's seen, what he's heard. A village, my dear Violette, is not a row of pretty flowerpots. And if we have a duck for dinner next Sunday it will be thanks to Gérard. He told me where to buy one. Shall we invite him to share it?"

"Yes, let's invite him."

Another evening, Maurice gave me the remainder of his exercise books. I read them avidly. I read about his childhood, the jobs he'd done, and about the brazen feats he had performed. I found him unjust toward Cocteau. I'll tell him so, I thought, I shall dare to tell him so. His bitterness distressed me. At last I was seeing the man himself as he told the story of his life. His biography has the bearing of a thoroughbred that knows how to take its time. The eighteenth-century style, that leaps out of the page at you. No and no again. The style is Maurice making a game out of his difficulties, it is Maurice proving himself stronger than style and bigger than mere literature.

"If we want people to go on thinking well of us we shall have to go to Mass, my child. Everyone goes to Mass on Sunday here."

It wasn't a mild attack of Roman Catholic fervor. It was simply a matter of protective coloration. And it was also the writer looking for fresh fields of observation. We would go to Sunday Mass. The doctor came to look at my sores. The treatment he prescribed! Night and morning, I had to moisten the scabs, take courage in both hands, and rip them off without hesitation. I had eight little lids to lift off every day. I closed my eyes, I stood the pain, my disease was exhibited. The puss at the bottom of the holes. Rose pink and white. Idiot, stop crying. Your calves are rose trees. Clean your roses.

"Why are you crying like that?" Maurice asked.

I was treating my sores in his workroom. The door was open. M.

Motté stuck his head through from the kitchen where he was preparing dinner. His big eyes were saying to Maurice: you're a man, you don't have these nasty female complaints, I'm very happy for you. My tears fell even faster because there were two of them.

"Calm yourself, Violette," Maurice said.

I flew at him: "Can't you see I have to dig into them, that I dig in and every day I have to dig deeper and deeper? I don't trust that doctor. Digging and digging like this. Having to do it oneself. It's horrible."

I poured what was almost pure alcohol into each of my little bowls of flesh. I wasn't allowed to hide my disease under dressings. I attracted the flies. That was another torture, watching for them and keeping them at bay.

I was walking along leaning on the young graduate's arm. We were going to meet Maurice for lunch. Maurice cried: "Ah ha," and stepped out of a hedge carrying a salad bowl. I was too aware of his worn-out shirt, his frayed pants, the holes in his shoes as he crossed the field.

"I've picked you some blackberries," he said to me.

"Bravo, Maurice! You've become the complete country-dweller," the young graduate said.

"We'll have them this evening, my dear, covered in fresh cream. That shall be our dinner."

Was he running short of money? I didn't want to think about it seriously.

*

We were the first to arrive for Mass. I dipped timid fingers in the holy-water stoup, and who was it I could see in the holy water? Maurice Sachs without teeth, laughing and snickering with a mouth full of gums. Maurice was naked and had frogs and toads embedded in his skin, all croaking. Maurice, stripped naked, covered in hair, was taking a hip bath in the holy water, swinging his feet and calves.

"Don't stand there crossing yourself forever," Maurice hissed in my ear.

"You mustn't sit in the pews," said an old countrywoman as clean as an egg still warm from the nest.

We followed her and she showed us to the small selection of battered chairs at the back of the church. Maurice opened my Bible. He began reading it, then unscrewed his fountain pen and started underlining phrases here and there. I sat suffering for the Bible I'd been given as a young girl, for the fineness of its paper being gouged by Maurice's pen point. There was M. Motté, spruced up and gaunt. There was the carpenter's little boy scuttling across in front of the altar. There was Mme. Champion, spruced up and gaunt. My Bible was open near the beginning, therefore Maurice was reading the Old Testament. What was he underlining? My sores were getting better, I ought to thank God. No hurry. In came Mme. Zoungasse, swathed in her long veil of humility, coming to present her talents to God and the Virgin Mary. Had she suffered some great misfortune, had she committed some terrible sin before making her entrance? The aisle seemed to grow wider. We hadn't noticed that the priest was already there, that the Mass had begun. The pedals squeaked, the harmonium moaned. Time to pray for Maurice. What should I ask. That he never leave me. I would have liked to be united to him there and then, so as not to leave him, and there I was, even in church, being forced to perform this comedy of free love. Ah! Mme. Zoungasse's return from the rail after taking communion, ah! those mystic sleepwalker's hands of hers. She wasn't going back to sit in her pew, she was going out to trail her pain and her communion with God through the woods and the forests. . . . I wondered why the church didn't burst out laughing and collapse on top of us all. The priest climbed into the pulpit, Maurice listened with folded arms, imitating the peasants. He gave me a bill of huge denomination and put another in the velvet bag himself when the collection was made. It was a folly. As we left church, "M. Maurice" won the old priest over completely.

Gérard was standing in the kitchen, one foot in front of the other, his arms hanging at his sides.

"This young boy has been waiting for you quite a while," M. Motté said with reproach in his eyes.

"Good morning," Gérard said, holding out his hand without looking at me, without raising his eyelids.

I sensed who was making those long lashes flutter so hard.

"I've put your duck in the oven," M. Motté said.

"Excellent, excellent," Maurice replied.

Gérard sat down in the place where Maurice always wrote. Legs crossed, arms around his knees, he listened to Maurice and gazed at him with the serious face of an adult. The necktie he'd put on, the knot loose because he didn't know how to tie it properly, his olive skin . . . He might have been an Oriental prince. Maurice was talking to him about Verlaine.

"I suggest we have a bottle of hard cider," Maurice said to M. Motté.

A knock at the door.

"Arnold!" Maurice exclaimed.

A young man of twenty-three appeared before us wearing blue overalls. His laughing, astonished Jewish face was further enlivened by the pieces of straw stuck in his curly hair.

Gérard was looking at the young man's comfortable espadrilles.

"I have to talk to Arnold," Maurice told us.

He picked up a book and handed it to Gérard. It was a collection of Guillaume Apollinaire's poems.

Gérard fled with his treasure, Maurice's door closed behind him.

I stayed stagnating in the kitchen; I wanted to follow M. Motté's example: he was attending to the duck in the oven, immersing one of his bottles of hard cider in a bucket of cold water. I couldn't move. Rejected by Maurice, rejected by Gérard, rejected by M. Motté, rejected by Arnold who didn't even know me. I couldn't recall a single embrace, a single moment of shared tenderness or abandon since we had arrived. I was living permanently on the defensive. I should have remembered the exercise books Maurice had given me to read and drawn strength and comfort from them, but I didn't remember them. Again, the sound of the chain, always the sound from the chain as the dog tried to work its way free. To run away, to go away and die of hunger with that emaciated dog . . . I should be free. Free of what? If I groveled at his feet . . . it was not impossible that he might say yes. His kindness, I would never risk it. A dunghill, such a coupling. I was farsighted, I would never ask for that. I was incapable of loving like Gérard, or forgetting myself like M. Motté. Gabriel, Hermine, Isabelle . . . I had remained a child who must be taken care of. An idiot woman jammed in neutral gear. Even if I'd had a friend of my own sex to visit me, it would have been no consolation. Seeing Maurice, hearing what Maurice had to say while the friend was visiting me. A praying mantis devouring herself. What was I to do?

The scent of their cigarettes seeped under the door. I caught a phrase here and there: you're eating, be patient. It's got to end. I'm fed up with it, they make me sweat for it. . . . The words Maurice and the young man were using steadied my nerves.

M. Motté was reading the local paper.

"The Russians are beginning to fight back," he commented.

He turned his head toward me. I saw a hero's courage in his eyes.

"Ah, if I was still young, my poor girl . . ."

". . ."

"Where is the young boy?" he asked.

Gérard came back just at that moment.

"I was reading in my room," he told M. Motté.

"That's as may be," said the old man.

The door opened.

"Come back whenever you like and don't lose heart," Maurice was saying.

Arnold was smoking greedily. He was radiating hope and health. He came over and gave us each a hearty handshake.

"I am dying of hunger. Let us eat, my children," Maurice said.

"Have you read *La Chanson du mal-aimé*?" he asked Gérard.

"I learned two poems," Gérard answered.

I was setting the table and looking at Gérard with his hands stuck deep into his pockets, magnificent in his loneliness and melancholy. The bread slipped from my hands. Gérard's immense, almond-shaped eyes had the power to drain away your energy.

M. Motté brought the duck and the bottle of hard cider to the table. Then he withdrew.

"It all looks quite perfect to me," Maurice said rubbing his hands together.

He dismembered the carcass of the duck, the cork from the cider bottle popped into the air.

"Do you know Arnold?" Maurice asked.

"I meet him sometimes," Gérard replied.

"Why don't you work on a farm like him?"

"Never," Gérard replied. "I don't understand them and they don't understand me."

"A fine excuse," Maurice said in a mocking tone as he poured some of the duck gravy onto Gérard's plate. "You'd always have enough to eat, you'd have hay to sleep on."

"Never," Gérard murmured. "I prefer my room."

"You call that a room? Well . . ."

"I can read there at night and I've got my candle," Gérard said.

Gravely, Maurice acquiesced in that.

"They say you're made of money," Gérard said, to change the subject.

"They're saying that we're made of money?" Maurice repeated. "That's perfect, absolutely perfect."

He was meditating on the possible profit to be reaped from such a reputation.

"My dear Violette," he said at the end of the meal, "you have dark circles under your eyes, you look tired. I would advise you to go and lie down with a book. Without weeping and without giving a performance of the first Mrs. Rochester in her attic."

I felt a hot wave of spite rise inside me because Maurice had taken me to task in front of Gérard. I raised my eyes to look over at Gérard. He was gazing at Maurice as we gaze at a chain of mountains in the dusk. The peaks exalt us and yet they are restful too.

". . . If you don't mind," Maurice went on, "I shall go and have a talk with this child in the shade of some tree or coppice."

There was nothing I could say. The careful way in which Maurice set about shaking me off upset me. Why did he depend on me? I always forgot his affection and friendship for me at those moments when I was convinced he was neglecting me, casting me aside.

Maurice picked up the book of Apollinaire poems again from the table.

"Are you ready?" he asked Gérard.

Gérard emitted a weird noise: a sob of happiness.

"Off we go!" Maurice said.

They went out.

I finished reading Maurice's last exercise book sitting on Gérard's chair, my free hand spread on the straw seat of Maurice's chair. I was making the most of what I had left. I closed the last exercise book and lay down on my bed in obedience to Maurice's instructions.

That Sunday evening, in my room:

"First I'd like to kiss you," I said to Maurice when he came in.

"Nothing could be more natural," Maurice replied. "Let us kiss one another, my dear."

Destructive beast, I thought to myself, needled by the expression "my dear," which I abominated.

Maurice leaned over my bed and deposited two of his little abstract kisses on my cheeks.

"I'm going to give you back your exercise books."

"As you like," Maurice said.

I leaped out of bed, I hugged him in my arms. He made no attempt to move.

"You'll catch cold," he said in a toneless voice, doubtless thinking this was an explosion of passion on my part.

I got back into bed and we drank a glass of calvados each.

"You've made it!" I said, handing my glass back to Maurice.

"Explain yourself," he replied.

"You've made it! You're a writer. You'd never really written anything till now, and now you've written a real book. I read it without pausing for breath. Believe me: it will make you. It's impossible for your book not to be a success. How happy it made me while I was reading it, how happy I still am. . . . What lucidity . . . I didn't think you were capable of writing this book, and now it's written."

Maurice Sachs was moved. I could see mistrust and joy fighting for possession of his face as he listened to me.

"Believe me."

"I believe you," he replied.

He sighed with contentment. We clinked our glasses together.

"May I make one criticism?"

"That goes without saying," Maurice answered.

"I would cut the passage about Cocteau. Cut it. . . ."

"Never," Maurice said.

"Why not?"

"Never. I suffered."

Maurice's face had hardened. I didn't insist.

The book written in those exercise books was published after the Liberation. It is called *The Witches' Sabbath*.

*

Next day, Maurice announced that he was intending to start doing business with some of the rich farmers in the neighborhood, that he was going to visit the Foulon place again where he had bought the duck, and charm Foulon, the biggest cattle merchant in the district, into helping him.

"You want to try and cheat them and they're the ones who'll end up cheating you. You think you're clever at these things, but they're cleverer than you are. We're not in Paris now. They haven't the time to be indulgent."

"So be it," Maurice replied. "A pity though. A man that rich . . ."

It had been a near thing.

He did go over to the Foulon place, but only to buy another duck, a half a pound of butter, and six eggs.

I bumped into one of the farmers' wives in the village square. She said: "I thought you'd left. The little boy who walks around with your gentleman, is he your son?"

I answered that we had no child; I refrained from adding: Gérard is becoming Maurice's child.

I told Maurice about my childhood, I talked to him incessantly about my mother without ever growing tired. I could see I bored him but I had to keep on because I was wooing him with my misfortunes. My misfortunes and I were winding ourselves around Maurice, but we could never be part of him.

Maurice had sent the fox jacket back to Paris, he had carried the package to the post office himself. Three and a half miles on foot. M. Motté watched sadly as Maurice pulled the string tight through its slip knot.

Every morning I went to give Mme. Bême warning that we wanted to have lunch at her place that day. Sometimes it was impossible because Nannan hadn't brought anything back. From time to time she sold us a joint of meat. If the meat was tough, next day Maurice would set about making his specialty: shepherd's pie. I prepared the mashed potatoes, M. Motté forced the handle of the meat grinder around, and Maurice, his dirty silk dressing gown girt about him, stubble on his chin, cupidity gleaming in his eye, went out searching for herbs in the kitchen garden; he laughed at the memory of a drag party he'd been to once with his friends, and the old man, without understanding, laughed at Maurice's laughter. Gérard arrived with energetic steps, his hair well combed, his clothes well brushed, his shoes badly polished. He distributed his three good mornings, then stationed himself in the middle of the kitchen to admire his friend, his father, his god. Maurice couldn't conceal his homosexual inclinations as he drew crisscross lines on the top of the shepherd's pie with the prongs of a fork. His little pouts, his bustling manner were beyond dispute. I watched him with a heavy heart. Gérard and M. Motté followed his decorative activities with the eyes of innocence.

Maurice began to remark more and more often that the air in Poitou was more bracing than the air in Normandy. The mists began. Autumn waited patiently in the woods. M. Bême had confided to Maurice that for thirty years he had been the head cloakroom attendant in the largest gambling club in Paris. Maurice got very excited. The suicides he'll have to tell me about! he said to me, the memoirs I'll be able to write for him!

Mme. Bême rose from her armchair. With her dainty feet in the sneakers that had been trodden down into mules, with her witty little feet, her plump little hands, her gray hair, very simply, Mme. Bême rose and went to join her husband beside the radio. They exchanged messages of love as they received the messages from London. They approved or criticized the various strategies. The customers were given good service when the news from the Anglo-French radio station was good, bad service when it was bad. M. Motté explained to me that he always judged how the war was going by watching M. Bême's face when he went around delivering telegrams to the farms. No one could forgive the Bêmes for living their own lives. It's terrible, they've beeen known to get up at ten o'clock. . . . Who is this mysterious Nannan they talk about? "You mustn't ask them," Maurice told me. We sat at their table to eat lunch and Maurice would buy vintage wine for us to share with them. He extolled the beauty of Paris to them, he fell in with their patriotism, he attempted to extract reminiscences from M. Bême. It was going to be difficult. M. Bême was suspicious. I sensed that they had guessed we weren't lovers. They were trying to discover what we were.

My life in the paradise of impossible love was obviously not satisfying to me because the state of my nerves was deteriorating steadily. Refused what any animal can find, I wallowed in sentimentality. I wept because the postman's little girl had frozen blue knees in the evening. She was four, she was in rags, you could see she was naked under her tatters. The branches of the apple trees, laden with fruit, were crawling in the long grass of the pastures, it was September, it was Maurice Sach's birthday. M. Motté, Gérard, and the young graduate were to be present at the festivities.

One night, I screamed and sobbed after talking to him for three hours about my unhappy childhood. "You shouldn't scream like that," M. Motté said to me in the morning. He was beginning to feel sorry for Maurice, he wanted to protect him from women. That's what I could read in his glassy eyes after I had screamed with my ovaries in the night.

Maurice refused to buy any shoes. He walked around in big, clumsy clogs and was quite satisfied. He said that he was becoming one of the villagers.

He read me the first twenty pages of what he'd written since we'd arrived. I interrupted him, laughing heartily:

"It's *Colette Baudoche*!"

"I agree with you. I'll write something else," Maurice replied with a laugh.

We continued to dine on milky coffee, bread and butter, egg custard, baked potatoes, and fresh cream. One evening I began to stamp and grind my teeth as I was breaking up the dry twigs to light M. Motté's kitchen stove. Maurice came out of the room where he was working, took the twigs from my hands, and told me that I was tired, that I ought to go to bed, that he would bring my dinner up to me. I obeyed without pleasure, I left the doors open. I listened.

"Leave that be, M. Maurice," the old man said. "I've got a way with fires."

Maurice began getting dinner. Annoyed at my own tantrums, annoyed at the way he put up with them, I lay bleeding. We ate dinner together in my room. I didn't desire Maurice. I desired the hell of our life together.

*

Maurice said to me next day: "Your unhappy childhood is beginning to bore me to distraction. This afternoon you will take your basket, a pen, and an exercise book, and you will go and sit under an apple tree. Then you will write down all the things you tell me.

"Yes, Maurice," I said, feeling upset.

He will read what I've written, he'll tell me it's no good, I said to myself at three that afternoon. I put the pen, the paper, and some blotting paper in my basket.

A tree to choose, a road to be taken. Why not begin with a good afternoon to Mme. Meulay? . . . The crossroads was waiting for me, the house was cool, Mme. Meulay was complaining in the lower part of the village, Gérard was waiting for Maurice. He was waiting to love Maurice in the Apollinaire poems Maurice would recite. Literature leads to love, love leads to literature.

I took the road alongside the stubble field. The cry came out of the earth. Larks, fireworks display spread over the earth, where were you? I was walking by heart, and with dry eyes I wept. Garlands of cattle sleepwalking beside the wire fences and the gates. I hid myself in the hedge, I saw a world at liberty. Write. Yes, Maurice. Later.

The mane was weeping over the eyes of the horse. He was the most diligent, the most self-effacing. The sow was too naked, the sheep was overdressed. A chicken was in love with a cow. She was following it, caged between four legs. Should I move on? I could never be tired of watching the foal following its mother. A heifer began to run. I waited for harmony to be restored before I moved on.

Lucid sparkles on the Métro steps, I have not forgotten you. The poem that swells my throat until it is as big as a goiter will be the poem I like best. Let me not die before the music of the stars is enough for me.

Sitting beneath an apple tree laden with green and pink apples, I dipped my pen in the inkwell and, with my mind a blank, I wrote the first sentence of *L'Asphyxie:* "My mother never gave me her hand." Light with the lightness Maurice had given me, my pen had no weight. I went on writing with the carelessness and the facility of a sailing ship blown before the wind. The innocence of a beginning. "Tell the paper about your childhood." I told the paper. The fury of a peacock in the meadow, its metallic chuckles, interrupted me. The peacock fell silent again, my pen lay at rest beneath the flight of two butterflies chasing one another. The birds suddenly stopped singing and then I sucked my penholder: the pleasure of foreseeing that my grandmother was about to be reborn, that I was going to bring her into the world; the pleasure of foreseeing that I would be the creator of my grandmother whom I adored, of my grandmother who adored me. To write . . . That seemed superfluous to me as I remembered my tenderness for her, her tenderness for me. I wrote to obey Maurice. I am afraid of damp. I stopped writing when I felt the grass wetting my skirt.

That evening, I showed Maurice my homework. He read, I waited for him to give me my good marks or my bad marks.

"My dear Violette, there is nothing left for you now but to continue," he said to me.

*

The evening before last, on my stone footbridge in the Vaucluse, the shooting star slid across the sky just at the moment when Richter let his hands fall from the keyboard. From my stone footbridge I can also see the flame of the holy sacrament at nightfall. It covers the little barred window of the church with fire. That is what was waiting for me when I suffered the pangs of love in churches. I counted the lighted candles, the tallest tapers, the tapers that lay extinct in their pool of tallow. I counted the women praying, I counted the blooms in the offerings of flowers, I counted the number of steps echoing over the flagstone floor. A tragedy, because I noticed an empty blue pack of Gauloises in one of the side aisles, another tragedy because I came across another empty pack outside the church door. Who was pursuing me with these empty cigarette packs scattered in my path? Who was this indefatigable foe? In Paris or here, when I have finished writing and walk out of the apartment building or strike out from the path over the hill, if I encounter a turd it destroys all my hours of work. That's what my pages are, it, him. Every turd I encounter is a torment every hour of the day. At night, the smell of them through the open window sneers at my next day's work. I shall write all the same. I want to be strong, like my mended basket hanging from the branch of a young oak, away from the ants, between the rocks where I am working. Yesterday I was sitting in X's basement. She combed my hair with her pocket comb. I told her that her comb in my hair felt like tenderness, that it was like kisses given to an old woman warming herself in the sun. How starved I must be! A thread. If it snaps I shall begin weeping again for a week, for months, for years. I shall blow my nose noisily, I will not weep.

*

We lit wood fires in our room, Maurice threw pine cones into the blaze; at midnight we ate baked apples covered with fresh cream. I sat facing him, he talked to me about Elie Faure, about Kant, about Plato, my cheeks were roasting. There was a jug warming. He thought I understood him because I was listening. I didn't dare ask him if Gérard was intelligent. He must have been because his capacity for suffering at the age of twelve was unlimited.

Maurice's birthday lunch was a success. Maurice, pleased with the way he'd set the kitchen table, was rubbing his hands, convinced that one year more was really quite a good thing after all.

"M. Motté is out in his hedge," I told them.

We went over to the window. M. Motté was wandering in and out of the bushes; he was picking something.

"Hey," he cried out from the kitchen doorway. (He shook Maurice's hand.) "This is the first time I've given anyone flowers," he said with a smile.

His bunch of flowers and leaves looked like the ones Maurice used to pick. M. Motté must have watched him arranging them in the vases.

The thunderclap:

"My dear, if you don't mind . . ."

"Don't call me 'my dear.' Please, please don't call me 'my dear'!"

"What a state of nerves you're in! You really must see a psychoanalyst. My dear Violette, if you want us to go on living here, you will have to go and make us some more money in Paris. I haven't a penny left."

"Why didn't you tell me before?"

So many glasses of calvados drained at a gulp, so many cigarettes gone up in smoke: the past was suddenly cutting my supply lines.

My head began to spin.

"Where do you expect me to find money?"

Maurice, for economy's sake, was now rolling our cigarettes in a roller.

"My dear, women can always find a way out of things. . . ."

"I won't be able to get any money. It's impossible."

Maurice gave me the cigarette he had just rolled: it was more tightly packed than the ones he usually made.

"Then we must go back to Paris and you will have to go back to your own home," he said.

His harshness was a ruse.

"I'll go, I'll try," I said.

I was ready to go through anything if only I could be allowed to go on living my obscure, insensate life with Maurice. I left next morning.

I was waiting for my connection, meditating on the platform of the station at L—, when a fat woman with a soothing manner accosted me.

"I know you. . . ."

"I don't know you."

"I can sell you some meat whenever you want any," she said.

The train came into the station. The fat woman laden with two tightly crammed bags was trotting along the platform. Men and women were leaning out the windows and shouting after her: "How are things, Charlotte?"

My room with its moldy, shut-up smell made me feel queasy. I rushed around to Louis Gervais, the hairdresser, like a young girl feverish for a glimpse of the young man she adores. The hairdresser loaned me ten thousand francs. When I got home, the concierge handed me a telegram from Maurice: "Come back quickly. Big wood fire waiting for you. A thousand loving thoughts." I became discouraged. I read ten thousand francs between each word. We wouldn't get far with a sum like that. That night, I took out my winter clothes, my white rubber boots. Maurice was expecting a trunk of books and clothes from the South.

Sitting in the bus taking me back to the village, I hid three of the ten thousand francs in the silver-studded, gray kid billfold Maurice had given me. I'll reveal my little store to him when we have nothing else left, I told myself. His prodigality filled me with panic now. I was hoping he'd meet me at the bus stop. No one. I recognized Didine. She was bent beneath the weight of a large carry-all. The countryside was fading. Points of gold were heralding the return of long evenings spent in kitchens and cow-sheds. An empire? A decline? A setting sun. I dropped my suitcase onto the kitchen floor and knocked at the door of Maurice's room. He didn't answer. I went in. I didn't recognize the room. Filthy, chaotic. Red wine spilled on the mantel and on the table. Maurice, with a dishcloth around his waist in lieu of an apron, was swishing some bowls and plates around in a basin of greasy water. Gérard was wiping.

"I wasn't expecting you so soon," Maurice said.

"Off you go," he said to Gérard.

I found his dependence on a woman distasteful.

He hugged me in his arms. His embrace put the finishing touch to my depression.

I gave him the seven thousand francs. The money I had handed over to him, the money I had hidden in my suitcase before going to bed, lay between us.

*

Every day the leaves with their washes of tawny gold, of rust, of purple, of copper, of bronze, of verdigris, of old rose, of orange, of plum, of ruby, of bilberry, held a new surprise for us. One day the dull thunder of cardinal red, the next day a clash of cymbals from a russet bush. We took walks out along the road to Notre-Dame du Hameau where there was a house we coveted; its tiny, languid blue towers filled us with excitement.

"I'd buy it," Maurice said, "I'd turn it into a luxury hotel, women patrons would come out from Paris and ride on my horses dressed in riding habits, or else in jockey suits. The people staying would give parties. . . . We would make a fantastic fortune. What?"

"Nothing. I was listening."

The storks had come back, the lake was thick with marsh hens once again. Maurice was at pains to tell me that the climate was more bracing in Poitou, that houses were easier to rent down there. We would get a really nice one, then we'd settle down to write without a worry in the world. He was going to find a house for us down there if he could get an advance out of the art publisher he was in correspondence with. I had no faith in his schemes.

Ten minutes later, I took his arm: "A little house in Poitou, Maurice?"

"I just said so."

"How will we find it, Maurice, this little house?"

"I'll go and look for it."

"And Gérard?"

"He'll go back to Paris."

"That's impossible."

"He'll get himself taken on at a farm."

"He doesn't want to."

"What is it you want me to say?" Maurice snapped impatiently.

All our unnecessary luxuries: a glass of calvados, a cigarette lit from the previous cigarette, a meal at the Bêmes'. What would become of us when Maurice had given away all the bills I'd brought back, the bills I'd hidden? Had he searched my suitcase? The bills were still in the same place. He had called me The Ant. I would be the disloyal Ant.

Maurice maintained that there was a mint of money to be made from anthologies. He suggested we compile an anthology of all the most beautiful love letters ever written, an anthology of all the most beautiful religious texts, an anthology of all the most erotic texts. He said we could make money by sending parcels to his friends: he would draw up a list. Why? We would be leaving soon for Poitou. I didn't understand, I didn't want to understand.

The post office where the clerk accepted parcels without asking questions was two miles from our village. Maurice wanted to walk there in clogs. He put his old shoes back on because I insisted. We sent a duck to Paris. He said we wouldn't do it again. He had some sort of gland trouble; the one trip had exhausted him.

He had a long conversation with Arnold. Arnold looked at me very sternly as he emerged from Maurice's workroom. Had they been discussing me? Was it because of the money I'd hidden? Because of my ill nature? Because of my nerves? Poor Arnold, who had been a jewelry salesman and now worked on a farm . . .

"Stop wearing that graveyard expression," Maurice said to me one evening.

I had been weeping night and day for the previous two days.

The art publisher sent a telegram. It was settled: Maurice was to go to Paris; I was to stay behind. I was afraid. Maurice alone in Paris, Maurice arrested in a Paris street. He was going to stay with Curly's mother. One week, just enough time to look around, raise some money, coax an advance out of the art publisher, then he would go down to Poitou. "That's where I shall find it again," he said. I listened, I was dying of grief inside. Every second before the time for him to leave was already a separation, a thousand separations as I stood with folded arms, with legs of jelly, with soaking handkerchief, and watched him pack and organize his imminent departure. He was calm, that made me sob even harder. I would have walked barefoot around the world to keep him. He was taking all his meager possessions with him. He put his toilet articles and his manuscript in a leather briefcase, he gave me back my Bible. I was dying because of his serenity. Women often die by slow degrees from men's equanimity. I died while he took great pains packing the duck for Curly's mother. His washing hadn't come back. He stroked my hair and went off to collect the laundry from Mme. Meulay. He did everything himself, he asked for no help. He was going to leave with Arnold's raincoat on his back, with Arnold's shoes on his feet. What a nice guy he is, Maurice said, they're the only pair he has and he won't let me send them back. There are great and immediate friendships sometimes that might easily pass unobserved. M. Motté had no idea what was going on. I chanted: Poitou, Poitou so as to make myself go numb.

Maurice went to bed first, I stood at the foot of his bed to chat a little while longer with him. The gentleness in his eyes filled me with terror. As if his destiny had crumbled into dust between my fingers.

He was to leave M. Motté's house the following morning at five, then he would walk as far as the little town where we had arrived the first evening. There he would wait for the bus to L—. It was raining that evening, the village was drowned in mists. M. Motté wished Maurice a good journey, he thought he was to see him again in four or five days. He was contemptuous of my red eyes and my wan face. That night, the whole village, the entire countryside mourned Maurice's departure with a great rain that would not stop. My grief, that night, called for no less than the great organs of the rain playing in the gullies and the water-butts.

My watch never once left the palm of my hand. Maurice had said good-by to me, he didn't want me to get up when he left. I got up, I went down in my nightgown. Hunched beneath the torrential rain, carrying his briefcase in one hand and the package of provisions in the other, bundled into his clothes rather than dressed, Maurice pushed open the gate with groping hands as he scolded me for getting up. I kissed his wet cheeks beneath the turned-down brim of his hat. I had never seen so much mist and so much rain until that morning. Maurice walked down the hill and disappeared into the mist. I said to myself: I shall never see him again, it's over.

Smashed with fatigue, dry-eyed, I went back to bed. I slept for fourteen hours.

❁
*

Two days later, the rumor reached me that Gérard was sick: jaundice. He had been more shaken by Maurice's departure than anyone.

I went into his awful little room for the first time. Four walls, an iron bedstead, a chair. Sitting up in bed, wearing his wretched pajamas, he looked like a child who'd been kidnapped. His eyes were dim with the bile. Without opening his mouth, he was asking me if I would like us to share our grief. I pulled up his bedclothes and told him that one must be careful not to get chilled when one has jaundice. I wouldn't sit down. The intensity of his love for the father he had found at last, then lost again, filled me with a disconcerting feeling of respect.

"Do you have any news?" he asked.

"It's too soon. You know he only left the day before yesterday."

"Yes, I know," Gérard said.

I shook his hand as I left. The nails were yellow.

M. Motté increased the rent; he told me that if I wanted to heat the downstairs room I'd have to pay him for the wood.

Go back to Paris? The idea never even occurred to me. I read over the list of Maurice's friends I could provide with food.

Now Maurice had gone, I was able to hide away from M. Motté and use my douche again. The doctor who treated me while I was staying at my mother's had told me it was necessary. Sitting in the darkness of the dilapidated kitchen, I waited for the saucepan of water to start bubbling, then to cool down. It was a disaster the first evening. I sank the feet of the chair into the eiderdown on my bed and placed the douche on the chair. Then I climbed onto the bed and squatted down. My posture was so ungracious, my condition so humiliating that I drew a sort of consolation from the fact. I lost my balance, the chair fell over, and the purple water spilled onto the eiderdown.

I stood killing time at Mme. Meulay's, reading her calendar from the year before. She will sell me all the eggs I want, I said to myself. Suddenly a ray of sunshine was rejuvenating the landscape, caressing a sloping pasture. Ungratefully, I left. Some bullocks in a paddock looked at me, their eyelashes overwhelmed me. It was spring in November. Oh, those vistas of blond beams! Now Maurice wasn't there I was beginning to see where I stood: in a village where the paths counted more than the inhabitants. Go back to Paris? I thought to myself. The tight, plump buds of the chrysanthemums were showing me the prosperity piled up in November barns. The caramel smell of the cider apples was wandering through the air, the angelus bells ringing in the distance were my fancies. They were ringing down there in my garden of orange blossoms. To become young again, to become light, to become strong. The change in me had to be celebrated. I treated myself to a calvados and a meal at the Bêmes'. And Maurice? Forgotten? Maurice was busy finding us a house.

The following week I received an envelope from Paris on which I recognized the writing of my concierge. I opened it and pulled out a postcard addressed, in a different handwriting, to my apartment in Paris. I was blinded by tears of rage.

On Sunday I took my Bible and occupied our usual place in church. I had promised myself that I would imitate Maurice even down to the intonations of his voice, so as to win over the village in the same way he had done. The church without him had no savor. My putting paper money in the velvet collection bag was simply a piece of mimicry: I promised myself I wouldn't do it again. I leafed through the Old Testament and discovered that Maurice had underlined all the passages that could be construed as having some connection with the deportation of the Jews and their extermination. During the elevation of the Host, I remembered a scene in Maurice's bedroom: we were talking at midday in front of the open window when we heard a clattering. A flock of a hundred or so sheep was coming toward us from the direction of Mme. Meulay's, all with their profiles toward us. The Jews, Maurice said sadly. He closed the window. But he, he could have waited the war out in the village. He should have waited, anything was better than going away as he had. Why had he written to me at my Paris address on a postcard? We could have parted and lived near each other at the same time. He in one house in the village, I in another. If it hadn't been for my concierge, the postman would have read the card, then the whole village would have known. The police closed their eyes to things, it was he who had told me so. Money? It was he again who had told me that we could send parcels and make a profit. I will always maintain that he could have waited out the war there in the village. He had thought only of himself and he had deceived me. Hamburg! He was mad. He thought that he would be stronger than they and that was folly. What was he expecting when he left for Normandy? If only I knew! It must have been lack of money that forced him to sign on as a voluntary war worker; after all, it would have been perfectly possible for him to seek refuge in Poitou without my knowing he was there. And then, the longing for travel was gnawing at him. His East, his Lebanon . . . The great writers who traveled. Flaubert, my dear. Gide, my dear. Lawrence of Arabia, my dear. If he had told me the truth before leaving me . . . I would have tried to understand him and make him change his mind.

When Gérard was convalescing, I went for a walk with him one afternoon. We ran into the young graduate; the wind in our backs was skirmishing with the trees.

"I was looking for you," he said. "No news," he added in a disheartened voice.

"I've heard. Maurice has signed up."

I showed him the postcard.

"Poor Maurice," he said. "Things can't have gone as he hoped. Where is he?"

"In Hamburg."

"He says he'll send you his address. That means it's not all over."

"And that trunk of his that's supposed to be coming . . ."

"So he didn't know he was going to volunteer! Will you go back to Paris?"

"I shall stay here. I'm going to send parcels."

"Be careful, it's dangerous."

Stay, stay. I won't lose Maurice a second time, Gérard's big eyes were saying to me.

I had moved into Maurice's workroom, I threw pine cones into the fire, the flames flickered up into the chimney. M. Motté half opened the door.

"Ah! I'm just saying good night," he said every evening.

In Paris, sharp cracking noises make me uneasy. I think there are enemies tormenting me or spying on me. But the explosions from my wood fire in the village . . . resolves, decisions, the crackling of the energy inside me. I sat writing my childhood reminiscences as fast as my pen would go, sheltered from the lashing gusts of rain, deep in night and solitude. I am a woman keeping vigil, a woman who is sufficient unto herself in the darkness of the countryside, I said to myself as I put out the fire before going to bed. I looked at Maurice's things. The mica box for watching the inside of an anthill, the wicker heart for curdling milk . . . I felt I was huge and sad like cold ashes.

I set my suitcase down in the middle of Maurice's worktable and counted my money. I had enough to buy a half-pound of butter for one of Maurice's friends.

One warm morning I walked over to visit Mme. Foulon. She was cleaning out a separator, she didn't say good morning. I knew about her tragedy. Her little boy had hanged himself at boarding school with his honeycomb towel. The day the cold body of her son was brought back to the farm, Mme. Foulon, without a tear, had milked the cows and cleaned the separator exactly as she was doing the day I visited her. Her nobility sprang also from her virility, from the ampleness of her figure, and from the limpidity of her gaze.

"What do you want?" she asked, brutally.

"I'd like a duck. . . . Your ducks are so good. . . . Maurice used to come to you. . . ."

"Why didn't he come today?"

"He can't. They've arrested him."

Silence.

"He wrote articles against them at the beginning of the war. They recognized him. They took him away."

Silence, silence.

"He's in Germany. He's been made to work for them."

The silence still continued. I waited, completely cast down.

She didn't believe my lie, they would none of them believe my lie. Where would I go? What would become of me?

Mme. Foulon brought me a half-pound of butter on a cabbage leaf.

"You must send him parcels," she said.

"Shall I be able to have a duck?"

"We'll see."

It took me three attempts to pack up my half-pound of butter properly. I picked out a name on Maurice's list of friends, wrote an accompanying note, and set out with a beating heart carrying my package. Hamburg, I said to myself quietly as I went along the road. I saw several peasant women cycling along with piles of parcels tied to their bikes.

Mine was the smallest.

"Register it," a slip of a woman said to me. "Then they'll get it tomorrow."

She was holding a whole pile of parcels in front of her, one on top of the other, all waiting to be sent.

"It's not absolutely necessary to register it. It's only small," the post-office clerk said to the little woman. "And it can't be foodstuffs any-way. . . ."

"It's butter!"

"Hush! I don't want to know that," the clerk said to me.

Two women in the line were chanting to one another about the unseasonable warmth of the weather, about the advantages of sending their rabbits with the skins still on.

Bring me luck, I said to the billfold Maurice had given me, when the receipt for my parcel was finally inside it.

I walked back to the village buzzing inside with hopes and future plans. I saw the piled-up parcels and the brown ringlets of the little woman again—a dead tree at the side of the road with curly branches.

That evening Gérard told me how bored he was, how he could find nothing to do but mend his bicycle all day. He called it his old crock. A poor child sacrificed by us all. He sat near the little table in front of the fireplace and warmed himself while I ate my dinner of café au lait and the white bread M. Motté sold me whenever he did a baking. He asked me to read him what I was writing. His eyes shone. I told him about the expeditions I was planning; he approved, and quivered in sympathy with my resolves. After giving me a manly handshake he left to go back to his little room, where he went on reading poems by the light of a candle.

"A letter, a package, and a money order," the postman cried, happy to have made me happy.

Maurice's friend thanked me for my initiative with some books and a sum of money. He was sending me what I longed to read: *The Diary of a Seducer* from Kierkegaard's *Either/Or*. He explained that his mother would like me to send eggs, meat, and another half-pound of butter. Things looked promising. I had begun, I was already a businesswoman, I had made a profit. The eggs? Mme. Meulay, forsooth. I set out without losing a moment.

Shutters closed, arms of the village cross wide open, Mme. Meulay wasn't at home.

M. Motté didn't leave his kitchen stove except to go to bed. He followed my comings and goings with a magnifying glass. I weighed more heavily on his house since Maurice's departure.

"You came and you didn't see me! I was out in the field. I was looking for my little chickens," Mme. Meulay said.

We chatted.

"Eggs are just unobtainable," I threw in at random.

Intoxicated by my own daring, I lit a cigarette in front of Mme. Meulay.

"Those that have eggs are those that have the grain to harvest," she said bitterly.

"And you haven't any at all!"

"Two dozen."

"How much do you get for them?"

"Oh I get a good price. You'd be wanting them for M. Maurice, I suppose? They'll break on the way, poor dear. How much will you give me?"

"Double. I'll pay you double for my friends in Paris."

"They're big eggs, mark you, they'll be pleased with them."

"Will I be able to have more later?"

"We'll see what we can do."

I paid her before viewing the merchandise.

"I'll pluck your ducks for you, you're a good soul," she said.

Yes, yes, money is good for the soul, it revives it.

"My ducks!" I said, bewildered. "What ducks do you mean?"

"Mme. Foulon's ducks. Now she, she has the means to raise them, you see."

"They're so hungry in Paris. . . . If only I could find some meat for them," I said as I made to leave.

I was playing my little comedy well.

"Meat is it? Mme. Bême knows all about that, with that crowd always at her place. . . ."

I rushed to visit Mme. Bême.

"Poor M. Maurice," Mme. Bême said. "Have you heard anything?"

"It's still too soon."

"Yes, you're right, it's still too soon," M. Bême agreed, confusing Maurice with the end of the war.

Mme. Bême was preparing what seemed to be no ordinary rabbit pâté: she told me that Nannan sold meat at Charlotte's house.

"Three houses along from ours."

"You can go up. They were kicking up a terrific shindy a moment ago," a blonde mother with a blonde baby on her arm told me.

It was complicated finding my way in. Up two steps, then a door off its hinges to open. The stairway squeezed at the end of a passage creaked and shook. I slipped. There was also the black rectangle of a missing tread to be negotiated. I knocked at the door at the top. I could hear paper rustling and flabby, thumping sounds. The door finally opened.

"I know you," cried the fat, soothing woman. "I know her, she was on the platform. . . . In the future you must give two knocks. Come in."

I went in. I was immediately and pleasantly overwhelmed by the heat. I sat down at the horseshoe table.

"Isn't she pretty, my daughter! That's my Pierrette there, madame."

"Be quiet," the young girl said.

"You're molded out of velvet," I told her.

Charlotte tipped back her chair and laughed happily.

"If you could hear the way she sings . . ."

"You talk about me as though I'm a doll!"

"You're prettier than a doll," Charlotte replied.

Made up, though she had no need of cosmetics, Pierrette was an ardent beauty. I looked at her, I was biting into a raspberry.

The young girl was humming the hit tune from *Rio Grande.*

"I came for some meat. . . ."

We moved closer together.

"Don't talk so loud," Charlotte said.

"You shout!" Pierrette said.

"How dare you speak to me like that! If my son-in-law were to find out . . ."

"Are you married?" I asked the child.

"I'm going to be. I shall soon be fifteen."

"About the meat. Do you think there's any hope?"

"How much would you want?"

They looked at me with avidity.

"Not very much at first," I answered, ill at ease. "I have friends I still have to write to."

"Nannan is out looking for some animals," Charlotte said.

"If you want some you shall have some, don't worry," Pierrette said.

I told Gérard everything that had happened.

*

There was a knock on my shutters at about half-past nine in the evening. I put down my pen and stubbed out my cigarette. I opened the door, the night poured into the kitchen. I went out: there was a man flattened against the shutters of my room.

"Are you Nannan?"

"Yes, I'm Fernand."

He followed me inside, then pulled open his summer jacket and produced a package.

"Your meat."

He unfolded the paper.

"Does it come up to expectations?"

"I'd be difficult to please if it didn't."

It was a slice of sirloin.

A piece of wood in the fireplace exploded. He looked toward it with the eyes of a little boy dazzled by fireworks.

"Cigarette?"

"Cigarette. How much do I owe you?"

"A light?"

"A light."

I lit my cigarette at the flame of his turquoise blue lighter.

"You've got a nice place here," he said.

He looked at my sheets of paper on the table.

"You working?"

"Yes, I'm writing. You still haven't told me how much."

He studied me: "We'll see each other again. Come around to the Bêmes', I go there."

I enjoyed watching the way he smoked.

"How fresh it is," I said, lowering my eyes to the meat.

"Marbled too."

The ash from his cigarette fell on the tile floor.

Aware of his error, he drew my attention to it deliberately with a motion of his chin.

"Will you bring me more of this beautiful meat?"

M. Motté came back into the kitchen. He was muttering testily to himself.

"I'll give you as much as you want," Fernand said in a low voice.

"Door ought to be locked this late," M. Motté said.

Fernand leaned against the door. He laughed noiselessly, displaying his two broken front teeth. He gestured over his shoulder with thumb bent back, pointing into the kitchen where M. Motté was clattering about in his clogs.

"Ah! I'm just saying good night," M. Motté said into Fernand's back.

I said good night to him as I usually did.

"Old skinflint," Fernand said in a low voice.

I made no reply.

"Shall I go?"

He leaped over to the little table with a single bound.

"I'm off. There are people waiting for me," Fernand said.

He opened the windows, then the shutters. He leaped out into the night.

If he were my lover, it would have been just like that, I said to myself as I closed the window again.

I searched in the hearth for Fernand's cigarette butt. Men like that never leave anything behind.

Out with the light, I said to myself, the moment has come for a review of this event. My fists pressed against my eyes, my breath restricted to the eye of a needle, the darkness in my veins and in my arteries, I span, I wove, I imprisoned the moments. Love at first sight is also a banquet. How pale he was, Fernand. Where did he get that youth of his, like a dog shaking himself as he runs out of the water? From his untrammeled vitality. The first time I met him, Fernand the slaughterer, was when I was warming my hands at the brazier of a chestnut vendor. In another life, it goes without saying. The wind was blowing on green throats in the wheat. That great wind, that bearer of gifts was Fernand. Was it a face? No, blows of a fist rather.. Heavy cheekbones, framework and architecture by the cartload. Pummeled from brow to chin. He's gone. Another day he'll bring me stars picked from the bramble branches along the paddock hedges. What was that flame in his eye? A bird as it waits. "Women should be slaves." Dear old Maurice Sachs. Tonight your axioms are my trampoline and I am dancing all alone. This evening I am Fernand's slave and, believe me, Maurice, it is no slavery. My flower was no longer my flower while I lived with you, Maurice Sachs. . . . A spider's web between the pages of your Plato. The conspiracy in Fernand's throat: the laugh in his voice as he talked. A man standing there, in silence: an adventure. His tattered pack of cigarettes, his two broken front teeth, his espadrilles the color of country roads when the dusk begins to howl.

Gérard told me that one rainy night, rolling with thunder and pierced by lightning, Fernand had come back on foot from a village a long way away with a live sheep on his shoulders. Waiting anxiously, the women had prayed for him. Then, so that the meat should have time to cool and the customers not have to leave empty-handed, Fernand had killed the sheep beside the stove as soon as he arrived, without warming himself or changing. He skinned it, ate, then cut it up.

*

I received a letter from Maurice. The pages had been withered by the crisscross pencil of the censor. He told me that he was getting up at five in the morning, then leaving the work camp with the others and being incarcerated until evening inside the cabin of a crane. The camp life suited him. At bedtime, the others came to ask him for advice. He also described his last evening with his editor in a Paris restaurant: he had paid for the meal. He asked me to send tobacco, his old shoes, food. Gérard was not forgotten. I read the letter through several times that same day.

Sunday, August 27, 1961. Opening of the hunting season in a village of the Vaucluse. I have changed my place. Hidden amongst the broom bushes I could be taken for a rabbit if the bushes moved. Here I am on the fringes of a pine wood, a game preserve in which the livestock is allowed to breed unmolested. The lavender has all been scorched, the hive is deserted. But I have known that floating hive over the mystic vapor of the lavender in flower when it was still full of life. The elegant stunt-flying of the light-winged birds. The feats of a bumblebee swinging on his trapeze from lavender stem to lavender stem. Happiness, that morning, was the weight of the insects and the birds on those flexible stems. Now the cicadas are singing in the distance, and that's how I prefer it. A crescendo of solitude at the end of the morning, and yet the smell of the pines is here to keep me company.

I had come back onto the sand on the hill above Jaux, I was eating my lunch, and at one o'clock in the afternoon I saw Vincent Van Gogh sitting against an olive tree wearing his market porter's straw hat. I could see him just as I could see my bread and my own hands.

Another money order, more compliments, and a list of Bernadette's friends. Butter, send us butter. I tore my hair. Where was I to find butter for them? Let us sit, let us talk this thing out, enormous udders, unseemly pendulums swaying beneath the herds. Where is this butter? The cows were sunk deep in their heavy dreams, they turned away from me as I passed by. Every pot of cream was a torture to me. Without butter I wouldn't be able to sell them anything, with butter I could sell them everything. I begged Gérard to keep his eyes open, to spy for me. I had to wait as patiently as I could for several days.

"It's off the beaten track, several miles away, but try. You mustn't be seen on the road. You might run into the inspectors and get picked up. You mustn't be seen by the stationmaster either, or by so and so, or so and so, or by Mme. this, or by Mme. that," Gérard told me finally.

I set out and the journey went to my head. I chose indecisive paths, sometimes hidden by swaths of old grass indifferent to the elements. I left the village behind me, I walked on with my basket and Maurice's basket slung on my arms, my hands stuck deep in my pockets, a cigarette in my mouth. My thirst for profit, my love of the country increased at every step. An orgy of pastureland. I skirted meadows, I crossed meadows, I crawled, I wriggled on all fours under bramble branches. . . . The dry cold lent beauty to my great nose. I sniffed the wind and sun with my weasel's snout. I stopped frequently to wrestle with poplar trees, I made my way around a silo. I patted a bullock. Would I make it? I asked the trees engraved with winter's dry-point on the sky. My lips slid over my wrist. That was where the country had imprinted its kiss on me. My thirst for butter, my thirst for gold when I glimpsed coppery leaves . . . The indifference of a horse standing alone in a paddock, that was my vitamins and my bath that morning. I was coming into the world with little wings on my heels. Cartier, Van Cleef, Mauboussin . . . That rusty juniper tree! Meadows of Normandy, green in winter, I drank you as we used to drink our Sandeman's port. All those avenues through the trees: so many organ pipes playing into the distance. The blue of the sky was an avenue. The wind rose into a region where the last leaves were quivering as I had quivered when I was sixteen.

I like long paths leading up to farms through haughty solitude, I like the muslin veil that comes from chimneys facing out on woods and undergrowth. I was almost there.

I walked into their paddock. A young girl was killing a rabbit. I called out to ask if it was all right to go in. She ran off with the rabbit; its head bumped flaccidly against the wall.

An old woman was beating a bunch of dry beans on the tiled floor.

"Oh my God! How you frightened me. Did anyone see you come in?"

She cut in again before I had time to speak.

"Why have you come to us? Who sent you?"

Her fright distressed me. It had been so gay, the bean pods exploding against the tiles, it was so gay, that transparent early day in winter.

I managed to explain that I was looking for butter. She went pale.

At that moment the young girl came in. She was wiping her hands on the apron around her waist printed with fresh blood.

"What's the matter, aunt?" she asked. "What's the matter with you?"

"She's asking for butter," the old woman said.

"Butter? Where do you think we're going to find butter for you?"

Then a man came in.

"Brother, she wants butter from us," the girl told him.

"Butter? Where do you think we could find butter?"

At that point another woman came in too, her apron filled with big, red apples. She almost curtsied to me. The polished surface of the scarlet fruit struck exactly the same chord as the glitter of the light between the bare branches of the trees.

"Mother, she wants butter," the girl said to her.

"Butter! We can sell you a rabbit. . . ."

A young man with a long Jesuit's face came in last.

"Son, she wants butter from us," said the woman.

"Butter, in the middle of the winter! It's like coming and asking for the moon," he said, unwinding his muffler.

There was fat heating in a deep frying pan; its smell made the kitchen more human.

Like an old robot, the aunt was walking around in a circle holding potatoes sliced ready for frying in a dish towel. The others applied themselves seriously to the business of eating. They took their places at the table. I sat down without asking permission.

"In Paris then, you have got a lot of friends there," the mother said.

"Let's see, what friends have I got in Paris? Lawyers, dress designers, playwrights, publishers. I also know some writers, some actors, some editors, some singers, some comedians. . . . They'll pay any price just to get food."

His dinner once demolished, the elder brother went out. The women breathed more freely.

I returned to the attack:

"You wouldn't have even a half a pound. . . . No?"

It was the girl who answered.

"Our cows are all in calf, and when a cow's in calf it doesn't give milk. Shall I show you the way?"

She weighed the corpse, all pink beneath its coating of ice. So many skinned rabbits every Saturday in Paris that I had looked at and not seen. The vociferous abandon of the open thighs held my gaze in a vise.

She calculated her price in a second and wrapped the animal in a piece of white cloth.

"I won't give you the skin," she said. "What would you do with it?"

"If you were to give me a big chicken instead!"

"Yes, chickens are allowed," the girl said.

She had put her apron back on, she walked across the farmyard like an amazon in her big rubber boots. She threw down some grain to attract the hen.

She caught it while I was eyeing a sumptuous cock.

"I kill them by cutting their tongues," she explained.

She cut its tongue. She worked sitting down like a cobbler.

"You must pluck it before you take it away. No one must know where it came from," the old woman said behind me.

"I don't know how to pluck it. . . ."

The girl was wrapping the head up in newspaper.

"I'll help you," the old woman said.

It was over: I could no longer see the open beak, that cruel little hole with the whole world's agony inside it. As the heart had given its rhythm to the creature's life, so the wings lent their rhythm to its death. It was over: it no longer seemed to be looking at me. That shutter lowering inside the eye meant that animals too feel the need for modesty in death. The wings beat less and less, the newspaper was soaked with blood. The corpse on our knees was stronger than a ghost. I was eating feathers, I was spitting feathers, I was tearing the skin, I was pulling at the spurs. At last, it was naked. My day had not been lost.

Gérard was waiting for me at a bend in the path.

"You took so long. . . ."

I told him all about it.

"I have a rabbit, I have a chicken. . . . But how much should I ask for them?"

"Listen," Gérard began, "last week I was repairing my bike in the railroad station. . . . There were people from Paris with suitcases waiting for the bus, and they were saying: 'I turned somersaults.' 'At that price you ought to turn somersaults, old boy.' Do you think they were talking about the prices they got for their food?"

"It's possible."

But what sum, what profit did that phrase "turn somersaults" represent?

"There've been all sorts of folk here asking for you," M. Motté said. "You must go up to Mme. Meulay's. Your washing is ready, she has something for you, the lady from Paris is waiting for you there, her daughter has come, Mme. Foulon has some ducks for you. Is that all? Yes, that's all."

I went back out immediately. I went up to Mme. Meulay's.

I had to listen to the usual refrain about the absence of happiness and the dearness of everything. How did she manage to wash in this freezing weather, standing in that wind in the half light?

"I can sell you four dozen," she said.

"Four dozen!"

"Yes, I've got my daughter's as well. You can decide the price, we don't know how."

I suggested a good price.

"You're not obliged to take them all," she added.

Away with you, old coquette!

I paid more for the eggs than the previous time.

"Your ducks in the fattening shed are in my way," Mme. Foulon said. "You can pay me and take them away with you."

"I can't pluck them tonight."

"They can spend the night on the floor."

"With their feet tied?"

"Just give them something to sleep on."

I went with Gérard to get some cigarettes from the woman who did my mending. She was waiting for me outside her little house besieged by hazel bushes. She took six packs out of the pockets of her long black skirt and I hid them in the pockets of my black topcoat.

The Bêmes' kitchen was full of Parisians and peasants.

"Fernand is looking for you," Mme. Bême told me. "Are you eating with us? I'm doing a boeuf à la mode."

"Nothing I'd like better," I replied with pleasure.

"Do you know where Nannan is?" she asked her husband.

"I'm waiting for him too," sighed Didine. "And the taxi'll be here in a quarter of an hour!"

"Us too, we're waiting for him," a couple said.

"And I'm the same as you. I'm waiting for him," a peasant said.

They were all smoking and drinking. Didine was eating her eggs. She blew her nose continually, in order, I am quite certain, to hear the click of her woman's weapon: the click of her handbag clasp as it snapped shut.

"I'm waiting for him too, for my boeuf à la mode," Mme. Bême said.

I asked for a slice of bread and pork pâté. Drugged by the warmth, the sound of their voices, the tobacco smoke, I hadn't the energy to take off my coat or my head scarf. I was turning over in my mind the costume I should wear to resell the stuff I'd bought. I'd put on my rabbit coat, then tie Maurice's dressing-gown cord around my waist. The others were looking at me as though I didn't belong. I was alone.

"Drinks all around!" cried Fernand as he walked in.

He removed his printed woolen scarf and wound it around M. Bême's neck. They all threw themselves upon him.

"Have you got any for me, Fernand? You promised me some."

"You told me you'd get me as much as I could carry, Fernand."

"I was counting on it, Fernand. I've had a lot of expenses this trip."

"Are you interested in a calf, Fernand? I can get you one. Milk-fed as well."

He wrapped his scarf around his right hand.

"How do you expect me to slaughter anything for you? Can't you see your slaughterer is wounded. No more dogs' dinners. Your dogs will have to go without their meat."

"Fernand . . . I already sent my telegram."

"The taxi's on its way, Fernand. Shall I come back tomorrow morning or shall I sleep here?"

Fernand unrolled the cloth from around his wrist as though it were a bandage.

"I was looking for you," he said to me.

The slice of bread and pork pâté dropped into my plate.

"Cigarette?"

"I've got one."

"Cigarette," he said sternly.

I took the cigarette he was offering me. He slid sinuously between the table and the bench.

"I'm slaughtering tonight. You'll all get your share. And you," he said to the peasant, "you say you've got a little something for me!"

"There's the calf but there's also the sheep," the peasant said. "What do you say?"

"I'll take it," Fernand said. "I know your farm, I know your livestock. Another drink all around! I'm a widower this evening. The girls are in Paris. Ah, I was only waiting for P'tit Paul, and here he is!"

"Evening all," said a short young man as he walked in.

"I'm slaughtering tonight and I'm counting on you," Fernand said to him.

"P'tit Paul is always where you are," M. Bême said.

Everyone left to complete their arrangements. The kitchen was empty. P'tit Paul sat down opposite Fernand.

"You wouldn't have a weed?" he asked, proud of his vocabulary.

Fernand threw a pack of cigarettes in his face.

"Keep it," he said.

"Can I?"

"That's what I said," Fernand replied.

"I'll buy a round," I said eagerly.

"I do the pouring," Fernand said. He picked up the bottle of calvados. P'tit Paul looked at me with tenderness in his eyes because I was giving Fernand something he liked.

"Mme. Leduc is going to be sending parcels to her friends," Fernand said.

"And why not?" Mme. Bême commented.

"They've got to keep their strength up somehow, our Parisians," M. Bême added as he turned on his radio.

"It's too early for the news, chicken," said Mme. Bême. M. Bême switched the radio off again.

"Now we have to run," Fernand told P'tit Paul. "I have the cleaver to see to, you have the knives to sharpen. I've got a new place. You'll see."

"I've got to talk to you about the hides," P'tit Paul answered.

He put his beret back on and pulled it straight over his smoothly combed hair.

I followed them outside. A pitch black night.

"The weather's on our side," P'tit Paul remarked.

"You were looking for me?" I asked Fernand.

P'tit Paul disappeared.

"I've reserved you the best cuts," Fernand said. "A leg, some cutlets . . ."

"A whole leg! How am I going to pack it?"

"We're eating at the Bêmes; after that you can come to my canary's."

"Your canary's?"

"To Pierrette's if you prefer. That's where I live. You've been there before. You'll have to hide your meat in the ditch when you go into the Bêmes'. Adiossa caballerossa," he called back laughingly, as though he were addressing himself to the night, his accomplice.

The door of the store opened a little way.

"My husband forgets everything," said Mme. Bême. "He's just told me there's a trunk waiting for you at the station."

Fernand was setting off home again with P'tit Paul. They were both whistling the tune from *Rio Grande*.

"Have you seen the mess they've left on my kitchen floor?" M. Motté asked. "I can't have that, it'll have to be cleaned up."

"I'll clean it up."

"And close the door properly when you go out."

"I'll close it properly."

I cleaned up the floor. I settled the ducks down for the night on one of my nightgowns. Fernand, I thought with a pang, is selling me the best cuts because someone has told him my "friends" are no paupers. And his rounds of drinks, you bitch, what about those? What about those best cuts you're going to turn somersaults with, slut? Prodigals take my breath away. I adore them and I clutch my billfold to me at the same time. Maurice's prodigality used to terrify me. Money was his headlong flight into the abyss. As soon as he had any he needed to free himself from it. His bizarre departure drowned in alcohol. The young graduate had described to me how Maurice had drunk fifteen or so glasses of calvados while waiting for the bus in the rain and the mist. I looked at my unhappy ducks lying on the nightgown; the bizarreness of their flattened beaks made them look too human. I seized hold of them and got back into harness. My head was full of songs as I walked up the hill toward Mme. Meulay's.

"You're in such a hurry, Mme. Leduc. . . . What a weight you've got there, Mme. Leduc. . . ."

The farmer's wife who lived next to the carpenter's shed was shining her flashlight in my eyes.

"What makes you think I'm in a hurry? I'm taking some ducks to be plucked. . . . Poultry is legal, isn't it?"

"My dear," she replied, "I didn't wish to pry. The only reason I stopped you was to offer you some bacon. . . . Would you be interested in a piece of salt bacon? People seem to think you're looking for that sort of thing."

"Thank you. I'll come around tomorrow evening."

Mme. Meulay was eating a supper of salt bacon and café au lait. She was perfectly willing for me to board out my animals with her, live and dead alike. She also promised to pluck the ducks. We parceled up her eggs. Then she opened the door of her pantry.

"A half-pound of butter," I cried in ecstasy.

I set off again for the Bêmes'. I hid my baskets in the ditch and slid my butter into my topcoat pocket so as not to be parted from it.

"P'tit Paul is eating with us," Mme. Bême said.

"Fernand wanted me to," P'tit Paul added, ill at ease.

He had prepared for the formality of the occasion by washing his face and hands.

Fernand came in by the door from the yard when I was expecting to see him arrive through the store. He was wearing a piece of black cloth pulled tightly over his head and knotted at the back in pirate fashion. He was biting tenderly at the stem of a rose held between his teeth.

"Is that how you're slaughtering tonight?" M. Bême inquired.

"Why not?" Fernand asked.

He warmed his back at the kitchen stove.

He performed a pirouette. The two ends of his headdress flicked the chimneypipe and P'tit Paul's neck.

"And now, one of your best bottles. All right?"

He sat down on the table, slid over toward me, and offered me a light.

"They say you're going to be married," Mme. Bême remarked.

"It seems I am," Fernand replied. He turned toward me. "You must come."

Leaning back against the wall, arms in the air, he kept repeating: "What a time we'll have beforehand, P'tit Paul. I shall stay drunk for three days."

He pushed back his plate. The muffled sound of his laugh sounded more like a sob.

"Eat, Nannan," Mme. Bême begged.

"Eat, Fernand," said P'tit Paul.

"I shall drink the blood," Fernand said.

M. Bême came up from the cellar.

"Here is my wife," Fernand cried, tearing the bottle from his hands.

The meal ended with rounds of calvados. Fernand burst into helpless laughter every time M. Bême said: "I have a horror of alcohol."

I went with P'tit Paul and Fernand to Pierrette's.

"I'll saw the bones for you," Fernand said as we arrived.

"How beautifully clean they've left it. . . ."

"That was all I needed," Fernand murmured. "I've forgotten my windbreaker."

"I'll go get it," P'tit Paul said.

"What a stink there'll be," Fernand said. "They'll be asleep."

He was envisaging the scene.

"Siddown," he said.

He began sawing the bone.

The rose fell onto the meat. I replaced it between his lips.

Two knocks on the door. P'tit Paul came in carrying his clogs.

"I ran into Toupin. The inspectors are around somewhere."

"I know Toupin," Fernand replied. "He's a pansy. He starts shaking if a leaf drops near him. I shall slaughter where I said I'd slaughter."

"That's what I think, I'm with you there," P'tit Paul said, delighted at the idea of sharing dangers with Fernand.

"Help me then," Fernand said. "We've got three hours ahead of us to bring back our little sheep."

My baskets were filling up with best end of neck and prime chops.

"Shall I put in the rose and the pirate hat for tonight?" P'tit Paul asked.

"That's right," Fernand said.

"Unless you prefer the topper, like the other day. . . ."

"You know I never wear the same one twice running. Had you forgotten?"

P'tit Paul placed the rose on the black cloth and laid them between the saw and the knives.

We stole down the stairs like thieves in the night; Fernand carried my baskets on his shoulders. They were already disappearing into the trees.

I staggered home, falling over my own feet. The village was asleep beneath its nightcap of shadows. Content with my day, with my evening, with Fernand, I called myself my little chick-chick, my little duck, my little hen. I looked at myself in the mirror, I saw the face of a woman beginning to succeed.

My heart began to molest me as soon as I got into bed. It was beating as though it would burst. I turned over, I sought respite from my right side, then from my left side, I gave vent to exaggerated sighs, I kicked violently at the bedclothes; anything to forget that muscle running wild inside me. I leaped out of bed, I looked at the time, right way up and wrong way up. I saw Fernand again, I was very sensibly in love. I fell asleep counting my profits and thinking of him.

Next day I applied myself to a lot of carefully worded letter writing, asking all my prospective customers for string, wrapping paper, clothes, and tin boxes. The postman brought me several letters from women I didn't know asking me for meat, fats, pâté, fresh cream, eggs, poultry, bacon. Gérard came in.

"Turning somersaults, I know what it is! Turning somersaults means selling for double what you paid."

"Plus postage," I added unhesitatingly.

"That I don't know," Gérard said.

He admired my parcels. Then he told me that the stationmaster wanted to see me about Maurice's trunk.

*

The post-office clerk gave me a letter from Sachs. A catastrophe: the tin with the leg of lamb in it weighed more than five pounds. The parcel was pushed back over the counter. I was ready to weep.

"Perhaps I can help you," said a man with a felt hat turned down over his eyes and a singsong voice.

The clerk gave me a look indicating that I should follow the man out.

"May I buy you a calva?" he asked.

"How can you help me? The parcel is too heavy."

"Come in here," he said. "What have you got in your package?"

"A leg of lamb," I replied after clinking glasses with him.

"Undo it," he said. He cut the string with his knife.

Some pieces of rusty iron wire fell out of the pockets of his corduroy jacket. He picked them up again quickly as I laid the lamb down on the marble.

"Prime quality," he remarked.

"A knife," he called.

The woman who ran the little café and store brought over a kitchen knife. He cut a slice off my leg of lamb.

"Your dinner," he said, offering it to me on the point of the knife.

I was exultant. He had gone straight to the heart of my little problem.

"Would you be interested in some fresh pork? Fernand will explain where I live. You can come and eat trout with us."

I discovered he had a finger missing when he grasped the handlebars of his bike.

I clutched Maurice's letter to me unopened every step of the way home, like a schoolgirl deliberately depriving herself of her first date. I selected a cradle of light in the depths of a hedge where I could read it in peace. It was a warm letter, a further installment in his description of camp life, his work as a crane driver, and his evenings with his friends. He was waiting for my parcel, he complimented me on staying on alone in the village.

It was the campaign chest of a dandy I opened in the humble railroad station. My hands dived into the silks, my nails dug into the initialed shirts, the satin, the tie silk, the brocade of the dressing gowns, the lawn and batiste of the handkerchiefs. A folded fan of bright sweaters and waistcoats, assortments of riding crops, of canes, of slippers, of shoes. Surprisingly, a pair of riding breeches. I helped myself, so that I would have things of his to remember him by. Here is an exact list of what I took: one shirt, for the initials M.S. embroidered on it; a dictionary; a book by Elie Faure; a three-page manuscript on the English painters. I have since given them all away, together with my Bible with his underlinings in it. I sent the trunk on to Curly's mother, and since she never received it the stationmaster insisted I put in a claim for loss in transit. I was awarded compensation. Ten thousand francs of the money in my suitcase belonged to Maurice Sachs.

That evening, the farmer's wife who lived next to the carpenter's shop sold me twenty pounds of salt bacon. The same evening, I presented myself at the pig-sticker's house: he was the son of the old woodcutter. Every day, this taciturn Breton peasant received a bonus: a superb joint of meat which he resold. My eyes goggled as he offered me long strings of sausages, slabs of pork pâté, coils of black pudding, slabs of lard. The pâtés lay dozing beneath their veils of fat. His prices were so low I would be able to triple them instead of just turning somersaults. He sold most of his provisions to the agricultural workers and local landowners. The money goes into that house and never comes out again, said M. Motté, obviously put out.

"Badly shaved? Hat over his eyes? Patched boots? Corduroy jacket? But he's the biggest poacher in the district, my poor girl," M. Motté explained.

I could expect hares and wild rabbits. As for trout . . . The poacher used to throw "spiders," big nets, across M. Lécolié's stream. How could one call it poaching when there were no more hunting and fishing licenses? "One day you'll be caught in a trap," M. Motté declared, his eyes frosting over with hope.

*

A year and a half passed: I became the slave of my baskets. But the slavery was good for me. My health became a thing of iron in the forge of my endurance, my perseverance, my dishonesty. Bent beneath the weight of my baskets, that is how I explored the resources that lay inside myself. Living dangerously: that meant carrying twenty pounds, thirty pounds, thirty-five pounds of butter along the paths, along the main roads in broad daylight. Mme. Bême began to grieve: I wasn't clearing my plate. How could I? My profits were devouring me. The more food I sent to Paris, the more I lost my appetite. How soon that time was left behind when I had prostituted myself by wiping their dishes, by entertaining them with lies, buffoonery, and bragging in order to obtain my first two pounds of butter. I rotted the moral fiber of the farmers with my offers, I betrayed the others who bought at lower prices. My tactics never varied. I walked in: the cows weren't giving milk. . . . I cut short their little speech:

"How much are you being paid now? From now on you shall have fifty francs a pound more."

They had refused me ten pounds, suddenly they were churning me twenty. The small operators, the ones who arrived in the morning and left again the same evening, the ones who didn't have a room to use as a warehouse, the ones who were watched for by inspectors on railroad platforms, the ones who were searched, the ones who had to pay their traveling expenses, the ones who were selling to people who earned as little as they themselves, began to hate me. I was pushing up the prices, I was snatching everything from under their noses, my customers were too rich. People came to my door to offer me hams, sheep, sides of pork. To refuse was to invite ruin; to miss a rendezvous, to be sick, meant losing a source of merchandise for good. The butter wouldn't wait, a competitor was there before you if you faltered for an instant.

I thought I would go mad with happiness the first month I made thirty thousand francs. I set out one morning of nightingales, of bindweed coiling its scent across the earth, and I walked along the road. I shall always remember the bird that celebrated my flood of money with its joyful modulations. At one in the morning, after I'd written some more of my childhood reminiscences or played bank at the Bêmes' café, I would unlock the catches of my silent, my divine companion: my fiber suitcase. I took out my bundles, I counted my tens upon tens of thousand-franc bills for the pleasure of counting, for the pleasure of poring over the numbers and the engravings, for the pleasure of pushing the pins through the money. Those bundles I coveted behind the bars of banks, I had them now, I possessed them, I was hiding them, I was storing them. They covered my letters from Maurice Sachs. What was it, this money I was at such pains to get? Pictures for me to look at. I had beeen absent-minded before, now I remembered everything: what each customer's letter had asked for and how much, the farmers I'd arranged to go and see, what time I was supposed to meet Fernand, the poacher, M. Lécolié, the mayor's wife, the mayor's daughter, Mme. Foulon, Mme. Meulay, the linen mender, the pork butcher, a middleman, another middleman. It meant six, ten, twelve miles every day with my sixteen, my twenty, my twenty-four pounds of food in my baskets. The result: I slept no better than before.

Once my rent had been paid, M. Motté remained completely unimpressed by the stock I brought into his house.

"What do you think of today's cut?"

He took the cut of meat in his hands and weighed it on his thickened fingers.

I waited for his verdict.

"Pah . . . ," he began to say, ruffling his white hair.

"You don't think much of it?"

He looked at me, staring as though I'd asked him a completely senseless question.

"Of that?" he said.

The meat swung from his fingers. M. Motté sniffed at it, inspected it.

"Well, it's meat, but that's all there is to be said. They've gypped you again, my girl. Here, you'd better have it back. . . ."

He lifted the lid of his big pan on the stove and filled his lungs with the scent of the potatoes dug from his own garden, the smell of the bacon from the pig he had fattened himself.

"The people in Paris are pleased anyhow. I get nothing but compliments."

"Give it here again!" he said.

He scratched his bronzed neck. That was where his concern for the truth always rankled him.

"It's been hacked to bits, it has no shape, it's not dressed properly. They'll have to make a stew of it."

I went back into my workroom with the meat. There were days when the abundance around me affected my sight. I saw great vipers of black pudding coiled around on themselves, I saw strings of choirboys' penises where there should have been tiny sausages, I saw dimpled virgins instead of short sausages, I saw dirty hailstones sprinkled on old shoes: my salt bacon. I saw my eyelashes stuck in the pork pâtés. I saw offerings of mandolins: smoked hams. I saw the butter exactly as it was: the protector I had always dreamed of. I weighed my goods, I didn't cheat, though sometimes I did dilute the cream with a little pump water. I tasted it, it was excellent, why shouldn't I do it again? I took my flasks to be filled, the mother and daughter sold me their first Christmas roses, plucked from their nest of snow. . . . Heavens above, as Laure used to say, how could I ever have imagined I would be living a life like this? . . . I had so many parcels to pack up that I lunched at midday off nothing put a piece of bread and some pâté; and even then I would leave them lying there on the table most of the time. My scissors, my string, my boxes, my wrapping paper absorbed all my attention. It was almost a sort of voluntary penal servitude. The postman came in, he handed me the money orders to sign, then looked the other way; he was incapable of jealousy. Leaving M. Motté's house was an agony. Everyone was waiting, spying, watching for me to emerge. My affability, my playful manner could not conceal the parcels I was taking to be mailed. The postman's wife and Gérard's landlady were my two most indefatigable pursuers. They didn't denounce me: they merely satisfied their public's thirst for gossip. I pulled myself together: I walked out with fatalistic courage. Mme. and M. Zoungasse nodded to me coldly. One glance was sufficient to express their disdain. I haunted the neighborhood farms with my white boots, my great strides, my worn rabbit-fur coat; people began to notice. Inquiries were started which luckily came to nothing and did me no harm. The police asked the carpenter: "Is she in the black market, that woman?"

"I don't know, I don't think so," he had replied.

"She's in the black market," the police insisted.

It was M. Motté who brought me the news. We agreed to keep it to ourselves. I was shaken by what he'd told me for an hour or two, then I plunged out along my paths with two horns on my brow: the two great fingernails of my rapacity. I had so many money orders to cash that I began having mail sent poste restante to the office in Notre-Dame-du-Hameau as well. The post-office clerk paid me when everyone else had gone. I would go back to the village, and if I wasn't going straight out on my rounds again I drank a few glasses of calvados at the Bêmes', hoping that my queasiness would disappear in their kitchen, that my appetite would come back. I stagnated, I sank down into myself; it was a delicious feeling, being so worn out and then letting myself go into a trance on a kitchen bench. I rested, according to the season, in the cool or in the warmth of two aging, disinterested lovers. A black marketeer asked me if I wanted to sell my business to him: my customers and my goodwill. People were saying that I'd made several million francs.

We were always laughing. The men who traveled up and down from Paris with their merchandise used to tell spicy stories. Unable to exercise their professions in wartime, or else unwilling to work for the enemy, they traveled back and forth and told tall tales to pass the time. Our illegal traffic also had its amorous side. The butter wasn't ready: that meant a night in a hotel with the latest girl friend and a reassuring telegram to the wife at home. Adultery proliferated, all forms of duty were in abeyance. Ungrateful, exacting, we criticized the peasants. They were selling in their own homes, they had no risks to run, no losses, no fines, no incidental expenses, they weren't searched in railroad stations, they had no parcels confiscated or smashed open, their nerves weren't always at breaking point or their hearts always beating too hard. Cycling twenty-five miles carrying eighty pounds of meat in one hand was mere daily routine. Kill a sheep, kill a calf, I can get it to the evening train, the black marketeer would say to the supplier.

The inspectors had their informers, the black marketeers had their grapevine, their oral broadsheet covering the adversary's plans, his tender spots, where he searched yesterday, where he would search tomorrow, together with portraits, character studies, and estimates of the degrees of severity or indulgence to be expected from individual inspectors. All this information was passed from mouth to mouth. What started as an illicit traffic soon became a brotherhood. Suddenly, the father of a large family made up his mind to join us: from then on he slaughtered a sheep every night in the kitchen of a rectory which he'd been given the use of by the village priest; there was only a wall between his nightly slaughter and the room where the priest took catechism classes. More middlemen sprang up than one could keep track of. They set up a market in the middle of a wood for the butter that the peasants were afraid to sell openly. Their customers commuted twice a day between Paris and the village. One of these middlemen sold me six hams inside which I found maggots writhing. I had to throw them away.

A year and a half had passed since Fernand, petrified beneath the waves meticulously crimped into his hair with a curling iron, came to collect me from M. Motté's on his wedding day. The white carnation in his buttonhole suited him less well than the rose between his lips. At the Bêmes', the phonograph was whining nasally. Pierrette, a model little bride, was tearing up her veil and giving pieces to all the guests. I danced a *paso doble* with the groom. P'tit Paul was yawning.

Wooed, worshipped, flattered, Pierrette was now receiving visitors in her bedroom. Wooden suitcases bumped against aluminum suitcases, plumbers' tool kits lay against hatboxes, a violin case was lying across the length of stovepipe into which the packages of butter would later be inserted one by one. I shall never understand how that rickety staircase didn't collapse. People swarmed up it in crowds to offer Pierrette materials, underclothes, curtains, bedcovers, eiderdowns, skirts, stockings, blouses, shoes, saucepans, facepowder, make-up, watches, bracelets, necklaces. They unwrapped them, unfolded them, and spread them out on the bridal bed. She would buy something, and then her appetite for frivolities satisfied, she would plunge back into the love story she was reading.

"Coffee!" he yelled.

Fernand had arrived with P'tit Paul and Arnold, who was now helping him as well.

"Where's Charlotte?" Fernand asked.

"Out collecting," Pierrette replied, without looking up from her dog-eared little book.

"Oh, that one!" Fernand said, looking pale and anxious.

Everyone was hanging on his every word.

"Is that coffee coming?"

Fernand fell onto his bed, his soaked espadrilles making marks on the bedspread. He took Pierrette's book and went on reading from the place where she'd left off.

The crowd of customers began to mutter.

"Pierrette . . . I'm thirsty . . . I've been walking for six hours," Fernand said in a bland voice.

The murmurs of the crowd grew louder.

At which, not taking his eyes from the book, Fernand said: "I tell you I'm going to bring it in tonight! If you're worried about getting it, you needn't be. I slaughter after midnight. Come back tomorrow morning. Is it my fault I'm being watched? Tomorrow morning . . . Why do you buy so many stockings, Pierrette?"

Fernand threw the stockings onto the floor, the crowd filed out with P'tit Paul at its head.

Pierrette served her husband his coffee, gently closed the door of their room, then asked me to tell her about the dresses I'd left behind in Paris, about my friends and the places I went with them. I invented. I was selling her high life at so much per yard. Everyone had guessed my feelings for Fernand, but they were all discreet and kind about it. What Charlotte and Pierrette weren't so happy about was my powers of endurance when we sat drinking together at the Bêmes'. I didn't go looking for him. I just met him there and I accepted the drinks he bought. He was a rake, but he was courageous too when he brought back a bullock twelve miles on foot across the fields in the darkness. "Fernand lets himself be led astray by his buddies," said his mother-in-law, "his buddies are always getting money out of him." No one ever got anything out of Fernand. He gave it. He often used to desert the conjugal bed after ten in the evening to come and play bank with us. P'tit Paul would arrive five minutes after him. I always won as much as I lost, and I wondered how Fernand managed it. I was in my seventh heaven when I had the bank, when I saw the money raining down into the plate. When I sat next to Fernand, if my boot happened to touch his espadrille, if his espadrille happened to touch my boot, we neither of us drew away. We played, we passed our cigarettes or the calvados bottle to each other without a glance. Our hands never knew what our feet were doing. I was happy living with him like that during the night hours and I was sincerely sorry for Pierrette. Pierrette? She's always asleep, Fernand told us. We parted at three in the morning. I walked home, I remembered Maurice climbing the grass bank and praying.

Sachs' best friend wrote to me. He lent me books, I sent him packets of pipe tobacco. Thanks to him I read Flaubert's *Letters*.

I was tired of my ragged appearance. I made a lightning visit to Paris. I bought a suit, a dress, and a blouse from Bruyère's and some shoes from Cazals. I tried them on in the room I used as a warehouse: it was a transformation. Next Sunday I paraded my new outfit at church; but I knew it was a mistake to flaunt my prosperity. People took me to be Sachs' girl friend. Scarlet woman, their eyes flashed at me, because they knew the young graduate was waiting for me at the Bêmes'.

I took Maurice's advice. The young graduate became my lover. A short-lived affair. We talked about Maurice. I went to visit Blaise in the town where he taught school; I stole furtively along a street still deep in slumber, I shut myself up for two days in his room, and we drank solidly while he cooked. The sleeping town cast a spell over me through the windowpane. Lying on the bed, our cigarettes in one hand, our glass of cognac in the other, we talked about his childhood, about the plays he was planning to write, about his mother for whom he was sacrificing himself. There were some tears, a scene or two, then it was all over. He still came to see me every week all the same, every Sunday at about six in the evening.

On Saturday afternoons I disinfected the long table and the furniture; I polished the floor, I cooked a few delicacies: an egg custard, a big turnover, a tart, a blancmange—something to offer Gérard, to M. Motté, to the young graduate. Gérard was beginning to look more and more like a gypsy. He wanted to go back to Paris because his mother was paying his board and lodging less and less frequently, because he loathed the peasants, because he refused, despite my efforts at persuasion, to work on a farm. Indifference, stupidity, avarice: which of these should I accuse myself of, I ask myself now as I look back. I hesitate to reply one way or the other. I didn't say to myself: I won't buy Gérard a bike, I won't pay for his board, I won't buy him a new suit. I never discussed it with myself. I didn't notice that there was a child near me, day after day, preparing to throw himself into the abyss.

I received a letter with a Rouen postmark. Who could be writing to me in that childish handwriting? I opened the envelope and found another envelope inside without any address. Maurice . . . He had written the following note on a little sheet of paper:

"My love,

You tell me that you are pregnant and that things are going badly for you. Would you like me to come and see you, would you feel better if I were by your side? Please answer. I kiss you my darling.

Maurice."

It knocked all the breath out of me.

Maurice was calling me "my love," Maurice was calling me "my darling." There is always a grain of truth in anything one writes, I told the bright wood fire. I read it again, I was quivering with happiness and gratified vanity. A child by that tedious woman who was always boring him to distraction with her childhood reminiscences . . . It was that Sunday afternoon in the café all over again. Even if it was not a genuine desire, Maurice wouldn't let it go. His darling, his love. The miracle had taken place: I had a homosexual at my feet. I felt light-headed with joy as I entertained the idea of his return, of all the money we could spend together. I wrote immediately to the doctor. He wrote out a certificate stating that I was pregnant and unwell, he signed it then flew away again. I kept the piece of paper for three days and nights, but I couldn't bring myself to send it. I no longer felt flattered. I was weighing the pros and cons, I was interrogating the flames flickering up the chimney. He will come back, you will love him, you will burn for him again, you will have to become a block of ice again. Can you have forgotten the barbed wire fences between you? Your long silences, your insignificance as he talked to you, as he will talk to you again, about Nietzsche, about Kant? It was killing you, remember, and it will start killing you again. Reflect. I sighed.

The three loops of my beautifully tied slip knots, where would they be? It was so good festooning myself with string, forgetting the curlers still in my hair. He would come back, I would crawl back into the ground again. He isn't responsible for the feelings he inspires in you, my little chicken. But he's my jailer all the same. My tongue would still be hanging out panting between the bars of the same great love. It is still hanging out now. Maurice was considerate. The chimes of midnight, and he would offer me a saucer of baked apple with cream. . . . Think back, think clearly, little bitch with your tongue out. He served you apples, but afterwards you felt more unhappy than a kitchenmaid when her master has given her a kick. My scissors falling on the floor, my ball of string rolling toward the door, the scoldings I give them, my pieces of cloth, my boxes, my tins, the bonds drawn tight between us with familiar and repeated gestures . . . My one o'clock in the morning . . . Greetings, night: yet another day well filled. And Violette goes off to lie like a draped statue in her bed. The pink penknife saying: "I'll see you in the morning," with its three gray eyes. Folding the sheets of fresh brown paper, cutting them with my penknife, what liberty. He would come back, I would have to say good-by to all the things I'd grown accustomed to. What would I be without them? The Bêmes' kitchen would no longer know me, the village would be cold, I should nod to Fernand from a distance on the paths. Would I dare to inhale the sweetish odor of my rabbit coat in front of Maurice Sachs? No, I wouldn't dare.

This great emotion springing up again irritated and frightened me at the same time. I was already poisoned by it. I had stopped going to the outhouse since the arrival of the letter. No, my buttocks were not a young man's buttocks. They demoralized me. But what did it amount to after all, this great emotion? What was it? It was unprofitable. Once Maurice had returned, my earnings would be so much dirty water going down a plughole. Ten months after his return we should be penniless again.

I read his note again. The real love letter was the doctor's certificate. I was stoking an inferno, my wood fire was a maddened blaze by ten in the evening.

Why hadn't he written quite simply: "Dear Violette, if you were to send me a doctor's certificate saying that you are pregnant by me it would make it much easier for me to get back to France"? I wept tears of rage, of fury, of despair. His trickery sickened me. "My love," a mockery. "My darling," a mockery. His proposal that he should get me with child came back to me in the way the taste of one's own vomit rises in one's gorge. There was no doubt that to Maurice my heart and his sperm were mere commodities of trade. I threw the certificate into the fire.

He wrote me a long letter two weeks later. He told me that he bore me no grudge, that he had "found a way around his difficulties." He didn't say exactly how. I believed him. In the letters that followed he described the sort of life we would lead together after the war. We would lunch together every day, we would go several times a week to the Comédie Française. He had scores of ideas about how I was to earn money. I would pay him the compensation money for the trunk and I would give him a part of my own profits since he had provided me with my village, my cows and milk, my rich Parisian clientele.

It took me fifteen years before I realized what it was I had thrown into the fire, before my regrets turned into remorse, into obsession, into persecution. It was a secret between Maurice and myself. While in Germany, he wrote *Portraits et moeurs de ce temps*. I am in it. I am called Lodève. If Maurice Sachs did really write that portrait, if someone didn't slip an extra sheet between Maurice's own pages covered with an imitation of his tiny penciled handwriting—he wrote the manuscript in a Hamburg prison—then he did bear me a grudge. The description of my face is a nightmare. How unhappy he must have been to have savaged my thankless face like that. How he must have been loved if someone was avenging him with that portrait.

*

I was waiting my turn in the post office of Notre-Dame-du-Hameau; a prisoner-of-war's wife clutched her child's hand tighter so as to protect it from the black marketeers.

"Fernand wants a word with you," the man with the turned-down felt hat sang softly in my ear. We went into the café.

Fernand was amusing himself with a windmill. The pink and orange celluloid sails were spinning as he tapped them with his fingers. Then he blew on it. Finally he stuck it in the buttonhole of his jacket.

"We have a proposition for you," the poacher said.

"Knock off," Fernand said to him.

The poacher smiled pityingly. "Five minutes ago you said yes. But you're right, there's no hurry. I met you once, Mme. Leduc, when it was snowing, late one evening. You wouldn't remember. You were following one of the paths through the woods, I was in among the trees. You were dragging your baskets along in the snow. You've been seen out in all weather. In short, there's nothing that stops you. . . ."

"Ice on the roads stops me. . . ."

"Yes, that's treacherous," Fernand put it.

The rounds of calva succeeded one another without any slackening in the pace. I bought the seventh. The poacher went out into the store to order it.

"Do you work with him now?"

"Have to," Fernand answered. "I hadn't any dough left to buy the animals."

"Can you tell me what I'm doing here?" I asked him.

"You're waiting to be sold a pig."

"A whole pig!"

"It's cheaper for you in the long run. We'll take it around to your place while M. Motté is out visiting."

Fernand bowed his head. Selling pork, that wasn't his kind of work.

"When do you want us to kill it for you?" the poacher asked when he came back.

It was so that I could go on drinking freely with Fernand that I accepted their offer.

"I'll take you back to the village on the handlebars of my bike," Fernand said to me after the fourteenth round.

We set off. Fernand pedaled slowly, the bike was zigzagging. I laughed, I couldn't stop laughing, and it was the first time I had ever laughed when drunk.

"No, Fernand, no . . ."

We had fallen off, Fernand dragged me into one of my favorite hedges. We exchanged the taste of alcohol in a long kiss.

"You'll be my mistress?" he asked, close to my ear.

I explained that it was impossible, that we couldn't deceive Pierrette.

"Let's get on then," he said.

He pedaled even faster, despite my cries of protest.

*

M. Motté was regaining his youth, there was fire in his cheeks after he had read the newspaper.

"The Russians," he kept saying, "are fighting like lions."

The Bêmes, more skeptical, were more interested in calculating the profit their country might be able to extract from this new state of affairs. I listened without taking part in their discussions. Blinkered by my own profits and my rapacity, my face grew longer as the others began to hope. I wanted to make more and still more money. Peace would mean stagnation for me again. I consoled myself vaguely with the thought that Maurice would be coming back, that he had scores of schemes in store for me. Some of my parcels were lost in transit, others were returned to me smashed open with the contents spoiled.

The rail service was becoming slower and slower, my customers began accusing me of sending them carrion. Gérard went back to Paris. I told him how unwise he was to do so, but he ignored my warning. Fernand was told in the nick of time that his house was to be raided: it was the kitchen of a vegetarian they searched. They apologized as they were leaving. Fernand went into hiding, then returned, determined to slaughter even more animals in the middle of the village square, to sell hundreds of pounds of meat in his raided kitchen.

Exhausted by the long walk to Notre-Dame-du-Hameau, I arranged with M. Lécolié that he should take me and my parcels with him in his trap whenever he drove in to the bakery next door to the post office. Like a sleepwalker because of her great age and her fatigue, Mme. Lécolié, tall and old-fashioned, reminded me of Fidéline. Their dairy: a grotto hung with hammocks of spiders' web.

Having retired from schoolteaching, M. Lécolié had got the idea into his head to become a farmer, despite his physical infirmity: his turned-in feet were always facing each other. How had he managed to work with the vigor of a young farm laborer, this man with two lumps of flesh where his feet should have been? When he was a young scholarship student and his hands were chapped, M. Lécolié used to lace up his orthopedic boots with his teeth. He told me about it.

M. Lécolié's indulgence toward Fernand, who slaughtered animals in his farmyard wearing a bowler hat, a sombrero, or a top hat, who hung animals from his trees to skin them and cut them up, who drank the blood and threw what he didn't drink over the grass, intrigued the peasants in the neighborhood. By night as well as by day, M. Lécolié was soaking up strength from the agility, from the daring, from the eccentricity, from the generous spirit of the young slaughterer as he made his farmyard into a stockyard not ten yards away from him.

"I'm going to show you what I did when I was young," he said to me one sunny day alive with festive bees.

We went through into the room next to his kitchen. The white cat with its red eyes plowed up my face with its claws, the eagle with spread wings was tearing my nostrils to shreds, the white owl and the tawny owl were blinding me with the headlights of their implacable eyes, the squirrel was gnawing at my breast, the fluffy Pomeranian was attacking my eyelids, the stag was impaling my belly with its horns. The animals M. Lécolié had stuffed were ferocious. Like the painter who succeeds in painting his own soul in a self-portrait, M. Lécolié had managed to transmit his cripple's bitterness and rancor even to the furry coat of a cat. Stag, doe, dog, owl, all were screeching their raging desire to live. M. Lécolié's face grew hard as he showed me the products of his youthful hobby.

Young, well fed, happy to be out, the little black horse trotted along with blissful regularity. I stepped down. Then we set off back again with the cover pulled over our knees. I left his trap as I used to leave a merry-go-round when I was seven: soaked with happiness. M. Lécolié was enchanted with my fifty francs.

Maurice's best friend wrote suggesting I go and stay with him for two days. I took some provisions, some pipe tobacco, and my old purse containing my money firmly attached to my slip with two safety pins. What a mentor my money was. I held myself as a cypress tree holds itself. Balustrades, lamp standards, and pylons bowed to me through the train window, bowed to the ground on the other side of the glass. I would have gulped down my own dung if it meant earning still more money and being even more like an infallible cypress tree. I was expecting to recognize Maurice's friend among the crowd in the station. Disappointment. I walked out into the street looking for him. Is it that man in the raincoat standing on the edge of the sidewalk? Noncommital face, gray face. His raincoat is the color of anguish, he is adrift inside his skin, that man over there. Is it he? Should I follow him? Should he follow me? Which of us is the cop? Which of us is the spy? This is becoming boring. Should I go back to the village or should I hurry over to the address Maurice gave me?

It must be him, because he's just the way Maurice described him. Harrowed and darkling. Which of us spoke first? A gap in my journey. He took my suitcase and led me off to meet his family. Maurice was the sole subject of our conversations. I remember their little kitchen, my undercooked chicken, my fevered consumption of red wine and cigarettes; I remember having tea with them in a Paris pâtisserie and a mirror in which I preened myself, proud of my suit, my shoes. I bought the biggest doll I could find for their little girl, and even that was another form of bragging. Unhappy creature, stripped, unfrocked by Maurice's absence! I wept at night for Maurice's friend. This abstract man excited me. My belly brayed its desire for his hand holding a volume of Hegel. I imagined this gentle, deep, uneasy, tormented, reflective being understanding Maurice Sachs and his distress of spirit, I imagined this remarkable teacher of philosophy as an indefatigable lover. I was accoutering an intellectual with the weapons of love and suffering because I was not the beneficiary of his attacks.

He took me into his library, a cozy citadel. He sat down at his desk, then offered me a chair. I told him I was writing my childhood reminiscences. There was a silence.

"What a big book," I said.

I was unable to take my eyes off the new book with its white Gallimard cover. The volume was lying in the middle of the desk on a blotter.

"That big book was written by a woman," replied Maurice's best friend. "It is Simone de Beauvoir's *L'Invitée*."

I read Simone de Beauvoir's name on the cover, then the title:

L'Invitée. A woman had written this book. I put it back on the blotter. I was at peace with myself.

The thought of Maurice's best friend continued to disturb me for a long while. I sent him several letters that read like the productions of an obsessed old maid. His replies didn't offend me. I believed that the exchanging of ideas had an aphrodisiac power, that an act of love is always better after one has fought either for or against Hegel. I believed it and I still believe it. Philosophic discussion is the promised land which I shall never attain. Things I cannot understand always fascinate me. Whenever I met him after that, full of despair at my inadequacy, I inevitably produced an impression of stupidity, muddleheadedness, and vanity. A sort of bluestocking made up mainly of runs.

*

Some of the other black marketeers advised me to take my stocks to Paris myself. I would lose less goods in transit and my customers would be better satisfied. I reluctantly decided to follow their advice. The railroad stations and grade crossings were being bombed. The trains were slow, the inspectors worn out by the strain and consequently very touchy. Some of the more fearful among us had already given up the game. Fernand decided that he too would go to Paris because he was spending all he was earning. That the great Fernand, who had plowed his way across the countryside on his bike, slaughtering animals with a bowler hat on his head and a rose between his teeth, scorning the dangers and the darkness, should now be forced to buy a railroad ticket and wait in line to board a train and heave his suitcases of meat up onto a luggage rack appeared to me as a fall from grace, a cause for melancholy. How was it going to end for us all? I made a big pastry for our first trip together and Fernand bought a bottle of good wine from the Bêmes, who were talking of selling their business. The victory they so much desired would also reduce them to bankruptcy.

One of the women from Paris sold me a suitcase. I packed it with sausages, eggs, pork pâtés, liver pâtés, veal, beef, mutton, cream, bacon, and butter. I hid Maurice's letters, I pinned my bankroll over my belly in a bath glove. I picked up my full suitcases: they were too heavy. Those who don't travel often know how heartbreaking such a moment is: putting back the books and possessions that cannot accompany you. Twofold heartbreak for a black marketeer when it's joints of meat that must stay behind. At last the moment came when I was climbing up into the bus with my fifty pounds of luggage and giving my performance of a lady traveling with just a scarf, a crêpe de Chine nightgown, and an angora pullover in case it should turn cold. At L— railroad station I met Fernand with "Gold Mouth," Didine, and found myself once more in my own world with the familiar expressions passing from mouth to mouth: it's so quiet on the platform we could play them our mandolins (our legs of lamb). Yesterday evening they let us through like buttercups, my chickadee. Cross my heart, they were picking lilies-of-the-valley at Meudon (no searches at the terminus in Paris). I walked out onto the platform weighed down not only by my cases but by the accumulated weariness of several years. Each of us was supposed to work his or her way into a group of innocent passengers. We wouldn't meet again till we were in the train corridor. *They* had been there early that morning, *they* might be coming back, Didine whispered to one of the railroad employees. I got scared. I would have given my suitcases away there and then if only I could have gone back and sat quietly peeling vegetables with M. Motté. The train came into the station. I had a vision of my butter, my joints, my eggs, my sausages under the slow wheels of the engine as it pulled out again. . . . I would go back to the village so much lighter than I came.

A first-class carriage drew up in front of me. I had a first-class ticket; this coincidence restored my courage somewhat. All the passengers were on the train when I managed to let my second suitcase fall on the second step up to the carriage door. An enemy soldier came out of his compartment; the chain and the silver badge on his chest terrified me. He pushed me, he knocked me back off the steps of the train. My two suitcases fell with me. Fernand, I yelled with all the strength of my lungs. Fernand, who must have been watching to see I was all right, ran up, picked up my bags, and shouted for me to follow him. The train was moving. Fernand disappeared inside it. I ran along beside the steps. A friendly black marketeer pulled me up and in. I found myself back with them all. I was weeping and promising myself inwardly that this journey would be the last. We ate the pastry and drank the Bêmes' wine. The passengers sharing the compartment with us were elegant but anemic looking: it was easy to see from the look in their eyes that we were the well-fed lower classes who had no right sitting on their comfortably padded seats. Fernand was cracking jokes, whistling, singing, yelling out obscene words for the hell of it. He was already spending his money. I played tunes of my own invention on a pocket comb with tissue paper around it. The tickle against my lips sent me into fits of helpless laughter. I stopped this game when we passed through a bombed area. The war did exist. Sequestered in our little village, a long way from the main highways, we had sometimes begun to wonder if it weren't a myth.

Fernand helped me down with my suitcases at the Montparnasse-Bienvenue station. "Get a load of him," he said to 'Gold Mouth'. A very dignified gentleman was walking along the platform with a suitcase trickling blood. A small pack fell from someone's shoulder, a bottle of cream smashed. The passenger fled, leaving his pack lying in a pool of cream. I still wrote to Gérard. Would he be at the station? He walked toward me. I didn't recognize him. Thin, pimply, uncouth in a pair of long trousers that made him look older, he shook my hand coolly. He offered to help me, but I refused: he was too weak and he was a Jew. I stopped every ten yards. I thought my heart was going to jump out of my mouth. It was interminable. I looked at the people on the street: unhealthy complexions and black circles under their eyes. I was trapped, imprisoned once more by my own and other people's misery. I went to call on Bernadette and sold her a pound of butter at cost price. A sacrifice. She warmed me up with a cup of tea and told me that she was counting on my bringing her more butter every time I came into town. I left her house with lead in my legs; now I had to start the rounds with my list of names. Five minutes later I was taking a room in a little hotel. "Leave your cases here," the manageress said.

"Not for the world," I answered. "They're my livelihood."

Paris seemed gayer again. Paris was under pressure, Paris was waiting for its deliverance.

With Gérard at my side, I presented myself at the door of my cream fanciers. I rang their bell with less assurance than I had written their name on the parcels. A man opened the door.

"I have your two pints . . ."

He realized what I meant and his face lit up. I followed him into the drawing room.

"I'm so sorry," he said. "My wife is out."

"Oh, I can wait!" I replied, because of the two canvases I could see on their easels.

My accommodating attitude was obviously an embarrassment to

him. He wanted to go on with his painting. He left the room. Did he paint two pictures at the same time?

"If you wouldn't mind coming this way . . . ," he said.

He moved around his own apartment like a discreet shadow.

We were introduced to his cook, very pleased with herself and her shining domain.

"Madame is anxious for fresh eggs and cream. She's expecting," she confided.

Which meant that she was going to be a mother. Gérard helped me close my suitcases again and the master of the house paid me in the drawing room. I had discovered from the cook that the mistress of the house painted too. I counted their money.

The trees and the hedges . . . the plumed clouds . . . the blue mists . . . the silence of pure oxygen . . . the feats of the nightingales . . . All that was no help in trying to forget what I was: a wet nurse and an errand boy.

The Seine two hundred yards away with its ever repeated, with my ever repeated standards of drooping ivy, with its quaint complement of passers-by. The trees were reflecting the sky, exactly as they do elsewhere. The tugs, the barges, the lighters, the barge captain's wife with her washing floating in the current, my work as I sink slowly into sleep. Time, the ages and the years, our river by the light of day. The eternity, the monotony of its handmaidens, of its varied raiment, the procession of dates in my history book that I never remembered. I bought a strawberry lollipop in winter, I gazed at you, at you the Seine, more diligent than your tiny tributaries, resting sinuously on your steep sloping banks. My unfailing one, my temptress, mirage of all my desired and bungled suicides. Roll by, roll on, my caravan, old, battered, resting house of waters. My fist, my brow, my miseries, my griefs. Gazing at the Seine, pondering on sorrows welling upward from the past. In glaucous troops my tattered miseries came floating up toward me, then drifted on again. I bought another strawberry lollipop, I went off to simmer with my fellows in neighborhood movie houses.

"There's the old doctor who wants the oxtails for his broth. We'd better go to his place next," I said to Gérard.

"I'd like to stop here for a moment first," Gérard replied.

We stopped, we gazed at the veil, at the imperceptible confetti of desolation over a Sisley landscape. The crumbling, the demoralizing rain of autumn in us. The galleries, the antique dealers, the print shops, were all displaying their rarities, as they had before the war. Nothing more unshakable in this world than trade.

"Did you remember my oxtail?"

"It is in my bag, monsieur."

This, an old man? An apricot tree in the sunlight. To live on, to endure, that is the essence of royalty. He didn't go out, he simply reigned there over his furniture, over his possessions. What was he saying? His egoism was comical. Eccentric. Aggressive.

A traveling player is what I am, a lute player with my leg of lamb, a slender young juggler with my sausages, a troubadour with my chitterlings, a conjuror with my liver sausages. I am entertaining, I am charming Whitebeard in his castle. Here is the oxtail for your soup; that's it, ask your lady-in-waiting to retire. What shall I dance before your court, great doctor? The dance of the hoarfrost on my pâtés. I can also dance the blood coughed out by eglantines, more briefly the delicate tints of my fresh-cut pork. You see, mother, I can be an underling in my grandfather's house and find it all amusing. See you next week, doctor.

And now for the real door-to-door delivery round.

"Yes, Gérard, yes, you'd better go home. Here, take these two sausages while no one is looking."

Two sausages missing from my rosaries. I am God since I am judging myself. The judgment is absolute as I give Gérard so little. Two sausages. A shiver of lucidity before the storm of destiny. Two sausages. A clear glimpse into the depths of my rapacity, the depths of my avarice, the abyss of my confrontation with myself, the vertigo of myself watching myself, my trial, my condemnation as I cut the string. After all, this child has a mother and a brother. This child has no one but me because I have the food to feed him with. Is that why I am so hard on misers? I hire out my own defects to others and they blind me. Help your neighbor. Did anyone help me when I was dying of grief! Along the tracks of all the tears once shed, I trotted on my way. Always remember number one, my mother said in her potted philosophy lessons.

It was my door-to-door deliveries that earned me my entry into the world of the trio. It was pure chance that led me into it in the first place. I was received by the keeper of a chaotic antique shop. He was tidying it up and complaining of the lack of space.

"I love cooking when I've got all the proper things to cook with," he said.

A melody that is always fresh to the ear of a saleswoman who sells all the proper things.

He was dusting off some opaline ware with a feather duster.

"How much is that one?" asked a mink that didn't even take the trouble to come inside.

It was the year of the opaline epidemic. Everyone had to have his blue vase.

I walked over to the display case with my great necklace of black sausages.

"I'll take it," he said.

The telephone was ringing, ringing.

"When I'm tidying up, I'm tidying up," he said without making any effort to answer it.

The surfaces of the tables looked like mirrors that were reflecting mahogany furniture.

The telephone continued to ring.

"Damn it all," he remarked to the bell.

Moving chairs, occasional tables, armchairs, cupboards is hot work. He took off his jacket and answered the telephone.

"No . . . nothing new this end. A few inquiries about prices. You're on your way home? I've someone in the shop who might interest you. Hurry back," he said into the telephone. Then, after hanging up, he turned to me: "My wife will be here in a moment with the Cat. They buy too much. Where am I going to put the things they've bought?"

"You have to have stock if you want to sell," I answered pontifically.

"Your hair looks as though it could do with a shampoo," he said, calmer now.

We both burst into hilarious laughter.

He liked me. I wondered what happened when he didn't like someone.

"Here they are!" he cried.

A little car, a toy, had drawn up in front of the opalines. His wife greeted me with imploring eyes as she rubbed the lenses of her spectacles.

"The Cat was extraordinary," she told her husband.

The Cat made his entrance. He was tapping an English cigarette nonchalantly against his cigarette case.

"I'll make tea for you," the husband told them.

"I'm going out to get the papers," the Cat said, without having noticed me.

"That's Romi," the husband told me. "Before the war he was a journalist. . . ."

Which meant that Romi wasn't exercising his profession during the Occupation.

"Have you felt the weight of her suitcases? Feel the weight of them. Shall we ask her to stay for a cup of tea?" he asked his wife.

She didn't hear him. She was consulting a small notebook with enormous concentration. She emitted a grunt of acquiescence.

Romi made a second entrance.

"Were you there before?" he asked, lifting his heavy eyelids as he looked at me.

"Cat, lend me your notebook," the wife said in a businesslike tone.

"Would you also like me to lend you my hat, my necktie, and my wallet?"

"Be serious, pussycat," she said.

He handed her his notebook.

"You look charming in that oilskin raincoat. Lugubrious, but charming," Romi said to me. "Cigarette?"

"Don't tease her," the wife said in a pleading voice, without lifting her eyes from the notebooks.

"I am depriving myself of my last cigarette, and you call that teasing her?" Romi rejoined.

"Take my wife's," the husband said.

"How long have you been playing the tradeswoman?" Romi asked.

He produced a very expensive-looking lighter for our cigarettes. A man who obviously possessed every modern convenience.

"I'm not playing! This is real work, believe me! But you're right: I didn't sell sausages before the war."

"Ah, so you sell sausages?"

"You're being idiotic," mumbled the businesswoman.

"I'll buy them," he said, "but I prefer roast beef."

"Children, the tea is ready," the husband said.

"I guessed you weren't a real tradeswoman by your oilskin and your long oily hair. You look almost like a Marcel Carné character," Romi said.

"Drink up your tea," the husband said to me.

"Don't listen to him," the wife added, meaning Romi.

"I used to know him, Marcel Carné. . . ."

"You see!" Romi exclaimed.

He was smoking with the narrowed gaze of a gangster.

I told them about my years as a culler of news items. I talked to them about Maurice Sachs, about the volume of childhood reminiscences I was writing. When I lifted my eyes, I surprised an exchange of approving looks between Romi and Andrée and Robert Payen. I was a novelty to them. Romi seemed enchanted by me. The wife was delighted because I was entertaining him. The husband was happy because his wife was pleased. Why did they call him "The Cat"? Because of his smooth brilliantined hair, because of his round, slightly plump, slightly feline face and his dimpled, priestly hands. The Cat always wore a hypocritical expression but in fact he was very forthright. Later, I was to see how roughly he could handle difficult customers.

Several hours passed. Romi talked to me about Rimbaud, about Lautréamont, about the postman Cheval, about Breton, about Huysmans. . . .

"He's crazy about the turn of the century," the wife told me.

"He collects picture postcards," the husband said.

"And newspaper clippings," the wife added.

Andrée and Robert Payen invited me to dinner that evening in their apartment. They drove me there in their car: Paris was taking me on its lap.

"What could possibly be more exciting than long black stockings?" the Cat asked as he gripped the steering wheel with his turn-of-the-century gloves.

Carrying two empty suitcases after having sold all the merchandise inside them was an intoxicating experience. Walking down the platform without any feeling of oppression, without a premonition of disaster, what bliss! The other black marketeers were indulging their obsession with sick jokes and lewd puns. I sat quite indifferent to such things, smiling up at the dappled sky with my profits against my belly and the memory of being liked. I was a writer, I had told Paris I was a writer. Bernadette wanted to read what I had written. So I would have to go on. Oh, what a pretty white cat with pale blue eyes I was as I let myself be cradled by the rhythm of the wheels! All the pork butcher's wares waiting for me in the country had a scent of jasmine.

*

They began canceling some of the trains, I was forced to get up early. One morning I left my bed at three in the morning after having stayed up until eleven the evening before packing my suitcases. Broken, exhausted, pleased with my own punctuality, I had to drag myself through that day step by step. Why did I get up so early? Why did I go on with it? I had proved to myself I could fend for myself, I had earned hundreds of thousands of francs. I never admitted to myself that I had in fact gained nothing, because the money in the bath glove over my belly was exactly that: nothing. I was a beast of burden, still determined to keep going despite the voice of the driver saying: rest now, you can rest now, my beauty. I must have been very unhappy to seek consolation in trials of endurance that amounted in fact to a form of self-punishment. I emerged from my room, feeling homesick for it already, conscious that it would stay behind me prolonging my night until daybreak. I groped my way down the banisterless staircase in the dark. God, beneath M. Motté's bedclothes, was still sleeping before dividing the light from the darkness. The kitchen: a womb filled with silence. The silence: a child being formed. Day in the belly of the night. Every object there was keeping watch behind the eyelid of the dark. The opulence and superfluity of the pendulum, time boiling inside every drawer of the sideboard. I walked into the room where Maurice had chattered, had laughed and smoked and written and talked. I switched on the light. Flowers, I thought as I looked at the two suitcases I had to carry. Suitcases full of flowers instead of suitcases full of sausages . . . I pondered this transformation, my brain was full of bubbles, I licked the calluses on the palms of my hands. The tick-tock of my watch against the harsh electric light . . . I buried myself in the old handkerchief, in the old rag that softened the handles of my suitcases. Enough tick-tock! I prefer the streetcar depot, my welcoming sheepfold after I have made love well. I lifted my suitcases, I stumbled, I fell onto the chair by the table where I wrote, I dozed off for two minutes. I set out, and to give a festive air to my departure, I switched on M. Motté's kitchen light before I left. And then, and then. I remembered the hermetic curves of the cabbages and the bowls of yellowness over their tops, I remembered whatever came to hand. The night offered nothing to my eyes, the night took nothing from me.

September 15, 1961. My persecution is a pretension on my part, since what I want is the world, the whole world set in my path in the guise of a pebble, a turd, a smell of excrement, a dirty newspaper, a bunch of crushed grapes, the ring of a spade—omen of death. I open my purse to put away my door key, what do I find? A five-franc piece in the compartment reserved for prescriptions, for tickets, and for the prayer I copied down to protect me in the street. Five francs. I haven't forgotten and I shall never forget the end of Jacques Becker's film. It is night. Modigliani is trying to sell some small drawings on the terrace of the Dôme. A stupid woman takes one and gives him a five-franc piece. Modigliani is radiant. The stupid woman hands the drawing back. Modigliani leaves the café, he crumbles in the night, he collapses onto a silk sheet of rain, he dies in the hospital. You don't see the connection, reader. Ten months ago, I sent a piece I had written to a magazine. It was to be published, it wasn't published, there was a good reason for the delay, it is to be published this month. This morning I don't think it will be, because of the five-franc piece that has appeared out of the blue. You're not Modigliani, say the dead branches on the rock. I'm not Modigliani, I wasn't paid for my piece before it appeared, and yet it is the same five-franc piece between the great Modigliani and the little Violette. The piece I wrote will not appear despite the letter I have read and reread again and again telling me that it will appear. I will keep you informed, reader.[1] Pity me if I put the five francs in my purse myself, or if there is someone trying to torment me. I have thought for years that someone is taking a revenge on me every day, is sucking my blood every day. "You will go from hornet's nest to hornet's nest," a friend once told me when she was telling my cards. First-class fortune-telling.

I lunched off a small tomato salad, a piece of very strongly spiced red sausage, a hard-boiled egg, a piece of Bonbel cheese, three crackers, and a melon picked the day before. You can't be all that unhappy. You couldn't eat that much if you were. You are wrong. I am feeding my unhappiness too when I feed myself. To eat my lunch weeping on a shoulder that would welcome the weight of my head. I asked for the impossible as I ate. Don't let's spoil the sun.

My journey at half-past three in the morning from M. Motté's house to Notre-Dame-du-Hameau—why start out so early? To escape the eyes of the inspectors, to avoid the eyes behind lifted curtains. I stopped every ten yards, and longed each time I stopped to be

[1] It did appear.

a horse unable to get up again. I would fall, I thought, the sirloin would return to the steer, the leg of lamb to the sheep, the eggs to their nests. The sky was all sadness. I had to hold my head tipped back a long time trying to find it, to recognize it. Comfortable cradle, the rancid smell of my old rabbit coat as I rubbed my chin against it. The day was gurgling in the throat of one of Mme. Champion's pigeons: a white-ringed sound beneath the down. I turned into the road leading to Notre-Dame-du-Hameau, I was afraid as I parted the night between the ditches, between the woods and the fields. The massacre, the passion of the wheel smashing through the water of the millpond. I was inhabited by moonbeams. I left the desolation of that sight behind me. Ideas? Thoughts? I was living the withdrawal of the bushes beside me. In front of the linen mender's cottage a leaf, detaching itself from the darkness, fell onto a branch. There are treasures in silence. The leaf fell at last upon the road.

I rested, I breathed in the cold and the freshness about me: the two scents of the day about to be born. Then I continued my advance between hedges of shapeless conspirators. I mustn't brush against the leaves. The sombreros are asleep. Is the turtledove about to waken? The light is pale blue, it is waiting, it is ready. What was that bunch of blackness I glimpsed? Will there be a mist at the railroad station? It's cold, shall I have early morning diamonds glistening on my ears? Who knows? The bunch of blackness is behind me. I'm afraid: the night is no longer covering me and I have so much to discover. We must walk quickly, we must keep going, we must make ourselves plural so as to face the darkness with less fear. Victory, a quiver in the hedge. Is the weight of a sparrow so heavy to support then? No transition, and suddenly a great stirring and rustling everywhere. Excitement, hopping, impatience. Dawn is not here, but the birds are celebrating it already, the light is a murmur in the ears before it can be seen: day is being born. I walked through Notre-Dame-du-Hameau. The village was asleep, the streets were waiting patiently. I made my way toward the station between its two hills, I drew near to the house. . . . For sale or for rent? I had no idea. Oh you cozy sheepfold, you piece of pastoral nonsense, I said to it, groaning with love for it because the post-office clerk's sheep were grazing on the grass slope opposite, just at the height my bedroom window would be if I had dared to buy it, if I had dared inquire.

The vine climbing its wall needed pruning, its shutters were tightly shut. The sun was warming the deserted house and thawing me into a desire for bustle and activity. There were rosebushes persevering there. My childhood laughter that I never had, my childhood laughter as I saw the upstairs windowpanes that needed cleaning. The warm smell of a gingham apron fresh from the iron was going to my head. I was outside it, I took the house into my arms, my bosom was as ample as the rising day. I was consoling myself for the house I shall never have, for the garden I shall never cultivate. I write it now with tears of blood: I shall never have my little house before I die.

I reached the station, I went around to one side of it, I retraced my steps, I recognized, thanks to a quiver of light between night and day, my rails and my stacks of wood. I had my particular spot, I had my own little ways. I thanked myself for having managed to carry fifty-five to sixty pounds a distance of two and a half miles. I was shivering despite all my efforts. I warmed myself in the musty odor of my coat. Then I slept with eyes wide open, my head between my knees, in the more vigorous smell of my woolen skirt. The day was breaking, the day had broken, I accused myself of being unfaithful. I watched the calm wisdom of the light slowly rising, the Gregorian chants moving between the trees in the distance: the daylight was like a sheet of beautiful paper. The countryside was awakening at a speed too swift for me to follow, there was smoke coming up from the chimneys. A footstep. Occasionally, a man on the road rubbing his hands together: he was chafing himself into existence. Impassive, the rails still lay lost in sleep. The train came into the station at seven. It was tiny, slow and diligent.

Sunday, September 17, 1961, in my little corner of the Vaucluse—is my state of persecution worse or better? A hint of burning paper in the air as I awake; the same thing the next day. I know: an unbalanced person's sense of smell invents things, it sees mirages. This is no invention of my sense of smell. A reminder of the letter from Maurice Sachs I burned? A reminder of the nullity of my exercise books with the blue tracery my pen lays on their pages with washable Parker ink? Or is it that my work is already so much smoke? Reader, you who are reading me, search, find me the answer. The situation has improved: Mme. D., my neighbor, has invited me to have lunch with her. Seventy years old. Discreet, brave, religious. A light presence. A practicing Catholic, but tactful. At eight o'clock this morning, Mme. D. was chopping up food in her kitchen for me.

My nice neighbors, M. and his wife, took me to visit Grignan: we went through the village of Grillon. The mistral was saucy with us on the terrace of the château: our skirts flew up, a priest turned away his head. What a terrace . . . Mme. de Sévigné got up in the morning, she had no need to set a foot outside her own home, there was all of Provence before her. Her room. If I had money to burn, I'd buy myself a fourposter bed with a tester. It would keep me safe from the noises and the eyes looking down from the ceiling. The château didn't speak to me, it didn't whisper. The wood floors were too brightly polished. There was no spittle lurking to confront me in Mme. de Sévigné's spittoon. But I remembered the expression powder blue for a vase. I softened at the sight of the *gavottes,* armchairs with a hood to protect you from drafts. They made me think of the turn-of-the-century beach chair in the film *Some Like It Hot.* If I were a furniture maker, I would sell my *gavottes* two by two just as pigeons are always sold at fairs.

*

I sank down into the warmth of the Bêmes' kitchen, into the warmth of M. Lécolié's kitchen. I rested, I amused myself, I educated myself in the trio's antique shop on Saturday afternoons. They were intrigued by my rabbit, which I called my rabbilet. They fingered my mangy coat. I loved it and I loved its leprous patches: we had lived together such a long time during those long quests after wealth in the rain and the storms and the snow. It was my companion in endurance. The trio called me their "little wild strawberry." That was a change for me. The customers came in and asked about this and that; I sat stagnant and overshadowed by Paris and its celebrities. Or else I bubbled, I frothed, I simmered, I exulted on Saturday afternoons. Paris and its celebrities were buying furniture. Music boxes were in fashion, everyone wanted new furniture since they had to stay home all the time now. Sitting beside the trio's teakettle, on the fringe of a chaos of telephone books, yardgoods samples, cookies, papers, and bars of chocolate, I was warm from top to toe in my big boots, in my rabbilet which I kept on from three in the morning till eleven at night; their electric fire under the table was so warm, so gentle and nice. With my nose resting on the sleeve of my molting coat, I watched out for Saint-Loups, for Swanns and Odette Swanns. From time to time I thought I recognized one. Beggars and shadows drifted in. The shadows were trying to sell albums, shawls, old parchments, fans. If the shadows sold their faded old possessions, they looked lighter as they drifted out. If they didn't sell them, they left us weighed down by the weight of one more disappointment. As for the beggars, they shut the door as they left with their heart's content. Romi would escape from the shop and come over to whisper scabrous but polished comments in my ear. I always missed the point and laughed in the wrong places. One day I arrived with a permanent wave that had gone wrong. "Well, here comes my little fuzzy-wuzzy friend," the husband said when he saw me. At lunchtime, he washed my hair for me in their bathroom. I watched him carefully preparing lunch in their kitchen and I saw what could be done with the meat they'd paid me for. They all three treated me like their baby during mealtimes. "Eat it all up," they said, making me accept as a gift what they had acquired from me as a purchase.

I had never used the back stairs before. Now I was becoming familiar with them, I liked them. They are narrow, but they aren't cold. Smells of soup, of roasting meat, of fritters, of frying potatoes, of tarts baking in ovens came to meet me and surrounded me. I greeted maids and housekeepers who returned my greetings. "Is business still good?" they asked as they were leaving for the shops or coming back home. Little by little, I became simply a living stone in their masters' courtyards. I was the woman who sold all the good things they couldn't go out and buy for themselves. They stood aside for me on the stairs.

There was one young butler-cook who liked me because my wares were varied and of good quality. He was soon to be married to a schoolteacher. I went in, I rejoiced in the lightness, the gaiety of his kitchen. Cutcha-cutcha-cutcha on the tiles around the sink, cutcha-cutcha-cutcha to the curtains, cutcha-cutcha-cutcha even to the refrigerator. The flowers on the table were always fresh, the apéritif he offered me was cool without being iced. He would go through that day's menu; I would recognize my cream, my butter, my poultry as he read the items out. What he wanted were his raw materials for next week's dinner. And there I was eating a piece of the cake that had been the grand finale to his yesterday's big dinner. He took me into the dining room and left me with the clumps of hydrangeas on the carpet. I appreciated immediately the window that had been enlarged to give a better view of the Seine. I had only to stretch out my hand and the river would be flowing through my fingers. Another apéritif? No thank you. I knew how to behave in a kitchen. I opened my suitcases and we got down to serious matters.

I also had a hard core of customers in the old doctor's sumptuous apartment building. They greeted me with open arms, they wanted me to tell them the story of my life and labors. I always added that I was a writer so as to add to my prestige.

*

"Tell me it won't be too small. . . ."

The surgeon pressed his hands together to help him think this over.

"That would be ridiculous," he said.

His big hands looked strong; his own was a very powerful one.

"It will look all right? You promise me?"

"Come, come, madame! I'm not a beginner, you know."

"No, of course not. Forgive me."

"I must photograph it," he said.

"Photograph it?" I said, bewildered.

"Follow me," he said more gently.

Standing up in his office, the surgeon scrutinized me. He was wasting his time with a half-wit, that was obvious.

"The plate is ready," he said.

Now his insistence was like a threat.

I followed him uneasily, as though everything were already lost. Burning hot from the ill temper inside me, I posed for him in a room full of filing cabinets and folders. I wanted to be separated from it; I didn't want him to give it back to me on a sheet of paper.

We went back into the office.

"Sit down," he said, as though we were at some serious court proceedings that had only just begun.

He didn't like me.

"Would you like it in a week's time?" he asked, putting his hands together again.

"In a week's time?" I echoed, taken by surprise.

"Otherwise I shall be forced to make you wait a month."

A month. A month in which I would have had it all to myself, entire and still my own as I walked into a bar, into a restaurant. I was going to miss it. It had been stuck on there a long time. It gave me momentum. It was my prow, it was the barge I sat in.

"A week from today at nine in the morning," he said.

I began to be afraid of the swabs, of the blood, of my funeral.

"Very well, in a week's time if that suits you," I answered, cowed.

But after all, there were no handcuffs on my wrists. I could disappear if I wished, I could go on wallowing in the mudbath of my miseries if I so chose.

"It will be twenty thousand francs."

The size of the sum restored my courage. I felt a sense of my own worth again. I saw a montage sequence of my suitcases, my baskets, my darlings passing in the distance.

I began all over again:

"It will be middle-sized? It will be straight? I'd like it rather taut, a little on the defensive. Only a little. Oh, a very little. A little child-like too. . . ."

"Madame, I've told you what it would be like. Do you have confidence in me?"

"Not much."

"Stand up!"

I obeyed. Being weak, being strong, hoping and despairing, all became a sort of excruciating calisthenics in his office. I was on my feet, I was in shreds. Because I wanted the impossible: to transform myself without yielding it up, without abandoning my familiar, good old moments of grief.

The surgeon was holding it in the palm of his hand. He was studying it.

"It can be done," he said, as though I had only just walked into his office, as though I had just explained what I wanted for the first time.

The expert hand fell away from it again.

"I shall be pleased with it?" I asked in a wan voice.

"Why shouldn't you be pleased?"

That conditional was the end of all discussion.

"I have suffered so much," I said.

He made no answer.

"In a week, then," I added as a way of escape.

I was not convinced by our handshake.

A diagnosis gives us a fresh lease on life. Our body too has a need for honesty. How ordered the world seemed when I found myself in the street once more. I began living with myself again as though we'd been parted for twenty years. I took pleasure in powdering my face, in looking at myself. My protuberance was no longer the instrument that had always tortured my head and my heart. I selected a pretext for not making up my mind: the size of the fee he had asked. The idea of a pretty face can upset any argument. To be attractive, oh, to be attractive and attractive until they carry you away on a bier. I went into a dream: myself drawing a charming smile from the man punching my ticket in the Métro. Me interrupting the absorption of the gourmets as I walked across the floor of a restaurant. Me blooming, radiant for the benefit of the schoolboys as they come out of school. Who is that little child who was playing and suddenly can't take his eyes off you? Your lover, my little one. Price: twenty thousand francs.

The evening before the date we had fixed, I packed my little bag in my hotel room. Bernadette telephoned, she asked me if I still intended to go through with it. I said I did: it wasn't true. I changed my mind a hundred times during the night of insomnia that followed. I interlaced my fingers and held it fast between my palms, I was snatching it back from the darkness. We'll grow old together, I said to myself, we'll go through life unnoticed and in peace, without stirring up cruelty and stupid mockery on every side. I went back through time to a turn-of-the-century sofa surrounded by a group of ninnies in evening dress, all sighing for a Poiret beauty. Those immense eyes, those soot-ringed ellipses, that turban, that pearl-hung bosom, why should they not be my bosom, my eyes, my fatal allure? Greedy-guts, I even wanted to lay in stores of beauty long out of fashion. I went to sleep finally at seven in the morning, having resolved not to lose one drop of my blood and to save my twenty thousand-franc bills.

The telephone rang.

"You asked us to wake you," said the manageress's voice.

I went to sleep again.

The telephone rang.

Bernadette was worried. I was already an hour and a half late. She would be in my room in ten minutes. If I could only get out of the hotel, get out of Paris . . . Numbed into nonexistence, my mouth full of fur, I put on my clothes without believing what was happening. Bernadette came in and scolded me. I left the hotel with death in my heart. I dragged myself into the clinic with Bernadette, who announced my arrival to the staff. A lady wearing a white veil led me into a room and told me reproachfully to put on my nightgown. Was I in a room, or on a raft that wasn't moving? Midday began chiming desultorily all around me. What was I to do? I left the room, I wandered down a deserted corridor in my nightgown. Nothing, no one. I walked on, haphazard, and without wanting to, without looking for it, I found myself in the operation room. Was this part of their plan? They ignored me.

"I'm here," I said.

They didn't answer.

I climbed up the steel steps and laid down as best I could, without them helping me. The surgeon, I recognized him when I was ready. I closed my eyes. I had promised myself I would.

"I've suffered so much," I said.

Under my lowered eyelids it was mainly the stars I was addressing.

"If you knew how much I've suffered . . ."

I surrendered myself to the noise of the steel containers, the noise of the syringes.

"They made fun," I said to the noises.

The first needle, suddenly, in my nostril. There, take that, since you've suffered so much, the needle said.

"They won't make fun any more, will they? . . ."

I was talking to my mouth as it began to collapse. There, take that too since you've suffered so much, said the second needle as it went into me.

"I'll be like other people. . . ."

"Don't talk," the surgeon said to me.

The nose, the nose I hated . . . it is suffering more than I am. I don't want this, I don't want this; I don't want to be separated from it. Stop the needles, stop them. I can't talk anymore. Third needle, fourth needle, I'm going away. It's a torture. How many needles? Ten? Twelve? I must try and count, I must. . . . How long will I go on suffering? I shall go away at the next nee . . . I am going. . . .

I woke up in a bed. The divine moment of awakening after an operation. We are intact again, I mean without a past. Then the suffering that is our creation returns to us once more. There was slime inside my dressings, I went to sleep again. That evening the surgeon came in to see me without so much as opening his lips. My pulse seemed to satisfy him.

I lived lying flat on my back, I learned to smile so that I could feel the threads holding my new nose together.

"I'd like to see it," I told the surgeon two days after the operation.

"It's too soon," he answered.

My hand continually brushed against the dressing, so as to sense what lay beneath, so as to be closer to my hopes. I got out of bed, I looked in the mirror at the shapeless cushion over the middle of my face. I was frightened by my little eyes, by the blue bruises under them. What a monster! I sighed. The dressings reassured me somewhat. There was a miracle sheltering behind those wads of cotton. I had only to be patient. The dressings would fall. . . .

The dressings fell. He gave me a mirror, he left the room.

I didn't recognize the old woman before me, the old woman with a big nose, the same one as before. A little less long? A little less ludicrous? It made me look older and harder.

The surgeon came back into the room later and asked if I was satisfied. I answered yes as though I were about to breathe my last.

The flesh was still swollen and bruised, there was still room for hope. I had no hope. I had become an object of horror to myself. I had paid twenty thousand francs in order to look like an ugly old lump of stone. I asked to be discharged from the clinic so that I could lose myself in my paths and my woods. He took out the stitches and told me I should protect it from the cold with a wad of cotton held in a handkerchief, this remodeled nose of mine. The hotel porter came to fetch me. He was simple and he was a saint. He coddled me in the Métro, in the street, in the café, without ever asking me why I talked all the time from behind a huge handkerchief. There were tiny pincers tugging at the stitch marks in my refashioned nostrils, but I could weep. As soon as I began to weep I found myself again, my self and my enormous nose, untouched. Bernadette complimented me on the results of the operation; I told her what I thought on the subject. Two days after being discharged from the clinic I was battling my way across the fields, two baskets in one hand and a wad of cotton in the other. The cold was intense. It was February if I remember correctly. I explained to everyone that a doctor had put one of the walls of a nasal cavity back into its correct position so that I could breathe better. Months passed, I liked my new nose less and less. I made a complaint; the surgeon showed me the photograph he had taken before the operation. A year later, I went into the Montana bar with Bernadette. She waved to Jacques Prévert. We sat down just a few feet away from his table. "It's her mouth, her eyes, her cheekbones they should have fixed," he said to one of his friends as he looked at me.

*

The letters from Maurice had stopped. He had told me almost nothing about his life after moving to a bachelor apartment in Hamburg. Then came the bombing of Hamburg. Was he still alive? He sent me a note, the last: "Don't torment yourself. I'm safe and sound." Today I say to myself: Is it possible that the man who drew that portrait of Lodève could have written me that reassuring note?

I was in the train with my suitcases full of meat and butter. We were approaching Paris. Suddenly there were English planes skimming the roof of the train. I leaped to my feet, I screamed in the compartment full of passengers. Two men's hands clamped down on my shoulders: no panicking. I sat down again and the hail began to fall on the roof of the train. Everyone threw themselves onto the floor. I began screaming again and trying to push my way under the seat. "Get a hold of yourself," said the woman on all fours next to me. The planes gained height again. The passengers resumed their seats; they sat and talked about the weather we were having, looking me up and down disgustedly as they did so. When I got back to the village I learned that the railroad stations were being closed. The cattle was drowning in grass, the farmers' wives were soaking their washing in milk. The price of food shot up like a rocket in Paris and sank to zero in the country. Gangs of cyclists appeared on the roads. People in the country were giving their butter to the pigs or throwing it onto the dungheap. I built up stocks in M. Motté's house, idle, completely at a loose end.

The maiden lady who played the harmonium informed me that Gérard had been arrested and taken away with his brother and mother. Gérard had often complained about his brother, the *zazou*. He had finally been arrested during a raid on a bar and forced to give his address. The enemy had then arrested the other two as well.

One afternoon of bright sun, of calm, of hollyhocks high in their ivory towers, just when I had finished gathering my day's quota of news from the wildly optimistic Bêmes and was preparing to fly off and disgorge it to M. Lécolié and his wife, I met Fernand, radiant with fresh linen and energy. He was "going up" to Paris with a load of butter on his bike. Everyone was afraid for him. "This is no moment to risk the roads," I said. "Be patient, it will soon be over." He shrugged his shoulders and went off to get ready for his journey. Fernand had always been pigheaded.

"There's never been a storm like the one there'll be tonight," M. Motté said at eight that evening.

The storm had been gathering since six. The navy blue sky was leaning lower and lower, ready to start lashing us. I sat raging with impotence beside my three hundred pounds of unsold butter. From time to time M. Motté opened the door of the room in which I sat being consumed by my own impatience. This is the end of your buying and selling, cried his round, glassy eyes, and I'm glad of it. M. Motté was letting me know that the war would soon be over, that he would be able to enjoy his own room again and leave the fresh meat of his own animals to grow cool in it. I powdered my nose, hoping to find succor in that simulacrum of frivolity. I went outside, I breathed the air deep into my lungs. The silence was heavy, the light was sinking fast. The distant vistas were making prophecies, then someone called my name in the center of the village. The old mayor's daughter was looking for me. A man she knew had arrived by car looking for butter. "If you give him half your stock, he'll take you into Paris this evening with all the butter as well," she told me. It was a steep price for a car-ride. She added that I had a half hour in which to make up my mind. I went back inside and suffered agonies at the thought of my bath glove bursting with thousand-franc bills. What if he were a bandit, what if he robbed me? . . .

The car drew up at half-past eight that evening in front of M. Motté's gate. Everyone was outside to watch me carry out my packages, which the motorist hid under a false floor in the car. We turned off by Mme. Meulay's and he asked me to help him find his way along the side roads that were impassable to military convoys. The enemy was beginning to retreat, especially at night. This disquieting request at the very beginning of our expedition increased my suspicions. What was the man like? I am searching back into my memory. I can find no record of either his face or his body. I was afraid of his hand when it left the steering wheel in order to change gear. The countryside was slumbering under the menace of the coming storm, the wind was away that evening. It was peaceful and it was a drama, this expectation of drama. The motorist swerved to avoid a little wild rabbit sitting in the middle of the road. His simplicity and silliness in that storm-laden atmosphere brought tears to my eyes. But I crossed my hands tightly over my gray cloth bag nonetheless: I was protecting my money. He refused a cigarette and that put me in a panic. He wanted as little as possible to do with me so that it would be easier for him to strangle me and throw me out of the car when he'd taken all my money. The calm of his face bore no relation to my fears. He didn't speak: he was intent on watching for gullies in the badly kept roads. The rain began falling thickly, in torrents. The countryside awoke from its slumber to exhale an odor of green leaves and steel. The motorist wound up his window to avoid the fury of the downpour. We were already driving along the bed of a stream, a muddy spray was splattering against the windshield.

"We'll have to stop," he said.

He drove off the road into a meadow with apple trees in it. He switched off the headlights, switched them on again, then cut the motor. He announced that it was impossible for him to go on driving in that deluge and that he was going to rest for a moment. His hands stayed on the wheel, he fell asleep to the sound of the rain as it settled down to a steady siege. He was asleep, an endless rain was thrusting its needles against the glass of the windshield. I passed the time by watching each drop burst into a star and rebound from the chrome trim.

For some while I had been growing accustomed to the muffled thunder of the convoys on a distant highway. Now I was listening to it, unending beneath the torrential storm. The plight of those soldiers, whether enemies or allies, was so lamentable that I was no longer making any distinction between a regiment, a deluge of rain, apple trees soaked with rain, and a streaming windshield.

I gave a start, I shook the sleeping motorist.

"Someone wants to speak to you. . . ."

The German officer in his streaming oilskin was waiting by the door. The motorist wound down his window and the officer saluted as though he had found himself face to face with another officer. The rain rebounded from that disciplined hand. He asked us in French how to get to a highway we didn't know, then thanked us with another salute. I didn't hear the squelching of his boots as he made his way back to the convoy. When the muffled thunder had stopped we set off again. It was a dismal dawn; all the other people on earth seemed to be dug in inside their houses.

"You'll soon be at our house drinking coffee," he said. "We're only fifty-five miles from Paris."

The sun didn't appear and the harvesters were enveloped in an impenetrable sadness.

His home at Ivry-la-Bataille left me cold. Yet it was a heart-warming scene of family life I had stumbled on. The grandmother was dressing her grandchildren, the young wife was in her robe mixing their breakfast food. We exchanged a few polite phrases and he insisted I stop and drink a cup of coffee. Then we set off again through the suburban streets, deserted but heavy with a sense of impending events.

When he'd put the car in his garage, he told me that he would drive me back as far as Ivry-la-Bataille that weekend.

The people in the streets said that the Métro stations would all be closed quite soon. There was a rising tide of cyclists: intrepid young girls, skirts billowing in the wind, satchels slung over their shoulders, were standing on their pedals as they swept by, free and fearless, as though bent on some important mission. Paris was a bird with folded wings along its tranquil streets. I passed thin people, wan people, undernourished people, and I envied them. The end of the Occupation was drawing near, they were about to reap the reward for all their deprivations. I was alone with my wad of money. "Withdraw into yourself, and stop pitying yourself," I said suddenly out loud, so that I would be doubly alone and doubly grotesque in a city that was beginning to hold its breath. The manageress of the little hotel told me that the room she kept for me every week wasn't available, that I would have to look elsewhere. I was aware that she was ridding herself of a black marketeer. I made no fuss. One of my customers in the old doctor's sumptuous building agreed to lend me a room with a bathroom and a kitchen. No, I wouldn't go back and live in Gabriel's room. I didn't want to see him again, I didn't want to see the miasmas of idleness rising around me once more. I sold my butter extremely quickly at an extremely high price.

*

I was sole ruler over a desert of asphalt roads, of meadows, of unharvested wheat, of country churches and spires, once I had alighted from the car that had brought me back out to Ivry-la-Bataille. I had forty-five miles to cover on foot. The cattle were gone, the people were hidden, the poultry and farmyard animals were all in eclipse. I was the first and last human being there in the anguish, the silence, and the misfortune of my country. I walked along at a good clip without saying good day, without saying thank you. To have lit a cigarette in that desert of trees, of gardens, of gravel heaps, of water towers, would have been too unseemly. The springs and brooks were occupation enough. I tried not to listen to the sound of the birds, to the songs they poured out from the heart of an implacable unawareness.

I turned into a narrow side road and noticed a little wood on the right filled with dappled brown and green tarpaulins. I imagined they were there to camouflage a munitions dump among the trees. There was a soldier with his rifle at the slope guarding the wood. He watched me as I advanced along the road toward him. I was walking on the other side of the road but I couldn't turn back. An officer appeared from among the trees, he watched me too. I guessed what was in their minds: I was a spy who had grown too bold. I was a solitary woman walking at a steady pace along the roads at a time when all the other civilians were living in their cellars, in their air-raid shelters. They opened their eyes wide. I walked past them without looking at them, without looking at the wood full of camouflaged ammunition. I heard the guard speak. He was talking to the officer in German. I saw between my eyelashes that he was aiming his rifle at me. Walking straight past them, clinging onto the horizon, making myself look like a Don Quixote in skirts silhouetted against the sky was my only chance of not being shot down at point-blank range. To live one's death. I lived mine as I waited for that bullet in my back. The officer replied to the guard. I understood, without knowing German, that I was not worth their bullet.

I walked from eight in the morning until seven in the evening without food, without drink, without a rest. By four in the afternoon I was being haunted by visions of the distance I still had to cover and kept going because I was afraid I might collapse entirely if I slowed down. My legs were swelling, my muscles were twisting over hot coals. I stopped in a big village. I had covered twenty-eight miles. My legs continued to swell as I sat in a restaurant. I nibbled at the food I'd ordered, and as I thought back to all the precautions my grandmother used to take when I was young and delicate, I summoned up enough energy for a smile. But I had to get to my feet when the meal was over. I gripped the table with both hands. My legs were red-hot bars of iron. It took three quarters of an hour of repeated effort before I succeeded in making them obey me. Bent double, I managed to drag myself to the room which a schoolteacher had lent me for the night. The throbbing in my calves kept up ceaselessly throughout a completely sleepless night. Powerful airplanes flew low continually over the roof. The next day it took me twelve hours to walk fourteen miles. On the third day, I spent six hours walking the last three. M. Motté gave a cry of surprise. The village thought I had vanished forever.

I became a celebrity as soon as it was known I was back; during the next few days I had to show my legs to a great number of visitors. Many were disappointed because my calves were not more swollen. I forgot my own weariness when I heard that Fernand was in a Paris jail; he had been arrested on a little side road. He was cycling along with a group of friends. They were all taking butter to Paris. An open car full of enemy soldiers had turned out of a crossroads, followed the group of cyclists, and fired over their heads to make them stop. They had all stopped except Fernand. The soldiers had fired into the air a second time as they chased Fernand. They caught him and took him away in the car, forgetting the others. The whole village was in a state of shock. Why hadn't he listened to me, that pigheaded boy for whom everyone was now weeping without tears?

My motorist came back to collect me with a second cargo of butter. He was anxious. We neither of us spoke, we didn't want to share our anxiety.

"It's raining over there," I said as we got close to Paris.

"No, I don't think it's rain," he replied.

Five minutes later, there were bullets riddling the wheat field beside us and planes hovering above us like crows. We got out of the car near a house. A woman was running toward a homemade air-raid shelter.

"Can we come in?" shouted the motorist.

"There's no room," she shouted back without looking around.

We threw ourselves flat on our stomachs in the wheat. Two minutes later the planes soared up and away again. I told him I was expecting to stay in Paris from then on: it was madness to be out in a car on the open roads. We learned later that what we had seen and heard was the final bombing of Trappes.

Two weeks later the Allies marched into Paris.

August 21, 1963. Quickly, reader, quickly, so that I can give you more of the old, familiar things: the soft ocean of the open country, the mown hay, the waves at rest with the far distance between them. They have been mowing, the lucerne is lying in the heat like a human body greedy for the rays that will tan it. Quickly, reader, so I shall still have time to give you what you saw when you first came. They have been plowing; the upturned earth is pale gray. And floating, not moving, above the tempest in the churned earth, a simple olive branch. A dead branch, satin textured, lighting another, scorched branch. Veiled sun, the concert of the leaves which began piano, piano; it is the wind making love to the trees. All the trees being wooed and responding to the soft arm stroking the harp. Every afternoon, at four o'clock, the summer submerges. August has been indecisive up till now and autumnal November weather often lays siege to us. Five o'clock, it is dark and the shepherd sets off home. With dusks, with mists strung between sterile broom bushes, the shepherd is wholly clad. He goes his way. He is pensive beside that sea of furrowed earth paler than the pale streaks in my hair. There are cicadas singing behind a windbreak, and I am sitting in the spot where I began my story. How am I to finish it? Is that all the story of my life? Should I say au revoir to you, reader, or should I say farewell? I do not know.

Let us go back to 1944. I am thirty-seven years old, the war is coming to an end. I shall simply vegetate as I did before if I live in Paris. Where should I live? M. Motté is dead, it seems, and I must fly from Normandy. Tomorrow I shall open the door of the room I had abandoned, I shall be holding my key in one hand and my divorce papers in the other. I have been scouting in the neighborhood. Gabriel, it seems, is going to marry again. . . . I heard the news, I smiled at the arch of time. There was a rainbow that smiled at me as well. Tomorrow I shall open the door of my room and I shall shut myself away. It was the wheat that made me go out walking in all weathers. The table on which I learned to write stories for a magazine is ready. Shall I keep the apartment? Shall I go on writing? Bernadette is taking my manuscript all over Paris, she wants it to be published. Maurice Sachs would have led me to the table, he would have opened the ball. What has become of Maurice? He is in Lebanon, he is in the East, he will come back one day when I least expect him. I have no doubt of that. He has nothing against me. He must just have run away. He is managing somehow in one of those countries he used to dream about. We will squander the money I earned, Maurice. What have I become in the past few days? A tradeswoman who has gone bankrupt.

I should buy gold. I don't dare to. The investments I make will wither, I sense it already, like the grass of the field. Paris will snatch it away from me, my woolen stocking, my passion. Paris frightens me. I fly from a flitting bat at every street corner. All my labor lost. The bat catches me, it stifles me inside its folding wings. Its velvet skin is my own idleness, is myself in Paris once again. Yesterday, I said to my mother as we came out of the movies: "Help me to find a job as a manageress somewhere, help me. I want to earn money." Will she help me? Earn money. But what have I earned up till now? I am so poor in Paris. . . . In the country, I was rich. I realize that, seeing all these chimneys and all this smoke. The beautiful money for which I would have eaten my own dung, what was it? The little flower, the golden button my shoe tried not to tread on. Oh the beautiful, the haughty golden sovereign of the dandelion in the field . . . That was what pushed up the value of my paper bills. It is comic and it is a matter for despair, my beige suitcase becoming the tomb of all my profits. Miser I am, miser I shall remain. I love everything without depth. And yet, reader, and yet. I give you without counting the tremulous sky arching over me on August 21, 1963, at half-past seven in the evening. That gentle pink has not even a suggestion of timidity. Believe me: I would bleed myself if that was the only way I could bring you this refinement of the palest sugared-almond pink. My love, I say to the subtle washes in the sky. At that moment God can hear me.

In the stock exchange they were shouting, they were yelling, while clouds passed overhead like Merovingian warriors, and I wanted to get rich during the war. I wanted to make my own way in the world. My own way where? Away from the disdain I imagined others felt for me. Society . . . to be someone . . . I like that, I liked that. As a black marketeer I did at least carve out a place for myself in the first rank. Fernand held out his lighter, we lit our cigarettes, and the grades of society crumbled. Where is Fernand? Will he come back? His laugh was sometimes like the cooing of a dove. Where is Maurice? Did I love him? I loved his intelligence, his sense of humor, his goodness, his radiance, his generosity. Separated from him, I no longer love his weaknesses, his miseries, his wounds. I wonder if I shall love another homosexual. Probably. To walk always on the same spot, that is my debauchery. I came into the world and I vowed to entertain a passion for the impossible.

1944. I am thirty-seven. I am almost forty. It's odd, I don't feel sad. I am getting older, therefore I shall suffer less and less. I have never had anything and I possess nothing now. I was forgetting: I had a child, it was a well-formed boy, so the doctor said. Gone into the abortionist's grape-trampling, my handsome child. Isabelle is in the Louvre. I shall go and see her. Hermine I see quite often. She had stature, yet she has grown in stature. The glow, the sunset, the beach more immense than all the countries in the world which I contemplate once more from the bridge of Arcole, that is Hermine. My mother is preparing to leave Paris forever. Our loves will be fire beneath the ashes. As for Fidéline, she is my little apple who keeps eternally. Julienne is moving to Provence. I am thirty-seven, I still have many years in which to weep. On Sundays I shall go for walks alone, I shall draw my tears from the springs, from the streams, I shall bite into the fruit of my desolations. That is the price of your egocentricity, my little one. Intelligent I am not, nor shall I ever become so. The crucial reckoning. Sainfoin, sand, mattress, tiles on the floor, now, in 1944, I am plunging deep into the abyss of onanism . . . the others all are gone.

I reflect: my wealth and my beauty in the paths of Normandy lay in the efforts I made. I kept going until I had what I wanted: I was existing at last. I was succeeding, and my courage led me astray. I toiled, and I forgot myself. What is it I love with all my heart? The country. The woods and the forests which I am beginning to value, which I shall leave. My place is with them and in them. I would be deceiving myself if I settled elsewhere. That is why I shall always be in exile. To grow old means to lose what one has. I have never had anything. I failed in the essential things: my loves, my studies. To love the light. I was sixteen once, and I preferred the glow of a candle on an open book. Now I am thirty-seven, and I prefer the sun on a white chalk cliff.

August 22, 1963. This August day, reader, is a rose window glowing with heat. I make you a gift of it, it is yours. One o'clock. I am going back to the village for lunch. Strong with the silence of the pines and the chestnut trees. I walk without flinching through the burning cathedral of the summer. My bank of wild grass is majestic and full of music. It is a fire that solitude presses against my lips.

SELECTED DALKEY ARCHIVE PAPERBACKS

CAROLE MASO, *AVA.*
LADISLAV MATEJKA AND KRYSTYNA POMORSKA, EDS., *Readings in Russian Poetics: Formalist and Structuralist Views.*
HARRY MATHEWS, *Cigarettes.*
The Conversions.
The Case of the Persevering Maltese: Collected Essays.
The Human Country: New and Collected Stories.
The Journalist.
Singular Pleasures.
The Sinking of the Odradek Stadium.
Tlooth.
20 Lines a Day.
ROBERT L. MCLAUGHLIN, ED., *Innovations: An Anthology of Modern & Contemporary Fiction.*
STEVEN MILLHAUSER, *The Barnum Museum.*
In the Penny Arcade.
RALPH J. MILLS, JR., *Essays on Poetry.*
OLIVE MOORE, *Spleen.*
NICHOLAS MOSLEY, *Accident.*
Assassins.
Catastrophe Practice.
Children of Darkness and Light.
The Hesperides Tree.
Hopeful Monsters.
Imago Bird.
Impossible Object.
Inventing God.
Judith.
Natalie Natalia.
Serpent.
WARREN F. MOTTE, JR., *Oulipo: A Primer of Potential Literature.*
Fables of the Novel: French Fiction since 1990.
YVES NAVARRE, *Our Share of Time.*
WILFRIDO D. NOLLEDO, *But for the Lovers.*
FLANN O'BRIEN, *At Swim-Two-Birds.*
The Best of Myles.
The Dalkey Archive.
Further Cuttings.
The Hard Life.
The Poor Mouth.
The Third Policeman.
CLAUDE OLLIER, *The Mise-en-Scène.*
FERNANDO DEL PASO, *Palinuro of Mexico.*
RAYMOND QUENEAU, *The Last Days.*
Odile.
Pierrot Mon Ami.
Saint Glinglin.
ANN QUIN, *Berg.*
Passages.
Three.
Tripticks.
ISHMAEL REED, *The Free-Lance Pallbearers.*
The Last Days of Louisiana Red.
Reckless Eyeballing.
The Terrible Threes.
The Terrible Twos.
Yellow Back Radio Broke-Down.
JULIÁN RÍOS, *Poundemonium.*
AUGUSTO ROA BASTOS, *I the Supreme.*
JACQUES ROUBAUD, *The Great Fire of London.*
Hortense in Exile.
Hortense Is Abducted.
The Plurality of Worlds of Lewis.
The Princess Hoppy.
Some Thing Black.
LEON S. ROUDIEZ, *French Fiction Revisited.*
LUIS RAFAEL SÁNCHEZ, *Macho Camacho's Beat.*
SEVERO SARDUY, *Cobra & Maitreya.*
ARNO SCHMIDT, *Collected Stories.*
Nobodaddy's Children.
CHRISTINE SCHUTT, *Nightwork.*
JUNE AKERS SEESE, *Is This What Other Women Feel, Too?*
What Waiting Really Means.
AURELIE SHEEHAN, *Jack Kerouac Is Pregnant.*
VIKTOR SHKLOVSKY, *Theory of Prose.*
Third Factory.
Zoo, or Letters Not about Love.
JOSEF ŠKVORECKÝ, *The Engineer of Human Souls.*
CLAUDE SIMON, *The Invitation.*
GILBERT SORRENTINO, *Aberration of Starlight.*
Blue Pastoral.
Crystal Vision.
Imaginative Qualities of Actual Things.
Mulligan Stew.
Pack of Lies.
The Sky Changes.
Something Said.
Splendide-Hôtel.
Steelwork.
Under the Shadow.
W. M. SPACKMAN, *The Complete Fiction.*
GERTRUDE STEIN, *Lucy Church Amiably.*
The Making of Americans.
A Novel of Thank You.
PIOTR SZEWC, *Annihilation.*
ESTHER TUSQUETS, *Stranded.*
LUISA VALENZUELA, *He Who Searches.*
PAUL WEST, *Words for a Deaf Daughter* and *Gala.*
CURTIS WHITE, *Memories of My Father Watching TV.*
Monstrous Possibility.
Requiem.
DIANE WILLIAMS, *Excitability: Selected Stories.*
Romancer Erector.
DOUGLAS WOOLF, *Wall to Wall.*
Ya! & John-Juan.
PHILIP WYLIE, *Generation of Vipers.*
MARGUERITE YOUNG, *Angel in the Forest.*
Miss MacIntosh, My Darling.
REYOUNG, *Unbabbling.*
LOUIS ZUKOFSKY, *Collected Fiction.*
SCOTT ZWIREN, *God Head.*

CPSIA information can be obtained
at www.ICGtesting.com
Printed in the USA
BVHW071506030319
541649BV00001B/5/P

9 781564 782892